EXTRAORDINARY
ENTREPRENEURSHIP

Extraordinary Entrepreneurship

The Professional's Guide to Starting an Exceptional Enterprise

Stephen C. Harper

WILEY

JOHN WILEY & SONS, INC.

For general information on our other products and services, or technical support, please contact our Customer Care Department within the United States at 800-762-2974, outside the United States at 317-572-3993 or fax 317-572-4002.

Wiley also publishes its books in a variety of electronic formats. Some content that appears in print may not be available in electronic books.

For more information about Wiley products, visit our Web site at *www.wiley.com*.

Library of Congress Cataloging-in-Publication Data:

Harper, Stephen C.
   Extraordinary entrepreneurship: the professional's guide to starting
an exceptional enterprise/Stephen C. Harper
     p.cm
Includes index.
   ISBN 0-471-69719-2 (cloth)
   1. New business enterprises. 2. Entrepreneurship.
I. Title
   HD62.5.H37337 2005
   658.1'1—dc22

                         2004013487

Printed in the United States of America

10 9 8 7 6 5 4 3 2 1

CONTENTS

1	**Essential Entrepreneurial Qualities and Capabilities**	1

2   What Type of Venture Do You Have in Mind?   35

4   Ventures that Capitalized on Market Gaps   101

7   Components of the Business Plan   203

ABOUT THE AUTHOR

Stephen C. Harper is the Progress Energy/Betty Cameron Distinguished Professor of Entrepreneurship at the University of North Carolina at Wilmington. He is also president of his own management consulting firm, Harper and Associates Inc. Steve has worked with entrepreneurs and executives for more than 30 years. He was cofounder of the Coastal Entrepreneurial Council and served as director of UNCW's Small Business Institute for 17 years. He has received numerous teaching awards. He also received special recognition for outstanding service by the U.S. Small Business Administration. During his career he has been cofounder and president of three economic development organizations and has served on the board of directors or advisory committees for numerous corporations and nonprofit organizations. He has also been a featured speaker at conferences throughout the United States sponsored by *Inc.* magazine.

Steve is the author of numerous books, including the national best seller *The McGraw-Hill Guide to Starting Your Own Business* (McGraw-Hill, 2003), *The Forward-Focused Organization* (Amacom, 2002), *The McGraw-Hill Guide to Managing Growth in Your Emerging Business* (McGraw-Hill, 1994), and *Management: Who Ever Said It Would Be Easy?* (Harper and Associates, 1983). His articles have appeared in national and international magazines. Steve served on the faculty at Arizona State University where he earned his Ph. D. He has also been a visiting professor in the executive MBA program at the Fuqua School of Business at Duke University.

FOREWORD

Imagine spending 12 years of grueling 80+ hour weeks, five years of which were spent working for a startup, seven years spent starting three companies, creating a team of trusted mentors, managing two successful exit events, assembling a network of fellow entrepreneurs, building a cadre of venture capitalists, and raising three rounds of venture capital with the ultimate goal of leveraging all of that aggregate knowledge to build a very large business.

Then one day you realize that someone has ingeniously captured and collected literally hundreds of years of entrepreneurial experience into an easy to read book?!? By my calculations, if Dr. Harper had written this book in 1992 vs. 2005, not only could I have saved 12 years of my life, but this book would have saved me 50,000 hours of work!

SERIOUSLY THOUGH...

Here's a quick recap of my personal entrepreneurial adventures and some of the experiences I've enjoyed mapped to concepts you'll find conveniently summarized for you in this book so you can learn from the deep experiences of others.

In 1992, when I graduated from North Carolina State University's engineering program with a Master's degree, I knew that someday I wanted to start my own business. Not just a small business, a *big* business—a home run, like a Dell or a Microsoft. I think the reason I had set my sights high was that I was raised around entrepreneurship. My father, Dale Wingo, started a business out of our house selling retail carpeting back-office systems that he ultimately grew to be quite large and sold to DuPont's Fiber/Carpet group.

As you can guess, growing up with the dinner conversation centered around the latest exciting hardware, software languages, hitting revenue targets, hiring salespeople, and other entrepreneurial exploits, I had the bug pretty bad going into college. But these were the days when entrepreneurship wasn't as widespread or accepted as it is now.

After graduating, I found myself on the horns of a dilemma with two job offers:

1. One from Motorola where my whole life was planned out. Move to Austin, start as a junior engineer and then progress through the Motorola "career ladder" for 10–20 years.
2. A startup in CT called Bristol Technologies started by an engineer I had met in a summer job. At Bristol, I would be the first nonfamily employee and there was no clear career path.

After much soul searching I talked to one of my professors and he convinced me to go the startup route.

- The Introduction and Chapter 1 will allow you to do the soul searching you need to do before embarking on an entrepreneurial journey of your own.

STARTUP EXPERIENCE

After three years at Bristol, I had some great experiences in what to do and some in what not to do and was ready to strike out on my own.

- Again, as you'll see in the Introduction and Chapter 1, entrepreneurs don't tend to "do well" working for other folks and crave the thrill and independence of entrepreneurship. Think of Chapter 1 as a litmus test and ask yourself: "Is this me?"

Stingray Software

From 1995 to 1998, I cofounded our first company, Stingray Software with two of my friends from graduate school: Aris Buinevicius is one of the best developers I've ever met and Dean Hallman is a true technological visionary. We were literally profitable from the first days and thus didn't need venture funding.

When we started Stingray, we decided that I would run the business side (what engineers jokingly refer to as "the dark side") of things with Dean and Aris running the technology side. At Stingray we developed software development software for software developers. We quickly grew to 75 people and a $12 million run rate, but realized we had a problem. We had chosen a somewhat small opportunity—probably about $20 million–$30 million total revenue opportunity size. Based on that information we decided to sell the business, which we did in 1998.

- Chapters 2 through 5 will help you avoid this pitfall by focusing you on larger opportunities and giving you the tools to evaluate the business ideas you do come up with so you can select a "home run."

At Stingray one thing we did "right" was to create a business plan that we stuck to and it was more of a "living" document versus something we wrote just before starting the company and looked at three years later. The plan gave us fiscal discipline as well as general focus discipline so we wouldn't chase odd opportunities, which is a trap that catches many entrepreneurs.

- Chapters 6 and 7 are the best treatment I've seen on business plans.

AuctionRover.com

In 1999, caught up in the Internet boom, Aris and I started an online auction search engine company (think Google for auction sites) called AuctionRover.com. This was to be our "home run" and as with any second effort we felt we had solved all of the problems with the 1.0 effort. Primarily we knew we were onto a marketspace that was already big and would be getting a great deal bigger—fast. This was clearly a $100 million + opportunity and we intended to own it.

Sensing that we needed to grow fast versus slow to capture the opportunity we funded the business with a sizable out-of-pocket amount and immediately started looking for venture funding.

Fortunately we were able to get several term sheets, but they were full of terms and terminology that were like Greek to me. In fact, I searched for weeks for any books or other information on venture capital and found nothing. I ultimately had to resort to talking with a handful of entrepreneurs and lawyers I could find that had actually gone through the process and every one had a different experience than I would have. Ultimately we closed a $3 million round, but what a learning experience that was.

- You will find Chapters 8 through 12 extremely valuable if you ever seek funding of any kind—especially venture capital.

Within six months we had our second version of the site live and surprisingly while we had no revenues yet we started to receive acquisition offers. We said no to the first several offers because we fully intended to grow this second business, do an IPO, and build a substantial billion-dollar business.

Ultimately we felt the dot-com bubble burst coming because of the insane valuations being placed on anything and everything dot-com and knew there would be a shakeout at some point. Serendipitously in early 2000 an offer came in from GoTo.com (now called Overture—part of Yahoo!) and we decided the value was right, the timing was right, and it was best to go ahead and sell the company.

ChannelAdvisor Corporation

For 18 months we rode out the dot-com bubble burst (dot-bomb) as part of Overture. In July 2001, opportunity knocked and we were able to buy back some parts of AuctionRover we had sold as well as some new ideas we had been working on over those 18 months and we spun out of Overture as ChannelAdvisor.

At ChannelAdvisor we provide software and services that help companies of all sizes (from single-employee microbusinesses to Fortune 100 firms like IBM and Motorola) harness the power of online marketplaces like eBay, Amazon, Yahoo! Shopping, Shopping.com, etc.

As of 2004 we have raised two venture rounds (again see Chapters 8–12) and we have our sights squarely fixed on eventually taking the company public and building that billion-dollar business.

- See Chapter 13 for information on the IPO process.

There's a saying in the software world that it takes three versions to get all the kinks worked out of the system; we're hoping that's the case with ChannelAdvisor, but only time will tell.

We've been working on ChannelAdvisor for three years now and occasionally when I've had a rough day, I'll pick up this book and scan through the Epilogue, Entrepreneurial Dos and Don'ts, for inspiration.

- The epilogue is a great way to spend 20 minutes and get yourself reenergized if you need a little "pep talk."

Hopefully this tour through my personal entrepreneurial adventures compared with the content of this book illustrates just how important and groundbreaking I believe *Extraordinary Entrepreneurship* is.

Now save yourself 12 years of hard work—read this book cover to cover and then go start your own adventures!

Scot Wingo
President and CEO, ChannelAdvisor
Serial Entrepreneur
2004 Entrepreneur of the Year for the Carolinas

PREFACE

Much of our American program has been the product of an individual who
had an idea, pursued it, tenaciously clung to it against all odds,
and then produced it, sold it, and profited from it

—Hubert H. Humphrey

You have taken a significant step toward being a successful entrepreneur. By opening this book, you have demonstrated your commitment to improving the odds that you will be prepared for many of the challenges that will come in your entrepreneurial journey.

This book is designed to give you an edge in the entrepreneurial journey, whether you are (1) at the "twinkle in your eyes" stage where you hear yourself saying "Someday, I'd like to start my own business," (2) at the "I'm not going to wait for someday" stage, where you have pretty well decided you are going to start your own business, or (3) at the "Just do it" stage, where you are going full speed ahead with preparing your business plan.

GOOD NEWS! THIS IS THE ERA OF THE ENTREPRENEUR

This is a great time to start a new venture. The 1990s signaled the transformation from the "Bigger is better" *Fortune* 500 to the "Newer is better" *Inc.* 500. The twentieth century placed a premium on gaining economies of scale. Yet mass production required considerable money, equipment, and other tangible resources to serve mass markets.

Although most established firms spend their time trying to find someone—anyone—to buy a product they have already produced, start-ups are free to explore emerging markets. The twenty-first century brings incredible opportunities for people who can create ventures to capitalize on the almost infinite opportunities that will emerge. In the years ahead, success will be contingent on the ability to sense what the market wants and the ability to provide satisfaction.

The twenty-first century will reward businesses that place a premium on brain power, perceptiveness, innovation, agility, and building alliances. New ventures have an advantage over established ventures because they do not have *legacy* systems. They aren't physically locked into all the fixed costs that bloat their cost structures. They aren't locked in the mental boxes that keep them from challenging the status quo and developing innovative products and services.

We are in an era of great change. An old Chinese curse goes, "May you live in times of change." People who are not prepared for change will be the casualties of change. Yet times of great change are times of great opportunities. Perceptive and resourceful people who are prepared to seize the moment can be the initiators and beneficiaries of change.

The marketplace calls out for new ideas, new products, new services, and new approaches. New ventures no longer have to live off the table scraps left by big businesses.

New ventures no longer have to eke out a meager existence in market segments or in locations that big businesses choose to ignore. Today, market segments are emerging that didn't even appear on yesterday's radar screen. Today, breakthrough technological advances make things possible that no one even dreamed of a few years ago. Today, information, capital, and services are available to start-ups that were not even available to mid-sized firms a few years ago.

The twenty-first century brings all new rules—if there are rules anymore! A number of entrepreneurs are challenging conventional wisdom. They are also thinking *outside the box*. One of the first challenges involves challenging the assumption that a business has to be big to be successful. While most of the twentieth century heralded big businesses, it is clear that businesses no longer have to be big to do big business! Now it is possible for a handful of people to operate a global business from virtually any place on the planet. Today, the keyboard has overtaken the boardroom. Today, financial markets, alliances, and joint ventures have eliminated the need for entrepreneurs to put up substantial capital investments. Today, the world is driven by ideas, innovation, and execution. If *America* was the land of opportunity in the twentieth century, then the *world* will be the land of opportunity in the twenty-first century!

Entrepreneurs should not be intimidated by big businesses. Economist Lester Thurow noted that as we entered the twenty-first century, of the 25 biggest firms in America, all but six either didn't exist or were small in 1960. Intel and Microsoft did not exist.[1] Many of the businesses featured on the cover of this week's *Fortune, BusinessWeek,* and *Forbes* were started by one or two people who saw an opportunity a few years ago and then developed a business that capitalized on that opportunity. For every established *Fortune* 500 firm there are a number of start-ups that are making their presence known and changing the way the game is played in the marketplace. For every IBM, there is at least one Apple, Dell, and Gateway. For every United Airlines, there is at least one Southwest Airlines or JetBlue Airways. For every Sears, there is an eBay. For every Barnes and Noble, there is at least one Amazon.com. For every Merrill Lynch, there is at least one Schwab. For every Anheuser-Busch, there is at least one Samuel Adams.

It's a Whole New Ballgame

Entrepreneurship is an equal opportunity employer. Entrepreneurs come in all shapes and sizes. They also come in all ages, nationalities, and genders. There was a time when one's pedigree may have affected where you went to school, whether you would be considered for a job, and whether you could get a business loan or attract investors. Today, your network of professional contacts may be more important than the diploma on your wall. Today, the "good old boy" elitist system has been replaced by a system where people are judged by their ability to make exciting things happen. Today, the world is wide open to people who want to start ventures that will make a difference.

Your attitude may be as important in your entrepreneurial journey as your aptitude. This is evident in the number of people who are leaving established firms to start their own ventures. It is also evident in the masses of people who have not left yet, but spend countless hours at work and at home contemplating whether they, too, should embark on the entrepreneurial journey. The interest in entrepreneurship is heightened by (1) the complete lack of job security by what were once considered life-time employers, (2) the relentless movement toward downsizing and outsourcing that is gutting employment at all levels of firms, (3) the frustration that comes from working for firms that are no longer in sync with new-world realities or their employees' ideas, and (4) having to work for a firm that does not value your ideas.

Yet the interest in entrepreneurship is not just the result of the growing "dark side" of existing enterprises. It is also driven by the explosion of irresistible opportunities in the marketplace. The myriad opportunities in almost every facet of the economy and every segment of every market serve as magnets drawing people to them who cannot resist the opportunity to seize them.

Welcome to the New Age Entrepreneur!

Entrepreneurs used to be seen as mavericks or egomaniacs who couldn't keep a job. Yet, many of today's entrepreneurs are different from the robber barons who built industries at the beginning of the twentieth century. Many of today's emerging ventures are creating considerable wealth for their employees and investors. They are also providing value-added products, services, and jobs.

Self-serving *lone entrepreneurs* are being replaced by team-oriented *wealth builders*. Progressive entrepreneurs recognize that to attract, motivate, and keep talent, they need to offer them a piece of the action. From an investment perspective, a number of recent start-ups have generated unheard-of wealth for people who worked for them and invested in them as they began their ascent. For example, Dell Computer's stock growth would shame the world's fastest-splitting amoeba. Bill Gates noted that his primary reason for taking Microsoft public was to provide his employees with a fast and easy vehicle for converting their stock into cash.

A number of entrepreneurs are bringing a breath of fresh air to the marketplace and to the workplace. They are changing the way the game of business is being played. Entrepreneurs are not relegated to building smokestacks near raw materials, nor do they have to be confined to congested urban areas. Many new ventures have considerable latitude as to where they can be located.

The rules of the game extend far beyond broadening location parameters. New Age entrepreneurs are rewriting the rulebook. In some cases, they are throwing out the rulebook for how businesses should be run. They are becoming the benchmarks for creating environments where people work hard and play hard.

New Age entrepreneurs recognize that firms succeed to the extent they are hospitable to the whole individual. They recognize that doing world-class work and having fun are not incompatible concepts. They recognize that commitment to one's work doesn't have to mean abandoning one's family. They recognize telecommuting, job sharing, flextime, and flexible fringe benefits may help attract talent. They recognize that casual, comfortable clothes may foster innovation. They recognize that calling people by their first names may foster an openness not found in the traditional starched-shirt environment. They recognize that a "first-come, first-parks" culture may be a more welcome environment than parking that is reserved for those whose position far exceeds his/her contribution to the firm in the past year.

They also recognize that businesses run on ideas and commitment, not bloodlines and college pedigree. Most importantly, these entrepreneurs recognize that bigger isn't always better. They recognize that *better*—whether it is in higher quality, quicker service, or more innovation—is better!

THERE ARE DEAL MAKERS AND THEN THERE ARE COMPANY BUILDERS

This might be a good time to note that this book is written primarily for people who want to build exceptional ventures rather than make a quick buck by creating a venture with the sole intent of selling it within two to three years. There are two types of entrepreneurs: deal makers and company builders. The "get in quick, make a deal, and cash out quick" strategy has its merits, but it is much more difficult to do today than a few years ago when the market succumbed to greed, temporary insanity, and "irrational exuberance."

During the late 1990s, funding for new ventures left prudence by the wayside. Venture capital firms threw money at almost any business that used the Internet or promised to bring some new technology to the marketplace. Some entrepreneurs were able to take their firms public before they were even profitable. Some ventures went public without sales or even products. There is even a story that three young Israeli entrepreneurs took themselves public so they would have the funds to develop product and service concepts that might generate profits some time in the future. In a sense, the young Israelis set a whole new standard—they were "taking their brains public"!

The time has passed when a raw idea developed by a totally naïve 20-year-old would be courted by a pack of venture capital firms. The days of irrational exuberance are gone, and hopefully they will not return. All of us will be better off if new ventures make money the old-fashioned way—by earning it.

The path for building an exceptional enterprise is different from the path for doing the deal. Building an exceptional enterprise requires making a commitment to the long-term. Building an exceptional enterprise means making a commitment to establishing systems and to building relationships. It does not involve cutting corners with your suppliers, customers, distributors, or employees.

Building an exceptional enterprise means making a commitment to finding markets that will last, hiring good people and giving them a chance to make a difference, and treating your suppliers and distributors as valued partners rather than as adversaries. It also means developing relationships with your customers that generate ideas for sustained growth. It means investing in tomorrow rather than doing financial smoke-and-mirror tricks that hype your financial statements to give the impression your business is worth far more than it is really worth.

If you are thinking about starting your own venture, then steer clear of the "get rich quick" schemes. Stay away from those who suggest financial sleights of hand. Resist the temptation to be an overnight sensation. If venture capitalists and investment bankers tempt you with the potential for incredible wealth in just a few years, make sure you do your own due diligence to ensure they are doing what is best for you and your venture. Although venture capitalists and investment bankers may play a valuable role in the evolution of high-growth ventures, remember that they see ventures as things in their portfolio that need to be harvested.

This book profiles the process for building an exceptional enterprise—not a "here today, gone tomorrow" blip on the radar screen. This book is about creating and building an exceptional business rather than cashing out! If you build a successful venture, suitors will come. Exceptional ventures attract investor interest and command top dollar. You won't need to put up an "enviable venture for sale" sign. Ironically, if you get to that point, you may envision putting up a "successful venture at work—do not disturb" sign.

The Party Isn't Over—It Has Just Begun!

Do not confuse the death of dot-com hype with the death of entrepreneurship. Most of the dot-coms that failed did so because their entrepreneurs did not know how to guide their firms through the rapids associated with a start-up, or their ventures were not built on a viable business model. Too many dot-coms were started by people who wanted to get rich quick rather than build a profitable and enduring venture. Too many were based on technology that did not have a market, or a half-baked Internet idea that tried to live off advertising revenue or venture capital rather than making money the old-fashioned way by offering products or services to people who are not having their needs met in an efficient, timely, or convenient manner.

When Bill Gates was asked a few years ago if he thought it was possible for today's start-ups to match Microsoft's success, he noted that opportunities like Amgen, Sun Microsystems, and MCI are still out there. He made another observation that may be more in line with people who are reading this book who don't have stratospheric aspirations. He noted, "You can hit the home run. But somebody can be quite wealthy creating a $20-million-a-year company."[2] While this book highlights a number of firms that have hit grand slams like Microsoft, Dell, and Federal Express, particular attention is directed at creating the $1 million to $20 million ventures that generate enough wealth and satisfaction to make all the time, anxiety, and money you will invest in building your venture to be worthwhile.

ENTREPRENEURSHIP IS ABOUT THE OPPORTUNITY TO DO SOMETHING SPECIAL

Entrepreneurship doesn't have to be just about the pursuit of wealth. The entrepreneurial journey can provide a never-ending set of challenges. It can also provide a great sense of personal satisfaction. New ventures can provide the marketplace with valuable products and services. They can also provide employment opportunities for people who want to be part of something they can be proud of.

Sometimes, the entrepreneurial journey can bring success that surpasses the entrepreneur's wildest expectations. For example, when Peter Karmanos and two others started Compuware in Detroit in 1973, their vision was not very lofty. When Karmanos reflected on his firm's astronomical growth and success, he stated that when they started Compuware, they were thinking, "If we could get up to 25 people, we could make a nice living." By 1999, the firm that was started with a personal tax refund had become the world's fifth largest independent software company. By 2003, the firm that started in a 600-square-foot office employed more than 15,000 people.

The excitement that can be found in the entrepreneurial journey is captured in the response Peter Karmanos made when he was asked why he didn't just retire when he reached the point when he had accumulated what he called "more wealth than he could possibly spend in his lifetime." Karmanos indicated that the challenges and rewards of entrepreneurship can be seen by watching a person playing a pinball game. He noted that when you get all the lights lit and the ball is hitting in all the right places, you start hearing the "pop, pop, pop" sound that indicates you are winning free games.

Karmanos observed that you will never see a pinball player walk away from the game when it is "popping." Ironically, he noted that when that game is finally over, the pinball player may not stay around to play all the free games he or she has won![3] For some entrepreneurs, *accumulating wealth* makes the popping sound. For others like Karmanos, the challenges of *creating an exceptional enterprise* and *providing what the market values* provide them with that wonderful popping sound!

Let the Adventure Begin!

This book profiles the entrepreneurial process of identifying business opportunities, evaluating potential business ventures, and developing a game plan for creating a venture from scratch. It identifies various qualities and capabilities that entrepreneurs need to have to increase the odds for success. It also highlights various challenges associated with starting a new venture. Before you begin the journey, however, you should step back and see if the entrepreneurial journey is really right for you. Being an entrepreneur has a lot of appeal, but it is not for everyone. The following "reader beware" caveats will give you a better idea if this book is for you.

READER BEWARE

This book isn't for people who want to start the typical "small" business. If you want to start a neighborhood bookstore, a one- or two-person bookkeeping business, or a frozen yogurt shop, then you should buy one of the books that helps people start a "small" business.[4] This book is for people who want to start a business that can grow and prosper ... a business that can generate wealth for the founder(s) ... a business that doesn't fear larger businesses ... a business that is an exceptional enterprise!

READER BEWARE

This book is for people who want to do more than start a business that is a copycat clone of a business that already exists down the street. Peter Drucker once observed that while a large number of people start businesses, few of them are true entrepreneurs. He noted that entrepreneurs bring something *new* to the marketplace that is valued; the rest of the people who start businesses are merely cloning something that already exists. This book is for people who want to create a business that stands out from the crowd ... a business that has significant competitive advantages ... a business that attracts customers because it is in tune with what the marketplace values ... a business that offers goods and/or services that fit the needs, wants, and desires of the new venture's target market.

READER BEWARE

This is not a textbook. It has been written to tell it like it is. It provides prospective entrepreneurs what they need to know. It doesn't waste time by providing table after table of government statistics. Nor does it not contain academic models or far-fetched ideas. It will not waste your time with various definitions of what is and is not a small business. If you are truly interested in starting a venture, then you aren't concerned with definitions and abstract models—you want guidelines, insights, and ideas!

READER BEWARE

This book does not devote countless pages to the principles of management or the need for business ethics. If you want to learn about *managing an existing business*, then take a management course or read a book about managing a business. This book is about the process of *starting an exceptional enterprise*. If you want to learn more about business ethics, then enroll in a class on business ethics. While ethical principles are crucial for establishing relationships and continued business success, this book doesn't devote a chapter to the ethical principles of entrepreneurship.

READER BEWARE

This book is designed for professionals who want to leave their current jobs to start a successful venture. It is written for people who have a professional background and who already understand the basic principles of marketing, accounting, finance, and management. This book is not designed to teach you about accounting, marketing, or finance. Instead, its pages are devoted to *applying* accounting, finance, and marketing principles and practices to the entrepreneurial process.

READER BEWARE

This book is not intended to be snobbish. It is not targeted to an elite group of people who want to be entrepreneurs. Instead, it is targeted to people who have benefited from being part of professionally run organizations where decisions are usually made after thorough analysis and where systems are in place to keep things from falling through the cracks.

READER BEWARE

This book is not written for the person who has limited business education and experience. People with limited business education should take classes on those subjects. Then, they should get a job with a well-managed firm so they can see professional systems at work *before* embarking on the entrepreneurial journey. Professionally managed firms tend to do things right the first time and continuously improve their product/serve offerings and operations so they are in tune with the marketplace. If you can identify an emerging opportunity and create a venture that can capitalize on that opportunity in an exceptional way by using professional systems, then you have a chance to be a very successful firm.

READER BEWARE

This book is tailored to fit the needs of two types of professionals. The first group is composed of people who are contemplating leaving good jobs with good companies to start their own ventures. The second group is composed of people who see opportunities that are not being tapped and who believe they can serve the marketplace better than existing firms. It is not designed for people who are looking for an easy way to make money or who think they can succeed by making the world adjust to what they want it to do.

Both of these target groups have something in common. They experience *entrepreneurial anxiety* on a daily basis. People in the first group have a lingering anxiety that comes with wanting to be one's own boss. The second group has a different type of anxiety. They live with the fear that someone else will capitalize on their targeted opportunity first. While the first group may be hesitant to take the plunge, the second group goes to work each day fearing the "window of opportunity" will close while they watch from the sidelines! These types of entrepreneurial anxieties are discussed in greater depth in the Introduction and Chapter 1.

If you are in the first group, then this book will help you analyze whether you have what it takes to start a venture. It will also help you learn more about the entrepreneurial process. If you are in the second group, then this book will help you analyze the opportunity that has captured your attention to see if you should drop everything to seize the moment.

CONCLUSION:
PREPARE YOURSELF FOR PERIODIC REALITY CHECKS

Entrepreneurs love to shake things up by not playing by the rules or by changing the rules! This book has adopted some of the unconventional approaches exhibited by entrepreneurs. Each chapter contains a number of *reality checks*. Entrepreneurs tend to be overly optimistic and look at the world through rose-colored glasses. While love may be blind, entrepreneurship calls for brutal honesty. More than 100 reality checks are provided throughout the book. The Epilogue also lists more than 600 entrepreneurial "dos and "don'ts.

This book's reality checks simply tell it like it is. If you want to gain insights into the entrepreneurial process, then have a magic marker ready to highlight the reality checks.

REALITY CHECK

Here is your first reality check. Proceed with caution as you read this book. No book on entrepreneurship can guarantee that your venture will be successful. There are too many uncertainties and too many prerequisites for success for it to be assured. This book directs your attention to doing the things that must be addressed to increase the odds of success. Your job in preparing for the entrepreneurial journey involves making sure (1) you are prepared for its challenges, (2) you are pursuing a viable and lucrative business opportunity, (3) you prepare a realistic plan for capitalizing on that opportunity, and (4) you garner the appropriate skills, capabilities, and resources so that your dream of having your own business becomes a profitable reality. If you believe this book is for you, then let the entrepreneurial journey begin! Customers today are more open than ever to new ideas.

It's an incredible time to start a new business or introduce a new product because people are eager to try new things.[5]

—Howard Schultz, CEO of Starbucks

END NOTES

1. Mortimer B. Zuckerman, "Creators of Prosperity" *U.S. News and World Report*, June 8, 1998, p. 64.

2. "How Can Somebody Not Be So Optimistic? *BusinessWeek*, "Reinventing America" special edition, 1992, p. 184.

3. Presentation at the *Annual Entrepreneurship Conference*, Duke University, February 6, 1999.

4. People who have limited business experience and education should read *The McGraw-Hill Guide to Starting Your Own Business* (McGraw-Hill, 2003). I wrote that bestseller for people who are interested in starting a small business.

5. Scott Smith, "Grounds for Success" *Entrepreneur*, May 1998 p. 124. Reprinted with permission of Entrepreneur Media, Inc.

ACKNOWLEDGMENTS

Inspired by true stories of countless entrepreneurs.

I want to thank all the entrepreneurs who have made this a great country. I especially want to thank the entrepreneurs I have known who have provided me with insights into the challenges in making their dreams a reality. People like serial entrepreneur Scot Wingo, CEO of ChannelAdvisor, who wrote the Foreword to this book, have been an inspiration to me and others who have contemplated "boldly going where no person has gone before."

This book was partly the result of a faculty reassignment grant provided by the Cameron School of Business at the University of North Carolina at Wilmington. The grant made it possible for me to devote a complete semester to providing the foundation for this book.

Numerous people provided valuable assistance in the development of this book. Four graduate students were particularly helpful. Eason Bryant, Donald Peterson, Lisa Eakins, and Brad Whitford helped in the analysis of interviews of more than 200 entrepreneurs. The interviews became the basis for the Epilogue, Entrepreneurial Dos and Don'ts. The entrepreneurial tips were the result of interviews conducted by my students in the last few years. They included the weekend executive MBA students in my classes while I was a visiting professor at Duke University as well as the MBA and undergraduate students enrolled in my entrepreneurship classes at the University of North Carolina at Wilmington. I truly appreciate the time and effort they put into the interviews. The Epilogue reflects only a fraction of their work and contribution. I also want to thank Janice Thomas for assisting in the proofreading of the prototype edition.

I also want to thank the Harvard Business School, *Inc.* magazine, *Business Leader,* and *Entrepreneur* magazine for granting permission to use material from their articles and/or books. I am particularly appreciative of the permission granted by Amar Bhidé (Columbia University), author of *The Origin and Evolution of New Businesses,* and its publisher Oxford University Press, Inc., Rob Ryan, author of *Smartups: Lessons from Rob Ryan's Entrepreneur America Boot Camp for Start-Ups,* and its publisher Cornell University Press, as well as John Wiley & Sons for granting permission to use material from *Angel Investing* (Copyright © 2000, Jossey-Bass) by Mark Van Osnabrugge and Robert J. Robinson.

My wife, Marshall, deserves a special thank you for putting up with me while I worked on this book and for being supportive of my career over the years. I would also like to thank Larry Clark, who as dean of the Cameron School of Business has been a champion for my career. Last, but not least, I would also like to thank Dan and Betty Cameron, as well as Bruce and Louise Cameron, for their support of the University of North Carolina at Wilmington. Their never-ending financial generosity and ongoing guidance have helped make it possible for me and other members of the faculty to grow professionally and enjoy our relationship with the university.

INTRODUCTION:

THE NATURE OF ENTREPRENEURSHIP

It is easy to find fault with a new idea.
It is easier to say it can't be done, than to try.
Thus, it is through the fear of failure,
That some men create their own hell.

—E. Jacob Taylor

It wasn't that long ago that entrepreneurs were considered to be mavericks, rebels, or even social deviants. They stood out because Corporate America was built on a foundation of loyalty and conformity. Big was better and economies of scale provided formidable barriers to entry. The last two decades, however, have placed a number of entrepreneurs in the limelight who have marched to the tune of a different drummer.

Today's entrepreneurs have been heralded for having the same qualities exhibited by this country's first colonists. The colonists had contempt for the way things were done, and they weren't afraid to break away from the establishment. The entrepreneurs who are heralded by the media created their own firms so they could be free to pursue new opportunities and try new approaches. They showed that bigger isn't always better and that the legacy systems and bureaucratic practices of most established firms can be like anvils that keep them from keeping pace with changes in the marketplace. Each day, entrepreneurs create agile new ventures that change the way the game is played.

America is known as the "Land of the free and the home of the brave." This country encourages individuality and self-determination. It also encourages people to "go for it." Entrepreneurship has become an integral part of this country's culture and economic system because it reflects the courage to break away from the pack and the desire to be the master of one's own destiny. Three statistics capture the entrepreneurial spirit in this country. First, 6.8 million households (7.2 percent of the country's total) include someone who is trying to start a business. Second, between 700,000 and 1 million new businesses are created each year. Third, at least 90 percent of the richest people in the United States generated their wealth through entrepreneurial endeavors.[1]

Few of this nation's most prominent entrepreneurs could have imagined in their wildest dreams they would become celebrities when they started their ventures, they would create so much wealth, or their firms would become household words. Exhibit I.1 illustrates the ability for entrepreneurs who have the ability to seize opportunities to generate substantial wealth. Each of the entrepreneurs has accumulated a net worth of at least $1 billion.[2]

Entrepreneur	Company	Wealth
Bill Gates	Microsoft	$46,000,000,000
Paul Allen	Microsoft	22,000,000,000
Larry Ellison	Oracle	18,000,000,000
Michael Dell	Dell Computer	13,000,000,000
Pierre Omidyar	eBay	6,900,000,000
Phillip Knight	Nike	5,800,000,000
Jeffrey Bezos	Amazon.com	5,100,000,000
Charles Schwab	Charles Schwab	3,200,000,000
Steven Jobs	Apple Computer	2,300,000,000
Bernard Marcus	The Home Depot	2,000,000,000
David Filo	Yahoo!	1,600,000,000
Jerry Yang	Yahoo!	1,400,000,000
Arthur Blank	The Home Depot	1,100,000,000

The list does not include the wealth that the late Sam Walton created with Wal-Mart. The total net worth of five members of his family is over $100,000,000,000.

EXHIBIT I.1   ENTREPRENEURIAL WEALTH IN THE UNITED STATES
Source: "The 400 Richest People in America", *Forbes*, October 6, 2003.

Obviously, the people on the list are not a representative sample of all the people who start ventures. They represent a fraction of 1 percent of all the entrepreneurs who have started ventures in the last few decades. Some of these entrepreneurs will go on to create additional ventures, some of them will lead their firms into the future, some of them will lose some of the wealth they have generated if the world changes and their firms don't, and some of them will be challenged by the next wave of entrepreneurs who consider the firms on the list to be "the establishment."

WHAT ARE THE CHARACTERISTICS OF SUCCESSFUL ENTREPRENEURS?

As more and more entrepreneurs are placed in the limelight, people try to find a common thread that sets entrepreneurs apart from the masses. One of the most interesting features about entrepreneurs is that they defy simple categorization or stereotyping. Some entrepreneurs create ventures for fame and fortune. Some embark on the entrepreneurial journey because they want to be their own boss. Some take the plunge because they see an irresistible opportunity.

Some entrepreneurs crafted their ventures with very deliberate plans. Others were tinkerers who weren't sure where the entrepreneurial journey would take them. Others were opportunistic and others were driven by the desire to make the world a better place. If you were to put together a formula for how to be a successful entrepreneur based on how some of the most noteworthy entrepreneurs got started, then it would have the following ingredients:

- Start in a garage: Steven Jobs and Steven Wozniak (Apple) and William Hewlett and David Packard (Hewlett-Packard)

- Drop out of college: Bill Gates (Microsoft), Michael Dell (Dell Computer), and Larry Ellison (Oracle)

- Get a marginal grade on your business plan while in college: Fred Smith (FedEx)

- Be irreverent: Richard Branson (Virgin Atlantic Airways, etc.)

- Have parents who can invest in your business: Jeff Bezos (Amazon.com)

- Notice that the world does not operate with banker's hours: Ted Turner (CNN)

- Get turned down for a funding more than 100 times: Howard Schultz (Starbucks)

- Have a mentor who is a successful entrepreneur: Tom Siebel (Siebel Systems) who worked in sales for Larry Ellison (Oracle)

Some people have even attributed some entrepreneurs' drive to start their own ventures to dyslexia. This condition may explain why entrepreneurs had trouble in school (did not fit in and thus had contempt for authority figures). It may also explain why they saw things differently from "normal" people.

REALITY CHECK

Wouldn't it be nice if all you had to do to start a successful venture was to drop out of college, walk out to your family's garage, have parents provide funding, and have minimal business experience? These factors do not assure success. These people succeeded in spite of their modest beginnings, not because of them.

ENTREPRENEURSHIP IS NOT FOR THE FAINT OF HEART

If entrepreneurship was a product, then the federal government would probably insist that it have the following warning label:

Entrepreneurship is not glamorous nor is it easy. There is no guaranteed formula for success. Few things will work as planned and venture capitalists will not be lined up to give you money. If you are successful initially, then competitors will try to steal your customers and they will not play by the rules. If you build it, customers may not come. If you do have customers, they'll probably never be satisfied and they sure won't be grateful. You may have to give your product away. Debbie Fields walked down the street giving her cookies away. You may have to almost pay prospects to become customers. The founders of Home Depot had employees give dollar bills away in the parking lot near their first store to get people to come in. Your employees and customers may become your competitors. You will have to accept terms or conditions from suppliers, distributors, and/or customers that are humiliating—and seem almost illegal. You may have to get a second mortgage on your home, personally co-sign every document, apply for a dozen credit cards to get the funds you need, and lie/withhold/fail to disclose to your spouse your level of financial commitment to the business. You will have to make promises that you're not sure you can keep and put a spin on your business's future to get people to quit their jobs and put their marriages, mortgages, and MasterCard balance in jeopardy to join your venture. You will become a stranger to your family and friends. You will lose sleep and become edgy because you will worry about things you never thought about when you worked for someone else. You will have to deal with wave after wave of rejections. You will be asked if you are kidding and your intelligence and sanity will be questioned by almost everyone you know.

You've got to be a little nuts to be an entrepreneur. The odds are stacked against you. For every successful entrepreneur, there are a handful of entrepreneurs who fail, throw in the towel by selling their ventures to someone who is as optimistic as they once were, or just shut their ventures down to pursue something else that will not require as much blood, sweat, and tears.

Entrepreneurship is like taking a never-ending roller-coaster ride in the dark. The journey will test your stomach with numerous ups and downs. It will test your stamina with unexpected twists and turns. There will be times when you feel like you are on top of the world and times when you feel like you have absolutely no control over your destiny.

MAPPING THE ENTREPRENEURIAL JOURNEY

If the preceding observations haven't killed your desire to embark on the entrepreneurial journey, then read on and learn how to improve the odds. This book is not intended to encourage or discourage you from taking the entrepreneurial journey. At times, it is intended to be a mirror. It provides you with the opportunity to take a look at yourself and what is involved in the entrepreneurial journey. The first part of the book addresses the challenges you will face, as well as the qualities and skills you will need for the journey. If you are satisfied you have what it takes to make the journey, then the rest of the book helps you map the journey.

This book highlights various facets of the entrepreneurial process. Each chapter provides guidelines and examples that should increase your odds for creating an exceptional enterprise. Each chapter also provides a number of valuable reality checks. This book captures in the following steps in the new-venture creation process.

THE NEW-VENTURE CREATION PROCESS

Step 1. Analysis of entrepreneurial preparedness (Introduction, Chapters 1 and 2)

Step 2. Market analysis (Chapters 2, 3, and 4)

Step 3. Identification of new venture opportunities (Chapters 2, 3, and 4)

Step 4. Evaluation of new venture opportunities (Chapter 5)

Step 5. Investigation of capability and resource requirements (Chapters 5, 6, and 7)

Step 6. Running the numbers (Chapters 5, 6, and 7)

Step 7. Analyzing risks, returns, and personal preferences (Chapter 5)

Step 8. Ranking potential ventures (Chapter 5)

Step 9. Selecting the opportunity to pursue (Chapter 5)

Step 10. Conducting the feasibility study and test market (Chapter 5)

Step 11. Developing the business plan (Chapters 6 and 7)

Step 12. Acquiring the resources (Chapters 8 through 13)

Step 13. Starting the venture (Epilogue)

Step 14. Managing the venture (Epilogue)

INCORPORATING THE ENTREPRENEURIAL TRIANGLE

Entrepreneurial success is contingent on the three major dimensions in the *entrepreneurial Triangle* profiled in Exhibit I.2. First, the entrepreneur must have the skills and capabilities to start and manage the new venture. Second, a gap in the market must exist that can be transformed into a new venture opportunity. Third, a sufficient amount of resources must be available to create the venture and to keep it running until it generates its own momentum. The importance and interrelatedness of the dimensions is reflected in the entrepreneurial triangle.

New venture success is contingent on having a sufficient level of strength in each area. It is also contingent on the *goodness of fit* for all three dimensions. The concept of having *critical mass* in physics applies to entrepreneurship. For the venture to have a successful launch, each dimension must exceed some minimum initial threshold for that dimension. The establishment of thresholds for each of the dimensions when evaluating possible venture opportunities is discussed in greater detail in Chapter 5. The thresholds can be plotted for each dimension in Exhibit I.2. The scale can then be used to depict whether all three of the prerequisite conditions exist for the venture under consideration.

The entrepreneurial triangle uses three tests to screen proposed ventures. The first test is the mirror test. It forces you to step back and see if you have what it takes from a skills and capabilities perspective. The second test is the market test. It asks whether the market opportunity being considered will be lasting and lucrative. The third test is the wallet test. It asks whether the venture has sufficient profit potential to justify the time and investment.

A few years ago, I was invited by the Louisville Chamber of Commerce to make a presentation on the challenges of entrepreneurship. In an effort to tailor my remarks to the audience, I put the image of a horse and a jockey on the screen. The audience was asked to identify similarities between the graphic art and entrepreneurship.

The audience quickly identified the jockey as the entrepreneur and the horse as the market opportunity. They had trouble seeing the *resource* dimension in the graphic art. I indicated that the resources were the support staff the horse needed before it entered the race. The jockey, horse, and support staff play integral roles in the horse race. If any factor is insufficient, then an unfavorable outcome is inevitable. For example, if the jockey lacks the proper skills, isn't familiar with the unique features of the track at the time of the race, and hasn't studied the competition for that day, then there is little chance for success. If the horse is not big enough to carry the jockey or strong enough to go the distance, then failure

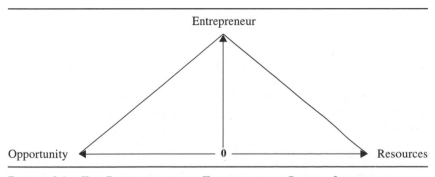

EXHIBIT I.2 The Entrepreneurial Triangle with Rating Scales

is inevitable. If the support staff doesn't do its job before the race in making sure everything is there when it is needed, then the odds for success are diminished. The same situation applies to the three dimensions of the entrepreneurial triangle. Each dimension plays a critical role in the success of the new venture.

WHICH DIMENSION IS THE MOST IMPORTANT?

The question is frequently raised about which factor in the entrepreneurial triangle is the most important. The easiest way to answer the question is to say, "They're equally important." When I asked the question in Louisville, the audience was almost equally divided between the jockey and the horse. Some thought the entrepreneur was the most important. Others thought the market opportunity was more important. Although few people considered the support staff to be the most important in the horse race situation, a few people indicated that resources might be the most important to the success of a new venture.

Each dimension of the triangle is important. The absence of any dimension violates the fundamental law of triangles; triangles have to have three sides! It doesn't matter how long two of the lines may be. Without the third line, there is no triangle. Yet the entrepreneurial triangle requires more than three lines. All three lines must be long enough to keep the triangle from having some bizarre shape.

The horse race illustrates the need for the three dimensions to fit together. First, imagine what would happen if the jockey didn't have the knowledge, talent, and strength needed to lead the horse out of the gate and to have it run at the right pace down the track. Without a skilled jockey, the horse might not even leave the gate. And if it does, it might run wild like a ball careening back and forth in a pinball game. When the horse crosses the finish line, it will probably be disqualified for violating race protocol. Second, if the horse (market opportunity) is not big enough to support the jockey (entrepreneur's personal aspirations and financial goals), then the jockey should not even suit up. Third, if the horse isn't fit enough (resources) to go the distance, then the horse and the jockey should stay home.

If you had to identify one dimension as being the most important, you might choose the need for a lucrative and lasting market opportunity. Joseph Mancuso has developed an interesting way of telling whether an individual really grasps what it takes to make a new venture work. He asks people which of four factors is both necessary and sufficient for starting a business. The factors are (1) money, (2) hard work, (3) an idea or product, or (4) customers.[3]

He found that people who work in businesses generally indicate one of the first three factors to be the most necessary. He found that veteran entrepreneurs, however, frequently cite customers as the most necessary. He observed, "An entrepreneur understands that while no business can get off the ground without money, a product, and a lot of hard work, customers are what will make or break the venture. If you've got customers, you will find the money, work the long hours, and make the business happen. Without them, you don't have a business."[4] Someone once observed: "Until you sell your product ... you are unemployed or doing a hobby!" Businesses imply sales—and hopefully profits.

Jon Vincent, president of JTV Enterprises, shares Mancuso's conclusions. He observed, "Have you ever seen a jockey carry a horse across the finish line?" If you are going to start a business, then make sure there is a substantial opportunity. If the opportunity is great, then the marketplace may give the entrepreneur a little slack in the start-up stage when a few things fall through the cracks. If the opportunity is great and the entrepreneur has sufficient skills and capabilities to capitalize on it, then the venture should be able to attract the necessary resources. If the opportunity is weak, then even a talented entrepreneur with a truckload of resources will probably see the venture whither and die.

Steven Jobs noted when he started NeXT Computer that if you are going to start a venture, then start one where there is a great opportunity. He noted that it takes almost the same amount of work to start a large business as it does to start a small one, so you might as well start one that can grow!

ENTREPRENEURS ARE LIKE EXPLORERS

This book stresses the need to boldly go where no one has gone before and to approach the entrepreneurial process in a professional and systematic manner. Entrepreneurship can be broken down into the following components in Latin:[5]

> *entre* means enter   *pre* means before   *neur* means nerve center

Entrepreneurs who want to create exceptional enterprises need to have the courage to enter new markets, to seize opportunities before other firms even see them, and to use the tools and techniques that are available for beating the odds. Tom Chappell, cofounder of Tom's of Maine, captured the essence of this book when he stated, "Entrepreneurship by definition is creating something new, discovering markets that no one thought were there, markets that will not be counted until the entrepreneur announces they are there."[6]

Starting a new venture is like crossing a minefield. The entrepreneurial journey is full of mines that can blow up in your face. First-time entrepreneurs should make every effort to learn from those who have beaten the odds. Most successful entrepreneurs attribute some of their success to what they learned from other successful entrepreneurs before they started their journey. Often, successful entrepreneurs can provide tips that prevent potential problems or reduce their consequences.

George Gendron, a successful entrepreneur and former editor for *Inc.* magazine, noted that research conducted on 27 start-ups profiled in *Inc.* magazine over the years lead to the following conclusions about successful ventures:[7]

1. The founder was ready, willing, and able to learn on the job during the start-up process.

2. The founder devoted an unusually large amount of time and effort to working with established suppliers and subcontractors.

3. The founder paid close attention to new entrants and potential competitors.

4. The founder positioned the venture right from the beginning so that he or she didn't have to spend a lot of time later on determining the business's identity.

5. The founder made sure he or she already had access to whatever capital is needed so he or she didn't have to spend a lot of time raising money.

6. The venture offered customized products or services that were designed or produced to order.

7. The founder chose a growth industry.

ENTREPRENEURS NEED TO IDENTIFY GAPS IN THE TRIANGLE

Drawing the entrepreneurial triangle for a proposed venture highlights two important issues. First, it shows the strength of each dimension. Second, it can be used to indicate whether each dimension has critical mass. Tedann Olsen, a marketing manager with SnowSports Industries America, noted, "The key is not only to have a good idea but to be in the market with the right resources at the right time."[8]

The entrepreneurial triangle is not expected to be an *equilateral triangle*, for two reasons. First, the base has two dimensions. Second, certain entrepreneurial situations require more resources than others. Starting a service enterprise may take far less capital than a manufacturing firm. Starting a software company may take far more technical experience in the field than starting a retail venture. Each entrepreneurial situation is unique. Mapping the entrepreneurial triangle for each situation enables the entrepreneur to analyze its uniqueness. It also helps the entrepreneur identify whether a gap may exist for each of the three dimensions.

The triangle may indicate that an *entrepreneurial gap* exists. Chapter 1 profiles various skills and capabilities entrepreneurs should have before starting a venture. The triangle may also indicate an *opportunity gap* or a *resource gap* exists. Chapter 5 provides numerous guidelines for evaluating market opportunities and resource requirements. Chapters 6 and 7 indicate how all three dimensions are addressed in the business plan. The remainder of this Introduction focuses on challenges entrepreneurs face in starting a venture and the need for the entrepreneur to start a venture that fits his or her needs, interests, and capabilities.

ENTREPRENEURSHIP INVOLVES VARIOUS TYPES OF PERSONAL CHALLENGES AND RISKS

Risk and entrepreneurship go hand-in-hand. Profit is defined as the reward for successfully taking business risk. The risk is compounded when you start a venture because there is little assurance that the venture will be able to attract enough customers to make a profit.

Two particular views about the propensity to change capture the nature of risk. Chris Argyris developed the first view. He differentiated the type of risk by placing risk into two categories: Anxiety I and Anxiety II. Entrepreneurship frequently elicits various anxieties. Anxiety I is the most common type of anxiety. It is the anxiety associated with the risks of doing something new. Anxiety I involves the risks associated with quitting your job, investing your own money in your venture, and having to make decisions you have never made before. Anxiety I arises from the risks that you may make a mistake and what you have to lose if you are wrong. One's perceptions of these risks may be a formidable barrier to embarking on the entrepreneurial journey.

Kurt Lewin's view about change and risk is reflected in his *force-field model.*[9] As a psychotherapist, he helped people change their behavior. His force-field model profiled in Exhibit I.3 (which modifies Lewin's model to incorporate forces that may affect entrepreneurship) views behavior as something that is in a state of dynamic equilibrium. The equilibrium exists when there are countervailing forces at play. According to Kurt Lewin, people tend to change when the forces supporting that change are stronger than the forces restraining the change.

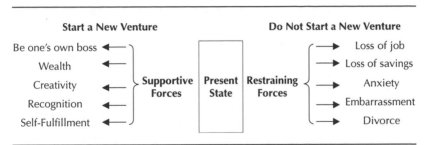

EXHIBIT I.3   LEWIN FORCE-FIELD MODEL

Anyone considering the entrepreneurial journey should have anxiety about the risks and unknowns. People who see more risks than rewards are not likely to embark on the journey. If they see the risk to be too great to commit the cash value of their life insurance to the venture and make the other associated commitments that need to be made, then they will not proceed. Conversely, if they see the rewards to be greater than the potential losses, the person may move ahead with the venture.

REALITY CHECK

It should be noted at this time that risks and rewards are always in the eye of the beholder. One person may consider quitting his or her job to be very risky. Another person may not consider that to be a restraining force because he or she was going to quit anyway or believes it would not take much time to find another job if the venture doesn't work out.

The *force-field model* views the decision to start a venture like a scale used for measuring two objects. When people are asked what holds them back from taking the entrepreneurial journey, they usually can provide a list of reasons. A thirty-something marketing vice-president provides a good example of Anxiety I. She had been thinking about starting a custom tile business *someday* for a number of years. When she was asked what was holding her back, she identified about 20 different reasons why she could not start her dream business. Her list of restraining forces included losing the steady income and the associated fringe benefits, uncertainty about making mortgage payments on her house, having young kids, and a number of other logical and socially acceptable reasons. When each restraining force was subjected to closer scrutiny, however, it turned out that the risks associated with each one could be addressed in a constructive manner via her marketability, having enough money in savings, and having a supportive husband. When all the restraining forces were addressed and she was asked what was really holding her back, she responded, "I am the reason I have not started my dream business!"

When she recognized it was her own apprehensiveness and not all the other reasons that was holding her back, she sat down to see if there was a way to reduce the risks associated with starting her business. She realized that she did not have enough information about the market and all the logistics associated with starting a custom tile business. She also realized she would not be able to do the research on a time-available basis.

She decided to approach her boss and see if she could negotiate a four-day week for 80 percent pay with full benefits. She knew she had valuable skills and her boss would rather have her there for four days than let her go and search for a new vice-president.

Her boss agreed to the proposal with the understanding that he could call her at home on Fridays if something came up.

She used her Fridays to analyze the market and to talk to potential suppliers, customers, and distributors. When she learned they were interested in her ability to make custom tiles, she devoted the next few Fridays to making some sample tiles. She found that having Fridays to work on her business concept gave her a chance to gather critical information and test her concept without having to quit her job. She was able to have her cake (test her business concept) and eat it (keep the security of her job, paycheck, and medical coverage), too. She then decided to launch her venture on a part-time basis to see if it really had potential. As her business picked up, she negotiated a three-day week and then a two-day week. She did not feel guilty about reducing her time with her employer because she spent a lot of it training her successor. When the successor was ready to take her place, she left the firm and committed herself to growing her venture.

The moral to the story is that by easing into the business, she was able to see if her dream venture met the thresholds for all three dimensions of the entrepreneurial triangle. She found her professional background provided her with the skills needed to start and manage that type of business. She found she had the artistic talent to design high-quality custom tiles. She found the custom tile business could be very lucrative and that it had the potential to be expanded geographically. She found she had enough money, equipment, contacts, and other resources to start the business.

Her market research indicated that customers will pay in advance for custom tiles. This would reduce her initial capital requirement and risk because her customers' prepayments would provide valuable working capital for her business. She also found that this wasn't just a hobby or a form of escapism for her—she had a passion for the business and the market wanted what she had to offer. Some people find that when a hobby becomes a job, it loses its appeal. It's like working in an ice cream store. After awhile, you don't even want to look at another scoop of ice cream. In her case, she found that the tile business was her *calling*.

Anxiety I can be viewed as what someone may have to lose or give up to start a business. This is also called *opportunity cost*. Michael Dell provides an excellent example of what can happen when there is minimal opportunity cost. He started selling computer equipment out of his dorm room when he was a freshman at the University of Texas. Before the end of the academic year he had sold more than $80,000 of equipment per month. His start-up PCs Unlimited became Dell Computer. He noted, "The opportunity looked so attractive, I couldn't stay in school. ... The risk was small."[10] He had only two opportunity costs. The first one involved the small amount of money he put into the business. The second one was that he would have to return to University of Texas the next year if it didn't work out. He didn't consider being a college student to be much of a penalty!

REALITY CHECK

You need to be objective about the realities of starting and managing a venture. Starting a venture is not a sprint; it is a marathon. It is not something you do over the weekend or for a month or two. You have to be committed to go the distance. It is easy to get caught up with the opportunities associated with starting and managing a new venture. You also need to take a hard look at the opportunity costs—what you won't be able to do as a result of starting the venture. Take a moment to ask yourself, "If my venture is a success, will I have any regrets for the 50 to 70 or more hours a week I will spend managing it? If you see yourself as having the time of your life, then there is no sacrifice or opportunity cost. If there are certain things that you wouldn't be doing that would cause you to feel some guilt (like time spent with your family, etc.) because you were not doing them, then you might not be ready for the journey.

REALITY CHECK

The impact that starting a new venture can have on one's psyche is highlighted by Tim DeMello when he was asked to reflect on the challenges of pulling the plug on a $175,000 job at the age of 27 to start Wall Street Games Inc. He stated, "It's not a job, it's not a career, it's a way of life. … When I started Wall Street Games, that was the loneliest period of my entire life. … It's one of the scariest things in the world to sit there with an empty legal pad and understand that nothing's going to happen unless I initiate it."[11]

REALITY CHECK

Don't expect divine guidance to know if you should start a venture or divine intervention to get you to actually do it. Don't expect to hear some voice from above say, "Now is the time!" The commitment to starting a venture can't come from your banker, your accountant, or your attorney … it must come from within! If you have to wait for someone to tell you that you should start a business, then don't quit your day job!

Anxiety II is entirely different from Anxiety I. Anxiety I is associated with the risk, consequences, and opportunity costs of doing something. Anxiety II is associated with the consequences of not doing something. The American culture is known for its *bias for action*. The following statements capture the attitude of some of the people who embark on the entrepreneurial journey.

- "Throw caution to the wind."
- "You only go around once."
- "You can't take it with you."
- "Time waits for no man."
- "Opportunity only knocks once."
- "He who hesitates is lost."

Anxiety II focuses on guilt and regret. It focuses on what life could have been like by not doing something rather than the risks associated with doing something. It is rooted in the questions:

- "What would my life have been like if I had … ?"
- "If I had bought XYZ stock at $10/share, then …!
- "I could kick myself for not …"

Anxiety II is reflected in the statement, "It is better to have tried and failed than to not have tried at all."

The following three examples highlight the power of Anxiety II. The first example illustrates how a decision not to seize the opportunity can haunt you. The second example illustrates the power to seize an opportunity. The third example shows what happens when Anxiety II is stronger than Anxiety I.

A few years ago a very successful restaurateur was asked to reflect on his career. Instead of smiling and talking about his restaurants, he shook his head and reflected on a call he got from a friend a few years earlier. His friend called one night and asked him if he would be interested in buying the franchise rights for two states for a new hamburger franchise. The friend indicated he could buy the rights for $100,000. The restaurateur noted there could not possibly be room for another hamburger franchise because McDonald's, Burger King, Burger Chef, and Hardee's dominated the market. When he asked what made the new hamburger franchise different, his friend indicated that the new franchise served square hamburgers! The restaurateur thought his friend was kidding, so he scoffed at the offer. The restaurateur indicated he would regret that decision for the rest of his life. He had turned down the opportunity to secure the rights to Wendy's franchises for two states!

Jeff Bezos utilized what he calls a *regret-minimization framework* to explain his decision to start Amazon.com. In 1994, at the age of 30, he came across a report projecting annual growth in Internet commerce at 2,300 percent. He projected himself into his 80s and asked what regrets he would have about his life. Ironically, he probably wouldn't remember all the things that seemed important right then on Wall Street. He realized that he would definitely remember that he'd ignored the emergence of the Internet just as it was happening. He believed that if he missed the emergence of the Internet, he'd have missed what he believed to be a "critical category formation time." Three months later, he walked away from being the youngest senior vice-president of D. E. Shaw, a Wall Street hedge-fund firm. Five days after reaching Seattle he set up Amazon.com in his garage.[12] Within five years, his stock in Amazon.com was valued in excess of $10 billion!

A thirty-something enrolled in an evening MBA program approached this author a few years ago to discuss what was on his mind. He indicated that for the last two months he had become obsessed with an idea for a new venture. I asked him if he was productive while at work in his job at a professional services firm. He indicated his concept kept him from focusing on his work. I asked him what it was like when he was with his girl friend. He indicated that he had to discipline himself to look like he was paying attention to her when he was actually thinking about his business concept. It was clear that he could not eat, sleep, or drink without thinking about his business concept. It was also clear that if he didn't take the time to do an in-depth analysis of the venture's prospects, he would be fired for doing lousy work, lose his girlfriend to someone who valued her, get sick because he was not taking care of himself, and never know whether the concept was really worth pursuing. He then committed himself to investigating the pros and cons of the venture. The research indicated that the idea had merit. It also put him in a position to recognize that he had more to lose by not pursuing the new venture than by starting it. These insights played an instrumental role in giving him the incentive to start the venture.

REALITY CHECK

This book is designed to help you determine whether an opportunity is worthwhile and if you have what it takes to beat the odds. If your venture concept has merit, then it will help you go from Anxiety I to Anxiety II. Anxiety II is reflected in the guilt that people have for not doing what they know they could or should have done. Henry David Thoreau captured the essence of Anxiety II when he observed, "The mass of men lead lives of quiet desperation."[13] There are times to think and there are times to act. When you get to Anxiety II, you are one step closer to transforming your dream into reality. You have a choice. Do you want to live a life of quiet desperation, or do you want to live a life where you seized the moment?

BEWARE OF ENTREPRENEURIAL MYTHS

There are a number of myths about entrepreneurs and the entrepreneurial process. They range from entrepreneurs are born and that entrepreneurship cannot be learned all the way to statistics that say only 1 in 10 entrepreneurs succeed. This section debunks a number of the myths.

Myth 1: Entrepreneurs Are Born Not Made

There is no *entrepreneurial* gene. Although people may be born with a high aptitude for learning, most people's lives are influenced by their surroundings. If your family has a lot of money, then that might help you get a better education, influence whom you may meet while at college, provide a source of initial funding, and provide a helpful network of contacts. Yet a number of prominent entrepreneurs have been classic Horatio Alger stories. Many came to this country with little education, money, or contacts. They created successful ventures through their ability to learn, resourcefulness, and never-ending commitment to making a life for themselves and their families.

Myth 2: Entrepreneurship Cannot Be Taught

Entrepreneurship is both an attitude and a process. Research indicates most people's basic values, personality, view of the world, and self-concept are established in one's formative years. One's attitudes are the product of one's experiences. Some experiences may build one's self-confidence, raise one's level of aspirations, and shape one's goals. Self-confidence has a direct impact on an individual's attitude toward risk and one's ability to make things happen. People can be encouraged by others to embark on the entrepreneurial journey, but the attitude to be an entrepreneur cannot be taught any more than ethics can be taught. People can be taught about the excitement of being an entrepreneur, just as people can be taught the need to be ethical—but this does not mean they will have the courage to be an entrepreneur or have the moral fortitude to act in an ethical manner when they are faced with a moral challenge.

When I was writing my first book on entrepreneurship my editor asked me to prepare a pencil and paper test so readers could find out if they are entrepreneurial. I indicated that people who know themselves should already know if they have what it takes to "boldly go where they have not gone before."

Desh Deshpande, who founded Sycamore Networks, put the decision to start a business in perspective. He stated, "When people ask me, 'Should I start this business?' my answer is no. You're ready when you don't need permission. You will be feverish about it. You will be like the kid who gets a bicycle but has to wait until morning to ride it because it's too dark. An entrepreneur knows what it's like to be made sleepless in anticipation of dawn."[14]

Chapter 1 does not provide a simple test but it does profile qualities that contribute to entrepreneurial success. Although the *attitude* cannot be taught, the *process* of entrepreneurship can be taught. Starting a new venture involves a series of steps. These steps are profiled in this book. They include market analysis, doing financial projections, developing a plan, raising funds, and making sure you have the right people in the right place at the right time. The process is not rocket science. It is fairly logical and uses tools and techniques that can be learned. Ironically, by learning the process people find there may be less risk to starting a venture than they originally thought. When they realize there is a market opportunity, that they have the needed skills, and they have the resources, their attitude about starting a venture may also change.

Myth 3: I Will Be My Own Boss

A lot of people start businesses so they can be their own bosses. Although you may own the business and have the title of president or chief executive officer, you will not be your own boss. If you have difficulty when your current boss tells you what to do and makes suggestions for how you can improve your performance, then you will probably have more difficulty dealing with customers who will suggest what you need to do differently. The customer may not always be right, but you have to put up with their suggestions, constructive criticism, and complaints. As a matter of fact, you will have to find a way to solicit their suggestions and thank them when they offer them. Without their input, you run the risk of being out of sync and going out of business. Remember, your customers can fire you. If you don't offer the market what it wants, you won't have a business to run.

REALITY CHECK

Entrepreneurship is an exercise in humility. Although you need to have confidence in your ability to make the right decisions and to make the right things happen the right way, there will be times when you will need to leave your ego at the door. Your employees, customers, suppliers, distributors, and even friends and family may be in a position to provide insightful and constructive criticism. It may be your business, but you do not have a monopoly on wisdom. You must be open to other people's ideas. You must also be willing to change what you are doing and try new things. If preserving your ego is more important than having your business fulfill its potential, then don't take the journey. A note of caution may help here. Although you must be open to others' ideas, you have to recognize the decisions are really up to you. If you fail, you cannot blame others.

Myth 4: Most New Ventures Fail

The statistic that 90 percent of all new ventures fail within the first five years is cited more than the pledge of allegiance in some circles. First, the statistic is not correct. The majority of firms that are started this year might not be around in five years. Some of them will fail, some of them will be sold, some of them will be shut down because they did not live up to their founder's expectations, and some of them will just fade away. Yes, there are risks, but they vary with the type of venture, the level of experience of the entrepreneur and the entrepreneurial team, how the venture is financed, and a whole host of other factors.

More than 800,000 businesses are started in the United States each year. A high percentage of these businesses are started by first-time entrepreneurs and people who have tried and failed before. Some of these people have no business starting a venture. Their lack of ability and/or lack of sufficient resources put them in a position where failure is almost inevitable. They are destined to fail before they even start their ventures. These people skew the *rate of failure* statistics so it looks like no one in their right mind should even consider starting a business. Their business is based on one or more unfounded assumptions or contains an unseen *fatal flaw* that cannot be fixed with all their blood, sweat, or tears! Other ventures will die a quick death because their entrepreneurs will fail to prepare them for various contingencies. They will be sold, shut down, or liquidated because they lose a key account, fail to collect sufficient receivables, or get out of sync with changing market expectations.

REALITY CHECK

Don't get caught up in the failure rates—your job is to change the odds.

The only statistic you need to know is that the odds for success should be stacked in your favor if you: (1) identify a lucrative and lasting opportunity, (2) have sufficient resources, (3) possess the right skills, (4) look before you leap, (5) develop a business plan, and (6) continually update your products, services, and skills so you maintain competitive advantages.

REALITY CHECK

People consider starting ventures for various reasons. There are good reasons and bad reasons for starting a new venture. Market opportunities represent the best reason. Starting a new venture to provide a product or service that the marketplace yearns for but has not been served may represent an excellent opportunity to beat the odds. When market demand exceeds supply, consumers are more forgiving of the types of mistakes made by new ventures.

Myth 5: I Can Always Start My Own Business

Being laid off or fired may be among the worst reasons to think about starting a new venture. These "reluctant" entrepreneurs tend to embark on the entrepreneurial journey for all the wrong reasons and they rarely have what it takes to succeed. If they got fired, then it may have been because they were unwilling or unable to keep up with changing job requirements. If they were laid off, then they may not have seen the layoff coming. Their lack of perceptiveness may cause them to miss key market changes with their new venture. In either case, they need to take out a mirror and do a personal reality check. The differences between people who really want to be entrepreneurs and reluctant entrepreneurs are similar to the differences in people who jog on a regular basis. Joggers generally fall into one of two groups. The first group jogs to get fit and to get the most out of their lives. The second group jogs because it is a form of escape. They jog to get away from things—they need time and space to get their lives in order. Those who do not have their mental house in order should not consider starting a new venture until they are mentally and physically fit!

Desh Deshpande noted that another way to prepare for this path is to be financially ready. He stated, "When you take a plunge like this, you have to be willing to say, 'I'm going to live on nothing for a certain period of time.' Either you are financially self-sufficient or you live a lifestyle that needs very little money."[15]

REALITY CHECK

Entrepreneurship is not in the same time zone as salaried employment. Starting a new venture should not be considered in the same list of alternatives that includes leaving one job to take a different or better position with one's present employer. Nor is starting a new venture in the same list of alternatives as changing employers or even changing one's profession. The transition from employment to entrepreneurship is not simple nor is it smooth.

REALITY CHECK

Entrepreneurship should not be considered as a solution to a mid-life crisis—even if a mid-life crisis occurs when one is in his or her twenties or thirties! George Dawson, who is president of Growing Your Business, notes, "The worst thing you can do is become an entrepreneur because you hate your present job."[16]

Myth 6: I Can Be an Entrepreneur Because I Have Been Successful in Corporate America

Being successful as a professional is no assurance that you have what it takes to be a successful entrepreneur. Ascending the organization chart of an established firm—whether it is a bank, a pharmaceutical firm, or a company that manufactures electronic components—is not the same as starting a new venture. Entrepreneurship takes different qualities, skills, and resources. Entrepreneurship is like a juggling act. A science teacher once noted that the best jugglers can juggle up to six objects at one time. Jugglers who try to keep more than six objects in the air may experience a mental shutdown. Entrepreneurship involves dealing with a multitude of factors at one time. As a professional in an established firm, you may have faced numerous challenges, but they usually were related to a specific facet of the firm's operations. Life for the entrepreneur, especially during the start-up stage, is characterized by different challenges that cover the whole business spectrum—and it can seem like trying to juggle 20 items at one time.

REALITY CHECK

Professionals may face an uncertain future. Working for a firm—even a *Fortune* 500 firm—no longer guarantees job security. Starting a new venture, however, involves even greater risks. Although the professional may lose his or her job, the entrepreneur is fully exposed. When a professional loses a job, he or she may go for weeks or months without a paycheck. When a new venture goes down, the entrepreneur may lose all of his or her tangible assets.

REALITY CHECK

Starting a new venture is far more challenging than launching a new product or service. People in the marketing field should not view starting a new venture to be just a little more challenging than introducing a new product or entering a new sales territory. Starting a new venture is far more comprehensive and it takes a broad range of skills. It also takes more time and more resources. A product manager may be risking his or her bonus, raise, or even job when a new product is introduced, but entrepreneurs frequently risk their homes, retirement plans, and personal bankruptcy when they start a new venture.

REALITY CHECK

The challenges of starting and operating a new venture tend to quickly overwhelm even those who were smitten with the prospect of having their own business.

Entrepreneurs don't work bankers' hours. Entrepreneurship is not a nine to five job. People considering starting their own business must be prepared to commit 70 to 100 hours per week to their venture. Entrepreneurs frequently put in 10- to 15-hour days six or seven days a week. Although most people believe that entrepreneurs put in these hours because they love their creations, it is clear that they primarily do it to keep their business afloat. They yearn for the day when their cash flow will permit them to hire additional staff so they can have a life away from work. An Australian entrepreneur who started a vineyard noted that he had taken only three days of vacation in the last four years.

NEW-VENTURE FACTS OF LIFE

There are a number of things to keep in mind when you think about the odds for starting a successful new venture. The *likelihood* for success varies as much as the *extent* that you are successful. The following figures represent a rough estimate of the degrees of success for the founders of the ventures started this year that actually beat the odds:

- A handful of ventures will create incredible wealth.
- About 5 percent of the ventures will generate substantial wealth.
- About 20 percent of the ventures will provide a sufficient level of profit in return for the entrepreneur's time, risk, and investment.
- 50 percent of the ventures started this year will provide enough return to keep them going from one year to the next.
- 25 percent of the ventures started this year will live a precarious type of existence.

REALITY CHECK

If you embark on the entrepreneurial journey then proceed with realistic expectations. Although Jeff Bezos, the founder of Amazon.com, may have been able to take his ideas for creating an *electronic portal* for selling books and other consumer products over the Internet, few entrepreneurs will see their businesses generate more than $10 billion in personal wealth within five years. For every super-nova like Intel and Amazon.com, there are hundreds of thousands of new ventures that just get by.

REALITY CHECK

Your focus should not be on avoiding failure or just making a profit. If you're going to take the entrepreneurial journey, then you should do it because you want to do more than just beat the odds. Your goal should be to create an *exceptional* enterprise. Your venture should put you in a position to enjoy the challenges of building an exceptional enterprise. It should also generate more than enough profit to justify the time and money you have invested in the business. Robert Townsend, the author of *Up the Organization*, once noted, "If you can't do it excellently, then don't do it at all. Because if it isn't excellent, it won't be profitable or fun, and if you're not in business for fun or profit, then what the hell are you doing here?"[17]

ARE YOU COMMITTED ENOUGH TO TAKE THE JOURNEY?

Starting a venture is more than a casual undertaking—it takes total commitment. The difference between going through the motions and being truly committed can be seen in a breakfast that includes eggs and bacon. The chicken may have participated in the meal, but the pig was truly committed!

The same distinction may be drawn between dating a person and marrying that person. Dating can be filled with fun and passion, but before you propose you need to be objective enough to do your own reality test. You need to determine whether it is the temporary infatuation associated with just a crush or whether it will stand the test of time. Carl Wallenda, the great high-wire performer, was once asked why he risked his life traversing the wire. He responded, "When I'm on the wire, I'm alive … everything else is waiting!" In the beginning, you may view the time you spend contemplating and starting your business to being *on the wire*. In most marriages, the excitement of the wedding and the honeymoon that follows tends to be short-lived. When the honeymoon is over, the work of maintaining a successful marriage begins.

Step back and ask yourself, "If I spend all my time trying to make my spouse happy, will I be happy? If you and your spouse have identical needs, then you will not be making any personal sacrifices doing what your spouse wants. The same applies to having your own business. You must be sure your new venture will truly meet your needs. Marriages have ended because of incompatibility and irreconcilable differences. The same can happen with your new venture. Remember, if you get divorced you may lose half of what you have. If your venture fails, you may lose all you have.

Calvin Kent noted, "An entrepreneur is someone who works 16 hours for himself or herself so he or she doesn't have to work 8 hours a day for someone else." It should be clear by now that your commitment to your business will be contingent on the satisfaction you get from it. If your venture fulfills your dreams, then there will be minimal opportunity cost or personal sacrifice. If it doesn't meet your needs, then it could be your worst nightmare.

Lanny Goodman of Management Technologies notes, "Your first order in starting a company is to design your business to satisfy your needs." He stresses the need for entrepreneurs to practice creative selfishness.[18] He recommends that entrepreneurs ask the following questions: (1) What do I want and need out of my life? (2) How can my company help me accomplish that? (3) What should such a company look like? and (4) How do we get it to look like that? He noted, "When your company doesn't fulfill your needs first, and balance the customers' and employees' needs with them, everything unravels. Either the business will just fall apart or you'll wind up with this sick, codependent, very toxic environment." He further stated, "It's tragic that our entrepreneurs—the people who put their butts on the line every day, the people who have the intelligence, drive, ambition, commitment, and courage should wake up one morning and realize they've created a monster that's devouring their life."[19]

As a professional, you may have had aspirations to make it to the top and be the firm's chief executive officer. When you start your own business you start at the top. You *are* the chief executive. When you start your own business you are also starting at the bottom. Until you hire someone else, you are also the labor force. You will have to do it all. There may come a time when you can delegate a lot of the "stuff" you don't want to do. And there may come a time when you can direct your attention to the things you really enjoy at work. But until then, every job is your job!

Although the person who wanted to start a custom tile business indicated it might be possible to test the concept on a small scale without committing considerable resources and quitting her job, most ventures that have considerable potential are faced with a window of opportunity that won't wait until it's convenient for the entrepreneur. Most market opportunities will require total immersion. John Chuang, of MacTemps Inc., noted, "Commit to the business—don't just do it on the side. If you have the vision and really believe in it, you should commit to it wholeheartedly."[20]

Talk is cheap. The same is true with dreams of starting your own business. Baseball is full of clichés. Two clichés apply quite well to those who dream about starting their own business. The first one is, "You've got to step to the plate." You must be willing to make the commitment. Nothing can happen until you actually step into the batter's box. The second is, "You can't steal second if you keep one foot on first base." You must be willing to put yourself at risk to be an entrepreneur. You must be willing to step out of your comfort zone before you can start the entrepreneurial journey.

REALITY CHECK

This could be called the *commitment check:* James Sheldon and Burt Alimansky provide an interesting reality check for entrepreneurs to see if they are committed enough to their venture for investors to commit their funds to it. They ask entrepreneurs, "If you were offered the opportunity to take a job with an investor's company for $200,000 a year, a lucrative bonus or stock option plan, and five weeks off for vacation each year, would you take it?" They note that if the answer is yes, then the investor knows that you aren't truly committed.[21]

CONCLUSION: ENTREPRENEURSHIP IS A DIFFERENT WORLD

The thrill of starting a venture for many entrepreneurs is often followed by a fondness for the good old days when they weren't on the *entrepreneurial high wire.* Many entrepreneurs yearn for the *corporate days* when they worked for someone else and they didn't have to worry about making payroll, when they took worry-free vacations, and when they had time for their families, hobbies, pets, and pleasure reading. In the corporate days when things didn't go as planned, your employer provided the staff and resources to help you get the job done. At the end of the day, you might have even been able to mentally and physically walk away from the day's challenges.

As an entrepreneur, you can't mentally walk away from your firm. It's always there. It's a part of you. When you are at home with your family, your business's challenges will be there with you. When you are on vacation (if you have the time and the money to take a vacation) your business's challenges will be there, too.

There isn't a switch to mentally turn your venture off. You can't leave work at work. You can't walk out and leave things for tomorrow, and you can't leave it for someone else to take care of. There will always be a multitude of things that need to be done, fixed, or prepared for—and it is all up to you to make sure they are addressed. There will be times when the challenges and frustrations seem like they are endless. For everything you complete, it will seem like there are five more things that must be done.

Before you begin the journey, you need to answer one of the most perplexing questions in life: "Do you work to live or live to work?" It is vital that you know whether your business is a means to an end or an end in itself. If you live to work, then you will need to have your mental and physical house in order. You will need to make sure everyone you value recognizes that your venture comes before everything else. If you work to live, then you will need to put your venture in perspective. You will need to find the type of venture that will give you the time, freedom, and income to do the things that matter when you are not at work.

REALITY CHECK

Make sure that those around you are supportive of your entrepreneurial journey and that they also benefit from it. New ventures are like a whirlpool; they drain all your time, energy, and emotions. Most entrepreneurs acknowledge they feel guilty about the limited time they spend with those they care about. Make sure your efforts to fulfill your entrepreneurial dream do not become a personal nightmare for you and those around you.

REALITY CHECK

Starting and growing a venture will strain even a good marriage. From a personal point of view, a divorce would be a major loss. From a business point of view, it could force you to divide up your assets. Since most businesses are undercapitalized, a divorce might also bring your business down. If your marriage goes down, where will the money come from to pay your spouse for the settlement? Your business will already be underfunded and your house will be mortgaged … and second mortgaged to finance your new venture. Recognize that you and your business can't afford a divorce. Do whatever it takes to keep your marriage and your business.

Chapter 1 identifies various skills and qualities that can be essential for starting a business. It also provides a foundation for inventorying your skills and assessing whether you are ready to embark on the entrepreneurial journey. By the time you finish Chapter 1, you should have a clear picture of the areas you will need to strengthen. It will also help you identify the types of people you will need to have on your management team to supplement your skills and qualities. If you are an *idea person* you may need to hire someone who likes dealing with the details and making sure nothing falls through the cracks. If you can't afford that person when you start the venture, then you will need to be sure you have systems in place that monitor operations carefully, because you won't naturally do it.

> *A lot of people have ideas, but few have the courage*
> *and persistence to see them through.*
> *A lot of people have dreams, but few have the ability*
> *to transform them into viable businesses.*
>
> —Stephen C. Harper

ENDNOTES

1. Mark Van Osnabrugge and Robert J. Robinson, *Angel Investing* (San Francisco: Jossey-Bass, 2000), pp. 11–14. Copyright © 2000, Jossey-Bass. This material is used by permission of John Wiley & Sons, Inc.

2. The Forbes 400 2003 list of the Wealthiest Americans, *Forbes,* October 6, 2003, pp. 272–284.

3. Joseph R. Mancuso, "Profile of a Winner," *Success,* December 1995, p. 14.

4. Ibid.

5. Joseph H. Boyett and Jimmie T. Boyett, *The Guru Guide to Entrepreneurship* (New York: John Wiley & Sons, 2001), p. xiii.

6. Tom Chappell, *The Soul of a Business* (New York: Bantam Trade Publications, 1994), p. 113.

7. George Gendron, "The Seven Habits of Highly Effective Start-ups," *Inc.*, March 1999, p. 1.

8. Christopher, D. Lancette, "Wide World of Sports," *Entrepreneur,* February 1999, pp. 142 and 144. Reprinted with permission of Entrepreneur Media, Inc.

9. Kurt Lewin, *Field Theory in Social Science: Selected Theoretical Papers* (New York: Harper & Brothers, 1951). Lewin's model has been modified to reflect forces that may affect entrepreneurship.

10. Jerry Main, "A Golden Age for Entrepreneurs." *Fortune,* February 12, 1990, p. 120.

11. Leslie Brokaw, "The Truth About Start-ups," *Inc.,* April 1991, p. 55.

12. Lesley Hazelton, "Jeff Bezos," *Success,* July 1998, p. 58.

13. Henry David Thoreau, *Walden* (New York; New American Library, 160), p. 10.

14. Desh Deshpande, "A Joyful Sleeplessness Says You're Ready," *Red Herring,* November 13, 2000, p. 240.

15. Ibid.

16. Jeff Morrow, "Secrets of a Start-up," *Success,* September 1998, p. 61.

17. Robert Townsend, *Up the Organization* (New York, Alfred A. Knopf, 1970), p. 58.

18. Michael S. Hopkins, "The World According To Me," *Inc.,* January 1998, p. 66.

19. Ibid.

20. Debra Phillips, G. David Doran, Elaine Teague, and Laura Tiffany, "Young Millionaires," *Entrepreneur,* November, 1998, p. 118. Reprinted with permission of Entrepreneur Media, Inc.

21. James Sheldon and Burt Alimansky, "8 Demons of Entrepreneurship," *Success,* March 1986, p. 57.

1

ESSENTIAL ENTREPRENEURIAL QUALITIES AND CAPABILITIES

The entrepreneur is not circumscribed by the walls of a job description or limited in what he may accomplish, by the insecurities of his superiors, or the necessity to wait until others ahead of him in the corporate pecking order retire. His field is wide open, and he can attempt whatever broken field running he is able to perform.[1]

—Leonard A. Batterson

Extra effort has been devoted in this chapter to identifying the qualities that entrepreneurs need so they can meet the challenges associated with starting a new venture. The analysis of entrepreneurial preparedness is the first step in the New-Venture Creation Process profiled in the introduction. Although the list of qualities may seem formidable and the list of challenges may seem overwhelming, this chapter is not intended to discourage you from starting a venture. Instead, it is designed to provide insights into the challenges of starting and running a new venture so you can decide if you are ready to take the journey.

This chapter focuses on five entrepreneurial issues.

1. It encourages you to take a good look at your skills and capabilities.
2. It encourages you to identify the skills and capabilities needed to start a venture.
3. It encourages you to identify gaps between the first and second areas.
4. It encourages you to identify areas that you can improve.
5. It encourages you to identify areas where other people will need to be involved in your venture to supplement your skills and capabilities.

These people may be members of your management team or employees. They could also be paid advisors (accountants, attorneys, insurance specialists, etc.), members of an advisory committee if you have one, or members of the board of directors. You may even choose to outsource certain skills and activities to an individual or firm.

STEP ONE: KNOW THYSELF!

Let's face it; most people are not cut out to be entrepreneurs. They don't have the temperament, experience, abilities, or resources to do what is necessary to create a successful venture. The first step in determining whether you have what it takes to start a successful venture is to step back and take an objective look at your skills and capabilities. You need to evaluate what you do know and what you don't know. You also need to know your strengths and weaknesses—and what makes you tick.

REALITY CHECK

If your definition of having a good life is working from nine to five and not making mistakes, then stay where you are and hope that the other people where you work are not so caught up in their comfort zones that your employer goes down in flames!

REALITY CHECK

Business relationships depend on trust. You need to pass the *mirror test*. If you have a checkered past (major litigation, bankruptcy, etc.) or there is any question about your integrity or mental stability, then forget starting your own business.

Amy Lingren, president of Prototype Career Services, located in St. Paul, Minnesota, offers the following list of questions for prospective entrepreneurs:

1. *What is my motivation?*
2. *What are my goals?* Every new business owner should have a clear idea of what he or she wants from the business. If your goal is income, you need to map out how much you want to earn and in what time period. If your goal is independence, you must define what it means to you. For some, it means freedom to work 80 hours a week at something they love. For others it means not working insane hours.
3. *What am I willing to give up?* Although most budding entrepreneurs have a clear picture of potential gains, they rarely understand what they will give up for their businesses. For example, your friendships and family life will definitely change as you become more absorbed in your new venture. Other sacrifices will include free time and vacations. Even your dignity, professional status, and physical comfort are up for grabs as you do everything from moving inventory to cleaning bathrooms.
4. *What is my work style?* Are you happiest working with a team or by yourself? To be happy, you must know your needs and work style before you choose the kind of company you will run.
5. *What is my timeline?* If you're currently unemployed, you may need an income as soon as possible. Whatever your start-up strategy, you need to choose a date to actually start and then develop a calendar of research and startup activities leading to that date. Without a timeline, you risk missing steps and starting too soon, or procrastinating until your excitement is gone.
6. *What is my budget?* You will need a revision in your household budget to reflect your first 6 to 12 months of business. What will your family do without your salary?[2]

This first step also includes taking a close look at your motives and aspirations. Why do you want to start a venture? Is it for fame and fortune? Is it to be your own boss and to have a sense of fulfillment? Fred Smith, founder of Federal Express, indicated that potential entrepreneurs need to decide if the venture is the thing they want to do with their time and their life more than any other thing.[3]

Check Your Motives

If your primary drive is to make a pile of money, then you may be among a small group of entrepreneurs. It is only recently that the desire to make millions has moved to center stage. The twenty-something dot-com entrepreneurs who thought they could rule the Internet seem to have been marching to the tune of a very different drummer. They had a mantra:

1. Develop some idea using Internet technology while working for someone else.
2. Quit your job to pursue your dream.
3. Have venture capitalists fight to invest in your business.
4. Go public.
5. Relax for the rest of your life.

Their lofty expectations and sense of infallibility were matched by the brevity of their timelines. Many wild-eyed young entrepreneurs believed they could do the whole set of actions in less than one year! David Arnoff, an associate of the Graylock Venture Capital firm, noted at a closing-fund dinner for a new company, "The celebration was a little dry as the VCs were the only ones at the table old enough to drink."[4]

REALITY CHECK

Beware of greed, get-rich-quick schemes, and take-the-money-and-run motives. If you are in it just for the money, then you will compromise key issues and cut too many corners. If you want to build an exceptional enterprise, then direct your time, attention, and resources to providing innovative products and services and creating an environment that attracts and rewards outstanding talent. And make sure your venture has systems that foster exceptional performance.

Show Me the Money

Entrepreneurs are driven by various motives. Some want to make a quick buck; others want to change the world. Steven Jobs, who cofounded Apple and then created NeXT, had very little interest in generating wealth. His desire to make computing user-friendly and to enhance the quality of education enabled him to attract great talent and create revolutionary products.

It has been observed, "Entrepreneurs and venture capitalists have forgotten what the Valley's business used to be: developing revolutionary technologies, bringing them to market, and building organizations that can, over the years, continue to create and sell stuff that can change the world."[5] It has also been noted, "If the founders of get-rich-quick startups were to study the history of the most successful tech companies, they'd find a recurring theme; money comes to those who do it for love."[6]

Richard Burnes, cofounder of Charles River Ventures, noted, "If you look at Bill Gates or Larry Ellison, money was not why they did it. They did it because they were driven to do it. ... They earned their wealth by painstakingly building their companies over many years."[7] Wilson Harrell, who founded over 100 companies, said, "Most entrepreneurs fail because they're not entrepreneurs in the first place. Entrepreneurs are a special breed, with the gate to their kingdom well guarded against the greedy and get-rich-quick schemers. Many knock, few are admitted."[8]

Ted Turner may have put the importance of money in perspective. He noted, "If you think money is a real big deal, ... you'll be too scared of losing it to get it."[9] When Turner figured out he was a billionaire, he thought whistles and bells would go off. He noted that nothing happened at all, and that having great wealth is overrated. He observed, "Average sex is better than being a billionaire."[10]

Most successful entrepreneurs are driven by the desire to create a venture that will make a difference. They want to use their talents and to make exciting things happen. The number-one reason people start a business is that they feel stifled. They feel their jobs are not taking full advantage of their talents. They're also looking for psychological freedom in what they do, and they're technically excellent at something.[11]

Technology-driven entrepreneurs (a.k.a. geeks) have never cared much about money; in fact, technology gurus on the Forbes 400 list, like Bill Gates and Steve Jobs, were always more concerned with dispensing utopia.[12] When Jobs was trying to get John Sculley to leave Pepsi to help him run Apple in its formative years, the deal was consummated when Jobs said to Sculley, "Do you want to spend the rest of your life selling sugared water, or do you want the chance to change the world?"[13] Tom Monaghan, founder of Domino's Pizza, noted, "Life is too precious to be wasted in doing work you don't love."[14]

The opportunity to be one's own boss and the master of one's destiny serve as the driving force for many entrepreneurs. The desire to be one's own boss, however, may not be the same as the desire to be the master of one's destiny. If the desire to be your own boss is based on wanting to have the freedom to try new things, then that desire can be a healthy attribute. If your desire is rooted in an aversion to having someone else being your boss, that could be entirely different. In the first case, some entrepreneurs live in a world where they are surrounded by things that can be improved. Their desire to seize opportunities and to improve products, services, and processes is stifled by the closed mindsets or bureaucratic tendencies that are characteristic of most established businesses. This causes many of them to start their own ventures. In the second case, people start ventures to get away from authority figures, rules, and procedures. In many cases, they cannot work for other people and have considerable difficulty complying with normal organizational practices. One entrepreneur noted, "I had to be my own boss because I can't work for anyone else."

REALITY CHECK

If you have trouble with other people telling you what to do and complying with prescribed guidelines, you need to recognize that your employees, customers, creditors, suppliers, distributors, and various government agencies will be telling you what to do. Being your own boss is an illusion—when you start a business you must be open to others' suggestions. There will also be times when you may want to think "outside the box," but have to accept the fact that you must operate "inside the box." If you are bull-headed and unwilling to solicit and consider other people's suggestions, then you may not be able to attract good people and learn from the marketplace.

Leonard Batterson noted that "Entrepreneurs are never entirely alike nor entirely different. They are driven by their own particular demons to attempt to create their own unique destiny. They are generally very uncomfortable with authority imposed from without, whether in the form of a corporation or the imposition of another's will. Many as children were unable to be true to themselves while attempting to conform and placate an overwhelming parent. Their characteristic hostility to authority, and the limitations they sense it imposes, is a response to these childhood chains."[15]

"Entrepreneurs are often misfits who simply don't mesh with the corporate culture. They don't fit in. Their independent ideas and vision and willingness to act decisively are not normal behavior at most corporations. Corporations move carefully, rationally when at their best, and mostly by consensus. Any new idea must be carefully sewn and gradually nurtured to survive the corporate political environment. Entrepreneurs are totally impatient with this process of consensus and accommodation."[16]

Before moving on, it may be worth taking a moment to address the question, "Is there a good age to be an entrepreneur?" The answer really comes down to this: The entrepreneur should be old enough to have the wisdom to not make naïve mistakes and young enough to have the energy needed to go the distance. This is an interesting paradox. There will be times when entrepreneurs need to have the patience to stay the course that comes with maturity and experience. Yet there will be times when they will need to have the youthfulness to take a leap of faith rather than to wait until all the data are in.

David Gladstone noted, "Venture capitalists believe entrepreneurs should be between the ages of 30 and 45. Younger than age 30 means that the entrepreneur lacks management experience or the knowledge needed to conduct a strong growth-oriented company. Older than 45 usually means he has the experience but lacks the drive and ambition."[17]

REALITY CHECK

Life is too short to wait. If you have the right skills, surround yourself with good people, have identified a lucrative opportunity, and can garner sufficient resources, then it is the time to seize the moment.

STEP TWO: DEVELOP THE "ENTREPRENEURIAL PROFILE"

The entrepreneurial profile represents a job description for the person who plans to start and manage a business. It highlights important skills, capabilities, and experience. Although the requirements may be different for different types of ventures in different markets, certain attributes are essential for most entrepreneurial journeys. Entrepreneurial qualities that play an important role in the success of the new venture are highlighted in the last two-thirds of this chapter.

STEP THREE: IDENTIFY THE "ENTREPRENEURIAL GAPS"

Kenneth Olm and George Eddy suggest that prospective entrepreneurs view the process of analyzing the extent that one has what it takes to be an entrepreneur to be similar to applying for a job. They encourage entrepreneurs to put together a resume and cover letter as if they are applying for the job of being a venture's entrepreneur. The résumé and cover letter should profile your skills, capabilities, and types of experience needed to attract quality people and capital. They suggest that you then put yourself in the position of the board of directors and review whether you are the right person to create the venture to meet the stockholders' needs.[18] You will need to also demonstrate you have what it takes to guide the venture through growth's minefields.

Although most entrepreneurs feel that preparing a resume may be a waste of their time, it serves two important purposes. First, it forces them to document what they have to offer. Second, they will need to provide this information to investors and/or the bank if they will be seeking external funding.

REALITY CHECK

Entrepreneurship is like lowering the water level in a river. When the water level is lowered, rocks (personal shortcomings) that used to be covered with sufficient water (in the corporate world) will make navigating and progress (entrepreneurship) more difficult. Take a look at your background and capabilities. Would you be qualified for the job? If not, which areas would keep you from being considered?

Step three focuses on three different entrepreneurial gaps. Gaps may exist in your personal qualities, areas of specialization or proficiency, and knowledge of the market. The *personal qualities* gap focuses on whether certain facets of your personality will be assets or liabilities for your new venture. This step tries to determine whether major gaps exist between your personal make-up and what it takes to start and lead a new venture. This chapter highlights a number of the attitudinal, behavioral, and perceptual factors that can play an integral role in the creation and management of a venture. These qualities range from tenacity all the way to a commitment to excellence. This step may indicate that your personal desire to make sure nothing goes wrong may actually deter the growth of the venture. A personal qualities gap may exist between your need to be in control and the need to delegate decisions and to build a team.

Step three tries to determine the extent that a *specialization gap* exists. Although the personal qualities gap may focus on certain personal attributes and challenges, the specialization gap looks for gaps in business skills. Most professionals spend their careers in one particular field. They work their way up one particular *functional silo.* Most established firms are organized along functional lines where people specialize in one facet of the firm's operations. Specialization has its merits in large organizations because it allows an individual to focus his or her attention in one particular area. The specialization, in turn, increases one's proficiency and productivity.

One's degree of specialization, however, can be a major drawback for someone who wants to be an entrepreneur. Starting a venture requires a broad range of business skills. The narrower your specialization, the greater the gap. The specialization gap can be monumental if your background is in government compliance or employee benefits. If your career has been in auditing, market research, human resources, or production scheduling, then you have your work cut out for you to broaden your skills and abilities.

Each of these areas may be important to your new venture, but they represent individual trees in the forest. To start a business, you need to know how the trees interact in the forest and how the forest fits into the overall marketplace! If you have a broad-based business education and have spent parts of your career in project environments where all facets of a business are at play at the same time, then the gaps may not be as great.

If you have little knowledge of finance, then you will not be in a position to develop financial projections, to identify potential cash deficits, and/or to raise funds. If you have little knowledge of accounting, then you will be ill-equipped to develop budgets that play an integral role in planning and controlling business operations. If you have little knowledge of marketing, then you will not be able to develop a marketing plan that will give your venture competitive advantages. If you have little knowledge and experience supervising people, then you will not have the finesse needed to attract, motivate, and lead your staff—which may be your new venture's most valuable assets.

The specialization gap has two other dimensions. First, people who have specialized in one particular area tend to see that area as the center of the business universe. People with a background in sales tend to believe that whenever a firm gets into trouble, the firm just needs to sell its way out of it. As someone once observed, "If you give a child a hammer, he or she will believe everything needs to be hammered." There will be times when cost control may be what is needed to improve the new venture's performance rather than more advertising, special promotions, price discounts, or sales incentives.

Second, entrepreneurs have a tendency to spend their time on areas they know best. Entrepreneurs who are unwilling or unable to let go of their past specialization may jeopardize their firm's future. They also tend to be reluctant to delegate those areas to other people. This can be detrimental because the entrepreneur has to spend his or her time managing the whole venture. Entrepreneurs have difficulty delegating things that they used to do before they started their ventures. If your career has been unidimensional, then you need to be aware of the tendency to have tunnel vision. You also need to be aware that you will be less likely to let your staff do what you did before you started the firm.

The specialization gap is particularly noteworthy in high-technology start-ups. "High technology entrepreneurs must learn to strike a balance between their dual roles as chief technologists and CEOs—and bring in help if their shortcomings become apparent."[19] The specialization gap raises the question of whether the entrepreneur should be the venture's chief executive officer. When Pete Bechtel, the founder of Cactus Group Ltd., was asked if he is the best person to be running his company, he indicated that he was not! He stated that his talents would be best used in developing accounts. This insight led him to hire a chief operating officer who could oversee ongoing operations. Bechtel was then free to lead the firm, to deal with strategic issues, and to develop accounts without being distracted by operational issues.

If you are not sure that you have the skills to be the lead entrepreneur, then it may be in your best interest to become part of a start-up or emerging venture that can use your specific skills. You will get a better feel for the challenges of starting and running a new venture by serving as a member of the management team of an emerging venture. You will also have a chance to broaden your knowledge of the other dimensions of the business. This interim step may be seen as an entrepreneurial apprenticeship. The time spent should provide valuable insights into whether you really want to embark on the entrepreneurial journey. It will also highlight skills and abilities that you will need to strengthen.

Step three also focuses on whether a *market knowledge gap* exists. Most entrepreneurs have experience in a particular industry. If your professional background was with one company in an industry that is different from the one in which you plan to start your new venture, then you need to recognize that a market knowledge gap exists. You will have to learn about the uniqueness and dynamics of the marketplace. You will also need to surround yourself with people who truly understand the practices and nuances of the market segments and corresponding competitors.

REALITY CHECK

The greater the difference between where you have been and where you are headed, the greater the risk of making mistakes. Know your shortcomings. Do something about them—or don't take the journey.

If you have an excellent working knowledge of the industry, competition, market segments, and regulations for the area you plan to start a venture, then the market knowledge gap may be minimal. Knowledge and insights play a key role in new venture success. If your competitors have a better grasp for what the market wants and have spent years perfecting their product/service offering and their operations, then it may be difficult for you to gain an immediate competitive advantage. Most markets show little mercy for newcomers who wing it or must resort to trial-and-error approaches because of their lack of

Have you started a venture before?	No	Entrepreneurial risk	Considerable risk
	Yes	Moderate risk	Market risk
		Yes	No
		Has anyone ever tried this type of venture before?	

EXHIBIT 1.1   ENTREPRENEURIAL/MARKET RISK MATRIX

knowledge or inexperience. Markets reward savvy entrepreneurs and leave naïve entrepreneurs little time to learn from their mistakes.

REALITY CHECK

We live in an ever-changing marketplace. You must be in sync with it. Yesterday's knowledge will not help you deal with tomorrow's challenges.

REALITY CHECK

Entrepreneurship involves various types of risks. The Entrepreneurial/Market Risk Matrix profiled in Exhibit 1.1 highlights four types and levels of risk. When you embark on the entrepreneurial journey for the first time, you are taking an *entrepreneurial* risk. You are doing something you have never done before. You are destined to make mistakes. When you create a venture to do something no other firm has done before, you are taking *market venture* risk. This risk involves trying to offer a product or service that has not been offered to a market that may not exist or that may reject your product/service offering right away. If you are taking the entrepreneurial journey for the first time and it involves doing something no other firm has done before, then you are truly testing the odds!

STEP FOUR: BRIDGE THE ENTREPRENEURIAL GAPS

Entrepreneurial gaps are inevitable. No individual can score "10" on every dimension. Most successful entrepreneurs still have gaps. It would be impossible for someone to have it all. There are not enough hours in the day to learn what needs to be known and to experience what needs to be experienced. If everyone waited until they had (1) adopted and internalized every personal quality, (2) developed expert-level knowledge of every functional area of business, and (3) gained extensive first-hand knowledge of the targeted industry/market, then no venture would ever be started.

It is recommended that you decide which skills you will need to develop immediately and which ones you'll want to strengthen over the course of owning your business. You should also ask yourself if you really want to learn these things.[20] If you don't want to learn these areas, then you should consider staying where you are or using your talents as a member of the management team rather than being your new venture's chief executive officer.

REALITY CHECK

It should be noted that one's personality might be the most difficult area to change. Your personality is the product of a lifetime's experiences. Some parts of your personality may even be affected by genetic factors. Psychoanalysts believe it may take two one-hour sessions per week for two years to produce major change, even when the client wants to change! The moral to the story is, "If you can't change your personality, then find a place where your personality can be an asset rather than a liability." For some people, that place is not an entrepreneurial place.

STEP FIVE: SUPPLEMENT YOUR SKILLS AND CAPABILITIES

No person has all the qualities that affect new venture success, nor could anyone be expected to develop them. What is important is that you take a good look at yourself, and make an effort to develop and strengthen the qualities that affect the likelihood of success. Then you need to surround yourself with people who possess the abilities you lack.

Some entrepreneurial gaps can be filled. For example, you can strengthen your knowledge about finance, marketing, and accounting. You can gain experience in managing people. You can research an industry's consumers, competitors, and distribution channels. The trick is to learn what you can, to recognize what you aren't going to know in time to start the venture, and to surround yourself with people whose talents supplement your knowledge, skills, and capabilities.

The era of the entrepreneur who flies solo is coming to an end. The entrepreneur may be the driving force in the creation of a venture, but it will take an exceptional team to build an exceptional enterprise. A few years ago, the actor Edward James Olmos made an insightful presentation to a college audience. He stated that America shouldn't be seen as a melting pot where diverse elements are thrown together to make a stew. He encouraged the audience to think of America's rich diversity as a salad.

The salad analogy can be applied to the need for the entrepreneur to bring people together with varied backgrounds, perspectives, skills, and capabilities. Like a chef preparing an outstanding salad, the entrepreneur identifies the critical ingredients, assembles them in the right quantity, and brings out each of their strengths by providing the right seasoning and dressing. Savvy entrepreneurs know their limitations, and they supplement their talents with people who can make the firm come alive via their insights and ideas.

Your people play a critical role in establishing competitive advantages. Kristen Knight, who started Creative Assets Inc., a Seattle-based staffing company that provides graphic artists, writers, Web designers, and other "creative types" for companies on the West Coast, noted, "Find and keep the best employees you can possibly afford, and create a vision they can buy into. Also know your weaknesses and compensate for them."[21]

If you are the world's greatest optimist, then you need to have someone on your staff who will keep your feet on the ground long enough to see the situation from all vantage points. This *reality-orientation* role is usually played by the board of directors or the firm's chief financial officer. The board should challenge the entrepreneur's key assumptions. The chief financial officer should run scenarios on spreadsheets to determine the impact of certain strategies on the firm's cash position.

If you are an "idea" person or someone who likes dealing with the big picture, then you need to have people on your staff who can ground you in reality. You will need people who thrive on the details that are the nuts and bolts of the business. These people will also play a crucial role because a venture's success is closely tied to the quality of execution. They may say, "That sounds good," but they will follow your idea with, "How do we operationalize it?" For example, if you think your firm can sell at least $5 million in its first year, they will add value to your venture by asking, "Who will be our customers, when will their orders come, what will the average purchase be, and when will the firm get paid?"

While these people may be a pain and slow you down, their questions will get you to look before you leap. They will make sure nothing falls through the cracks. And they will make sure your exuberance is not irrational. If you love to identify new opportunities and develop new products, then you need to have someone on your staff who can take your ideas and flesh them out. People who have the ability to follow up on your ideas can be worth every dollar you pay them. Without these people, you will get wrapped up in so many logistical issues that you will not have the time to be the venture's "chief executive officer."

Warren Buffett stresses the need to surround yourself with people who supplement your *circle of competence.*[22] Bill Gates also indicated that it is essential that you do not surround yourself with people who are just like you. Bill Gates noted that Microsoft's cofounder Paul Allen played a crucial role in Microsoft's development because he challenged Gates's ideas.[23]

Systems can also play a key role in a new venture's success. Few ventures start with a complete management team. It is for this reason that you need to make every effort to attract people from the beginning who possess the types of personalities that make for a rich salad. If you can't afford to hire people with the qualities and experience to supplement your skills, then you will need to be sure systems are established to supplement your skills and personality. If you are not likely to run scenarios, then you need the type of planning software that runs three different sales projections. If you are prone to procrastinate, then you need systems in place that identify key milestones and deadlines. If your staff supplements your skills and personality and if you have systems in place that foster good management practices, then things will be done that you wouldn't do.

Kristen Knight provides an excellent testimonial for the need to have management systems in place. When she reflected on her background and biases, she noted, "Being focused on the sales and marketing side of the business, I overlooked the vital role of the less interesting functions of accounting, technology, and database systems. It was expensive, and at times, an embarrassing lesson (payroll and receivables mistakes), but I now realize the importance of setting up systems you can grow into. I also learned to surround myself with the best vendors and staff I can afford."[24]

PERSONAL QUALITIES THAT CAN MAKE A DIFFERENCE

There is no single personality profile of successful entrepreneurs. Entrepreneurs come in all shapes and sizes. They have varying levels of business experience and education. Bill Gates, cofounder of Microsoft, Steven Jobs, cofounder of Apple, Fred DeLuca, cofounder of Subway, Fred Smith, founder of FedEx, and Jeff Bezos, founder of Amazon.com, are as different as they are similar.

Entrepreneurs don't need to have superhuman powers. They do not have to be able to run faster than a speeding bullet or to jump over tall buildings in a single bound. The job description, however, for the entrepreneur is as multifaceted as a diamond. The remainder of this chapter profiles various personal qualities and capabilities that can enhance a new venture's chances for success.

Entrepreneurs Don't Have To Be Inventors

It may be helpful to start this discussion by differentiating the role of the inventor, the entrepreneur, the leader, and the manager. Many people are hesitant to take the entrepreneurial journey because they have not invented a breakthrough product or service that revolutionizes the way people live or work. This is known as the *inventor myth.* Entrepreneurs don't have to be inventors. The world is full of people who are not having their needs met. The world is also full of inventors who come up with fascinating products and services. The entrepreneur adds value to the marketplace by finding a way to bring these two groups together for a profit. The strength of the entrepreneur is his or her ability to sense a market gap and transform it into a new venture opportunity. Chapter 4 profiles dozens of entrepreneurs who identified a gap and relied on the inventive talents of others to develop the products, services, or systems for filling that gap.

Although entrepreneurs don't have to be inventors, it does help if they have some degree of innovative ability. They may have to find a new way to a deliver a product, just as Fred Smith did with Federal Express, or an innovative way to provide a service, just as Pierre Omidyar did when he created eBay. In some cases, entrepreneurs don't have to be innovative at all. If you have the ability to create an organization that attracts creative people and capitalizes on their talents, then you don't have to be innovative. In a sense, your role as the entrepreneur is like the role played by the symphony conductor. Symphony conductors do not play the instruments, but they create an environment where beautiful music fills the air.

Inventors rarely become successful entrepreneurs. While they relish the challenge associated with solving a particular problem, most inventors lack the business skills and capital needed to take their inventions to the market. Inventors also tend to fall in love with their inventions. They lack the objectivity needed to determine the invention's true value. They frequently get caught in the "If you build a better mousetrap, the world will beat a path to your door" fallacy. They have trouble understanding why people don't buy their revolutionary products.

Walt Hobbs provides a good example of an inventor's preoccupation with solving a problem. He wanted to create a product that would help women who lived with "inconsiderate" men. Walt Hobbs spent three years developing a hydraulic device called "Seat Down" that automatically lowers the toilet seat. His invention lowers the toilet seat 90 seconds after the pedal has been pressed that raises it.[25]

A number of inventions are marketable, but they never make it to the marketplace because their inventors are not willing to let anyone else have a piece of their action. They want to manufacture their product and control every aspect of marketing it. Their desire to run the show and to get 100 percent of the profits for their blood, sweat, and tears puts them in a position where their inventions never leave the launch pad.

Their unwillingness to sell or license their product to an entrepreneur (or existing firm) who can take it to the marketplace means that they have no revenue for their invention. Everyone loses in this situation. The inventor does not receive any money in return for his or her efforts. The inventor also loses because the money could serve as seed capital for developing additional products. The market also loses because consumers do not have the opportunity to buy innovative products.

REALITY CHECK

Inventors should spend their time inventing. They will be better off leaving the *business side* of inventing to people who are as good at *doing business* as the inventor is good at inventing.

A few inventors are able to acquire funding via government technology grants. But their lack of business acumen frequently keeps their "wow" products from achieving their true potential. Inventors need to recognize that there may be a substantial opportunity cost when they try to handle the "business" side of an invention. Every moment they spend trying to raise money, manufacture the product, and establish distribution outlets could have been spent developing other inventions! The moral to the inventor story is, "A reasonable piece of a big-revenue pie is better than 100 percent of a no-revenue pie."

Inventors usually underestimate what is involved in taking their idea to market. Nothing is ever as simple as it seems. Marilyn Searcy provides a good example of what happens when even a simple innovation has a head-on collision with the real world. She invented a product called "It's a Keeper" that hooks onto a ladder and holds either a two- or a five-gallon paint can.

When Marilyn Searcy set out to be an honest-to-gosh inventor, she pictured herself right up there with Alexander Graham Bell, Thomas Edison, and her father's favorite hero, Benjamin Franklin. The Fremont woman imagined a type of paint-caddy product that would let a person work on a ladder without dropping or spilling anything or running up and down the ladder. Marilyn Searcy noted, "It was so simple in design, I figured it'd be nothing to manufacture." She added, "Just a few minutes and I'd be on my way to inventor's heaven. ...[26]

Her experience is a reality check for anyone who has ever considered a "new" idea and thought, "I should do this." At that point, Marilyn Searcy applied for a patent to protect the product. She noted, "I thought I had reached and cleared a major milestone." As the weeks and months progressed, she found out she needed much more than a product idea; she needed a business license, a seller's permit, incorporation, checking accounts, product insurance, business and marketing plan, UPC bar-code symbol, graphic artist, packaging, a logo and brochures, and more.[27]

Then she found out the real meaning of crisis. The shop she was using did not have the CNC bender (a computerized machine that pushes wire through wire) she needed to go into huge production. "I didn't even know what a CNC bender was," she says. "I had orders coming in and couldn't fill them. I went through two shops and contacted hundreds all over the country. People told me to go overseas, but I wanted to keep the product right here in the United States." But she says the whole thing is an eye-opener. "I can understand why there aren't more entrepreneurs out there—it's just too hard." She says. "I was not prepared, nor did I suspect the toll all this takes on you. I never suspected that my little idea would turn into something that would keep me awake nights, cost me a minor fortune, and throw me headlong into the dog-eat-dog world of business."[28]

REALITY CHECK

Although some inventors may have the desire to run the ventures that bring their inventions to the marketplace, they need to step back and ask, "Is this the best use of my creative talent?" and "Am I the best person to be running the new venture?" Passion and creativity are noteworthy qualities, but it takes more than passion and creativity to launch a successful venture.

Inventors may suffer the same shortcomings as perfectionists. Their drive for perfection has two major drawbacks. First, they will not launch the product until it is perfect. Timing and quality play key roles in determining whether a new product will be successful. The product must be in sync with when the window of opportunity is open. If the product misses the window, then the whole venture could be left out in the cold. The same applies to the product's level of quality. Quality is defined by consumer expectations, not by the inventor. Inventors may be so infatuated with improving one feature of their product that they lose sight of what is important to consumers. Kenneth Rind as a venture capitalist noted, "We never invest in an inventor. Almost by definition, he only wants to improve his invention and isn't interested in the business as a business."[29]

Second, the product has to meet needs that are not being met at all or well enough in the marketplace. It doesn't matter how innovative the product may be or how many patents it has; if the product doesn't appeal to the market, then it will die of neglect.

Inventors frequently have two other shortcomings. They tend to be very secretive—even paranoid. They are reluctant to provide critical information to prospective investors because they are afraid they will steal their ideas. Inventors also tend to be reluctant to spend money on promoting their products. They believe, "If you build it, people will come." However, Elbert Hubbard once noted, "Parties that want milk should not seat themselves on a stool in the middle of the field in hopes a cow will back up to them." Inventors need to recognize, "Without sales you do not have a business."

Entrepreneurs Need To Be Entrepreneurs

While inventors may fall in love with their products, entrepreneurs tend to fall in love with the prospect of creating a venture to capitalize on a market opportunity. Inventors relish the challenge of solving some technical problem. Entrepreneurs thrive on the challenge of creating ventures that fill market gaps.

The entrepreneur's ability to identify an opportunity and transform it into a profitable business has been the fuel for the fires of free enterprise. Perceptiveness and resourcefulness set entrepreneurs apart from inventors and dreamers. Joseph Mancuso, president of the Center for Entrepreneurial Management, stated, "To be a true entrepreneur, you have to be more than a dreamer: You have to be a doer, too. Fantasies don't sustain entrepreneurs; action does."[30]

The entrepreneur's perceptiveness also includes the ability to sense when the "window of opportunity" may be opening. By scanning the market's horizon, their mental radar screen is able to identify opportunities when they are just beginning to emerge. This gives them lead time to find a way to fill the gap. The lead time may enable them to be a first mover. Jeff Bezos's ability to sense the opportunity early and his commitment to sell books over the Internet gave Amazon.com a two-year head start over Barnes & Noble. By 1998, Amazon.com was doing eight times the Internet sales of Barnes & Noble.[31]

A few entrepreneurs have become masters at developing entrepreneurial ventures. They surround themselves with people who thrive on filling the gaps in the marketplace. These entrepreneurs form internal entrepreneurial teams and provide them with the resources to run free. They also create an untethered environment that encourages people to scan the environment for emerging opportunities. Their firms become "incubators" for hatching new products, new services, and new ventures. They also seek alliances with other firms that will produce symbiotic relationships.

REALITY CHECK

You can't know it all. There are too many hats to wear and too many issues to address. This is why entrepreneurial teams are so important.

The best entrepreneurs are connoisseurs of talent. Robbie Hardy, who founded two software companies and an investment firm, notes, "The team is everything. Ninety-nine percent of entrepreneurs can't do it all on their own. They need partners and teams. One of the highs for me is creating teams." Her people skills are evident in her ability to know what people can do best and empowering them to make the most of their talents. She also knows what she does best and what she doesn't, and enthusiastically shares responsibility and power. Hardy believes her team of people is a primary reason her firms have flourished.[32]

REALITY CHECK

If you are starting the venture with an entrepreneurial team, don't expect each member of the team to be as committed as you. At any given time, at least one member of the entrepreneurial team will feel that his or her circumstances warrant individual treatment. That person may not be willing or able to commit additional time and money into the enterprise. That person may lose interest or the willingness to take on additional financial commitments or expansion risks.

Entrepreneurs Need To Be Leaders

Leadership has been defined in many ways. As the new venture's leader, the entrepreneur represents the electricity that makes the enterprise come alive. Jeff Bezos shed light on the role the entrepreneur plays in creating an exceptional enterprise. He indicated you have to (1) bring together a talented and diverse group of people, and (2) attract them by giving them the opportunity to build something important, to improve customers' lives, and to change the world in some fundamental way. He also noted that great people should also be owners, and they are, through Amazon.com's generous stock option incentives.[33]

Jeff Bezos also stressed the need for entrepreneurs to consistently articulate what is to be achieved. According to Bezos, "You can have the best people, but if they're not moving toward the same vision, it's not going to work."[34]

Entrepreneurs as leaders need to take the long view, see the big picture, establish a clear set of priorities, and make sure the firm keeps moving ahead. Jeff Bezos noted that within the overall vision there are hundreds of smaller ones. As the firm's leader, there are times when the entrepreneur needs to demonstrate brutal triage. In those instances, you have to say, "No we don't this, that, and that; we're going to focus exclusively on these three things."[35]

Entrepreneurs Need To Be Managers

While inventors, entrepreneurs, and leaders are frequently given celebrity status by the media, managers seem to be the Rodney Dangerfields of the corporate world. They get no respect! Yet managers play an essential role in organizations. Bezos highlighted the importance of good management when he was asked if his success was simply the result of being in the right place at the right time. He responded, "I think ideas are easy—it's execution that's hard. If you and I were to sit here for an hour and scribble on this chalkboard on the wall, we could come up with a hundred good ideas. The hard part is making them work, and there are several key components in that."[36]

Managers play a crucial role in the success of an emerging venture. They design systems and monitor operations to make sure things go smoothly and nothing falls through the cracks. Managers make sure quality is up to standard, expenses are within budget, and deadlines are met. Managers make sure the organization gets the optimal use of its limited resources.

Kenneth Olm and George Eddy stressed the need for a new venture to have quality management from its inception. They noted, "A new entry in a highly competitive market lacks the time to develop itself managerially; that could take years. If it is to succeed, it must begin with the requisite talent."[37] Jeffry Timmons also stressed the need for entrepreneurs to have strong managerial skills. He stated, "Entrepreneurship is the know-how to find, marshal, and control resources (often owned by others) and to make sure you don't run out of money when you need it most."[38]

Howard Schultz, CEO of Starbucks, notes, "The ability to recognize limitations in yourself is what determines whether you have a great idea that can become a great business. You can't keep your finger on the pulse of all the issues you'll face; no one person can do everything. Entrepreneurs are bold thinkers, but they're usually not detail-oriented. You need the self-esteem to hire people who are smarter than you and give them the autonomy to manage their own areas. Surround yourself with great people and get out of their way.[39]

Chris Evans, who created Accipiter, a software company, recognized the need for good management. He hired a chief operating officer because management was critical to his firm's growth. He noted, "My strong suit is not management. I needed a detail-oriented individual to manage the day-to-day operations while adhering to my values."[40]

Rob Ryan, who established a boot camp for aspiring entrepreneurs in Montana, feels the ability to establish a team is crucial. He believes an entrepreneur must be able to balance his or her own weaknesses with others' strengths. According to Rob Ryan, the team is the first company element investors assess. Investors know that a hardy team can overcome staggering obstacles, quickly whip up new products, outsmart competition, recover from problems, and make impressive investor presentations.[41]

REALITY CHECK

A new venture's success is contingent on being able to do the right things the right way at the right time. No lender will agree to finance a venture that is understaffed in needed skills.[42]

TYPES OF ENTREPRENEURS

Rob Ryan groups prospective entrepreneurs into seven categories. Each category reflects different aspirations, attitudes, and qualities. Each category also has a corresponding likelihood of creating a successful new venture. Rob Ryan refers to prospective entrepreneurs as "Wanna-bes." He noted that lots of people have a germ of an idea and are convinced that they can turn it into a gazillion-dollar business.[43]

Rob Ryan notes that often Wanna-bes can transform themselves into successful entrepreneurs—but only if they are willing to work hard. A lot of the Wanna-bes he deals with frequently make the classic mistake of not differentiating between the *idea* of a business and the actual *building* of a business. In coming up with a good idea, they think they have already done the hard part of building a company. In fact, what they have done is equivalent to finding their sneakers before running a marathon—they're still not even at the starting line. They haven't built a prototype or gotten feedback from potential customers.[44]

Prospective entrepreneurs fall into one of the following seven categories:[45]

1. *The Quickie Wanna-Be.* This person uses a get-rich-quick business model that has no clear-cut application and no value proposition. Their ideas or models lack sustainability for 10 to 20 years. They are the entrepreneurs who set up websites to get "eyeballs" but not sustainable profits. They tend to take the company public ASAP, manage the stock for maximum valuation, then sell their stock. These companies represent ideas that are in search of money; they aren't *real* companies.

2. *The Wonderful Wacky MBA.* They dance around the conference room whipping out tons of charts and quotes to prove that the market is humongous. In immature industries, nobody knows what they are talking about. If the industry is mature, there are entrenched leaders.

3. *The Send Money Wanna-Be.* They believe all they need to do is get a big venture capital (VC) check in the bank, then everything else will fall in place. These entrepreneurs have it backward. Money follows those who do the right things. These entrepreneurs need to bootstrap during the start-up stage. Entrepreneurs need to spend their time talking to customers rather than running around looking for investors. If you get interested customers, then you might get interested investors.

4. *The Dreamer Wanna-Be.* They are visionaries who are rarely blessed with detailed information or management know-how. If you are in this category, you could admittedly be the next Michael Dell or Bill Gates. But it is more likely you'll end up tinkering in your garage forever. The problem with visionaries is that most of the time they aren't doers. Rob Ryan noted, "They love to sit in a room and think about their great idea or spend hours telling their bored friends all about it. But they don't know how to snap out of the dreamer mode and turn their glorious idea into something real. Even if they do, big dreams usually come with big problems, and these Wannabes aren't always the type to figure out how to work around them."[46] Remember, ideas are like belly buttons; everyone has one.

5. *The One-Stripe Zebra Wanna-Be.* This is a company that is built around a single function in a very narrow market. Perhaps it's even an interesting and viable product, but it's not a wide-enough stripe to support a sustainable company.

6. *The Technoid Wanna-Be.* Technoids are smart about their technology but not always clued in about what it takes to run a business. They need a predictable revenue model and a management team with a track record of working together.

7. *The Guts and Brains Wanna-Be.* They've got the guts to plunge into the real world, even if there is a lot of scary stuff out there. They dig in and do their homework. Sure, they'll get rejected and ignored at first, just like the other Wanna-bes. But this team keeps going. They've got faith in themselves and their business.

    The Guts and Brains Wanna-bes are like the Eveready bunny. They just keep going, and going, and going. They have their act together and are positioned to beat the odds.

Wanted: An Entrepreneur For All Seasons

Michael Dell noted that entrepreneurs come in two basic styles. One is the deal junkie who restlessly seeks new ventures and new markets. The other is the optimizer, who starts with a good idea and then tirelessly executes on that idea.[47] If you were asked which of these two approaches is best, you should answer, "both." Success is the product of great ideas and great execution. The best entrepreneurs are hybrids. They have the innovativeness to come up with new things to do and new ways to do things. They have the entrepreneurial ability to create a venture that can bring revolutionary products and services to market. They have leadership skills to inspire people to do things they have never done before. They also have the management skills to keep their ventures from being derailed by the never-ending challenges that can shut a firm down in a heartbeat.

KEY ENTREPRENEURIAL QUALITIES

Entrepreneurs have gone from being labeled *business misfits* to being heralded for their pioneering spirit. A romantic view of entrepreneurship has grown out of new ventures that have taken on the Goliaths of industry. Ted Turner's CNN took on the major networks. Richard Branson's Virgin Atlantic Airways took on British Airways. Steven Jobs and Steven Wozniak's Apple Computer took on IBM. Steven Jobs even flew the skull and crossbones over his Mac unit's building to symbolize the swashbuckling nature of his venture.

Media coverage of entrepreneurs may give the impression that starting a venture is a romantic endeavor. Yet entrepreneurship also has its low points. Entrepreneurs have more than their share of sleepless nights. New ventures live a precarious type of existence. Even when Amazon.com enjoyed its highest valuation, Bezos told his staff "to wake up petrified and afraid every morning." [48]

Wilson Harrell indicated entrepreneurs are members of *club terror*. He said it is "a private world filled with monsters sucking at every morsel of your being ... [where] there can be no sleep ... just wide-awake nightmares."[49] Harrell noted that being an entrepreneur was similar to his experience in World War II when he was shot down behind enemy lines. He noted that club terror for entrepreneurs comes with having the cash to make payroll, staying up to review accounts, trying to keep your creditors at bay, and having to deal with the challenges no one imagined—death, accidents, building inspectors, vandalism, weather, stock market, skyrocketing oil prices, loss of good employee to become a competitor, and so forth.[50]

Entrepreneurs Have a Vision for What Can Be

Most successful entrepreneurs are driven by a vision for what is possible. They share George Bernard Shaw's observation, "Some men see things as they are and say, why? I dream things that never were and say, why not?" While the world may see the world as it is, entrepreneurs see what it can be.

Steve Schussler created Rainforest Café because he had a vision for the type of restaurant Walt Disney would have created. He combined animatronics with a spectacular interior to create a spectacular restaurant. When executives at Disney finally got around to thinking about the restaurant that should be part of their Animal Kingdom Theme Park, rather than create their own restaurant from scratch, they asked him to put one of his restaurants on the Disney property.

Although some people have the courage to take the road less traveled, entrepreneurs with vision are willing to take *the road yet to be traveled*. Stephen Rebello, as capital strategies editor for *Inc.* magazine, noted that "Visionaries have the capacity to see what others can't (or won't) and the courage to bring their vision to life. Truly successful people have the ability to see new paths and the power to persuade others to follow. ... Through a combination of smarts, bravado, innovativeness, luck, common sense, and insight, they often win fortunes, create legends, inspire imitators, and sometimes become household names."[51] When Ray Kroc saw the McDonalds brothers' drive-in fast food hamburger restaurant in California, he had a vision for what was possible. Thomas Monaghan's vision for delivered pizza was the basis for Domino's. Fred Smith's vision for overnight delivery was the basis for Federal Express. Howard Schultz's vision for a place people could go each day for a break from boredom was the basis for Starbucks' fantastic success.

Entrepreneurs Are Perceptive and Demonstrate a Kaleidoscopic Perspective

Entrepreneurs have the mental dexterity or kaleidoscopic perspective to look at a market situation and see what others cannot see. They also have the mental dexterity to see how one business opportunity may lead to other opportunities. Stig Leschley demonstrated a kaleidoscopic perspective when he recognized there might be numerous opportunities within every business opportunity. While Jeff Bezos was focusing his attention on selling new books, Stig Leschley started Exchange.com, an on-line seller of used books. He sold it seven months later to Amazon.com for $200 million.[52] Michael Dell demonstrated mental dexterity when he realized that he could not gain retail distribution for his fledgling enterprise. He viewed the problem as an opportunity and then explored the idea of selling direct to consumers.[53] Dell's success can be attributed, in part, to his ability to look at situations from various vantage points and his ability to design systems that make things possible that established firms did not consider to be possible or profitable.

Entrepreneurs Are Venturesome

The job description for being an entrepreneur may contain many dimensions, but few dimensions are as important as the ability to take initiative. John Johnson, founder of *Ebony* magazine, says entrepreneurs need to be "responsibly daring."[54] His comment captures the notion that entrepreneurs are modern-day explorers. Entrepreneurs must be prepared to enter doors of uncertainty, to travel unmarked paths, and to navigate uncharted waters.

Entrepreneurs revel in the opportunity to introduce new products and services. Entrepreneurs personify the prelude to *Star Trek*—they are willing to "boldly go where no one has gone before." Bezos noted, "I am entranced by the idea of the impossible (being) achieved."[55]

Entrepreneurs See Opportunities Where Others See Problems

The kaleidoscopic perspective also applies to seeing opportunities where others see problems or nothing at all. Akio Morita, cofounder of Sony Corporation, enjoyed telling the story about two shoe salesmen in Africa. According to Morita, "Two salesmen ... find themselves in a rustic backward part of Africa. The first salesman wires back to head office: 'There is no prospect of sales. Natives don't wear shoes!' The other salesman wires: 'No one wears shoes here. We can dominate the market. Send all possible stock.'"[56]

Ironically, sometimes entrepreneurs see opportunities that are right in front of them and others. The old saying, "If it was a snake it would have bitten you right in your face," applies to a number of interesting opportunities. Dr. Francine Vogler had been a flight surgeon for an air evacuation service that went out of business. When a friend fractured a hip in Italy and wanted to return to the United States, Vogler called transport companies and was told the project would involve chartering a jumbo jet for more than $200,000. She eventually managed to bring her friend back on a commercial jet for $15,000. Her ability to sense a gap in the market served as the basis for creating AIRescue International. She employs a staff of on-call physicians, nurses, and respiratory therapists who respond to pleas for help in leased jets outfitted with lifesaving medical equipment. They have earned the reputation for transporting the untransportable.[57]

Dr. Roy Archambault, who founded Xero Products LLC, also demonstrates how the world is full of opportunities for those who recognize gaps in the marketplace. His patients frequently asked him what they could do to keep their casts from getting wet. Mothers were particularly frustrated with the lack of any way to keep casts dry. They knew it was nearly impossible for kids to keep their casts dry.

Dr. Archambault knew there had to be a better way to keep casts dry than covering it with a garbage bag and taping it closed, which is what most people resorted to due to the lack of anything better. He had been very enterprising while going to medical school to pay his bills, so he investigated ways to keep casts dry. He developed a product using molded latex that surrounds the cast. The product provides a watertight seal around the cast when the air is removed from the latex cover. One model is designed to keep a hand cast dry. Another model covers a cast on one's foot. Dr. Archambault has heard from numerous mothers who thank him for "saving their family's vacation." His watertight cast cover is now sold in 20 countries.

Two things make these preceding two ventures noteworthy. First, Dr. Vogler and Dr. Archambault were certainly not the first people or even the first doctors to be confronted with the corresponding problems. What made them different was that they did something about the problem. Lots of people see a gap in the marketplace, but few take the initiative to do something about it. The problems/gap between what was available and what consumers really wanted had been there for years or even decades. Second, neither Dr. Vogler nor Dr. Archambault had to be physicians to sense to opportunity or to seize it. It was their entrepreneurial spirit that prompted them to transform the gap into an enterprise that delights its customers. Countless others were confronted with the same problems, but they lacked the perceptiveness, motivation, or ability *to boldly go where no firm had gone before.*

Entrepreneurs Live at the Edge

When entrepreneurs take the path yet to be traveled and boldly go where no firm has gone before, they operate where there are no experts, no paths, no certainties, no fail-safe market studies, no trade associations, and no maps. When you are at the edge, you don't have a lot of data when confronted with make-or-break decisions. When you are at the edge, starting a venture may involve taking a leap of faith due to the absence of complete information.

Entrepreneurship is like living a life without a safety net—it is thrilling and dangerous—where misjudgments are punished ruthlessly.[58] The best entrepreneurs are not risk seekers, but they know risk is something that comes with the territory. The precarious and fragile nature of new ventures also creates a sense of urgency where time is of the essence. They look at life as if it is sand in an hourglass. Once the hourglass is turned, there is no way to reverse the flow of sand. They see every moment as a moment that benefits the venture or as a moment that was lost. A line from the movie *The Doctor* captures the sense of urgency. When a doctor approaches a young woman who is dying of cancer and tries to make light conversation, she tells him, "I'm dying and you are wasting my time."

Entrepreneurs Have the Ability to Make
Good Things Happen—in Spite of the Odds

Entrepreneurs approach challenges with the *Apollo 13* "Failure is not an option" mentality. Michael Egan, who started Alamo Rent-a-Car, noted that as an investor he looks for entrepreneurs who can "marry a good idea to good business practices, follow through on those practices, make mistakes, and overcome them without letting those mistakes bury them."[59]

Entrepreneurs Thrive in Times of Uncertainty

Times of great change are also times of uncertainty. Uncertainty implies risk, because you are not sure what is possible and what the probabilities of various possibilities may be. Some people freeze when faced with uncertainty. Most people, especially professionals, try to reduce or eliminate uncertainty by collecting information about the situation they are facing. Entrepreneurs capitalize on change by acknowledging the ambiguity, accepting the risk, and seizing the moment. They know that opportunity is always present in the midst of crises, turbulence, and change.

Entrepreneurs recognize that they do not have the luxury of operating with a "ready, aim, aim, aim, and then fire" mentality. When you are at the edge and time is of the essence, you may have to fire without having much time to aim. They know they need to take whatever information they can muster, do a quick analysis of it, make assumptions for what could be, and then make a timely decision. Steven Jobs demonstrated the ability to constructively deal with uncertainty when he formed NeXT Computer. While no one in the industry thought they could do what they were proposing, he believed his firm was fortunate to be presented with such an opportunity and that it would be a sin not to pursue it.

Amar Bhidé noted that five factors help differentiate winners from the also-rans:

1. Lack of differentiating technologies or concepts
2. Lack of personal traits such as open-mindedness
3. Unwillingness to make decisions quickly
4. Inability to cope with setbacks and rejections
5. Lack of skill in face-to-face selling[60]

Bhidé also noted that entrepreneurs really don't know what works until they actually try it. Entrepreneurs cannot objectively evaluate their relative ability to serve amorphous customer wants without actually starting the venture and launching the product. He also noted that if Bill Gates and Paul Allen had spent the time to do a competitor or market analysis, they might have missed the boat, since several other programmers were trying to develop BASIC for MITS's (a small Albuquerque start-up) Altair at the same time.[61]

According to Bhidé, entrepreneurs deal with uncertainty by using discovery-driven planning and adaptive execution. *Discovery-driven planning* involves plotting a direction into an uncertain future and redirecting as reality unfolds. This type of planning calls for speed, the capacity for rapid response, and insight. Speed is important because opportunities are fleeting. Insight is important because people have to act on inadequate, sketchy information.[62] *Adaptive execution* involves capturing the opportunity without falling prey to many of the pitfalls of high uncertainty. The key concern in adaptive execution is that new and changing business models imply new customers, competitors, and competencies. This forces entrepreneurs to operate with a much higher ratio of assumptions to knowledge than most people may be accustomed to.[63]

Henry Schact, former CEO of Lucent Technologies, noted that it is better for entrepreneurs to be "roughly right" than to consume time developing an analytically correct, but slow answer. This facet of entrepreneurship may be similar to two situations in football. When time is of the essence, the quarterback may have to call the play at the line of scrimmage as he looks at configuration of the opposing defense. Barry Sanders, the great NFL running back for the Detroit Lions, illustrated the need to be able to make decisions on the spot. His ability to adjust to what was happening in realtime made him one of the greatest running backs of all time.

Entrepreneurs Have a Tolerance for Turbulence

Entrepreneurs need to be able to deal with turbulence that comes with times of change and uncertainty. Today's marketplace resembles the white water of a rapids more than the serenity of a placid lake. A lot of people deal with uncertainty by trying to cope with it. Entrepreneurs do more than cope with it; they deal with turbulence in a proactive manner. Entrepreneurship at its best involves thriving in turbulence. Rob Ryan noted, "The true entrepreneur doesn't see change as something to fear or even merely has tolerance for change. Instead, he or she has an appetite for it, recognizing that change is what brings opportunity."[64]

In combat—the ultimate form of turbulence—soldiers need to keep cool under fire. Entrepreneurs need to keep cool when things get rather chaotic. They need to be able to land on their feet. Jeff Bezos admits to being a change junkie.[65] Amar Bhidé noted, "Differences in the capacities to adapt to chance events and to execute strategies for acquiring resources apparently play important roles in separating the winners from the losers."[66] He also noted, "Entrepreneurs who effectively adapt to unexpected problems and opportunities and who persuade resource providers to take a chance on their start-ups can influence their luck. … Savvy entrepreneurs know there are times to follow procedure and there are times to break the rules. They know that changing times often call for organized chaos."[67]

"Entrepreneurs go insanely fast. Look into the eyes of a great entrepreneur, and you'll see him or her parallel-processing more thoughts in a moment than most people do in a day. They consume data as if it were their first drink after 30 days in the desert. They remember everyone else's jobs, because the real fun is in getting their hands dirty. Entrepreneurs don't manage companies into life; they race their visions into reality."[68]

REALITY CHECK

If you are a perfectionist, then you will have to recognize that a fixation on perfection in times of turbulence can be like a straightjacket. Entrepreneurial ventures thrive on experimentation and improvisation. Firms that expect perfection when things are in a state of flux actually kill the creative spirit. Perfection takes twice as long as excellence. In many instances, things just need to be done. According to Wayne Baty, "Nothing is going to send a start-up to the bottom faster than a perfectionist type of personality. The day-to-day process of running a new business is never orderly, and the problems that come up never lend themselves to orderly solutions."[69]

REALITY CHECK

If you are a control freak, then you will have to loosen up. Entrepreneurs are never in control of the employees. Most new ventures live a precarious existence, teetering at the edge of oblivion in their early years. If you believe you can do everything better than everyone in your venture or feel that you must oversee and check—and recheck—everything before any decision is made or anyone does anything, then you will undermine your people and jeopardize your venture's success. "People who are overly concerned with being in control also have little tolerance for subordinates who think for themselves."[70] New ventures will only grow to the extent their entrepreneurs give their people a chance to grow.

Entrepreneurs Need Confidence to Take the Plunge

Entrepreneurs tend to have a higher level of confidence in their ability to make things happen than most people. They also tend to rely less on what others do and to care less about what other people think. Confidence plays a key role in entrepreneurship because you have to believe you can make things happen that you and possibly no one else has ever done before. Confidence gives entrepreneurs the courage to take the first step in a long journey. It also gives them faith that they can meet the challenges they will face and deal with the barriers that stand between them and the fulfillment of their vision.

Confidence for entrepreneurs is two-dimensional. It applies to the belief in oneself and the belief in one's venture. Successful entrepreneurs believe passionately in what they are doing. The negativism of others only strengthens their resolve. At heart, they believe that things will just turn out right in the end.[71] Howard Schultz noted, "People will shut you out. They'll regard you with suspicion. They'll undermine your self-confidence. They'll offer you every reason imaginable why your idea simply won't work."[72]

Confidence is rarely an all-or-none issue. If you have little confidence, then you will not try anything new. If you have too much confidence, then you could be reckless. The key is to have enough confidence to try what should be tried and enough common sense to not grasp for things beyond your reach. Confidence is not the same as cockiness or being egocentric. People do not want to associate with people who are arrogant or so wrapped up in themselves that they cannot work as part of a team. They do, however, want to be part of endeavors that are led by people who can make good things happen.

People who believe in their ability to make things happen usually have a track record for making things happen. "Though the first leap into business can be a scary one, most entrepreneurs have shown the aptitude for enterprise sometime in their past." [73]

Confidence usually has its roots in competence. Desh Deshpande, cofounder of Sycamore Networks, noted, "Prior success, confidence, and the ability to sell are absolutely vital to becoming an entrepreneur, and can be cultivated. The things that have helped me are a track record of prior successes, a well-rounded skill set, and a deep knowledge of the market. In fact, it was a track record in the industry that gave me the confidence to start a business. While at Motorola in Toronto, I expanded a small multiplexing division into a $100 million business. Creating that business gave me the confidence I needed to become an entrepreneur. It also gave me the freedom to work in different areas of the company to broaden my skills."[74]

REALITY CHECK

While this book is designed to help people with a professional background start a new venture, it should be noted that having a professional background might inhibit taking the entrepreneurial plunge. Your training and skills have taught you to minimize risk by operating within the box and playing it safe so you do not rock the boat. Entrepreneurship implies accepting risk and creating turbulence by *making* waves. Starting a venture has far more unknowns and risks than making a minor modification in a firm's product that has been on the market for a number of years. Entrepreneurship also implies being willing to put yourself at risk. People who have been very successful in a corporate environment tend to be reluctant to pull the plug on things even after they have outlived their usefulness. The more successful you become, the more you have to lose from an ego and financial perspective if you embark on the entrepreneurial journey.

Confidence is related to one's attitude, just as it is to one's ability. Entrepreneurs embody Ferrari's slogan, "If you can dream it, we can make it." If entrepreneurs had a national anthem, it would include the lines:

Just because it hasn't been done does not mean that it cannot be done.

and

Just because no one has done it does not mean that I cannot do it.

Entrepreneurs see opportunity in every problem and seek a solution when faced with every setback. Ironically, if entrepreneurs don't know that something can't be done, then they don't know they can't do it. Entrepreneurs succeed when others won't even try. They try because they don't know that what they want to do can't be done.[75]

Here is an example of that kind of spirit. Years ago, a student working on his Ph.D. came in late to class one day looking frazzled. When the professor asked him why he looked so tired, he responded that he had been working through the night on the homework assignment from the previous class. The student indicated he was hesitant about even continuing the class because he had only been able to solve one of the problems that was listed on the blackboard. When the professor realized the student had arrived late for the preceding class, he told him that the list on the board was not a homework assignment ... it was a list of mathematical problems that had yet to be solved by anyone in the world. The student did not know they were impossible. He created an optimization algorithm to do what no one else had been able to do—ever!

Entrepreneurs appear to be driven more by their aversion to missing an opportunity (Anxiety II) that was profiled in the Introduction than their fear of failure. Leonard Batterson noted, "They don't like to fail, but it is not necessary for their survival not to fail. ... The entrepreneur rarely consciously considers the possibility of failure. He is engaged in creating the future."[76]

When Walt Disney was asked about the risks associated with starting a venture, he responded, "I look at it this way: I've been broke five times in my life. One more time won't hurt."[77] The risks associated with Anxiety II help explain why people start ventures. Instead of seeing the risks associated with starting a venture, entrepreneurs see the opportunities that would be lost if they failed to seize the moment. For example, when Steven Jobs, the cofounder of Apple Computer, and Fred Smith, the founder of Federal Express, reflected on the success of their ventures, they claimed they did not consider them to be very risky. Both knew there were corresponding needs/opportunities and that it was inescapable that someone would capitalize on each of them.

Risks are an integral part of doing business. Yet entrepreneurship means taking calculated risks; it doesn't mean being reckless. Savvy entrepreneurs know that operating without a plan is like walking the high wire without a net. Jeff Bezos once indicated, "The high wire never seemed impossible to me."[78] It is heartwarming to see that Michael Dell, Bill Gates, Paul Allen, and other entrepreneurs had the courage to seize the moment and go where no one had gone before. They changed the way we live and work.

REALITY CHECK

The difference between being heralded as a genius versus being labeled as an idiot can be a fine line. Mark Twain observed, "The man with a new idea is a crank—until the idea succeeds." If they had not been successful, then the efforts of Steven Jobs, Fred Smith, and Jeff Bezos would have been seen as folly and subjected to the exclamation, "Anyone with a brain would have known it wouldn't work." Monday-morning quarterbacking is common for people who have never taken and will never take the entrepreneurial journey.

Entrepreneurs Are Opportunistic and Have Contempt for the Status Quo

Robbie Hardy notes, "Entrepreneurs make things happen because they're not satisfied with what they've seen in the marketplace or there's something they need and can't get."[79] Her attitude was reflected in why Professor Dr. Ing h.c. Porsche created his automobile company. He stated, "You must look beyond what has been done before. ... I couldn't find quite the car I dreamed of ... so I decided to build it myself." This quality appears to be inherent to the American culture. This country was founded by people who wanted to create a new way of life. The willingness of entrepreneurs to challenge the merit of almost everything, when combined with a recent desire by American consumers to try new products and services, has fostered a culture where opportunistic entrepreneurs can flourish.

Robbie Hardy also echoed the nonconventional nature of many entrepreneurs when she reflected on her years in established organizations before she shed her shackles and became an entrepreneur. She stated, "I was a success in spite of myself when playing the corporate game for 22 years. I knew I thought about things differently, approached problems differently, and didn't get off on the same things."[80]

Contempt for the status quo is evident in what Joseph Schumpeter labeled *creative destruction.* His concept noted that the marketplace evolves when individuals and organizations create new models that replace less effective, existing models. Niccolo Machiavelli noted in his book *The Prince*, "There is nothing more difficult to take in hand, more perilous to conduct, or more uncertain in its success, than to take the lead in the introduction of a new order of things." It is apparent that one of the things that sets entrepreneurs apart from the crowd is their commitment to create a new order. Entrepreneurs are marketplace revolutionaries. They look for sacred cows and slaughter them. They change the way the game is played by providing breakthrough innovations or by breaking the rules.

Entrepreneurs Are Open-Minded and Quick to Learn

While an earlier section may have indicated entrepreneurs rely more on themselves than others, this does not mean that entrepreneurs should not solicit others' ideas or isolate themselves from the world around them. The best entrepreneurs make an effort to keep an open mind. They are not like a lot of male drivers who will not ask for advice when they are lost. They make an effort to interact with people who have different viewpoints and perspectives. They are also willing to try new approaches.

Their open-mindedness is also apparent in their willingness to revise their mental models and forecasts because of the uncertain nature of their markets and their limited initial planning. In rapidly changing markets, unforeseeable developments can make previously sound assumptions obsolete.[81]

The best entrepreneurs are quick studies. They know that windows of opportunity will open and close swiftly. They also know that nothing—not consumers or competitors—stands still. Their open-mindedness, perceptiveness, ability to learn, flexibility, and agility enable them to see things before others do and to turn on a dime when the situation calls for new things to do and new ways to do things.

Bob Young, cofounder of Red Hat, also noted that entrepreneurs are thieves. Although Thomas Edison said innovation is 10 percent inspiration and 90 percent perspiration, Young believed innovation is 1 percent inspiration and 99 percent theft! Although Young might not have been advocating actual theft, he did recognize that the solutions to some problems might already exist.

Bob Young observed that many entrepreneurs are also like mental sponges. Their eyes are always open to new ideas. Their ears are always listening for new ideas. Entrepreneurs who have an open mind, who scan the horizon for ideas developed by other people, and are able to develop innovative solutions by synthesizing their ideas may be in a position to capitalize on market opportunities.

REALITY CHECK

No one has the advantage of experience in new and emerging markets. When everything is new, people who cling to old ways of doing business are destined to fail. Entrepreneurs have an advantage over most established organizations when they enter new markets. Established firms not only have legacy systems and assets, they also have legacy mindsets. Entrepreneurs do not have the same shackles. They do not have to sever the past before they journey into the future. When things are new and everything is changing, the ability to learn quickly, to decide quickly, to implement quickly, and to change again quickly can provide considerable competitive advantage. The entrepreneurial dimension was captured in the film *The Carpetbaggers*. When the young entrepreneur was asked what he knew about plastics, he responded he didn't know anything, but in 30 days he would know as much about plastics as anybody.

Entrepreneurs Must Be Focused and Decisive

Entrepreneurship is not for the faint of heart, nor is it for those who have a tendency to be indecisive. Kenneth Olm and George Eddy observed that "the successful entrepreneur is the one who first detects and seizes a profitable opportunity … he may not make a comprehensive market survey, but he'll know when to move boldly and quickly."[82]

Entrepreneurship involves making decisions and taking action. Entrepreneurs know that you don't make decisions to make decisions; you make decisions so you can initiate actions that will help you achieve your objectives. Their vision for what the firm should become and their clear sense of priorities enables entrepreneurs to size up the situation and to make decisions quickly.

Although entrepreneurs must make strategic decisions about the nature of the business, the markets it will serve, and the products and services it will offer, the vast majority of decisions are operational in nature. Some days, life for an entrepreneur resembles life in an emergency room. Entrepreneurship is a lot like triage, where important decisions must be made without the benefit of complete information and the time to do extensive research and analysis. This doesn't mean that entrepreneurs should not be diligent, or systematic, or base their decisions on information. It simply means that entrepreneurs cannot afford to succumb to paralysis by analysis.

Most executives who work in established firms are like economists and meteorologists. Economists love to report all sorts of statistics for what the economy has done, but they are rarely willing to bet their jobs on a forecast. Meteorologists have a similar propensity to avoid making commitments. They may offer a forecast, but few of them would actually bet their jobs on their ability to predict what will happen for each of the next seven days.

The best entrepreneurs know how to balance diligence with their bias for action. The saying, "No more prizes for predicting rain; prizes only for building arks," captures the distinction between analyzing a situation and doing something about it. The best entrepreneurs seem to know when the risk of having the world pass them by is greater than the risk associated with not having complete information. This does not mean they fly by the seat of their pants or rely solely on their gut feeling. They actively seek and use whatever information and techniques may be available, but they know when the time for analysis stops and the decision to start the venture begins.

REALITY CHECK

Starting and running a business involves making thousands of decisions. Some people do not have a track record for making good decisions. When faced with a decision, they either freeze and cannot make a decision or they make bad decisions. In some cases, they didn't even realize that a decision had to be made! If you have trouble making decisions, then you will find the entrepreneurial journey to be a painful one. Paralysis, by analysis, can be fatal in a world that can pass you by while you are still processing data.

Entrepreneurs Must Be Committed

The difference between the willingness to make commitments between entrepreneurs and economists and meteorologists was highlighted in the eggs and bacon breakfast story in the Introduction. Entrepreneurs must make numerous commitments each day. Each commitment creates a responsibility to another person or organization to make something happen. Bill Morris, former president of Holly Ridge Foods, places a premium on personal commitment. He has strong feelings against hiring MBAs. He noted that while most MBAs are willing to commit their employer's funds (other people's money), few of them are willing to ante up and put their own funds on the line.

Entrepreneurs have to be truly committed to making their venture an exceptional enterprise. Commitment is particularly important when things get tough. In those times, it is easy to compromise the integrity of the venture. You will be tempted to cut corners, to make commitments you know you cannot keep, and to hire people you know you should not hire. Howard Schultz, CEO of Starbucks, noted, "You have to have a great tolerance for pain! You have to work so hard and have so much enthusiasm for one thing that most other things in your life have to be sacrificed."[83]

Entrepreneurs must also be able to generate a high level of commitment by the other people in their venture. Ross Garber observed, "Entrepreneurs are wonderfully crazy. Most of the great entrepreneurs that I've known have been a bit nuts. They believe so deeply in their ideas that they never say die. They will work without food, sleep, or money until the market says, 'Yes!' They can motivate a group of employees to believe in what they're doing and will attack competitors as if exacting revenge for an insult to their mother."[84]

REALITY CHECK

The challenges of entrepreneurship put a premium on being mentally and physically fit. You will need to have the courage to do the right things when things get tough. If you are trying to reduce your stress and simplify your life, then do not take the entrepreneurial journey. If you don't have the energy to hang in there when things get tough—and they will—then do not leave the comfort zone of your current job.

Entrepreneurs Must Have Passion and Selling Skills

It should be clear by now that you cannot talk about entrepreneurship without talking about risk. Yet most of the attention has been directed to the risks that entrepreneurs take when they start a new venture. Ironically, any time a new venture is created it creates risk for other people and organizations. Banks and investors may be approached for funding. Suppliers will be approached for various products and services. Distributors will be sought to make the products and services available to consumers. Each of these groups will incur risk when they deal with a new venture.

Two other groups—employees and customers—will also be vulnerable. They take considerable risk when they get involved with a new venture. New ventures succeed to the extent they are able to get people and organizations to change their behavior. The entrepreneur's job involves getting them to take the risk that comes from doing business with an untested venture. The more the entrepreneur can reduce the risk for the other parties, the greater the likelihood they will change what they are doing. In a sense, the entrepreneur must create a situation where Anxiety II is greater than Anxiety I for prospective customers and employees.

The same situation applies to attracting quality people. Prospective employees must find the risk and consequences for not joining the new venture to be markedly higher than the benefits they are receiving in their current jobs. Entrepreneurs must make switching worthwhile and as risk-free as possible for the prospective customers as well. Entrepreneurs need to show prospective customers they have their act together, the venture's offering is markedly better than their current suppliers, and that it is going to be around to meet their needs for some time. The ideal situation would be for prospective customers to feel they would be crazy not to do business with the new venture and that they should drop their current product/service providers in a heartbeat!

Your new venture must give prospective employees a truly compelling reason to quit their present jobs. "Attracting successful, powerful, capable people to work in a new venture takes sales ability and conviction. By their nature, capable people are already gainfully employed and in high demand. Your ability to attract top talent is a function of how committed and passionate you are about the endeavor and how well you're able to communicate that to others. People will not sacrifice their stable lives to come to a venture if the founder doesn't seem committed or sure. They must be sold on the idea that they will realize long-term gain for their short-term sacrifice."[85]

Entrepreneurs Need to Be Persistent, Tenacious, and Resilient

Lazy people cannot be entrepreneurs. Leonard Batterson noted that entrepreneurs "are always working and planning their next move, examining the risks in their decisions, and acting, always acting."[86] Time and again, entrepreneurs have to go the extra mile. Howard Johnson, founder of Howard Johnson Company, observed, "Most projects that fail do so simply because their initiators just do not keep doggedly at them—all too often, they give up just short of the goal."[87]

David Gladstone noted that if you look at the track record of a successful entrepreneur, you will certainly find lucky breaks. He noted, however, that the lucky breaks seem to come when the entrepreneur is exerting a tremendous amount of energy to succeed. Gladstone believes that success can be attributed to 10 percent luck and 90 percent hard work.[88]

The entrepreneurial journey is fraught with peril, and success rarely occurs overnight. Persistence helps entrepreneurs stay the course.[89] Jake Burton, founder of Burton Snowboards, provides a good example of the value of being persistent. He began his entrepreneurial career in the garage of his Londonderry, Vermont, home. He stated, "I came close to bailing several times. If I hadn't been so persistent, it wouldn't have ever happened. In the early days, we had to create demand for the product." By 1999, his firm employed nearly 500 employees.[90]

Manfred F.R. Kets de Vries, a psychoanalyst, has observed, "Many entrepreneurs seem to be driven by a magnificent obsession, some idea, concept or theme that haunts them and that eventually determines what kind of business they choose to be in."[91] This obsession can be healthy if it is kept in balance. John H. Johnson, founder of *Ebony* magazine, indicated that he tried 14 different circulation methods for *Ebony* before he hit on the method that finally put him over the one-millionth mark.[92] His persistence gave him the staying power needed to keep experimenting.

Resilience is different from persistence and tenacity. Resilience helps entrepreneurs go the distance by giving them the ability to recover from setbacks. Resilience helps entrepreneurs pick themselves up when they get knocked down. Persistence helps keep entrepreneurs in the game when others feel overwhelmed by myriad challenges associated with starting a venture. Tenacity helps entrepreneurs find a way when their efforts are blocked. Leonard Batterson noted that even the best-laid plans go wrong. Developing and nurturing of a new technical business is a fragile endeavor. Most companies are at some time in the valley of death.[93]

Jay Van Andel, cofounder of Amway, noted, "Running a business is a matter of pressing on in spite of an unending series of unexpected problems."[94] There will be times when the problems seem like waves crashing against swimmers near the shore. Some people will avoid going into the water because they don't want to get knocked down. Some people will stay in the shallows for a while before retreating to the beach from the relentless waves. A few people look at the onslaught of waves and say, "Bring it on."

Earl Graves, founder of Black Enterprise, noted that entrepreneurs need to have a junkyard dog mentality. He noted, "Like the junkyard dog, they hang on no matter how much they are shaken, cursed, beaten, and kicked because they are focused on the task at hand."[95] Amar Bhidé noted that life for entrepreneurs frequently boils down to the ability to handle various annoyances and setbacks. He indicated that unreturned phone calls, long waits in reception rooms, and canceled appointments are par for the course.[96] Mike McCue, cofounder and CEO of Tellme Networks Inc., noted, "Starting up a business is like being in a long sparring match."[97] Herb Kelleher, who played a key role in the creation of Southwest Airlines, spent years in court battles before Southwest Airlines was able to make its first flight. His legal background and unwillingness to give in to the bullying strategies of a number of major airlines were valuable assets.

REALITY CHECK

Jim Valvano's "Never give up" slogan as Coach of North Carolina State University's basketball team may be inspirational to those who have cancer or may be facing any type of other challenge, but entrepreneurs need to recognize when their persistence has been replaced by bullheadedness. Persistence, tenacity, and resilience can be faults if you are unwilling to let go when something doesn't work or where success just isn't going to happen. When taken to the extreme, they become the basis for a fixation or even an obsession that can control your life. Jeff Schwartz's comments as he reflected on the failure of his Remarkable Moments, shed light into what happens when the entrepreneur's tenacity can backfire—when the entrepreneur is not willing to let go and pull the plug on a venture that is going down—to cut one's losses. At 43, Schwartz had committed the last five years of his life to his venture, which offered framed photographs of athletes that allow the consumer to press a button and hear the athlete's words about the event captured in the picture. Ironically, what bugged Schwartz the most wasn't that he started his venture or that it had failed. He regrets that he didn't pull the plug three years earlier when he started going without paying himself, before he had burned another $100,000 of his own money, before his wife quit the PTA and other community activities because of the business's demands, before he had raided his kids' college funds."[98]

Entrepreneurs Need to Be Aware of the Impact They Have on Their People

The best entrepreneurs are connoisseurs of talent. They recognize their own shortcomings and surround themselves with people who bring strengths to the firm. Entrepreneurs also need to create an environment where people can flourish. New ventures grow to the extent their entrepreneurs attract people with various perspectives, encourage the free exchange of ideas, welcome constructive criticism, and nurture the entrepreneurial spirit. Batterson noted, "Working within an entrepreneurial company can be hazardous, particularly if the entrepreneur does not allow the same degree of freedom and creativeness to his employees as he himself demands."[99]

Some people are great at creating ventures. Other people are great at growing emerging ventures. "Great entrepreneurs make lousy managers. They tend to be horribly impatient and don't let people in the organization act on their own. Their energy and passion turns outsiders into believers, but it scares people on the inside. They problem-solve out loud and then watch helplessly as their organization reacts by going to work on each hare-brained idea. If this sounds like you, congratulations. Now let go so your company can take off."[100]

Entrepreneurs Should Use the Talents of People Outside the Firm

Robbie Hardy stresses the importance of getting advice from outside the firm. According to Hardy, "I think a lot of business people take their advisors and service providers for granted. But forging strong partnerships with your accountant and attorney is really important, because they provide that third dimension. They are key to your success, and you should treat them as well as you do the others in your company."[101]

In addition to her service providers, Hardy packed her board with people from outside the company. She believes outside members will reduce the tendency for management to have a myopic perspective. She noted, "These people can keep you out of trouble. They ask a lot of questions because they don't know your business. And that's what makes them so valuable. They give you an outside perspective even when you don't want to hear it ... Boards keep you honest."[102] She also created a technical advisory board to keep a keen focus on real-world requirements for system management capabilities. The board provided technical guidance to the Intrasoft development team on product direction and features, as well as feedback.[103]

Never Underestimate the Value of Experience

People who are embarking on the entrepreneurial journey for the first time should make every effort to have experienced people on their management team. People with experience can help the venture hit the ground running. They should also make every effort to select people with experience to serve on their advisory boards. Experience is like a sixth sense. It gives people the ability to read between the lines and to see what is missing in a situation. They may also have foresight into what may be over the horizon, see around corners, and see walls before they appear.

First-time entrepreneurs also should seek the counsel of successful entrepreneurs. People who have started a number of successful ventures can help you reduce the need for trial and error. They can help you get it right the first time. They know there are times that require immediate action and they know there are times for patience. They know there is never a wrong time to hire the right person. They know if the right person walks in the door, you hire him or her even if you don't have a position for him or her at that time. They know job descriptions can constrain workers. They know everyone in the firm needs to view himself or herself as vice-president of customer relations.

Veteran entrepreneurs also know you need to expect the unexpected. They know that Murphy's Law, "Whatever can possibly go wrong will—and at the most inopportune time," is a fact of entrepreneurial life. They have learned that things take longer than you expected. They have learned that suppliers don't always ship what you ordered. They have learned that contractors rarely meet deadlines. They have learned that the accounts with the most money frequently are the hardest ones to collect from and the slowest to pay. They have learned that you never have all the money you need to do the things that need to be done. Although it is impossible for veteran entrepreneurs to know about everything that can affect your venture, they can help you keep your venture out of the "I wish I had known …" minefield.

CONCLUSION: I DO NOT HAVE SUPERHUMAN POWERS!

This chapter identified various entrepreneurial qualities and challenges. It should be recognized, however, that the requirements will vary with the type of venture being created. Each market and each venture will require certain skills, qualities, and resources. Service firms may require considerable interpersonal skills for employee and customer relations. Manufacturing firms may require considerable technical skills. Firms that are created to serve emerging markets or "operate at the edge" require different skills than firms that operate in more mature industries. The primacy of skills will also vary with the stage of evolution for the venture.

Chapters 3 through 7 will address the need for "goodness of fit" between the entrepreneur's (or entrepreneurial team's) skills, capabilities, and resources and the challenges associated with the specific venture that is being considered. If you are feeling a little inadequate right now, then don't be discouraged. Remember, no person has all these qualities. Olm and Eddy noted, "The entrepreneur must realize at the onset when the enterprise requires more skills than he possesses, and not try to go it alone. He should not deceive himself that he will be able to figure it out later."[104] Entrepreneurship involves more than creating a new venture; it also involves creating a management team. This is why it is so important for you to attract people who will supplement your skills and capabilities.

Your team's skills and capabilities and your venture's resources represent the basis for establishing the competitive advantages that represent the lifeblood for any business—especially a new venture. If you can't do it better, quicker, cheaper, or in a more convenient manner than your competitors, then how do you expect to create and maintain customers?

To every man there comes in his lifetime that special moment when he is figuratively tapped on the shoulder and offered that chance to do a very special thing, unique to him and fitted to his talent; what a tragedy if that moment finds him unprepared or unqualified for the work that could have been his finest hour.

—Winston Churchill

ENDNOTES

1. Leonard A. Batterson, *Raising Venture Capital and the Entrepreneur* (Englewood Cliffs, NJ: Prentice Hall, 1986), p. 109.

2. Amy Lingren, "Questions for Budding Entrepreneurs," *Wilmington Star-News,* March 23, 1997, p, 3-E.

3. *Forbes: Great Minds of Business* (New York: John Wiley & Sons, 1977), p. 49.

4. Anthony B. Perkins, "Greed and Lack of Management Plague Our 'New Economy'," *Red Herring*, December 1999, p. 21.

5. Jason Pontin, "Affluenza," *Red Herring*, January 2000, p. 320.

6. Justin Hibbard, "For Love or Money?," *Red Herring*, January 2000, p. 114.

7. Ibid.

8. Wilson Harrell, "Swapping Principle for Profit Will Not Pay Off in the Long Run," *Atlanta Business Chronicle*, January 31, 1997, p. 1D.

9. Joseph H. Boyette and Jimmie T. Boyette, *The Guru Guide to Entrepreneurship* (New York: John Wiley & Sons, 2001), p. 16.

10. "The Wit and Wisdom of Ted Turner," *Across the Board*, July–August, 1997, p. 13.

11. Hattie Bryant, "Start-up Smarts," *Success*, April 1997.p. 45.

12. Anthony B. Perkins, "The Pussification of Silicon Valley Continues," *Red Herring*, December 1998, p. 14.

13. John Sculley, *Odyssey* (New York: Perennial, 1987), p. 90.

14. Tom Monaghan, *Pizza Tiger* (New York: Random House, 1986), p. 7.

15. Batterson, *Raising Venture Capital and the Entrepreneur*, p. 101.

16. Ibid., pp. 101 and 102.

17. David Gladstone, *Venture Capital Handbook* (Englewood Cliffs, NJ: Prentice Hall, 1988), p. 63.

18. Kenneth W. Olm and George G. Eddy, *Entrepreneurship and Venture Management* (Englewood Cliffs, NJ: Prentice Hall, 1985), p. 41.

19. Heather Page, "High Hopes," *Entrepreneur*, March 1999, p. 132. Reprinted with permission of Entrepreneur Media, Inc.

20. Lingren, "Questions for Budding Entrepreneurs," p. 3-E.

21. Debra Phillips, G. David Doran, Elaine Teague, and Laura Tiffany. "Young Millionaires," *Entrepreneur*, November 1998, p. 125. Reprinted with permission of Entrepreneur Media, Inc.

22. Public Television Special featuring Bill Gates and Warren Buffett.

23. Ibid.

24. Phillips, Doran, Teague, and Tiffany. "Young Millionaires," p. 125. Reprinted with permission of Entrepreneur Media, Inc.

25. John Wall, "Familial Flush," *Insight*, vol. 6, 1997, p. 68.

26. Joan Jackson, "Invention Taught Her She's a Ms Fields, Not an Edison," *San Jose Mercury News*, December 20, 1996. p. 5F. Copyright 2002 © San Jose Mercury News. All rights reserved. Reproduced with permission.

27. Ibid.

28. Ibid.

29. James Sheldon and Burt Alimansky, "8 Demons of Entrepreneurship," *Success*, March 1986, p. 57.

30. Joseph R. Mancuso, "Profile of a Winner," *Success*, December 1985, p. 14.

31. Lesley Hazleton, "Jeff Bezos," *Success*, July 1998. p. 60.

32. Margot Carmichael Lester, "1997 Top Gun," *Business Leader*, January 1998, pp. 16–22.

33. Hazleton, "Jeff Bezos," p. 60.

34. Ibid.

35. Ibid.

36. Ibid.

37. Olm and Eddy, *Entrepreneurship and Venture Management*, p. 54.

38. Jeffrey A. Timmons, "Growing Up Big: Entrepreneurship and Creating High-Potential Ventures," *Texas A&M Business Forum*, Fall 1985, p. 11.

39. Scott Smith, "Grounds for Success," *Entrepreneur*, May 1998, p. 123. Reprinted with permission of Entrepreneur Media, Inc.

40. Kristen Tyler, "An Entrepreneur's Dream: One Company and Two Liquid Events," *Business Leader*, January 1999, p. 28.

41. Rob Ryan, *Smartups: Lessons from Rob Ryan's Entrepreneur America Boot Camp for Start-Ups* (Ithaca: Cornell University Press, 2001), p. 27. © 2001 by Rob Ryan. Used by permission of the publisher, Cornell University Press.

42. Olm and Eddy, *Entrepreneurship and Venture Management*, p. 53.

43. Ryan, *Smartups: Lessons from Rob Ryan's Entrepreneur America Boot Camp for Start-Ups*, p. 15.

44. Ibid.

45. Ibid., pp. 16-26.

46. Ibid., p. 19.

47. Richard Murphy, "Michael Dell," *Success*, January 1998, p. 50.

48. *60 Minutes* interview, CBS, February 3, 1999.

49. Wilson Harrell, *For Entrepreneurs Only* (Hawthorne, N.J.: Career Press, 1994), p. 18.

50. Ibid., p. 19.

51. Stephen Rebello, "Visionaries," *Success*, February 1998, p. 39.

52. Mark Van Osnabrugge and Robert J. Robinson, *Angel Investing* (San Francisco: Jossey-Bass, 2000), p. 16. Copyright © 2000, Jossey-Bass. This material is used by permission of John Wiley & Sons, Inc.

53. Richard Murphy, "Michael Dell," *Success*, January 1998, p. 52.

54. Olm and Eddy, *Entrepreneurship and Venture Management*, p. 29.

55. Hazleton, "Jeff Bezos," p. 60.

56. A. David Silver, *Entrepreneurial Megabucks: The 100 Greatest Entrepreneurs of the Last 25 Years* (New York: John Wiley & Sons, 1985), p. 17.

57. Megan McCorriston and Dina Ingber Stein, "20/20 Foresight" *Success*, February 1998, p. 48.

58. Charles Burck, "The Real World of the Entrepreneur," *Fortune*, April 5, 1993, p. 62.

59. Stephen Rebello, "Visionaries," *Success*, February 1998, p. 39.

60. Amar V. Bhidé, *The Origin and Evolution of New Business* (New York: Oxford University Press, 2000), p. 19.

61. Ibid., pp. 59 & 60.

62. Ibid., p. 7.

63. Ibid., p. 6.

64. Ryan, *Smartups: Lessons from Rob Ryan's Entrepreneur America Boot Camp for Start-Ups*, p. 27.

65. C-SPAN "American Perspectives," May 19, 2001, *www.c-span.org*.

66. Bhidé, *The Origin and Evolution of New Business*, p. 89.

67. Ibid., p. 19.

68. Ross Garber, "Founder Knows Best and Other Startup Myths," *Red Herring*, January 2000, *www.redherring.com*.

69. Sheldon and Alimansky, "8 Demons of Entrepreneurship," p. 56

70. Manfred F.R. Kets de Vries, "The Dark Side of Entrepreneurship," *Harvard Business Review*, November–December 1985, p. 162. Reprinted by permission of *Harvard Business Review*.

71. Boyette and Boyette, *The Guru Guide to Entrepreneurship*, p. 33.

72. Howard Schultz and Dori Jones Yang, *Pour Your Heart into It: How Starbucks Built a Company One Cup at a Time* (New York: Hyperion, 1997), p. 332.

73. Mancuso, "Profile of a Winner," p. 14.

74. Desh Deshpande, "A Joyful Sleeplessness Says You're Ready," *Red Herring*, November 13, 2000, p. 240.

75. Boyette and Boyette, *The Guru Guide to Entrepreneurship*, pp. 30 & 31.

76. Batterson, *Raising Venture Capital and the Entrepreneur*, p. 102.

77. Bob Thomas, *Building a Company: Roy O. Disney and the Creation of an Entertainment Empire* (New York: Hyperion, 1998), p. 190.

78. Hazleton, "Jeff Bezos," p. 60.

79. Carmichael Lester, "1997 Top Gun," pp. 16–22.

80. Ibid.

81. Bhidé, *The Origin and Evolution of New Business*, p. 99.

82. Olm and Eddy, *Entrepreneurship and Venture Management*, p. 41.

83. Scott Smith, "Grounds for Success," *Entrepreneur*, May 1998, p. 126. Reprinted with permission of Entrepreneur Media, Inc.

84. Ross Garber, "Founder Knows Best and Other Startup Myths," *Red Herring*, January 2000, *www.redherring.com*.

85. Deshpande, "A Joyful Sleeplessness Says You're Ready," p. 240

86. Batterson, *Raising Venture Capital and the Entrepreneur*, p. 107.

87. Timothy Patrick Cahill, *Profiles in the American Dream: The Real-Life Stories of the Struggles of American Entrepreneurs* (Hanover, MA: Christopher Publishing House, 1994), p. 37.

88. David Gladstone, *Venture Capital Handbook* (Englewood Cliffs, NJ: Prentice Hall, 1988), p. 256.

89. Christopher, D. Lancette, "Wide World of Sports," *Entrepreneur*, February 1999, pp. 142 and 144. Reprinted with permission of Entrepreneur Media, Inc.

90. Ibid.

91. F.R. Kets de Vries, "The Dark Side of Entrepreneurship," p. 160.

92. Olm and Eddy, *Entrepreneurship and Venture Management*, p. 41.

93. Batterson, *Raising Venture Capital and the Entrepreneur*, p. 123.

94. Jay Van Andel, *An Enterprising Life: An Autobiography* (New York: HarperBusiness, 1998), pp. 16–18.

95. Earl Graves and Robert Crandall, *How to Succeed in Business Without Really Being White: Straight Talk on Making it in America* (New York: HarperBusiness, 1997), pp. 123–126.

96. Bhidé, *The Origin and Evolution of New Business*, p. 106.

97. "First Impressions," *Fast Company*, June 19, 2001.

98. Jerry Useem, "Failure: The Secret of My Success," *Inc.*, May 1998, p. 68.

99. Batterson, *Raising Venture Capital and the Entrepreneur*, p. 106.

100. Ross Garber, "Founder Knows Best and Other Startup Myths," *Red Herring*, January 2000, *www.redherring.com*.

101. Carmichael Lester, "1997 Top Gun," January 1998, p. 21.

102. Ibid., p. 22.

103. Ibid., p. 21.

104. Olm and Eddy, *Entrepreneurship and Venture Management*, p. 53.

2

WHAT TYPE OF VENTURE DO YOU HAVE IN MIND?

The world stands aside for the person who knows where he or she is going.[1]
—John Naisbitt, author of *Megatrends*

Chapter 1 emphasized the need to take an objective look at yourself to be sure you have what it takes to embark on the entrepreneurial journey. This chapter builds on that foundation by profiling different types of ventures. Part of being an entrepreneur involves having a grasp for your level of ambition. Starting a business so you can be your own boss is entirely different from starting a business that has the potential to be in the *Fortune* 500.

Most new ventures will fall into one of five broad categories:

1. Lifestyle ventures
2. Modest ventures
3. Promising ventures
4. High-growth ventures
5. Revolutionary ventures*

These ventures vary in their potential for growth, their rate of growth, the level of skills and experience the entrepreneur and entrepreneurial team will need to have, the amount of resources that will be needed to start and grow the venture, and their ability to attract funding. The ventures also vary in terms of the extent that they lend themselves to formal planning, how innovative they will need to be to be competitive, and the degree of risk associated with them. Each of the five types of venture tends to have a different type of strategy for competing in the marketplace.

---

*These categories were developed by Amar Bhidé. Many of his ideas are incorporated into this chapter and other chapters. His ideas are used with his permission and the permission of Oxford University Press, Inc. I have added some of my own thoughts to each of Amar Bhidé's categories.

LIFESTYLE VENTURES: AN ALTERNATIVE TO WORKING FOR SOMEONE ELSE

Most of the 800,000 businesses started this year are destined to be small businesses if they survive the start-up stage. These ventures play an important role in the marketplace because they provide various products and services, especially at the local level. Although their founders may have dreams of them being very successful, it is unlikely that they will have more than a few employees.

Most new ventures are lifestyle businesses. They represent about 80 percent of all businesses in the United States. While some of these businesses may provide a comfortable lifestyle for their founders, most merely provide a hand-to-mouth type of income. Some of their founders keep them going even if they could make more money by working for someone else. For some people the desire to be one's own boss may be greater than the desire to earn a living.

Lifestyle ventures tend to be copycat businesses. They rarely have a major competitive advantage. They also tend to operate in a limited geographic market where they compete against other lifestyle firms or small franchises. The typical lifestyle business starts small and stays small due to the founder's lack of skills, his or her limited growth aspirations, the lack of competitive advantages, the lack of access to additional resources, and/or the lack of market opportunity.

Many lifestyle entrepreneurs prefer to keep them small so they are manageable. Their small size of operations acts like a comfort zone for them. They know their limitations and stay within their abilities, risk tolerance, and resources. They may even recognize the time and risks associated with taking their ventures to the next level exceed their potential benefits. Their primary concern is to have their own business and to keep it going. Even though their ventures may not be very successful, working for someone else and not being able to do something they really enjoy doing are not acceptable alternatives to them. In some cases, the lifestyle entrepreneur's focus is merely to create a job for himself or herself.

The beauty of most lifestyle ventures is their simplicity. They do not require a lot of capital or extensive business experience. Yet the ease of entry and the minimal need for resources means that they can face a lot of competition. They often survive because they are competing against businesses that also lack competitive advantages. While a few lifestyle businesses may provide great customer service or have a very desirable location, most are similar to the other lifestyle ventures in the same markets. The lack of differentiation and the presence of other businesses limit their ability to charge higher prices. This keeps them from being very profitable. When a truly formidable competitor like Wal-Mart enters their territory, they are usually blown out of the water.

The difference between *popularity* and *profitability* was highlighted in a study of *Inc.* 500 firms by Amar Bhidé. None of the firms he interviewed were involved in the types of businesses that made the "Most *popular* start-ups" list compiled by County Data Corporation (CDC).[2] The list included restaurants, beauty salons, construction firms, and cleaning services. Although the CDC's list of the 20 most popular fields account for about a quarter of the start-ups formed in the United States, they might not hold the promise for much profit or growth. The types of firms that have made the *Inc.* 500, however, have demonstrated considerable profit and sustained growth.

REALITY CHECK

Remember, there is no pleasure when your business is losing money and you have to liquidate your personal assets in what could be nothing more than an exercise in futility.

If you want to combine business and pleasure, then make sure the business will make a sufficient profit to cover your time, effort, and risk. Although some types of lifestyle businesses make more money than others, few make a significant profit.

REALITY CHECK

Lifestyle businesses may be appropriate for people who have modest financial goals. If you want to travel a lot, build a pension so you can retire early, or contribute to a child's or grandchild's college fund, then starting a lifestyle business is probably not the way to go.

MODEST VENTURES: VIABLE VENTURES BUT NOT THAT PROFITABLE

Modest ventures represent about 15 percent of all businesses. They grow beyond the typical lifestyle business. Their entrepreneurs balance keeping their ventures going while striving to keep them growing. Unlike most lifestyle ventures, modest ventures may generate a reasonable income for the entrepreneur. Modest ventures fall into three categories. The first and largest group is composed of businesses that are better than most of the lifestyle businesses they are competing against in the marketplace. Their founders approach them as businesses rather than just an alternative to working for someone else.

The second group usually starts out with the intent of being lifestyle businesses, but market demand rather than the entrepreneur's ambition pulls them to a higher level of business activity. These businesses experience what may be considered "reluctant or even accidental growth." They grow by default rather than by plan. Although their entrepreneurs do not want to commit more time or money to the business, they allow their businesses to grow. They recognize that if they do not grow other businesses may take their customers.

The third group is composed of modest ventures that, at best, stay modest ventures because their founders do not have the skills needed to enable them to keep growing. Growth is avoided because it may bring challenges beyond the entrepreneur's level of skills. Like most lifestyle entrepreneurs, they prefer to stay in their comfort zone. Their unwillingness to make any changes and venture forward is referred to as *management by Braille*. They will only deal with things within their immediate time horizon and reach. Unfortunately, their founders choose to maintain the status quo rather than to venture ahead when they encounter problems. Their lack of a growth plan and corresponding lack of commitment to improving their businesses on a continuous basis usually causes their downfall. In a sense, their complacency and tendency to take their customers for granted opens the door for other entrepreneurs who are more in sync with market needs and who will commit the resources to creating and maintaining customers for a profit.

Most successful modest ventures can be characterized by their "incremental" competitive strategy. They try to maintain or enhance their competitive position by making periodic improvements. They may grow by expanding their territories and/or improving their products and services. They also tend to be open to ways to improve their people and operating systems. Most modest ventures live by the credo *improve or die*.

Most modest ventures avoid situations where they have to compete against larger businesses. They stay close to home and operate in relatively small market niches. Most choose to compete in terms of customer service. Their limited funds keep them from being aggressive. Their lack of innovation keeps them from gaining a major competitive advantage.

> ### REALITY CHECK
>
> Modest ventures can be very challenging. The marketplace shows no mercy for those who are not committed to being competitive. Entrepreneurs have to be savvy to the ever-changing marketplace and willing to keep their ventures positioned so they will not be blown out of the water by larger firms that have more resources and other emerging ventures that have the agility to capitalize on their competitors' shortcomings or emerging opportunities.

PROMISING VENTURES: CAPITALIZING ON HOSPITABLE MARKETS

Promising ventures represent about 4 percent of all ventures. Promising ventures have numerous characteristics that separate them from lifestyle and modest ventures. The following eight characteristics are particularly noteworthy:

1. Intent
2. Focus
3. Incrementalism
4. Execution
5. Hospitable markets
6. Scale
7. Scalability
8. Proximity

First, they are created with the *intent* to be a force in the local or even regional marketplace. Their founders want to create a business that will generate a level of wealth and stature that is not possible in a lifestyle business or even a modest venture.

Second, they *focus* their attention on being the best they can be in a particular market niche. A good way to look at promising ventures is to draw the parallel with high school wrestling. High school wrestling divides wrestlers into various weight divisions so that the wrestlers compete against students their own size. The best wrestler in that weight division is likely to win the match. In most cases the best wrestler in a weight division will be able to beat the wrestlers in lower weight divisions. Promising ventures operate with the same principle. They are very good at what they do in the markets they serve. They keep growing because they attract customers from less competitive ventures and they don't try to compete directly with large businesses.

Third, they use a more aggressive *incremental* strategy for attracting and keeping customers. Their founders recognize that they will have to be better than their competitors if they want to capture their customers. Once started, they continue growing by making continuous improvements and/or through occasional innovation. It is interesting to note, however, that if they are innovative in their products, services, or processes, they tend to be a second or third generation of the products, services, or processes. They are better at improving on another firm's innovation than creating a first-generation innovation.

Most promising ventures make up for their lack of true innovativeness through their ability to continuously improve and to execute well. They know that if they are consistently better than their competitors in regional and local markets, then they will create and maintain customers for a profit. Tom Smith captured this attitude when he was president of Food Lion, a successful regional grocery chain. When he was asked why his firm was so successful, he stated, "We're 1 percent better in 1,000 different things."[3] Smith's emphasis on being better by making improvements rather than trying to be highly innovative characterizes the competitive strategy used by most of the promising ventures. In baseball, you can score a run by having a number of successive hits or by hitting a home run. Most promising ventures focus their attention on getting hits.

Fourth, their ability to enter a market and to continue growing by satisfying their customers and capturing their competitor's customers can be attributed to *execution*. The ability to out-execute one's competitors is directly related to the quality of the management team and the systems the management team use to make sure things do not fall through the cracks. A number of the firms that have made it to the *Inc.* 500 list got there by entering markets that had been around for some time and that were served by lifestyle or modest ventures. The founders of the promising ventures captured substantial market share by professionalizing operations that used to be rather amateurish.

Domino's and Subway provide two classic examples of what can happen when a new venture enters the market with the ability to execute well. Neither business is very complicated. Domino's provided an alternative to risking your life driving to get a pizza. Subway provided a healthy alternative to fast-food hamburgers and french fries. Both ventures have grown because they developed well-orchestrated systems for providing or delivering a good product to market segments that were not having their needs met well. Their strategies, systems, and resources, when combined with a rapidly expanding market, enabled both ventures to keep growing. As their markets evolved, they demonstrated their ability to provide a continuous stream of improvements to keep pace with the changes and to deliver their products and services in an efficient manner with minimal glitches. Both firms went on to become high-growth firms when they made the commitment to become national and then international firms.

Fifth, promising ventures operate in *hospitable markets*. They seem to thrive in markets where they can be successful without having to be exceptional. Markets are considered hospitable when three particular conditions exist. First, they are large enough to support numerous small- to mid-sized ventures. Second, the markets are growing. When the pie (market) is growing, then each piece of the pie (overall sales per market share) also grows. This minimizes cutthroat competition for customers. Third, they tend to be niche markets. Their markets and their firms are not large enough to attract larger firms. This means that promising ventures do not have to compete against firms that have economies of scale, major distribution clout, or dozens of MBAs trying to develop competitive strategies that will blow their competitors out of the water. When these three conditions exist, good firms can make a reasonable profit and really good firms can make a very respectable profit. Most of the *Inc.* 500 entrepreneurs interviewed by Amar Bhidé indicated their businesses generated a positive cash flow within months of launch.[4]

Firms operating in hospitable markets do not have to operate "at the edge." Hospitable markets do not require large investments in capital, wow technology, brilliant people, or highly sophisticated systems. Hospitable markets don't require patents or other types of intellectual property, breakthrough innovation, or unique products. Most service markets are very hospitable. Amar Bhidé's research indicated that 90 percent of *Inc.* 500 companies don't offer a unique product or service. Their success can be attributed to the hospitable nature of the markets they compete in.[5]

Promising ventures appear to be well suited for playing straight poker where there are no wild cards. Their markets seem to be very straightforward. Promising ventures are very successful because they know how the game is played and they play it well. Promising ventures seem to recognize growth opportunities when they arise in their markets. They are successful because they position themselves to capitalize on those opportunities. Promising ventures are successful because they are acutely attuned to their targeted market niche and do a better job serving it than their competitors.

Sixth, their relative size or *scale* of operations is another distinguishing feature. Their founders tend to sense that there may be an optimal size for their ventures. When their ventures achieve the critical mass needed to be competitive, their founders are not preoccupied with being a lot bigger. They direct their attention to being better and grow only when it will help them get better. They also know that growing too quickly is like "driving beyond your headlights."

Entrepreneurs of promising ventures know their limits. They avoid getting into a head-to-head battle with the Wal-Marts of their world. Promising ventures reflect the saying, "The one-eyed man rules in the Kingdom of the Blind." Although they may be better than their immediate competitors, they recognize they do not have the depth of talent, systems, and resources to dominate large markets or to compete directly against the Goliaths of their industries. When they do choose to compete against larger businesses, then they make a deliberate effort to develop strengths that attack the larger competitors' weaknesses.

Promising ventures frequently make the *Inc.* 500. Their sustained rate of growth clearly outpaces modest businesses. The 25 fastest-growing firms in the *Inc.* 500 in 2003 had an average rate of growth for the last five years of 8,250 percent. The top 25 firms had an average sales of $60 million, 251 employees, and had been in business for eight years.[6] American Biophysics, which sells a mosquito-killing machine, topped the list with 25,615 percent growth in five years and $54 million in sales.[7]

The rate of growth for *Inc.* 500 firms illustrates the differences between innovation and improvement. Research by Amar Bhidé indicated that making incremental improvements and execution may be all that it takes in some markets to have a competitive advantage. In fact, execution might be more important than being innovative. Bhidé found that the typical *Inc.* 500 company starts with products or services that are similar, at least in their tangible attributes, to the products or services offered by other companies. Of the 100 *Inc.* founders he interviewed, only 6 percent even claimed to have started with unique products or services. Nearly 60 percent said that identical or very close substitutes were available for their product or service. The rest of the *Inc.* 100 entrepreneurs interviewed indicated slight to moderate differences between their offerings and those of their competitors.

Another study of *Inc.* 500 founders indicated only 12 percent of the founders attributed the success of their companies to "an unusual or extraordinary" idea. Almost 90 percent reported their success was mainly due to "exceptional execution" of an ordinary idea.[8] Bhidé's research also found that *Inc.* 500 ventures were successful because they were niche players. He found that fewer than 5 percent of the *Inc.* 500 start-ups he studied competed against large *Fortune* 500-type companies.[9]

Seventh, *scalability* contributes to the success of most promising ventures. Domino's and Subway succeeded in the beginning because they really weren't taking on Pizza Hut or McDonald's. Instead, they were providing an alternative—offering something that McDonald's and Pizza Hut were not providing. Scalability was critical to their initial success. Neither business had to start off on a national scale so they did not require much capital. By starting on a small scale, they had the time and the opportunity to get their act together. Their small scale also let them stay under the radar of Pizza Hut or McDonald's until they had established brand identity.

Scalability has another advantage. Being able to start on a small scale in most cases permits the venture to be internally funded. Having a low initial capital requirement enables many founders to finance their ventures by themselves. As their ventures grow, they may be able to finance their growth through retained earnings. The typical *Inc.* 500 company studied by Bhidé started off with less than $30,000.[10]

Eighth, *proximity* may influence the type of venture started. Founders of numerous promising ventures usually do not reflect the prelude to *Star Trek*. They don't "boldly go where no one has gone before." They tend to start businesses in fields where they have worked. This is known as the *proximity effect*. Most of the founders imitated someone else's ideas that they often encountered in the course of a previous job.[11]

McDonald's and Starbucks Coffee Company demonstrate how proximity can make a difference. While both firms have become major international businesses, their growth can be attributed to someone stumbling across them and who saw what they could become. Ray Kroc did not start McDonald's. He worked for a company that made malt mixers. He noticed that a small restaurant in California was buying far more mixers than other restaurants. When he was on vacation in California, he stopped by to learn what made McDonald's so different. When he visited the drive-in restaurant, he was amazed at the level of business generated by one store. He then bought the rights to McDonald's from the two McDonald brothers.

Howard Schultz also benefited from the proximity effect. When he worked in marketing for Starbucks it was a small coffee-bean distributor. While on vacation in Italy, Schultz observed how people flocked to neighborhood coffeehouses. When he returned to Starbucks, he presented his idea for establishing retail stores to the owners. When it was clear that they did not want to go the retail route, Schultz bought Starbucks and created what some consider to be "the third place" people go (other than work and home) on a daily basis.

Although promising ventures can be very challenging, they also can be fairly lucrative. They are real businesses making real profits. Many promising ventures can be very rewarding from a return on investment perspective, because they do not require a relatively large investment. Many promising ventures can generate profits that make it worth quitting even a high-paying job.

While promising ventures may be smaller and make less profit than high-growth ventures, they have four major advantages over high-growth ventures:

1. They tend not to have outside investors; the business is still *your* business.
2. They operate in markets without considerable uncertainty. They tend to serve markets that are already established.
3. They are not competing against firms that can blow them out of the water.
4. Major innovation is not critical.

Promising ventures can do well if they are consistently better than their competitors. Conversely, many high-growth ventures live at the technological edge. If they don't have the latest "Wow!" technology, then they crash in flames.

REALITY CHECK

It is easy for a promising venture to get *delusions of grandeur* and to grow too fast. Promising ventures succeed only to the extent they keep getting better at what the market values and avoid competing with the Goliaths.

HIGH-GROWTH VENTURES: PROFESSIONAL MANAGEMENT IS ESSENTIAL

High-growth ventures represent about one-tenth of 1 percent of all ventures. They are the one-in-a-thousand businesses that are truly exceptional. The better promising businesses might make it into the *Inc.* 500; a few high-growth ventures might make it into the *Fortune* 500 and be among such notable firms as Amazon.com, Dell Computers, and Southwest Airlines. The odds might make it seem like it would be nearly impossible to start a high-growth venture, but two things may be going in your favor. First, the vast majority of start-ups and existing ventures are not positioned to capitalize on the high-growth opportunities. Their founders either don't have the ambition or they don't have the vision, talent, or the resources to capitalize on them. Second, there are a lot of high-growth opportunities out there. There have never been as many opportunities as there are today. Perceptive entrepreneurs live by Peter Drucker's observation, "Within every problem there lies at least one disguised opportunity." Big problems provide big opportunities, and firms that catch the opportunity waves early are in a position to experience dramatic growth.

The founders of promising firms should be commended for their willingness to embark on the entrepreneurial journey and for their ability to develop competitive advantages in their corresponding niche markets. Yet it should be apparent that most of them recognize their limitations. Their success is partly due to their competing against similar ventures in hospitable markets, where being very good is good enough to make a difference. Few promising ventures, however, are positioned to capitalize on high-growth opportunities, and few promising ventures can compete with high-growth ventures that enter their markets. Exhibit 2.1 profiles some of the differences between promising and high-growth ventures.

Dimension	Promising Venture	High-Growth Venture
Founder's skills	May have worked in that field	Extensive experience in field
Ambition	Reasonable profit	High return on investment
Entrepreneurial experience	First start-up	May be serial entrepreneur
Management team	None to limited	In place or soon to be there
Search for opportunity	Proximity	Active and open search
Competitive strategy	Incrementalism and execution	Innovation and execution
Funding	Internal	May attract outside funding
Systems	Generally available	Professional or state of the art
Market orientation	Best of similar firms	Market leader
Scale	Small to moderate	What ever it takes to dominate
Growth objective	Bottom part of hockey stick	Handle of hockey stick

EXHIBIT 2.1   PROFILES OF PROMISING AND HIGH-GROWTH VENTURES

High-growth ventures are considerably different from promising ventures. They are different right from the start and they continue being different throughout their evolution. Most high-growth ventures are created to be high-growth ventures. They are created because the founder identified a lucrative opportunity or developed a new product, service, or process with considerable potential. Founders of promising ventures usually stumble across an opportunity as a result of proximity. A study of *Inc.* firms revealed that only 7 percent had done a systematic search for business opportunities.[12] Founders of high-growth ventures usually do a more systematic analysis of the market in their effort to identify potential opportunities.

The two types of ventures also differ in the amount of planning that goes into their launch and growth. Amar Bhidé's research indicated that 41 percent of the *Inc.* 500 entrepreneurs had no business plan at all, 26 percent had just a rudimentary plan, and only 28 percent wrote a full-blown business plan.[13] Business plans are an essential part of any start-up because they will reduce trial and error. They can also help accelerate growth. They are particularly important if the venture is to involve complexity, grow quickly, face stiff competition, raise outside capital, and attract talent. The relative lack of a business plan by even promising firms indicates the founders did not have either the knowledge of how to do one or the willingness or discipline to take the time to prepare one.

They may also get away with not developing a business plan if they can fund their ventures internally. Entrepreneurs of promising ventures may also get by without having a plan if their competitors also fail to plan for the future. Their success without a business plan to guide them may be attributed to operating in hospitable markets and doing a better job than their competitors who also did not operate with a well-developed business plan. With promising ventures, using the "just do it" approach to launching their ventures and being very good may be good enough to make a profit—until a firm enters the scene that approaches every facet of business in a more proactive and professional manner.

High-growth ventures live a much more precarious existence than promising ventures. They tend to operate at the edge of technology or face more formidable competitors. These conditions require a higher level of entrepreneurial prowess and professional management. Their existence may be even more precarious if they are seeking angel or venture capital funding.

Many entrepreneurs of promising ventures use the old approach of just jumping in when starting a venture. Hoping for the best will not be enough, however, to start and manage a high-growth venture. Professional management is important because high-growth ventures usually compete against firms that have professional management. Professional management is particularly important if the venture will be seeking external funding.

Some entrepreneurs go boldly into the night like a moth irresistibly attracted to a flame! Entrepreneurs of high-growth ventures need to demonstrate a more deliberate "look before you leap" approach when starting a venture. Professionals approach decision making in a more systematic manner, develop a network of value-added individuals, seek advice from other professionals, and base decisions on data rather than gut feelings. Professionals recognize that each situation is unique. They gather data, analyze it, explore alternatives, choose the best course of action, develop a plan, and then implement it to make things happen. Amar Bhidé's research indicated that more than half of the founders of *Inc.* 500 firms did not consult with a lawyer and three-quarters did not develop any marketing materials. It also revealed that only 4 percent of the *Inc.* founders Bhidé interviewed found their business ideas through systematic research.[14] This may explain why promising ventures do not become high-growth ventures.

REALITY CHECK

The preceding paragraphs are not intended to be criticisms of *Inc.* 500 ventures. Promising ventures play a crucial role in our economy. They create jobs and provide quality goods and services at competitive prices. They also demonstrate the entrepreneurial spirit is alive in almost every community. The preceding paragraphs merely reflect that there are opportunities for even higher levels of growth if you are positioned to operate on an even higher level in more challenging markets. *Inc.* 500 ventures can be very successful but few are formidable or truly exceptional. They don't have the skills, systems, and/or resources to dominate medium to large markets. They cannot, for instance, contemplate high-volume production where they would have to incur substantial costs in advance of the realization of revenues. Their small scale and lack of capital minimize their chances for attracting major funding. Instead, most of them operate in niche markets where they cannot realistically expect million-dollar profits. They succeed because they do not need much working capital or up-front investment in R&D, manufacturing facilities, or marketing. They also succeed because they do not have to confront large rivals. Most of the *Inc.* companies studied by Bhidé started off by serving local markets or a small number of customers with specialized needs.[15]

REALITY CHECK

It is possible for a high-growth venture to succeed, at least initially, without professional management if the market is very hospitable and the venture offers a superior product. Microsoft was created without much deliberation. When Paul Allen and Bill Gates developed Microsoft's first product, they did not do any market research or competitor analysis first and they did not even write a business plan.[16] Starting a venture and getting outside funding usually require a higher level of management sophistication. Bhidé observed that few individuals start with the ideas and human capital necessary to secure VC funding. He noted that Bill Gates probably could not have received VC funding in the beginning.[17] Microsoft's management team at that time was untested and the market was too uncertain to garner external funding.

REALITY CHECK

Professional management needs to be put in perspective. Approaching things in a systematic manner has its merits, but it should not be taken to its extreme. Some people are so risk averse that they are unable to make a decision. They succumb to paralysis by analysis where they want to postpone a decision until they know it is right. They operate with a "ready, ready, ready, aim, aim, aim … but never fire" mentality. They want complete, accurate, and timely information so they will not make mistakes. Entrepreneurs need to recognize they will never have all the information they would like before having to make important decisions—including starting a venture. Entrepreneurship implies risk because you will not have perfect information. Entrepreneurship, however, does not call for reckless abandon. Successful entrepreneurs indicate they were willing to take calculated risks.

REALITY CHECK

This book emphasizes the need for and benefits associated with approaching the entrepreneurial process from a professional perspective. You should exercise caution against "paralysis by analysis" and preoccupation with being an extremely "professional organization." Systems and procedures are nice but you also need to have the emotion that ideas bring to seize the moment and the creative juices flowing to foster innovation. The need for having "professional systems" must be put in perspective. John W. Gardner, who founded Common Cause, observed, "Human beings are forever building the church and killing the creed."[18] Professionalism and entrepreneurial activity are not two ends of the same continuum. The key to success is finding a way to professionalize your venture without losing the energy and spirit of entrepreneurship.

Innovation is one of the main differences between promising ventures and high-growth ventures. High-growth ventures rely on innovation in their effort to capture customers and become market leaders. Although promising ventures tend to rely on incrementalism, high-growth ventures bring breakthrough innovation to the marketplace. If their innovation is not the type of first-generation that creates a market and enables them to be market makers, then it is the type of innovation that takes the market to the next level and leaves other firms behind that are less innovative. In both instances, their innovation has strategic impact on the market by either bringing new customers into the marketplace, capturing market share, or increasing the importance of the product or service to present consumers.

High-growth ventures frequently introduce *killer applications* or *category killers*. Their innovations are so much better that they blow all the other firms out of the water. The pursuit of a killer app is similar to the strategy used by pharmaceutical firms. Pharmaceutical companies, for example, try to develop new drugs that will gain FDA approval. When the FDA approves a drug, it acknowledges that the new drug is superior to all the drugs of that type already on the market.

Promising ventures stand out in their markets because of their ability to execute well. High-growth ventures, however, are exceptional enterprises because they combine innovative products, services, and/or processes with excellent execution. Their rate of growth also attracts outside investors. Angels, venture capitalists, corporate partners, and/or strategic allies want to get a piece of their action. These investors tend to become involved very early in the venture's evolution because the venture needs to move quickly to capitalize on the opportunity and capture that market. It is not unusual for high-growth ventures to attract millions of dollars in venture capital.

The ability of high growth-ventures to attract outside funding is contingent on numerous factors. If the entrepreneur/team do not appear to be able to capitalize on the opportunity, then there will not be external funding. If the entrepreneur/team look solid, but the opportunity does not appear to be lucrative, then there will be little chance for outside funding. If a strong entrepreneur and management team are in place and the opportunity for substantial returns is there, then outside funding will usually be there.

Promising ventures may have the potential to be profitable, but they rarely have the potential to make substantial profits. They rarely have high-growth potential because the niches they serve are too small to be very lucrative, the entrepreneur/team have limited depth and ability, or they do not have the level of innovation needed to blow other ventures out of the market.

For a high-growth venture to succeed over an extended period of time, three criteria must be met:

1. The market must be large enough to permit a high level of sales and profitability.
2. The entrepreneur/team must be savvy enough to make sure the venture is properly positioned and executes well.
3. It must be innovative enough to attract new customers.

In short, the high-growth ventures also tend to be high-risk ventures because they live at the edge. For people to be willing to risk their money, they must believe the ventures can generate high returns. If investors believe the level of risk exceeds the expected level of returns, then they will not be willing to commit their funds to the venture.

High-growth ventures also make every effort to ensure they are not one-hit wonders that characterize "here today, gone tomorrow" ventures. They are relentless in their effort to provide what the market wants and to do it in such a manner that no other firm can touch them. They constantly improve their systems and people so they do not leave the door open for potential competitors.

Many of today's household brands/products like Dell, Microsoft, Southwest Airlines, and Subway either did not exist or were relatively unknown a few decades ago. When you combine great people with great ideas and great execution with sufficient resources, then the world may beat a path to your door! Funding plays a crucial role for high-growth ventures. It fuels the start-up and sustains the growth. If you have the perceptiveness to spot an opportunity when no else sees it and have the ability to bring together a team of people who have the ability to turn your vision for a great company into a reality, then the money will follow.

REALITY CHECK

If you have heard there is not any money out there to invest in emerging ventures —that is not the case. Investors no longer throw money at wild-eyed 20-year-olds who map out some idea on a cocktail napkin that has not been subjected to any type of reality check. There is money out there looking for ventures that make sense and that are positioned to take off. The key to getting funding is to show you have what it takes to make it happen, that a substantial and lucrative market opportunity exists, and that your firm is or can be markedly superior to existing firms and potential entrants.

REALITY CHECK

Good news! First movers in a forgiving/hospitable market don't have to be great. Dell Computer and Apple Computer were created by young people who saw a gap and created businesses to turn the gap into a business opportunity. These firms didn't have deep management teams or the most sophisticated systems. But as they grew and sought external funding, they recognized the need to professionalize their firms to attract investors and to be competitive against other firms. For example, Apple Computer recognized that while cofounder Steven Jobs might have been highly creative it needed to bring in a veteran executive to guide Apple's growth in an increasingly competitive marketplace. Apple recruited John Sculley from Pepsi because he had extensive experience competing against large firms and was fascinated with technology. He helped Apple craft a strategy for sustained growth and professionalized its systems. He also tried to ensure that Apple would continue growing by having innovative products in its pipeline. Emerging ventures that did not professionalize their firms fell by the wayside.

REALITY CHECK

It would have been interesting to see what would have happened if Dell, Apple, and Microsoft really had been started with a professional management team from the beginning. That is what this book is about. It stresses the need to combine professional business skills with emerging business opportunities!

REALITY CHECK

Few businesses are overnight successes, for three reasons. First, when you are at the edge few things are certain. You need to find out what works and what does not work. This requires experimentation and adaptation. The road to success is rarely a straight path. It tends to be a path with curves and setbacks as you navigate uncharted territory. Second, it may take years to develop the competencies and sufficient assets (scale) needed to serve and ultimately dominate the market. Third, you may need to wait for the market to take off. The rate of growth for a high-growth venture is contingent on the size and rate of growth of the market as well as the venture's ability to capitalize on the market opportunity. Every market is unique. Some windows of opportunity open slowly and stay open for an extended period of time. Other windows blow wide open and then close almost as quickly as they opened. Rolling Stone, Calvin Klein, Waste Management, and Wal-Mart started without much capital or a lot of fanfare. They did not exhibit hockey-stick growth* for quite a while. It took those companies decades to develop the assets and organization that eventually made them the leaders in their fields.[19]

---

*Hypergrowth is usually described as hockey-stick growth. The lower part of the stick reflects moderate growth. The handle, however, is shaped with a greater slope.

REALITY CHECK

Windows of opportunity are like waves. You will need to anticipate when the right wave will appear on the horizon, put yourself out there so you can catch it early, be positioned to ride it to the fullest, and kick out before it gets too crowded or it crests just before it crashes on the shore.

REALITY CHECK

High-growth ventures require capital to grow. Sales revenue and retained earnings will not be enough to fund a high rate of growth. Unless you are sitting on a ton of money, you are going to have to give up some of the firm to angels and/or venture capitalists fairly early in its evolution to enable it to be a high-growth venture.

REALITY CHECK

Even if your venture falls short of being the one in a thousand, it will be well worth the effort. Even being a one-in-a-hundred type of venture will still make it all worthwhile. The venture will still generate a very respectable level of wealth and distinction.

REVOLUTIONARY VENTURES: ROLLING THE DICE TO CHANGE THE WORLD

Revolutionary ventures are rare. They appear once or twice in a decade. Revolutionary ventures embody economist Joseph Schumpeter's concept of creative destruction. They try to create a whole new business model by breaking all the rules through radical innovation. Revolutionary ventures either create a whole new game or change the rules so much that existing firms are not positioned to stay in the game unless they undergo radical change.

Revolutionary ventures capture the essence of entrepreneurship. They require perceptiveness, guts, outstanding management, highly persuasive marketing, a keen sense of timing, breakthrough innovation, vast resources, and time. Perceptiveness is crucial because the entrepreneur must either be able to see the opportunity before others (even potential customers) see it or sense a way to capitalize on the opportunity in a revolutionary manner if others have already seen it. Guts play a crucial role in starting a revolutionary venture because of the uncertainty associated with it and the skepticism that others will express about such an idea.

Starting a revolutionary venture takes more than commitment and passion; it must border on being an obsession. The people involved in creating the venture must be exceptional if they are to do what has not been done before. They must have the ability to make the right things happen the right way the first time. They must also be able to improvise ways to do what has not been done before and have the finesse needed to deal with various stakeholders.

Marketing and communication also play a key role in starting a revolutionary venture. The entrepreneur/team must be able to identify what the marketplace really wants (even if potential customers cannot articulate their needs) and to deliver the right product/service offering, at the right price, and through the proper channels of distribution. Effective communication is critical in the marketing efforts because consumers may need to be educated on the merit of using the revolutionary product or service. It is a lot easier for people to make minor modifications in their habits than it is to change what they have been doing for quite some time. The greater the difference between what they have been doing and what the revolutionary product or service requires them to do, the greater the need for communication, finesse, perseverance, and patience. The same applies to attracting suppliers, key personnel, distributors, investors, and allies. Again, the world will beat a path to your door only if they know where your door is and they believe it will be well worth their time, money, and effort.

Timing plays a key role in starting a revolutionary venture. If the venture is started before the market is ready, then there will not be sufficient revenue to cover the initial outlay and ongoing expenses. If the venture waits until the demand is clearly there, then another firm may preempt it or garner the benefits that usually go to first-to-market firms. The success of revolutionary ventures is contingent on the ability to (1) sense the opportunity before it is visible, (2) position the venture to seize the opportunity when the window opens, (3) capitalize on it when it does open, and (4) make sure that the venture keeps in sync with the market as it evolves.

Revolutionary ventures are not possible without breakthrough innovation. Innovation can be in terms of technology, products or services, and/or business processes. The innovation must be able to "wow" potential consumers by doing something that they didn't think was possible.

Revolutionary ventures are also rare because they are not scalable. They cannot provide their level of products or services unless they have considerable size from the very beginning. The lack of scalability is one of the things that separate revolutionary ventures from high-growth ventures. Although Home Depot, Amazon, eBay, Dell, and Southwest Airlines have become exceptional enterprises, they fit the high-growth venture profile more than the revolutionary venture profile. The same applies to Microsoft and Wal-Mart. They did not have to be started on a large scale. They were able to start small and grow. This made it possible for them to be started without a substantial initial investment. They were able to scale up quickly when the market embraced their products or services. Federal Express and Iridium are profiled as revolutionary ventures below because they captured the need to operate on a large scale from their inception in their effort to provide what had not been possible until then.

The issue of bigness also applies to the need for substantial returns to cover the substantial risks that come with attempting to create revolutionary ventures. Revolutionary ventures have to offer the opportunity for very large profits to justify the substantial investments. Revolutionary ventures take a substantial amount of up-front investment to deliver breakthrough products or services and for the necessary infrastructure to support sizable operations while waiting for the level of demand and revenue needed to get the venture on its feet. Those who invest in revolutionary ventures know that if they don't work out, they will be total losses.

Time plays a key role in revolutionary ventures for two reasons. First, it takes considerable time to analyze the market, to determine the necessary logistics, to develop the systems that allow them to make, deliver, and service the breakthrough product or service. Few things are simple when you try to do something that has never been done before, especially if it is to be done on a large scale. Second, revolutionary ventures are rarely overnight successes. It takes time for people to learn about the product service, to communicate its merits, to get people to try it, and then to get people to buy it. It may take more than a decade before the venture even begins to generate the type of return needed to justify the risk associated with it. Management must be prepared to go the distance and the venture must be funded to go the distance.

Fred Smith's concept for providing overnight delivery represented a radical departure from the way things were done. Smith had to demonstrate the potential for securing a significant share of an untapped $1 billion market to raise the capital for launching Federal Express. Fortunately, a study by A.T. Kearney revealed a large untapped air freight market for priority cargo.[20]

It took Smith about eight years from the time he conceived of a business that would provide overnight delivery to the time it became operational.[21] It also required considerable resources. Federal Express was a revolutionary venture because it could not do what it needed to do if it had just a couple of planes. When Federal Express's Falcon jets flew into Memphis the first night, they carried a total of six packages to a facility that was designed to handle 10,000 packages per hour. Federal Express was on the brink of bankruptcy for several years. It took more than 27 months—not the 6 originally estimated—to build the volume of business needed to cover fixed costs.[22]

Unfortunately, Iridium is an example of an unsuccessful revolutionary venture. It was a bold effort to provide a wireless phone system to almost every part of the globe via a network of satellites. While Iridium's plan was visionary, it also demonstrated the risks and potential for incredible financial losses if things don't work out. When you try to change the way the game is played and boldly go where no firm has gone before, your products need to be truly innovative, your management team must be savvy to the challenges that will arise, you must have the systems in place so you can execute your strategy well, the market must embrace the revolutionary product, and you have to have resources in reserve to weather the glitches, delays, setbacks, and surprises that are inevitable.

Iridium was not the only firm that failed in its efforts to bring a whole new business model to the marketplace. Peapod and Webvan serve as painful financial examples that revolutionary approaches are not assured success even when established firms commit their money, technology, and systems to their venture. Webvan and Peapod tried to bypass conventional grocery stores by providing delivered groceries from warehouses to residences. Their strategies were not incremental. They incorporated the latest information technology and supply chain logistics. Some of the top firms in their field were allies. They also attracted institutional investors. Although the concept may sound simple, the ability to *deliver* (pardon the pun) in an exceptional fashion to a large number of homes in major metropolitan areas was a formidable challenge.

REALITY CHECK

The preceding information on revolutionary ventures is intended to illustrate there is a tremendous difference between being a high-growth venture and a revolutionary venture. Having dreams and ambitions can be healthy and provide considerable motivation, but make sure your reach does not exceed your grasp.

FACTORS AFFECTING NEW VENTURE SUCCESS AND GROWTH

It may be helpful at this time to highlight some of the factors that affect a new venture's ability to grow and its corresponding profitability. Some factors are internal to the venture, including the quality of the entrepreneur/team, whether the venture has any major innovations, and financial resources. Other factors including the nature of the market and the extent and sophistication of competition are external to the venture. The following sections profile factors that should be considered when deciding the type of venture to start.

Scalability: Can the Venture Be Started in a Small Scale?

While promising ventures may enjoy sustained growth, their growth tends to be in regional markets or in niche markets in larger markets. High-growth ventures are different from promising ventures because they are usually created to become major players in large markets or dominant players mid-size markets. Fortunately, most high-growth ventures do not have to be started on a large scale.

High-growth ventures are usually characterized by a hockey-stick growth profile. They are scalable. Scalability provides the opportunity to start small and to test the market without committing substantial resources or taking major risks. Scalability allows you to experiment, to find out what works, to get it right, and then to "ramp up" operations to serve a growing market. A number of *Fortune* 500 companies started with niche opportunities that they could exploit without having much capital or having to face large competitors.[23]

Scalability allows you to get your people and systems in place. It also affects your ability to attract the capital needed to place the venture in a high-growth mode. Scalability is like testing the temperature of the ocean with your big toe, rather than having to jump in with both feet. It allows you to get some customers, to get referrals from those customers, and to learn if there may be additional uses/markets/users. It also gives you time to get your distribution network established and for your advertising to take effect. If these work out, then you may be able to create a "demand pull" situation where customers seek out your firm rather than your firm relying solely on seeking out customers. Starting small also gives you a chance to get your firm's act together before it appears on a larger, more formidable competitor's radar.

Scalability plays a major role in deciding what type of venture to start for numerous reasons. If the venture can be started on a small scale, then you are minimizing your financial risk. You have a chance to see if the market values your product/service and to modify your approach and systems so they are in sync with internal and external realities. As the firm gets its act together, it can "ramp up" its operations by (1) the entrepreneur investing more money in it, (2) the management team investing in it, (3) securing a loan, (4) bringing in outside investors, or (5) using a combination of these funding sources. Starbucks provides an example of a firm that did not ramp-up its retail operations until the timing was right. It poured its first cup of coffee in 1971 and did not open its second outlet for another 16 years.[24] When Howard Schultz took over Starbucks in 1985, he embarked on the growth journey that has made it a daily experience for many people. Between 1990 and 2003, Starbucks opened more than 6,300 outlets.

Starting small allows you to determine if there are major economies of scale. If the costs for producing the product or providing the service go down dramatically with larger volume, then larger firms will have a significant cost and pricing advantage over new firms that start on a small scale. Price might not be the only factor in determining which products or services customers buy, but a significant price disadvantage can really hurt a new venture's ability to attract customers.

Three particular things need to be noted about economies of scale. First, there are no economies of scale when it comes to managing a firm. It takes a lot more skill and talent to manage a larger firm. Second, there are few economies of scale for ventures that provide a service. The number of people usually has to increase in proportion to the level of sales. There are situations, however, when software may be used as a substitute for labor to provide certain economies of scale. Third, if you outsource production and distribution of the product, then you may get the benefits of lower costs without having to establish large-scale facilities.

If you have limited resources and do not expect to be able to bring in additional resources from a loan or issuing stock to others, then you will need to look for the type of venture that does not require substantial resources from the beginning. This does not mean that your venture is destined to stay small. If the firm can generate profits on a small scale, then you may be in a position to reinvest the profits so it can grow larger.

Some ventures need to operate on a fairly large scale from the beginning to succeed. They either need a massive infrastructure to provide the product or service or they need to serve a large geographic area to provide the product or service. The need for large-scale operations is not necessarily a bad thing. Large scale can minimize competition, especially new entrants. If you are able to secure the funding to start the venture on a large scale, then it may put you in a situation where you have considerable advantage.

Newness Can Affect Growth and Risk

Newness occurs in numerous ways. It can apply to the newness of the market, the level of experience for the entrepreneur/team, and the relative newness of the venture's products/services/processes. This section will address the first two areas. The relative newness of the venture's products/services/processes will be discussed later in the chapter. The newness of the entrepreneur/team and the market can be depicted in the Degree of Newness Matrix profiled in Exhibit 2.2.

The entrepreneur's and team's level of experience affect the venture in various ways. The entrepreneur and team's level of experience can be viewed in three ways:

1. Do they have experience in the positions they will have in the new venture? This includes whether any of them have started a venture before.
2. Do they have experience in that industry?
3. Have they worked together as a team before? If they have this level of experience, then they should be able to hit the ground running. If they haven't, then they will have to go through a *feeling out* process.

REALITY CHECK

While individual resumes may be impressive, new ventures need to have people who can work together. Some people are like oil and water; they do not mix well. Generally speaking, the greater the degree of newness for the three factors, the greater the challenge and associated risk for the venture.

Newness of Team		Moderate risk	High risk
	High	Moderate risk	High risk
	Low	Low risk	Moderate risk
		Low level of ambiguity	**High level of uncertainty**
		Newness of Market	

EXHIBIT 2.2 DEGREE OF NEWNESS MATRIX

The degree of newness of the market has considerable bearing on a new venture. If the market is in its formative stages, then there are a lot of uncertainties. New markets are characterized by uncertainty about (1) the level of demand, (2) who will actually be the consumers, (3) whether there are numerous segments, (4) price sensitivity, (5) what other firms may be attempting to serve the market, and (6) what will be the most important areas for establishing competitive advantages. Forecasting the overall level of demand and the venture's corresponding market share is particularly challenging in a new market. The questions: "How quickly will the window of opportunity open?" "How soon will demand take off?" and "How long will the window stay open?" are difficult to answer.

The degree of newness of the market will be important in two other ways. First, newness can also affect how forgiving consumers may be to the various glitches that may occur by your firm. Consumers tend to be more forgiving in new markets than in established markets. In new markets, if the consumers have been waiting for the products or services to be offered, then they might be almost delighted when a firm finally provides what they have been looking for. This is why it can be so beneficial to be the first mover or first to market.

Forgiving markets provide some latitude by allowing you to learn what works and what does not work. Domino's didn't have to be great when it started delivering pizza. It just needed to deliver a good-tasting pizza in a reasonable time at a fair price. If Domino's' marketing mix did not meet the market's expectations, then it would have been inviting in competition. As the market becomes less forgiving and other firms enter the scene, firms that do not have their acts together will drive their customers away by giving them reasons to look for firms that get it—and get it right!

Planning versus Adaptation Paradox

This chapter highlights numerous paradoxes. Questions are raised about whether ideas are more important than execution and whether innovation is really more important than continuous improvement. The issue of whether planning is more important than adaptation can also be added to the list. There is no question that planning plays a crucial role in the success of a new venture. Planning has always been important and it will continue being important in the years ahead. Planning increases a venture's chances for success because it encourages firms to "look before they leap" and to take the mental journey before taking the physical journey. Planning also reduces the likelihood that things will fall through the cracks.

Planning is not that difficult when things are fairly predictable. If you know what the market wants and what competition will be offering, then developing a plan to gain a competitive advantage may not be that difficult. Yet the days of predictability have been replaced with turbulence and uncertainty. The marketplace changes from one moment to the next. Consumer interests, needs, and desires can change overnight. New competitors can enter the scene and change the way the game is played without even appearing on the radar. A few established firms may even wake up from their sleeps of mediocrity and try to be more entrepreneurial.

It was not that long ago that plans were comprehensive, detailed, and linear. They were comprehensive because they tried to include every facet of an operation. Each dimension of the plan was highly detailed. Every *i* was dotted and every *t* was crossed. Most plans were linear. They simply added another dot to the linear series of dots. They reflected a philosophy of doing more of the same in the future.

Turbulence and discontinuous change make it difficult to develop a plan. Planning used to follow an *analyze-plan-implement* cycle. Today, plans may need to be modified the same day they are implemented. Someone once noted, "In combat, your plans must be modified as soon as the first shot is fired."

Adaptation can be defined as the ability to change what you are doing to reflect current realities and evolving possibilities. It is built on the premise, "If you cannot *predict* the future, then you must prepare for it." Adaptation is not the same as being reactive. If it is done right, then it can be proactive. It places a premium on being able to anticipate what the future may hold and positioning the venture so that it will benefit from the changes. Alan Kay, who worked for Apple Computer, captured the proactive nature of adaptation when he stated, "If you can't predict the future, then create it."

Adaptation is not the opposite of planning. Entrepreneurs still need to develop plans. You cannot afford to sit around waiting to see what happens and then adjust to it. Some marketplaces lend themselves more to planning. Mature markets tend to be less turbulent than emerging markets. In mature markets, most of the firms have demonstrated their strategies for attracting and keeping customers. They also operate in specific segments. The number and nature of competitors is far from certain in an emerging market. There is also a lot more experimentation when markets are in their formative stages because firms are trying to find out what works. Instead of the *analyze-plan-implement* cycle, firms have to use an *analyze-plan-implement-learn-adapt* cycle.

Planning is particularly difficult when it has to deal with uncertainty and complexity. Most large and established firms have an aversion to dealing with things where there is limited information. They develop formal systems and procedures for analyzing situations and evaluating alternatives. They also have committees that review plans and strategies. New initiatives tend to be subjected to even closer scrutiny. Although the systematic analysis that precedes decisions may seem very professional, it also slows established firms down and causes them to avoid entrepreneurial behavior where the results are far from certain.

Firms that develop formal plans tend to miss windows of opportunity when they open. They also tend to be slow in entering emerging markets. When things are changing quickly, the ability to sense quickly what is happening, to develop action plans quickly, and to implement the most appropriate action plan quickly can make the difference between catching a great wave versus watching it from the beach.

Adaptation can range from simply being agile enough to adjust to a changing situation as it is happening all the way to making a deliberate effort to anticipate what may happen and positioning yourself to capitalize on the change before it happens. Agility is an important quality today. As the world changes, the ability to change with it is crucial. The ability to anticipate what may happen, however, gives the firm an edge over less-perceptive firms. The ability to anticipate and the agility to change what you are doing on a moment's notice go together like innovation and improvement.

REALITY CHECK

It would be great if the firm could have breakthrough innovation all the time, but that is not likely, so it should also be striving to improve what it is doing so it remains competitive. It would be great if the firm could anticipate emerging opportunities before every other firm, but that is also not likely, so it needs to continuously adapt to the world around it so it does not get out of sync.

New ventures that are entering emerging markets need to operate like explorers. William Lewis and Meriwether Clark developed plans, but they also recognized that they would be exploring uncharted territory. They tried to anticipate various situations and have the resources available to meet the corresponding challenges. They also knew they would have to live off the land. Lewis and Clark started their journey with about a 1,000 pounds of trinkets to trade with the Indians in exchange for goods and services.

Lewis and Clark knew they would encounter numerous decision junctures. This is why they sent scouts ahead to survey the territory ahead of them. The scouts could not travel every possible path in advance, but they would reduce the trial and error process for the expedition. Lewis and Clark, like Christopher Columbus before them, succeeded where others failed because they (1) were willing to boldly go where no one had gone before, (2) anticipated various situations, (3) were agile and resourceful enough to change their plans when the situation was not what was expected, and (4) had sufficient resources to go the distance and to deal with adversity.

Explorers who started their journeys without a game plan, who didn't use scouts, who didn't know how to read the territory for clues to what may lie ahead, and who were not agile enough to change what they were doing did not live to be heralded in history books.

When you are exploring new markets you are not taking the road less traveled; you are taking the road yet to be traveled. There are no maps, road signs, global positioning systems, or motor clubs to help you find your way. You will be on your own. Your ability to chart a course and to make the appropriate changes will determine whether you move forward or fall by the wayside.

Bhidé believes an *opportunistic adaptation strategy* may be very worthwhile for emerging ventures. He notes that in lieu of extensive planning, entrepreneurs have to rely on adaptation. The opportunistic adaptation strategy can then be seen as a process where an entrepreneur starts with a sketchy idea of how he or she wants to do business based on a set of tentative hypotheses about the market. The entrepreneur then revises the hypotheses rapidly through a series of experiments or adaptive responses to unforeseen responses and opportunities.[25]

Opportunitistic adaptation can be summarized as

- See a gap in the market.
- Develop a strategy to bridge the gap.
- Test it out.
- Learn from the market's response.
- Modify your strategy.
- Test it out.

It is very similar to Sony's practice of rapid prototyping. Instead of spending months in R&D, Sony tries to get a working prototype into a test market within five days so that it can gauge its appeal and learn from potential customers. The prototype is modified quickly and then subjected to another round of reality testing. Bhidé noted that more than one-third of the *Inc.* 500 founders he interviewed significantly altered their initial concepts, and another third reported moderate changes.[26]

Entrepreneurs facing uncertain conditions have to deal with ambiguity. They must have the courage to choose a course of action without complete information. They must also have the humility to be willing to modify that course of action or to adopt a new one if the situation warrants it. An entrepreneur interviewed by Bhidé likened the process of starting a business to "Jumping from rock to rock up a stream rather than constructing the Golden Gate Bridge from a detailed blueprint."[27]

Opportunistic adaptation is not the same as reckless abandon where the venture is simply launched into the market with minimal forethought. Opportunistic adaptation starts with a game plan and then adjusts it as the venture learns more. As noted earlier, plans are helpful because they encourage people to ponder what the future may hold and to identify what may be the best strategy for capitalizing on a targeted market opportunity. Plans also let you know when things are not going as planned so that we can change what we are doing. If awareness is a prerequisite for change, then plans can foster agility rather than inhibit it.

REALITY CHECK

Planning is not the same as preparation. Planning tries to foster foresight and reduce uncertainty. Preparing, however, tries to deal with uncertainty. There will be times when planning may be very effective and times when the level of uncertainty makes detailed and comprehensive planning an exercise in futility. The key is knowing the difference and having the skills, information, and systems to handle the corresponding situation.

REALITY CHECK

You should view planning more as a process that points the venture in a certain direction rather than to an exact destination. In a sense you are trying to move your firm to a zip code rather than an exact address. Planning and preparing are like fishing. You may have an overall game plan, but you also need to be prepared to try different baits and move to different spots as you search for schools of hungry fish. If you simply plan to go to one spot and drop anchor in hopes that a fish will bite your line, then your odds of having fish for dinner might not be very high. You will increase the odds when you go in with an open mind and are willing to modify your plans to fit the conditions as they evolve.

REALITY CHECK

Planning reduces a venture's flexibility. When you implement your plan you are committing resources. Preparing implies deliberately keeping resources in reserve so you can adapt to the dynamics of a situation as it unfolds. Preparation thereby involves having a general sense of direction, being able to go with the flow, and mastering adaptive opportunism. If you are the type of person who likes being in control and having all the *i*s dotted, then find an opportunity that will provide you the time and data needed to develop detailed plans. If you thrive in uncertain situations and are very resourceful, then look for the type of opportunity that will capitalize on your talents.

REALITY CHECK

Planning is like hiring people. You may have been very systematic in the process of hiring the person whom you think will do the best job. Although that person may look great on paper and you may have been very diligent in doing reference checks, the truth of the matter is that you really won't know about that person until he or she starts working for you. The same is true with your strategy for attracting customers. You won't know if it really works until you actually begin implementing it. It is only when you begin implementing your plan that you will be in a position to learn what works and to tweak it—and what doesn't, so you can modify it, drop it, or replace it with a strategy that should work better.

REALITY CHECK

When you are at the edge, you will have to make judgment calls—and you will make mistakes. You will have to experiment with products, services, and processes. There will be trials and there will be errors. And there will be times when you have to improvise. This isn't necessarily bad. Your series of experiments may yield "lateral opportunities." When you are pursuing something, you may find a related opportunity that has even more potential. The opportunity may not be visible if you are on the outside. Once you embark on the entrepreneurial journey and start interacting with customers, suppliers, and distributors, the opportunities may become visible. If you view your venture as a customer-problem-solver, then you may encounter prospective customers who say, "Could you do this?" Some of today's most successful ventures traveled a rather circuitous route rather than in the straight line characterized in their original plan/strategy. What they are doing today bears little resemblance to what they were doing when they embarked on their entrepreneurial journeys.

REALITY CHECK

Do not mistake the *preparing strategy* to be the same as winging it. They are entirely different. The preparing strategy takes perceptiveness, decisiveness, and fluidity. It involves preparing for various possible situations. It also recognizes that if you cannot anticipate the future, then you must be agile enough to proactively adapt to it as it invades the present.

Barriers to Entry and Competitive Advantages Can Make a Difference

The issue of scale was profiled as a potential barrier to entry. Other factors can also serve as barriers to entry for new ventures. Free enterprise is defined as a situation where there are minimal or no barriers to entry. Few markets are totally free to new entrants. Barriers may include access to certain resources including raw material, having certain skills, patents or copyrights, licenses, certain software, and access to certain distribution channels. If you are not able to secure certain talent, then that could impede your venture's ability to create and maintain customers. Location can even be considered a barrier to entry. If the venture needs a certain location, then the inability to secure it could stop a new venture in its tracks.

Legal barriers to entry can also inhibit new competitors. If a firm cannot get a license to a certain process, patent, or other form of intellectual property because another firm has exclusive rights to it, then that firm may not be in a position to enter that market.

Some barriers are financial in nature. They can be dealt with if enough money is provided. For example, some suppliers require a minimum order size before they will do business with a new venture. The same applies to securing talent. If you provide the right compensation package (salary, bonuses, stock options, fringe benefits, etc.), then people may be willing to quit their jobs to join your new venture team.

The extent the venture needs to have significant and sustainable competitive advantages also affects the degree of challenge associated with starting a venture. As noted earlier, if the market is very forgiving, then the firm may not need to be exceptional in what it offers. Few markets, however, are forgiving for very long. A new venture's success is contingent on how much better it is than the other firms on the things that matter to its target market(s). If the existing firms are already in sync with what the market wants, then the new venture will need to be markedly better on the things that matter for consumers to even consider switching to the new venture. The degree of dissatisfaction and the degree the venture can be better than existing and potential firms will influence a new venture's success.

Brand loyalty can also play a significant role in a new venture's ability to enter a market. If brand loyalty for the existing firms is high, then consumers are less likely to even consider another venture—especially a new venture. This is particularly true with a relatively unknown venture/brand. The extent to which the market is composed of people who really enjoy trying new things (a.k.a. innovators) and people who quickly follow the lead of others (a.k.a. early adopters) will also influence a new venture's ability to crack a market.

REALITY CHECK

If the market has formidable barriers to entry and requires a number of substantial competitive advantages to garner consumer interest, then it may be better to consider another market. If consumers have indicated major dissatisfaction with existing firms and your venture can provide a markedly better offering and has the resources to address any barrier to entry, then you may proceed. If you have the ability to create barriers to entry for potential new entrants and raise the bar for the existing firms, then you should proceed with utmost vigor.

REALITY CHECK

If you have a major advantage that threatens large, established firms, then be prepared to do battle in court or in the marketplace. It is not unusual for another firm to violate your patent rights or do things that can be construed as restraint of trade (predatory pricing, filing injunctions, putting pressure on distributors and suppliers to not do business with you, etc.) which make it difficult for your firm to succeed. Although these practices may be clearly illegal, they may be hard to enforce or you could be tied up in court for years. New ventures rarely have the time or the money to win these battles. Assume that the better your firm is, the greater the likelihood you will become the target of these actions. Be prepared for them and have resources on the sidelines so you can go the distance.

Investment and Uncertainty

The amount of money needed to start and grow the venture has considerable bearing on the type of venture to start. The amount of capital needed to start the venture is important for at least two reasons. First, it can be a barrier to entry. Second, the initial capital requirement will affect whether the founder will be able to fund the venture. All things being equal, the larger the initial capital requirement, the greater the need for external funding.

The ability to get external funding is directly related to the degree of risk associated with the new venture. External funding is particularly difficult to secure in the start-up stage. Once the venture is up and running, it may be less difficult to attract external funding. The degree of uncertainty is related to the degree of newness, the extent and nature of competition, as well as the maturity and profitability of the market. It is also affected by the risk of technological obsolescence, government regulation, and economic volatility.

REALITY CHECK

If you are considering starting a venture that will have to deal with highly uncertain situations and require a substantial investment, then you may need to (1) have enough money to fund it yourself, (2) do what you can to reduce the amount of money needed, and/or (3) find ways to decrease the degree of uncertainty so you can lower the risk as well as attract funding from other sources.

It is interesting how some of today's great firms would be plotted on a 2×2 investment-uncertainty matrix with high and low cells for each dimension. Steven Jobs and Steven Wozniak formed Apple with a minimal investment. Paul Allen and Bill Gates started Microsoft with minimal investment. People today might say they were taking a big risk in starting a computer hardware or software business. Risk, however, is in the eye of the beholder. None of them considered what they were doing to be taking much risk. They were very young and had few personal or financial obligations. They had little to lose if their ventures failed. Jobs and Wozniak were operating out of a garage, so they had minimal overhead. Gates and Allen could find a job developing software for someone else or start another venture.

Janice Joplin sang a song during the Vietnam War era that included the lyrics, "Freedom's just another word for nothin' left to lose."[28] When you don't have to put much money into your venture and you can find another job that pays well if things do not work out, then there is really little risk to starting a venture.

Potential Return on Investment and Time to Get Profitable

People who have owned boats say there are two great days when you own a boat. The first great day is when you buy the boat and put it into the water. The second great day is when you sell it and are free of all the hassles! Boats are often described as "holes in the water that you pour money into." Launching a new venture can engender similar feelings.

Veteran entrepreneurs note two significant milestones in starting a business: getting to the points where you have positive cash flow and are actually making a profit. Yet you don't start a venture to achieve positive cash flow or profitability. You start a venture to generate a return on your investment that justifies the time, effort, risk, sleepless nights, cases of antacids, strained marriage, distance between you and your kids and friends, vulnerability of your mortgage, and last but not least, all the money you put into it.

New ventures vary in terms of their potential return on investment and the time it will take to generate a return on the investment to make it all worthwhile. Ventures that offer, at best, a minimal return on investment should be avoided unless you want to start a lifestyle business or already have more money than you will possibly ever need. The lack of profitability and positive cash flow will affect your ability to secure a loan, and the lack of a sufficient return on investment will affect your ability to attract investors.

REALITY CHECK

It is surprising how many people do not set a return on investment objective when they consider starting a venture. They want to start a venture that is profitable, but fail to set a return on investment (ROI) target. You should set a threshold return on investment well before you begin exploring potential ventures. The threshold will be particularly helpful when you screen potential opportunities.

The amount of time it takes to get a reasonable return on your investment affects a venture's attractiveness. Ventures that have the ability to generate a high return on investment within a short period of time are vastly preferable to those that may take five, seven, or ten years. The time factor is like being out in the cold or having to hold one's breath. People don't want to do either for an extended period of time. Things become far more uncertain as you extend the time horizon into the future. The potential for a high return on investment will not appeal to many investors if they have to wait for an extended period of time. Most investors want to get their money back with a substantial return within three to five years. The time lag between the development of a revolutionary new product and its commercialization can be quite long. Philo Farnsworth invented the television in 1927, but it would be a number of decades before it would generate it first dollar of revenue.[29]

REALITY CHECK

People will expect some degree of specificity if you are courting their time and/or their money for your new venture. Avoid using the words *someday* and *substantial* when seeking talent, bankers, and investors.

Entrepreneurship captures the risk-reward ratio. People are willing to accept a high level of risk if they believe they will get a return that more than justifies the level of risk. Ideally, the venture will (1) not require much investment, (2) generate an incredible return on that money, (3) generate the return within a year or two, and (4) continue generating that return for at least a decade.

REALITY CHECK

Most people believe the greatest degree of risk occurs when you quit your job and start a venture. In reality, the risk may be greater after the venture is up and running. When you start a venture, most of the people involved recognize the risk and are prepared to take it. As the venture grows you will hire more and more people. The prospect of your venture having major setbacks or even failing will cause you to have sleepless nights—not just because of what you may lose, but because so many people's livelihood is dependent on the success of your venture. You will feel responsible for them so be prepared to feel their weight on your shoulders.

Innovation and Execution Characterize the Exceptional Enterprise

People frequently ask, "Which is more important: the quality of the idea or the quality of execution?" If you want to create an exceptional enterprise, then the answer is *both*. If the new venture is to create and maintain customers for a profit, then it needs to be better on the things that matter most to its target market. Focusing on what your target market wants will give you more of an edge than focusing on what is offered by the firms already in the marketplace. To be better, the firm has to be different. This is where innovation comes in. Being different via innovation is not enough; for innovation to matter, it must create a sustainable competitive advantage and be valued by your target market.

Innovation can occur in various areas and levels. It can be in the firm's products, services, and/or processes. It can also range from the "Wow, you can really do that!" that comes with a breakthrough innovation all the way down to the placement of a complimentary change counting machine in its lobby by Commerce Bank in its efforts to get customers to actually enjoy coming inside.[30] Conversely, most established firms rate high on the yawn meter. They make great targets for new ventures that are innovative on an ongoing basis on all fronts. Most people in established firms are conservative because they believe innovation is risky. They believe making minor modifications to be a far safer strategy. Two ads, however, capture the need for innovation. An AIG ad stated, "The greatest risk is not taking one." A U.S. West ad stated, "If you don't make dust, you eat dust!"

Execution is important when introducing innovation. Forgiving markets may allow a few glitches but exceptional firms minimize the chance that even these glitches will occur. They think things through, anticipate where things can go wrong, and prevent potential problems. Execution is also important when it comes to the more mundane things that have to be done. Execution involves taking existing business practices to a new level and executing them better.

Exceptional firms do an extraordinary job with what most firms consider ordinary. Wal-Mart, Dell Computer, and Southwest Airlines grew partly because they were exceptional in their ability to do the blocking and tackling side of business. Wal-Mart mastered inventory ordering and control. Dell Computer made it easier to order a computer over the Internet than buying one at a retail store. Southwest Airlines designed a system to get an airplane in and out of the airport gate far quicker than any other airline.

Although these firms were very innovative, they were also masters of execution. Ironically, the little things can make a big difference in a firm's bottom line. Bhidé noted that profitability can be more a function of tactical and operational ability (hustle) than of superior long-term strategy.[31] A regional fish market provides an example of how it can separate itself from the pack by just doing a few things better than other firms. Every Friday when its inventory level is higher than expected for certain types of fish, its staff searches its database to identify customers who have purchased that type of fish in the past. The staff then calls those customers to let them know that they have their favorite fish and that they can filet it and have it ready for them on their way home so that they will not have to wait in line. That fish market's use of modern information technology to do what other fish markets don't even think about doing has contributed to its growth, success, and notoriety.

Murphy's Law, "If any thing can go wrong, it will—and at the most inopportune time!" tests every firm's ability to execute its plans, strategies, systems, and tactics. Complexity and scale create formidable execution challenges. Exceptional enterprises find ways to simplify everything and use systems that provide information so variances can be identified early and kept to a minimum.

REALITY CHECK

The ability to do things the right way only has merit if you are doing the right things. If you are not in sync with what the market wants, then doing something better that no one values is like rearranging the deckchairs on the *Titanic* or having a perfectly packed parachute on a submarine.

REALITY CHECK

In your zeal to excel at execution, make sure that you do not make the venture rigid and bureaucratic. Emerging ventures need to be agile so they can change with changing conditions. Do not allow execution to be a fixation or obsession to the point that it jeopardizes your firm's innovativeness and vitality. Do not let skeptical "How can this be done?" voices deter "What can we do that will make a real difference?" voices.

REALITY CHECK

The degree of innovation affects how good your execution must be. Although innovators and early adopters may not be very picky when an innovation is introduced, the honeymoon ends as the market matures. When competitors enter the scene to steal your thunder and prospective customers (a.k.a. the early majority and late majority) enter the scene with particular expectations, continuous innovation and flawless execution can give your venture a formidable competitive edge.

REALITY CHECK

A lot of people believe mature markets offer limited opportunities for new ventures. They believe the market is the exclusive domain of the established firms. Mature markets, however, may be what air force pilots call "a target rich environment." Established firms tend to grow complacent and arrogant. They operate with an "If no firm rocks the boat, then we will all do just fine" mentality. This is particularly true with second- and third-generation firms. If the existing firms are getting fat by doing a mediocre job, then you are not taking a major risk by taking them on. If you are innovative and execute well, you may even be able to charge a little more (or less, via efficiencies and systems) by providing a better product and/or higher level of service.

Innovation and Improvement: Two Dimensions for Gaining a Competitive Advantage

Innovation can take many forms. It can be in the development of a breakthrough product or service. It can also be the development of various processes. It can also be in how a venture markets its products as well as how it handles customer inquiries. Amazon.com was innovative by making it possible for people to access all sorts of information about books that no retail sales clerk could know. Amazon.com also made it possible for people to order books without going to a store and to have them delivered to one's home or office. Although other established firms had been offering books for decades, Amazon.com was innovative because it also offered information and convenience.

Most people confuse invention and innovation. Invention is when you create a first-generation product or service. Innovation usually involves developing a second- or third-generation of a product or service. It may also involve doing something that already exists differently. Pringles was innovative when it developed potato chips that are stackable and packaged in a canister to prevent breakage. Innovation, thereby, may involve combining two or more things that have not been combined before. Providing peanut butter and jelly in a single container or in a prepared ready-to-eat sandwich is innovative if no one else has done it before. Innovation usually involves perceptiveness more than raw creativity.

Numerous innovations are the result of "lateral transfer," where you take something that already exists in one industry and introduce it for the first time in another industry. Although it is not clear which industry was the first to offer a drive-up window, it is clear that at least one firm in a number of industries was innovative when it was the first to offer it in its respective industry. The West Coast funeral parlor that offered drive-up visitation was truly innovative!

The need for a new venture to be truly innovative varies from market to market. If the market is composed of established firms that are innovative and proficient at execution, then the new venture may need to provide a breakthrough level of innovation to attract customers. Fortunately, most markets do not require breakthrough innovation. New ventures may be successful if they sense what the market wants and can provide it in a more innovative manner.

Innovation and improvement should not be seen as end points on a single continuum. They need to be seen as separate dimensions. In some cases, a firm may be able to gain an edge without having a truly innovative product, service, or process. A number of firms started off by offering a fairly generic product but built competitive advantages by making continuous improvements. Some of the improvements involved the product's design. Other improvements may have made it easier to use or lowered its price.

Lucrative opportunities may exist for new ventures if they find a product or service that is considered a commodity and improve on it. The firm that can make the "supposed" commodity more convenient, better, easier to use, or more attractive may leapfrog established firms that have taken it for granted and fallen asleep at the wheel. Henry Ford's, "They can have their car in any color as long as it is black" mentality was also demonstrated by the color selection in the first desktop computers, cell phones, and numerous other products. New entrants offered more appealing designs and selection of colors.

REALITY CHECK

There is no such thing as a commodity. Water is no longer just water and coffee is no longer just coffee. If you can improve on the products or services other firms offer and put your brand on them, people who value the difference will reward you.

Richard Branson has a track record for combining innovation and improvement. He looks for markets where existing businesses have become complacent by taking their customers and markets for granted. He jumps into the market with incredible bravado and takes it to a new level. He created Virgin Atlantic Airways to provide air travelers an alternative to British Airways. He created Virgin Records to showcase new musical groups. Branson's "status quo killer" attitude when combined with innovation, continuous improvement, and execution have redefined or changed the competitive playing field for numerous industries.

OPERATING AT THE EDGE: THE INNOVATION PORTAL

It should be clear by now that innovation can play a significant role in the growth and success of an emerging venture. Most of the attention so far has been directed to developing and offering leading-edge products and services. This is only half of the equation. The question still remains, "Who will you be offering the leading-edge products and services to?" Corporate obituaries are full of ventures that developed a "wow" technology. They died on the vine while waiting for customers to buy it. Entrepreneurs need to recognize that they don't have a business unless they have paying customers. Growth is possible only to the extent that more people buy the product or service or if existing customers increase the amount that they buy.

The innovation portal profiled in Exhibit 2.3 not only reflects the need to be out front; it also stresses the need for leading-edge providers to look for *leading-edge users*. The innovation portal captures the essence of entrepreneurship. New ventures grow to the extent that they find a gap in the market and fill it. Firms that develop a technology without a clear idea of who will buy it are playing Russian roulette. They operate with a "here's something great; someone buy it" mentality. These firms may be very innovative, but they are not truly entrepreneurial. Entrepreneurship starts with a market orientation—by identifying needs that are not being met enough or at all. The innovation portal illustrates the need for a new venture to locate leading users and to find out what they want, and then to work closely with them to provide what they want—and will pay for.

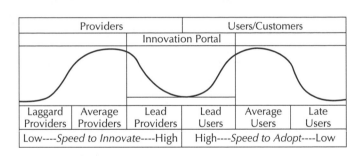

Providers			Users/Customers		
		Innovation Portal			
Laggard Providers	Average Providers	Lead Providers	Lead Users	Average Users	Late Users
Low----*Speed to Innovate*----High			High----*Speed to Adopt*----Low		

EXHIBIT 2.3   INNOVATION PORTAL

Leading-edge users come in various forms. Sometimes they are large firms that are looking for something to meet their needs. Sometimes, however, they are emerging ventures that need something to enable them to grow. A leading-edge user may serve as a "beta site" where the leading-edge provider can experiment with a potential customer. Beta sites are a great way to learn what works and to get the bugs out before actually launching a new product or service.

The leading-edge user may want to form an alliance with the leading-edge provider. If the leading-edge user is a large firm, then it may commit funds, personnel, equipment, and other resources to your new venture's new product or service development efforts. Beta sites and corporate alliances can give the new venture a considerable boost. They may be the lead dominos that help set in motion a string of subsequent customers.

CONCLUSION: IN SEARCH OF GOODNESS OF FIT

Finding the right venture to start is contingent on a number of factors. Two of the most critical factors are: (1) "What type of business will have the greatest chance for success?" and (2) "What is the optimal size for the business I want to start?" Both questions are tied to the talents and resources you are able to bring to the venture. Some people are very talented and are committed to surrounding themselves with other talented people. They look for opportunities that will capitalize on their talents. Other people know their limitations and prefer to do things alone and within their reach.

Some people welcome the challenge to do exciting things and thrive in times of turbulence and uncertainty. Other people have little tolerance for risk and look for fairly stable situations. Some people are very innovative because they have contempt for the status quo. They are constantly experimenting with new ways to do things and looking for new things to do. Other people are tweakers. They like fine-tuning things that are already in the mainstream. Some people want to create an exceptional enterprise. They are like the baseball players who swing for the bleachers every time at bat. Other people want to just start a business as an alternative to working for someone else. In baseball, they would be happy to just get a single.

Entrepreneurship involves risks and rewards. There is a right size and type of business for almost anyone who is prepared to take the entrepreneurial journey. The key is taking a close look at yourself and not reaching beyond your grasp. Some people do not have what it takes to be successful entrepreneurs. They are destined to fail because they don't have the ability or because their ideas are totally out of sync with market realities. They will not be able to create and maintain customers for a profit. Other entrepreneurs and ideas have the potential to be the best of the best. They will not only be able to attract and maintain customers for a profit, they will also attract investors and other talented people who want to join them in their entrepreneurial journey.

Know your strengths and limitations and make sure your venture is in sync with your talent, resources, and ambition. If you are just looking for the opportunity to be your own boss, then look for the type of opportunity that lends itself to a lifestyle business. If you are looking for having a handful of people work with you and want to have some disposable income, then look for the type of opportunity that will allow you to have a modest venture. If you are looking for the challenge that will allow you to be better than local businesses, then look for an opportunity to start a promising business. If you have the ability and can attract the resources to dominate mid-sized or substantial segments of even large markets, then look for an opportunity that has the potential for you to start a high-growth venture. And if you are one of the few people each decade who has the ability to put together a world-class team and to attract vast resources to launch a revolutionary venture, then brace yourself to boldly go where no entrepreneur has gone before!

> *A choice confronts us. Shall we feel our foundations shaking,*
> *withdraw in anxiety ... if we do ... we shall have surrendered*
> *our chance to participate in the forming of the future.*[32]

—Rollo May

ENDNOTES

1. John Naisbitt, *Megatrends* (New York: Warner Books, 1988).
2. Amar V. Bhidé, *The Origin and Evolution of New Businesses* (New York: Oxford University Press, Inc., 2000), p. 30.
3. Presentation at the "Growth Companies: America's Rising Stars" Conference, sponsored by *Inc.* magazine, July 11, 1988.
4. Ibid., p. 29.
5. Ibid., p. 30.
6. *Inc.* 500 special Fall 2003 issue published by *Inc.* magazine. Data collected from throughout the book. Volume 25, issue 11.
7. Ibid., p. 38.
8. Bhidé, *The Origin and Evolution of New Businesses,* p. 32.
9. Ibid., p. 40.
10. Ibid., p. 141.
11. Ibid., p. 32.
12. Ibid., p. 54.
13. Ibid., p. 54.
14. Ibid., pp. 53 & 54.
15. Ibid., pp. 39 & 40.
16. Bill Gates, *The Road Ahead* (New York: Penguin Books, 1996), p. 18.
17. Bhidé, *The Origin and Evolution of New Businesses,* pp. 147 & 148.
18. John Gardner, *No Easy Victories* (New York: Harper Colophon, 1968), p. 45.
19. Ibid., p.16.
20. Ibid., p. 172.

21. Ibid., p. 168.

22. Ibid., p. 176.

23. Ibid., p. 42.

24. "Brand Building," *Business 2.0,* July 2002, p. 35.

25. Bhidé, *The Origin and Evolution of New Businesses,* p. 53.

26. Ibid., p. 61

27. Ibid., p. 18.

28. From the song, "Me and Bobby McGee"; lyrics by Kris Kristofferson.

29. Frazier Moore, "Inventor in the Picture at Last," *Wilmington Morning Star,* June 14, 2002. p. 3-D.

30. Chuck Salter, "The Problem With Most Banks Is That They Abuse Their Customers Every Day. We Want to Wow Ours," *Fast Company,* May 2002, p. 84.

31. Bhidé, *The Origin and Evolution of New Businesses,* p. xvi.

32. Rollo May, *The Courage to Create* (New York: Bantam Books, 1976), p. 11.

—————————————— **3** ——————————————

IDENTIFYING NEW VENTURE
OPPORTUNITIES

*Entrepreneurship is the knack for sensing opportunity where others saw chaos,
contradiction, and confusion.*[1]

—Jeffrey Timmons

If you feel you have the necessary qualities and capabilities or believe you can develop
them or can surround yourself with people who have the necessary qualities and capabilities (Step 1 in the new-venture creation process) and have identified how ambitious a venture you want to start, then you are ready to proceed to the next steps in the entrepreneurial
journey. It is now time to analyze the market (Step 2 in the new-venture creation process)
and identify problems or gaps (Step 3 in the new-venture creation process) that may represent opportunities for creating a venture that will use your capabilities and fulfill your
desires.

NEW-VENTURE CREATION PROCESS

Step 1. Analysis of entrepreneurial preparedness
Step 2. *Market analysis*
Step 3. *Identification of problems and gaps*
Step 4. Evaluation of new venture opportunities
Step 5. Investigation of capability and resource requirements
Step 6. Running the numbers
Step 7. Analyzing risks, returns, and personal preferences
Step 8. Ranking potential ventures
Step 9. Selecting the opportunity to pursue
Step 10. Conducting the feasibility study and test market
Step 11. Developing the business plan
Step 12. Getting the resources

67

Step 13. Starting the venture

Step 14. Managing the venture

REALITY CHECK

You may be tempted to skip this chapter if you already have a particular type of business in mind. You should read it because people who embark on the entrepreneurial journey frequently commit one or two of the following mistakes:

Mistake 1: *They start a business selling products or services that they like.*

Mistake 2: *They start a business where they live or where they would like to live.*

MISTAKE 1: "ENTREPRENEURSHIP BY BRAILLE"

It might be human nature for people to want to start a bookstore if they like to read or to start a restaurant if they like to cook or eat certain types of foods. If you do this, then you will be starting a business in search of customers. Just because you read lots of books or dine out often, don't assume the world shares your interests and will beat a path to your door.

You have a much better chance of being successful if you create a venture to serve customers in search of a business. The difference between starting a business in search of customers and creating a venture to serve customers in search of a business is the difference between sales and marketing. In most sales situations, the product has already been made; the salesperson's job is to find someone to buy it. Marketing begins with the marketplace. It tries to determine what people want. The firm then develops the products or service to meet the market's unmet needs.

Entrepreneurs must embrace the marketing concept. You must provide what the market wants; don't try to get the market to buy what you like. Entrepreneurs who are perceptive and flexible are far more likely to succeed. Entrepreneurs who try to change the market to fit their view of the world will have as much success as trying to stop an outgoing tide.

People who make mistake 1 are demonstrating *entrepreneurship by Braille.* That is, they only consider business opportunities that are within their reach—only things that they know and like. Personal interest has a place in the entrepreneurial process, but it needs to be postponed until the evaluation stage when financial worthiness and perceived risk are also used as criteria for evaluating and ranking potential new venture opportunities. If you limit Step 2 and Step 3 of the entrepreneurial process to products and services you enjoy, then you will be unduly restricting the number of opportunities you can consider.

The world is full of business opportunities. It would be a shame if Step 2 and Step 3 were built on a very narrow foundation. Step 2 and Step 3 work best when they incorporate the basic premises of brainstorming and decision theory. Brainstorming is designed to generate as many ideas as possible by postponing the evaluation of ideas until after they are generated. Brainstorming also recognizes that new ideas may be generated in the process. One new venture idea may generate a serendipitous new venture idea that would not have surfaced without an open mind and a nonevaluative process.

Decision theory states that a decision can only be as good as the best alternative. Effort needs to be taken early in the process to generate as many new venture ideas as possible. Steps 2 and 3 work best when they are not restricted to one's immediate world. Mistake 1 is frequently committed by people who want to turn a hobby into a business. It would be great to get paid for doing things that you have had to pay for as a hobby. The high failure rate of first-time start-ups can be attributed to people who don't have the prerequisite skills and who start businesses that were their hobbies.

REALITY CHECK

Most hobbies should remain hobbies. This book is written for people who want to start businesses that can beat the odds. If your hobby-turned-business does not fare well, then you may not have any money left to enjoy that hobby. If you start a business where there is a lucrative opportunity, then you may have the time and money to enjoy a number of hobbies!

Disclaimer to Mistake 1. There are situations when you can create a business selling what you like. Some of the examples on the following pages demonstrate that people's personal interests in computers, music, books, and travel provided them with insights into market gaps that became opportunities for successful ventures. In most of the instances, however, the entrepreneurs approached the gaps in a fairly systematic manner. Chapter 4 profiles those who succeeded rather than those who should never have started the journey. Remember, the explorers who were smart enough to make it back were the ones who made it into the history books; countless others either didn't make it back or returned with little to show for their efforts.

MISTAKE 2: ASSUMING CUSTOMERS WILL COME

A number of people want to start a business where they live or where they would like to live. Like mistake 1, this is natural. Starting a venture is like trying to catch fish. You are far more likely to catch fish if you know where they are, when they eat, and what they like to eat. You need to position your venture so it provides customers what they want when they want it. Don't expect the customers to come to you. The key is to locate your business where there are customers in search of a business. Again, perceptiveness and flexibility are key ingredients for success.

Disclaimer to Mistake 2. There are situations where it may be possible to start a venture where you live or where you would like to live. There is a story about a man who loved snow skiing and wanted to start a business where he could ski. Fortunately, he recognized that he should not restrict his search for a potential new venture to skiing-related businesses. Instead, he went to one of his favorite ski towns west of Denver to see if he could find "customers in search of a business." He decided to sit in a chair at one of the entrances to the ski town to watch what types of businesses operated in that town. His approach to analyzing the market may not have been very sophisticated, but it did identify a "gap" that was worth pursuing. He noticed that early each morning a truck from a Denver-based audiovideo store would enter the town. The truck would then leave the town at the end of the day. One day, he followed the truck to find out where it was going.

He learned that a number of the hotels were renting audiovideo equipment for meetings and conferences. The hotels were outsourcing the audiovideo equipment and corresponding support services to a business located in Denver. He studied the situation and concluded that there were no real barriers to entry for him, that it wouldn't take much money to start a similar business, and that by being in the immediate area he could eliminate the need for the lengthy and cost-prohibitive 180-mile round-trip from Denver each day. The entrepreneur set up his venture with a simple division of labor. His staff would be hired from people who lived nearby. He would spend his time developing accounts and overseeing the operation. His staff would deliver, set up, and operate the equipment.

The ski-enthusiast entrepreneur was able to have his cake and eat it, too. He was able to start a business where he wanted to live, and by working early or late in the day, he was able to get a fair amount of skiing in as well. His success can be attributed to his perceptiveness and flexibility. He didn't set up a business doing his hobby; he started a business where there was a gap between what was being provided and what could be provided. In this case, personalized service, greater reliability, and lower costs provided his new venture with significant competitive advantages. The entrepreneur recognized the hotels did not want to provide the audiovisual equipment. They had enough challenges in running their hotels. They also did not want to worry about whether the equipment would be stuck in the snow somewhere between Denver and their facilities.

THE DOOR IS WIDE OPEN FOR ENTREPRENEURIAL VENTURES

There is an old saying about advertising, "Only half of it works; the problem is that before you spend your money on it, you don't know which advertising is in that half." The same may be true with new ventures; there are numerous opportunities out there—the trick is knowing which ones will justify the time, effort, money, and risk. This chapter identifies numerous avenues for identifying new venture opportunities. Chapter 4 profiles entrepreneurs who had the mental dexterity to see the problems as business opportunities and who then created ventures that filled gaps in the marketplace. Numerous examples are provided in Chapter 4 because they demonstrate how perceptiveness helps identify new venture ideas. The examples may also help you generate ideas for your own venture. Chapter 5 addresses how to determine which opportunities have enough merit to start.

Peter Drucker once noted there is never a bad time to hire the right person. The same philosophy may apply to whether there is a right or wrong time to start a new venture. Obviously, some times are better than others, but opportunities exist in every possible economic situation and every industry.

It is natural to be hesitant to start a venture in lean economic times or in turbulent times. The opening quotation for this chapter, however, captures the essence of entrepreneurship: Entrepreneurs don't wait for things to happen; they make things happen! The best entrepreneurs are able to identify lucrative opportunities. They also have a keen sense of timing. Michael Dell noted, "I think there are opportunities everywhere. The question is, which are the right ones, and which are the ones that will make a success? The simple answer to the question, 'How do you do this?' is, you find a really large market—or one that's going to be large—that's inefficient, and you come up with a breakthrough way of delivering value to customers that nobody has ever done before."[2]

It is difficult to find fault in Dell's observation. Yet Chapter 2 noted there are a lot of lucrative opportunities out there, and most do not require breakthrough innovation or massive markets. Lucrative opportunities exist in services, retailing, and manufacturing. They also exist in providing goods and/or services to individual consumers, businesses, and government agencies.

IS THERE AN IDEAL BUSINESS SITUATION?

Prospective entrepreneurs frequently ask, "Is there such a thing as an ideal business situation?" William Sahlman noted, "The best business is a post office box to which people send cashier's checks."[3] It is not likely that you will be able to start that business. An ideal business, however, would have certain characteristics that would give it an edge in the marketplace and provide considerable financial return. The following characteristics are particularly noteworthy:

- *Category killer or killer application.* The product or service would be so superior in meeting the target market's needs (in the target market's eyes) that consumers would not even consider any other business. The product or service would not be 10 percent better, faster, more convenient, or less expensive. It would be at least twice as good, fast, or convenient—and be offered at less than half the price of what is currently available.

- *Right in front of your eyes.* The product or service addresses something that is not obscure. It makes people say, "Why didn't I think of that!" It is ironic in a world that nearly worships new technology how some low-technology or no-technology ventures are so successful. Examples of low-technology or no-technology products and services include a latex glove or boot developed and marketed by Xero Products LLC that keeps plaster casts dry, or changing the oil in boats by Naut-a-Care Marine Services while they are in the water. These and other ventures are profiled in Chapter 4.

- *Not price sensitive.* The product or service is targeted to people or organizations that have enough money to buy it without any hesitation.

- *Little relationship between cost and pricing.* You can price according to what consumers are willing to pay, and there is a big difference between what you can charge and your costs.

- *Minimal initial personal investment.* The venture either requires only a modest investment or outside investors are lined up who will be delighted to put up all the money for only a fraction of the ownership and management control.

- *Pent-up demand.* Customers have been asking, "Is there a business out there that can …?" for quite a while. They will be grateful that you have created a venture to meet their needs, interests, and desires. You will not need to advertise much, have a sales force, or take the time to educate consumers on the merit of your product or service.

- *Lasting window of opportunity.* Demand is not subject to fluctuating economic conditions, and the product or service is not a fad or subject to technological obsolescence. Customers will be around to purchase it again and again, or there will be wave after wave of customers entering the market.

- *Addictive.* It is like the microwave, cell phone, laptop, PDA, and Post-it notes. Your customers cannot imagine what life would be like without it.

- *Competitive edge.* You have a proprietary position that gives your firm a sustainable competitive advantage. You have a patent, an exclusive situation/agreement/source of supply, distribution channel, business process, particular skill, or something that gives you an advantage that cannot be matched by any other firm. Your edge also serves as a major barrier to entry.

- *Temporary legal monopoly.* If all of these factors came together, then your business would be the closest thing to being a legal monopoly. It is like the *Hagar the Horrible* cartoon strip that shows a bunch of people at the edge of a cliff being chased by an enemy tribe. When they ask Hagar how much he wants for his ladder, he responds,

"$10 million." If it were the ideal business situation, instead of contacting the Justice Department for being an abusive monopoly, your customers would be delighted that you were there and would welcome the opportunity to give you their money.

REALITY CHECK

So much for wishful thinking. It is highly unlikely that you would find an opportunity or be able to create a venture that would have most of these characteristics. So let's take a look at how real people can identify real opportunities.

IDENTIFYING BUSINESS OPPORTUNITIES: RAISE YOUR "OPPORTUNITY ANTENNAE"

Entrepreneurial success is contingent on numerous factors. Two factors are particularly important. First, you need to start with a good opportunity. The best entrepreneurs have the ability to see opportunities that other people don't see. Second, you need to make sure your business has the ability to capitalize on the opportunity for a reasonable profit. The best entrepreneurs are observant, perceptive, open-minded, and innovative, and they have a keen sense of timing. Their ventures are positioned to capitalize on opportunities, and they execute their plans well.

The first step in identifying new venture opportunities involves having an "external orientation." Prospective entrepreneurs need to have their eyes, ears, and minds open to what is happening in the world around them. Lillian Vernon noted, "Wherever you find yourself and whatever you are doing, keep your mind open to ideas for products or services that might satisfy needs. Also, watch for ways to improve what is already on the market."[4]

Market changes create entrepreneurial opportunities. Changes in technology have created incredible opportunities for ventures that can tap the Internet and use the power provided by databases. Changes in societal values are affecting how people want to spend time at work and their leisure time. Changes in government regulations create opportunities for new products and services. Numerous firms have been created to enhance safety and reduce pollution. Entrepreneurs who identify trends or gaps early and create ventures to cultivate and capitalize on these and other changes may be in a position to beat the odds.

CHANGE BRINGS CHALLENGES—AND NEW VENTURE OPPORTUNITIES

Peter Drucker noted, "The entrepreneur always searches for change, responds to it, and exploits it as opportunity." Change has always been a fact of life. Today, we are surrounded by change on all fronts. Yet we are now in an era where the rate of change, the magnitude of change, and the breadth of change are unprecedented.

We are getting hit by wave after wave of dramatic change. Social change is altering what we value and how we want to spend our time. Technological innovation is changing the way we live and work. Certain government agencies are increasing the regulation of certain facets of life, while other agencies are deregulating other facets of life. Economic and political change is opening doors to global commerce that have been off limits for decades.

Paul Saffo, director of Institute for the Future, noted that while the dot-com bubble may have burst a few years ago, use of the Internet goes unabated. He believes wireless connectivity will change the way people live and work. He noted, "The fundamental question to ask is, 'Okay, in a world where people are carrying the Internet in their pockets, what can I deliver to them that they want?' That's a big space."[5]

Gary Hoover, founder of Bookstop Inc. (which is now part of Barnes & Noble), has an entirely different perspective about technology. He expresses caution because it is difficult to build a company that will last because technological advantages last only a short period of time. He believes, however, the aging of baby boomers will provide exciting opportunities in financial services, health services and health-related things, travel, and education. He believes the health services field is full of opportunities because it is full of problems. He also believes that as the baby boomers age, they will have a lot of time and money on their hands. The baby boomers will be in search of constructive ways to use their time and money to be healthy and to stay healthy.[6]

Bob Johnson, founder of BET Holdings II Inc., the parent company of Black Entertainment Network (now owned by Viacom), also believes the aging of the population will provide considerable opportunities. He noted, "If I were going to start a business today, I would start one aimed at the growing-older generation: a medical facility that focuses on total wellness. It's a health club and leisure product—almost a country club— that you can join. Two things we know absolutely: the population is getting older, and the older population is living longer. If you assume that's the case, what are these people going to do to remain active? If you can ever combine active and healthy, that's a market for you."[7]

Aging baby boomers will provide an almost unlimited number of opportunities for businesses that are in sync with their recreational, leisure, educational, and health needs, interests, and desires. Many of the boomers' lifestyles in retirement will be markedly different from the lifestyles of the generations that preceded them. If they have the time, the health, and the money, then they may seize the moment with the same vigor that they pursued their careers. They will not "go slowly or gently into the night." They will not want to be restricted to only the vanilla, chocolate, and strawberry alternatives of yesteryear. Many will look for the opportunities to travel and learn. They will look for opportunities to expand their brains and horizons.

Paula E. Chauncey, who founded Être LLC, a financial services advisory firm serving individuals and businesses, stated, "The boomers are going to redefine what it means to be 50, 60, 70-plus."[8] She also noted, "The 77 million baby boomers born between 1946 and 1964 have driven consumer purchasing patterns in the United States since birth, and they will continue to do so till death do them part. And that's where some very interesting business opportunities lie, if you want to get crassly commercial about it. As the first boomers turn the corner at 50, the gestalt is becoming, "What's the second part of my life about? What do I really want to do with my life, and how do I figure out financially how to make that possible?"[9]

Entrepreneur magazine recognized people with limited business experience and information will look for helpful guidelines when they want to start a particular type of business— particularly a lifestyle business. It offers a number of guides (*www.smallbizbooks.com*) for people who want to start various businesses, including a restaurant, a medical claims billing service, a gift-basket service, a bed and breakfast, a home inspection service, a consignment clothing store, an executive recruiting service, a personal concierge service, a wedding consultant service, a child-care service, and a mail-order business.

These changes and countless others will create gaps in the marketplace that can be transformed into new venture opportunities. Businesses that can find new ways to do things and create new things to do will be the beneficiaries of change. It is amazing what can happen when preparation meets opportunity!

THE MARKETPLACE IS EXPLODING WITH ENTREPRENEURIAL OPPORTUNITIES

Each problem represents a gap between what exists and what people would like. Steps 2 and 3 in the new-venture creation process encourage entrepreneurs to listen to the market in search of gaps. Each gap should then be stated as a problem that needs to be solved. Attention is then directed to identifying potential business opportunities that may be related to each problem. The market gap business opportunity matrix in Exhibit 3.1 indicates that a single gap when framed as a problem may result in the identification of numerous business opportunities.

Gap analysis begins with looking for a chorus of people or businesses that exclaim:

"If only there was a business that ... ." or

"I wish I could buy a product or service that ... ."

These gaps represent the "market pull" nature of entrepreneurship where customers are looking for businesses that can fill gaps in the marketplace. Existing businesses frequently expand their operations to serve customers who ask them if they can provide products and services to fill gaps in their own operations. It is impossible, however, for existing businesses to keep in touch with everything the market wants and to serve every need.

Entrepreneurs should keep their antennae tuned to gaps that are not being filled by existing businesses. Scott Cook, founder of Intuit, noted that entrepreneurs should look for opportunities to change people's lives and invent new ways to help people out in ways that they have never been able to be helped before.[10]

Entrepreneurs should also be listening for a second type of exclamation:

"There has to be a better way to ... "

This exclamation represents the "innovation push" nature of entrepreneurship where someone sees a gap between what is and what is possible. Sometimes, the creation of a venture was not planned. Numerous well-known ventures were started with the personal observation, "You know, I could do it better!" Three Dog Bakery was developed by two guys (who had three dogs) who realized dog biscuits might not be very healthy. They developed a line of dog treats that are healthier. Auntie Anne's Pretzels was also the result of dissatisfaction with pretzels already on the market.

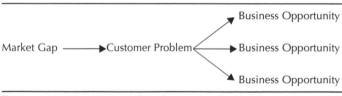

EXHIBIT 3.1   MARKET GAP BUSINESS OPPORTUNITY MATRIX

Entrepreneurs do not have to be consumers or even in the business of providing that type of product or service. They make things happen by going out and developing (or acquiring) the "better way" that offers the market a much higher level of value and customer satisfaction.

It is ironic that technology not only serves as the basis for solving problems; it also creates all new problems and business opportunities. Cellular phones and desktop computers serve as excellent examples. Cell phones provided mobility that conventional phones lacked. While the ability to move freely provided a significant advantage over conventional phones, the increased number of users and uses for cellular phones brought concerns about potential injury from the sound waves, the potential for distraction while driving, and theft. Each of these problems spurred the development of new products and services. Personal computers have spurred the development of thousands of problems or gaps. Physical problems ranging from glare to carpel tunnel syndrome spurred the development of various products and services.

Both the market pull and innovation push approaches represent viable avenues for identifying opportunities that exist today and that will appear soon on the horizon. These opportunities will provide a target-rich environment for today's and tomorrow's entrepreneurs.

DEVELOPING A KALEIDOSCOPIC PERSPECTIVE CAN HELP IDENTIFY OPPORTUNITIES

Mental dexterity plays a key role in the entrepreneurial process. As noted in Chapter 1, most entrepreneurs are not inventors and do not need to be inventors. The key to entrepreneurship is the ability to see a gap in the market and to transform it into a viable venture. The ability to see what others don't see and to make things happen are what set, successful entrepreneurs apart from the inventors, the dreamers, and the spectators.

Prospective entrepreneurs should make every effort to develop a *kaleidoscopic perspective*. They need to be able to look at situations from various vantage points. By looking at a market situation from various vantage points or angles, prospective entrepreneurs may see things that others don't see. "The real challenge is recognizing that an opportunity is buried in the often-conflicting and contradictory data and signals, and the inevitable noise and chaos in the marketplace. Often the skillful entrepreneur can shape and create opportunity where others see little or nothing."[11]

Changing one's vantage points is like twisting a kaleidoscope. You see something new with each turn. The kaleidoscopic perspective is captured in the question, "What is half of 8?" Most people will rely on the math they learned in elementary school to give them the answer of "4." People who have a kaleidoscopic perspective will respond "0, 3, E, and 4." The kaleidoscopic perspective will provide additional answers because it looks at the question from multiple dimensions. If you cut 8 in half laterally, then one half becomes 0! If you cut 8 in half vertically, then it becomes a 3 or an E!

Adopting a kaleidoscopic perspective will provide prospective entrepreneurs with new images of the marketplace. It will give you the ability to see things from different perspectives and to see things differently. Kaleidoscopic thinking ultimately gives prospective entrepreneurs the ability to see things others don't see, haven't seen, or can't see. David Gumpert and Harold Stevenson noted, "To capitalize on an opportunity, entrepreneurs must know the territory they operate in, then they must be able to recognize patterns as they develop."[12] The ability to see patterns enables prospective entrepreneurs to see what is missing or what might be possible.

EXAMPLES OF MARKET GAPS THAT WERE FILLED
BY PERCEPTIVE ENTREPRENEURS

Fred Smith did not come up with the idea of overnight delivery through divine intervention. He found in his first business venture that he could not get reliable and timely delivery of spare parts. Fred Smith believed there was an untapped market for overnight shipping that would "absolutely, positively" get it there! He created Federal Express to transform the market gap into a business opportunity.

Anthony Desio was so frustrated waiting in lines at the Post Office that he created Mail Boxes Etc. to provide a better alternative. He figured he could provide quicker service and offer various related products and services. His venture also would be valuable to people who moved around a lot or who were out of town a lot who needed to have their mail delivered to a specific place.[13]

Mary Kay Ash found that no company was teaching women how to care for their skin, so she created Mary Kay Cosmetics. Anita Roddick found that women were frustrated with having to spend a lot of money to try cosmetics so she developed The Body Shop so women could buy cosmetics by weight or bulk. Her approach allowed women to try a sample or purchase a product in a trial size container. Women were more willing to try The Body Shop's products because they did not have to throw a lot of it out if they didn't like it. Roddick also noticed that consumers were becoming more concerned about the environment. Her stores allow customers to get refills. This strategy not only reduced cost and waste, it also provided the incentive for customers to return to the store.

Inc. magazine periodically provides a list of hot start-ups. Each of the following businesses demonstrates there are a variety of opportunities in the market today. Cranium Inc. was created by Whit Alexander and Richard Tait. They recognized there was a gap in the game market. They developed the board game Cranium to challenge both sides of the brain. KaBloom Ltd. was created to become the first superstore for flowers. Its founder, David Hartstein, who had worked for Staples, observed in trips to Europe that people purchased fresh flowers as often as they bought fresh bread. His research also indicated that people who were not affluent bought flowers. Jeremy Kraus who started Jeremy's Micro-Batch Ice Creams applied the beer industry's microbrew strategy to ice cream by making ice cream in small quantities and selling it in limited editions.[14]

The need for information has created opportunities for numerous new ventures. Steve Birnbaum found there was a major gap in the Disney experience. Although the Walt Disney staff may have done a monumental job designing and building Walt Disney World in Orlando, it did not do a comparable job in providing tourists with the information they needed to truly enjoy the park. Tourists were overwhelmed by the scale and complexity of the site. Disney provided maps, but tourists wanted to know how to get the most out of the park. In addition to directions, tourists wanted tips about what was worth doing and what would make a great vacation at Disney. Birnbaum created a guide that provided valuable tips and insights for people visiting Disney World.

Nina and Tim Zagat, like Steve Birnbaum, found that tourists, business travelers, and locals yearned for insightful information about restaurants in specific cities. They created guides for numerous restaurants and nightlife in various cities. In 2002, their restaurant guide for New York sold more than 650,000 copies.[15]

The need for guides to fill information gaps is also evident in the numerous *Dummies Guides* and *Idiot's Guides* that have been published. Some of the guides like *Philosophy for Dummies* help distill vast amounts of information. They are like Cliff's Notes for people who are not in school and who don't want to take a lot of time to get an overview of a subject. Some of the guides are similar to Steve Birnbaum's guide to Walt Disney World. They do what the manufacturers did not do—they make it easier for the consumer to use the product. Microsoft, like Disney, could have—and probably should have—provided guides that were truly written for lay people. Yet it is often difficult for the developer of a product—which knows the intricacies of a product—to be truly empathetic of its potential users. Entrepreneurs who recognize consumers do not have ESP may be in a position to capitalize on information gaps.

The use of technology in providing potential customers valuable information and insights has served as the basis for numerous ventures. Companies have been created to provide virtual tours of cities, stores, and houses. Two savvy college students created a venture to help various bars and nightclubs market the bands that would be playing in their establishments. When one of the students asked bar owners what they wanted to provide potential customers on their Websites, they indicated they wanted the names and schedules for the bands that would be playing in the next few weeks. When he asked potential customers what they *really* wanted, they said they wanted to know "in real time" whether the place was jumping!

They then set up a series of cameras that streamed live pictures of the bar and dance floor on that business's Website. Potential customers could decide which establishments to go to based on what was happening at that moment. Entrepreneurs who provide virtual tours have gone well beyond the Yellow Pages. They demonstrate the value of being customer-centric. They let their customers' eyes do the touring rather than letting their fingers—or feet—do the walking.

The preceding businesses provide a very small sample of ventures that were created in the last few years to capitalize on various trends, technological breakthroughs, and/or needs. Chapter 4 contains dozens of additional examples of ventures that were created by entrepreneurs who had the mental dexterity to see opportunities where others merely saw problems.

TECHNIQUES FOR IDENTIFYING BUSINESS OPPORTUNITIES

There are dozens of ways to identify potential opportunities. Some techniques are very simple. Other techniques are more comprehensive. The following techniques may help you identify new venture opportunities.

Ask People to Identify Areas Where Their Needs Aren't Being Met

It is ironic how many prospective entrepreneurs spend untold hours, days, weeks, or months trying to come up with an idea for a new venture. Fred Smith, Mary Kay Ash, the Zagats, and Steve Birnbaum didn't need to be rocket scientists to identify the opportunities that served as the basis for their ventures. Entrepreneurs don't need to come up with Nobel Prize–winning flashes of brilliance. Often, all they need is that "blinding flash of the obvious!" The world is full of problems, so all prospective entrepreneurs need to do to generate a list of new venture ideas is to actively look around, observe gaps, listen to what people are complaining about, and ask people to identify gaps that they want filled.

Focus Groups Can Identify Gaps and Solutions

Focus groups can provide a good avenue for generating ideas for new products and services. Bringing people together to talk about "gaps" in their personal and professional lives can provide interesting insights. By providing some direction, people may identify things that bother them. By probing even deeper, you may even get them to articulate additional gaps or frustrations. Like peeling back layers of an onion, they may identify "It may not be possible, but it would be great if a product or service could be created that would ..." areas. The list of problem areas that is generated can then be analyzed by the group to identify gaps that could serve as the basis for creating new ventures.

Reverse Brainstorming: Contempt for the Status Quo

Focus groups frequently use brainstorming to identify problems. They may also be used to generate creative solutions to specific problems. *Reverse brainstorming* represents an interesting twist to the creative process. Reverse brainstorming is a technique that encourages participants to be highly critical, rather than highly creative. Participants are encouraged to either identify problems or gaps in the marketplace or to identify drawbacks, problems, or shortcomings with a particular product or service. Once the problems or gaps are identified, attention can then be directed to finding out what is wrong with it (the situation, product, or service) and how it can be improved.

A reverse brainstorming group may be asked to identify problems or gaps in various areas. They may be asked to identify problems in an area as large as financial services. They could be asked to reverse brainstorm a particular product like peanut butter. They could be asked to identify problems in a particular situation like traveling by air for an extended period of time. Reverse brainstorming may identify gaps in financial services that are available and how they are provided. Reverse brainstorming may identify drawbacks with the flavor, packaging, and color of peanut butter. Reverse brainstorming may identify frustrations encountered while waiting for planes, getting ground transportation, and with personal hygiene.

The identification of problems may serve as the springboard for creative brainstorming sessions where participants may come up with more customer-centric financial services, better tasting or easier to apply peanut butter, and innovative ways to make air travel more enjoyable and productive. Prospective entrepreneurs may use the "there must be a better way" type of thinking to identify areas where a new venture may be able to develop a competitive advantage over existing firms. Numerous entrepreneurs and established firms have enjoyed considerable success by identifying existing products that rust, warp, fade, and/or shrink. Then they develop innovative products that reduce or eliminate these problems. The strategy of replacing one material with another has served many firms well. Examples abound for firms that transformed wooden products into metal products. Ironically a number of firms developed a competitive advantage over these firms by taking the metal products and making them out of plastic or some composite.

Howard Head offered metal skis to a world that used wooden skis. He used the same strategy when he offered metal tennis rackets to a world that was accustomed to wooden tennis rackets. Ironically, metal skis and tennis rackets were replaced by skis and rackets made of plastic and/or composites.

A significant part of Rubbermaid's marketing strategy is based on challenging the status quo. Rubbermaid's product development team scours the planet looking for products that are made of wood or metal. They look for opportunities to make those products better and/or less expensive by forming them out of plastic. When they looked for opportunities to replace metal products that rust, Rubbermaid questioned why garbage cans, residential mailboxes, and children's lunch boxes had to be made of metal. The kaleidoscopic perspective and contempt for the status quo attitude explain why Rubbermaid develops more than 1,000 new products each year.

The world is full of other products that have challenged the status quo. Pringles potato chips were developed because consumers really didn't want to pay for *chips* of chips. In-line skates were created because someone challenged the status quo of skates that used four wheels in a rectangular format. The Walkman was created because Sony believed it was possible to have high-quality sound in a small portable unit.

The kaleidoscopic perspective encourages people to ask the following questions:

1. Can it be made out of different material? (Rubbermaid—plastic birdhouses)

2. Can it be made smaller? (Sony—Walkman)

3. Can it be made larger? (Calloway—Big Bertha golf club and Prince Tennis Rackets)

4. Can the package make it better? (Pringles—potato chips)

5. Can trash be transformed? (FCR Inc.—processing old newsprint into insulation)

6. Are there other uses? (Arm & Hammer Baking Soda—refrigerator air freshener)

7. Are there other users? (Pacific Bio Systems—microwave for medical use)

8. Are there ways to increase the usage rate? (Florida orange juice—cocktails)

9. Can it be combined with something else? (Laundromat and cocktail lounge)

10. Can it be more convenient? (Amazon.com—24 hours a day, 7 days a week)

11. Can it be available to more people? (Southwest Airlines—discount air fare)

12. Can it be done quicker? (Federal Express—overnight almost anywhere in the world)

13. Can it be made to last longer? (Ziebart—automobile rustproofing)

14. Can we make it possible for people to do it for themselves? (Home Depot—home improvement)

15. Can it be made to be more attractive? (Tweedies Optical—eyeglass frames for kids)

16. Can it be made quieter? (Noise Cancellation Technologies—neutralizes sound waves)

The kaleidoscopic perspective encourages prospective entrepreneurs to

- Take things that smell and remove the scent (Febreze odor remover)

- Take things that don't smell and give them a pleasing scent (fabric softener sheets)

- Take things that taste bad and make them tasteless or tasteful (antacid, mouth wash)

- Take things and make them disposable (lighters, cameras, cell phones, long-distance-phone cards)

- Take things that look bad and make them less noticeable or attractive (toilet brush caddies)

- Take something that is not readily available and make it available and convenient (cheap, high-quality printers that scan, fax, and copy)
- Take something in the maturity stage of the product life cycle and bring it to life (Sony Walkman)

The list of ways to improve on the status quo is almost endless. In many cases, entrepreneurs come up with ideas via what can be called a *blinding flash of the obvious*. They come up with products and services that cause others to exclaim, "I should have thought of that!" It is amazing how long it took before a sports bra was developed for female athletes. When Brandi Chastain took her jersey off to celebrate the United States woman's soccer team's victory in the World Cup on television in 1999, that was the first time some people saw a sports bra. What a blinding flash of the obvious. Men had worn athletic supporters for centuries. Why did it take so long for someone to create an athletic supporter for women?

REALITY CHECK

Coming up with what you consider to be a better way to deal with a drawback in the marketplace doesn't mean consumers will embrace it. Women have complained about how pantyhose seems to be subject to Murphy's Law. Pantyhose have the propensity to get a run when women are away from home. An inventor thought that he had come up with the ultimate solution. He developed a three-legged pantyhose where a third leg was rolled up next to the panty-part of the panty hose. His logic was that if one leg got a run, then the wearer could roll up the one leg and roll out the one that had been rolled up as a contingency plan. There are two morals to this example. First, it might be worthwhile to test market a prototype with potential consumers. A lot of ideas sound good in theory but die in the marketplace. Second, you have to be better to succeed in the marketplace ... and to be better, you have to be different. Remember this, however, "If you are different without being better, then you surely won't have a leg up on competition!"

Matrix Charting May Reveal Interesting Insights

Matrix charting is a systematic method of searching for new opportunities by listing important elements for each product or service along two axes of a chart and then asking questions regarding each of these elements. The answers are recorded in the relevant boxes of the matrix. By asking various questions entrepreneurs may be in a position to come up with creative new product or service ideas. Questions may include: What can it be used for? Where can it be used? Who can use it? When can it be used? How can it be used?[16]

The Big Dream Approach Encourages Unbounded Thinking

This approach encourages entrepreneurs to "dream" or "think big" about a particular problem and its solution without any constraints. It encourages entrepreneurs to be bold and to ask the question, "What change would change everything?" Like brainstorming, every possibility is recorded and investigated without regard to all the negatives or the resources required. This allows an idea to be considered until it is developed into a workable form.[17]

The people who toyed with providing full video capability using wireless Internet technology into a cell phone or personal digital assistant, when existing businesses were just transmitting voices or providing simple data storage and retrieval, were using the *big dream approach*. They explored what could happen if they could "make the impossible possible."

Free Association and Paired Comparison May Provide New Insights

These two techniques are similar in that they try to get people to see things in a different light. Free association tries to get people to state what immediately comes to mind when a word is said. The word may be related to a product, service, need, or market. The words that pop up via free association may provide insights into gaps or potential improvements.

Paired comparison is a bit more structured than free association. A product or service may be paired with one or more unrelated words. Attention is then directed to generating insights or ideas from the two things. If an entrepreneur was looking for ways to improve a cell phone, then a list of words may be paired with *cell phone* one by one. If the word *tomato* was put into a paired-comparison with *cell phone*, someone may take the red of the tomato and suggest that cell phones be provided in different colors—including red. This might sound simplistic, but consider how long it took for cars, computers, and cell phones to come out in a variety of colors so consumers could actually have a choice! Interesting things can happen when people are encouraged to think thoughts that no one may have thought before!

The "Slice of Life" Approach Can Identify Opportunities

The slice of life approach to identifying gaps is similar to the focus group. Richard White noted in his classic book, *The Entrepreneur's Manual,*[18] that you can find opportunities in almost any aspect of life. He uses the example of looking at problems encountered by adults. This approach asks a sequence of questions that resemble a decision tree, where the response to one question leads to another question that is based on the response to the preceding question. For example, White divides adult life between work and leisure. If you choose to focus on the leisure side of adult life, you then choose between weekend leisure and weekday leisure. If you choose weekday, then you choose leisure time *before* or *after* work. If you choose *after* work, then you choose *before* or *after* dinner. You then investigate the types of problems adults have during that time.

White found that numerous problems exist for many adults during that interval. The list includes fatigue, heavy traffic, tired feet, rumpled and clinging clothes, needing to take the dog out, and so on. He found that hundreds of problems exist during the brief "adult/leisure/weekday/post-work/pre-dinner" time interval.[19] Each of these problems may represent a multitude of new product or service opportunities.

How we deal with food provides an interesting example for how the slice of life approach can be applied. For example, we can look at food from various vantage points, including (1) how we plan our meals, (2) how we prepare our meals, (3) how we eat our meals, (4) how we clean up after our meals, and (5) how we store our food before and after our meals.[20] A multitude of products have been developed over the years to address each of these facets. Microwave ovens, TV trays, TV dinners, and plastic containers are just a few examples. As noted earlier, a few innovative firms like Peapod and Webvan made a gallant effort to eliminate having to go to the grocery store altogether. By using the Internet, database technology, state-of-the-art inventory management systems, and innovative storage systems, they tried to find a way to save people time and effort.

Market research indicated a significant number of people would be delighted to spend 10 percent more for their groceries to have Saturday morning free to "enjoy life." Research also indicated that this service might not cost more because people will be less likely to buy snack foods and other impulse items if they don't have to go into the store. Unfortunately, the research did not translate into profitable ventures for Peapod or Webvan. This example demonstrates there may be a big difference between being able to identify a gap and being able to create a profitable business to capitalize on it. Nevertheless, a number of ventures are still trying to find a way to do it profitably—the market is just too big to be left alone.

The slice of life process could be used for other aspects of life including (1) adults traveling on business from Pacific Rim cities who plan to do business within three hours of their arrival in the United States, and (2) people who had long layovers who wanted to spend their time doing something other than shopping, eating, watching television, and so on. A perceptive entrepreneur found that a number of people traveling on business from the Pacific Rim to the United States, unlike people traveling from Europe to the United States, would like to have a chance to freshen up before meeting their U.S. contacts. The entrepreneur found that many of the travelers would welcome the opportunity to take a shower, have their clothes pressed, take a quick nap, have a message, or just have a few moments to themselves to realign their atoms.

Another perceptive entrepreneur found that people on long layovers in the United States would welcome the opportunity to turn idle time into recreational time. He created a venture that offered an indoor driving range that also videotaped the person's swing. Ironically, the original concept of hitting a plastic ball against a net or screen has been replaced by interactive videogame technology that simulates actual golf holes.

The slice of life approach can be applied to objects as well as people. For instance, you could look at the various facets of powerboat use. The process may narrow down to the problems associated with powerboats that are between 15 and 25 feet long that are stored on their trailers after summer is over. A perceptive entrepreneur found that a number of boat owners were frustrated because they would have their boats cleaned, but then the boats would become dirty from falling leaves and air pollution. Boats on trailers also had the tendency to become homes for various insects, birds, and so on. The entrepreneur created a business that would not only clean the boat at a competitive rate; it would also shrinkwrap the boat. The simple process that uses special wrap, a vacuum, and a heat gun takes a nominal amount of time, but offers a considerable advantage and it keeps the boat from having to be cleaned again at the beginning of the next summer.

The Market-Area Saturation Approach Asks, "What's Missing in This Picture?"

The market area saturation approach tries to identify whether a gap may exist for a certain type of business in a specific geographic area. People are frequently heard saying, "A town of this size should have ... ." The market area saturation approach is based on the premise that for a town with X number of people, there should be Y number of businesses of Z type. When I moved to Wilmington, North Carolina, in 1976, I was asked by a number of businesspeople what I thought the town with a 100,000 metropolitan base lacked. My list of gaps included a number of businesses such as a high-quality men's clothing store, delivered pizza, a French restaurant, and more restaurants with a view of the river, waterway, or ocean. I found the gap in the delivered pizza market to be particularly noticeable because the town hosted a community college and a state university. I wasn't surprised when Thomas Monaghan started Domino's so people in my community and elsewhere could enjoy pizza without having to risk their lives, driver's licenses, and insurance coverage by going out to eat pizza.

The market-area saturation approach provides a quick and somewhat cursory way of analyzing whether an opportunity may exist for a certain type of venture. It uses industry or government data to determine whether a specific geographic area may not have enough businesses of that type. This approach may be used for retail and service organizations like convenience stores, veterinarians, dry cleaners, movie theaters, water slides, and fast-food restaurants.

The Census of Retail Trade indicates the number of inhabitants for various types of businesses. If you want to know if there may be an opportunity for a bookstore in a town with 100,000 people, then you would compare the number of bookstores in that area with the number of inhabitants to determine the degree of saturation. If the census data reveal that there are 26,000 people per store and that there already are five bookstores in that town, then the market may offer little opportunity for another bookstore unless you will be markedly superior than the businesses already serving the market or a particular geographic location exists where prospective customers are not being served. McDonald's and Starbucks incorporate saturation data when they are looking for locations for additional outlets.

REALITY CHECK

The market-area saturation approach, however, needs to be used with caution. Its simplicity has major shortcomings. It fails to consider the size and strength of existing businesses. Your analysis may indicate the city has only four bookstores and the census data indicates it may handle six bookstores. The census data may not consider the size, competitive strength, location, and financial success of the four existing bookstores. The census data also fails to take into consideration the level of income and education of the population and whether it is a suburb of a major metropolitan area that has a number of bookstores. It also fails to consider the impact of mail order, the increasing use of online bookstores like Amazon.com, and publishers' Websites. If you use this approach, then supplement it with additional research into the uniqueness of the market area. This approach is best suited to products or services where the convenience of purchase and location are important.

The Competitive Matrix May Reveal Market Gaps

The competitive matrix depicted in Exhibit 3.2 may be helpful in identifying if there are gaps in particular markets. If the prospective entrepreneur has already decided the nature of the product or service and the geographic area where he or she plans to start a business, then the matrix will help profile how well existing businesses are meeting consumers' needs. The matrix can also be useful if the prospective entrepreneur is considering different businesses in various locations.

The overall market is divided into its corresponding segments. Segmentation may be based on usage rate, income level, geographic area, or a combination of factors. A matrix is then constructed for each segment. Key factors are listed as rows and businesses already providing those goods or services are identified in the columns. Each segment may place a different value on a particular dimension, so that segment's weight (relative importance) is stated in the box inside each matrix cell.

A market gap exists for a segment when what is offered by existing businesses (the first number in the calculation at the bottom of each cell) is less than what consumers in that segment want (the second number in the calculation). Prospective entrepreneurs should pay attention to dimensions that consumers in that particular segment consider to be very important and are not being served well. Particular attention should be directed to gaps with at least two points of separation, which are noted by double asterisks. Gaps with only one point of separation may be filled by existing businesses without much effort. Gaps of at least two points will usually require a significant change in a business's strategy. Each asterisk in the matrix indicates that that business is not meeting that segment's expectations. If a whole row has asterisks, then the matrix indicates none of the existing businesses are meeting that segment's needs. Figure 3-2 indicates that significant gaps exist between the level of customer service and the level of quality offered by the existing firms and what is sought by consumers in that segment. Figure 3-2 also indicates (1) only one of the existing firms offers the type or level of services sought by customers in that segment, (2) only one of the existing firms provides the caliber of facilities and atmosphere sought by customers in that segment, and (3) the prices charged by four of the firms are considered high by customers in that segment.

Competitive factor	Business #1		Business #2		Business #3		Business #4		Business #5	
Price	* $3 \times 4 = 12$	4	* $1 \times 4 = 4$	4	** $2 \times 4 = 8$	4	$4 \times 4 = 16$	4	* $3 \times 4 = 12$	4
Quality	** $3 \times 5 = 15$	5	** $3 \times 5 = 15$	5	** $2 \times 5 = 10$	5	** $3 \times 5 = 15$	5	** $2 \times 5 = 10$	5
Selection	$4 \times 3 = 12$	3	$4 \times 3 = 12$	3	$3 \times 3 = 9$	3	$3 \times 3 = 9$	3	$4 \times 3 = 12$	3
Promotion	$3 \times 2 = 6$	2	$4 \times 2 = 8$	2	$2 \times 2 = 4$	2	$4 \times 2 = 8$	2	$2 \times 2 = 4$	2
Services	* $4 \times 5 = 20$	5	$5 \times 5 = 25$	5	** $2 \times 5 = 10$	5	** $3 \times 5 = 15$	5	* $4 \times 5 = 20$	5
Customer Service	** $3 \times 5 = 15$	5	** $3 \times 5 = 15$	5	** $1 \times 5 = 5$	5	** $3 \times 5 = 15$	5	** $3 \times 5 = 15$	5
Facilities/ Atmosphere	* $3 \times 4 = 12$	4	$5 \times 4 = 20$	4	** $2 \times 4 = 8$	4	** $2 \times 4 = 8$	4	* $3 \times 4 = 12$	4
Location	$3 \times 3 = 9$	3	$4 \times 3 = 12$	3	* $2 \times 3 = 6$	3	* $2 \times 3 = 6$	3	$3 \times 3 = 9$	3
Relative strength of this segment	101		111		59		92		94	

Rating of the business on this factor ⟶ # × # = #

\# ⟵ Importance of this factor to this segment

Combined score for the extent the business meets the segment's needs and the importance of this factor.

↖ Importance of this factor to this segment

* Indicates a gap exists between what this business offers and what this segment wants.

** Indicates a significant gap exists between what this business offers and what this segment wants.

EXHIBIT 3.2 COMPETITIVE MATRIX REFLECTING GAPS IN THE MARKETPLACE

Referrals and the Trend Toward Outsourcing Open Entrepreneurial Doors

While many of the opportunities provided so far may be for consumer products and services, business-to-business activities may provide some of the best opportunities for new ventures. Amar Bhidé's research into firms that have been in the *Inc.* 500 indicated most of the *Inc.* 500 companies were serving other businesses rather than consumers.[21]

People who are already in business may be a great source for new venture opportunities. They may identify gaps or deficiencies that exist with their suppliers and in their distribution system. They may also indicate product and service opportunities that they have identified that their businesses are not going to pursue because the opportunities are either outside their present operations or because they would force their business to grow beyond their comfort zone.

It is fairly common for a business that is very good at providing a particular service to be approached by a customer to provide a service that they want to outsource or that they will need in the near future. Both of these instances may represent opportunities for creating a venture if the business that was approached is not interested in the proposition. These requests could range from doing a newsletter all the way to the other end of the spectrum, where the business wants someone to store all the parts, assemble the product, and ship it to their customers for them.

All of these situations may represent opportunities because there is at least one customer in search of that business. As noted earlier, if you define your business as a customer problem solver, then referrals may generate a number of new venture opportunities.

ACQUIRING IDEAS VERSUS INVENTING THEM

This book emphasizes the merits of creating a business to serve customers in search of a business rather than starting with a product in search of customers. A number of entrepreneurs start their entrepreneurial journey by trying to find products and then trying to find customers. The *product-first approach* may involve buying or licensing the rights to a product that was invented by someone else.

Entrepreneurs may also start their journey by buying or licensing products that have been developed by companies that do not plan to take them to market. You should check your employer's inventory of products to see if it has any products that have potential but have not been offered to the market. Supposedly, Steven Jobs benefited from innovations he saw when he visited Xerox's Palo Alto Research Center. He found the mouse and the graphic interface to be particularly intriguing. Sometimes entrepreneurs will acquire the rights to a product that has been on the market but has fallen out of favor with that firm. This is what is known as the *Lazarus effect,* where an entrepreneur may bring a product back to life.

The search for products may include a review of publications that list products that can be acquired. A number of services publish information on a wide variety of patents and products available for licensing. The National Technical Information Service that is part of the U.S. Department of Commerce is a helpful source of information. Inventors frequently showcase their products so they can get feedback, establish contacts, and explore the degree of interest by others in licensing or acquiring their products. The U.S. Patent Office (*www.USPTO.gov*) provides considerable information on its Website.

INPEX (*www.inventionshow.com*) also provides information on inventions and new product expositions.

If the entrepreneur takes the *market-first approach* and has identified a need for a specific type of product, then he or she may follow a similar process to see if a product or process already exists. Remember, entrepreneurs don't have to be inventors. There is little reason for you to spend the time reinventing the wheel when you may be able to (1) license the rights to the wheel, (2) gain access to it by forming an alliance with the firm that developed it, or (3) buy it from the person who invented it. If you find a product, service, or process that already exists that will give your start-up a competitive advantage, then it may be worthwhile for you to acquire the rights to use or own it.

Obtaining the right to manufacture a product based on a patent may be the only way to get into a particular market. The Haloid Company provides an excellent example of how acquiring the rights to a product or process can represent a breakthrough opportunity. The Haloid Company was a small manufacturing firm when it learned about a revolutionary photoduplicating process invented by a professor at the University of Chicago. The invention was developed by Battelle Memorial Institute. The Haloid Company secured the license to manufacture and distribute the new product. The Haloid Company then changed its name to become Xerox Company.[22]

REALITY CHECK

Acquiring the rights to a product or a process is not a risk-free proposition. You need to beware of numerous factors before signing on the dotted line. First, you may be getting access to a product that will let you get to market quicker than if you had developed it yourself, but make sure a market really exists for the product and that the product has a competitive advantage. Remember the three-legged pantyhose; being different doesn't always mean being better. Second, don't assume that that patent or license is iron clad. It is fairly easy for someone to skirt patent protection by modifying a key component. Third, if you acquire a license to a product from another firm, you may not be able to secure exclusive rights to it. Fourth, the cost for the rights may exceed the benefits. Acquiring the rights may open doors that you couldn't open on your own, but make sure in advance that there are sufficient returns on the other side of the door to justify the price you have to pay for the key!

ALLIANCES AND JOINT VENTURES CAN OPEN ENTREPRENEURIAL DOORS

Alliances and joint ventures with other firms are gaining popularity with entrepreneurs and established firms. These approaches to doing business attempt to foster a symbiotic relationship where each firm benefits from the other firm. An alliance usually involves two or more firms working together on a common issue. They may share people, funds, data, and/or facilities. One firm may have an innovative product but lack the sales force or distribution channels to get it to market. The other firm may then agree to promote the product through its sales and distribution network. The first firm benefits because it doesn't have to commit its limited resources to marketing efforts. The second firm gets to broaden its product offering without having to spend time and money on research and development.

Alliances tend to be less formal than joint ventures. A joint venture involves the creation of a new entity. Alliances tend to be more like a relationship that is built on trust and sharing rather than legal forms. Alliances usually arise when two or more firms want to try something out. Instead of getting bogged down in legalese, they agree to explore the merit of a certain concept or business relationship. The flexibility of alliances permits firms to experiment.

Entrepreneurs are finding that alliances may help them get over some of the hurdles in the start-up stage when they have limited resources. They let the entrepreneur focus on what he or she can do best. Allies can provide crucial core competencies. Chunka Mui, co-author of *Unleashing the Killer App: Digital Strategies for Market Dominance*, noted, "If there's something you don't have—a certain skill or a certain function—you can use technology to form a partnership (or alliance) with someone else to get it, and when you don't need it anymore, you end that partnership (alliance) … There's no need to build a large organization in order to compete.[23]

Virtual corporations represent alliances taken to the extreme. It is possible for an entrepreneur to create a business that operates in global markets that does millions of dollars in business without any other employees. By forming alliances or outsourcing every business activity, the entrepreneur is focusing on the essence of entrepreneurship. Virtual ventures epitomize identifying a gap and creating a venture to capitalize on that opportunity for a profit. Like the old Greyhound Bus Lines' ad that said, "Leave the driving to us," virtual entrepreneurs are finding ways to leave almost everything to other firms that can do certain activities better, cheaper, quicker, or in a more convenient manner.

FRANCHISES MAY OFFER NEW VENTURE OPPORTUNITIES

Acquiring the rights to products and/or processes can also be achieved by becoming a franchisee or by buying a complete business. When you become a franchisee, you are acquiring the rights to do business with a certain name in a certain way. You pay certain fees to get certain benefits. In a sense, you are buying someone's formula for success. Franchises are popular for people who are not pure entrepreneurs. The franchisor identifies the market opportunity and usually develops the systems (advertising, accounting, inventory, and so on) for capitalizing on the opportunity.

Jon Vincent, president of JTV Enterprises, provides an excellent example of how going the franchise route might be particularly rewarding. He recognized early in his career that his strength was in developing and overseeing business operations. He left the identification of emerging opportunities to people who have the ability to sense an opportunity at an early stage. His strength was identifying franchises that would fare well in territories he knows from first-hand experience. In a sense, he used the "what's missing in this picture" approach to identify gaps that franchises could fill in those territories. The foundation of his business was built on acquiring franchise rights for geographic areas that are not being served well or at all. He started with Domino's franchises and then added Steak-Out and Gloria Jean's Gourmet Coffees. He added franchises when there was sufficient opportunity and sold off franchises when their potential seemed to be waning.

REALITY CHECK

Franchises come in all shapes and sizes. Some have a great track record and some should be avoided. The principle of *caveat emptor* (let the buyer beware) applies to franchises as it does to any other avenue for acquiring rights that may expedite starting a venture. If you are considering going the franchise route, then make sure you seek advice from an attorney that specializes in franchises.

SOLD! BUYING A BUSINESS TO CAPITALIZE ON AN OPPORTUNITY

Buying an existing business also represents an avenue for capitalizing on a business opportunity. In some instances it may be better, quicker, or less expensive to buy an existing business than it would be to start a venture from scratch. Buying a business may be the best way to get your foot in the door in certain areas. Some suppliers are reluctant to do business with a start-up. If you want to offer a particular brand and the supplier is reluctant to provide that brand, then you may have to acquire a business that carries that brand. If you need a specific site to gain a competitive advantage, then you may have to acquire the business that owns that site.

Victor Kiam became a national celebrity when he went on national television with his ad, "I liked their razor so much that I bought the company!" He bought the company that made Remington electric razors because he thought the market had greater potential than was being realized by the existing firms. He also believed he could make the company even better. If you are in a position to bring new ideas, new approaches, and new resources into a market that has grown a bit stale, then buying an existing business may be worthwhile.

Buying out an existing business has advantages and disadvantages. When you buy a business, you are acquiring a business that is up and running. Customers are accustomed to doing business with you, operating systems are in place, employees have experience, and financial information is available that profiles the firm's performance. These factors represent goodwill.

REALITY CHECK

When you buy a business, you can never be sure in advance of what you are getting. You may be paying a premium because the business is up and running. You may also be taking a nightmare off the seller's hands. Remember, if the deal seems too good to be true, it probably is. In almost every business sale there is an optimist and a pessimist. The seller believes he or she should get out while the going is good. The buyer always believes he or she can make it even better. If you are considering acquiring a business, then make sure you explore all the possibilities and hire an accountant and attorney who are experienced in business acquisitions to help you through the minefield.

KEEP A NOTEBOOK OF POTENTIAL ENTREPRENEURIAL OPPORTUNITIES

Some prospective entrepreneurs are very patient and deliberate when looking for new venture opportunities. Other prospective entrepreneurs jump at the first opportunity they come across. This book emphasizes the benefits of approaching the entrepreneurial process in a systematic manner. Although it cautions against *paralysis by analysis,* it should be clear that the best way to beat the odds is to start with a lucrative business opportunity. If a decision can only be as good as the best alternative available, then effort should be made to ensure the pool of new venture opportunities is a fertile one.

Prospective entrepreneurs should create a notebook with two sections. The first section can be titled "Problem Inventory." This section lists needs that are not being met well or at all. It identifies customers in search of a business.

The second section can be titled "Neat Product/Service Ideas Inventory." This section identifies products or services in search of customers. This section contains two subsections. The first subsection lists cool product or service concepts. These concepts represent innovative approaches whose time may not have arrived yet or that are in very rough form and need considerable work. The other subsection lists products or services that have not been introduced to the market or that may have the potential to be used in other markets for other uses. This subsection might provide the prospective entrepreneur with the incentive to look for market segments that would value particular products and services.

Richard Branson is a classic serial entrepreneur. It seems as if his opportunity antennae are always engaged. He carries around a black notebook to record his notes on conversations, observations, and ideas he thinks he can put to use.[24] Gary Hoover, who has started numerous businesses including Bookstop Inc. and Hoover's Inc., has a list with about 70 business ideas on it. He indicated, "Hopefully not a day goes by that I am not investigating opportunities and passions.[25]

BROADEN YOUR PERSPECTIVE: OPPORTUNITIES ARE OUT THERE

Most people see the world as full of problems. Entrepreneurs see it as a world full of opportunities. Successful entrepreneurs recognize that if you want to identify opportunities, then you have to get out of your comfort zone. Successful entrepreneurs have their opportunity antennae out so they can see opportunities before others see them and/or to see them because they look at the world from a different perspective. If they can see the future first, then they have a head start on others. If they can see opportunities where others see problems, then they can transform them into profits.

Entrepreneurs need to open their eyes and to see the world from differing perspectives. Entrepreneurs will see more opportunities if they broaden their travels, reading, contacts, and thoughts. People who travel and observe the world around them will be able to spot trends earlier than others. Perceptive entrepreneurs in the Midwest and East Coast frequently travel to the West Coast to see how people live and work. The West Coast may be a good barometer for what may be in vogue a year or more later in the Midwest and on the East Coast.

Someone once said, "You are what you read." If you want to spot emerging opportunities, and be a successful entrepreneur, then you will need to read magazines and electronic data sources that will open your eyes to the changes that are presently taking place as well as those that may be on the horizon. If you want to minimize the chance that you will be guilty of entrepreneurship by braille, then you must read outside your usual comfort zone. I recommend reading *Inc., The Futurist, Red Herring, Technology Review, Fast Company,* and *Entrepreneur,* in addition to the usual suspects of *BusinessWeek, Fortune, Forbes,* and the *Wall Street Journal.* I also suggest that you spend the afternoon at the largest bookstore or library in town scanning all the magazines that you never knew existed. Who knows— the best new venture opportunity may be lurking in a magazine that you have never read before.

Prospective entrepreneurs would do well to develop an information network composed of a wide variety of people who think and talk about new ideas, new products, new technology, and new businesses.[26] Attending entrepreneurship conferences, business expositions, and trade shows can be eye-opening experiences. Establishing a network of idea people and successful entrepreneurs can be very helpful. Chris Evans, a young entrepreneur, has started and sold a number of successful technology-related businesses. He noted, "My ideas are rarely original. In talking with others, they tell me something that triggers connections."[27] Remember, your business cannot be any better than the need or gap that it is created to serve. By broadening your perceptual field and perspective you will be in a much better position to spot the best opportunity.

Entrepreneurs can be more than problem solvers; they can be problem seekers. Elbert Hubbard observed, "Parties that want milk should not seat themselves on a stool in the middle of a field in hopes a cow will back up to them." The same applies to new ventures that are trying to attract customers. Prospective entrepreneurs who want to be problem seekers and problem solvers need to stop what they are doing, raise their opportunity antennae, look around, and listen for people who are not having their needs met.

Wilson Harrell, who started a brokerage business to sell products in military bases in Europe, suggested scanning the horizon for "irritants." He noted that entrepreneurs should find out what bugs people and then find a way to remove the irritant.[28] The greater the irritant, the more people will seek someone who can help them out. Lucrative opportunities exist when the irritant is strong, and where consumers have not been able to have it addressed by any other firm, and they are willing to spend considerable funds to be rid of the irritant.

Irritants may be particularly good opportunities for a new venture because people are willing to try almost anything or any business—even a new business—to have their needs met. Two sayings capture the irritant situation. The first is, "When confronted by a gale, take any port in a storm." The second is, "People dying of thirst have little brand loyalty." Ironically, consumers frequently thank businesses that deal with irritants. They are glad to pay them for their products or services and treat the businesses as if the businesses were doing them a favor!

REALITY CHECK

Some businesses and consumers just *satisfice*. They are not that discriminating. They are in their comfort zone. They are not actively looking for the best or even the better. Don't offer them what they are not willing to pay for. Look for consumers who are dissatisfied. Don't target consumers or businesses that seem to be satisfied with present vendors or are brand loyal for emotional reasons.

REALITY CHECK

People who are unsure of themselves or the alternatives usually minimize risk by going with the established brand or their present supplier. Look for consumers who have the guts or need to try something new.

REALITY CHECK

Look for leading-edge users who are actively looking for better or truly innovative products or services. They are always in an active search mode.

REALITY CHECK

Look for markets where demand exceeds supply. Some of those people will have to try new businesses.

Looking around can be a fairly simple process. For example, Richard Worth walked through grocery store aisles to see what may be missing. He noticed that in spite of all the cookies on the shelves, there were no sugar-free cookies. He developed a line of sugar-free cookies and called them Frookies! Looking at what is available may also indicate weaknesses in present firms. Successful entrepreneurs make it a practice to visit their competitors' stores and shop their businesses in order to discover what their competitors are doing wrong and what they are doing right.[29]

Michael Dell looked around and realized he could make a computer quicker, less expensive, and tailored to customers' needs. As he looked for opportunities, he was bold enough to look at the market leader's strength and try to find a way to exploit it as a weakness.[30]

David Neeleman looked around and realized that flying had become a modern nightmare. He noted that even the best airlines were rude, cramped, slow, and expensive. His process for creating a customer-centric airline started when his team made a list of the worst things about flying. The list of problems led to the creation of JetBlue.[31]

REALITY CHECK

Copying will not cut it. If you aren't markedly better, cheaper, or more convenient, then you may be swimming against the current.

REALITY CHECK

Expect retaliation when you try to steal another firm's thunder. When you awaken a sleeping giant, unlike David, you are going to need more than a slingshot to survive.

Prospective entrepreneurs can learn from the perceptiveness and boldness exhibited by Wilson Harrell, Richard Worth, Michael Dell, and David Neeleman. Numerous opportunities exist in mature markets where existing firms take the market for granted and no one wants to rock the boat. Established firms are often arrogant. They mistake repeat purchases for customer loyalty. When established firms grow complacent, they unknowingly put out the welcome mat to new ventures that are in sync with the market and are committed to delighting their customers.

When a pharmaceutical contract research organization (CRO) was looking for opportunities, it directed its search to improving products that had been around and had not been changed by their manufacturers for decades. The firm asked consumers what they did not like about the products they were using. It found that even though one over-the-counter product had been on the market for years, most customers did not like its taste. Evidently the manufacturer of the product was more concerned about its efficacy than its taste. This is similar to Listerine mouthwash. People thought mouthwash had to taste bad for it to be killing germs. Before long, Scope and other mouthwashes were introduced by firms that realized consumers wanted a strong product with a refreshing taste.

The CRO, without contacting the manufacturer, then developed a more pleasing flavor for the product that consumers preferred by a wide margin. The CRO then approached the manufacturer with the data reflecting discontent, the new flavor, and an offer for the proposal to buy the new formulation. The perceptiveness and innovativeness of the CRO can serve as a good lesson for prospective entrepreneurs.

Numerous other avenues are available for finding out if consumers are dissatisfied with what is available and are willing to try something new. Some entrepreneurs will dangle some bait in the water to see if someone bites. They place an ad in a trade magazine to see if people express an interest. Others will demonstrate a prototype in a trade show to see the level of interest. Scot Wingo, cofounder of Stingray Software, used chat rooms to find out what frustrated certain software users. He then tested the level of potential interest when he sent out a message, "If ... was available, would you buy it?" When his employer failed to express an interest in developing the product, he started his own venture.

Looking around for opportunities could also include three other dimensions. First, look for various facets of something. Every need, product, and/or service has multiple facets.

Explode the facet and look to see if there are spin-offs that may serve particular market segments. Second, check out previous market failures that might be approached differently or that may be more appropriate with a different target market. The product or service may have been good, but it may have been premature or executed poorly. Third, explore how a product or service may be used in a completely different way and/or by a completely different target market.

The Proximity Effect: Where You Are Can Lead to Interesting Opportunities

Although this book emphasizes the merit of having a kaleidoscopic perspective and doing a fairly broad search, numerous ventures have been started merely as a result of where their corresponding entrepreneurs were and what they were doing at that point in time. Proximity is particularly noteworthy when it comes to one's work. Some entrepreneurs identified new venture opportunities. Other entrepreneurs did not have their opportunity antennae up. The opportunities they ultimately pursued merely bumped into them.

Amar Bhidé's research indicated that many of the *Inc.* 500 companies were started by someone who was working in another business who saw a small niche opportunity. The niche opportunity was either one the company he or she was already working for was already taking advantage of, or one in which a supplier or customer was involved. The entrepreneurs left their employers and then created a venture. Ironically, Bhidé's research also indicated that the entrepreneurs were successful even though they jumped in with very little preparation and analysis. He attributed their success to (1) having firsthand knowledge of the profitability of that opportunity and (2) doing pretty much what someone else is already doing, but doing it better and faster.[32]

Although the development of Post-it note sheets may not be a truly entrepreneurial endeavor, it shows what can happen when there is a need that is not being met by existing products and someone makes the effort to do something about it. Post-it notes began its new product development journey when Art Fry, who sang in the choir, was frustrated with trying to keep notes in his hymnal for what hymns would be sung in a particular service. Art worked for 3M, so he asked the people in R&D if they could come up with a product that would stick but not stick forever.

Entrepreneurs can learn from Art Fry's perceptiveness and his effort to solve a problem faced by people around the world. Post-it notes were a real windfall for 3M when they were introduced in 1981. Their sales exceeded the revenue for Disney's Magic Kingdom in Orlando. They also served as the basis for numerous related products. Within three years, 3M had added 22 other follow-on products to the Post-it line.[33] Fry demonstrated how proximity can open doors to opportunities, how having the attitude that there has to be a better way, and how networking with people who can develop a solution can lead to outstanding success.

Most companies are not as open-minded as 3M about exploring new product and service ideas. Bob Zider, as president of the Beta Group, a firm that develops and commercializes technology, noted that most companies are reluctant to explore different product and service concepts and their "not invented here, or we're not in that business" mentality may, in fact, contribute to entrepreneurial endeavors by people who do not get the support experienced by Art Fry. He noted, "Companies typically invest in and protect their existing market positions; they tend to fund only those ideas that are central to their strategies. The result is a reservoir of talent and new ideas, which creates the pool for new ventures."[34]

The proximity effect has contributed to the creation of numerous ventures. Clarence Birdseye came up with his concept for frozen packaged foods when he was on a government-sponsored expedition early in the twentieth century. He noticed how Eskimo fishermen could delay cooking their catches for days by having the fish freeze in the open air after they were caught.[35]

Linda Kellogg is a good example of the proximity effect. As head of human resources for Venture Law Group in Menlo Park, she organized a number of the firms' office moves and openings. She recognized that start-ups and other rapidly growing firms could benefit from her expertise. She then founded Start-up Resources, which manages everything from finding and furnishing office space to setting up benefits and payroll systems. Kellogg observed, "[Even the sharpest entrepreneurs] don't know how to go about actually starting a business. They spend too much time checking out used-furniture prices and not enough time on recruiting and product development. Or they might hire two or three employees before even thinking about setting up a workers' compensation system," something Kellogg says can be done in an hour.[36]

The proximity effect may serve as a springboard for other entrepreneurial opportunities in at least four other ways. First, if your employer has a list of ideas that it decided not to pursue, then you may consider starting a venture that will take these ideas to market. These product ideas (1) may be in a relatively raw form that your employer has decided not to flush out, (2) may have been flushed out but do not fit your employer's product/service mix, (3) may not have a sufficient market to meet its minimal volume requirements, or (4) could also be in the form of a request for something specific from one of your employer's customers that your employer has decided to pass on.

REALITY CHECK

If you are considering starting a business that will capitalize on an idea, product, service, or process that you learned about while you were working for a firm, contact an attorney who specializes in intellectual property law to make sure you cannot be accused of stealing that firm's intellectual property.

Second, if your employer is looking for ways to reduce overhead, employment, and money tied up in assets, then you may consider proposing that your employer outsource that activity to a venture to be formed by you. Third, if your employer is complacent or you are tired of suggesting ways to improve its competitiveness, then you might consider starting your own venture. If your employer and its competitors are mediocre, then you may be able to rule the marketplace.

REALITY CHECK

If you are hesitant to take this option, then consider your fate if you stay with your current employer. You will not have your job for very long because someone else will notice the gap and create a venture to steal your employer's thunder. If this happens, then you'll be out of work and kick yourself for not taking the entrepreneurial plunge. Remember anxiety II ... the risk associated with not starting a business?

Fourth, one's contact with suppliers and people involved in the channels of distribution may also provide clues to what is missing and what can be done better.[37]

"If This Company Won't Do It, Then I Will ... ."

Few firms offer the market exactly the product it wants; even fewer firms delight their customers. At any given time, most consumers are in search of a business that will better meet their needs. Repeat purchases should never be confused with customer satisfaction and loyalty. Most ventures in today's *Fortune* 500 were started by people who were employed by a large firm in the past. They quit and formed their own ventures because they had new product or service ideas that were not embraced by their employers. Some of their ideas may not have fit their employer's product/service portfolio. In other cases, however, their ideas were directly related to their employer's product/service mix. It is ironic how in just a few years one or more frustrated employees may become a formidable competitor. This was the case when Jobs and Wozniak left Hewlett-Packard to form Apple Computer.

REALITY CHECK

If you leave one firm to start or work in another, make sure that you abide by your nondisclosure statement or noncompete agreement if you signed one. You also need to make sure you cannot be accused of theft or be subject to litigation by your employer. Make sure you do not take any trade secrets, customer lists, employee manuals, or any other written or electronic material that may be considered your employer's property.

Don't Wait for Downsizing: Initiate a Preemptive Strike

The growing trend for businesses of all sizes to downsize their operations by outsourcing all but their core competencies has caused a number of people to start ventures. Chunka Mui, co-author of *Unleashing the Killer App: Digital Strategies for Market Dominance*, believes the next wave of entrepreneurial start-ups will provide services to companies that are getting smaller.[38] Outsourcing opens the door for employees to become entrepreneurs. New ventures can be created to provide the goods and service that used to be done in-house. A number of perceptive people did not wait for the time when they would be put on the street because their firm chose to outsource their jobs. They initiated a "preemptive" strike by approaching their firm with a proposal to spin off their division, department, or service. Instead of being employees, they would create a venture that would be a supplier of those products or services for their "former" employer.

The concept of being a supplier to your former employer has numerous attributes. The first attribute is that you already have a customer. This will help your cash flow. It may also help you get funding for your business. Banks and investors are more willing to provide funding if the firm has a commitment from a customer for a certain amount of business. Your former employer may even be in a position to provide seed money, make a partial payment for goods or services in advance, or provide favorable payment terms. Your suppliers, in turn, may provide you with better terms than they would for a start-up that doesn't have any accounts yet.

REALITY CHECK

Becoming a supplier to your former employer may have a major drawback. Your former employer may be reluctant to work with you if you are also going to be calling on its competitors. Your former employer may want an exclusive service agreement with you. An exclusive service agreement will be great in the first year if it will provide a substantial amount of business. An exclusive agreement, however, forces you to put all your revenue eggs in one basket. This gives your former employer a lot of power over you and it keeps you from actively courting other accounts that may be more lucrative down the road.

REALITY CHECK

If your company is downsizing its operations, then it may be because the industry is saturated or declining. You may be better off taking your skills to an emerging market where your new venture may have a better chance for success.

REALITY CHECK

Some of the best opportunities lie at the edge of existing markets or in emerging fields. As noted earlier, if you only look for opportunities where you live and/or work, then you will limit your search to what you already know. A broader search may take you to areas that are less familiar, but these areas may represent virgin territory where there is little competition because no one has the knowledge, capabilities, and resources.

LOOK AHEAD

Howard Schultz noted, "The best ideas are those that create a new mindset or sense a need before others do."[39] The ability to see an opportunity ahead of its time and to capitalize on it was captured in Wayne Gretzky's approach to the sport of hockey. When he was asked why he was successful in the National Hockey League, he noted that most players skate to where the puck is; he skated to where he thought it *would be*. Some people define luck as what happens "when preparation meets opportunity." Entrepreneurs know it is up to them to not rely on luck. They know their success will be directly related to the extent they are prepared to capitalize on an opportunity. They know that if you spot the opportunity early enough, then you may have time to develop the skills and acquire the resources to be the first to capitalize on it. Remember, the first five letters of *entrepreneur* mean "to enter."

Those who see the future first will be in a better position to capitalize on what it will bring. Envisioning the future gives entrepreneurs valuable time to gather information, to develop a game plan, and to conduct trials to see what people really want. This lead time gives their firms an edge over firms that are more reactive.

Envisioning the future incorporates the concepts of anticipatory management. Anticipatory management tries to identify what the future may hold. It also reduces the likelihood of being blindsided by new realities. Most people either live in the present or cling to the past. Most people are also prone to cling to mental models that may keep them from seeing emerging realities. A number of well-known people misread the future when they made the following comments:[40]

Heavier than air flying machines are impossible.

—Lord Kelvin,
British mathematician, physicist, and
president of the British Royal Society, 1895

Who the hell wants to hear actors talk?

—Harry M. Warner,
Warner Brothers Pictures, 1927

We don't like their sound. Groups with guitars are on the way out.

—Decca Recording Company executive,
turning down the Beatles in 1962

I think there is a world market for about five computers.
—Thomas Watson, Chairman of IBM, 1943

There is no reason for any individual to have a computer in their home.
—Ken Olson, President of Digital Equipment Corp., 1977

Envisioning the future does not take clairvoyance. It involves a commitment to mentally breaking away from the present and a willingness to look to the future with an open mind. It also involves looking for trends and running "What if?" scenarios. Ironically, a lot of what the future holds is already set in motion. Envisioning the future in many cases is nothing more than recognizing the inevitable. It is not a matter of whether certain things will happen; it is just a question of when they will happen. Maya Angelou noted, "The horizon leans forward, offering you space to place new steps of change."

Prospective entrepreneurs who regularly ask, "What is next and what will come after that?" may be in a position to capitalize on emerging opportunities. Entrepreneurs who envision the future will be in a position to be market makers or first movers. Entrepreneurs should try to anticipate what today's customers will want in two to three years as well as what customers entering the market two to three years from now will want.

Anticipatory management enables firms to evolve and keeps entrepreneurs from taking the market for granted. Michael Dell demonstrated his entrepreneurial talent when he created a business to sell low-priced customized computers directly to the consumer. He also demonstrated anticipatory management when he started selling his products over the Internet.

Anticipatory management recognizes that success comes from having the right answers at the right time. Entrepreneurs incorporate anticipatory management when they are able to offer products and services that can solve customer problems. Yet, anticipatory management has more than one level. The first level involves coming up with the answers to today's questions. The second and higher level involves identifying the questions that will be asked in the near future so you have time to answer them. The third and ultimate level is having the answers to tomorrow's questions before anyone else, including tomorrow's consumers, even know the question!

Steve Schussler benefited from sensing a gap in the market, having the opportunity to develop something truly unique, and being in the right place at the right time with the right product when a special window of opportunity opened. He recognized that a number of people wanted more than just a meal when they went to a restaurant—they wanted an experience. He asked himself, "What would Walt Disney do if he started a restaurant today?" He developed the Rainforest Café that combined animatronics, plants, and an outstanding menu. When the Disney staff was trying to figure out what restaurant should be located at Disney's new African Safari Theme Park, they found the Rainforest Café had exactly what they were looking for.

Schussler saved Disney considerable time and effort because it did not have to design that restaurant from scratch. He demonstrated anticipatory management by having what Disney wanted before Disney even knew it wanted it!

LISTEN AND ASK

If new ventures succeed to the extent they are customer problem finders and customer problem-solvers, then it is clear that entrepreneurs should make a point of listening to the market—and their customers when their ventures are started—on a regular basis. Michael Dell noted, "Companies that are successful today—and perhaps, more importantly, companies that will be successful tomorrow—are those that can get closest to their customers' needs."[41] Yet listening to the market may not be enough. Entrepreneurs should go out and ask people what they want, what would improve their work or personal lives, and what they would be delighted to buy if it was available.

REALITY CHECK

Listening to the market is productive most of the time. There may be times, however, when interviews, focus groups, and so on have limitations. When you ask people what they would like, they tend to think about what is currently available and suggest incremental improvements. They also tend to be preoccupied with the present rather than what they may need in the future. This situation tends to result in tweaking rather than innovation. Finally, talk is cheap. There may be a big difference between what people say and what they will do.

MOST LARGE AND ESTABLISHED COMPANIES ARE NOT ENTREPRENEURIAL

Entrepreneurs should have their opportunity antennae tuned in for new markets and market niches. New markets have limited information and their future is hard to predict. Market niches are good targets for new ventures because they may be too small to appeal to larger firms or they may require the ability to tailor one's offering beyond what most established firms are willing or able to do.

Amar Bhidé noted, "Established corporations and professional venture capital funds expend considerable resources on evaluating and monitoring their investments. They tend to avoid investments in niche opportunities whose profit potential isn't large enough to cover their fixed evaluation and monitoring costs. Therefore the bootstrapped entrepreneur in a niche market faces direct competition mainly from other undercapitalized businesses."[42]

Established firms are usually reluctant to enter markets until the window is clearly open and offers large returns. Established firms also prefer to operate within established markets rather than explore new and untested markets. Their avoidance of uncertainty causes them to wait until the image is large and clearly defined on the radar screen before they do anything about it. Bhidé observed that a popular business heuristic exists for established businesses that suggests that selling to existing customers is more profitable than cultivating new customers, and maintaining customer loyalty is less costly than adding new customers.[43] Successful entrepreneurs have found lucrative opportunities are often at the edge of the radar screen.

REALITY CHECK

When you are operating at the fringe of the radar screen or in a niche market, you really don't know how much demand there will be. Sometimes the only way to find out is to introduce the product or service and see what happens. This is what the entrepreneurial risk-return ratio is all about.

CONCLUSION: THE DOOR IS WIDE OPEN
FOR ENTREPRENEURIAL VENTURES

There are "pockets of opportunity" in good times as well as bad times. One of the keys to entrepreneurial success is the ability to find the right opportunity. Lucrative opportunities exist throughout the marketplace:

- There are opportunities in high, low, and no-technology fields.
- There are opportunities for new ventures to make their mark by introducing break-through products, services, or processes.
- There are opportunities for new ventures to gain a competitive advantage by being a bit better than existing firms and through flawless execution.
- There are opportunities to be first movers.
- There are also opportunities in maturing markets.
- There are opportunities for new ventures that provide a personal touch in a techno-logical world.
- There are also opportunities to use technology to solve problems caused by technology.
- There are large markets with room for newcomers.
- There are also niche markets where new ventures can thrive.

Identifying the opportunities does not take rocket science or ESP. In some cases, it involves seeing what others have not seen. In other cases, it is merely seizing what appears to be an obvious opportunity. Marshall Loeb, editor of *Fortune* and *Money,* noted, "Profitable ideas can be monumental or mundane." Most of the opportunities do not require considerable capital or a proprietary position. In many cases, new ventures can gain an edge by just being a little bit better on the things that matter.

Entrepreneurs can benefit from the story about two barefooted campers who see a bear coming toward them. When one camper sits down for a moment to put on his jogging shoes, the other exclaims, "You can't outrun a bear!" The first camper responds, "I don't need to outrun the bear, I just need to outrun you!"

Prospective entrepreneurs can learn something from surfers. They need to see waves early, paddle out to catch them, catch them before they get crowded, and have the skill to make the most out of them. They don't need to be the first rider of the wave to have a long ride. If they get in early when demand exceeds supply or when the firms already there are not in sync with the market's interests, then they may "be able to outrun the other campers."

Jann Wenner, founder of *Rolling Stone,* recalls that when he launched the magazine in 1967, "It was the beginning of a new era of rock and roll. The nature of what musicians and bands were doing was changing. They began to really take themselves seriously, and we wanted to write about these serious, meaningful things. There was a big cultural shift taking place. We were at the beginning of it. We caught it, we withstood it, and we rode it. *Rolling Stone* was not the first or the only rock and roll magazine of the time."[44]

Only that day dawns for those who are awake.

—Henry David Thoreau

ENDNOTES

1. Jeffrey A. Timmons, "Growing Up Big: Entrepreneurship and Creating High-Potential Ventures," *Texas A&M Business Forum,* Fall 1985, p. 11.

2. Thea Singer, "What Business Should You Start?," *Inc.,* March 2002, p. 71.

3. William A. Sahlman, "How to Write a Really Great Business Plan," *Harvard Business Review,* July–August 1997, in Annual Editions Entrepreneurship 99/00, p. 129. Reprinted by permission of *Harvard Business Review.*

4. Lillian Vernon, *An Eye for Winners: How I Built One of America's Greatest Direct Mail Businesses* (New York: HarperCollins, 1996), p. 6.

5. Thea Singer, "What Business Should You Start?," *Inc.,* March, 2002, p. 75.

6. Ibid.

7. Ibid.

8. Ibid., p. 72.

9. Ibid.

10. Kaufman Foundation Website, *www.entreworld.org.*

11. Timmons, "Growing Up Big: Entrepreneurship and Creating High-Potential Ventures," p. 11.

12. Howard H. Stevenson and David E. Gumpert, "The Heart of Entrepreneurship," *Harvard Business Review,* March–April 1985, p. 88. Reprinted by permission of *Harvard Business Review.*

13. Craig E. Aronogg and John Ward, *Contemporary Entrepreneurs: Profiles of Entrepreneurs and Businesses They Started, Representing 74 Companies in 30 Industries* (Detroit: Omnigraphics, 1992), p. 127.

14. Ilan Mochari, "Mind Games," *Inc.,* July 1999, p. 36.

15. Tom Loury, "The Zagat Guide to Just About Everything," *BusinessWeek,* December 9, 2002, p. 44.

16. Robert D. Hisrich and Michael P. Peters, *Entrepreneurship* (New York: McGraw-Hill, 1998) p. 182.

17. Ibid.

18. Richard M. White, *The Entrepreneur's Manual* (Radford, NJ: Clifton Book Company, 1977).

19. Ibid., p. 57.

20. Edward M. Tauber, "Discovering New Product Opportunities With Problem Inventory Analysis," *Journal of Marketing,* January 1975, p. 69.

21. Amar Bhidé, "How Entrepreneurs Craft Strategies That Work," *Harvard Business Review,* March–April 1994 in Annual Editions Entrepreneurship 99/00, pp. 62–73. Reprinted by permission of *Harvard Business Review.*

22. Kenneth W. Olm and George G. Eddy, *Entrepreneurship and Venture Management* (Englewood Cliffs, NJ: Prentice Hall, 1985), p. 61.

23. Leigh Buchanan, "Killer Apps," *Inc.,* May, 1998, p. 94.

24. Joseph Boyett and Jimmie Boyett, *The Guru Guide to Entrepreneurship* (New York: John Wiley & Sons, 2001), p. 37.

25. Thea Singer, "What Business Should You Start?," *Inc.,* March 2002, p. 75.

26. Olm and Eddy, *Entrepreneurship and Venture Management,* p. 62.

27. Kristen Tyler, "An Entrepreneur's Dream: One Company and Two Liquid Events," *Business Leader,* January 1999, p. 27.

28. Boyett and Boyett, *The Guru Guide to Entrepreneurship,* p. 45.

29. Ibid., p. 78.

30. Michael Dell and Catherine Fredman, *Direct from Dell: Strategies That Revolutionized an Industry* (New York: HarperBusiness, 1999), p. 82.

31. Jan Mount, "For Creating an Airline Fit for Humans," *Inc.,* April 2004, p. 144.

32. Bhidé, "How Entrepreneurs Craft Strategies That Work," pp. 62–73.

33. Amar Bhidé, *The Origin and Evolution of New Businesses* (Oxford: Oxford University Press, 2000), p. 129.

34. Bob Zider, "How Venture Capital Works," *Harvard Business Review,* November–December 1998, in Annual Editions Entrepreneurship 99/00, p. 138. Reprinted by permission of *Harvard Business Review.*

35. Mike Hofman, "Birdseye's View," *Inc.,* November 2001, p. 184.

36. Karen Dillon, "The Plug and Play Office," *Inc.,* July 1999, *www.inc.com.*

37. Olm and Eddy, *Entrepreneurship and Venture Management*, p. 59.

38. Leigh Buchanon, "Killer Apps" *Inc.,* May 1998, p. 94.

39. Howard Schultz and Dori Jones, *Pour Your Heart Into It: How Starbucks Built a Company One Cup at a Time* (New York: Hyperion, 1997), p. 77.

40. Christopher Cerf and Victor Navasky, *The Experts Speak* (New York: Pantheon, 1984), pp. 172, 182, 208, 209, and 236.

41. Michael Dell and Catherine Fredman, *Direct from Dell: Strategies That Revolutionized the Industry* (New York: HarperBusiness, 1999), p. 200.

42. Bhidé, *The Origin and Evolution of New Businesses,* pp. 42 & 43.

43. Ibid., p. 135.

44. Ibid., p. 46.

4

VENTURES THAT CAPITALIZED ON MARKET GAPS

The gap between reality and possibility is the entrepreneur's playing field.
—Scott DeGarno, Editor of *Success* magazine[1]

Entrepreneurial opportunities are everywhere. This chapter profiles entrepreneurs who saw opportunities and made their mark on the world around us. Some entrepreneurs changed the way we work; others changed the way we live. Numerous examples of entrepreneurs are provided for three important reasons. First, they demonstrate that people from all walks of life have started ventures. Second, they demonstrate that new venture opportunities are abundant in no-tech and low-tech areas as well as high-tech areas. Third, they demonstrate that sometimes, successful ventures were started because their founders merely "bumped" into the opportunities rather than through an extensive and lengthy search.

It would be nice to believe that all the entrepreneurs followed a step-by-step process for identifying various opportunities. A number of the examples, however, demonstrate that the systematic process may be the exception rather than the rule. It turns out that many people who became entrepreneurs happened to be in the right place at the right time. They were in situations where they realized that a gap existed in the marketplace or that there must be a better way to do what people were doing.

REALITY CHECK

You have a choice—you can wait to bump into an opportunity or you can be proactive and systematically search for a lucrative and lasting opportunity.

Ironically, most of the entrepreneurs were not the first to see the gap or opportunity. Other people may have seen the gaps or opportunities before them. The difference between the people who were the first to see the gaps and the entrepreneurs who created ventures to serve them is that the entrepreneurs knew what to do when they recognized the opportunities. They showed that entrepreneurial success is not the result of being lucky: It occurs "when preparation meets opportunity." As in fishing, occasionally an unprepared person will get lucky when an errant fish swims by and gets its lip caught on the hook. Entrepreneurs beat the odds by preparing in such a way that luck has little to do with catching fish! They deliberately search for a school of hungry fish and catch them by offering them a tantalizing bait. The examples provided in this chapter demonstrate that entrepreneurship is not *rocket science*. They also show that amazing things can happen when preparation meets opportunity!

REALITY CHECK

The examples are not intended to be company endorsements, nor are they provided as examples of entrepreneurial best practices. Some of the businesses have gone on to greatness; others have faded into the shadows. Some have been acquired by firms that wanted to buy a future; others did not stay in sync and left the door open for entrepreneurial competitors.

ENTREPRENEURIAL PERCEPTIVENESS CREATED SOME OF TODAY'S HOUSEHOLD NAMES

Some of today's popular businesses began when an entrepreneur looked around, listened to the market, found customers in search of a business, and had the mental dexterity to turn the problem into a business opportunity. In many cases, the entrepreneurs created ventures that addressed issues that have affected millions of people.

Problem = Complicated tax form → Opportunity = H & R Block

Almost every adult in the United States knows about H&R Block. Henry and David Bloch (they chose to use "Block" for their business's name) listened to the market and heard people who were frustrated with having to prepare their own taxes. A large number of Americans did not know how to prepare their returns, wanted a second opinion so they could sleep at night, or wanted to find some way to reduce their tax obligation. The Blochs found that people would be willing to pay a small fee if reliable tax preparation could be provided at convenient times and locations. H&R Block handles more than 11 million tax returns filed each year in the United States.

Gap = Lack of first-class, conveniently located day-care → Opportunity = KinderCare

Perry Mendel, like the Bloch brothers, recognized that changes and challenges can produce great opportunities. He kept hearing parents of young children expressing frustration over the lack of first-class day-care facilities. He researched the census data for the growing trend in preschool-aged children who needed day care. He also studied the existing state of day care in the South. He found that most day-care businesses were run out of people's homes. Existing facilities were not conducive to handling large numbers of children. He also found that most locations were not conveniently located for the parents.

Mendel's research found there were large numbers of parents who were still in search of a day-care business that met their needs. He believed that a professionally managed day-care business could be set up to offer first-class facilities that were located on the way to and from work. He also believed that by providing the latest toys and offering nutritious meals for a price no higher than traditional mom-and-pop backyard day-care businesses, he could capture a large share of the market. Mendel's perceptiveness paid off. His KinderCare became one of the largest day-care businesses in the world.

Gap = Lack of quick, convenient restaurants → Opportunity = McDonald's

Gap = Lack of variety in desserts in fast-food places → Opportunity = Baskin & Robbins

The list of businesses that were created to capitalize on gaps in the market is almost endless. The list includes Ray Kroc, who upon visiting the drive-in restaurant run by the McDonald brothers in California, recognized that people all over the country were more mobile and that they wanted a way to get a "convenient" meal. Kroc franchised the idea and the rest is history! The list also includes Burton Baskin and Irv Robbins, who recognized that the American public might want more than three flavors of ice cream.

The following businesses might not be as well known as H & R Block or KinderCare, but they share a common beginning—they were created when their founders saw a gap and created a business to fill it:

- *Aqua-Vox, Inc.* Michael Benjamin found that one of the most frustrating aspects of scuba diving was the inability to communicate with other divers while underwater. He developed a device that sells for $100 that permits underwater communication.

- *My Own Meals, Inc.* Mary Ann Jackson was able to turn a night-time routine into a lucrative business. She recognized that one of the most cumbersome aspects of being a parent involves preparing a child's lunch for school. Her company was the first to market packaged meals for kids aged 2 to 10 on a large scale. The entrees, which originally retailed for less than $3.00, are pressure-cooked and vacuum-sealed in plastic pouches.

- *Tweedies Optical, Inc.* Tweedy Prager encountered a problem finding appropriate eye glasses for her three-year-old twins. She found most kids' eyeglasses were merely "downsized" versions of adult frames. She started her business to market a line of "spiffy specks" eyeglass frames that are attractive and fun to wear. Her line of frames for kids from 4 to 8 years old was so successful that she developed a line of frames for kids between 9 and 13.

- *Abt Enterprises.* Nancy Abt came to the conclusion that there must be a better way to help people cool off in the heat of summer. She developed and received a patent for her product, *The Cool Advantage*. Her product holds blocks of foam that are soaked in salt water. When the blocks, which are in polyurethane insulating bags, are frozen, they are colder than regular ice. Her product comes with a cloth cover seamed with Velcro strips, which allows people to wear it while playing tennis and other sports. Nancy then explored how her unique product could help solve problems for other people. She found that people might be able to use it in certain jobs. She also found that it might be beneficial for people with certain health problems like multiple sclerosis.

PICK AN AREA AND IDENTIFY POTENTIAL OPPORTUNITIES

Anthony A. Martino, Kurt Ziebart, Arthur Peterson, and Francis Keery demonstrate the value of trying to identify new venture opportunities systematically. Anthony A. Martino and Kurt Ziebart chose to start their businesses in the auto industry because they believed it offered numerous opportunities. Years later, Arthur Peterson and Francis Keery chose the health care industry because it was evolving rapidly and billions of dollars were being spent on health care each year. They knew market gaps would generate incredible opportunities.

These entrepreneurs incorporated Step Two and Step Three of the new-venture creation process (see the Introduction) in their effort to identify opportunities. They listened to the market and identified gaps that could serve as the basis for creating new ventures. The four entrepreneurs looked at various dimensions of an industry in search of gaps where people's needs weren't being met at all or well enough. By exploding an industry into various dimensions, they believed they would find opportunities to pursue. Although they might have limited their search to a particular industry, their minds were open to the types of products or services to offer, as well as where they should locate new ventures. Exhibit 4.1 illustrates how car problems can become business opportunities.

Anthony A. Martino demonstrated the ability to study an industry, to find multiple gaps, and to transform problems into new venture opportunities. Years ago, he recognized that the United States is a society of car owners. He realized he didn't have the capital to manufacture automobiles, so he investigated various facets of the U.S. auto industry in search of gaps or problems that could be transformed into business opportunities. He found that auto transmissions had a tendency to break down after the warranty expired. He also found that local service stations specialized in selling gasoline and that new car dealerships specialized in selling new cars. It turned out that neither type of business did a particularly good job repairing or replacing transmissions! Martino then founded AAMCO (which incorporates his initials of AAM).

In 1972, Martino realized there must be other business opportunities that were disguised as market problems. Again, he listened to the market. He found that cars had a propensity to get into accidents. Sooner or later, most people get into an accident that requires bodywork and repainting. He found that few businesses specialized in this side of auto work. As with transmissions, he found customers were in search of a business. When he had to select a name for his business, he merely reversed his initials and founded MAACO. Millions of automobiles have been painted by MAACO.

Martino's efforts to create new ventures to serve customers in search of a business were without limits. He listened to the market and found people were not having their needs met by existing businesses when it came to having their cars tuned and oil changed. In 1981, he started SPARKS Tune-Up Centers. His new ventures offered a "one-price" tune-up and oil change with a warranty. He also tried to end the mystery surrounding auto service centers by allowing customers to view the work while it was being done.

Kurt Ziebart was another person to see the almost unlimited opportunities created by the millions of automobiles on the roads today. In the 1960s, Ziebart recognized the desire by car owners to keep their cars longer as a way of beating inflation. He found, however, that cars in many parts of the country would rust out before the engines wore out. He compared existing businesses with consumer needs. He found customers in various parts of the country were in search of a business that would let them postpone buying their next car by a few more years. People in cold climates wanted their cars treated to keep the road salt from damaging them. He also found customers in search of rustproofing who lived near the ocean because the salt spray also accelerated rust. He created Ziebart Rustproofing Centers. His business would extend the life of a car by a few more years for a few hundred dollars. Ziebart's outstanding cost–benefit ratio, convenient locations, and one-day service proved to be a formula for success.

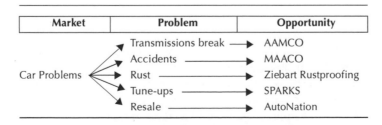

EXHIBIT 4.1   CAR PROBLEMS BECOME BUSINESS OPPORTUNITIES

Wayne Huizenga noticed that the used car business was highly fragmented and lacked professional systems. He took what he learned about tying together garbage haulers into Waste Management and created AutoNation. AutoNation sells various brands of new and used cars.

Arthur Peterson and Francis Keery believed the health care industry offered numerous opportunities. They started their entrepreneurial journey by listening to the market and then looking for gaps that represented new venture opportunities. While Peterson and Keery knew the health care industry offered various opportunities, they narrowed their search to hospitals. They went from one area of the hospital to the next, looking for areas where people's needs were not being met well enough or at all. They knew that the words, "I wish someone could develop a product that ..." might identify a product or service gap that could be transformed into a new business.

Their search revealed various gaps. One gap, however, caught their attention. They recognized a problem encountered by medical personnel in every hospital. Their research revealed that it usually takes doctors 10 minutes to wash their hands and arms before surgery. Not only was the process time consuming, it was painful and did not provide the level of cleanliness desired by the surgeons.

Industry: Health Care → Area: Hospitals → Field: → Surgery →

Problem = Pre-surgery scrubbing → Opportunity = Pacific Bio Systems

Peterson and Keery founded Pacific Bio Systems Inc. to develop an automatic hand-washing machine called the *stat scrub*. With this revolutionary product, doctors place their hands and arms into "sleeves" that clean them in less than two minutes. The machine is not only pain free, it does a much better job of eliminating bacteria.

Peterson and Keery illustrate the merit in starting a business that serves "customers in search of a business." They didn't start with a business in search of customers. They also demonstrate that if you develop and offer a product that is quicker, better, and in a more convenient manner than what is on the market, then you can garner considerable market share. Once their product demonstrated its ability to fill a gap in the health care industry, they investigated whether firms that manufacture chemicals, pharmaceuticals, and computers were also in search of a business that has a product that can provide quick cleaning.

"PROXIMITY" PLAYS A KEY ROLE IN IDENTIFYING MARKET GAPS

The proximity effect reflects the tendency for ventures to be founded by people who happened to be in a situation where they recognized an opportunity. Their proximity to the situation via their work or personal lives enabled them to see gaps that could be transformed into business opportunities. Research indicates that in some fields 90 percent or more of the founders start their companies in the same marketplace and industry in which they have been working.[2] The high incidence of people starting businesses related to their work is not surprising because people are more likely to see a gap where they spend a considerable amount of their time.

REALITY CHECK

Chapter 3 noted the propensity to start ventures where you live and/or work and/or in a field you already know. Some of the best opportunities lie at the edge of existing markets or in emerging fields. You should deliberately broaden your search for opportunities by exploring areas outside your comfort zone. The broader the search, the greater the number of gaps that will be identified. The greater the number of gaps, the greater the probability the best opportunity will be found.

Health Care Gap: Contain This!

In 1994, Dan Tribastone was working as a registered nurse in an orthopedic operating room. He recognized a serious shortcoming in the operating room. During orthopedic surgery, the body part undergoing reconstruction is constantly flushed with water. The spent fluid is collected in small containers. An operation could produce 75 to 100 liters of fluid, which required 25 to 35 canisters. Nurses were constantly having to disconnect and reconnect containers. Nurses typically had to make 150 to 200 connections to the waste fluid connectors during every single procedure.

He thought the problem could be fixed by buying larger containers, but after scouring RN trade magazines he realized such a container did not exist. So he requested samples from container manufacturers he located in the Thomas Register of American Manufacturers (*www.thomasregister.com*). Tribastone noted, "I got dozens of samples, most of which collapsed from the vacuum pressure. But finally I was able to find a steel container that held up. I added two connections ports and started to use them at work. The containers were a big hit in the operating room. They cut the number of connections to a fifth of what it had been."[3]

In 1995 he decided to place a small ad in *Operating Room Nursing Journal*. When he got $1,000 in orders, he was convinced he had a winner. He worked in his basement workshop building the product after working in the operating room in the daytime. When he explained to a doctor why he was so tired, the doctor thought he had a wonderful idea. That week the doctor set him up with an investor, and by 1997 Tribastone started selling the product—a disposable 3.5 gallon Omni Jug canister priced at $25 from his new company, Waterstone Medical in Falls Church, Virginia. By 2001, his firm had sales of $5 million.

One of Tribastone's biggest advantages was that he truly understood how customers would use the product. He noted that sales were a lot easier to generate when customers realized he came from the operating room trenches. At a trade show, nurses immediately recognized he wasn't a smooth-talking sales rep, but was really one of them.[4]

Health Care: Are We Covered?

In 1996, Tod Loofbourrow realized that he and his wife had no idea about what their health insurance covered for their daughter's delivery and tests, as well as his wife's extended stay in the hospital. He realized he and his wife weren't the only people who didn't have a good understanding of how health and dental plans worked, or of the benefits and human resource policies employers offered.

Loofbourrow had a background in knowledge-based systems. He explored the idea of using the Internet to give people the ability to obtain dynamic, personalized, real-time information from their companies' HR departments, health care companies, and benefits systems. He then committed 12 years of savings to start Authoria and fund its first year of operations. His firm took off because of its ability to provide accurate and timely information at a time when people have considerable anxiety. By 2001, with a few rounds of venture capital financing, Authoria had 225 employees with nearly 8 million people using its line of products.[5]

Health Care: Language Translation in the Emergency Room

Dr. Charles Lee, M.D., a Korean-American physician, recognized a gap in the market while working at a hospital. When he was called by another department to translate for an "Asian" patient, he found he could not help because the patient was Vietnamese. He and the other medical staff, along with the patient, were helpless. Dr. Lee, who also had a background in software, founded Polyglot Systems in 2001 to help health care providers communicate with non-English speakers, and vice versa. The firm's first product, ProLingua 24/7, is a multilanguage translation system for emergency rooms.[6]

Health: Be Careful about the Air You Breathe

Rider McDowell and Victoria Knight-McDowell recognized people are increasingly concerned about the air they breathe—especially when they are in crowded and confined spaces. They created Knight-McDowell Labs to produce and market a tablet that provides instant protection for anyone venturing into such germ-infested environments as schools, hospitals, and airplane cabins. Their product, called *Airborne* (it functions like a surgical mask strapped across one's face), is an effervescent tablet that dissolves in water. Airborne, which sells for $5 to $8, is the result of experimenting with different combinations of vitamins and Chinese herbs bought at San Francisco Bay area natural food stores. It qualifies as a dietary supplement and sells at airport gift shops, Web, and its 800 number.[7]

Technology Gap: Expand Bandwidth!

New ventures are frequently started by employees who see the world differently than one's employer or others in the industry. Desh Deshpande, while working at Cascade Communications, the company he founded, saw that companies, including Cascade, were working too hard to make the best use of the bandwidth they had. He observed that their focus was on quality of service only. It was as if the firms were rationing oil rather than drilling new wells or seeking alternative fuels. He then cofounded Sycamore Networks to create an abundance of bandwidth that could sustain the networked economy. Sycamore Networks then set out to increase bandwidth via innovation in optical networking. The firm's strategy included delivering it where and when needed with software intelligence. Deshpande's strategy won the backing of venture capitalists, a world-class team, and it first customers.[8]

Technology: When Does the Movie Start?

One day Andrew Jarecki, a young venture capitalist, failed to buy movie tickets ahead of time and kept on getting busy signals from the movie theater. He realized there must be a way to make money from his frustration. He had always been interested in marketing and movies. In 1989 Jarecki and a friend Adam Slutsky saw an article about a Los Angeles team developing an interactive automated movie guide. Jarecki flew them to New York. The four of them then founded MovieFone. The firm's 777-FILM line offered free, instant access to movie listings and previews and is now operational in 30 cities. By 1997, the firm's annual revenue exceeded $15 million—mostly from advertising revenues.[9] America Online acquired MovieFone in 1999 for $388 million. At the time, MovieFone served 100 million moviegoers. Its listings included 17,000 screens in 42 cities.

Technology: Paging Mr./Ms. ...

Dave Miller was sick of hearing customers complain about the level of service in his restaurant. Determined to remedy this situation, Miller wanted to create a device that would let servers know that their orders were ready. He turned to an engineer friend, and the vibrating pager was born. In 1988, Miller and his two partners went to the national restaurant trade show in Chicago and sold $70,000 worth of pagers to other restaurateurs. Their paging firm, J Tech, has more than 40,000 accounts and revenue over $20 million.[10]

Information: Linking the New World to the Old World

Bill Weimer recognized that there might be a business opportunity when one of his friends—who was chairman of a Web-based digital consumer-electronics vendor—expressed frustration getting his company's name out there. His friend also noted that online advertising was not enough. Weimer set up focus groups to learn how consumers were affected by advertising. The focus groups indicated that Internet users visited the URLs they saw in print or traditional media much more than ones they saw in banner ads. He created The Net's to develop Sunday newspaper inserts for Web sites wishing to advertise economically off-line.[11]

Information: Market to Niche Groups

Jon Segal found that in large cities, pro and college teams push high school sports off the news pages. He created SchoolSports Communications Network LLC to build an advertising-supported media company with print and Web products devoted to local coverage of high school sports. Students pick up the free magazines at their schools.[12]

Environment and Convenience: "Boating Is Supposed to Be Fun!"

Don Drysdale was expecting guests on his yacht on July 4th to watch the fireworks. Suddenly, the word *full* lit up on his marine toilet. He recognized that he certainly wasn't the only boat owner who needed to have the toilet serviced in a timely and convenient manner. He contacted Dan and Harry West, who owned Aqualube Inc. They had a boat that drained system fluids without mess or environmental damage.

Drysdale saw the potential (like Ray Kroc did when he saw the McDonald brothers' drive-in restaurant) for providing the service on a national basis. Drysdale persuaded Dan and Harry West to join him in creating Naut-a-Care Marine Services Inc. The franchise provides custom-designed watercraft that offer numerous services including oil changing, steam cleaning of marine bilges, and maintenance of closed-loop systems.[13]

The statistics for the market are impressive. There are about 17 million inboard boats in the United States, and most of their owners hate wasting precious boating hours on such unfun activities as oil changes. Caroline Ajootian, director of consumer affairs for The Boat Owners Association of the United States, says "Boats require more maintenance than automobiles do, but there's nothing like Jiffy-Lube that can be found in harbors across the country."[14]

Dogs, Dogs, and More Dogs: It's a Dog's World

The following examples demonstrate that humans may not be the only market that offers entrepreneurial opportunities. "Man's best friend" has proven to be a source of numerous ventures.

How Much Is that Biscotti in the Window?

Dan Dye and Mark Beckloff's love for their pets and their awareness of the lack of nutritional value led them to make their own dog biscuits. One of them received a biscuit maker for Christmas. They found they could make more biscuits than their dogs could eat. They took their extra biscuits to a flea market and sold all they had made. At first, they made biscuits by moonlighting. Then they set up a retail store. Soon after that, they were invited to PETsMART's headquarters, where they were offered the opportunity to set up Three Dog Bakery boutiques in PETsMART's superstore. They also expanded into catalog sales, franchises, and a show on cable television.

Beware of My Dog

Beth Marcus was walking her dog one night and almost got hit by a car. She was certainly not the first person to have had such an experience. Marcus was different from most people. She was a consultant at Reflective Technologies Inc., a maker of glow-in-the-dark fabric called IllumiNite. Reflective Technologies was targeting strictly joggers who ran at night. Marcus demonstrated lateral thinking by investigating whether a product targeted to one set of users might appeal to different set of users. She recognized that dogs represented a whole other opportunity. She created Glow Dog Inc. to sell light-reflective clothing for pets and people who walk them. Her firm got a real boost when it was able to get a listing in PETsMART's catalog. Glow Dog Inc.'s products include collars and rain slickers.[15]

Fasten Rover's Sealbelt!

In 1995, Carl Goldberg had a personal experience with his dog that prompted him to create Ruff Rider LLC. When his dog almost lost his life by flying through his car's front windshield in a car accident, he vowed he would never put his dog at risk again. With the guidance of his veterinarian, he created the Ruff Rider canine vehicle restraint system. The restraint harness is available in numerous sizes. Goldberg believed the market was not just in his mind. He noted, "There are 26 states with laws stating it's illegal to transport a living animal over the road in a moving vehicle in a way that [might] cause tortuous injury or death."[16]

Food and Drink: The Opportunities Are Unlimited

Food and drink are like the confluence of two large rivers. The first river carries an incredible amount of money. The second river carries an incredible amount of consumer diversity. When these two rivers meet, entrepreneurial opportunities abound. The following examples represent just a few of the ventures that have been created from the ever-growing and ever-changing marketplace.

Forget Tea and Cola—Give Them Juice!

When Tom Scott and Tom First graduated from Brown University, they did not have any grand plans for their lives. All they had was a 19-foot Boston Whaler. One night during the winter when they had nothing else to do, one of them made his own concoction of fresh peach juice in a blender. Within five minutes, they decided to sell juice off their boat the next summer. They noted, "To us, juice was a generically packaged product—not very good. We were juice freaks, always drinking it because we worked outside and were hot, and you can't keep drinking Coke. So we asked the question: Why don't other companies' juices taste like this?"[17]

They started selling fresh "Nantucket Nectars" from their boat and out of a little store-front they opened. Their observation that people might want to have drinks available while they were in their boats and that people may value an alternative to the usual colas served as the springboard for their venture. By 1998, eight years after it was started, Nantucket Nectars had grown into a $50-million-a-year business.[18]

Mixing Food and Play: "Play Dough? No, Cookie Dough"

Susan Pasarow and Jill Schiff were not like the dog or food people profiled in the preceding examples. They knew they wanted to start a business. They were entrepreneurs in search of an opportunity rather than people who through their proximity happened to see a gap. They initially worked on creating a cookie-decoration kit. When they added some food coloring to some cookie mix, they found their kids went wild over the Play-Doh-like cookie dough. It turns out their dough can be played with, sculpted, molded, and even baked and eaten. They started Van Gogh's Kitchen Inc. in 2000 to offer Get Kookie—a colored cookie dough for kids. Get Kookie is available in a variety of grocery stores nationwide and has been sold on QVC and in 1,000 Wal-Mart Supercenters and Super Targets.[19]

Food: "Offer Premium When They Have Only Tasted Regular"

Areti Skalkos had already started a dry-cleaning business when she realized that there might be more to life than making money doing people's clothes. Skalkos had been giving her best customers bottles of extra-virgin olive oil from her family's grove in Greece. The customers raved so much about the superior taste of the olive oil that in 1995, she, along with Sally Williams and Bonnie Henry, formed Hellas International Inc. in Salem, Massachusetts, to import olive oil. They located an olive-oil supplier in Greece and a bottle manufacturer in Italy. Their strategy involved creating their own brand and becoming their own distributor. They wanted to sell the best oil in the best packaging directly to specialty stores. They bought a list of 5,000 specialty store buyers for $30.00 and called about 30 stores per day. Although their firm only generated $15,000 in sales in its first year, their persistence paid off. By 1997 sales were projected to be over $1,700,000 with a profit of over $150,000.

Convenience: "Hey Buddy, Can You Spare Some Change?"

Jebs Molbak moved often, and found that he always had a jar of coins that he had to move with him. He also realized that it took him nearly an hour to roll the coins so he could cash them in. He figured there must be a more convenient way to turn coins into cash. So he and a friend interviewed about 1,500 people outside supermarkets to see if other people were frustrated. His research also indicated there are about $7 billion (about $30 per person) out of circulation in the United States.

Molbak then oversaw the development of the Coinstar machine. The machine uses a patented mechanism to count as many as 180,000 coins before automatically calling for service via the central computer network. Coinstar's screen shows consumers a running total of the coin count; and displays advertisements of its host store. When the machine has finished counting the coins, it prints out vouchers redeemable for goods or cash, less a "convenience charge," at the store's checkout counters.

Coinstar manufactures, markets, and operates machines located in grocery stores nationwide. By 1998 Coinstar, which is traded on the NASDAQ, had close to 5,000 machines in operation in grocery stores throughout the United States. The average amount deposited is $40. At that time, Coinstar had been contacted by 20 foreign countries about exporting modified versions of its machines overseas.[20] By 2003, Coinstar had more than 11,000 units in supermarkets.

Convenience: "Couch Potatoes Need All the Help They Can Get"

Steve Perlman recognized most people are not technologically gifted. If most people have trouble programming their VCRs, then they would not embrace surfing the Internet over their TVs. He created WebTV Network, an easy-to-operate set-top box that allows people to surf the net for information and access e-mail. When WebTV's box was launched in 1996, it was marketed as "Internet for the rest of us." Microsoft purchased WebTV Network in 1997 for $425 million in cash and stock.

Sports and Recreation: Out with the Old, In with the New

Scott Olson, Jake Burton, Mike Sinyard, and Roger Adams created ventures to capitalize on the country's growing interest in recreation and exercise. Their youth, when combined with dissatisfaction with existing products, provided the impetus to create new forms of recreation. All four entrepreneurs demonstrated the value of perceptiveness, innovation, and perseverance. They started with a half-baked idea, re-cooked it, and made it into a mainstream product, sport, or industry.

At the age of 19, Scott Olson walked into a sporting goods store and found a pair of roller skates in the back. The skates weren't typical because each skate had four narrow wheels rather than the usual blade. He reworked the skates and pondered the idea of using them for street hockey rather than as roller skates. A couple of years later, Olson founded Rollerblade.[21]

Jake Burton transformed the concept of a surfboard into the snowboard. He began his entrepreneurial career in the garage of his Londonderry, Vermont home. By 1999, his firm, Burton Snowboards, employed nearly 500 employees.[22]

Mike Sinyard, founder of Specialized Bicycle Components, developed a prototype for the first mountain bike. He market tested his "Stumpjumper" until he got it right. In 1998, 60 percent of all bikes sold in the United States were mountain bikes.[23]

Roger Adams grew up in a roller rink. His whole family was involved in some form of roller skating. He noticed that kids were into inline skates, skateboards, and bicycles and believed there had to be an opportunity for something new. He started tinkering in his garage, and after a few days he had created Heelys, a shoe with a removable wheel in the heel. In 1998, he formed Heeling Sports Inc., an athletic footwear company. By 2001, sales reached $25 million.[24]

Recreation and Sports: "I Need Streamlined Water!"

New ventures are often created as a result of a gap identified through one's hobby or recreational endeavors. Vinu Malik had been competing in triathlons for years. In 1998, he recognized a problem that became a business opportunity. The bottles he and other triathletes carried to stay hydrated were large and cumbersome. He figured he could develop a better water system for athletes. He developed a system that featured four small, flat bottles that attached to a belt. His system was superior to existing systems because the weight of the water could be spread out around the runner's waist. He also curved the bottle spouts in one direction so they would face away from the runner's body.

Malik recruited his brother and started Fuel Belt Inc. in Cambridge, Massachusetts, for $5,000. They started selling their product on the Web and ran a little ad in *Triathlete*. They sold $25,000 worth of products in the first three months. In 1999, they continued doing sales on the Web while still holding their full-time jobs. They also were able to get a few retail stores to carry their product. By the end of that year, sales had grown to $50,000. In 2000, they decided to jump in with both feet. They quit their jobs, filed for patents, improved the product design, incorporated, and set up their business structure. In 2001, they approached the official board of the Ironman Triathlon to see if they could license the Ironman name for their product. They not only got the license to use the Ironman name, they were also allowed to state their Fuel Belt is the "official worldwide Hydration Belt of Ironman." By 2002, their Fuel Belt was carried in 500 running stores in the United States and 1,000 stores worldwide.[25]

Fuel Belt's success can be attributed to many things. Malik's first-hand experience enabled him to identify a gap. His ability to develop a superior product to fill it and to gain the Ironman license helped foster brand identity. The series of events contributed to interest among retailers in carrying the product.

Travel: "I Only Need a Few Square Feet."

Amy Nye ran across an opportunity at the age of 17 when she was in London's Heathrow Airport. She was tired of listening to the music she brought with her for her Walkman. When she stopped at a shop at the airport that sold tapes, she found the prices were sky-high. That moment marked the beginning of her "music-store-in-the-airport" concept. Nine years later, the financial analyst started AltiTUNES which sells CDs, tapes, portable electronics, and videogames to weary travelers. Nye knew that space at terminals would be expensive and hard to find, so she decided to have her businesses operate out of "movable but permanent looking" kiosks that only needed 200 square feet of unused space.[26] Alti-TUNES now has retail outlets in dozens of airports.

Travel: "Help, I Need to Get Away from It All!"

In 1976, Mike Thiel bought a cabin in New Hampshire. He planned to rent it as a summer getaway, but he had trouble finding renters. He observed, "There wasn't a good mechanism for renting out properties like this." He then devised a "club" to bring together homeowners and would-be renters. His concept grew into Hideaways International Inc., which charges membership fees for owners and renters. His firm publishes a booklet to entice travelers with villas and condos all over the world that are located away from the maddening crowd. Hideaways has more than 20,000 members and its annual revenue exceeds $4 million. Thiel, who travels all over the world looking for private homes to list, noted that he has had numerous offers from major players to buy his firm, but that he is "having too much fun" to sell it.[27]

Safety: Get Me Out of Here!

Andrew Ive found as a student living in a dorm while attending Harvard Business School that having an escape ladder would give him peace of mind. When he tried the two different ladders he bought, he found they were difficult to unfold and too flimsy for his 215 pounds. At that moment, he knew there was a gap in the market. He and Aldo DiBerlardi built an aluminum-runged ladder in their product-development course as a class project. Their ladder was twice as strong as a steel-runged ladder. Andrew Ive, Aldo DiBalardino, and Kevin Dodge created X-It Products LLC to make and sell home-safety products. Their product line includes an escape ladder that folds up to the size of a two-liter soda bottle and a fire extinguisher as light as a can of hair spray.[28]

Environment: It's Too Late to Build an Ark!

While watching TV coverage of Midwestern floods in 1993, Stacey Kanzler was shocked to see military personnel filling sandbags by hand. She noted, "I couldn't believe we didn't have a machine that sewed multiple sandbags simultaneously." Kanzler, who had experience working at her husband's earth-moving business, used her imagination to quickly dream up an automated sandbagging machine. In two weeks, the National Guard was testing some prototypes. It is estimated that the "Sandbagger" does the work of 40 people—and the subsequent, motorized Sandbagger is five times faster than that. "Many times we are credited with helping save communities." Her firm, Sandbagger Corp, now does worldwide sales.[29]

Kanzler demonstrated the value of being observant, having a kaleidoscopic perspective, and using a little ingenuity in bringing solutions to market. Her success demonstrates that entrepreneurs are different from most people. She wasn't involved in any facet of the sandbagging operation. She wasn't one of the thousands of people who were getting drenched and exhausted on the shoveling line. Surely, a number of people on the line had to be mumbling, "There's got to be a better way." And Kanzler wasn't employed by one of the businesses that provided the sand or the bags. You would think people in those businesses would be saying, "There's got to be a better way." She demonstrated true entrepreneurial acumen by turning a serious and recurring problem into a profitable venture.

Clothing: "Do We Have to Wear Green?"

Sue Callaway didn't even plan to be an entrepreneur. As a nurse, she wondered why hospital "scrubs" had to be such a bland, hospital green. She spent some time trying to make more fashionable scrubs for herself. A year later, Sue, with her husband and two friends, started S.C.R.U.B.S. in 1992.[30]

Electronic Commerce: A Brave New World

The accelerating rate of change creates opportunities for those who can create change and for those who can harness its power. In times of great change, the initiators of change will be its beneficiaries. The greater the change, the greater the opportunities for entrepreneurs who are in tune with the change. Entrepreneurs who are perceptive, flexible, and innovative will be the beneficiaries of the change. "The real challenge is recognizing that an opportunity is buried in the often conflicting and contradictory data and signals, and the inevitable noise and chaos of the marketplace. Often, a skillful entrepreneur can shape and create opportunity where others see little or nothing."[31]

The information revolution can be seen as a series of waves. Each wave brings opportunities. Numerous ventures were started by entrepreneurs who saw the first waves on the horizon and positioned themselves to ride them. By being the first information technology wave riders, they were able to write the rules for how information technology would be used and how the e-commerce game would be played. The following examples demonstrate how entrepreneurial prowess, when combined with technology and a keen sense of timing, can change the way we live and work.

Amazon.com: One Statistic Can Change the Retailing Game

It is interesting to note that Amazon.com got its start with one statistic. In 1994, when Jeff Bezos was a 30-year-old hedge fund manager in New York, he ran across the projection that e-commerce would grow by 2,300 percent. Bezos was amazed that something could grow so much. He noted that nothing usually grows that fast outside of a Petri dish.[32]

Bezos decided to create a venture that would ride the e-commerce wave. Yet to ride the wave, he had to determine which products or services would work. In the three months preceding his arrival in Seattle, Bezos had drawn up a list of 20 products that could be sold on the Net. The list ranged from clothing to gardening tools. Bezos then researched his top five product markets. He used a number of criteria including the size of the relative markets to evaluate the potential of each product. The price point was another criteria. He wanted a low-priced product because he wanted the product to not be so expensive that it would intimidate the first-time buyer. He also wanted a wide range of products to be available to the customer. He felt that the larger the product base, the greater the opportunity for him to utilize information technology to separate his firm from conventional businesses. Bezos chose the book market because it represented an $80 billion worldwide market, the price of books was reasonably low, and he could use the power of the computer to organize and enhance product selection.[33]

Amazon.com made books available to everyone through its geographic reach, customer service, product breadth, and around-the-clock hours. Consumers were no longer limited to what was available at the nearest mall. For millions of consumers that didn't have a mall within 20 miles, it became their mall. Customers could also be provided information that surpasses even specialty shops that pride themselves on knowing their customers.[34]

eBay: From Garage Sales and Flea Markets to Cyberspace

The formation of eBay can be traced back to a comment made by Pierre M. Omidyar's girl-friend. She had a passion for collecting Pez (candy) dispensers. She complained about how hard it is to buy and sell Pez dispensers. Omidyar realized that if a business could link buyers and sellers of items via the Internet, then the whole world could be an electronic market-place. In 1995, he decided to start a cyberspace flea market where anyone could sell almost anything to anybody. Within three years, eBay was running over 400,000 daily on-line auctions. eBay, unlike most e-commerce firms, made money from the start.[35] eBay now provides a vehicle for manufacturers to sell their products to other businesses and individuals.

Yahoo! Bringing Order Out of Chaos

David Filo and Jerry Yang were working on their doctorate when they realized the World Wide Web was a tangled mess. While the Web had a lot of interesting sites, there was no system enabling people to find the sites they wanted in an easy, orderly way. They created a search engine that made finding the right site as simple as typing in the right keywords. Yang noted, "We were one of the first to (try to organize the Web) and we did it better than anyone. ... This company really isn't about technology; it's about solving people's basic needs for efficiency, effectiveness, and simplicity. From that standpoint, we're really like a lot of other companies."[36] Within four years, Yahoo! Inc. had a market valuation of over $25 billion. Years later, Google.com challenged Yahoo!'s market dominance because of its ability to cite the most frequently sought sites.

Chris Evans: Surfing Multiple E-Commerce Waves

Chris Evans became a serial entrepreneur by riding more than one technology wave. His ability to sense consumer needs and to develop timely products has enabled him to start numerous ventures. He formed his first company, DaVinci e-mail, after attending the 1985 COMDEX show. He sold DaVinci for millions. He then founded Hotlinx to publish catalogs on the Internet. When he saw the benefits of targeted advertising versus traditional saturation advertising on the net, he created Accipiter to target ads to specific individuals. Evans's ventures had a common theme ... to make money without having to sell a product on the Net. He noted, "I decided I wanted to sell the picks and the shovels of the Internet gold rush rather than mine for gold."[37]

OPPORTUNITIES ALSO EXIST IN THE SOFTER SIDE OF TECHNOLOGY

John Nesbitt noted in his classic book *Megatrends* that we are in a high-tech and high-touch world. He noted the increasing use of technology will also bring an increasing need for the personal touch. The following ventures illustrate that technology waves also have a softer side to them.

Internet Crossing: When in Rome, Do as the Romans Do

Jeffrey Herzog observed that most companies that do international commerce do not take into account the customs, values, and traditions of different areas of the world. He created Internet Crossing (*www.internetcrossing.com*) to help companies avoid potential cultural embarrassments. Internet Crossing developed a program called eCulturation to help companies overhaul their Web site's color scheme, imagery, and slogans to make them friendlier to a country's consumer mindset.[38]

ValiCert: Creating a "Virtual Gallery"

Yosi Amram took a page out of eBay's notebook by founding ValiCert. He noted, "iTheo was designed to put artists directly in touch with buyers, bypassing the inefficient gallery channel. The challenge was to overcome the risks involved for both sides and creating a trusted transaction environment."[39]

ENTREPRENEURS RELISH THE OPPORTUNITY TO CHANGE THE RULES OF THE GAME

Sometimes entrepreneurs do more than ride the waves of change; they make waves. Entrepreneurs change the way the game is played by breaking the rules or making new rules. Entrepreneurs practice Joseph Schumpeter's notion of creative destruction. They take on established businesses, almost daring them to keep them out of the game. Many entrepreneurs made their mark by shaking up industries that operated like gentlemen's clubs. Some entrepreneurs changed the game through their nimbleness; others garnered customers via outstanding customer service. Other entrepreneurs reconfigured markets by bringing state-of-the-art practices and processes. The following ventures illustrate how entrepreneurs changed the way the game is played.

Dragon Systems: Avoiding Paralysis by Analysis

Established firms have a tendency to get caught up in analyzing situations to the point that the world passes them by. The weakness of big companies represents an opportunity for entrepreneurial ventures to seize the moment.

The evolution of Dragon Systems provides one of the best examples of how a David start-up can compete against a modern Goliath. Jim and Janet Baker took their knowledge of voice-recognition systems and artificial intelligence that they had honed while working on their doctorates at Carnegie Mellon to IBM's Thomas J. Watson Research Center in 1975. According to Janet, "IBM is an excellent research institution and we enjoyed working there, but we were eager to get things out into the marketplace and get real users."[40] IBM's management considered their desire to get to market to be premature, so in their frustration with being constrained, they left. In 1979, the Bakers joined Verbex, a Boston-based subsidiary of Exxon Enterprises, where Jim became vice-president of advanced development and Janet became vice-president of research. They were involved in Verbex's continuous speech effort. Three years later, Exxon decided to get out of the speech recognition business. In 1982, with no venture capital, two preschool-aged kids, and a big mortgage, the Bakers founded Dragon Systems. The couple ran the company from their living room, and figured their savings could last 18 to 24 months. The Bakers attribute part of Dragon's success to not heaping the company in debt and not selling a stake in the company. Instead, they insisted that salaries and expenses had to be paid out of revenue. They were also committed to focusing their attention on solving real-world problems with current technology.[41] Dragon Systems went on to become a major player in the voice-recognition software field. At times it had about 40 percent of the market. Lernout & Hauspie acquired Dragon Systems when it saw its high adoption rate. ScanSoft then acquired Dragon Systems from Lernout & Hauspie.

Richard Branson: Shaking Up Existing Markets

Few people can match Richard Branson for creating new ventures, his flair for promotions, or his ability to develop brand identity. By the age of 47 he had started more than 150 ventures. His parent company has become a multibillion-dollar enterprise. Nothing gets him more excited than taking the establishment—whether it is the music, transportation, financial services, or cola industry. He attributes his success in part to entering markets where things have been done the same way for a long time—and then doing things differently.[42]

1-800-Auto Tow: Professionalizing Fragmented Industries

Numerous new ventures have gained considerable market share by professionalizing their operations. This approach seems to work best in industries that are operated by "mom and pop" businesses. Vince Gelormine was fascinated with Wayne Huizenga's success in transforming trash collection and video rentals into substantial national enterprises. He researched various fields and found that the auto-towing industry was very fragmented. His research revealed that among the 40,000 towing companies, only a few hundred had more than 40 trucks. He also found that less than one-half percent had automated dispatching.[43]

Gelormine's research then led him to check out a number of towing companies. He noted, "It was like chaos. The wife is on two telephone lines, both with call waiting. She's also working the radio. She's handwriting notes, fumbling with maps, making sure addresses are correct. The radio is blaring static."[44] Gelormine envisioned a company that would unite the smaller players into a consolidated entity. His firm would then automate, standardize, systematize, and routinize tow truck operations for firms in its network. His plan also included using artificial intelligence to make the best use of trucks in an area.[45]

Staples: Cater to Those Who Are Ignored

Thomas Stemberg provides a good example of how you can stumble across a great opportunity when you may not even be looking for one. He went out one Friday afternoon to buy some office supplies. When he got to the small office supply store he found that it had already closed for the day.[46] He recognized that small businesses were at a disadvantage when they wanted to buy office supplies. While large businesses had people who handled purchasing on a full-time basis, people who owned small businesses had to do their own purchasing.

Stemberg also believed that small businesses would welcome a business that helped them be more competitive and profitable by lowering the cost of their supplies. He also believed small businesses would welcome the opportunity to buy a wide variety of products from a firm that would provide more convenient hours. The inability to buy a few office supplies marked the beginning of Staples.

Research Triangle Consultants: Offer the Whole Package

After working in the corporate world for more than 25 years, Jeff LeRose decided in 1991 to pull the corporate rip cord and start his own venture. He started Research Triangle Consultants when he realized there was a gap in the e-commerce market when it came to integrating diverse software applications. He established a vertically integrated software and services firm that provides full-service solutions for clients with much of the work being done at RTCI's office rather than at the clients' sites.

LeRose observed, "Other people can do pieces of what we do, and they do it with contractors and consultants. Normally, they don't have the full-time permanent people that know how to do the work. ... We have all the pieces in-house." With more than 30 different specialized software products in-house, RTCI can duplicate the clients' systems and do all the work off-site, as opposed to having to send people on-site for the whole project. This assures quality and fosters a higher level of cost-effectiveness for it clients. RTCI's 900 percent growth rate over five years put it into the 1997 and 1998 *Inc.* 500.[47]

Starbucks: Taking an Established Industry to a Whole New Level

New ventures may be in a position to jumpstart a tired industry. Howard Schultz, CEO of Starbucks, attributes much of Starbucks' success to its ability to transform the everyday occurrence of drinking a cup of coffee into a valued experience. According to Schultz, "Customers don't always know what they want. The decline in coffee drinking (in the United States over the years) was due to the fact that most of the coffee people drank was stale and they weren't enjoying it. Once they tasted ours and experienced what we call the "third place"—a gathering place between home and work where they were treated with respect—they found we were filling a need they didn't know they had."[48]

ADOPTING A KALEIDOSCOPIC PERSPECTIVE

Sometimes new ventures are created when entrepreneurs look at a problem or situation from various vantage points. Kaleidoscopic thinking may enable an entrepreneur to take a concept and apply it to a different segment. The following examples highlight how business opportunities may arise when ideas are applied from one situation to a different situation.

Air Surveillance Corp.: Stay Away from the Obvious, Look for Niches

When most people think about the need for home security, they think about wealthy suburban areas. Don Fletcher recognized people who live in rural areas may also need security. He observed, however, that estates, ranches, and farms did not lend themselves to conventional "ground" security methods because they may be located a distance apart. Fletcher already had a security business, so he knew the distance between clients was both time and cost prohibitive. As a pilot, however, he recognized that he could cover far more territory by plane. He then bought a two-seat Cessna to do aerial surveillance. The plane gave him the ability to serve 500 to 600 clients. In 1996, he realized that the concept could be applied to other geographic areas, as well. He then founded Air Surveillance Corp. to franchise the business concept.[49]

Radiant Systems: One Venture Can Lead to Another Venture

Dean Debnam started his entrepreneurial career early. At the age of 17, he started growing plants in a greenhouse. Then he got into the heating business by looking for ways to save energy in his greenhouses during the energy crisis in the 1970s. He started Radiant Systems in 1989 to sell industrial greenhouse heating equipment. His venture eventually manufactured its own line of heating equipment.

Debnam recognized that he should not limit his product to greenhouses. He then began to penetrate the car wash market. He noted, "We started putting heaters in car washes to keep them from freezing with the doors closed. It used to be, when it got to freezing, the car washes would just close. But people still want to wash their cars at 0 degrees and –10 degrees. So we started to develop products to do that. Debnam sees his company to be a "solutions" provider. His company has evolved to meet client needs. In addition to its own line of heating equipment, Radiant Systems manufactures overhead doors, radiant tube car-wash heaters, and polycarbonate car-wash doors. He observed, "In each industry, there's a set of problems, and if you can solve the problems, then customers will pay you for them."[50] Radiant Systems' 600 percent growth rate in five years put it in the *Inc.* 500 in 1997.

America's Finest Pasta Sauces: Embracing the Concept of "Opportunity Transfer"

Todd Holmes and Louis Amoroso II created Beer Across America, a mail-order beer-of-the-month club, in 1991. By 1997, the business they started for $20,000 had been transformed into a venture with sales of $30 million.

They did not know, however, that their business would serve as a model for David Gamperi. While pursuing his MBA at DePaul, he explored the merit in creating a club that sends members jars of the best pasta sauces in the United States each month. In 1994, he formed America's Finest Pasta Sauces after developing a business plan for the concept as a course term project. He sold his house, cashed in his 401K, borrowed $25,000 on his credit card, got loans from family and in-laws, and secured a $100,000 SBA loan to start his venture. His Pasta Sauce of the Month Club sends two jars of meatless sauce with two bags of pasta imported from Italy for $19.95 a month. The sauces are made from recipes of some of the country's most popular restaurants. The restaurants sign a release for five years. In return for participating, the restaurants get a royalty and the opportunity to sell their sauces through their restaurants for $8.95 a jar.

Capital Concierge Inc.: "Geographic Transfer" May Beat Reinventing the Wheel

Perceptiveness may be more valuable than innovation in some cases. Numerous entrepreneurs have merely taken an idea that has been successful somewhere else by someone else and introduced it to an untapped market.

After reading about a corporate concierge business in Los Angeles, Mary Naylor decided to try the concept in Washington, D.C. In 1987, she began the business with a $2,000 loan from her mother and started cold calling prospects. She noted, "Everyone needs everything yesterday." This is particularly true with lobbyists and attorneys. Fortunately, her first client was a well-respected firm. Naylor notes, "That was my stamp of approval." By 1995, her firm, Capital Concierge Inc., had nearly $5 million in revenue and employed more than 100 employees in more than 80 buildings.[51]

Trakus Inc.: Looking for A and Finding B

Kaleidoscopic thinking can pay off if you find the window of opportunity fails to open. This is what happened to Trakus Inc. Eric Spitz, fresh out of MIT's Sloan School of Management, joined two engineering grads to build a system that would track the movements of supermarket customers. By outfitting the carts with transmitters, the trio hoped to show supermarket managers where shoppers spent the most time. They found, however, that their product would be too expensive for the low-margin grocery business.

The team then brainstormed how and where their technology might be of value. They were looking for markets that valued specific information involving movement. They recognized that providing information about athletes may be a better use for their technology. They developed the Electronic Local Area Positioning System, which collects performance data in real time during a game. Trakus Inc.'s devices, when imbedded in athletes' helmets, transmit data providing a wealth of new statistics about the game. Trakus's data provides statistics and digital images. Coaches and broadcasters get precise information on an athlete's speed, acceleration, and impact with other players or objects, and create digital replays of key moments.[52]

REGULATION AND DEREGULATION

Almost every change in government regulations creates new product and new service opportunities. The Occupational Safety and Health Act and the Environmental Protection Act created thousands of opportunities for new products and services that would help individuals and organizations comply with new statutes. Tremendous opportunities emerged for entrepreneurs who had innovative ways to fulfill recycling statutes. Deregulation also created numerous opportunities. Changes in the regulatory environment have one significant difference over most changes in the marketplace. They usually take a few years to be enacted. This has its advantages and disadvantages. It gives the entrepreneur a lot of lead time to get ready. The lead time also gives competitors time to get ready. The following example illustrates how one entrepreneur created a venture to capitalize on changes in the regulatory environment.

Reno Air: Who Says Flying into Reno Is a Gamble?

More than 200 firms filed for permission to fly since the industry was deregulated in 1978. Joe Lorenzo started his entrepreneurial journey by looking for a market where jet service had deteriorated, but where there was still latent demand for it. Lorenzo found a market gap in Reno, Nevada. He noted, "Reno was a gem: poor jet service, outrageous prices, and plenty of casinos and Lake Tahoe resorts to assist the airline's marketing department." Lorenzo then leased a few jets and developed a relationship with American Airlines to give it added strength.[53] American Airlines acquired Reno Air in 1999.

INTERNATIONAL OPPORTUNITIES

Numerous entrepreneurs have found that there is no shortage of opportunities if you can span national borders. The following examples provide a very small sample of what is possible.

The Vietnam Business Journal: Return to Vietnam

Kenneth Felberbaum capitalized on a different form of deregulation. In 1993, he took a trip to Asia to look for trading opportunities. He stopped in Vietnam, which was then under a mandated trade embargo by the United States. Although some U.S. businesses were working with Vietnamese companies in anticipation of the embargo's end, he found that many deals fell through because foreign companies didn't understand the business and cultural environments in Vietnam. He returned to New York, where he began publishing a newsletter about doing business in Vietnam. The readership grew when the embargo was lifted in 1994. In that year, he transformed his newsletter into a full-blown magazine, *The Vietnam Business Journal*. The magazine generates more than $1 million in revenue and attracts worldwide advertisers with a circulation of more than 25,000 copies.[54]

American Tours International: Coming to America

Noel Irwin-Hentschel, CEO of American Tours International (ATI), created the largest inbound tour operator in the United States. In 1977, at the age of 24, she recognized a gap in the tour market. She noted, "Early on I saw a void in bringing tourists to the United States—in selling America. Until then, everybody was focusing on sending people the other way." She started ATI with $5,000 and a $2,000 credit card loan. By 1998, ATI had become the biggest *Visit USA* tour operator in the country, with more than $150 million in revenue.[55]

Lucille Roberts Health Clubs: "Girls Just Want to Have Fun"

Lucille Roberts, who started Lucille Roberts Health Clubs (for women), recognized that there may be an opportunity to export a popular type of American business to Europe and other parts of the world. She noted, "They're 10 years behind us because they're still smoking and eating dead animals. ... They'll catch up though (to the need for health).[56] By 1998, she had 50 centers.

CONCLUSION: THE POSSIBILITIES ARE LIMITLESS!

This chapter has described dozens of examples of ventures that were created to fill voids in the marketplace. Some of the opportunities involved state-of-the-art technology; other opportunities only called for the ability to do something better than firms that had grown complacent.

It seems that almost every problem is as multifaceted as a diamond. It also seems that the solutions to most problems create new gaps or problems. The ability to digitize information led to the question about what to do with the original paper documents. New ventures sensing a new problem seized the moment by offering ways to shred, recycle, or even store the original paper documents in more secure places.

The entrepreneurial journey will be more fruitful if it is embarked with both eyes open and an equally open mind. Perceptiveness will enable you to see where windows of opportunity are about to open. Agility, resourcefulness, and a keen sense of timing will enable you to seize the opportunity.

In every economy, there is one crucial and definitive conflict—the struggle between the existing configuration of industries and the industries that will someday replace them.[57]

—George Gilder

ENDNOTES

1. Scott DeGarno, "Wanted: A Company President," *Success,* June 1997, p. 2.
2. Jeffry A. Timmons, "Growing Up Big: Entrepreneurship and Creating High Potential Ventures," *Texas A&M Business Forum,* Fall 1985, p. 12.
3. Don Debelak, "I Needed That," *Entrepreneur,* May 2002, pp. 127–128. Reprinted with permission of Entrepreneur Media, Inc.
4. Ibid.
5. Tod Loofbourrow, "My Company Was Born in the Delivery Room," *American Venture,* July 2001, pp. 29 and 31.
6. Cal Chang Yocum, "Durham Software Firm Translates for Medical World," *Triangle Tech Journal,* August 2003, p. 1.
7. Michael J. Hofman, "A Cure for Cabin Fever," *Inc.,* July 1999, p. 48.
8. Desh Deshpane, "How to Find the Right Niche," *Red Herring,* December 18, 2000, p. 212.
9. Hagar Scher, "Refer Madness," *Success,* October 1997, p. 22.
10. Frances Huffman, "A Page In History," *Entrepreneur,* September 1997, p. 18. Reprinted with permission of Entrepreneur Media, Inc.
11. Ilan Mochari, "Circular Logic" *Inc.,* July 1999, p. 42.
12. Michael J. Hofman, "Reads Like Teen Spirit," *Inc.,* July 1999, pp. 44–45.
13. Michael J. Hofman, "Changing Oil in Troubled Waters," *Inc.,* July 1999, p. 44.
14. Ibid., p. 45.
15. Michael J. Hofman, "A Spot in the Dark," *Inc.,* July 1999, p. 38.
16. Gisela M. Pedroza, "Road Dogs," *Entrepreneur,* May 2002, p. 112, Reprinted with permission of Entrepreneur Media, Inc.
17. "Two Men and a Bottle," *State of Small Business,* 1998, pp. 60–64.
18. Ibid.
19. Gisela M. Pedroza, "Color of Money," *Entrepreneur,* May 2002, p. 112. Reprinted with permission of Entrepreneur Media, Inc.
20. Mark Reily, "Counting Change," *Bottom Line*–Personal, February 15, 1998, p. 4.
21. David Carnoy, "Sporting Chance," *Success,* January 1998, p. 49.
22. Christopher, D. Lancette, "Wide World of Sports," *Entrepreneur,* February 1999, pp. 142 and 144. Reprinted with permission of Entrepreneur Media, Inc.
23. David Carnoy, "Sporting Chance," *Success,* January 1998, p. 49.
24. April Y. Pennington, "Healing Art," *Entrepreneur,* May 2002, p. 164. Reprinted with permission of Entrepreneur Media, Inc.
25. Debelak, "I Needed That," *Entrepreneur,* pp. 127 and 128.
26. Kristen Dunlap Godsey, "Terminal Velocity," *Success,* October 1997, p. 12.
27. Hagar Scher, "Refer Madness," *Success,* October 1997, p. 22.
28. Ilan Mochari, "A Winning Exit Strategy," *Inc.,* July 1999, p. 47.
29. Debra Phillips, G. David Doran, Elaine Teague, and Laura Tiffany, "Young Millionaires," *Entrepreneur,* November 1998, p. 119. Reprinted with permission of Entrepreneur Media, Inc.
30. Ibid., p. 121.
31. Timmons, "Growing Up Big: Entrepreneurship and Creating High Potential Ventures," p. 13.
32. Lesley Hazleton, "Jeff Bezos," *Success,* July 1998, p. 58.
33. Ibid.
34. Heather Green and Seanna Browder, "Cyberspace Winners: How They Did It," *BusinessWeek,* June 22, 1998, p. 158.
35. Ibid., p. 154.

36. Gayle Sato Stodder, "How to Build a Million Dollar Business," *Entrepreneur,* September 1997, p. 106. Reprinted with permission of Entrepreneur Media, Inc.

37. Kristen Tyler, "An Entrepreneur's Dream: One Company and Two Liquid Events," *Business Leader,* January 1999, pp. 26 and 27.

38. Alex Perez and Jeffrey Herzog, "Clarity Across Cultures," *Business 2.0,* February 20, 2001, p. 33.

39. Alex Perez, "What Troubled or Failed Dot-Com Seemed Like a Solid Business Model?" *Business 2.0,* February 20, 2001, p. 33.

40. Ibid., p. 61.

41. Simson L. Garfinkle, "Enter the Dragon," *Technology Review,* September/October 1998, pp. 61 and 62.

42. David Carnoy, "Richard Branson," *Success,* April 1998, pp. 62.

43. DeGarno, "Wanted: A Company President," p. 2.

44. Ibid.

45. Ibid., p. 4.

46. Thomas Stemberg, *Staples for Success* (Santa Monica: Knowledge Exchange, 1996), p. 28.

47. Amy Nelson, "The Triangle Inc. Well," *Business Leader*, February 1998, pp. 32–33.

48. Scott Smith, "Grounds for Success," *Entrepreneur*, May 1998, p. 124. Reprinted with permission of Entrepreneur Media, Inc.

49. Carol Steinberg, "Go West," Success, June 1997, p. 89.

50. Amy Nelson, "The Triangle Inc. Well," *Business Leader,* February 1998, pp. 30–31.

51. "Entrepreneurs Across America," *Entrepreneur*, June 1995, p. 97. Reprinted with permission of Entrepreneur Media, Inc.

52. Emily Barber, "Upsetting the Stats Quo," *Inc.,* July 1999, p. 48.

53. Ronald Lieber, "Beating the Odds," *Fortune,* March 31, 1997, p. 88.

54. Phillips, Doran, Teague, and Tiffany, "Young Millionaires," p. 123. Reprinted with permission of Entrepreneur Media, Inc.

55. Ivor Davis, "Patriot Gains," *Success,* May 1998, p. 61.

56. Stephen Rebello, "Visionaries," *Success,* February 1998, p. 42.

57. Craig R. Hickman and Michael A. Silva, *Creating Excellence* (New York: Plume, 1984), p. 175.

5

EVALUATING NEW VENTURE OPPORTUNITIES

Perceptive people can identify market opportunities.
Inventive people can develop products and services.
But it takes an entrepreneurial type of person
to create a venture that can do both for a profit.

—Stephen C. Harper

Steps 2 and 3 of the new-venture creation process resemble the top of a funnel. They attempt to identify a large number of new venture opportunities. Both steps incorporate the two basic rules of brainstorming. They try to generate as many ideas as possible and resist the temptation to evaluate them. It is assumed that this open-mindedness will lead to the identification of opportunities that would not have surfaced if screening parameters were established from the beginning.

NEW-VENTURE CREATION PROCESS

Step 1. Analysis of entrepreneurial preparedness
Step 2. Market analysis
Step 3. Identification of new venture opportunities
Step 4. **Evaluation of new venture opportunities**
Step 5. **Investigation of capability and resource requirements**
Step 6. **Running the numbers**
Step 7. **Analyzing risks, returns, and personal preferences**
Step 8. **Ranking potential ventures**
Step 9. **Selecting the opportunity to pursue**
Step 10. **Conducting the feasibility study and test market**
Step 11. Developing the business plan
Step 12. Getting the resources
Step 13. Starting the venture
Step 14. Managing the venture

This chapter provides a systematic framework for determining the relative merits of the new venture opportunities identified in Step 3. Steps 4 through 10 profile a process and set of criteria for evaluating and ranking new venture opportunities. The questions posed in this chapter represent a series of screens inside the funnel. Opportunities that meet specified criteria will pass through the screens. Opportunities that fail to meet the criteria are dropped from consideration. Although the chapter might seem like it focuses on what separates the good, bad, and the ugly, it is really directed at identifying opportunities that have the potential to be exceptional enterprises.

This chapter focuses on finding the best opportunities. These will be opportunities that optimize the risk/return ratio. Attention will be directed to identifying lasting and lucrative opportunities. Attention will also be directed to reducing the risk associated with starting a venture that could fail. This chapter does not, however, try to eliminate risk. Entrepreneurial decisions involve taking calculated risks. The only way to eliminate the risk of new venture failure is to not embark on the journey altogether.

This chapter encourages entrepreneurs to look at opportunities objectively and to be diligent in analyzing their relative merit. New venture success is contingent on the extent you can create and maintain customers for a profit. Accordingly, success will be contingent on whether (1) there is a true market opportunity, (2) you can develop a strategy that attracts customers and fosters a sustained competitive advantage, (3) you can execute your strategy well, (4) the venture can be profitable, and (5) success can be sustained.

This chapter may be frustrating because it raises so many tough questions. It is unlikely that you or even your management team (if you have one) will be able to identify all the questions—and even more unlikely that you and your team will have all the answers to the corresponding questions. This is why it is so important that you enlist the help of others who either have traveled the entrepreneurial journey or have helped entrepreneurs in their journey.

First-time entrepreneurs should make a deliberate effort to find a mentor who will ask the tough questions. First-time entrepreneurs should establish an advisory board at this stage. The advisory board should be composed of people who can provide various perspectives when analyzing various opportunities. Members of the advisory board may also be in a position to identify potential mines and avoid them as you prepare to enter the entrepreneurial minefield. The people on the advisory board may be considered for the actual board of directors if you decide to start a venture.

SCREENING NEW VENTURE OPPORTUNITIES

This step raises the question of whether a new product, process, or service idea represents a legitimate foundation for a viable business. Prospective entrepreneurs need to call an emotional time out so they can be objective in their analysis of the relative merit of each opportunity. Thomas Zimmerer and Norman Scarborough stress the need for entrepreneurs to have a reality check at this point in the entrepreneurial process. They observed, "Unsuccessful entrepreneurs tend to have one thing in common; they view every great idea they have as an opportunity. Successful entrepreneurs also tend to have one thing in common; they have developed an uncanny ability to separate the opportunities from the chaotic sea of ideas. Too often, aspiring entrepreneurs become enchanted with a new idea or product that they feel can be the solution the world is waiting for. However, experience has shown that if a business is based on a solution without a problem, the business will soon have a problem with no solution."[1]

By now, you may have even identified a number of gaps in the market. It is now time to determine which opportunities have merit. The process for evaluating opportunities is similar to the process used in selecting candidates for a position in an organization. Before a position can be filled, the job needs to be analyzed to identify the most important dimensions. A job description is then drafted that identifies the required skills and capabilities. The job description serves as the basis for evaluating each applicant.

Veteran recruiters do not start the candidate screening process by trying to find the best applicant. Instead, they look for candidates who fail to meet the minimum expectations. Applicants who do not meet all the criteria are dropped from consideration. The Pareto 80/20 Principle tends to apply to the initial screening. Most applicants are quickly screened out because they fail to meet at least one of the criteria. This gives recruiters the time needed to do a more in-depth analysis of the remaining candidates. The in-depth analysis includes reference checks as well as an investigation of each candidate's qualifications, his or her potential, and the likelihood the candidate will fit in with the firm's corporate culture.

The evaluation of new venture opportunities follows a similar process. Entrepreneurs must have a crystal clear grasp for what they want from their new venture. If you don't have clearly articulated expectations, then you will lack the criteria needed for evaluating the opportunities generated in Step 3. Without clear criteria you will waste time considering ideas without merit. Criteria are like the strike zone in baseball. The strike zone provides the batter with a mental picture of when to swing and when to ignore the pitch. The same applies when it comes to evaluating new venture opportunities. Particular attention should include the acceptable degree of risk, the demands on your time, the profit potential, resource requirements, and any other factor that may affect venture attractiveness.

The Opportunity Screening Funnel depicted in Exhibit 5.1 profiles the process where opportunities that are being considered are reviewed according to a successive set of criteria.

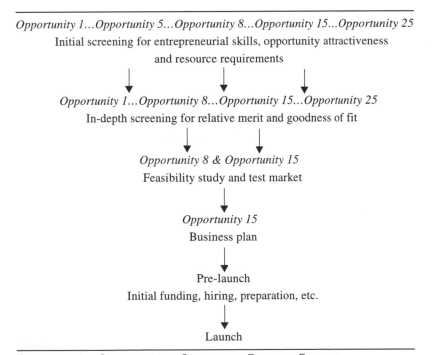

Opportunity 1...Opportunity 5...Opportunity 8...Opportunity 15...Opportunity 25
Initial screening for entrepreneurial skills, opportunity attractiveness
and resource requirements

Opportunity 1...Opportunity 8...Opportunity 15...Opportunity 25
In-depth screening for relative merit and goodness of fit

Opportunity 8 & Opportunity 15
Feasibility study and test market

Opportunity 15
Business plan

Pre-launch
Initial funding, hiring, preparation, etc.

Launch

EXHIBIT 5.1 OPPORTUNITY SCREENING PROCESS FUNNEL

A threshold must be established for each criterion. Opportunities that fail to meet any threshold are dropped from further consideration. At first, each opportunity is evaluated on its *absolute merit*. Opportunities that meet or exceed all the thresholds are then analyzed to determine their *relative merit*. The analysis of each opportunity's relative merit provides the basis for ranking the opportunities. The relative merit may be affected by the perceived risk, financial worthiness, and personal preference. If the criteria are specific and challenging, then one opportunity may stand out from the others. The relative weighting of these factors is addressed later in the chapter, that applies various screens for evaluating opportunities.

The highest-ranking opportunity is then subjected to closer scrutiny to determine the validity of some of the assumptions associated with it. A feasibility study may be conducted to determine if the product, process, or service can actually be provided. The top product, process, or service is then test marketed to determine if the prospective target market embraces it. The development of a prototype and the use of a test market will also be discussed later in this chapter. If the opportunity clears both of these hurdles, then a business plan is developed to address all the pieces in the new venture puzzle. The business plan is described in Chapters 6 and 7.

Evaluation Thresholds and Critical Mass

The Introduction to this book indicated that three key dimensions of the entrepreneurial triangle must exist for a new venture to be successful. The importance and interrelatedness of the three dimensions is reflected in Exhibit 5.2. New venture success is contingent on having a sufficient level of strength in each area. Success is also contingent on the goodness of fit of all three dimensions.

The concept of having critical mass in physics also applies to the creation of new ventures. For the venture to have a successful launch, each dimension must exceed some minimum initial threshold. For example, if the initial capital requirement for a venture under consideration (Opportunity 8 profiled in Exhibit 5.3) is estimated to be $220,000, then the threshold would reflect that amount. If the entrepreneur has the ability to access up to $400,000 in debt and equity financing, then the resource dimension of the triangle would clearly exceed the venture's resource threshold.

The same evaluation process would take place with the relative attractiveness of the opportunity and the extent that the entrepreneur and the management team have the necessary skills and capabilities. A margin of safety exists to the extent the actual level for each of the three dimensions exceeds its corresponding threshold. It should also be understood that it is rare that one dimension can make up for the lack of critical mass in any other

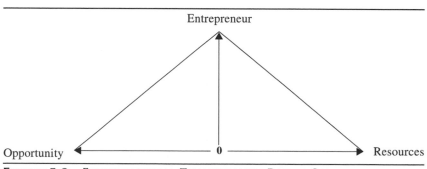

EXHIBIT 5.2   ENTREPRENEURIAL TRIANGLE WITH RATING SCALES

dimension. If you have enough money, you may be able to hire talented people. Although money may not be able to solve all problems, it can reduce new venture risk. The triangle in Exhibit 5.2 indicates the relative strength and threshold for each dimension.

The triangle in Exhibit 5.3 indicates that the requirements for all three thresholds are met or exceeded for the opportunity that is being analyzed. The opportunity is particularly attractive and the entrepreneur appears to have little difficulty raising the necessary resources. The margin of safety for both of these dimensions will provide a buffer if things do not go as well as expected. The availability of resources could even help the financial attractiveness of this venture. The availability of capital, particularly equity, could lower the interest rate of debt financing if a loan is sought.

The triangle in Exhibit 5.4 indicates two significant deficiencies in the entrepreneurial triangle for Opportunity 5. The attractiveness of this opportunity (15 percent) fails to meet or exceed that threshold (18 percent). This is usually the case when a new venture is considering a market that may be saturated. Intense price competition tends to lower profit margins. Even if the firm is able to capture a reasonable market share, its margins may not be able to generate a sufficient financial return. Exhibit 5.4 also indicates that the resource requirements (520 K) exceed the resources available (400 K) for the venture. The entrepreneur/team may consider committing more of their resources and/or seeking additional resources from outside sources. The lack of financial attractiveness of this opportunity, however, would limit the merit of such an effort. It should be noted that even if the opportunity was more attractive from a financial perspective, additional funding might dilute the return on investment (due to a larger investment base) unless the additional resources generate a commensurate increase in the financial returns.

The entrepreneurial triangle provides an overview of the three prerequisites for new venture success. Certain facets of each dimension may have their own thresholds. For example, each dimension may then be a composite of the corresponding facets and thresholds. The attractiveness dimension may have thresholds for the rate of market growth, differential advantage, gross margin ratio, and internal rate of return.

The remainder of the chapter provides a list of questions that can be used to provide a more in-depth evaluation of the opportunities that made it through the initial screening. It would be easy to be overwhelmed by all the questions, but keep in mind that the questions play a key role in clarifying the issues that are the foundation for the whole book. It is said

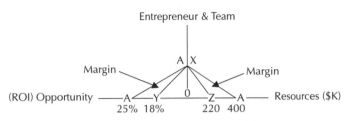

Entrepreneur & Team

A = *Actual level* of skill and experience for that entrepreneur/team, projected return for that opportunity, and resources available for that venture
X = *Skill and capability threshold* (what the entrepreneur and team will need)
Y = *Opportunity threshold* (minimum return on investment required by the entrepreneur/investors)
Z = *Resource threshold* (amount of money required for that opportunity)

EXHIBIT 5.3   ENTREPRENEURIAL TRIANGLE FOR OPPORTUNITY 8

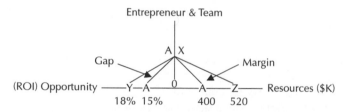

A = *Actual level* of skill and experience for that entrepreneur/team, projected
    return for the opportunity, and resources available for the venture
X = *Skill and capability threshold* (what the entrepreneur and team will need)
Y = *Opportunity threshold* (minimum return on investment required by the
    entrepreneur/investors)
Z = *Resource threshold* (amount of money required for that opportunity)

EXHIBIT 5.4   ENTREPRENEURIAL TRIANGLE FOR OPPORTUNITY 5

that in ancient times, all roads led to Rome. In the entrepreneurial journey, all the questions posed in this chapter lead to the six principal entrepreneurial questions:

1. Do the entrepreneur and team have the ability to create and manage the venture?
2. Is there an identifiable gap in the marketplace?
3. Does the gap represent a viable business opportunity?
4. Will the venture be able to attract the necessary resources?
5. Will the venture be able to bridge the gap and have a competitive advantage?
6. Will the venture generate a sufficient financial return to justify the risk?

Reflections: What Can Prospective Entrepreneurs Learn from the Original Wave of Dot-coms?

Before moving on to evaluating prospective opportunities, it may be worthwhile to take a look at why numerous dot-coms failed. Someone once noted that failure is a great teacher. Although it is true that we can learn from our failures, it might be better to learn from other people's failures! The first wave of dot-coms in the latter 1990s helped clarify what it takes for new ventures to succeed. For every eBay, Amazon.com, and Yahoo!, there were dozens of Pets.com, Eve.com, and Mortgage.com dot-coms that failed.

The period that was characterized by "irrational exuberance," in the words of Federal Reserve Chairman Alan Greenspan, was a time when entrepreneurs and investors failed to differentiate solid business models from hare-brained ideas, bona fide demand from wishful thinking, a well-thought-out business plan and strategy from notes scribbled on a cocktail napkin for a nebulous concept, and the ability to execute from improvising on the fly. It was a time of recklessness when people forgot all business sense. It was a time when tons of money chased after a lot of bad ideas. It was like a feeding frenzy with little meat. What were entrepreneurs and investors thinking?

In retrospect, the first wave of dot-coms demonstrated what can happen when new venture opportunities and proposed ventures are not subjected to reasonable evaluation and scrutiny. Evaluation is intended to separate true value propositions from ill-conceived concepts. Evaluation is intended to separate lucrative and lasting opportunities from aberrations, mirages, and hallucinations. In many cases, entrepreneurial efforts could be summed up as much to do about nothing. Their field of dreams, "If we build it they will come," turned into a field of nightmares for all involved. The marketplace is not forgiving. In the long run, it will not reward those who start ventures on blind faith.

The victors were markedly different from the vanquished. The victors identified and capitalized on real market opportunities. The victors had a game plan that enabled them to address business realities. The victors had sufficient resources to go the distance and to deal with the turbulence. They recognized the need to have capable management teams, as well as access to sufficient capital to keep them afloat until their revenue stream could sustain operations and fund growth.

The vanquished were launched by entrepreneurs who were seduced with technology that could not deliver on its promises or that did not solve a real problem. Many of the vanquished failed to differentiate *eyeballs* (Website hits) from revenue. Some of the vanquished failed to differentiate revenue from profitability. Some of the vanquished had too little money from the beginning; others spent money as if they could print it at will.

The victors found the pockets of profitable fire associated with the Internet; the vanquished in their recklessness suffocated in the Internet's smoke. The moral to the first wave of dot-coms is really nothing new: "There is only one way to make money—you have to earn it." For a venture to succeed, it has to offer products and services that people value in ways that are clearly superior to competitors in a manner that generates sustained profitability.

Although the team that started Pets.com thought it would succeed because "pets can't drive," it failed because it spent too much on advertising and consumers did not consider it to be a compelling alternative to conventional businesses. Webvan and Peapod, like Pets.com, tried to deliver regularly purchased items. They tried to deliver groceries through sophisticated distribution and information systems (with the help of some well-respected firms), but their inability to deliver positive cash flow and profitability led to their demise.

DrKoop.com. provides another example of a good idea that failed to become a profitable venture. Alex Perez noted, "Either it wasn't a good enough business model, its formula for success was flawed, its management was unable to manage it, or its capital structure was too massive to enable profitability."[2] Kurt Long, CEO of OpenNetwork Technologies noted, "The idea that a person can privately seek unbiased medical information from one of the most respected names in medicine remains compelling. It is unfortunate that it could not find the economic model for ensuring its ongoing viability."[3] Although DrKoop.com was able to generate considerable investor and consumer interest when it was conceived, its inability to make a commensurate financial return led to its demise.

Although Elingo may not have generated the same level of fanfare as the preceding failures, it also shows that having a neat idea does not guarantee new venture success. Guy Gecht, CEO of Electronics for Imaging, noted, "I thought the idea behind Elingo to provide translation services over the Internet was a great way to leverage one of the Net's great strengths—the ability to transfer bits of information, as opposed to atoms or hard goods."[4]

Most of the dot-com failures can be attributed to hitting the market too soon or too late, not being big enough to gain economies of scale, having insufficient demand, and/or having market research that did not differentiate between interest and intent. Their inability to generate sufficient cash flow expedited their demise. In many cases, there wasn't a compelling reason for customers to try their product/service or to switch from existing firms. In many cases, the dot-coms died because of unexpected occurrences such as technical glitches or the introduction of a killer application from a new competitor. In many cases, they self-destructed because their assumptions did not bear out. Their management teams were insufficient, incompetent, or inexperienced. They died because they couldn't get crucial suppliers or distribution outlets, additional funding, or cash flow to cover a higher-than-expected burn rate.

Rita Gunther McGrath and Ian MacMillan, who wrote *The Entrepreneurial Mindset*, profiled a number of the reasons Amazon.com survived in a world where many dot-coms perished. They noted that Jeff Bezos's new venture was based on a carefully articulated business concept. They attributed much of Bezos's success to his analysis of consumer and technological trends. The trends indicated that it would be possible for Amazon.com to provide the information and products consumers valued. Research indicated that personal computers were becoming more common at home. Research also indicated people were becoming more willing to buy products over the Internet.[5] Amazon.com succeeded because it was the right firm at the right time with the right capabilities. It had a solid business model and Bezos's team executed it well. Amazon.com has continued to succeed (and defy its critics) due to its ability to sense consumer wants and offer products and services that provide value in a timely manner.

The future for Internet-based or Internet-related businesses may be even more challenging than in the past. More sophisticated consumers and rapidly changing technology have raised the bar for new ventures as well as businesses already operating in cyberspace.

IT'S TIME TO APPLY VARIOUS SCREENS FOR EVALUATING THE OPPORTUNITIES

Numerous screens need to be used when evaluating opportunities. The screens focus on entrepreneurial prowess, the strength of the opportunity, the extent the proposed venture can generate a competitive advantage, financial worthiness, projected risk, personal preference, and feasibility issues. Each of these dimensions will be addressed in the remainder of this chapter.

Entrepreneurial Analysis

By now, you should have determined if you have what it takes in general terms to be an entrepreneur. You need to recognize that the skill, capability, and experience requirements of the entrepreneur and management team will vary with each opportunity. Certain opportunities will require extensive technical knowledge and experience. Other opportunities may have a much lower threshold. Higher skill and experience levels create a greater barrier to entry for potential competitors. If the entrepreneur and team have extensive knowledge and experience in the field of opportunity, then the relative strength of their capabilities may also be reflected in a high rating for opportunity attractiveness because the team should provide a potential competitive advantage. The strength of the entrepreneur and team may also enhance the resource availability rating because the firm has critical human resources.

Attractiveness of the Opportunity

Thomas Zimmerer and Norman Scarborough noted that many would-be entrepreneurs are obsessed with the notion that if they have a great idea, success is guaranteed.[6] It has been said that the difference between a good idea and a viable business is, "Unsuccessful entrepreneurs usually equate an idea with an opportunity; successful entrepreneurs know the difference—a novel idea is not the same as a sound business concept anchored to a marketable idea."[7] The attractiveness of the opportunity reflects a combination of two principal factors. First, the evaluation looks at the size and nature of the gap in the marketplace. The evaluation of this dimension also addresses the new venture's ability to serve that gap through its products, services, and processes. Second, it looks at the financial attractiveness of the opportunity.

Timing and Opportunity: The Dynamic Duo

The business opportunity screening process is intended to help you distinguish between neat ideas and truly worthwhile business opportunities. It is also directed to identifying opportunities that have lucrative and lasting profit potential. If you want to create an exceptional enterprise, then you must be able to differentiate opportunities that have considerable potential from those that are no more than short-term blips on the radar scene. Earlier chapters noted that opportunities are like race horses. If you want to win the race, then you need to have a horse that not only is faster than the others, it also has to have the ability to go the distance and outperform its competitors.

Entrepreneurial success depends on identifying the right opportunity and seizing it at the right time. The window of opportunity concept captures the relationship between timing and opportunities. From a timing perspective, if you get to the window well before it opens, then you have to wait. If you get there after it has been open for a while, then you may find yourself competing with numerous other firms. You also run the risk of entering as the window is closing. From an opportunity perspective, you do not want to pursue an opportunity with limited potential or that will only be open for a brief period of time. Your analysis must be directed to identifying windows of opportunity where you can have a decided timing advantage and that have the potential to open wide enough and long enough for your venture to create and maintain customers for a profit.

The ability to recognize a potential opportunity when it appears and the sense of timing to seize it as the window is opening, rather than slamming shut, is critical. "Another way to think of the process of creating and seizing an opportunity in real time is to think of it as a process of selecting objects (opportunities) from a conveyor belt moving through an open window, the window of opportunity. The speed of the conveyor belt changes, and the window through which it moves is constantly opening and closing. That the window is continually opening and closing and that the speed of the conveyor belt is constantly changing represent the volatile nature of the marketplace and the importance of timing."[8]

Chapter 2 drew the parallel between creating a new venture and surfing. Opportunities are like waves. If you want to get a great ride, then you need to catch the right wave at the right time. The Timing/Opportunity Matrix profiled in Exhibit 5.5 illustrates the need to evaluate opportunities as surfers judge waves. Like surfers, you should be looking for opportunities that can provide a long and rewarding ride.

Timing	**Good**	Short ride/limited thrill	Great & lasting ride
	Bad	A lot of effort/no ride	Marginal ride
		Limited **Exceptional**	
		Opportunity	

EXHIBIT 5.5   TIMING/OPPORTUNITY MATRIX

Surfers scan the horizon for waves that are about to form, position themselves to catch the waves, get a great ride, and kick out before it crashes on them as it nears the shore. Entrepreneurs need to identify windows of opportunity before they open, position their ventures to capitalize on the opportunity at the right time, and make sure they do not stay too long in a saturated market experiencing intense price competition and waning demand.

Entrepreneurs need to determine if the opportunity is real and lasting or if it is nothing more than a passing fad. Some opportunities are as perishable as fruit. Although they may garner a lot of attention like the Y2K info-tech crisis, they are short-lived. Some opportunities may stick around for a while and then fade. You need to determine if the opportunity is here to stay. Your analysis of the windows of opportunity should also include an analysis of the potential for substitute products or services to leapfrog the need for your product or service. The development of substitute products can make even a relatively new product obsolete. Although the Pony Express captured the spirit of adventure in the Wild West, it lasted just over one year. The telegraph made it obsolete for most markets. More recently, the proliferation of e-mail has had a dramatic effect on the need for fax machines.

If the window is just opening, then it will need to stay open for a number of years so you can harvest it. The first year may provide revenue, but it could take two to three years before you earn a profit and generate positive cash flow. Hopefully the market will stay open for at least 5 to 10 years. Additional time will give you the opportunity to position your venture to harvest new segments as they emerge. Additional time may also give you the opportunity to find ways to increase the usage rate, to find new uses for your products and services, and to develop subsequent generations from them.

If your preliminary analysis indicates that the window of opportunity may not be opening for some time, then the corresponding venture should be put on hold until the timing will be more favorable. One of the skills that characterize successful entrepreneurs is in the ability to hold onto their ideas over time, not necessarily moving on them right away, but not forgetting about them, either. Rita Gunther McGrath and Ian MacMillan note that a simple way to hold onto good ideas whose time may not be quite ripe is to create an opportunity register that profiles potential new venture opportunities.[9]

Opportunity/Strategy Analysis

When Steven Jobs was starting NeXT Computer, he noted that entrepreneurs should look for big opportunities because it takes almost as much time to start a small business as it does to start a business that has considerable growth potential. Rob Ryan, author of *Smartups,* put Jobs's observation in an interesting way when he noted, "Don't rob delicatessens—rob banks, that's where the money is."[10] Venture capitalists frequently judge prospective investments according to whether they can generate at least $100 million in sales. For this to be possible (assuming the venture can capture about 10 percent of the overall market), the overall market would have to have the potential to support $1 billion in sales. If the business can make 10 percent profit on sales and the venture capital firm has 30 percent ownership (given a $3 million investment), then the venture capital firm would be getting a 100 percent return on its investment per year. Few opportunities have the potential to provide this kind of return.

Amar Bhidé encourages entrepreneurs to look at opportunities in a little different light. Rather than seeing an opportunity as a single entity, he suggests looking at it to see if it can be seen as a number or series of opportunities. He suggests looking for opportunities that may actually be the lead domino in a series of opportunities where one opportunity leads to the next or as a path that has many off ramps. The dominos and/or off ramps capture Bhidé's concept of adaptive opportunism where entrepreneurial firms get themselves into the market and then adapt themselves to opportunities that appear in front of them.[11] As noted earlier, many of the firms that have made the *Inc.* 500 over the years have adapted to market opportunities.

Some of today's most successful firms illustrate the merit in being first into a market and then exploring growth opportunities. Dell found that selling custom-made computers directly to individual consumers could be a springboard for selling printers, monitors, and servers. eBay found out that established firms, not just individual consumers, would use its online auction system to buy and sell products. Amazon.com found that it did not have to change its DNA when it realized that it was a very effective vehicle for selling music and movies.

Although the preceding examples illustrate that capturing a large part of a large opportunity can be lucrative, they also indicate how difficult it can be to estimate the size, nature, longevity, and profitability for an emerging market. Michael Dell, Pierre Omidyar, and Jeff Bezos believed there was an opportunity for each of their ventures, but none of them perceived how big their markets would be or how large their firms would become.

These three examples illustrate another interesting point: Sensing an opportunity is of little value unless you can capitalize on it. Each firm sensed a wave (market opportunity) as it was beginning to form, caught the wave early (established brand identity), established good systems, and evolved by positioning themselves (by keeping their eyes open to customer needs) so they could catch related waves as they began to form.

Each of these examples illustrates two other critical ingredients for new venture success. All three firms developed strategies that were designed to give their firms a competitive advantage and they executed the strategies well. Finding the right window of opportunity is important—but being able to gain a sustainable competitive advantage may be equally important. It's like being given the opportunity to be a designated hitter in baseball. Standing in the batter's box is of little value unless you are able to hit the pitch!

A new venture will be able to create and maintain customers for a profit only to the extent it is able to offer the market a compelling reason to buy its products and service. Its strategy must also keep current and potential competitors at bay. Chapter 2 profiled various types of ventures. Numerous successful ventures entered an established, yet fragmented industry. They created and maintained customers by professionalizing their operations. Kindercare was successful when it entered the child daycare marketplace because it professionalized what had traditionally been a mom-and-pop type of business. Firms that use incremental and continuous improvement strategies try to be at least a little better than their competitors on a number of dimensions.

High-growth ventures, however, utilize a much bolder strategy for creating and maintaining customers for a profit. They try to capture the market through major innovation. They come in with a bang and they try to keep competitors out by leaving little room for them. Rob Ryan calls this strategy, "Sucking the air out of the room." According to Ryan, "A market lead is not enough to fend off the hordes of competitors that will come at you. And they will come. You can't prevent copycats; they're part of the landscape of capitalism. You have a choice—you can cruise along as you always have, or you can go into the *suck mode*. I'm talking about sucking the air right out of the room. Don't leave your competitors anything to breathe. In suck mode you make it difficult for established companies to recover and very expensive for start-ups to compete. This is what people don't like about Bill Gates. He sucks the air right out of the room. Nobody can breathe when they're standing next to Microsoft, and eventually they just quit trying."[12]

Although it might be possible to create a successful venture by offering products or services that are slightly better than the firms already serving that target market or by having business processes that give your venture a competitive advantage by being a little faster, more convenient, or less costly, the more your venture is able to provide a significant value proposition, the greater its potential to be an exceptional enterprise. Exceptional enterprises seem to have at least two things in common. First, they identify markets where customers are dissatisfied with the current state of affairs. They focus their attention on target-rich environments. Second, they *wow* the market by providing a superior offering.

Pip Coburn, as a global technology strategist with Warburg Dillon Read, stressed the difference between a solution to a problem and a solution looking for a problem. A business needs to be sure it is providing a real solution to a real problem.[13] According to Coburn, a solution is defined as a genuine answer to a legitimate problem, and a problem is defined as a genuine need of a customer. He also notes three other points that can apply to new ventures. First, the marketplace is dynamic. Solutions and problems change as the needs of customers and the solutions change over time. Second, those who correctly forecast the migration paths may have significant opportunity. Third, when demand is real, equity investors should have more downside protection if product delays occur.[14]

If new ventures are viewed as *customer problem solvers,* then new venture success will be contingent on whether there is in fact a problem that customers are compelled to solve and whether the venture can offer those consumers a superior solution to their problem. The New Venture Opportunity Matrix profiled in Exhibit 5.6 encourages entrepreneurs to differentiate between situations that may provide opportunities for new ventures and situations that should be avoided.

Entrepreneurs should avoid Quadrant 1 in most situations. Chapter 1 distinguished between inventors and entrepreneurs. It was noted that many inventors frequently get so caught up in creating products that they develop products where no need exists. Inventors may be excited about their creations, but if no one in the marketplace finds any value in their inventions, they do not generate any revenue. Someone once noted, "In business, nothing happens until someone places an order."

This book encourages prospective entrepreneurs to look for situations where customers are in search of a business. Quadrant 2 profiles the situation where a *market gap* exists. If the new venture can offer what consumers want, then it should be in the enviable position of having a temporary legal monopoly. Entrepreneurs should exercise caution, however, by making sure (1) they truly offer what prospective customers want, (2) the venture will provide a worthwhile return given the risk associated with being a first mover, and (3) they recognize other firms will enter the market when they see a market exists.

		Is there an existing need?	
		No	Yes
Are products or services already provided by existing businesses?	No	Quadrant 1 No present opportunity: Potential opportunity if market evolves.	Quadrant 2 Market gap exists: Make sure it is worth the effort before entering.
	Yes	Quadrant 3 Exercise in futility: Much to-do about nothing.	Quadrant 4 Uphill climb: Make sure you can provide a sustainable competitive advantage.

EXHIBIT 5.6 NEW VENTURE OPPORTUNITY MATRIX

Quadrant 3 profiles the situation that may occur when businesses do not look before they leap. This was particularly true in the irrational exuberance associated with dot-coms at the turn of this century. In many cases, entrepreneurs thought they could bring something (like a new way of handling data or the opportunity to order a product such as 100 pound bags of dog food over the Internet that few people even wanted via retail stores) to the market without verifying the need for such a product or service. The situation became even worse when other firms jumped on the bandwagon. Entrepreneurs need to recognize that 100 percent of a market that does not exist produces absolutely no revenue.

Quadrant 4 may provide opportunities for entrepreneurs if they have their acts together. New ventures can enter existing markets if they can meet needs that are not being met fully by the firms already serving the market. If the new venture can provide products and/or services that are less expensive, better quality, quicker, and/or in a more convenient manner, then they may be able to attract customers. If the new venture can bring a killer application via breakthrough innovation to the marketplace, then it may be able to capture significant market share. This strategy may also be worthwhile if the new venture tailors its offering to market segments that are not being served well or at all. In any event, entrepreneurs who pursue opportunities in Quadrant 4 should make sure their ventures have sustainable competitive advantages and that the need they are targeting will not be short-lived.

Although the matrix cautions entrepreneurs against starting ventures to enter Quadrant 1, entrepreneurs should differentiate between situations where no apparent need exists and situations where people have not articulated their problems well. There is a difference between the absence of a genuine problem and a problem that has not been articulated by the consumer.

Gary Hamel and C. K. Prahalad, who wrote *Competing for the Future*, differentiate articulated and unarticulated needs.[15] They note that if you ask people to identify their problems, they usually identify frustrations with deficiencies in existing products or services. If you probe deeply, however, people may reveal needs that have not been articulated. They believe these needs may represent significant opportunities.

The issue of timing comes in here again on two fronts. If you can get consumers to articulate their unarticulated needs to the point where they will actively seek solutions and you put your venture in a position where it can offer them a genuine solution to their newly articulated problem, then you may enjoy a temporary legal advantage. Timing can also play a role if you try to anticipate future problems. You should not focus your attention exclusively on existing windows of opportunity. You should also scan the horizon for windows that may appear in the very near term. Windows that are on the verge of opening may be far more lucrative than windows that are already open. Consumers' needs evolve over time. New consumers also enter markets. The Future Positioning Matrix profiled in Exhibit 5.7 can help you identify opportunities.

Future **Products/ Services** Present	Future product/service "development" opportunities	Wide-open future opportunities
	Current product/service offering	Gaps in current product/service offering
	Present	Future
	Customers	

EXHIBIT 5.7 FUTURE POSITIONING MATRIX

If you can anticipate future needs and position your venture to offer a genuine solution when consumers start their search for a solution, you will have a temporary legal monopoly. By blending the 2×2 matrices, you may be able to identify market opportunities. If you can provide superior solutions to genuine needs, then your venture may be in a very lucrative sweet spot. Rob Ryan noted, "Successful companies don't just roll out new products; they crack whole new markets. The role of the CEO is to create chaos of a specific kind—the creative chaos that leads to new ideas or leverages your old core technology into a new market."[16]

WHAT DOES THE OVERALL MARKET LOOK LIKE?

Entrepreneurs should take a close look at the current and projected status of the window for the opportunity being reviewed. The following questions can help the evaluation process:

- Is there truly a market?
- Is the market definable?
- Can demand be measured?
- Can customers be identified?
- Are customers reachable?
- Are channels of distribution in place?
- Is the market new and amorphous?
- How long will the market opportunity last?
- Is the market mature?
- Is the market likely to change dramatically?
- In what ways is the market likely to change?
- Are there clearly identifiable market segments?
- Is the market composed of naïve consumers or sophisticated consumers?
- Is the market at the interested stage, or the "I'll pay you cash now!" stage?
- Are firms successful that are already serving the market?
- What are the qualities that characterize the most successful firms in the marketplace?
- Are existing firms trying to serve the whole market, or are they targeting specific niches?

Questions about your product/service idea:

- Do we have a proprietary position?
- Will people buy it?
- Will enough people buy it for the venture to make its financial targets?
- Can we provide and deliver it?
- Can we do it efficiently?
- Can we maintain a competitive edge?
- Will we be a pioneer or a tweaker?
- Are we going after a large market or a niche?

- Can we readily access and serve the customers?
- Does our product/service lend itself to trialability?
- Will the market need to be educated?
- Will there be switching costs for prospective customers?
- What is the degree of loyalty?
- How forgiving will the market be of our mistakes or glitches?
- What is the slope of the learning curve to create a competitive advantage?

What is the Nature and Duration of the Window?

Entrepreneurs need to recognize that the window is unique. The size of the window and the speed at which it opens and closes will vary with each opportunity. The extent the window is visible in advance will also vary. The window for some opportunities will open wide and stay open for an extended period of time. Other windows remain open for a brief period of time.

If you get to the window before it opens, then you will have committed resources and tipped your hand about what you plan to offer the market to potential competitors. A number of ventures died on the vine because they had too little capital to hold them over until the window opened and provided them with a revenue stream to cover their outlays. Being late also has its consequences. If the new venture tries to enter after more perceptive firms have established their competitive positions and market share, then that firm will have an uphill battle. Its revenue stream will be contingent on the firm's ability to take customers from the other firms.

Being first to market is important for new ventures because it means you have the whole market to yourself. In a sense, you have a temporary legal monopoly. Being first to market requires considerable skill. It is like trying to hit the bull's eye of a target when the target is barely visible. You have to see the opportunity *before* other firms. You have to sense what the market wants *before* the market even knows exactly what it wants. You must have the people and resources in place *before* the window opens. You have to develop the goods, services, processes, and distribution capabilities *before* the window opens.

The rewards of being first to market can be considerable. Success is contingent on being in the right place at the right time with the right capabilities. First-to-market firms don't have to be perfect. The market tends to be somewhat forgiving in the beginning. The market's first customers are usually so anxious to buy anything that will satisfy their pent-up needs that they will buy almost anything. When Domino's delivered the first pizzas, expectations were much lower than today. At that time, most college students and other pizza lovers would be satisfied if the pizza was delivered within an hour, was reasonably warm, was not stuck to the carton, and cost less than $20.00! First-to-market firms also have the opportunity to have their brand become synonymous with the industry. Second-to-market firms rarely gain the distinction and publicity of first-to-market firms.

As the market matures, it gets saturated with competitors. Firms that are late to enter or that have minimal competitive advantage frequently become desperate in their efforts to attract customers from competitors. They will engage in price competition even if it means that they will lose money. They will try to get customers at any price so they can have some revenue to cover expenses. Mature markets are like quicksand. Firms without a significant competitive advantage are destined to sink into oblivion. The more they flail in desperation, the faster they go under.

The most successful firms get to the window just before it opens. They offer the market what it wants. They modify their products, services, and processes to meet market demand when it changes. As the market grows, they identify segments that represent niches where they can gain additional temporary legal monopolies by being the first to serve them. And finally, they sense when the window for that opportunity is closing so they can get out before it closes on them. They then reallocate and redirect their resources to windows that are about to open so they can delight a whole new set of customers who will be in search of a business!

The following questions can help in the evaluation of the opportunities under review:

- How long will the window of opportunity stay open?
- What is the opportunity's overall potential?
- Is the market susceptible to seasonality?
- Is the market susceptible to business cycles?
- Is the opportunity based on a real need or just a want?
- What is or will be the nature and extent of competition?
- Will the market provide niche opportunities?
- What is the ratio of firms entering the market to the number exiting the market?
- How volatile is the market?
- Is the market susceptible to sudden shifts?
- Are there any forces that could cause the window to be slammed shut?
- Are there major barriers to entry?
- What are the threats?
- Is the market susceptible to changing government regulations?
- Is the market susceptible to technological breakthroughs and obsolescence?
- Is the industry susceptible to litigation?

First Mover Advantage: The Jury is Still Out

The merit in being the first-to-market firm has recently come under closer scrutiny. This book has emphasized the benefits of being the first firm to enter the window of opportunity when it opens. Yet being the first will not guarantee success. Trying to be first to market has numerous risks.

- The window may never open.
- It may open but much later than expected.
- It may be slow in opening.
- It may not open as much as expected.
- Your offering may not be in sync with consumer needs.
- Competitors may enter sooner than expected.
- Competitors may actually enter the market with superior offerings.

Firms that try to operate at the leading edge might find themselves at the bleeding edge. Like the pioneers who tried to settle the American West, first timers might encounter various types of problems. First movers usually have to bear the burden of research and development costs. First movers usually have to spend more money on advertising and educating the market. First movers may find that prospective consumers do not embrace them. First movers may find that distribution channels either do not exist or are reluctant to do business with them. Second and subsequent movers have the opportunity to learn from the first mover's mistakes. They may also benefit from the first mover's education of the market. Second movers and other fast followers may be able to leapfrog the first mover within a short time. Norm Brodsky, who has founded numerous ventures, noted, "I never want to be first in a market. There is nothing more expensive than educating a market."[17] He also noted, "I want an industry that is antiquated. I'm talking about a business in which most companies are out of step with the customer. Maybe the customers' needs have changed and the suppliers haven't paid much attention. Maybe they're not up to date on the latest technology. In any case, there has been a change and the industry hasn't followed it."[18]

Firms that plan to be first movers need to proceed with both eyes open, for at least three reasons. First, they need to make sure the window is in fact going to open by doing good market research. Second, they need to time their launch so they do not have to wait too long. Established firms have the luxury of having existing products provide revenue for them while waiting for their new products to take off. For new ventures, however, each day without revenue puts the venture one day closer to bankruptcy. Third, they must not assume being the first mover is all the advantage the firm needs to succeed. Bill Boulding, a professor at Duke, conducted research into first movers. He noted, "I think the overriding conclusion from this research is that it's dangerous simply to think you have a first-mover advantage and that 'I'm first; therefore, I'm going to do better.' It's not just enough to be first; you need to be first with some kind of additional protection [and] some kind of sustainable advantage [such as] a patent on [your] product."[19]

REALITY CHECK

Although being first-to-market may provide a real rush, winning is about who crosses the finish line first. Don't let your ego and eagerness to be first to market cause you to enter a market prematurely. Remember the immortal words of Ernest and Julio Gallo, "We will serve no wine before its time."

REALITY CHECK

If you are first to market, don't let your arrogance keep you from continuing your efforts to do whatever it takes to maintain a competitive advantage.

What is the Nature of the Target Market?

Although the nature of the overall market is important, the target market for the firm is what matters most. Entrepreneurs need to direct their attention and resources to one or more market segments. They cannot afford to take a *shotgun approach* to the market. They need to adopt a *rifle approach* that targets one particular segment of the market that is not having its needs met at all or well enough. This focus will enable the firm to tailor its products, services, and processes to that segment's specific needs and expectations.

Each segment also represents a window of opportunity. Each has a different size, degree of profit, and duration. Some segments can be inviting and lucrative. Other segments can be like minefields where one false step can mean disaster. Entrepreneurs need to identify the segment within the overall market that represents the best opportunity for the new venture.

The questions posed about the overall nature of the market when combined with the following questions may shed light on the nature of the target market:

- Is this a one-time or repeat type of purchase?
- How lucrative will this segment be?
- What factors are critical to satisfying consumers?
- What is the frequency of purchase?
- What is the extent of brand loyalty for the companies already serving the segment?
- Is there price sensitivity?
- What is the size and strength of suppliers? Do the suppliers have power over their customers?
- What is the size and strength of distribution channels? Do distribution channels have bargaining power?

Three other points should be stressed about market opportunities. Norm Brodsky noted the importance of finding a lucrative niche. He stated that having a niche is critical to every start-up, but not for the reason most people think. It has to do with the high gross margins you must have so your start-up capital lasts long enough for your business to achieve viability. If you're a new kid in town, you can't compete on price because you'll go out of business. However, you do have to have customers. That means offering them more value at the going rate.[20]

Amar Bhidé noted that entrepreneurs must be willing to seek out profitable niches wherever they are. He noted that entrepreneurs must be willing to prosper in a backwater; dominating a neglected market segment is sometimes more profitable than intellectually stimulating or glamorous market segements. Niche enterprises can also enter the land of the living dead because their market is too small for the business to thrive but the entrepreneur has invested too much effort to be willing to quit.[21]

Rita Gunther McGrath and Ian MacMillan encourage entrepreneurs to look into the prospects for expanding into additional market niches. They note that products or services that can be spread across multiple markets may be significantly better than products or services that will live or die in one market.[22]

What is the Competitive Situation?

No firm operates in a vacuum. The presence of competition and the potential for additional competitors can play a significant role in determining whether a new venture thrives or if it barely survives. The ideal situation for a new venture would be to be the only firm serving a lucrative market. Yet even under the best conditions, monopolies are short-lived. Firms that fail to stay synchronized to the market's changing needs leave the welcome mat out for other firms to enter the marketplace with even better products, services, or processes.

The stage of the product life cycle (i.e., the relative maturity or saturation of the market) has a major impact on the nature of competition. The first consumers (frequently called innovators) are not as particular as the early adopters and early majority that enter the scene with the passage of time. The early adopters and early majority become consumers when the risk and uncertainty of trying a new product or service are reduced by the innovators.

If you are first to market and offer a credible product or service, then you will be afforded some latitude in your pricing strategy. As the market matures, consumers can choose from numerous firms. Firms with a limited or no competitive advantage have little choice but to lower their prices in an attempt to attract and keep customers. Their efforts to maintain a revenue stream usually result in declining profits. If these firms are unable to restore their competitiveness by other means than lowering their prices, then they may remain viable. If not, then it is just a matter of time before they go bankrupt. Serious repercussions also arise if your competitors expected the market to grow more than it did. Firms with excess capacity frequently lower their prices to boost volume so the facilities will not be idle. Firms that enter the market late frequently face intense price pressures as a result of the overcapacity.

Markets that are growing represent the best opportunities for two reasons. First, these markets are like a pie that is growing. Each firm will grow if it merely maintains its share or slice of the market. Second, additional segments or niches may emerge. Each emerging segment has its own particular needs and expectations. These segments are like new waves. Entrepreneurs who can identify these waves when they are being formed and who can tailor their venture's products and services to the emerging segment will enjoy a temporary legal monopoly. The best type of competition is to have no competition!

The size and nature of the firms in the market can also affect the success of a new venture. If the competition is *fragmented,* then no single firm is in a position to determine the rules for how the game will be played. If one particular firm has significant market share and a large supply of resources at its disposal, then that firm may have bargaining power over the distribution channels and with suppliers. This may give the firm a significant cost and distribution advantage. This is why it is so hard to compete against Microsoft. Brand loyalty can also affect new venture success. If the firms in the market have high brand loyalty, then a new entrant will have more difficulty attracting customers.

Other factors may also make it difficult to enter a market. At least one major business publication requires that a business be in existence for three years before it will allow that firm to advertise its products. Distribution channels may also represent a major barrier to entry. New ventures that are trying to offer products through retail outlets frequently encounter difficulty getting their new products on the retail shelf. For example, getting a new product on a grocery store shelf may be one of the greatest challenges in the world of business.

How Distinct Will Your New Venture's Market Offering Be?

If your new venture's products and services are not markedly better, more affordable, or more convenient than what is already on the market, then you should not even consider entering the market. Success is not contingent on being different; it is contingent on being better. If the market doesn't value the difference, then you have no competitive advantage. Uniqueness does not guarantee success. If your offering is distinctive in the areas that really matter, then it may be able to attract customers.

The degree of distinctiveness can have considerable impact on the firm's pricing strategy. The ability to charge higher prices without reducing demand provides that firm with a better profit margin. Higher margins enable the firm to achieve break-even volume quicker. Quicker profitability reduces new venture risk.

Entrepreneurs need to show some restraint and humility when they are developing their products and services. As they say, "The proof of the pudding is in the eating." If you believe that you have developed the greatest thing since sliced bread, then you need to step back and do a reality check to see if you are truly ahead of the pack. A recent article noted, "The more intuitively obvious your idea, the higher the likelihood that someone else is working on it as well, so even at step one there may be multiple players."[23] Richard Shaffer of Technologic Partners stated, "The *herd instinct* sometimes causes investors and entrepreneurs to seize simultaneously on the same good idea and proceed to trample it in the ensuing stampede."[24]

The problem is not that good ideas are bad but rather that good ideas may be too good. "The idea may be so intuitively obvious that the playing field becomes crowded with opponents, the message gets overhyped, expectations balloon out of control, and a hot idea becomes a flash in the pan."[25] Business writer Scott Kirsner noted, "The first law of business is that every good idea gets taken to excess."[26]

"The entrepreneur adds value through innovation in the marketplace. The successful entrepreneur uses product, process, or service innovation to exploit change. Innovation is the instrument that empowers resources to new ends, thus creating value. The enduring strength of an entrepreneurially driven economy is the continuous creation of value. Thus, in evaluating an idea, the individual must determine if the idea represents a significant innovation in the marketplace, or is it simply a different way of doing the same thing."[27]

The ultimate distinctiveness is called a *killer application*. Killer apps have the ability to change the way people live and work. They are so superior to what is on the market that they blow the competition out of the marketplace. Many entrepreneurs consider their products or services to be killer apps. This can be a mistake. Entrepreneurs frequently become so ego-involved with their products or services that they cannot see them objectively. The market, not the entrepreneur, determines whether a product or service is a killer app.

The following questions provide insight into the factors that might affect the success of the new venture's market offering:

- Is the market easy to enter?
- What are the barriers to entry?
- How much lead time do we have?
- How long will it take for competitors to enter the market?
- Do competitors have deep pockets to retaliate?
- How long will it take for competitors to match our offering?
- How have existing firms responded to competitive attacks in the past?
- What distinguishes our product from what is already out there?
- Does our new product, process, or service create value for the purchaser/consumer?
- Does our new product, process, or service make everything on the market obsolete?
- To what extent is the market satisfied with existing products and services?
- Will the product change the way people live and work?
- How sophisticated is our product or service?
- How sophisticated is the target market?
- How different is our new product, process, or service from what people are currently using?

- Is our new product, process, or service going to require people to change their habits?
- Is our new product, process, or service easy to learn how to use?
- Is our new product, process, or service easy to use?
- Will targeted consumers need to be educated on the merit of our new product, process, or service and how to use it?
- Will links in the distribution network have to be educated in the product/service and how to use our new product, process, or service?
- Are there significant switching costs involved for potential customers?
- Are there significant switching costs involved for potential distributors?
- How large is the market?
- How much market share can we gain?
- Is the market growing?
- Will everything have to be perfect to attract customers?
- Will we be seeking virgin customers?
- Will we have to steal customers from other firms?
- What is the extent of brand/institutional loyalty for existing firms?
- What are the target market(s) characteristics?
- What is the growth potential for the target market(s) and related segments?
- What is the profit potential for the target market(s) and related segments?
- Is the customer the same person as the consumer?
- What are the differences in potential for domestic and foreign markets?
- Do we have a proprietary position?
- Can we provide a high level of quality and be the low-cost provider?
- Are there substitutes?
- Can the customer do it without us? Are our customers potential competitors?
- Are there any fatal flaws that could kill acceptance of our product or service?
- Can a technological breakthrough make our product or service obsolete overnight?
- Are there other potential segments of users for the product or service?
- Are there ways to increase the usage rate by consumers?
- Are there other uses for the product or service?
- Are there potential spin-offs for the product or service?
- Can sales of our new product, process, or service be facilitated by the Internet?
- Is it possible to establish alliances with suppliers?
- Is it possible to establish alliances with distributors?
- Is it possible to establish alliances with competitors?
- Who really is the gatekeeper in the purchase decision for the product or service?
- What is the nature and extent of government regulations?
- Do we need government approval before our new product, process, or service can be offered to the public?
- Are there any regulatory changes on the horizon?
- Are channels of distribution established and interested, particularly in foreign markets?

- Will we be vulnerable to litigation, particularly for product liability?
- Can our new product, process, or service be made?
- Can a prototype be made to test production feasibility and for test marketing?
- Will we have to provide service after the sale?
- Will we have to provide a warranty?
- How easy is it to exit the market and/or business?

The preceding list of questions can be overwhelming, yet they need to be addressed. They provide a broad view of the factors that need to be considered while the new venture is determining which markets to enter and the products and services it needs to offer. The extent the firm is able to gain a competitive advantage will have a significant impact on the firm's profitability.

FINANCIAL DIMENSIONS

New ventures will be successful to the extent they create and maintain customers for a profit. The window of opportunity, target market, competitive situation, and market offering will affect the new venture's revenue stream. The revenue stream is not an end in itself. A number of firms sell themselves into bankruptcy each year. The income statement's top line is important, but its bottom line will determine whether the firm fulfills its investors' expectations and its obligations to its creditors. Profits are the fuel for paying off loans, paying dividends, investing in new product development, improving the firm's processes, rewarding the firm's human resources, and for building the value of the firm.

Each opportunity needs to be evaluated in terms of its profitability, cash flow, and return on investment. Although a threshold may be established for the overall level of attractiveness, the threshold for the market gap and financial attractiveness may vary with each opportunity. Opportunities that require a substantial investment may have a higher threshold than opportunities that place fewer resources at risk.

Scalability may be an important factor when evaluating ventures. It describes the extent the venture can be started on a small scale and then expanded in manageable increments. Bhidé noted that entrepreneurs who have limited funds should favor ventures that aren't capital intensive and have profit margins to sustain rapid growth with internally generated funds. In a similar fashion, entrepreneurs should look for ventures with a high margin for error, simple operations, and low fixed costs that are less likely to face a cash crunch because of factors such as technical delays, cost overruns, and slow buildup of sales.[28] Fred DeLuca, cofounder of Subway Restaurants, captures the nature of scalability in the title of his book, *Start Small, Finish Big*.[29]

The Return on Investment/Investment Base Matrix profiled in Exhibit 5.8 illustrates four different combinations of return on investment and the amount of capital required to start the venture.

Return on Investment	High	Sweet spot/jewel	The next big thing	
	Low	Lifestyle business	Hole in the ground	
		Minimal		Considerable
		Investment Required		

EXHIBIT 5.8   RETURN ON INVESTMENT/INVESTMENT BASE MATRIX

Entrepreneurs who want to get a significant return on their investments should direct their attention to creating ventures that have the potential to provide a lucrative return on their investments. *Sweet spot/jewel* opportunities may be the most appealing opportunities. They provide high yields yet require a minimal investment.

Sweet spot/jewel opportunities, however, may have two relative drawbacks. First, if they do not take a significant investment, then there may be few barriers to entry for potential competitors. If you have a proprietary position that prohibits competitors, then you may be in a very enviable position. Second, there may be situations when the return on investment may be high in percentage terms, but the yield in absolute dollars may not be enough in real dollars to satisfy your overall yield objectives. For example, a venture that generates a 1,500 percent return on a $1,000 investment will only yield a $15,000 profit. That would be a great return if it was an investment in a stock, but it may not be enough return in absolute dollars to justify all the time and effort you will devote to starting and running a business. Opportunities that have sweet spot/jewel potential that can generate lucrative returns in relative and absolute dollars should be sought.

The *next big thing* type of opportunities can also be appealing, but they usually have a substantial initial capital requirement. They may also require a regular infusion of capital to get them to the point where they dominate a substantial market.

Lifestyle ventures have merit for people who are looking for an alternative to working for someone else and who are not ambitious from a financial standpoint. Hole-in-the-ground ventures are to be avoided. They require substantial investment but provide minimal, if any, return on investment. They are like pleasure boats. Most people who have owned a boat describe their boats as a hole in the water that you pour money into. Many boat owners consider the term *pleasure boat* to be an oxymoron!

The classic return on investment formula divides the level of profit by the investment. The formula permits different opportunities to be compared to one another. It also provides a good basis for establishing a threshold for evaluating opportunities. You will need to determine the appropriate threshold for your new venture. The most common financial threshold is the rate you could get for an investment with a moderate risk. If you believe you could get a 10 percent return in a relatively risk-free investment, then why should you risk your whole investment in a new venture that would provide a lower return? If you will be seeking additional investors, then the threshold must be high enough to attract their attention.

The threshold is usually a few points above the rate you could get for a safe investment. The threshold may be anywhere from 12 to 15 percent. If bond yields are high or the stock market is climbing, then the threshold may need to be higher to cover the opportunity cost of investing in the venture and to attract outside investors. When the threshold is raised, opportunities that do not generate a higher level of profit per dollar invested are dropped from consideration.

Profit margin is actually the result of two margins. The first margin is gross margin. Gross margin is determined by subtracting the cost of the goods sold from sales. The cost of goods sold includes what you paid for the products you sold or the payroll expenses for the people who provided the services if you are in a service business. The gross margin is influenced by your firm's cost structure. It is also influenced by its ability to charge what the market is willing to pay. As noted earlier, the ideal situation is for a new venture to have a temporary legal monopoly. This gives the firm considerable latitude in pricing its products or services.

Kenneth Olm and George Eddy noted, "Profit margin potential depends on a number of factors. The first and most critical is the existence of a strong market for the product/service.

The second is the ability to differentiate the product in the mind of the consumer so that intense competition is not encountered. Another important consideration is the ability to isolate yourself from intense competition by patents, copyrights, or geography."[30] Having a temporary legal monopoly or even a significant competitive advantage does not mean you should skim the market by charging an outrageous price. Such a strategy could generate considerable ill will from consumers. It would also invite competition.

The *operating* expenses also affect the firm's profit margin. If you do not control regular operating expenses (salaries, rent, advertising, etc.), then the profit margin will be reduced. Perceptive marketing can enhance your gross margin, but it will take savvy management to keep the other expenses in line. This is why the skills and experience of the entrepreneur and the management team are so important. Their skills and experience will help them know where money should be spent and where it must be controlled. Managing growth is like having your foot on the accelerator. Successful entrepreneurs are able to differentiate between too little, too much, and just the right amount of selling and administrative expenses.

It would be time and cost prohibitive to do an in-depth analysis of the financials for every opportunity under review. You need to come up with estimates of the level of sales, the associated expenses, the resulting profit, and the corresponding investment for each opportunity. You do not need to develop full-blown projections; ballpark figures will be sufficient to determine if the opportunity exceeds the threshold. If you are reviewing just a couple of opportunities at this stage, then you may consider running three different sales scenarios for each opportunity. You would run best-case, most-likely, and worst-case sales projections for the first five years.

The sales projections serve as the foundation for the corresponding profit and return on investment estimates. Each of the opportunities would then be ranked to determine their financial strength. This approach may also be helpful in determining the degree of risk for each opportunity. Opportunities that exceed the threshold with even their worst-case scenario are particularly noteworthy. Robert Morris Associates' (RMA's) *Annual Statement Studies* and numerous business magazines provide useful financial benchmarks for profitability and return on investment. Service businesses that usually require small capital investments usually generate higher profit margins. The following questions provide valuable insights when evaluating the financial worthiness of each opportunity:

- What is the return on investment threshold?
- What is the initial capital requirement?
- What is the projected return on investment?
- How much money do I have available to invest?
- Are there areas where I can reduce costs constructively via the learning curve?
- What is the assets-to-sales ratio? (This indicates how much money will be required to support growth.)
- What is the gross margin to sales ratio?
- What is the net profit margin to sales ratio?
- What is the break-even point?
- What is the burn rate? (daily cash outlay to keep the business running)
- What is the cash flow?
- How soon will the firm achieve positive cash flow?

- Is the financial side of the firm easy for bankers and investors to understand?
- What are the financial risks?
- How forgiving are the financials?
- How easy is it to cash out of the business?

Each opportunity should be evaluated for at least its first five years of operation. Profitability in the first year is not as critical as cash flow. Few firms make a profit in the first year. Cash flow is critical from the beginning, however, because it is the lifeblood of the new venture. Too many new ventures die on the vine because they run out of cash. The ideal situation would be for the new venture to have a hockey-stick or J-shaped growth curve and substantial margins. Opportunities that can maintain a 20+ percent annual growth rate, have at least a 10 to 15 percent profit on sales after tax, and generate a 20 to 25 percent return on investment will help justify risking your time and money.

Veteran entrepreneurs frequently reflect on what would be the ideal situation from a financial perspective when starting a new venture. They list such factors as the ability to make an extraordinary return on a minimal investment, the ability to generate positive cash flow and profitability right away, minimal loss if things do not work out, ease of cashing out, and a steady stream of people who want to buy the venture that will give you an incredible gain.

It was once noted that it takes seven years to find out if the venture is truly successful and less than two years to find out if it is a loser. The time to reach profitability and positive cash flow is important because it reduces your financial vulnerability. The ability to generate a favorable position is also important because it makes it easier to sell the venture if you find your talent and interests are more in starting ventures than managing them. The longer it takes the venture to generate solid financial returns, the greater the risk. Patrick Duffeler, who founded Williamsburg Winery, started his venture with the prospect of going seven years before it would generate any sales revenue. He noted, however, that if the venture did not generate a profit, at least he could spend the rest of his life liquidating the inventory!

The time frame and return on investment are important for another reason. Both factors will influence how much time and money you may be willing to commit to the venture. If your goal is to build an exceptional enterprise and own it for some time, then you will look at the financial worthiness of various opportunities from a long-term perspective. If you want to cash out within a few years, then you will need to direct your attention to opportunities that generate favorable financials right away. The time frame and the amount of money required for the venture may also affect your evaluation of various opportunities. Kathleen Allen, author of *Bringing New Technology to Market,* noted that if you have developed a highly innovative product or service and are not committed to the long haul and/or have limited funds, then you should consider licensing or selling it to another firm rather than doing it all yourself.[31]

IDENTIFYING EACH OPPORTUNITY'S RESOURCE REQUIREMENTS

Each opportunity will require a different set of resources. The resources may include materials, equipment, skilled labor, intellectual property, and money. Some opportunities will be very capital intensive. Some of the opportunities that require substantial resources may be able to reduce their resource needs through outsourcing, joint ventures, by forming alliances, or by leasing. Other opportunities may require few resources. Low- or no-tech firms require fewer resources because they might not need sophisticated equipment and require little training. Service organizations also tend to require fewer resources.

Resources need to be viewed as more than logistical necessities. They can provide the new venture with competitive advantages. Resources are like time. It was once noted, "With time all is possible, without it nothing is possible." You need to identify the resource requirement for each opportunity. You then compare each opportunity with your resource threshold. The resource threshold will be influenced by the money you have at your disposal. Your money may be leveraged to bring in additional investors and loans. The financial attractiveness of the opportunities that are being evaluated will also affect the amount of capital that can be raised. Opportunities that offer high returns with low risk will attract more money and other critical resources. The following questions help in the evaluation of the opportunities under review:

- What is the resource threshold?
- What resources will be required to start the venture?
- What is the cost of the resources?
- Will additional resources be required after the start-up stage?
- What resources do I have at this time?
- Is there a resource gap?
- What skills and capabilities do I need to acquire via hiring?
- What is the level of availability for key talent?
- What resources can be acquired by having additional investors?
- What resources can be acquired by loans?
- What resources can be obtained through leasing?
- What resources can be obtained through licensing?
- What resources can be obtained through alliances?
- What resources can be obtained through joint ventures?
- Are there any intellectual property considerations?
- Is the computer hardware and software required readily available?
- Can I secure the needed licenses, permits, zoning?
- Can the firm develop intellectual property?
- What will it take to protect the firm's intellectual property?

The resource audit for each alternative can be revealing. It may reveal that the resource requirements for some opportunities exceed what is available. You may find that a firm in the marketplace has the patent or an exclusive license agreement to a product, process, or technology that you needed to capitalize on that particular opportunity. The resource audit may indicate that certain types of equipment are not available or affordable. It may also reveal that certain types of talent are in such short supply that the firm would be vulnerable if it could not attract and keep those people. "In addition to the typical demands of running a business, tech entrepreneurs have a whole different set of issues to deal with when growing their companies. With today's shortage of technical workers, they must find creative ways to retain employees who could quit and find a higher-paying job the very next day."[32] The resource audit may also indicate that the firm would have to do extensive training and/or hire union workers.

What Happens if None of the Opportunities Exceeds the Three Thresholds?

It is possible that none of the opportunities under consideration achieves sufficient critical mass for launching a new venture. If this is the case, then you have three choices. Your first alternative is to start the process all over and scan the market for opportunities that have recently emerged or that you may have originally missed. The marketplace is changing so quickly that gaps are constantly occurring that represent new venture opportunities. If you are truly committed to the entrepreneurial journey, then you should consider the time invested so far as a learning experience rather than as a waste of your time.

The second alternative involves lowering the threshold for one or more of the three dimensions in the entrepreneurial pyramid. You need to be objective and ask yourself if the thresholds were realistic in the first place. Some entrepreneurs are so risk averse that they set the thresholds too high. These entrepreneurs want to have their cake and eat it too. They want the market to be attractive and the financials to be so lucrative that there will be little risk.

Opportunities should be evaluated according to their risk/return/degree of challenge ratio. The entrepreneur's sense of achievement also varies in proportion to the degree of challenge and risks associated with creating each type of venture.

Some entrepreneurs are so fixated on starting a venture—any venture—that they rationalize away their original thresholds. They lower the thresholds until one of the opportunities achieves critical mass. If the thresholds are lowered because they were unrealistically high, then such an effort may be appropriate. If the thresholds are lowered out of desperation, then the entrepreneurial journey should be stopped at this time.

Entrepreneurs who let their emotions preempt the need to systematically and objectively analyze the new venture situation are usually the ones who drive up the failure rate. If you hear yourself saying, "I've already made up my mind, don't confuse me with the facts," then prepare yourself for a very unpleasant journey. The need to maintain objectivity is one of the reasons you should have an advisory board from the beginning of your entrepreneurial journey. If the advisory board is composed of people who are experienced, objective, and candid, then they will provide the dose of reality needed to keep you from boldly going where you *shouldn't* go.

The third alternative is to pack up your tent and end your entrepreneurial journey. You may be like a number of people who looked and didn't leap! You may have found that what you were looking for wasn't available or that you did not have the skills or resources needed to take the plunge. To not venture forward is not to have failed; it may be the smartest thing to do. Some things shouldn't be forced. Entrepreneurship is one of those things.

RANKING THE OPPORTUNITIES

Let's assume that a few opportunities have made it through the screening process. Now, it is time to look at the opportunities from a relative point of view. If resources are available and the entrepreneur and team have the necessary skills and capabilities, then the evaluation process comes down to (1) financial attractiveness, (2) projected risk, and (3) personal preference. The remaining opportunities can be rated on a 10-point scale for each of these three criteria.

Each type of stakeholder may place a different weight on each of the factors. Sophisticated investors place little value on the emotional appeal of the opportunity. They look at each opportunity's financial worthiness and how it fits their overall investment portfolio.

Investors look for opportunities that will provide significant capital appreciation with an acceptable risk. Less sophisticated investors may place a personal preference fudge factor on opportunities that are in their zone of familiarity. Although they may not admit it, most people would rather invest in something that has emotional appeal such as a minor league baseball franchise, rather than a worm farm or a medical waste disposal business.

Bankers look at the degree of risk in their evaluation of a loan application. Each loan request is reviewed to determine inherent risk and ability to pay off the note. Although bankers do not focus their attention on the opportunity's ability to generate considerable wealth, they do place a premium on business opportunities that will borrow larger amounts of money to finance additional growth.

The entrepreneur's personal preference is rarely left out of the evaluation equation and the final decision. Personal preference should be considered at this stage. Personal preference can be weighted to reflect how important it may be to the entrepreneur. Most entrepreneurs place a high weight on personal preference. Because they will be investing their blood, sweat, and tears in the venture as well as their own money, they tend to place a premium on opportunities that fit their personal interests. If they like to travel, entertain, and products that make a difference in people's lives, then they may place a premium on opportunities that supplement financial rewards with nonfinancial rewards.

The desire to do something that fits the entrepreneur's interests and desires may far outweigh their concern for wealth and aversion to risk. Steve Schussler, who created Rainforest Café, may be one of the best examples of the role that passion plays for an entrepreneur who is driven to see his dream for creating a Disney-like family restaurant realized. His passion for his venture gave him the resilience needed to face all the challenges and to bounce back from all the setbacks associated with turning his concept into reality. Most people would have thrown in the towel when faced with just a fraction of the situations he encountered in the years he devoted to developing his innovative restaurant.

Risk, financial worthiness, and personal preference may vary from industry to industry. The rate of technological change and obsolescence place most firms in a very precarious position. Some industries can be lucrative for the firms that are in sync with market realities. Some industries allow some leeway for firms that seem to have questionable standards and practices. You should step back and ask yourself if you are willing to take that level of risk, commit the level of resources to capture lucrative gains, and whether you want to put yourself in a situation where the firms you may be competing with or the customers you may be serving may have questionable standards.

In the Opportunity Rating System profiled in Exhibit 5.9 the entrepreneur then assigns a weight to each of the three criteria that reflects its relative importance. The weight factor can range from 1 to 5. The rating for each opportunity on a 10-point scale for each of the three criteria is then multiplied by the weighting factor. The example indicates the relative rating of two opportunities.

Criteria and Weighting	(%)	Opportunity A	Opportunity B
Financial Worthiness	40% or 0.4	0.4 × 8 rating = 3.2	0.4 × 7 rating = 2.8
Degree of Risk*	40% or 0.4	0.4 × 6 rating = 2.4	0.4 × 8 rating = 3.2
Personal Preference	20% or 0.2	0.2 × 8 rating = 1.6	0.2 × 7 rating = 1.4
Total	100%	7.2	7.4
* Higher ratings indicate lower levels of risk			

EXHIBIT 5.9   OPPORTUNITY RATING SYSTEM

The *all things considered* nature of the overall rating system enables all the opportunities to be ranked that met the threshold requirements. Opportunity B has a higher overall rating than Opportunity A. Although B might not be as lucrative as A, its lower level of risk outweighed A's financial worthiness. The lower level of risk also outweighed the higher personal preference rating of Opportunity A.

IT'S TIME TO DETERMINE IF THE MARKET TRULY VALUES YOUR PRODUCT/SERVICE CONCEPT

Most of your analysis until now has been at a fairly superficial level. Now it is time to do a more in-depth analysis of whether consumers are in search of a business and whether your product/service concept is truly in sync with their needs.

There are various levels of market research. Each level is intended to reveal a particular type of information. The following steps capture the multiple iterations of market research.

1. *Initial market research.* This is when you listen to the market to see if there are gaps where people's needs are not being met well or at all.

2. *Identify and articulate a particular need.* You tighten up the general gap into a more specific need.

3. *Develop a preliminary concept.* You develop a preliminary product/service concept to meet the need.

4. *Market research round two.* You go back into the marketplace to ask prospective consumers and distributors about their perceptions of your product/service concept.

5. *Learn from the market research.* Analyze the comments and suggestions made by potential consumers and distributors.

6. *Modify your product/service concept to incorporate what you learned.*

7. *Test market the modified product/service concept again in the market.*

8. *Take what you have learned from the market and develop a basic prototype.*

9. *Test market the prototype to see how potential consumers and distributors like it.*

10. *Modify the prototype given what you learned from the market.*

11. *Possibly test market the modified prototype again to see if potential consumers and distributors like it.*

12. *Take what you have learned from the test market and forecast the corresponding level of the sales.*

Market research is a multi-iterative learning process. Each level should provide valuable insights into what consumers really want and whether your product/service meets their needs. The first three steps of market research were completed as you went into the ranking process that compared the opportunities that made it through the screening process. The remaining steps will be covered in the following sections.

The ranking system should have identified the best opportunity for the new venture. The opportunity has to clear two hurdles, however, before you go much further. Almost all of the evaluation stage has been centered on researching the merit of each opportunity. Now it is time to see if the targeted opportunity has the potential to actually fly. It is time to determine if the timing is right and if the market is ripe. It is time to do a test market to see if the product or service is valued enough by the target market. It is also time to do a technical and logistics study to determine if the product and service can actually be provided.

The hurdles will indicate if the opportunity is at the green-light stage in the entrepreneurial stoplight where all systems are go for developing the business plan. The hurdles might indicate that the targeted opportunity is at the yellow-light stage where you may need to proceed with caution. The yellow-light stage indicates that some issue(s) need further investigation to see if changes can be made to turn it into a green light. If the issue(s) cannot be resolved, then that opportunity should be dropped from consideration.

The hurdles might indicate the targeted opportunity is at the red-light stage. Two situations can produce a red light. A red light might occur if a number of minor issues exist that cast a shadow of doubt on the viability and merit of the opportunity. A red light might also occur if a fatal flaw is found. Although the analysis of an opportunity is not intended to look at minute details, it may identify one or more fatal flaws. Fatal flaws are issues or factors that automatically drop the opportunity from consideration. Fatal flaws may include a crucial assumption about the market not holding up to a reality check. A closer look may reveal that the window of opportunity may not open for a number of years. It may also indicate that another firm is on the verge of introducing a killer app that wasn't on the radar screen when you started evaluating the list of opportunities. A closer look may also indicate there are just too many bugs to be worked out before you can bring the product or service to market in a timely fashion.

Your analysis may reveal that the challenges associated with the targeted opportunity may not be formidable. You may find that the opportunity is not as complicated as it appeared when it was originally identified. You may find that it actually appeals to your interests and that when you learned the jargon, you were able to learn about the technology and market conditions. You might find that a trade association offers a wealth of information and services for people who plan to start a business in that industry. You might find that professional organizations have departments to help their clients. Some accounting firms, legal practices, staffing firms, banks and other financial institutions have specialists in certain industries. You might also find that key technical people that need to be hired are readily available.

The remainder of this chapter is directed to getting information so you go from the present concept stage to the point where you know whether you should prepare a business plan or drop that opportunity altogether and explore other entrepreneurial opportunities.

Market Research Round Two

The first round of market research may have revealed that there was a gap in the market. This round asks more probing questions to learn more about what consumers want and how they perceive your product/service concept. Don Debelak noted the importance of conducting market research, especially if you are the inventor of the product or service. Debelak noted that inventors usually don't have the same buying motivations as most consumers.[33]

Not all ideas catch on. What might seem logical to the inventor might not be embraced by others. Although inventors may live by the saying, "If you build a better mousetrap, the world will beat a path to your door," entrepreneurs should still conduct research to see if consumers are looking for a better way to get rid of mice, whether consumers consider the trap to be better, and if they will buy it. As noted in Chapter 2, Walt Hobbs spent three years developing Seat Down—a hydraulic device that automatically lowers the toilet seat. Hobbs wanted to create a product that would help women who lived with inconsiderate men. The device lowers the seat 90 seconds after the pedal has been pressed that raises it.[34]

Two cautions need to be raised before proceeding with the following steps. First, market research is not a science. Market research information is not always accurate. What people say and what they do can be different. Second, there are no perfect products or services. You must recognize that your product/service cannot be all things to all people. Your venture's success will be contingent on the extent it meets the target market's needs and has a sustainable competitive advantage. If you try to make it perfect, then you will probably never launch it because you will be constantly making changes in response to market feedback or your desire to make it perfect. Remember, the key is to offer the market a product/service that is markedly better and valued—it does not have to be perfect.

Round two is directed to gaining insights from potential customers and distributors by asking them perceptive questions. You want to know if there is a genuine need and what you will need to offer your target market to give them a compelling reason to buy your product/service offering. This step attempts to probe problem–solution issues. Round two may use various market research techniques for gaining useful insights. You may consider sending a one-page product/service specification sheet to some prospects and asking them for their comment about its merit and how it could be improved to make it more appealing to them. You may also consider surveying people at trade shows, contacting user groups, and/or conducting focus groups to learn what they want and where existing businesses are not meeting their needs.

Round two may also include strategies for gaining insights from potential consumers about your concept to see if potential consumers see your product/service concept as a solution to their problems. As noted in Chapter 3, Scot Wingo's background in information technology helped him notice that a number of users of a particular software package were very frustrated about its inability to provide a user-friendly approach to their problems. He sent a message to the chat room that asked, "If a product was introduced that could—would you buy it?" His inquiry brought forth a tsunami of interest in such a product. When his suggestion to his employer that that firm pursue such a product fell on deaf ears, he quit his job and cofounded Stingray Software to provide the market what it wanted. He found that if you can provide customers with a way to solve problems in ways that will enhance their profits and/or competitiveness, then they will find a way to buy the product or service. He also found that they will not be that sensitive to the price if you can provide the product/service ASAP. Ideally, your research will indicate your target market believes your product/service will change their lives or enhance their firm's profitability.

A number of the firms that have made the *Inc.* 100 list are business-to-business enterprises. Many *Inc.* 100 founders attribute some of their success to their solicitation of customer (including prospective customer) input and their willingness to modify and, in some cases, tailor their firm's offerings to their customers' desires.

Learning from the Market Research

Round two market research can be seen as an out-of-body experience for the entrepreneur. It forces the entrepreneur to seek real information from real consumers about their needs and the entrepreneur's concept. Many entrepreneurs fall in love with their product/service concepts. They believe the world has a need for them, and that consumers will be delighted with their product/service offering.

Round two represents a crucial and timely reality test for the entrepreneur. Some entrepreneurs are reluctant to do the market research because they do not want to take the time or spend the money to do it. Some entrepreneurs are reluctant to do it because they are afraid that someone will steal their idea. Some entrepreneurs don't do it because they have already made up their mind and don't want to be confused with the facts.

Unfortunately, round two can be a Catch 22 for numerous reasons. There is no doubt that you need to learn as much as possible about the market and to reality test your concept. Yet, you also need to recognize that you are shooting at a moving target that can be fairly amorphous. As noted earlier, the best way to reduce risk is to learn as much as you can about the situation before making a decision. This is what venture capitalists call due diligence. Market research attempts to get complete, accurate, and timely information. You need to recognize, however, that you will never have complete, timely, and accurate information. Prospective entrepreneurs need to recognize there is a time to think, a time to analyze—and then there is a time to take the entrepreneurial leap. Prospective entrepreneurs need to recognize that there is a time to decide and a time to act. The quest for perfect information which leads to certainty when coupled with the aversion to making mistakes can stop the entrepreneurial journey in its tracks. Gary Hoover, founder of Bookstop Inc. (now part of Barnes & Noble, Hoover's Inc.) noted, "I'm a big numbers guy but I also know there is a place for intuition. You can't get paralyzed by analysis. I love analysis, but you need to know when to stop it and say, 'Yeah, there's something here' and roll with it. You've just got to do that."[35] Exhibit 5.10 profiles the role that information plays in decision making.

You should use market research techniques, yet you should also recognize that conventional market research techniques have a number of drawbacks. First, market research techniques take time and money. Second, the information you gain from them may be as perishable as today's news. What people say they want and what other firms offer tend to change over time. Here is another Catch 22. If you listen to what consumers say and make the changes, then you run the risk of making changes that accommodate today's concerns rather than directing your attention to what consumers will want when you actually bring the product/service to market. Third, there may be a big difference between what consumers say and what they will actually do. Fourth, consumers may not be in a position to articulate their needs or imagine what might be possible.

The first and second drawbacks are fairly self-explanatory and have already been addressed. The third and fourth drawbacks warrant additional discussion. The third drawback can be addressed if you design a good test market program. The fourth drawback needs to be considered when you conduct market research. A number of firms have found that consumers may not grasp the merit of various products or their widespread adoption. David Packard, cofounder of Hewlett-Packard, noted that market research conducted when black-and-white printers were new and not sophisticated clearly showed that customers were not looking for color printers.[36] If your product is sufficiently new or different, such as Ted Turner's CNN, Pleasant Rowland's American Girl Collection, Mary Kay Ash's skin-care classes, Land's instant camera, and Morita's Walkman, then it is unlikely that traditional market research will be of much help.[37]

Akio Morita, cofounder of Sony, indicated, "Our plan is to lead the public with new products rather than ask them what kinds of products they want. The public does not know what is possible, but we do. So instead of doing a lot of market research, we refine our

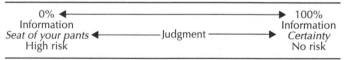

EXHIBIT 5.10   ROLE OF INFORMATION IN DECISION MAKING

thinking on a product and its use and try to create a market for it by educating and communicating with the public."[38] Sony used this mentality when it introduced the Walkman. Most people thought there would be little interest in portable tape players. By introducing a high-quality tape player for joggers and other target markets, Sony found there was, in fact, considerable interest in such a product. Morita noted, "I do not believe that any amount of market research could have told us that the Sony Walkman would be successful, not to say a sensational hit that would spawn so many imitators."[39] He noted that when you ask people what they want, they tend to cite minor modifications in what is available. Most consumers are not able to envision breakthrough innovations. Entrepreneurs may need to be a bit more cautious than Sony, however, because Sony has a whole portfolio of products. Sony, unlike a startup, does not have its future tied to one product.

Market research may be a multi-iterative process where one round of market research leads to new insights that are incorporated into the product/service concept. The modified product/service concept is then subjected to another round of market research to see if it is more appealing to the target market. As noted earlier, while you may be tempted to do round after round of market research to improve your product/service concept and to reduce the risk, you need to move ahead with the test market of the product/service. Entrepreneurs need to remember the immortal words of Noah when he stated, "The time for predicting rain is over; the time for building arks has begun."

IT'S TIME TO TEST MARKET YOUR PRODUCT/SERVICE

The test market represents a trial run. Unlike the first two rounds of market research, which look for feedback on a product/service concept, the test market usually involves presenting a prototype to a group of potential customers or distributors.

The test market does two things. First, it indicates the level of interest in the product or service the firm plans to offer the target market. Second, it may provide useful feedback. Test markets frequently provide insights into distribution preferences, price sensitivity, quality perceptions, and service-after-the-sale expectations.

It is important that you get some reading on the level of consumer interest in your proposed product/service because very few new products are commercial successes. Testing a well-documented product/service concept, or better yet, an actual prototype, can provide valuable feedback. Wilson Harrell, an entrepreneur and publisher of *Inc.* magazine, offered two interesting ways to gauge consumer response to your idea. His "Well, I'll Be Damned Test" encourages entrepreneurs to show a proposed product or service to 20 objective people. It will be even better if they can actually sample your product or service. If most of them don't say, "Well, I'll be damned!" or "Why didn't I think of that?" stop right there. However, if most of the people you ask say the magic words, you're on the right track. Harrell's "Would You Buy This Product?" test involves tabulating the responses to the question, "Would you buy this product?" Take 100 percent of the for-sure answers and 50 percent of the maybe answers. If that total is more than 50 percent of the answers (of the people who responded), you have a fighting chance; 65 percent is okay; more than 85 percent is great.[40]

Test marketing can be done in numerous ways. The key, however, is to get the product/service in front of potential consumers and distributors. The test market should also provide insights into the relative positioning of the product or service in relation to the other products and services in the market.

Entrepreneurs have developed rather ingenious ways to learn about the target market's level of interest in a product or service. Some entrepreneurs will run an ad in a magazine to see what type of response it generates. Vinu Malik, who developed a revolutionary bottle system for holding water for runners, ran an ad for his new product before he had perfected it to see if people were interested.[41] Other entrepreneurs will take a prototype to a trade show to see if it generates interest and orders. A test market may involve letting a select sample of potential consumers use your product/service for a couple of weeks as mini-beta sites.

Rob Ryan stressed the value of beta-testing it in a few different market segments to learn which applications have the strongest potential for development and growth.[42] By testing the product/service with various consumers, you may find opportunities may not be where you initially expected to find them. Some of the consumers may suggest ways to modify the product/service to fit their particular needs. They may even identify different uses, applications, and/or distribution avenues for the product/service. Ryan noted that a common mistake made early in the start-up process by entrepreneurs who have an interesting core ability or technology is that they frequently develop it into the wrong product and/or aim it at the wrong market.[43] It may be worthwhile to test market the prototype with more than one target market. He also noted that entrepreneurs should be open to the possibility that the customer might take your product or service in an unexpected direction.[44]

Honda provides an excellent example of what can be learned when you get the prototype in the hands of potential consumers. When Honda test marketed its original line of motorcycles, it found that consumers were not impressed with it. One prospective customer in California took it home and rode it off the street on trails. Honda found that the motorcycle had far more appeal if it could be modified as a scrambler—or what would later be known as a dirt bike.

Your test market efforts may also benefit if they include suppliers and distributors. They may be in a position to provide useful feedback and suggestions. By talking to people in the distribution channels, then entrepreneurs can get a better idea of whether they have a killer app or just an incremental improvement.

Test marketing should indicate if the product or service gets the target market's attention, if the target market is interested, and if the target market will actually buy the product or service. Test markets may be particularly beneficial if the product is markedly different from what is currently on the market. "Make sure your products are unique, but not so different that your customers don't know what to make of them."[45]

The test market should indicate whether potential consumers place your product/service in the "nice to have," "like to have," or "must have right now!" category. The test market should indicate how compelling the product/service is as well as how sensitive consumers are to the price of the product/service.

REALITY CHECK

Expect people to say, "It's a great idea; of course I'd buy it." Good intentions don't guarantee sales. Talk is cheap. Talk to the decision makers—the people who do the buying. Ask them If this was available right now at $x would you buy it, or could I send an invoice?

Rob Ryan emphasizes the importance of making sure the market research and test market are directed to the right people. He encourages entrepreneurs to make a list of the top target markets. The entrepreneur should identify the top three market leaders in each target market. The entrepreneur should then get an insider to steer the entrepreneur to the right person. He noted that when the entrepreneur gets a meeting with each person to talk about the product/service idea, the entrepreneur should leave the PowerPoint at home. Instead, he recommends sharing your idea and letting that person talk, because sometimes the best ideas pop up at the end of the meetings. Ryan stresses the need to ask about what problems can the product solve and how it can be changed to fit the prospect's needs exactly. He also encourages the entrepreneur to be prepared to say when the product will be ready for delivery—if the customer wants to place an order.[46]

Three examples help illustrate the role that test marketing can play in the decision to commit resources. Years ago, film studios used to invite people to a prerelease screening of a new movie. The studio would then call the neighbors of the people who attended the screening. The studio asked them if they had heard about the film from a neighbor, and if the neighbor had liked the film. The studios then plotted the extent that the people talked to their neighbors about the film. The test market resembled a stone being dropped in a pond. The films that had the biggest favorable ripples were likely to generate the highest levels of viewership. The premise was that people frequently tell others about films they liked or disliked. Word-of-mouth recommendations can be a good barometer of market acceptance.

In the 1990s, Lee Iacocca conveyed the level of market response he wanted for the new models he wanted Chrysler to develop. Iacocca said he was tired of offering cars that the majority of people surveyed liked. He indicated that there are a lot of cars on the market that were offered by Chrysler's competitors that people liked. Iacocca told his new car development team to come up with cars that cause people to drop what they are doing and chase them down the street so they can buy them! The *drop everything and buy the product on the spot* criteria provided valuable feedback about the level of interest when a prototype was tested in the market.

Rob Vito developed ezAUDIO, a transmitter and receiver box that delivers sound through speakers plugged into a wall socket anywhere in the house, no matter where the stereo is. Myr Jones, who helped perfect the technology, noted that at trade shows, "People would see it and still not believe it." [47]

Prototypes can play a key role in test marketing and technical testing. The sooner a prototype of a product or service can be developed and tested, the better. One software firm runs various tests before it introduces new products or updates to its current products. For example, the firm brings potential customers into a specially equipped room to try its latest prototype. Cameras monitor the people's eyes to determine if they are able to follow the instructions for booting up the software and running the program. Eye movement indicates when the user doesn't understand the instructions and when the program is not running smoothly. The firm's goal is to make its software so user-friendly that there are no breaks in the action. Its test markets provide valuable feedback on the level of satisfaction with the software and whether the product is free of technical glitches. The firm even studies the ease of opening the shrink-wrapped box so that it isn't a source of frustration for its customers.

Entrepreneurs need to remember that the purpose of test marketing is to learn as quickly as possible about how prospective consumers view the product/service. This is not the time to try to develop the perfect prototype. W. Keith Schilit noted, "A trend among better managed entrepreneurial companies has been to adhere to a philosophy of developing a pilot project (or prototype), testing reactions, refining the product, and then getting it out to the market shortly thereafter. This will enable you to obtain some preliminary indication of customer appeal—something that investors require—and to perfect the product or service when you eventually market it on a larger scale." [48]

Test marketing may also be a multi-iterative process. If the feedback suggests major changes in the product/service, then it may be worthwhile to test the modified product/service to see if it actually garners a higher level of interest. Again, entrepreneurs need to resist the temptation to do round after round of test marketing. The key is to do rapid prototyping, rapid learning, and then rapid turnaround by testing the modified prototype.

If the prototype is considered to be significantly better than what is on the market, then it may be better to err on the side of getting to market too early rather than a little late. The longer you wait for actual product launch, the greater the chance that another firm will steal your thunder or that consumers may change their preferences. Improving the prototype has value but make sure you do not succumb to paralysis by analysis. The test market should address the following questions:

- Do people really want the product or service?
- What is their level of interest?
- Are there enough customers out there who will buy the product?
- Can they tell the difference between the firm's planned offering and products and services already available?
- What price are they prepared to pay for the product or service?
- How do they want to buy the product?
- How frequently would they buy the product or service?
- What brand do they currently buy?
- Are there other users for the product/service?
- Are there other uses for the product/service?

REALITY CHECK

Market research and test marketing should be handled in a discrete manner. In your zeal to gain insights try to operate below competitors' radar. There are trade-offs between getting information and letting potential competitors know what you are doing. J. William Gurley noted, "When you declare yourself king, you annoy the really big kings in neighboring lands. Jealous of the attention you're receiving, they direct their great assets and focus their business development on your space. Before you know it, there are 15 companies committed to the market—and your product is still in beta testing."[49] This is one of the reasons why rapid prototyping and rapid test marketing are encouraged. By learning quickly and incorporating what you have learned in the shortest period of time, the quicker you can launch the venture. The sooner you can get the product/service into the market, the greater the head start you have over competitors.

It's Time for the Dog Food Test

It has already been noted that entrepreneurs in general and inventor entrepreneurs in particular tend to be less than objective when viewing their proposed product/service offering and its corresponding market acceptance. Most entrepreneurs think customers will beat a path to their door and open their wallets to reward the entrepreneurs for how they have changed their lives.

Venture capital firms have developed their own jargon for evaluating the relative merit of new product/service ideas. They call it the *dog food test*. They want to know if the dogs (targeted customers) will actually eat (buy) the dog food (proposed product/service).

Rob Ryan's Dog Food Test

Rate each of these categories with a number from 1 (worst) to 10 (best):

1. Idea – Is it sufficiently developed to have customers? That's a 10. If it is still in the dream   stage, it's a 1.

2. Customers – Is the idea aimed at *paying* customers? Rate their potential from 1 to 10.

3. Money – Is it clear how the business makes money now (not ten years from now)? If it's a very clear, easy-to-explain model, give it a 10.

4. Application – Is there a clear business problem that the product solves? If so, it's a 10. If it's just kind of fun to have, it's a 1.

5. Uniqueness – It ranks a 10 if the solution is unique. Give it a 1 if it's merely a variation on some existing theme.

6. Value – Is the value proposition extremely clear? Does it save a measurable amount of money? Then it's a 10.

7. Barriers – Does the product, once built, throw up sufficient barriers to entry? If the barriers   buy the company about a year, it's a 10. Lower the rating for less time.

8. Strategy – Does the product or service directly impact the customer's bottom line? Or is it just nice to have? (For example, customer relations management is strategic – a 10. Training internal people on Office 2000 is important, but not strategic – a 5 or 6.)

9. Competition – Are lots of others doing the same thing? The fewer the competitors, the higher the score.

10. Scalability – Once your customer adopts the product or service, will it spread rapidly to other customers (or other parts of the company, if your client is a corporation)? The faster and more places it spreads, the higher the rating.

Reprinted from Rob Ryan, *Smartups: Lessons from Rob Ryan's Entrepreneur America Boot Camp* (Ithaca: Cornell University Press, 2001), p. 37. Copyright © 2001 by Rob Ryan. Used with permission of the publisher, Cornell University Press.

EXHIBIT 5.11

Rob Ryan has developed an interesting dog food test for entrepreneurs who may be seeking venture capital funding.[50] Although the test profiled in Exhibit 5.11 is designed to see if a new venture has the growth potential to attract venture capital funding, it provides entrepreneurs with a useful framework or reality check for judging the potential for most new ventures.

Ryan indicated that you want to know whether the dogs will rip open your product/service box, if the dogs will yawn at it, or if there are even any hungry dogs at all. He also noted that there's nothing like having a list of potential customers who are chomping at the bit for your product who provide signed purchase orders or better yet—cash up front! [51]

Estimating Demand

Although market research and test marketing provide insights into how prospective consumers see your product/service, they also provide a foundation for doing an initial forecast of demand. Robert Hisrich and Michael Peters noted, "The determination of market demand is by far the most important criterion of a proposed new product idea. Assessment of the market opportunity and size needs to take into account such factors as the size of this potential market in dollars and units, the nature of the market with respect to its stage in the product life cycle (growing or declining), and the share of the market the product could reasonably capture. Current competing producers, prices, and marketing policies should also be evaluated, particularly in terms of their impact on market share of the proposed product. The new product should be able to compete successfully with products already on the market by having features that will meet or overcome current and anticipated competition. The product should have some unique differential advantage based on an evaluation of all competitive products filling the same consumer needs."[52]

If market research and test marketing reveal that targeted customers consider your product/service to be markedly superior from a price/quality perspective to what is available, then you might be able to forecast demand in market share terms as a percent of the overall market.

Market research and test marketing may play an even more important role if your venture will be launching a revolutionary product/service to a market that is just emerging. In this situation, you will be looking for information that will help you forecast the number of consumers and the number of products or amount of services they may purchase from your firm. Wilson Harrell's "Well, I'll be damned!" or "Would you buy this product?" tests may provide some insights into the level of interest in prospective customers. Indications that consumers want it now and have minimal sensitivity to price and potential for addiction may also help when developing the sales forecast. Of course, nothing beats signed purchase orders as a basis for forecasting demand.

How to Use Market Research to Look Before You Leap: An Example

Stephanie Kellar provides an excellent example about how the systematic analysis of an opportunity may be worth the time and money. Like many entrepreneurs, she stumbled across an opportunity via personal experience. Her entrepreneurial journey started when her eyelash curler pinched her face. In 1995, she set out to invent a better eyelash curler that would reduce the likelihood for pinching and minimized the chances for overcurling lashes. She found close to five million eyelash curlers are purchased each year. She was confident her new product would have an adequate user base. She decided to start by finding out whether other potential users had the same complaints about eyelash curlers. She used a Usenet newsgroup called alt.fashion to gather information and to see how anxious people were to switch to a new product. She noted, "I didn't want to tell people what I was doing so I would pose questions like, 'Has anyone had problems pinching their face with an eyelash curler?'" She got input from more than 100 people. The overall consensus was that the eyelash curlers currently on the market clearly had problems. Kellar was sure there was a great opportunity. Next she decided to make a pilot run of products so she could ensure the product was right. She also noted, "The biggest mistake people make is to put a product on the market before it's ready." In 1996, she produced a small run of eyelash curlers and gave test units to about 50 of the users she had met through Usenet to see if they felt her innovative eyelash curler actually delivered the results. The product testers suggested a few adjustments, which she made.[53]

Kellar did a patent search at the Boston Public Library to research past patents (*www.uspto.gov*) on eyelash curlers. After finding that other inventors hadn't really pursued her approach to the problem before, she applied for and was granted a patent in 1999. She noted that she wanted to do the patent herself so she could see all the improvements people had proposed, just as much as she wanted to see if anyone had already patented her idea.[54] She launched her product in 2000. By 2002, she had her product, Lashpro, which retails for $19.00, in 50 high-end stores. Her growth strategy also targeted mass-merchant accounts and beauty supply shops to carry her product.

Kellar illustrated the role the Internet can play in gaining insights into consumer perceptions. Usenet, an online bulletin board system that lets users post what they have to say in ongoing discussions about specific topics, is a great market research tool if you can find a newsgroup that fits your product category. To access Google's extensive Usenet directory, log on to *www.google.com* and enter Usenet as a search term. Another site that you can use to find the right newsgroup is *www.ii.com/internet/messsaging/newsgroups*, to search through 18,000 newsgroups.[55]

TESTING PATENTABILITY AND MARKET ACCEPTANCE

Numerous organizations are in a position to provide useful feedback and assistance on the relative merit of a new product. Two independent nonprofit organizations are particularly noteworthy that can help evaluate the marketability of your idea. The Washington Innovation Assessment Center's (WIAC), Pullman, Washington, analysis includes research and development, marketing, performance and implementation, and legal protection. WIAC's analysis pays particular attention to the product's manufacturability and the complexity of the research necessary to bring the product to a market-ready stage. WIAC even estimates the probability for the new product's success.

The Wisconsin Innovation Service Center (WISC), Whitewater, Wisconsin, evaluates the product using three criteria: competition, demand, and industry trends. WISC also does an online search to see what patents may already exist for that type of product. Both organizations also publish guides. WISC publishes *Innovation Guidebook,* which is full of answers for first-time inventors' common questions. WIAC publishes *Tips and Traps for Inventors,* as well as *Marketing Your Invention.*

Both organizations analyzed Tomima Edmark's Halo hat that is made of rain- and sun-resistant fabric. WISC reported that Edmark's Halo appeared to be a unique, useful, and feasible product. The WIAC report indicated that the Halo should be targeted to the "general market and that it had a 70 percent chance for success."[56] Arthur D. Little Enterprises Inc., based in Cambridge, Massachusetts, also reviews ideas through its Innovation Assessment Program.[57]

IT'S TIME FOR A TECHNICAL AND LOGISTICS TEST

If the product or service concept is embraced by the target market, then it is time to move to the next hurdle. A feasibility study needs to be conducted to determine whether the product or service the firm plans to offer can actually be provided to the target market. The following questions should be raised to increase the likelihood that your product/service can be provided to your target market:

- Are distributors really willing to carry it?
- Are suppliers really willing to provide the various components?
- Can you get that location?
- Are the key people committed to joining the venture team?
- Do you have any unfair advantages, exclusivity?
- Is there an available supply of labor?
- Will employees have to be trained?
- Will labor conditions affect your ability to attract talent?

- Will your business be the target for unionization?
- Can a working prototype be made?
- Can the actual product be made?
- Can the actual product be made economically?
- Can the actual service be provided?
- Can the actual service be provided economically?
- Can the processes be designed and tested at this time?
- How long will it take to make the product?
- What are the potential bottlenecks?
- Can the process be tested earlier so there is time to get the bugs out?

The greater the degree of innovation and complexity, the greater the need to do a technical and logistics test. Heather Page noted that a high-technology venture, especially one that will rely on providing products or services exclusively through the Internet, is subject to unforeseen circumstances well beyond an entrepreneur's control.[58]

VULNERABILITY ANALYSIS

The analysis of an opportunity would not be complete without a vulnerability analysis. You should look at the opportunity from a 360-degree or kaleidoscopic perspective. Although the screening process may have looked at the nature of the market opportunity, your competitive advantage, financial worthiness, and a whole host of other factors, you need to look around to see if there may be any other risks that should be analyzed. Vulnerability analysis encourages you to scan the environment and run scenarios to identify potential threats.

Particular attention should be directed to assumptions or conditions that could become fatal flaws. These factors could include changes in the weather, competitive entry, breakthrough innovation, a major change in government regulations, and so forth. The outbreak of war in the Middle East can send shock waves through the world economy. The outbreak of a contagious disease like SARS can have a devastating impact in various businesses. Evidence of Mad Cow disease can send shock waves for firms that are tied to meat-related products.

Even specific circumstances can have adverse effects on specific businesses. A new venture that is designed to provide emergency road service in the Northeast could risk bankruptcy if the first winter is mild. Integrated Medical Resources, which was founded in 1990, is an example of how a venture can be vulnerable to external forces. Integrated Medical Resources grew into a national chain of clinics that specialized in diagnosing and treating impotence. Integrated Medical Resources, Inc. was started when Troy Burns, an internist, recognized that the number of cases of impotence would likely rise as the baby-boom generation approaches retirement age. The company grew and even went public. Integrated Medical Resources, however, took a major hit when Viagra became available. Many prospective patients bypassed Integrated Medical Resources' clinics and went directly to their primary-care physicians or urologists for prescriptions of Viagra.[59]

Life can be described as a series of events. Each event has its own corresponding probability and consequences. Vulnerability analysis helps reduce the likelihood you will be blindsided by events that can derail your new venture. Vulnerability analysis may not eliminate every possible risk, but it may help you position your venture so it can avoid certain risks. It may also reduce the likelihood or adverse impact of risks that cannot be avoided. Remember, however, that the only way to eliminate business risk is not to go into business. The key is to keep your eyes open, to anticipate the unexpected, and to be prepared to deal with almost anything. That is what due diligence is all about.

REALITY CHECK

Ted Turner captured the role that risk plays when embarking on the entrepreneurial journey. He noted, "Business is full of lawyers and advisors, and you've got to remember, whatever you're doing, these guys are trying to keep you from getting burned. That's their job. So if you get a new idea, don't expect everybody to say, "Let's go." You're the one who says that."[60]

CONCLUSION: INSIGHTS IDENTIFY OPPORTUNITIES AND REDUCE RISK

The saying, "You've come a long way, baby," is applicable at this point in your entrepreneurial journey. Hopefully, your market research, test marketing, and feasibility analysis indicate that a lucrative and lasting opportunity exists. Hopefully, the data and preliminary projections indicate that your venture will have a competitive advantage and that consumers are excited about your product/service offering.

If the issues raised in this chapter indicate all systems are go for the highest-ranking opportunity, then the time has arrived for you to begin preparing the business plan. The business plan plays a significant role in the entrepreneurial journey because it represents an in-depth analysis of the targeted opportunity as well as the strategy to be used in creating and maintaining customers for a profit. The business plan also includes a complete set of financial projections, identifies how the venture will be funded, and addresses the legal form of organization.

If it seems like you have answered a lot of questions and learned a lot about the opportunity you have reviewed so far, then brace yourself for the next round of analysis. A lot of homework still needs to be done about the industry and all the other factors that may influence whether your venture can beat the odds.

Some prospective entrepreneurs try to do the next round of analysis on a part-time basis by devoting their evenings and weekends to learning more about their targeted opportunity. Some prospective entrepreneurs actually proceed by starting their venture on a part-time basis and try to learn as they go. If they find the idea has merit, then they quit their jobs and commit themselves to the venture on a full-time basis. And some prospective entrepreneurs jump in with both feet. When Jim Lowe and Polly Nelson got to this point, they quit their jobs and took one year to take courses, read trade information, and complete their preliminary evaluation of the targeted opportunity. Then they conducted an in-depth analysis of the industry before they decided to go ahead with Hog's Head Beer Cellers, a mail-order gourmet microbrew business. Their in-depth analysis included talking to nearly 1,000 specialty breweries across the nation.[61]

Opportunities multiply as they are seized; they die when neglected.
Life is a long line of opportunities.[62]

—John Wicker

ENDNOTES

1. Thomas W. Zimmerer and Norman M. Scarborough, *Entrepreneurship and New Venture Formation* (Englewood Cliffs, NJ: Prentice Hall, 1996), p. 80.

2. Alex Perez, "What Troubled or Failed Dot-Com Seemed Like a Solid Business Model?," *Business 2.0,* February 20, 2001, p. 33.

3. Ibid.

4. Ibid.

5. Rita Gunther McGrath and Ian MacMillan, *The Entrepreneurial Mindset* (Boston: Harvard Business School Press, 2000), pp. 18 & 19. Reprinted by permission of Harvard Business School Press.

6. Zimmerer and Scarborough, *Entrepreneurship and New Venture Formation,* p. 83.

7. Jeffry A. Timmons, "Growing Up Big: Entrepreneurship and Creating High Potential Ventures," *Texas A&M Business Forum,* Fall 1985, p. 13.

8. Jeffry A. Timmons, *New Venture Creation* (New York: McGraw-Hill, 1999), p. 84.

9. McGrath and MacMillan, *Entrepreneurial Mindset,* p. 6.

10. Rob Ryan, *Smartups: Lessons from Rob Ryan's Entrepreneur America Boot Camp for Start-Ups* (Ithaca: Cornell University Press, 2001), p. 38. Copyright © 2001 by Rob Ryan. Used with permission of the publisher, Cornell University Press.

11. Amar Bhidé, *The Origin and Evolution of New Businesses* (Oxford: Oxford University Press, 2000), pp. 18–19.

12. Ryan, *Smartups,* p. 144.

13. Pip Coburn, "Learning to Live with Hype," *Red Herring,* July 2000, p. 410.

14. Ibid.

15. Gary Hamel and C.K. Prahalad, *Competing for the Future* (Boston: Harvard Business School Press, 1994), p. 103.

16. Ryan, *Smartups,* p. 61.

17. Norm Brodsky, "The Three Criteria for a Successful New Business," *Inc.,* April 1996, in Annual Editions Entrepreneurship 99/00, p. 48.

18. Ibid.

19. Nicole L. Torres, "First Come, First Served," *Entrepreneur,* June 2002, p. 140. Reprinted with permission of Entrepreneur Media, Inc.

20. Brodsky, "The Three Criteria for a Successful New Business," p. 48.

21. Amar Bhidé, "How Entrepreneurs Craft Strategies That Work," *Harvard Business Review,* March–April 1994 in Annual Editions Entrepreneurship 99/00, p. 69. Reprinted by permission of *Harvard Business Review.*

22. Gunther McGrath and MacMillan, *The Entrepreneurial Mindset,* p. 20.

23. J. William Gurley, "Got a Good Idea? Better Think Twice," *Fortune,* December 7, 1998, p. 216.

24. Ibid.

25. Ibid., p. 215.

26. Scott Kirsner, "Guerrillas in the Midst," *Fast Company,* January 1999, p. 134.

27. Zimmerer and Scarborough, *Entrepreneurship and New Venture Formation,* pp. 80 & 81.

28. Bhidé, "How Entrepreneurs Craft Strategies that Work," p. 68.

29. Fred DeLuca, *Start Small, Finish Big* (New York: Warner Books, 2000).

30. Kenneth W. Olm and George G. Eddy, *Entrepreneurship and Venture Management* (Englewood Cliffs, NJ: Prentice Hall, 1985), p. 58.

31. Elaine Pofeldt, "The Success Start-up Guide," *Success,* March 1999, p. 62.

32. Heather Page, "High Hopes," *Entrepreneur,* March 1999, p. 132.

33. Don Debelak, "Want Some of This?" *Entrepreneur,* June 2002, p. 127. Reprinted with permission of Entrepreneur Media, Inc.

34. John Wall, "Familial Flush," *Insight,* June 1997, p. 68.

35. Thea Singer, "What Business Should You Start?," *Inc.,* March 2002, p. 72.

36. David Packard, *The HP Way* (New York: HarperBusiness, 1995), p. 120.

37. Joseph H. Boyette and Jimmie T. Boyette, *The Guru Guide to Entrepreneurship* (New York: John Wiley & Sons, 2001), p. 155.

38. Akio Morita with Edwin M. Reingold and Mitsuko Shimomura, *Made in Japan: Akio Morita and Sony* (New York: E.P. Dutton, 1986), p. 79.

39. Gene Landrum, *Profiles of Genius: Thirteen Creative Men Who Changed the World* (Buffalo: Prometheus Books, 1993), p. 195.

40. Wilson Harrell, *For Entrepreneurs Only* (Hawthorne, NJ: Career Press, 1994), pp. 67–74.

41. Don Debelak, "I Needed That," *Entrepreneur,* May 2002, pp. 127–128. Reprinted with permission of Entrepreneur Media, Inc.

42. Ryan, *Smartups,* p. 60.

43. Ibid., p. 36.

44. Ibid., p. 56.

45. Leslie Brokaw, "The Truth About Start-ups," *Inc.,* April 1991, p. 60.

46. Ryan, *Smartups,* pp. 47–51.

47. Jay Finegin, Can Big Business Be Built on Breakthrough Products?," *Inc.,* November 1996, p. 17.

48. W. Keith Schilit, *The Entrepreneur's Guide to Preparing a Winning Business Plan and Raising Venture Capital* (Englewood Cliffs, NJ: Prentice Hall, 1990), p. 48.

49. Gurley, "Got a Good Idea? Better Think Twice," p. 216.

50. Ryan, *Smartups,* p. 37.

51. Ibid., p. 9.

52. Robert D. Hisrich and Michael P. Peters, *Entrepreneurship* (New York: McGraw-Hill, 1998), p. 183.

53. Don Debelak, "Want Some of This?," *Entrepreneur,* June 2002, pp. 126–127. Reprinted with permission of Entrepreneur Media, Inc.

54. Ibid.

55. Ibid., p. 127.

56. Tomima Edmark, "Testing Your Wings," *Entrepreneur,* June 1998, p. 125. Reprinted with permission of Entrepreneur Media, Inc.

57. Kristen Dunlop Godsey, "Invention Intervention," *Success,* June 1997, p. 14.

58. Heather Page, "High Hopes," *Entrepreneur,* March 1999, p. 132. Reprinted with permission of Entrepreneur Media, Inc.

59. Mike Hofman, "Impotence Clinic Flops in Wake of Viagra," *Inc.,* May 1999, p. 23.

60. Christian Williams, *Lead, Follow, or Get Out of the Way* (New York: Times Books, 1981), p. 14.

61. Pofeldt, "The Success Start-up Guide," p. 60.

62. B.C. Forbes, *The Forbes Scrapbook of Life* (New York: B.C. Forbes & Sons Publishing Co., 1976), p. 134.

6

DEVELOPING THE BUSINESS PLAN

Businesses that fail to plan are planning to fail.

—Peter Drucker

Now that you have identified the type of business opportunity you want to pursue, it is time to begin preparing your business plan. Even though you have a general idea of the kind of business to start, numerous questions remain unanswered. When people complete the process described in Chapter 5, they often feel they do not need to prepare a formal business plan because they know what goods or services they want to offer to the one or more market segments they plan to serve. Getting to this point may have taken a lot of time, effort, and thought, but a lot of decisions still need to be made. Preparing a business plan helps to identify questions you need to answer. It also provides a framework and timetable for its implementation.

The probability of being successful in starting a new business is directly related to the extent your business plan is accurate, complete, and reflects realities. Accordingly, it will take considerable time and effort to prepare a useful business plan. It may take at least four months to prepare a business plan for even the simplest *new* business. A note of caution also needs to be brought up at this time. Some people believe they do not need to prepare a business plan if they don't need to borrow money, bring in a partner, or attract investors. This is a mistake. A business plan is not the same as a request for funding; it is your blueprint for building a successful business. You need to have a plan even if you don't need financing because you are the primary audience for your business plan.

Your initial analysis from Chapter 5 may have indicated there is an opportunity for a new venture, that you should be able to develop a competitive advantage, and that there should be a sufficient return to justify the time, risk, and investment. The time has arrived for you to take a much closer look at the venture's feasibility and financial merit. This chapter focuses on why the business plan is so important to the success of the venture and why it needs to be grounded in reality. Chapter 7 profiles the various components of the business plan.

THE ROLE OF THE BUSINESS PLAN

Developing a business plan forces you to do an in-depth analysis of the issues and factors that will play a crucial role in the success of the venture under consideration. Most of the analysis described in the first five chapters has taken place on a fairly conceptual level. The business plan is important because it serves as a reality check. The process of developing a business plan puts the venture concept through a comprehensive and systematic CT scan so it can be seen from various vantage points.

The preparation of the business plan marks an interesting change in the role the entrepreneur plays in the creation and development of a venture. Until now, you have been doing what entrepreneurs do. Your time has been spent identifying an opportunity that has merit. Until now, your perceptiveness and innovativeness have played a key role in identifying the opportunity and developing a way to capitalize on it. Now, research and managerial prowess become critical determinants in whether your venture will have a successful launch. At this point, you must become the venture's chief executive officer.

The screening process profiled in Chapter 5 was helpful because it provided a general framework for evaluating and ranking alternative opportunities. This chapter emphasizes the need for closer scrutiny. The business plan will help you determine whether you should really start the venture. The more comprehensive the analysis and detail of the plan, the lower the likelihood that you will encounter surprises, oversights, and setbacks.

Anyone who tries to build anything, especially something as complicated as a business, without having a blueprint is courting disaster. It is true that a business plan may help you secure funding for your business, but it is important for two other reasons. First, your plan allows you to take the mental journey before you commit resources and take the physical journey. It identifies specifically the *who, what, when, where, how much, why,* and *how* of your proposed venture. The plan may indicate your venture will require much more money, that its break-even point is much higher, or that there is too much competition. Developing the business plan forces you to look before you leap, before quitting your job and before taking a second mortgage on your home.

The process of developing the plan indicates the critical elements, the necessary time-line, the initial capital requirement, and the likely level of profitability. It should also indicate the inflection points where major events or growth occurs and how the firm will deal with them. The plan thereby identifies critical issues including financing, staffing, product introduction, and so forth.

Second, your business plan is a reflection of your ability to manage. If you do not have the patience, perseverance, skill, and information needed to prepare a business plan, then you probably lack the ability to start and manage a new business.

The process of developing a business plan incorporates the Three *I*'s of planning. Planning forces you to make *inquiries* into what could affect the venture. The inquiries provide *insights* into what may be needed. The insights, in turn, provide the basis for *initiatives* that will need to be taken to enhance the firm's chances for success. Accordingly, the process of planning may indicate the need to find innovative ways to raise money, to form alliances, and to provide incentives to attract people to your venture.

REALITY CHECK

The process of developing the business plan might reveal that it will take more money or that it will be at least two years before the business generates a positive cash flow. It might indicate that the firms already serving the market have a dominant proprietary position or that the location you need is not available. The plan might reveal that vendors won't deal with you unless you pay up front or that their minimum order requirements are well beyond your venture's needs. Finally, the process of developing the plan might reveal that you don't want it bad enough to do all the research and analysis that is needed to start a venture.

The business plan plays a critical role in the success of a new venture because it takes a closer look at the resource requirements and the associated risks. It challenges assumptions by conducting additional research and it puts initial estimates to the test by forcing you to develop more detailed projections. The business plan transforms preliminary sales estimates into pro forma income statements, cash flows, balance sheets, and financial ratios. It also transforms preliminary time estimates into timelines, critical paths, and milestones.

If the business plan gives the new venture the green light, then it serves as the blueprint for launching the venture. If it indicates there may be a fatal flaw, then the plan has served its purpose—it kept you from taking a journey that was destined to fail.

Yes, You Really Need To Prepare a Business Plan!

Most entrepreneurs are not into planning. They face two dilemmas when they get to the stage where they have to develop a business plan. Their first dilemma is related to their lack of patience. Most entrepreneurs are anxious to transform their ideas into reality. Their desire to make things happen can put them in harm's way. When they see the window of opportunity opening in front of them they want to seize the moment. They know market opportunities, like time, will not wait for anyone. They hear a voice inside exclaim, "He who hesitates is lost!" The lack of patience causes many entrepreneurs to leap before they look. Their desire to "boldly go where no one has gone before" frequently becomes a journey into oblivion. Entrepreneurs who do not take the time to think things through are the ones who drive up the new venture failure rate.

The second dilemma arises because entrepreneurs frequently lack the business skills needed to prepare a comprehensive plan for their new venture. Their dreams, ideas, concepts, and ballpark estimates may have kept them going until now, but developing a business plan forces them to roll up their sleeves, crunch numbers, and come up with specific answers to probing questions.

REALITY CHECK

Most entrepreneurs welcome the prospect of developing a business plan as much as people welcome a root canal. If the data were available, if it took less than 10 hours, if it was similar to what they have done before, if all the questions were already identified, and if all the questions had certain answers, then developing a business plan would not be that difficult. If they could call a timeout and stop the world long enough to collect the data and develop the plan, then most entrepreneurs would develop a business plan. If it was fun and entrepreneurs had a staff of experts at their disposal, then developing a business plan would be welcomed rather than dreaded so much.

REALITY CHECK

Let the truth be told. Most entrepreneurs start their ventures without a business plan. If you ask for a copy of their plan, most entrepreneurs will find a way to change the subject. This is because they don't *have* a written plan. Mostly, they have rough concepts in their heads rather than actual plans. Your plan needs to be the product of deliberate effort, and it needs to be in writing.

REALITY CHECK

Developing a business plan for a new venture is not the same as developing a plan for an established company in an established market. Planning in established businesses is like tuning a piano. Developing a business plan for a new venture is like designing and building the first piano. Planning something for the first time not only takes a lot of time, it tends to take even more time than anticipated. When Steven Jobs started NeXT Computer, he noted that he had forgotten how hard it was to start a company. This is particularly noteworthy because he started NeXT with a lot of the people who had worked with him on the Macintosh while at Apple.

Developing a Business Plan Takes Commitment

First-time entrepreneurs frequently ask, "Do I really need to do a business plan?" Some first-time entrepreneurs even cite examples of firms that were started without a formal business plan. This question doesn't even deserve an answer. Of course you need a plan. Would you take a trip without knowing where you wanted to go, when you wanted to get there, and how much money you would need? Creating even the simplest venture involves hundreds of decisions. Planning identifies the questions that need to be answered. Planning also identifies areas where there is uncertainty and risk. Planning may not give you all the answers, but it will reduce the likelihood of being blindsided. You will never be in total control of your venture's destiny. Planning gives you an edge so you will be better prepared to deal with the factors beyond your control.

Although preparing a business plan does not guarantee new venture success, not doing one places the new venture in jeopardy. A study by Donald Sexton and Phillip Van Auken indicated that 80 percent of the unsuccessful entrepreneurs in their sample had no formal plan when they opened their business. Their study also revealed that 60 percent of the unsuccessful ones had done no market research at the outset of their ventures.[1]

Developing the business plan is the first real test of your commitment to starting a new venture. Doing a business plan is like fraternity hazing—only those who are truly committed will be willing to take the time, to deal with the hassles, to do the research, and to roll up their sleeves to do what needs to be done. There is no glory and there is no glamour to doing a business plan—it is work! It is a time when you have to temper your passion with reality. It is a time when you have to turn your fantasies into facts.

Developing a business plan is a moment of truth for the entrepreneur and the new venture. Few people welcome the prospect of committing the weeks or months needed to develop a business plan. Mark Deion, a business planning and strategy consultant, notes "If writing a good business plan scares you off, then maybe you should think about a less challenging occupation than entrepreneurship."[2] Nancy Russell, a business development officer at the Money Store in Irvine, California, noted that while entrepreneurs may come in all shapes and sizes, "they all roll their eyes when I tell them they have to do a business plan."[3] Mark Van Osnabrugge and Robert Robinson noted that crafting a good plan is a difficult task, usually involving weeks (if not months) of endless drafting and rewriting.[4]

One recent article stated that most entrepreneurs are afraid to plan. Bruce Posner, senior writer for *Inc.* magazine states, "Planning strikes terror in their hearts because it threatens their mystique about themselves. They *like* flying by the seat of their pants and keeping others blindfolded. Once they invite outsiders into their own private world—in writing, no less—the mystery is gone. All of their underlying assumptions can be examined and questioned by employees and others; under scrutiny, these assumptions might unravel, leaving the emperors with no clothes. They might have to admit that they have no *idea* where they are going."[5]

Business Plan Is a Reflection Of the Entrepreneur

Developing a business plan demonstrates whether you think like a businessperson. How you approach the business plan indicates how you will manage the venture. If you are thorough in developing the business plan, then you will probably be thorough in making decisions after the business is launched. This thoroughness is the strength of the professional entrepreneur. It separates the purely intuitive, flying by the seat of the pants, "I've already made up my mind—don't confuse me with the facts" type of entrepreneur from the professional entrepreneur who looks before he or she leaps.

For example, the business plan is a reality check for most inventors. If their eyes go blank when they ponder sales forecasts, cash flow, and the hundreds of other business questions, then they should seriously consider licensing their ideas rather than trying to run a new venture on a trial-and-error basis.

A plan must demonstrate mastery of the entire entrepreneurial process, from identification of opportunity to harvest. He notes that crafting a business plan that thoroughly and candidly addresses the ingredients of success—people, opportunity, context, and the risk/reward picture—is vitally important to the success of the venture.[6]

REALITY CHECK

New ventures are the Rodney Dangerfields of the business world—they don't get much respect. Harvard Professor William Sahlman observed, "The real-world often prefers not to deal with start-ups."[7] Bankers rarely lend money to start-ups. Investors also prefer firms that have an established track record. Suppliers usually place purchasing or credit limits on new ventures if they even do business with them. Potential customers usually wait for the new venture to show it's real before they seriously consider buying its products or services.

If you want your venture to be taken seriously, then you must take the business plan seriously. You will be judged by the quality of the new venture's business plan. A professional business plan can open doors for you. For example, one first-time entrepreneur who wanted to start a gourmet food store and café found that the firm leasing the desired retail site was reluctant to do business with a start-up. When she provided the leasing agent with a copy of her business plan that indicated she (1) had managerial experience, (2) had taken numerous business classes, (3) had researched similar successful ventures in other cities, (4) had a letter of commitment from the primary supplier, and (5) had sufficient capital, the agent went from being reluctant to being excited about the business. The business plan provided credibility and demonstrated she was not the typical naïve first-timer.

The preceding example demonstrates the power of a business plan. Entrepreneurs who take the time to develop plans that provide the answers to critical questions are starting their ventures off on the right foot. Conversely, entrepreneurs who fail to do sufficient research develop business plans that raise more questions than they answer. In these instances, the lack of preparation can seriously jeopardize the venture's ability to achieve the critical mass needed for a successful launch.

Entrepreneurs are like explorers. Entrepreneurs boldly go where no one has gone before. They must make a deliberate and systematic effort to collect information about what may lie ahead. They must prepare for the unexpected. They must also have the ability to modify what they are doing when their plans do not produce the results they expected.

Explorers like Lewis and Clark have been heralded for their accomplishments for centuries. Yet they were among the few who were successful. Countless others did not find what they were looking for or never made it back. The most successful explorers had more than luck on their side. In most cases, they were better prepared and they began their journey with sufficient resources to deal with the challenges they could not have foreseen.

Entrepreneurs need to expect the unexpected. They need to recognize that it usually takes twice as much time and twice as much money as they originally expected. They run *what if?* scenarios in advance and then they make sure they have enough time and money to deal with the various contingencies. Although they may encounter obstacles and face setbacks in their schedules, they are positioned to go the distance.

Amy Nye provides an interesting example of how having a plan may not assure a smooth start-up. Most people would assume setting up kiosks at major airports to sell CDs would be a relatively simple proposition. She found that creating her ALTI-TUNES's kiosks was anything but simple. According to *Forbes,* she was stunned when airport officials at LaGuardia rejected her construction plan, color scheme, building materials, and placement of lighting.[8] Complying with the various regulations doubled her construction costs and delayed the opening of that kiosk by three months. Fortunately, she turned that setback into a learning experience. She took what she learned from the LaGuardia experience and simplified the design of the kiosks so they could be installed quicker in subsequent sites. ALTITUNES's next two kiosks opened on time and on budget.

Nye's setback in launching her business demonstrates the value of developing a plan. Developing a business plan should be like taking a mental journey before you take the physical journey. The process of developing a plan should force you to identify the critical issues. Business plans are worth their weight in gold if they enable you to prevent problems that could jeopardize the venture. The business planning process forces you to think things through, to get the facts rather than to rely on assumptions, and to do reality checks on critical issues. In Nye's case, a few more mental reality checks when preparing for her first site may have saved her valuable time, frustration, and money. Although no plan can anticipate every possibility, a thorough planning process will reduce the likelihood that you will be blindsided.

Jay Conrad Levinson coined the term *guerrilla entrepreneurs* to represent entrepreneurs who have their act together and who are positioned to deal with ever-changing realities. According to Levinson, "Guerrilla entrepreneurs always operate according to a plan. y know who they are, where they are going, and how they will get there. They know anything can happen and deal with the barriers to success because their long-term have foreseen them and offer ways to surmount them."[9]

BASICS OF THE NEW VENTURE BUSINESS PLAN

Dun and Bradstreet found mismanagement to be the number-one reason for venture failure. Planning is an integral part of management. "Planning is really no more or no less than another word for good management."[10] If knowledge is power, then planning provides the information that gives the business plan the ability to beat the odds. Information and preparation reduce uncertainty and anxiety. By putting your game plan in writing, you identify key assumptions and risks. You also identify the early warning signals that indicate things are not going as expected.

REALITY CHECK

Most entreprenurs may have a game plan in their head, but they don't have a real business plan. If it's not in writing, then it's not a plan. If it isn't the product of systematic analysis, then it's not a plan. If it can't be handed to someone else to implement, then it's not a plan. If it doesn't highlight the four or five critical factors for success, then it's not a business plan.

REALITY CHECK

First-time entrepreneurs, by definition, have never done a business plan for a start-up before. This elevates the usual anxiety associated with doing a business plan. Anytime you have to do something you have never done before you experience anxiety. Yet entrepreneurship involves being prepared to go where you have not gone before. Let's take a closer look at the anxiety and reluctance associated with doing a business plan. As noted earlier, most entrepreneurs don't want to take the time to do all the planning stuff. In reality, it isn't the amount of time that planning takes that bothers most entrepreneurs, it's having to find answers for questions that you haven't had to answer in detail, it's having to state your assumptions and reality-test them, it's having to run the numbers for the ideas that have served you well, and it's having to develop price schedules, make monthly cash-flow projections, and identify specific suppliers that hurts!

REALITY CHECK

Most first-time entrepreneurs today are tempted to hire someone else to put in the blood, sweat, and tears frequently associated with preparing and writing the business plan. You have to be the primary architect of the plan. You are the one who will be making the decisions when the venture is up and running. You have to know the business inside and out. If you are tempted to delegate the development of the plan to someone else, then you should think about delegating the whole business to someone else! If you are only an idea person, then don't try to start a venture. You may be better off making money by selling your ideas to people who have the desire and ability to plan, create, and manage ventures.

REALITY CHECK

First-time entrepreneurs cannot rely on ESP when people ask them, "What type of business do you plan to start?" You must be able to describe the business in detail. You have to be able to tell what products or services you'll provide, and to whom. You have to be able to discuss the market and your competition. "If you can't explain your venture in 25 words or less, it's probably not a good idea."[11]

REALITY CHECK

Flying by the seat of your pants won't cut it. Telling others, "Trust me, I know what I'm doing," won't cut it. Having a proprietary position without a plan won't cut it. Believing you really won't have competition won't cut it. Assuming that competition will not retaliate won't cut it.

THE NATURE OF PLANNING: CONSTRUCTING A BUSINESS MODEL FOR THE VENTURE

The first thing entrepreneurs need to know about developing the business plan is that the goal is not to develop a plan; it's to develop a plan that when implemented will achieve the desired results. Planning is basically a process that identifies a set of actions, when implemented, that have the best chance to go from Point A, a concept, to Point B, the establishment of a venture that meets the entrepreneur's expectations.

Although the plan is intended to be comprehensive, it would be impossible for any plan to cover every possible detail, nor should it attempt to do so. The plan incorporates the Pareto 80/20 rule. It should provide an in-depth analysis and discussion of the few (20 percent) things that are of paramount importance and an overview of the numerous (80 percent) factors that play a less important role in the success of the venture.

Planning involves asking the tough questions about what will it take to be successful. Nearly every plan for a new venture is based on four or five key assumptions or factors. The plan must identify the factors and put them into perspective. The overall plan can be viewed as a business model that identifies the various pieces and how they fit together. The plan should identify why the business should succeed. The process of developing a business plan might reveal that the numbers just don't work or that there is a fatal flaw in the business model. For example, entrepreneurs with a great product discover that it's simply too costly to find customers who can and will buy what they are selling.[12]

The business plan should address four fundamental and interdependent issues. First, the plan should highlight the people who are going to be involved in the venture. The plan should profile the entrepreneur, the management team, the board of directors, the advisory board (if one is set up), and the people (attorneys, accountants, etc.) or firms that will be serving in an advisory capacity. Second, the plan should profile the opportunity and demonstrate that it is attractive and sustainable. This part of the plan would identify the target market to be served and how the firm plans to create and maintain a competitive advantage. Third, the plan should profile the context in which the venture will operate. The context includes the factors over which the firm has little, if any, control. Contextual factors include government regulations, economic conditions, and the competition. Fourth, the plan should profile the risks and rewards associated with the venture. The plan should identify everything that can go wrong and what the firm will do to prevent or address each of the risks.[13]

Some of the most successful firms have used very simple business models. Amazon.com, for example, was built on the assumption that people would welcome the opportunity to buy various products over the Internet rather than through conventional retail outlets. Federal Express was based on the assumption that a number of people and businesses wanted overnight delivery of parcels. Ironically, the ability and resource requirements needed to sell products over the Internet or to provide overnight delivery services were far greater than the simplicity of each venture's business concept. Ventures that start with the right competencies and sufficient resources have a marked advantage when they have a head start over established firms.

The model for the business would be incomplete if it didn't include three other components. The plan should also include how the firm will deal with competitive retaliation, how it plans to grow, as well as its exit strategy. The plan needs to demonstrate that the new venture will not fall prey to the here today, gone tomorrow syndrome. The plan should profile how you will attract customers from existing businesses and what it will take to delight them so they become ambassadors for your venture. It will also need to indicate how your marketing strategy will change to meet the challenges of new competitors as well as respond to the competitive responses of existing firms. The plan should also indicate whether the venture will be offering additional products and services, expanding into other markets, entering into a licensing agreement, doing a joint venture, seeking alliances with other firms, and/or acquiring other ventures. Finally, the plan should indicate if the firm plans to be acquired, go public, or be acquired.

The Business Plan Puts Things In Perspective

The process of developing the business plan helps you look at the new venture from various dimensions. The process encourages you to adopt a bifocal perspective of the venture. Having a bifocal perspective means that you address strategic and operational issues. Yet the business plan is not the typical strategic plan. Nor is it the typical operational plan. It is strategic in the sense that it forces you to address the issues that will make or break the new venture. The plan must identify your five-year vision for the firm and how it will get there. It must also provide enough details so little falls through the cracks as you try to fulfill the vision.

The plan must identify what is important and what is urgent. The plan must identify what the yeses and nos are for the myriad decisions that must be made. The plan must also indicate the various priorities. No new venture has unlimited resources, so the plan must differentiate between the must-dos, should-dos, and like-to-dos.

The plan will also need to indicate the timeline for the new venture. The clock for new ventures runs quickly, so you will need to know what is essential and what can be postponed. You'll also need to know which activities need to be addressed in a sequential manner and which actions need to be done concurrently. The timeline will also need to reflect major milestones for sales, cash flow, expansion, and other key events.

The plan should include a chronological list of the 10 to 15 most critical actions you will need to take during the next six months and the hurdles that need to be overcome in order to convert your idea into a real opportunity. Jeffry Timmons also noted that it is a good idea to have another person review what you have listed and adjust the list if warranted.[14]

The plan must also demonstrate that the new venture is environmentally consonant and internally consistent. The plan must indicate that the new venture is in sync with economic conditions, will use the latest technology, is savvy to the labor market, and reflects government regulations. The plan must also indicate that the various components of the new venture are in synch with one another. The plan must show how capital expenditures will be funded and that sales will be supported via personnel, advertising, and inventory.

Documentation, Documentation, And More Documentation

Ignorance is not bliss when it comes to starting a new venture. What you don't know can hurt you. Research and documentation force you to deal in facts rather than fantasies and assumptions. They allow you to test drive your projections and assumptions to see if they hold up.

Your sales projections will need to identify the number of customers, the location of the customers, the average purchase, seasonality, and the amount of sales in receivables. The plan will have to project the number of employees, the wage rates they will be paid, and the benefits program you will offer them. It will also need to document the management team's qualifications, capabilities, and experience.

The plan will also need to include cash flow, the average amount of inventory, and profit as a percent of sales. In addition, the plan will need to provide documentation that vendors, distributors, and prospective customers will do business with you. It will also have to demonstrate that the firm has a competitive advantage and that the projected rate of growth is realistic.

The Business Plan Provides Focus

Some things have to be done well; other things just need to be done. The key is knowing which things are critical and need your ongoing attention. If the plan is prepared well, then it will identify the bull's eye of the new venture's target. The plan should identify what the venture needs to do to start off on the right foot, as well as what it needs to do to be positioned to fulfill its three- to five-year vision. The business plan should provide focus for every key decision and essential actions. When you know what business you're in, who is in your target market, and what you need to do to delight them, then the firm is less likely to drift or to be seduced by various short-lived opportunities.

The business plan targets performance and provides a basis for measuring success. When you establish goals, timelines, and budgets, you are also establishing an early warning system for your firm. These indicators function like the gauges on your car's dashboard. Your sales goals are like the speedometer. They let you see if your daily and weekly sales are meeting projections. Your budget is like the odometer. It tells you if your sales are covering your expenses. Your cash flow statement is like the gas gauge. It tells you if you are burning too much fuel. Each of the gauges lets you identify variances so that you can modify your plans and operations to get back on track.

REALITY CHECK

It will be impossible for you to monitor every dimension of the firm at every instant in time. You must identify the truly critical performance measures and monitor them closely.

A carefully crafted business plan will allow you to do management by exception. Your plan should identify the key metrics that serve as performance gauges for your venture. Each metric should have a corresponding range of performance that is considered acceptable. For example, if sales are projected to be $400,000 per month, then you might establish an acceptable sales range of plus or minus $20,000. If sales exceed $420,000 or fall below $380,000 for the month, then you have an exceptional variance. The presence of an exceptional variance indicates that your assumptions were off base or that your plan is not going as expected.

Exceptional variances usually require a change in the plan. If sales are higher than expected, then you will have to synchronize your support systems to ensure that the firm is able to meet higher levels of demand. If the system is not recalibrated, then you run the risk of making commitments to customers that cannot be honored. Although you may want to celebrate the high levels of sales, you want to be sure you are not jeopardizing customer goodwill. Conversely, lower than expected sales means that you may have to take a hard look at the effectiveness of your advertising, sales efforts, pricing strategy, and/or the competitiveness of your products or services.

The breadth of the acceptable range for each performance metric will be contingent on its relative impact on the performance of your new venture. The acceptable range will also be affected by how long it will take to correct an exceptional deviation and the costs associated with making the correction. Areas that have a high probability of deviation and that have the potential for serious consequences should be monitored frequently. They should also have narrow acceptable ranges.

Identify the Drivers of Success

The business plan for a new venture is not designed to cover every minute detail for every operational issue. Instead, the business plan has two primary dimensions. First, it should identify the areas that are critical to the success of the new venture. Second, it should describe how the issues will be addressed.

The plan must separate the substantive issues from all the other issues that are part of the operational plan. It is easy for the entrepreneur to get bogged down in all the stuff that goes into an operational plan. Operational logistics and details will play an important part in the success of the venture and they will have to be addressed. What matters most at this stage, however, is that you direct your attention to the drivers of success. Your time is limited and the world continues to change so you must direct most of your attention to the things that matter most. At this time, you should ask. "What are the five most critical things for the successful launch of the venture?" Then you should ask, "What are the five things that can kill the venture if they are not addressed?" These two questions represent only 20 percent of the issues that need to be addressed in the development of the plan, but they may make up 80 percent of the plan.

Scot Wingo is a living testimony to the value of developing a sound business plan. As cofounder of Stingray Software (he later founded ChannelAdvisor), Wingo stresses the role that a business plan can play in providing focus. He noted that he had a plan from day one. His plan not only identified what needed to be done, it also kept the firm from veering off course. Wingo also notes that the plan plays an instrumental role well after launching the new venture. He noted, "Don't underestimate how fast you can grow."[15] Because his firm had a plan, Stingray Software was able to expand operations and add products to capitalize on growth opportunities.

Wingo also demonstrates how easy it can be for the management team to get so caught up in ongoing operations that it loses sight of the need to do planning on an ongoing basis. He noted that for the first three years they were implementing the three-year plan—Stingray Software was growing so rapidly that they didn't have the time to do annual updates.

Rapid growth rarely occurs without consequences. Firms that grow beyond their plans are driving beyond their headlights. When reflecting on the early years, Wingo noted, "We kept underestimating our growth. We outgrew our accounting system very quickly and we outgrew our Internet service provider very quickly."[16]

When planning is done right, it increases the probability that you get it right the first time. Wingo notes, "If I had to do it over again I'd go with better systems, I'd start off with a lot more money for systems and infrastructure, and I'd get audited financial statements every year. I would also hire for energy and enthusiasm rather than just skills. I'd get people right out of school who like challenges and will work 16-hour days."

Wingo noted that having worked in a start-up before was very beneficial. His previous employer had 50 employees so he felt comfortable when his firm grew up to 50 employees. But when his firm went beyond 50—he was in all new territory! Although people and personalities are important in the beginning, you also need to have systems in place so that it has a growth plan and infrastructure in place if the firm is successful.

REALITY CHECK

Scot Wingo noted, "Don't assume that all the time and effort you spend in the planning process will produce a flawless plan. It doesn't matter how smart or careful you are. There will be major flaws in your first business plan."[17] Accept the fact that it is virtually impossible for reality to match the plan. Your assumptions about initial sales, the amount of receivables, the speed of collections, initial capital requirements, supplier dependability, competitive retaliation, seasonality, and so on, will not be totally accurate.

REALITY CHECK

It would be easy to conclude that the time spent in planning is a waste because the world is changing rapidly on all fronts. Some entrepreneurs exclaim that the world changed so much while they were developing their plans that they could not implement their plans once they were drafted. It is better to have a plan that needs to be modified than not to have a plan at all.

REALITY CHECK

Joseph Mancuso, as director of the Center for Entrepreneurial Management, noted, "Nobody ever volunteers to give you a copy of their business plan, even when they're successful, because 9 out of 10 times that plan didn't come true."[18] This does not mean that developing a business plan is an exercise in futility. Without a plan's projections, milestones, budgets, and so on, you would not be in a position to know that other things are not going as planned. Your plan can be seen as a performance assessment tool. It serves as a scorecard for your venture. Its timeline with milestones allows you to measure progress. A plan will help identify when things need to be changed before it is too late. Although your plan may have been modified as soon as your venture is launched, it will serve as a useful springboard for making the changes.

Awareness is a prerequisite for change. One entrepreneur who prefers to remain anonymous recognized that if a plan had the proper metrics it could serve as an early warning system. She noted, "When I started my business, having a business plan made it easier for me to respond quickly! I was able to determine what wasn't going as planned—to find out why—and to fix it!"

Separate the funding from the plan

Too many people focus on the role the plan plays in raising funds. Most discussions, articles, and books about business plans focus on the role funding plays in the creation and growth of a new venture. Although funding may play a critical role in the creation of a new venture, it must be put in perspective.

Business plans are like performance reviews. Performance reviews work best when they separate the review from the merit increase. Performance reviews should be designed to improve future performance; if they focus almost exclusively on merit pay issues, then too little attention will be directed to doing what needs to be done to enhance future performance. You develop a business plan to increase the odds for new venture success, not just to attract funding. If you demonstrate there is an opportunity and that you have the ability to create and maintain customers for a profit, then you should have a higher probability of attracting funds!

Three important points need to be kept in mind. First, remember you are the most important reader of the business plan. You develop the business plan so you have a blueprint for building a successful venture. Funding might be an important part, but it is only one part of the blueprint. Second, entrepreneurs who have sufficient personal funding may conclude that since they do not need any outside funding that they do not need to prepare a business plan. Again, you develop the business plan to increase the chances for success.

Ironically, having sufficient personal funds to start a venture could backfire. Seeking investors or bank financing forces you to identify the opportunity and to articulate how you plan to capitalize on it. Their review of your plan may reveal flaws that you missed. A thoroughly developed plan also provides financial benchmarks that will help you manage your investment better. When you project cash flows, income statements, and key ratios, you are establishing benchmarks for measuring the financial performance of the firm.

Third, having enough money to finance your own venture may also contribute to financial inefficiencies. Although most entrepreneurs have to resort to bootstrap funding, they will admit that their diligence and frugality made their firms razor sharp. Because they had limited funds, they had to be more diligent and resourceful. If you have deep pockets, then you may be tempted to buy fixtures and equipment rather than lease them. Today's ventures need to be able to change what they are doing to stay in sync with the changes in the marketplace. Leasing permits the emerging venture to make changes. Leasing also lets you keep some of your resources in reserve for future uses.

If you have sufficient personal funds, then you may also fall prey to the *wheel of retailing*. The wheel of retailing refers to the tendency for retail (and other types of businesses) to get caught up in buying things that add little value to the products and services they offer. They get caught up in image and accoutrements, when they should be keeping their eyes on delighting their customers. They get caught up in carrying inventory rather than finding ways to enhance stock turn. They spend their money on furnishings rather than streamlining the order and delivery process.

REALITY CHECK

The business plan must not be seen as a way to separate unsuspecting investors from their money by hiding the fatal flaw.[19]

Business Plans, Like Entrepreneurs, Come In All Shapes And Sizes

Developing a business plan for the first-time entrepreneur is particularly frustrating. It's like a student who asks the professor how long a term paper should be and how many references it should contain. The professor usually says that it should be long enough to do the topic justice and it should have enough sources to illustrate that it was thoroughly researched.

The length, breadth, depth, detail, and supporting documentation of the business plan are contingent on the nature of venture. The details of the plan will vary with who is the intended audience. Certain readers want certain details. The difficulty in preparing the business plan will also vary with the situation. The easiest type of business plan to develop is one where the proposed venture will offer only a minor modification of existing products or services in an established market that has not changed much, where the data are readily available, competition is fairly predictable, and almost everyone is successful. If the market is growing and the existing firms have become rather complacent, then it might not be that difficult to develop a plan to give your venture a competitive advantage.

It is far more difficult to develop a plan if your venture will be the first to market in a new field where your product or service is untested, the size and nature of the market is uncertain, and the technology is very complex. When things are uncertain and things are changing at a break-neck pace, then planning becomes very difficult. When things are changing, then time is of the essence. Time is also of the essence if major firms are eyeing the market. The challenge of planning is magnified if the venture will involve a substantial amount of money and fixed assets. The greater the need for outside funding, the greater the need to provide potential investors and creditors with information and documentation.

The creation of a winery provides an interesting example of the dynamics associated with developing a business plan. The business plan for a winery must address numerous critical dimensions. First, you have to identify a market opportunity. Next, you have to create a superior wine. Then you have to develop a distribution network to get the wine to the marketplace. Getting the right vines and finding the ideal location for growing the grapes is enough of a challenge. When you try to build a facility that uses an assortment of equipment from around the world, that adds to the challenge. The challenge is particularly noteworthy when you realize that it will be at least seven years before you can sell your wine.

THE PLAN EVOLVES THROUGH A NUMBER OF ITERATIONS

Developing a business plan may involve a number of iterations. The venture-screening process described in Chapter 4 evaluated the business concept according to certain criteria. The analysis of the market opportunity and the concept's merit can be viewed as building blocks for developing a very preliminary business plan. Developing the actual business plan takes the process much farther. Each iteration represents a gate. Each iteration raises questions that require additional information and documentation. If the proposed venture passes through the series of planning gates, then the plan should be implemented.

The entrepreneurial team should treat the new venture as a series of experiments. "Before launching the whole show, launch a little piece of it. Convene a focus group to test the product, build a prototype and watch it perform, or conduct a regional or local rollout of a service. Such an exercise reveals the true economics of the business and can help enormously in determining how much money the new venture actually requires and in what stages."[20]

Gary Lim of Syracuse University's Entrepreneurship and Emerging Enterprises program captured the need when the entrepreneur is early in the process to keep focused on the few things that really matter. He stated, "Sometimes you don't need anything more than a three-page map of where you want to take your business."[21] He states that all you need to do is sit down, ask yourself the following questions, and write out the answers:

- Where do I want to take this business?
- Can it make money?
- What is my market?
- What do I do if it doesn't sell like gangbusters?
- Who is the competition?[22]

The preliminary plan represents the first iteration of the business plan. It flushes out key issues, clarifies key assumptions, and addresses the i's without having to dot them and the t's without having to cross them.

The first iteration of the business plan should also answer four key questions:

1. What is the concept?
2. How are you going to market it?
3. How much do you think it will cost to produce and deliver what you're selling?
4. What do you expect will happen when you actually go out and start making sales?[23]

GOING FROM THE PRELIMINARY PLAN TO THE COMPREHENSIVE BUSINESS PLAN

The preliminary business plan serves as the foundation for a more comprehensive version of the plan. The comprehensive business plan is different from the preliminary plan on two key dimensions. First, it is far more thorough. It tries to dot every i and cross every t. Although the preliminary plan may have incorporated estimates and generalizations, the comprehensive business plan must be reality based as much as possible. Preliminary sales estimates for the first few years must be replaced with pro forma financial statements that reflect best-case, most-likely-case, and worst-case sales scenarios. The rough estimate of the venture's initial capital requirement must be replaced by a cash flow analysis that incorporates accounts payable, accounts receivable, amortized loan payments, inventory requirements, and so forth.

Second, the comprehensive plan is developed for more than just the entrepreneur's benefit. The comprehensive plan may be developed for other stakeholders. It will influence whether the entrepreneur will be able to attract (1) prospective members of the management team, (2) people who will invest in the venture, (3) bankers who will provide loans with reasonable rates and terms, (4) suppliers who welcome the opportunity to work with the firm and who will provide favorable credit terms, and (5) customers who will want to do business with the firm.

If the entrepreneur tries to attract interest and develop a relationship with targeted stakeholders without a comprehensive plan, then he or she is likely to encounter little interest. A comprehensive plan that demonstrates the venture's ability to seize an opportunity will open doors for the new venture. A plan that generates more questions than answers will cast a shadow of doubt on the entrepreneur's ability to start and manage a new venture.

THE COMPREHENSIVE BUSINESS PLAN WILL REQUIRE ADDITIONAL BRAIN POWER

Developing the comprehensive business plan usually involves considerable research and analysis. Although the entrepreneur may have been the only one involved in the step-by-step process of identifying and evaluating alternative business opportunities, development of the comprehensive business plan should involve the people who will be involved in the venture if it is started. Various people can play a key role in the development of the plan and the launch of the venture. Their depth of knowledge and perspectives can provide insights that will increase the venture's chances for success.

Find a Mentor Who Will Help You Shoot the Rapids

Many successful entrepreneurs note that having a mentor before starting their ventures and in its earliest days contributed to their success. The process of starting a venture can be very lonely and frustrating. Having someone whom you can call or sit down with who can serve as a sounding board can be extremely helpful, especially if the management team has not been formed.

Successful entrepreneurs usually are the best mentors. Their experience and breadth of perspective can help the first-time entrepreneur in almost any decision situation. The mentor's primary role is to help the entrepreneur put things in their proper perspective. The best mentors avoid making decisions for the entrepreneur; instead, they ask probing questions, challenge assumptions, and/or encourage the entrepreneur to explore other alternatives. Objectivity and candor play a key role in a mentoring relationship. The mentor must be able to share his or her thoughts freely. The entrepreneur will benefit from a mentor if he or she has a genuine interest in getting assistance, values the mentor's views, and welcomes constructive criticism.

Mentors play a very different role from the other sources of assistance. They assist the entrepreneur because they want to help the entrepreneur succeed. They are rarely paid for their services, yet they may invest in the venture at some time. The key to mentor relationships is that the mentor be available for assistance on short notice. The entrepreneur may seek their assistance over the phone or over lunch. In some cases, the entrepreneur may be looking for just a quick impression of some issue. In other cases, the entrepreneur may be looking for advice on hiring a member of the management team or sources of funding. The length of time for mentor assistance can range from some assistance during the period prior to start-up all the way to continued assistance as a member of the board of directors.

Mentors usually come from three areas. Mentors are frequently businesspeople the entrepreneur knows and respects. In some cases, a mentor may be referred to the entrepreneur via an accountant, banker, or an attorney. Entrepreneurial organizations may be an excellent place to network with entrepreneurs and service providers.

External Advisors/Service Providers

Professional advisors may play a key role in the development of a business plan. The need for professional advisors depends on the entrepreneur's knowledge, the depth and breadth of the management team, and the nature and complexity of the proposed venture. It should be clear by now that it is impossible for any entrepreneur to know all that needs to be known about starting and running a venture. Even if the entrepreneur had extensive experience, there are not enough hours in the day to review every situation and to stay abreast of recent developments in the field of accounting, commercial law, insurance, banking, and other business practices.

The relationship played by external advisors and the management team may resemble the "Which came first, the chicken or the egg?" question. The answer is that the entrepreneur should contact external advisors as early as possible in the process of starting a venture. Professional advisors may be helpful sources of information. They may also identify potential pitfalls that should be avoided. The best way to select advisors is to ask successful businesspeople whom they recommend—then interview at least three for each area—if you select the attorney first, then ask that person whom he or she recommends and make that one of the people you interview.[24]

REALITY CHECK

The use of professional advisors is a litmus test of the entrepreneur's commitment to doing things right and willingness to pay for quality assistance. People who have a professional background are accustomed to using professional services. People with strong egos rarely seek the advice of others and are usually reluctant to pay others for their services. Although you might not relish paying for their services, if you recognize the need for professional advice and are willing to commit some of your limited capital to pay for it, then you have made a big step toward starting your venture off right.

Certified Public Accountant

Many first-time entrepreneurs underestimate the assistance that a CPA can provide prior to start-up. The selection of your accountant is directly related to the preceding reality check. If you are committed to creating an exceptional enterprise, then you need to make sure you are starting off on the right foot. Do not try to save a few dollars by hiring a bookkeeper rather than a CPA.

You start the process by selecting the right accounting firm. This is important for three reasons. First, certain accounting firms have accountants on their staffs that specialize in entrepreneurial ventures. The largest accounting firms have departments that specialize in the formation and growth of entrepreneurial ventures. You want to have an accountant that truly grasps the challenges associated with starting a new venture. These firms can also help you in your search for funding and talent.

Second, you should not put all your eggs in one basket. If you go with a small accounting firm, then you may have to scramble for a new accountant if that accountant is no longer available. Third, you and your venture will be judged by other potential stakeholders—particularly investors—by the accounting firm you use. Although it might cost a little more for the premium accounting firm, you will be sending a signal that you are committed to getting the best advice.

Ironically, using one of the premier accounting firms might *not* cost you more money. If your venture has considerable growth potential, then you may be able to negotiate a lower rate for the first year or two. Most accounting firms are willing to lower their rates if they want to have the inside position when you grow. The rates charged by premier firms may not be more expensive than smaller firms. Accounting firms that specialize in entrepreneurial ventures are in a better position to provide you with advice, so they do not have to charge you to learn. Their fees are also worth the money because they are more apt to provide the right advice, rather than wing it.

Many entrepreneurs enter business without any real appreciation of the value of external advisors. They use them out of necessity or desperation. Unfortunately, many businesses fail—not because the business lacks potential, but for other reasons. Two of those reasons can be the failure to get good, practical advice when such advice is needed and the receipt of bad advice.[25]

The accountant can help you set up the best method of accounting for your business.

The accountant may help you maintain your monthly financial reports, prepare payroll tax reports and W-2s, prepare your taxes, and do an audit if is it is required by a lender. Your accountant can also help you establish controls to prevent theft or embezzlement—which is a concern for every business.[26]

It should be clear that you should select an accounting firm that can help you succeed. The top accounting firms function more like consulting firms than traditional accounting firms.   Select the firm that can improve your decisions and performance.

Legal Counsel

You should demonstrate the same amount of diligence in selecting a law firm as you do in selecting an accounting firm. The right legal counsel will provide useful advice and reduce your risks. You should look for a law firm that has attorneys who specialize in entrepreneurial ventures. They will be in a position to recommend the right legal form, file the appropriate legal documents, and advise you on how to run the business so it follows proper meeting, decision, and reporting requirements.

Attorneys who specialize in entrepreneurial ventures can be particularly beneficial if your proposed venture involves intellectual property. Attorneys can provide advice on copyrights, trademarks, patents, contracts, leases, and hiring practices. Like accountants, it may be possible to negotiate lower initial fees if your venture has the potential to grow dramatically and use the firm's services in the future. It may be worthwhile to ask other entrepreneurs which firm they would recommend. If you have selected an accountant, then your accountant may suggest a law firm.

Bankers

Bankers can be very helpful when you are evaluating opportunities and developing your business plan. Most of the larger banks, like accounting and law firms, have people on their staffs who specialize in entrepreneurial ventures. These specialists may be called commercial loan officers or business bankers. Although most banks and bankers are noto-riously skeptical about new ventures, the bankers who specialize in entrepreneurial ven-tures have a better understanding of the challenges associated with creating a business. Unfortunately, most banks will not loan start-ups any money. Instead, they usually wait until a business is actually up and running before they will consider providing it with a loan. Yet, business bankers are usually willing to provide useful advice before you start your venture because they want the venture to do its banking with them. Business bankers have access to key operating ratios for certain types of business.

Consultants

Consultants may need to be hired to provide advice in areas where the entrepreneur does not have sufficient knowledge. This is usually the case if the management team has not been formed yet or if the team does not have a person with a sufficient level of knowl-edge in that area. If you are going to seek the services of a consultant, make sure you hire a consultant who is in sync with entrepreneurial ventures and your particular type of business. There are consultants for just about every aspect of business and every type of business.

Some entrepreneurs have found it more worthwhile to seek the advice of other entre-preneurs than full-time consultants. Iris Shur and Jean Sifleet wanted to start a shop sell-ing furniture and home accessories on consignment, but they recognized their limited experience and expertise could jeopardize their venture's success. They approached Jan Hess and Sarah Powers, who had started the Stock Exchange, a consignment store, 15 years earlier. Hess and Powers agreed to spend a day with Shur and Sifleet teaching them the ropes. Their fee was $1,500 and Shur and Sifleet had to sign an agreement to not set up their store within 30 miles of the Stock Exchange. Shur and Sifleet learned how to choose an ideal location, how to identify good workers, and where to advertise. They also got lessons in merchandise appraisal, bookkeeping, and store layout, as well as the idio-syncrasies of the consignment business. Shur noted, "If we didn't learn from somebody else, it would have taken us a lot longer to get to where we are now."[27]

Insurance Advisor

First-time entrepreneurs should seek the advice of a couple of commercial insurance pro-viders as early as possible. They can identify key business risks and indicate how they can be addressed. They can also identify the type and amount of coverage your venture should have to cover property and casualty, hospitalization, medical, business interruption, prod-uct liability, and various other risks. Insurance products are now so diverse and complex that it is difficult to find one agent who has the requisite expertise in all these areas to give you the right product at the best cost. It is preferable to seek out agents that specialize in the areas of coverage you need.[28]

Management Team

There is no point in beating around the bushes—if you want to create an exceptional enterprise, then you must have an exceptional management team. The days of the lone wolf entrepreneur are over. There are just too many challenges that must be addressed for one person to make all the decisions. You need to create the management team as soon as possible.

The role of the management team in developing the business plan, however, also presents an interesting question. Entrepreneurs face the dilemma of whether they should assemble the key people and then develop the plan or develop the plan and then get the key people to implement it. The answer is both.

If the management team is to be composed of people who will also be principal investors, then they will find it in their best interests to be involved from the beginning. Tom Weldon, principal founder of Novoste Corp, a medical devices company, provides an interesting perspective for when the comprehensive business plan should be prepared. He says most entrepreneurs write a business plan way too soon, producing little substance and dubious projections. He notes that it is important to have the company running with the top people in place first.[29] This echoes the chicken-or-the-egg nature of the dilemma. The process of developing the business plan will indicate the need for certain skills, abilities, and levels of experience for the management team. These characteristics and qualities will then serve as the basis for recruiting the management team. Conversely, if the entrepreneur waits until the team is in place, then its members' insights could play a major role in the development and refinement of the comprehensive business plan.

If the prospective team hasn't been identified and won't play an integral role in the development of the comprehensive business plan, then the entrepreneur should seek advice from other people so he or she won't be the sole architect of the plan. This is why it is so important for the entrepreneur to have a mentor, his or her set of professional advisors in place, or an advisory committee from the beginning.

The team must be assembled from both a defensive and offensive point of view when it is put together. From a defensive perspective, you need to identify your own shortcomings and hire people to fill in the managerial blanks. If you have a technology background, then you need to be sure you are the right person to be running your venture. Overseeing new product development may be the best use of your talents. If you are really good at marketing, then you may need to bring in someone right away who is strong in accounting or operational matters. In any event, you cannot afford to build your team on a *when time or when money is available* basis. Your business plan should identify the skill and experience areas that are important to your venture's success and how they will be addressed.

Second, as you address the managerial gaps to be filled, you need to make sure that you have strength in the dimensions that are most critical to the success of your venture. You may not be able to afford a blue-ribbon management team, but it pays to have battle-tested people in key positions. This is particularly true if you will be seeking investors or a loan from a bank. William Sahlman noted that he is like many investors when he reviews a business plan. He said, "I always read the resume section first. Not because the people part of the new venture is the most important, but because without the right team, none of the other parts really matters. Investors value managers who have been around the block a few times."[30]

The business plan should candidly describe each team member's knowledge of the new venture's product or service; its production processes; and the market itself, from competitors to customers. It also helps to indicate if the team has worked together before. If the new venture is run by people well known to suppliers, customers, and employees, their enterprise may be brand new, but they aren't.[31]

A high-quality management team will enable your venture to hit the ground running. People with experience know about the big and little things that make a difference. Experienced people are in a better position to know what works and what doesn't. Their experience may have taught them to expect the unexpected. Their extensive experience may also enable them to open doors with important vendors, distributors, lenders, and investors.

If your team is composed of people who were with very successful firms, then their pedigree will also help. If your venture is in the high-technology field, then having an individual who is an expert in that field on your team, as a member of your advisory committee, your board of directors, or as a consultant will enhance your venture's credibility.

Tod Loofbourrow, founder of Authoria Inc., a business providing information services, noted the importance of having experienced people on the management team. He noted, "If I started Authoria over I would hire a senior executive even sooner. Three years ago, if we had had the world-class senior staff that we have today, we'd be much farther ahead than we are now in the market. It's difficult to recruit executives when your company consists of six people in an apartment still developing the product, but it's so valuable to have deep experience on staff. It's also critical to be extremely choosy in hiring members of the team. Every time we compromised to get a job filled earlier, we regretted it. Building a world-class senior team is hard, time-consuming work. We succeeded most significantly when we hired people with incredible experience in their field. The enthusiasm of a start-up environment breeds the temptation to build the team fast, but a bad hire is far worse and more time consuming than leaving an empty chair at the table until you recruit the right candidate."[32]

REALITY CHECK

Make sure you check out every prospective person. There are too many examples of entrepreneurs who were too easily impressed with resumes. This is one of the times that it may be worth using an executive search firm. Executive search firms will be responsible for attracting qualified applicants and checking them out to be sure they are what they say they are.

Advisory Committee

First-time entrepreneurs are finding that it may be well worth their time to establish an advisory committee when they are exploring various business opportunities and developing their business plan. Starting a venture can be like walking through a minefield. The advisory committee can help you reduce the likelihood that things will blow up in your face. Having an advisory committee is like a having a group of mentors at your disposal.

The beauty of the advisory committee is its flexibility. You can select people to serve on it who have the skills and experience you need to supplement your skills. The advisory committee can also meet as often as needed. You can convene the committee to challenge your perceptions and assumptions as you approach a decision junction or if you are facing a more immediate issue.

Advisory committees have become more common due to the increase in lawsuits directed at boards of directors. People whom you would like to serve on your board of directors may be reluctant to serve on your board because they may not be willing to accept the liability that comes with being on the board. Board members are considered trustees for the stockholders. A stockholder may sue the board if the stockholder believes the board did not fulfill its corresponding fiduciary responsibilities. Directors may also be the targets of other litigation. Advisory committees do not have comparable vulnerability because they do not make decisions. They merely provide advice. In theory, if you do not make a decision, then you cannot be liable for the decision that was made. Some advisory committees are called *advisory boards,* but it is much safer to call them *committees* so they are not seen as decision-making boards.

If you choose a noncorporate legal form for your new venture, then you should still consider setting up an advisory committee to provide advice on key decisions. In any event, your advisory committee should be composed of successful businesspeople.

Entrepreneurs frequently ask how they can get professionals to serve on an advisory committee. One of the amazing things about new ventures is that a number of professionals have a keen interest in helping them. Helping emerging ventures is like vicarious parenting. A number of professionals seem to admire entrepreneurs who are out there on their own putting everything they have on the line. The same is true for veteran entrepreneurs. They want to help those who are embarking on the entrepreneurial journey for the first time.

If your business idea has merit and you have a genuine interest in getting their advice, then it usually is not that difficult to get three or four professionals to serve on your advisory committee. You may offer to pay them a modest honorarium, but their desire to help usually keeps this from being an amount that outweighs the benefits from having an advisory committee. The key is to ask people who are in a position to provide good advice. People who have experience in meeting the challenges you are about to face and people who have a broad perspective are the most valuable. They can open your eyes to things you haven't thought of and they can reduce the likelihood that you will be blindsided by something that could set you back.

Advisory committees can play a valuable role when you are developing your business plan. Advisory committees are particularly beneficial when the entrepreneur has limited experience and does not expect to have a management team in place when the venture is formed. Once the venture gets up and running and the team is established, then you may convene the team less frequently. People should be recruited to serve on the committee based on the nature of the challenges you expect to face. As the venture evolves, you may ask different professionals to serve on the committee.

It is strongly recommended that the advisory committee be established while the venture is in the concept stage. The advisory committee will not only keep the entrepreneur focused on the critical issues, but its members' insights and experiences may prevent the entrepreneur from making a number of mistakes.

Matthew Reich, who founded The Old New York Brewing Company, exemplifies the situation encountered by a number of entrepreneurs. He stated, "You don't know what it's like in the trenches until you're in the trenches."[33] He planned to spend about $2 million to own and build a brewery, but he paid nearly $4 million just to lease and modify a structure. He had to pay a dollar a case more for glassware than he expected. Bottle suppliers would let him buy only $12,000 worth of bottles on credit. The rest had to be cash. He learned the hard way that every construction firm pays bribes, that buyers expect special deals, and you do whatever you have to do to buy your way into an account. He believed New Yorkers would buy a beer brewed in New York. He found that most of the consumers who live in New York could care less where the beer is brewed.[34]

The advisory committee may be seen as a skeptical ally. It should ask the questions that need to be asked and challenge key assumptions about competition, suppliers, and the ability to attract customers and personnel. Murphy's Law, "If something can go wrong, it will," is particularly applicable to new ventures. Although veteran entrepreneurs and other professionals (accountants, bankers, attorneys, etc.) who may serve on your advisory committee may not know all that you'd like them to know about your business, they usually know that you should not expect things to go as planned. They know that suppliers don't always deliver what or when they are supposed to. They know that contractors rarely make or keep a commitment. They know that you can't count on the weather. They know that if something needs to be inspected then a different inspector will not approve whatever it is because of his or her own interpretation of the code.

REALITY CHECK

Don't set up an advisory committee because you read about its merits here. If you set up an advisory committee, then look for people who will challenge your ideas. Leslie Brokaw notes, "It's shocking how infrequently entrepreneurs seek advice. There ought to be a rule: Before you start a business, find 10 smart people who know the industry and ask them: How am I going to screw up?"[35]

The people on the advisory committee are not there just to be cynics. They may also be a source of ideas and contacts. They can also be helpful in exploring possibilities. As long as they are not put in a position where they may have a conflict of interest, they should be willing to share their thoughts and their time.

Technology Advisory Committee

If your product/service is related to technology, then you should consider setting up a technology advisory committee. Sometimes it is called a *board* rather than a *committee,* but it may be advisable to call it a *committee* rather than a board so it is not considered a decision-making unit with corresponding liability. A technology advisory board is different than an advisory committee because it focuses exclusively on technology-related issues rather than ongoing business issues. The technology advisory committee should be composed of people who are at the leading edge of your industry. They may be from the supply, distribution channels, or ultimate consumer side. They may also be academic researchers or people who are considered at the leading edge of your field.

Edward Welles noted that technical advisors might suggest future products worth developing. He also noted that a technology committee composed of thought leaders could legitimize a company. Tom Weldon says he would have set up one even with a low-tech business. Even if an investor has never heard of a company or its founder, he or she might have heard of its technical advisors and be suitably impressed. It may be possible to pay members of the advisory committee in stock.[36]

Board of Directors

Every corporation is required to have a board of directors. In an ideal world, the board would be composed of outside professionals who could add considerable value to the firm. Unfortunately, most boards do not add much value. People who serve on them either do not have the time or the knowledge to provide substantive assistance to the direction of the venture. If the board is composed of the same people who are part of the management team, then it will rarely offer new insights. They will just satisfy legal statutes that the board must meet to conduct corporate business.

Robbie Hardy, who founded two software companies and an investment firm, noted that most entrepreneurs don't want a board of directors and because of this, they don't surround themselves with professional and successful people. Many entrepreneurs don't know how to build a fully functioning professional board. She noted, "Instead of carefully researching board candidates, they pick friends, yes men, people they heard speak at conferences, or just about anyone who will offer them funding."[37]

REALITY CHECK

Your venture's success will be directly related to the quality of decisions that are made. You cannot do it all. If you have the right board, then it can help you be a better manager. If you consider having a board to be a waste of your time, then you should step back and ask yourself if you should be the one running the venture. Leading an emerging enterprise involves soliciting ideas from people who know what you don't, listening to their views and constructive criticism, and capitalizing on what they have to offer.

REALITY CHECK

The board of directors cannot be approached on a time available basis. Setting up a board, orienting the board, and working with the board can take at least 10 percent of your time. If you don't see the time and their questions as an investment in your venture's future, then step back and ask yourself if you should really be running the venture.

The board of directors has considerable rights and responsibilities. The board of directors must make decisions about securing debt, paying dividends, acquiring assets, selecting and compensating the chief executive, as well as selling the firm's assets or the firm as a whole.

The board acts in a trustee (fiduciary) capacity for the shareholders. The decision-making role of the board mandates that the board exercise considerable diligence in all of its decisions; most of the people who would add value insist that director and officer liability coverage be in place to protect them.

If a person you are seeking for a board position is reluctant to accept that vulnerability, then he or she may be willing to serve on your advisory committee. Having an advisory committee in addition to the board of directors may be worthwhile if the board is composed of investors. You may also consider setting up a separate advisory committee if the people elected to serve on the board by the stockholders do not have what you need in a board. Since the board is elected by its stockholders (who may be outside investors) it may be made up of people who do not have the breadth of perspective, the depth of business knowledge, and the connections needed to provide insightful advice to you and to fill gaps in the management team. Robbie Hardy noted that in her industry, the boards of directors are investors—and just because they have money doesn't mean that they can help (advise) you. The formal board of directors will satisfy legal requirements. The advisory committee will then provide value-added business advice and help you be sure you are pointed in the right direction.

Your board should have at least one person on it who has started a business from scratch and guided its growth for at least five years. This person may keep you from committing many of the classic mistakes made by first-timers. When you're fighting from the trenches, you don't have the general's view from behind the lines. There are obstacles and opportunities that won't be apparent to you, only because your point of view is distorted by the fog of war.[38]

Ted Weldon sought balance and credibility when assembling his board of directors. In addition to three members of the management team, he recruited two outside members from the local community. Weldon was new to the Atlanta area, and he considered local members a wise strategic move to raise his firm's profile in Atlanta and to widen his own network of professional contacts.[39]

A board can do much to probe your thoughts on the business and point out what you need to see.[40] One of the best ways for the board of directors to help you is to have them prequalify your business spending. Weldon suggests that before every prospective purchase the board should ask three questions:

1. Is this expenditure necessary right now?
2. Will this make money or cost money?
3. Is there a cheaper way to accomplish this (outsourcing, leasing, etc.)?[41]

Ross Garber, cofounder of Vignette Corporation, offers the following advice to entrepreneurs when forming their boards:

- You and your board should agree in advance on what you control and what they need to approve. This will avoid future surprises when you have a big deal, financing, or a management hire to finalize.
- Pay a lot of attention to the personalities and backgrounds of your board members to ensure they will be able to work together in difficult times and over the long run.
- Although you should count on them to listen well and help you think through all the options, you should not expect them to have the same intimate understanding of your markets that allows you to make the final decision.
- Most of all, remember that you are the CEO, and you are the one being paid to run the company, take the risks, and make the big decisions. Use your board as advisors, but don't wait for someone else to do the world's hardest job for you.[42]
- In summary, the people who serve on the board and the extent the board provides direction and oversight will reflect whether you are committed to having a professionally managed enterprise.

AVOID PARALYSIS BY ANALYSIS

This book encourages you to approach the entrepreneurial process in a systematic manner, to gather as much information as possible in analyzing the market, and to develop a solid business plan. Don't let your desire to create the perfect business plan keep you from actually starting your venture. As noted earlier, entrepreneurs need to recognize that there is a natural rhythm for new ventures. Starting a venture is like catching the right wave where judgment, timing, and adaptability are essential. There is a time to analyze, a time to plan, and a time to act. If you try to address every issue to the last detail, then the wave may pass you by.

Success for some ventures will be tied to whether they have a comprehensive plan that dots every *i* and crosses every *t*. Success for other ventures will be tied to their ability to get into the market quickly and then adapt constructively to the marketplace. These ventures may only need a skeletal plan that highlights the key issues and addresses them in fairly general terms. Bhidé noted, "In ventures based on hustle rather than proprietary advantages, a detailed analysis of competitors and industry structure is rarely of much value. The ability to seize short-lived opportunities and execute them brilliantly is of far more importance than a long-term competitive strategy."[43]

Entrepreneurs need to recognize that the law of diminishing marginal returns applies to the time invested in the planning process. There comes a time when the insights gained from planning decline relative to the time invested in planning. Bhidé noted, "In setting their analytical priorities, entrepreneurs must recognize that some critical uncertainties cannot be resolved through more research. Resolving a few big questions—understanding what things must go right and anticipating the venture-destroying pitfalls—is far more important than investigating many nice-to-do matters. The entrepreneur has to live with critical uncertainties, such as the relative competence of rivals or the preferences of strategic customers, which are not easy to analyze."[44]

Jeffry Timmons noted, "Remember that the plan is not the business and that an ounce of can-do implementation is worth two pounds of planning."[45] He also noted the preparation time/opportunity cost nature of the time spent on planning when he stated, "Don't waste time writing a plan when you could be closing sales and collecting cash."[46]

The plan must not be set in stone. "A business plan must not be an albatross that hangs around the neck of the entrepreneurial team, dragging it into oblivion. Instead, the plan must be a call for action, one that recognizes management's responsibility to fix what is broken proactively and in real time."[47]

THE BUSINESS PLAN MUST BE A LIVING DOCUMENT

No entrepreneur is all knowing, and no business plan is flawless. Although business plans attempt to identify what needs to be done to enhance the odds for success, no plan can predict what the future holds. Life is full of surprises. As once noted, "The only thing that is certain about the future is that it is uncertain."

The words "This plan is subject to change" should be printed on the cover of every business plan. Business plans for new ventures must be flexible and evolve with the times. Plans need to adapt to new challenges or the realization that assumptions don't reflect reality. Erik Larson notes, "The real world has a way of quickly awakening companies from the paper dreams in their business plans."[48] Jay Conrad Levinson noted, "Guerrilla entrepreneurs reevaluate their plans regularly and don't hesitate to make changes in them."[49]

Bhidé noted, "Business plans lead such brief but important lives, like training wheels and booster rockets. Businesses cannot be launched like space shuttles, with every detail of the mission planned in advance. Initial analyses only provide plausible hypotheses, which must be tested and modified."[50]

REALITY CHECK

"Nothing happens according to the plan, and what's worse, things happen in discrete bundles, not in small increments. Sales and most expenses come in lumps, the timing of which is unpredictable at the start. The lesson: Don't count on your cash projection; plan for the worst."[51]

THE BUSINESS PLAN EMPHASIZES HITTING THE TARGET, NOT HITTING THE BULL'S EYE!

Business plans have come under attack for three specific reasons in the last few years. The first criticism is the world is changing so rapidly, it makes it more difficult to plan for the future. The second criticism is that plans need to be more realistic. Instead of trying to hit a specific point in the future, they should shoot for a general destination. The third criticism is related to the second criticism. It stresses the need for plans to be more flexible. Instead of being linear, they should be more adaptive and opportunistic.

The first criticism has already been addressed. Although planning may be more difficult, the rate and nature of change make planning for the future more important than ever. The second criticism has merit because too many established firms are fixated on hitting a specific sales target, a specific return on investment target, and/or market share target.

The third criticism is also based on the new realities. The venture may do a lot better if it adopts an opportunistic adaptation strategy instead of a rigid strategy. Although entrepreneurs need to avoid being seduced by short-term opportunities and *here today, gone tomorrow* fads, they need to recognize that they might not really know what works and what does not work until they launch their ventures. A number of the most successful ventures in the last decade grew because of a suggestion made by a customer, supplier, or distributor. In many cases, their growth was the result of a customer asking, "Can you do this for us?" Entrepreneurs need to keep their eyes and ears open for opportunities that may present themselves.

Being an opportunity-driven venture is more likely to succeed than a venture that says, "We are in the business of XYZ and we don't care if the grass is greener over there—we have made up our mind—don't confuse me with the opportunities." Your business plan should not be a straitjacket that keeps your venture from exploring emerging opportunities. Bhidé noted, "Entrepreneurial adaptations result from imaginative responses to unforeseen events."[52] He also noted, "A significant proportion of successful ventures develop entirely new markets, products, and sources of competitive advantage. Therefore, although perseverance and tenacity are valuable entrepreneurial traits, they must be complemented with flexibility and willingness to learn. Entrepreneurs should be willing to exploit opportunities that didn't figure into the initial plan."[53]

The need for defensive adaptation applies when things do not go as planned. Many of the companies *Inc.* magazine has watched over the years were noteworthy because of their the ability (1) to recognize and react to the completely unpredictable, (2) to use enough managerial sense to plan and anticipate, yet enough street savvy to know when things are going wrong, and (3) to be flexible, and not just in response to the wrong customers or selling through entirely the wrong channels.[54]

The need for adaptability, whether it is the result of an unexpected opportunity or an unanticipated problem, means that your venture needs to be perceptive, to have early warning systems, and to be able to adapt to new realities. What needs to be done to succeed under ever-changing conditions may be more important than what was planned. Success in the years ahead may be more contingent on the venture's ability to act like a SWAT unit than a rigid *Fortune* 500 firm. "You can write a plan that makes your business look fabulous and gets the money, but you can still go broke." For example, Jake Holmes of Stowe Canoe got into trouble when he lost his largest customer to bankruptcy.[55]

THE BUSINESS PLAN SHOULD PROVIDE A COMPELLING REASON FOR CREATING THE VENTURE

The business plan should be seen as a call to arms. It must provide a compelling reason for starting the venture. It must also provide a compelling reason for customers, suppliers, distributors, investors, and personnel to seek out the venture. Desh Deshpande encourages entrepreneurs to reach for the stars. He noted, "Dare to dream. Big ideas capture the imagination of investors and customers."[56] He cautioned entrepreneurs, however, to be pragmatic dreamers by making sure your reach does not exceed your grasp. He noted, "Your big idea may be a disruptive technology that will change the world, but at the start you may need to concentrate on a smaller entry point into the market. Find a product that allows you to enter the market and generate revenue first, then work your way up to the startling idea that transforms the planet."[57]

Bhidé noted that entrepreneurs should treat everyone whom they talk to as a potential customer, employee, or supplier, or at least as a possible source of leads down the road.[58] Your business plan should indicate why your venture should be perceived as the provider of choice, the employer of choice, and the investment of choice. It should convey why customers should stop buying from their current providers and do business with your venture. The plan should indicate why targeted customers should call you up, why they will want your goods/services, why they will want them now, and why they will not be price sensitive to what you have to offer. If you want to be the provider of choice, then your plan must indicate why your target market will be delighted to do business with your firm.

Entrepreneurs need to recognize that while they are risking their time and money, customers, investors, bankers, suppliers, distributors, and prospective personnel are also taking a risk if they become involved in new ventures. Customers take a risk when they switch to a new venture. Investors commit funds that could be put into other investments. Suppliers run the risk the new venture may not be able to pay its invoices. Distributors' reputations are tied to their ability to provide what their customers want. If a new venture is unable to meet its commitments or goes bankrupt, then distributors may also suffer.

Entrepreneurs must be very effective salespeople if they want to get the other stakeholders to accept the risk in doing business with a new venture. The business plan can play a valuable role by clarifying what the venture plans to accomplish as well as a compelling reason for others to jump on the new venture's bandwagon. The entrepreneur needs to show how the benefits of being involved in the firm far exceed the possible risks. Your business plan should answer the following questions:

- If you were a commercial banker would you lend it money? Would you welcome the opportunity to make it part of your loan portfolio?

- Would you want to work there?

- Would you quit your job to join the management team?

- If you were a private investor would you take a second mortgage to invest in it?

- Would you sell your GE or Merck stock to invest in it?

- Would you want to be a supplier for the firm?

- Would you consider the firm to be a key prospect?

- Would you grant the firm favorable terms?

- If you were in the channel of distribution for this type of product/service, would you seek this firm out to carry its products?

- Does your firm have a core competency that would prompt firms to seek you out to be part of a strategic alliance?

REALITY CHECK

Your venture will be competing for customers, talent, and funds. We live in a word full of alternatives. You must be the leading salesperson for your venture, and your business must be the vehicle for converting window shoppers into committed stakeholders. If you do not have the skills to promote your business, then you should not be the one to lead it.

THE BUSINESS PLAN SHOWS HOW YOU PLAN TO DEAL WITH RISK

The Mass Mutual ad, "You cannot predict the future, but you can prepare for it," captures the position that entrepreneurs need to take in dealing with risk. Classic *SWOT analysis* has helped managers for decades analyze the world around them. Managers have developed corporate strategies by identifying their firm's *strengths* and *weaknesses* as well as the external environment's *opportunities* and *threats*. Entrepreneurs need to use SWOT to identify current and prospective threats. The threats can include changing economic conditions, competition, government regulation or deregulation, technology, weather, consumer tastes and buying patterns, and so forth.

Although entrepreneurs cannot predict the future, they can run scenarios to identify possible futures. Scenarios are like mental radar. They can provide insights into what may be on the horizon as well as in the neighborhood. Scenarios help identify what may be possible. Effort should then be directed to identifying the probabilities such events may occur. The consequences (both favorable and unfavorable) should then be identified.

Risk analysis can be seen as a form of anticipatory management. By asking *what if?* questions, you may be in a position to develop contingency plans for dealing constructively with situations that could hinder your venture's success.

Anticipating possible events is of little value if you are not in a position to deal with new realities when they could jeopardize the venture's success. You need back-up plans and you need resources in reserve that can be employed to deal with the situation. Contingency plans need to be developed when (1) the consequences of your plan being derailed are high, (2) the probability of the detrimental event(s) is too high, and/or (3) both situations exist.

Insurance obviously plays a key role in how you deal with risk. You can buy insurance coverage for almost any type of situation or event. Your 360-degree analysis of your venture's risk should provide insights into which risks can be handled through preparedness and which risks need to be covered by insurance. Insurance policies and coverage are tied to probabilities and consequences. You should do what you can to reduce the risks and the consequences—and get insurance to cover the things that could truly jeopardize your venture.

Rob Ryan made an interesting observation that applies to how you approach preparing your business plan and dealing with risk. He observed, "The harder you work, the luckier you get."[59] Your business plan should indicate how the management team has positioned the firm to increase the likelihood good things will happen as well as decrease the likelihood bad things will occur. William Sahlman noted, "All opportunities have promise: all have vulnerabilities. A good business plan doesn't whitewash the latter. Rather, it proves that the entrepreneurial team knows the good, bad, and the ugly that the venture faces ahead. The plan must unflinchingly confront the risks ahead—in terms of people, opportunities, and context. What happens if one of the new venture's leaders leaves? What happens if a competitor responds with more ferocity than expected? What happens if you lose your source of raw material?"[60]

SOFTWARE IS NOT THE PANACEA

When entrepreneurs are confronted with the challenges associated with developing a business plan they are tempted to look for easier and quicker ways to prepare the plan. They either run down to the office supply store to check out the latest software package for developing a business plan for new ventures or they call around to see if they can outsource the plan to some consulting firm.

Inexpensive software packages are available for preparing business plans. These plans may save you some time because they are formatted to look like a sophisticated business plan. A closer look reveals that most software packages are nothing more than a set of templates wrapped around an electronic spreadsheet. The templates are nothing more than a bunch of words in a text format where you fill in the blanks. The software may ask a number of very important questions, but you still have to come up with the answers to the questions.

The same applies to the spreadsheets. Although they may contain certain formulas for subtracting expenses from revenue to figure profit and monthly cash flow, spreadsheets merely manipulate numbers. You still have to do research and analysis to figure out what numbers go into the corresponding calculations. You still have to estimate first year's sales on a monthly basis. You still have to estimate market share. You still have to figure out when price discounts will need to be offered to offset seasonality. You still have to estimate inventory requirements and payroll. You still have to estimate the percent of sales that will be in receivables. You still have to figure what amount you will need to spend on advertising as well as when and where it will be spent. You will also have to figure what will be the content of the advertising.

Accordingly, you still need to put all the critical information into the software. Software packages and spreadsheet are not like funnels. Developing a plan and projecting financial results involve more than just pouring a lot of data in one end and getting a flawless business plan or income statement out at the other end. A software-driven plan will only be as good as the data that you put into it. If you put in questionable estimates and faulty assumptions, then the software will give you rough financial statements. If you miss the sales estimate by 30 percent, then the income statement, cash flow projection, and balance sheet will all be way off. Mark S. Deion, a business planning and strategy consultant, noted, "Some software packages generate the same payroll numbers each month, even though the numbers of days in each month varies." He says that one way bankers look for sloppy numbers is by checking month-to-month financials.[61]

The only real advantage of software is that electronic spreadsheets can run various scenarios once you have entered key data. Electronic spreadsheets enable you to see the effect that varying levels of sales have on expenses and profits. Your plan should run the best-case, most-likely case, and worst-case revenue scenarios each of the first five years. These scenarios can reflect the consequences of different prices, different cost structures, and different financing packages on the firm's income statements and balance sheets. Electronic spreadsheets can also indicate the impact that varying levels of sales, accounts receivable, and collection periods can have on cash flow.

RESIST THE TEMPTATION TO OUTSOURCE
THE BUSINESS PLAN

The plan will take considerable time and it will be the source of considerable frustration. Nevertheless, you must be the primary architect of the plan. You have to know the plan inside and out. You can and should use the services of professionals (accountants, attorneys, etc.) where they can provide guidance and insights, but that doesn't mean that you should outsource the development of the business plan to a consultant even if you have an abundant supply of money.

Outside professionals may help clarify alternatives and provide initial assistance, but you are the one who is going to make the thousands of decisions that will determine whether the venture thrives or dies.

The need for you to be the principal architect—rather than software packages and consultants—is particularly evident if you are seeking external financing. It is generally recognized that banks don't lend money to businesses. They lend money to people who will make the right decisions that, in turn, will pay off the loans. Investors may be even more concerned about the entrepreneur's ability to make the right decisions because investors are at the end of the line when trying to recover their money if the business goes down. Timothy Dineen, founder of Leprechaun Capital, notes, "Investors can spot canned business plans a mile away. The most important thing a venture capitalist is looking for is quality management. You can sabotage your credibility with some of those [business plan software] packages."[62] Entrepreneurs should recognize one of the facts of financing, "The slicker the packaging, the weaker the plan." If the bankers and/or investors suspect that your plan was drafted by a consultant, then don't be surprised if they devalue its contents.

THE TIMELINE FOR PREPARING AND WRITING
THE BUSINESS PLAN

The timeline begins once the opportunity screening process has identified the best opportunity to pursue. It should be understood that the process of developing the business plan does not guarantee that the venture will be created. The process of developing the plan may indicate that the opportunity has insufficient financial merit to justify the risk, the time is not right, or that a fatal flaw exists. The venture also may not be launched if key resources, including personnel and/or funding, cannot be obtained.

The development of a business plan is not the same as writing the business plan. Developing the business plan involves considerable research and analysis. The opportunity screening process involved very preliminary estimates. The opportunity was merely a business concept at that stage. The development of the business plan, however, requires an in-depth analysis of the factors that will be essential to a successful launch. The process of writing the actual business plan begins when the research and analysis is completed. The research and analysis that were an integral part of developing the plan provide the documentation needed for the plan when it is written.

The following 24-step list profiles how the process for developing the business plan fits into the overall scheme of things that precede the decision to start a new venture:

Step 1. Clarify the financial and nonfinancial objectives for the venture.

Step 2. Analyze the industry and corresponding context.

Step 3. Analyze the market gaps.

Step 4. Analyze the market segments.

Step 5. Analyze the competition.

Step 6. Identify the target market.

Step 7. Analyze the target market's gaps.

Step 8. Identify the product/service/technology needs.

Step 9. Identify the product/service/technology offering.

Step 10. Develop the product/service/technology offering.

Step 11. Identify the operational and logistical requirements.

Step 12. Analyze the operational and logistical requirements.

Step 13. Identify the management team's necessary capabilities.

Step 14. Identify the skill and experience requirements for the board of directors and advisory committees.

Step 15. Develop the overall business strategy and timeline.

Step 16. Identify the key risks and develop the corresponding contingency plans.

Step 17. Prepare the financial projections.

Step 18. Identify the financial requirements.

Step 19. Determine whether the venture will meet the objectives set in step 1.

Step 20. Identify funding sources.

Step 21. Write the business plan.

Step 22. Have the board of directors and/or advisory committees review the business plan.

Step 23. Incorporate the board of directors' and/or advisory committee's feedback and recommendations into the business plan.

Step 24. Present the business plan to corresponding stakeholders.

CONCLUSION:
PREDICTING RAIN VERSUS BUILDING ARKS

The business plan should provide insight into whether the opportunity under consideration has merit, as well as identify the factors that must be addressed for the venture to capitalize on the opportunity. The business plan should also serve as a flexible blueprint for creating the venture.

No plan will be fail-safe and no amount of planning can foresee every eventuality. The key to the planning process is to force you to look before you leap, to get facts rather than to rely on assumptions, to recognize the prerequisites for success, and to do what you can do to increase the likelihood your venture will succeed.

Part of me relished the fact that so many people said my plan couldn't be done.[63]

— Howard Schultz
Founder of Starbucks

ENDNOTES

1. Kenneth W. Olm and George G. Eddy, *Entrepreneurship and Venture Management* (Engelwood Cliffs, NJ: Prentice Hall, 1985), p. 50.

2. Brian McWilliams, "Garbage In, Garbage Out," *Inc.,* August 1996, in Annual Editions Entrepreneurship 99/00, p. 139.

3. Ibid., p. 136.

4. Mark Van Osnabrugge and Robert J. Robinson, *Angel Investing* (San Francisco: Jossey-Bass, 2000), p. 364. Copyright © 2000, Jossey Bass. This material is used by permission of John Wiley & Sons, Inc.

5. Bruce Posner, "Real Entrepreneurs Don't Plan," *Inc.,* November 1985, p. 129.

6. Ibid., pp. 123–126.

7. William A. Sahlman, "How to Write a Really Great Business Plan," *Harvard Business Review,* July–August, 1997, in Annual Editions Entrepreneurship 99/00, p. 124. Reprinted by permission of *Harvard Business Review.*

8. Colleen Mastony, "Turbulent Takeoff," *Forbes,* May 3, 1999, p. 94.

9. Jay Conrad Levinson, "In the Trenches," *Entrepreneur,* June 1998, p. 110. Reprinted with permission of Jay Conrad Levinson.

10. Joseph R. Mancuso, "Profile of a Winner," *Success,* December 1995, p. 14.

11. Susan Hodges, "One Giant Step Toward a Loan," *Nation's Business,* August 1997, in Annual Editions Entrepreneurship 99/00, p. 121.

12. Sahlman, "How to Write a Really Great Business Plan," p. 125.

13. Ibid., p. 128.

14. Jeffry A. Timmons, *New Venture Creation* (New York: Irwin-McGraw-Hill, 1994), p. 154.

15. Interview with Scot Wingo, March 9, 1999.

16. Ibid.

17. Ibid.

18. Erik Larson, "The Best-Laid Plans," *Inc.,* February 1987, p. 60.

19. Sahlman, "How to Write a Really Great Business Plan," p. 131.

20. Ibid., pp. 130 & 131.

21. James Morrow, "Secrets of a Start-Up," *Success*, September 1998, p. 66.

22. Ibid.

23. Brodsky, "Due Diligence," p. 26.

24. Edward O. Welles, "15 Steps to a Start-Up," *Inc.,* March 1994, pp. 72–80.

25. Curtis F. Tate, James F. Cox, Frank Hoy, Vida Scarpello, and W. Woodrow Stewart, *Small Business Management and Entrepreneurship* (Boston: PWS-Kent Publishing, 1992), p. 118.

26. Ibid., p. 122.

27. Shane McLaughlin, "Mentors for Hire," *Inc.,* December 1998, p. 121.

28. Tate, Cox, Hoy, Scarpello, and Stewart, *Small Business Management and Entrepreneurship,* p. 123.

29. Welles, "15 Steps to a Start-Up," p. 78.

30. Sahlman, "How to Write a Really Great Business Plan," p. 124.

31. Ibid.

32. Tod Loofbourrow, "My Company Was Born in the Delivery Room," *American Venture,* July 2001, p. 31.

33. Erik Larson "The Best-Laid Plans," *Inc.,* February 1987, p. 63.

34. Ibid.

35. Leslie Brokaw, "The Truth About Start-Ups," *Inc.,* April 1991, p. 56.

36. Welles, "15 Steps to a Start-Up," pp. 72–80.

37. Cara Cunningham, "How to Build Your Own Board," *Red Herring,* October 30, 2000, p. 209.

38. Ken Elias, "Why My Business Failed," *Wall Street Journal,* October 11, 1994, in Annual Editions Entrepreneurship 99/00, p. 75.

39. Welles, "15 Steps to a Start-Up," p. 74.

40. Elias, "Why My Business Failed," p. 74.

41. David M. Anderson, "Deadly Sins," Entrepreneur, August 2001, p. 109. Reprinted with permission of Entrepreneur Media, Inc.

42. Ross Garber, "Board Management Made Easy," *Red Herring,* July 2000, p. 390.

43. Amar Bhidé, "How Entrepreneurs Craft Strategies That Work," p. 71.

44. Ibid., p. 70.

45. Jeffry A. Timmons, *New Venture Creation* (New York: Irwin-McGraw-Hill, 1994), p. 154.

46. Ibid.

47. Sahlman, "How to Write a Really Great Business Plan," p. 131.

48. Larson, "The Best-Laid Plans," p. 63.

49. Jay Conrad Levinson, "In the Trenches," *Entrepreneur,* June 1998, p. 110. Reprinted with permission of Jay Conrad Levinson.

50. Bhidé, "How Entrepreneurs Craft Strategies That Work," p. 71.

51. Elias, "Why My Business Failed," p. 74.

52. Amar Bhidé, *The Origin and Evolution of New Businesses* (Oxford: Oxford University Press, 2000), p. 67.

53. Bhidé, "How Entrepreneurs Craft Strategies That Work," p. 73.

54. Brokaw, "The Truth about Start-Ups," p. 54.

55. McWilliams, "Garbage In, Garbage Out," p. 139.

56. Desh Deshpande, "How to Find the Right Niche," *Red Herring,* December 18, 2000, p. 212.

57. Ibid.

58. Bhidé, "How Entrepreneurs Craft Strategies That Work," p. 73.

59. Rob Ryan, *Smartups: Lessons from Rob Ryan's Entrepreneur America Boot Camp for Start-Ups* (Ithaca: Cornell University Press, 2001), p. 145. Copyright © 2001 by Rob Ryan. Used with permission of the publisher, Cornell University Press.

60. Sahlman, "How to Write a Really Great Business Plan," pp. 128 & 129.

61. McWilliams, "Garbage In, Garbage Out," p. 136.

62. Ibid.

63. Howard Schultz and Dori Jones Yang, *Pour Your Heart into It: How Starbucks Built a Company One Cup at a Time* (NewYork: Hyperion, 1997), p. 65.

7

COMPONENTS OF THE BUSINESS PLAN

*There is no single omission that bodes worse for a start-up's future
than the lack of a business plan.*[1]

—David Anderson

Your ability to seize a particular opportunity for profit is directly related to the quality of your business plan. Business plans for new ventures are a bit of a paradox. They need to be comprehensive, yet they should not be so comprehensive that they impede the launch of the venture. It should be long enough to address major issues, yet it should not be too long. It should capture the fundamental idea that drives the creation of the venture, yet the plan may have to be changed dramatically after the venture is launched. It should be prepared primarily as a roadmap for the entrepreneur, yet other stakeholders will look to the plan to answer their most pressing questions.

First-time entrepreneurs frequently ask, "How long does the plan have to be?" The length, depth, and breadth of the plan will depend on numerous factors. The answer may be, "It has to be long enough to address the issues that will influence the venture's success." Anything less than that and it is just a concept paper. Anything much longer than that will mean that precious time has been taken that could have been invested in actually launching the venture. Remember, there is a time to plan—and then a time to act. Recognizing the difference between the two can have a dramatic effect on a new venture's likelihood for success.

THE PLAN MUST FULFILL ITS PURPOSE

The plan serves as a blueprint for building a new business. Although the issues to be addressed in the business plan are fairly standard, the depth that each area is addressed will vary, depending on the situation. If the business will be very complex and subject to a variety of potential problems, then the plan may need to be more comprehensive in its preparation. It will also need to include more details. If the business is very straightforward and involves only being slightly different from existing businesses, then it may not need to dot every *i* and cross every *t*. In this case, much of the fine-tuning decisions may be made during the launch process.

The length of the plan will be directly related to how comprehensive it needs to be, as well as the need for specific details. If the plan is expected to play a key role in attracting investors, securing a loan from a bank, gaining support from suppliers and/or distributors, or establishing an alliance with another firm, then it may need to be tailored to the expectations of each of the potential stakeholders.

Most business plans should not exceed 40 to 50 pages of content. Supporting material may be provided in the appendices. Most stakeholders are concerned about a few salient issues. They do not need to know every detail. Most financial projections should be provided as tables that highlight financial issues. Projected cash flow, as well as line-item income statements and balance sheets, can be provided in an appendix devoted to financial issues. The same applies to marketing and operational issues.

Venture capitalists, for example, want to know about the team, whether there is a proprietary position, and if the business has the potential to be harvested for significant capital gain within a few years. If prospective employees, suppliers, and distributors want to review the plan, they usually just want to see if the team has its act together and is worth the time and effort before agreeing to work with the venture.

REALITY CHECK

As you start preparing your business plan and feel the urge to make it the most comprehensive plan ever written, remember that Sun Microsystems' business plan was only 12 pages long.

The business plan should have four basic components:

1. Start with a general overview of the business.
2. Discuss how the business will create and maintain customers.
3. Provide a set of financial projections that indicate the level of profit the business is expected to make in its first few years of operation.
4. Profile key operating issues.

Mark Van Osnabrugge and Robert Robinson note that the business plan should be clear, professional, and well balanced. It should be short and concise. It should get to the point as briefly as possible, summarizing the product, credentials of the management team, the financing sought and reasons why, the achievements of the venture to date, expected milestones, and exit strategies.[2] The plan should also be written in the third person.

REALITY CHECK

Most entrepreneurs fall in love with their product/service/process offering. Beware of the tendency for overinfatuation. The same applies to the tendency to exaggerate the team's capabilities, the superiority of the venture's product/service/process offering and competitive advantages, and financial projections. Don't make claims that cannot be supported by sound data. Confidence supported by objective data can gain interest; arrogance and exaggeration, however, can turn off any interested stakeholder. Frederick Adler has reviewed more than 3,000 business plans over the years. He calls them *Dreams of Glory*.[3]

COMPONENTS OF THE BUSINESS PLAN

Most business plans follow a common outline. Some plans go into more detail describing the marketing strategy; others go into more detail in describing operational protocol.

Exhibit 7.1 is a business plan outline that identifies most of the items that should be addressed in a business start-up. The remainder of this chapter is devoted to briefly profiling the major components of the business plan.

Cover Page

The cover page identifies the name of the venture, the name and address of the contact person (usually the entrepreneur), and a statement of confidentiality (see Exhibit 7.2).

Confidentiality: The Nondisclosure Agreement

You should make a deliberate effort to minimize the likelihood that anyone will use the contents of your business plan to compete against you or to aid a competitor. A sheet should be attached to the front of the business plan that contains the *copy number* of that business plan and a statement that the information provided in the report is confidential and proprietary. The recipient should sign and date the sheet. The sheet should also note that the plan is to be returned by a specific date. You should keep a log of who has a copy of the plan, the date they received it, and whether it has been returned. It is not unusual for someone to request permission to have his or her financial advisor/accountant review the plan. The sheet should indicate that permission has been granted for that individual to review the plan and that he or she acknowledges the confidentiality/noncompete conditions. The sheet should also include a section for the reader's signature and date of receipt. Exhibit 7.3 provides a sample confidentiality agreement.

Cover page

Confidentiality page

Executive summary

Financing request—if seeking a loan or investors

Table of contents

General Description of the Venture:

Venture objectives

Opportunity

Context

Industry

Overall strategy

    Target market(s)

    Competition

    Competitive advantage(s)

Management team (background, qualifications, experience, and organization chart)

Ownership structure

Funding structure

Advisors

    CPA

    Attorney

    Banker

EXHIBIT 7.1 BUSINESS PLAN OUTLINE

Legal form

Alliances

Stages of growth

Marketing Section:

Target market

Analysis of competition

Market offering/competitive advantage

      Product/service strategy

      Price strategy

      Promotion strategy

      Distribution strategy

Proprietary position

Market share

Financial Section:

Financial Projections

Sources and uses of funds

Stages of funding

      Initial funding

      Expansion funding

Operational Issues:

Timeline, key milestones, and critical path

Hours of service

Key logistics

Facilities

Equipment

Availability of labor

Supplier Relations:

Risks and Responses:

Key risks

Contingency plans

Insurance

Succession plan

Exit/Harvest Strategy:

Conclusion:

Appendix:

Resumes of the management team, board of directors, and any other key personnel

Detailed financial projections

Supporting documentation

      Letters from potential suppliers

      Letters from potential customers

      Letters from potential distributors

EXHIBIT 7.1   BUSINESS PLAN OUTLINE *(CONTINUED)*

INTER-GALACTIC ENTERPRISES INC.
(A business plan for the creation of an electronic information services company)

Prepared by

Dragor Stravinski, Founder and Chief Executive Officer
Inter-Galactic Enterprises Inc.
123 Park Avenue
36th Floor, Suite 26
New York, New York 10021
v = (505) 555-4567
e = *igeinc@ige.com*
September 15, 200X

Copy #X of 25 copies

EXHIBIT 7.2 SAMPLE COVER PAGE[a]

[a]The sample cover sheet and executive summary are for a hypothetical company.
Any similarity to an actual venture is unintentional. Also, the nondisclosure and
confidentiality agreements as well as the private placement disclaimer are
provided in an abbreviated form. An attorney who specializes in intellectual
property should be consulted so the agreements are drafted properly.

REALITY CHECK

Don't be surprised if a venture capitalist, angel, investment banker, or prospective member of your management team balks at the need to sign the sheet. Professionals by their very nature frequently have reservations about having to acknowledge anything other than the fact that they have received the plan. They feel that having to sign a nondisclosure and noncompete agreement challenges their professional integrity.

REALITY CHECK

It is hard to enforce the confidentiality/noncompete agreement unless you have tangible proof that a person violated the agreement. The best practice is to check the readers out in advance and to go with people who are trustworthy, even if they have a policy against signing the statement.

---

1. It is agreed to by the following party_____ that the information included in this plan (including, but not limited to, product plans, marketing strategies, trade secrets, costs, pricing information, performance features, studies, reports, objectives, customer information, dealings, arrangements, financial projections, and any other information about the venture) is considered confidential.

2. Any use or disclosure of the confidential information other than expressly provided in this Agreement shall be deemed a breach of this agreement.

3. Recipient agrees to maintain the confidential information in confidence, take reasonable steps to prevent disclosure of the confidential information to any third party, and not to copy, divulge, sell, or otherwise disclose the confidential information.

4. Exclusions: This agreement shall not apply to information for which the Recipient can substantiate, as evidenced by documentary proof that such information was known by the recipient prior to the time it was disclosed, the information was in the public domain at the time it was disclosed to the recipient, or becomes publicly known through no wrongful act of Recipient.

EXHIBIT 7.3 SAMPLE OF CONFIDENTIALITY AGREEMENT

(This is a simplified disclaimer statement)

PRIVATE PLACEMENT DISCLAIMER

This business plan does not constitute an offer to sell or solicitation of an offer to buy any securities other than the securities offered hereby. The information contained in this plan is confidential and is intended only for the persons to whom it is transmitted by Inter-Galactic Enterprises Inc. Any reproduction of the contents, without prior written permission of Dragor Stravinski, is prohibited. The information set forth herein is believed by the company to be reliable. It must be recognized, however, that predictions and projections as to the company's future performance are necessarily subject to a high degree of uncertainty, and no warranty of such projections may be subject to legal penalty and place you and the issuer hereof in direct violation of state and federal securities laws. This copy is to be returned to Inter-Galactic Enterprises Inc. on request.

EXHIBIT 7.4 SAMPLE PRIVATE PLACEMENT DISCLAIMER

If the business plan is being used as a formal solicitation of investment, then the title page should include a statement of the financing sought. If the business plan is being used to seek a loan, then the cover page may indicate the amount sought, its duration, and intended use of funds. Exhibit 7.4 provides a statement that should be included on the cover page if the plan is seeking investors.

Executive Summary

A business plan begins with an executive summary. The executive summary is one or two pages in length and captures the essence of the proposed business venture. Even though it appears at the beginning of the plan, it is usually written after the rest of the plan has been completed.

The executive summary serves an important purpose. It forces you to articulate the basic ingredients of your business venture. The executive summary is often called the *elevator pitch*. It can be viewed as what you would say if you had 30 seconds (the length of an elevator ride) to tell someone about your business.

REALITY CHECK

First-time entrepreneurs find describing their proposed venture to be a real challenge. Some entrepreneurs describe their ventures in too general terms. They state, "I plan to start a business using leading-edge information technology." Other entrepreneurs tend to get too wrapped up in describing the product, service, or process. Identify what it is and how it is better than what is already on the market. A more in-depth description can be provided in the text of the plan.

It is not unusual for bankers, potential investors, suppliers, or friends to ask you about your proposed venture. The executive summary provides a concise description of your business. The executive summary profiles the proposed business in terms of the management team, its legal form, the specific market(s) to be served, the business's competitive advantage(s), its projected rate of growth, how it will be financed, and the projected return to its owner(s).

The executive summary should not be a litany of generalities. It should contain the vital facts about your business and reflect the research that went into preparing your business plan. If it is done well and represents a solid business proposal, anyone who reads it will want to read the entire business plan.

If the plan is being used to seek investors, then the executive summary should provide answers to their questions about why they should invest in the new venture. Particular attention should be directed to how the product/service is superior, that a substantial market exists, that the management team has the ability to capture a significant market share, and that the exit financials are compelling. Exhibit 7.5 provides a sample executive summary.

INTER-GALACTIC ENTERPRISES INC.

Inter-Galactic Enterprises Inc. will specialize in providing patient and employee-relations software applications and services to medical service organizations. It will be formed as a corporation in the state of New York. The management team will be headed by IGEI's founder Dragor Stravinski, Susan Markowitz, Evan Smith, and Joyce Stevens. Mr. Stravinski's background includes serving as co-founder of VXG Enterprises, which was acquired by Thompson & Grand Inc. in 2003. Susan Markowitz will serve as chief technology officer. Ms. Markowitz has extensive experience in software development. Her most recent experience was as CTO with Amalgamated Medical Systems. Evan Smith will serve as chief financial officer. Mr. Smith was CFO for Mountain States Medical Services. Joyce Stevens will serve as chief marketing officer. Ms. Stevens was vice-president of marketing for Pacific Medical Interactive Systems. The management team has more than 50 years of managerial and software experience.

Inter-Galactic Enterprises Inc. plans to introduce its first software package within six months. The software is targeted to mid- to large-scale medical organizations. IGEI anticipates launching a second software package for smaller medical organizations at the beginning of its second year. Updates of each of the software packages will be launched on an annual basis. IGEI also expects to increase its revenue and profitability by developing and providing customized patient and employee-relations information technology solutions to larger medical organizations.

Inter-Galactic Enterprises Inc. plans to target medical organizations in New York and New Jersey in its first year. IGEI already has letters of intent to purchase its software from three mid-sized medical organizations in New York and one large medical organization in New Jersey. IGEI plans to expand its marketing into other Eastern states in its second year. IGEI plans to serve clients throughout the United States by its fifth year. Major medical organizations in foreign markets will also be targeted after the second year.

Inter-Galactic Enterprises Inc.'s management team and core employees will focus on the development and marketing of IDEI's proprietary software applications and consulting services. Most of IGEI's operations will be outsourced. Trans-India Software Solutions will oversee code development. Pacific-Korean Systems will oversee software packaging, shipping, training assistance, and customer relations.

Inter-Galactic Enterprises Inc.'s initial board of directors will be composed of the founding four members of the management team, Dr. Elliott Suder, who is an expert in information technology, Ms. Tracy Cutter, who is a former CEO of Consolidated Medical Services, and three directors nominated by outside investors.

Inter-Galactic Enterprises Inc. projects sales for its first year to be $2,000,000 with a resulting loss of $500,000. Sales for the second year are expected to increase to $4,000,000 with a profit of $450,000. Sales are projected to increase to $25,000,000 by the fifth year with a profit of $5,000,000.

Inter-Galactic Enterprises Inc. has an initial capital requirement of $2,500,000. The management team will be investing a total of $1,000,000 in IGEI. The additional $1,500,000 will be sought from outside investors. The management team will have 60 percent of the outstanding common stock. Initial outside investors will have 40 percent of the outstanding stock. Unissued stock may be used for additional rounds of funding and for stock options for current and future employees.

EXHIBIT 7.5 SAMPLE EXECUTIVE SUMMARY[a]

[a]This is an abbreviated executive summary. The names provided in the example are fictitious. Any similarity to actual names or companies is unintentional.

Table of Contents

The table of contents should identify each section and corresponding page number. It is not unusual for an interested stakeholder to take a section of the plan and have someone else review it. Venture capitalists may have a financial analyst check the financial statements for validity and accuracy. They may also have an expert review the technology if it is a critical component of the venture's proposed competitive advantage.

GENERAL DESCRIPTION OF THE VENTURE

This part of the plan highlights some of the key points for the venture. Some of the information—particularly marketing-related information—in the general summary is described in more detail later in the plan. The brief profiles at this point give the reader more information than what was provided in the executive summary. If the profiles are appealing, then the reader may read the whole plan. The general overview is designed to identify unique points about the venture as well as the factors that will influence the venture's success.

Venture Objectives

The plan should indicate the primary objective(s) for the venture. If the venture is being created to go the distance, then the plan should indicate the vision for 5 to 10 years. Particular attention should be directed to overall worth, capital appreciation, and so forth. If the venture is being started so the original investors can *cash out* in three to five years, then the plan should reflect how it will be positioned for acquisition by another firm, a management buyout, or even an initial public offering. The targeted cash-out value of the venture should also be noted. In any event, the objectives should include a time component indicating when the vision should be accomplished.

The Opportunity

The business plan must do an excellent job profiling the opportunity because the business's success will be tied to the size and financial merit of the opportunity. The plan should indicate if the market is already established or if it is just emerging. It should also note how much the market is growing, how long it will last, whether it has numerous lucrative segments, as well as the extent and nature of competition.

If you are seeking investors, then the plan must demonstrate that the opportunity is attractive and compelling. "Investors look for large or rapidly growing markets mainly because it is often easier to obtain a share of a growing market than to fight with entrenched competitors for a share of a mature or stagnant market. Smart investors try hard to identify high-growth potential markets: That's where the big payoffs are. Many investors will not invest in a company that cannot reach a significant scale ($50 million in annual revenues) within five years."[4] If the venture will be trying to seize a technology-based opportunity that tends to be short-lived, then the plan should demonstrate how the team can make a good return while the opportunity lasts.[5] The opportunity section must analyze and demonstrate how the opportunity can grow and the new venture can expand its range of products or services, its customer base, or geographic scope. It should also note if there is the potential for highly profitable ancillary spin-offs.[6]

Context

New venture opportunities exist in context of the economy in general and the specific marketplace in particular. The business plan should show how the context supports the new venture. Contextual factors include the state of technology, government regulations, demographics, and economic conditions. The plan should also show how the management team plans to deal with the situation in a proactive manner if the context changes.

Industry

This section of the business plan should profile the overall industry your venture will be operating in. It should profile whether a few firms dominate the industry as well as the challenges firms may face in the next few years. Particular attention should be directed to whether it is directly related to the business cycle, the rate of technological change, the major segments, and the effect of foreign firms. Industry sales for the last three to five years as well as the projected rate of growth should also be noted. The description will be particularly important if it is an emerging industry. Investors may need to be educated about industry attributes. The profile will also need to indicate the industry will provide a favorable environment for your new venture.

Overall Strategy

The plan should provide a brief profile of the target market, the competition, and the firm's competitive advantages. The marketing part of the plan will provide more detail.

Management Team

The plan must identify the entrepreneurs and management team's strengths and qualifications. Particular attention should be directed to whether they have experience in that industry, whether they have previous start-up experience, and if they have worked together before. Each of these factors represents a real plus for the venture. Each key person's resume should be provided in the appendix.

Experienced teams can hit the ground running. They should be able to handle the inevitable setbacks that can tear apart novice teams. A strong team will give the venture considerable credibility. It will also help the venture attract funding. Jeffry Timmons noted that if you ask venture capitalists what are the three most important success factors for a high-growth venture their answer would be, "(1) the lead entrepreneur and the quality of the team, (2) the lead entrepreneur and the quality of the team, and (3) all of the above."[7] Edward Welles noted, "Although venture capitalists may read just 2% of all business plans they see, they always note who is running the company."[8] Timmons also noted that most successful entrepreneurs went through an apprenticeship. They accumulated 5 to 10 years' or more of general management and industry experience prior to their first start-up.[9]

REALITY CHECK

Your resume and the resumes of the other key people should indicate some stability in each person's employment background. People whose resumes indicate a propensity to jack rabbit—jump from one employer to the next—even if they were good jobs—may raise eyebrows about whether they will stick around and see things through.

If the entrepreneur and team do not have experience, then the entrepreneur must find a way to bring in experienced talent. The strongest start-ups were led by people with experience in their industries. Companies started by people new to their fields didn't fare as well. It's all about respecting the marketplace—why waste time and money managing from ignorance? You have to know your business, and if you don't, you'd better find someone who does.[10]

The plan should include an organization chart. The chart should indicate who has already committed to join the venture as well as the positions that need to be filled. The plan should also indicate what the organization chart should look like in three to five years.

The plan should also indicate the compensation packages for the entrepreneur, management team, and any other key people. Particular attention should be directed to the number of shares of stock owned and eligibility for stock options.

Ownership Structure

The plan needs to indicate the overall ownership structure for the venture. A table should profile the number of shares owned, the type of stock held, and corresponding ownership percentage of the venture. The table should note the board of directors and any outside investors. This section should also indicate if there are any warrants, convertible debentures, and types of stock. This section should indicate eligibility for stock options as well as the number of shares available for future issuance. The table should also note if some of the stock has been issued or bartered in return for goods and/or services. Law firms, public relations firms, consultants, and other service providers may agree to charging lower fees in return for stock. Accounting firms are prohibited from accepting stock in exchange for services.

Funding Structure

The plan should profile how the venture will be financed. Attention will be directed to the sources of debt as well as the amount to be invested in the business.

Advisors

The plan should identify the people and firms who will be serving as professional advisors for the venture. If an advisory committee is formed in addition to the board of directors, the plan should indicate their responsibilities as well as their background. The plan should also identify the bank that will be providing financial services.

Legal Form

The plan should identify the venture's legal form. There are many things to consider when you select the legal form for your business. Fortunately, you may be able to change the legal form after you start your business if you meet certain requirements. Nevertheless, you should give this decision the time and attention it deserves from the very beginning. The legal form for your business will affect your initial capital requirement, your ability to raise money, your personal liability, how profits/losses will be reported and treated, the tax obligations you will incur, the corresponding cash flow for your business, and how you conduct your business. You may find it helpful to ask your attorney and accountant, "Which legal form will be most appropriate in three to five years?" This will give you a good idea which legal form should be selected to start your business. Businesses that are expected to grow and need additional funds are usually formed as corporations. Most medium-sized businesses and nearly all large businesses are corporations.

A venture may be formed as a sole proprietorship, partnership, or corporation. Most new businesses are formed as sole proprietorships. This is because most businesses are started by people who want to start lifestyle businesses. As noted in Chapter 2, many people start businesses as an alternative to working for someone else. This book does not focus on lifestyle businesses, whether they are proprietorships or partnerships. Instead, it is directed to high-growth ventures. For this reason, this section of the business plan will be directed primarily to the corporate form of organization. If you are planning to start a lifestyle business, then you should seek the advice of an attorney and an accountant about which legal form may be best for your situation.

Each type of legal form has advantages and drawbacks. The sole proprietorship is easy to form and costs very little to establish. A sole proprietorship, however, is not a legal entity. It is just an extension of the proprietor. This means that the business's incomes or losses are reported with the owner's personal income tax returns. The biggest drawback to a sole proprietorship is that the owner has unlimited personal liability for the business's operations. Any claims against the business by creditors or other claimants are directed at the proprietor. It is for this reason that it is advisable for the venture to be formed as a corporation.

A number of businesses are formed as partnerships. Partnerships are usually formed because the entrepreneur does not have sufficient money or skills. Partnerships are not very difficult to form. Unfortunately, like sole proprietorships, they are not considered legal entities. They are considered to be extensions of each of the partners. Each partner may be held personally liable for any claims made against the partnership. To make matters worse, any single partner may be held liable for the full claim. One's liability will not be limited to one's ownership share. If you are considering going the partnership route, then seek legal advice and make sure you draft a comprehensive partnership agreement that describes the rights and responsibilities for each partner. Partnerships are also cumbersome because the addition or deletion of a partner for any reason may result in the discontinuation of the partnership. This may make it very difficult for a partnership to seek additional funding. Finally, partnerships tend to be very precarious. Most partnerships cannot handle interpersonal dynamics. Most partnerships are formed by friends and/or family members. Starting and operating a business will test and strain even the best relationships. People who have observed partnerships consider them a *disaster waiting to happen.*

Limited partnerships are different from general partnerships. They are formed to limit the personal liability for most of the partners. They are called *limited partnerships* because the *limited* partners cannot lose any more than what they invested in the venture. This benefit exists because the limited partners' involvement is limited to investing in the venture. Limited partners are not allowed to be involved in business activities in any manner. It should be noted that not everyone has limited personal liability. At least one person must be a general partner. The general partner is responsible for all the business's decisions and assumes unlimited personal liability. Most limited partnerships are formed to do a specific business deal. Real estate developments are frequently structured as limited partnerships.

Before moving on to the corporate form of organization it may be worthwhile to discuss limited liability companies (LLCs). LLCs have gained popularity recently because they have some of the merits of partnerships and some of the benefits associated with corporations. They cost less to form and maintain than corporations. They also limit one's liability to what he or she has invested in the venture. Although there are a number of distinctions between LLCs and the other legal forms, the most important point about them is that they provide limited liability for their owners. Unlike sole proprietorships and partnerships, no one has unlimited personal liability.

LLCs do not have partners or stockholders; their owners are called *members.* LLCs do not issue stock or have partnership shares; they have ownership *interests,* which are identified in the LLC's *articles of organization.* The limited liability does not come without its drawbacks. Members cannot freely transfer their ownership interest. Transfer of ownership usually requires unanimous written agreement by the other members. The duration for the venture may also be limited. Most LLCs cannot operate for more than 30 years. The relative newness of this legal form and the variation in statutes from state to state mean that you will need to seek the advice of an attorney who has extensive experience with LLCs for that state. You should also consult with a CPA about taxation and how Social Security and Medicare obligations should be reported.

Corporations represent about 20 percent of all businesses in the United States. They differ from proprietorships and partnerships in many ways. First of all, a corporation is considered a *legal entity.* The corporation is treated as something separate from its owners. If a corporation is sued, defaults on its loans, or goes bankrupt, then the shareholders' losses are limited to what they invested in the business. This means that the stockholders have limited liability.

If you choose the corporate form for your venture, you may still be personally liable for its affairs. Banks and other creditors may expect you to personally cosign any loans or other business agreements. Most new corporations are started and operate without an abundant supply of cash. For this reason, the power company, phone company, and some of your suppliers may ask the major stockholders to personally guarantee credit obligations if the corporation becomes insolvent.

The stockholders can be personally liable for the actions of the corporation for at least two other reasons. First, if the firm fails to conduct its affairs as a corporation, then it may be treated as if it were a proprietorship or partnership. The stockholders, through the firm's board of directors, must adopt bylaws, conduct regular meetings, elect officers, and keep records of the meetings. If they fail to do so, then the Internal Revenue Service or other creditors may request that the courts declare the owners of the business to be held personally liable for claims. The other instance of unlimited personal liability for the stockholders exists when they are involved in any criminal activity when conducting the corporation's affairs. This type of situation is rare, but it is clear that the owners' personal liability is limited only if they behave in the appropriate and legal manner.

The corporate form is appealing because it limits the stockholders' legal and financial liabilities. Yet the corporate form has three major drawbacks. First, it takes more money to start a business as a corporation. The incorporation process tends to cost hundreds to thousands of dollars. Second, it takes more time and paperwork. You must file your articles of incorporation with the secretary of state in the state where you plan to conduct your business, register the firm where its principal office is to be located or its real estate is to be held, elect directors, establish bylaws, issue stock, conduct meetings, and keep formal records of corporate decisions. In some states, certain types of businesses (law, accounting, medical practices, etc.) may not be able to be formed as corporations so the owners maintain a higher level of personal liability. In these cases, they are formed as professional services partnerships.

The third major drawback to the corporate form is in the area of taxes. Profits are subject to *double taxation.* The corporation will pay a federal tax on each year's profits to the Internal Revenue Service. Most firms are also required to pay a state income tax on their profits. The corporate income tax is the first wave of tax imposed on a firm's profits. The second wave occurs if the corporation's board of directors decides to distribute any of that year's profits left after state and federal taxes are paid as dividends. Stockholders are obligated to pay federal and state personal income taxes on dividends they receive from the firm. As you can see, the benefits of limited personal liability come at the cost of double taxation.

A major advantage of the corporate form over partnerships and sole proprietorships goes back to the fact that a corporation is a legal entity. Whenever a partner or sole proprietor dies, the business also ceases. In a similar fashion, whenever a new partner is added or a partner wants to leave, a new partnership may need to be formed. This is not the case with the corporate form. If someone wants to become an owner of a corporation, then that person buys stock. Sale of stock transfers ownership from seller to buyer. Stockholders can come and go without affecting the legal status or operations of the firm. Moreover, if the corporation needs money to expand its operations or pay off debt, it may be possible to raise funds by selling additional stock.

The laws pertaining to the formation and conduct of a corporation vary from state to state. Statutes vary in terms of the minimum number of directors, officers, and stockholders. It should be noted that in most states one person can own all the stock in a corporation. If you plan to be the sole owner, then make sure that every aspect of the business's operations (checking accounts, etc.) are separate from the personal side of your life.

The Subchapter S (Sub S) or S corporation represents a special type of corporation that may appeal to people who plan to start a business that will have a limited number of stockholders. The Sub S corporation is frequently referred to as *the corporation that is taxed like a partnership or proprietorship.* This is not exactly the case, but there are some similarities.

Your accountant should be in a good position to identify the merits of forming your business as a Sub S corporation and whether your state recognizes Sub S status. Your

CPA should also be in a position to analyze the difference in tax rates between a regular corporation and a Sub S corporation. Corporate tax rates and personal tax rates are not the same.

The first thing that needs to be recognized about a Sub S corporation is the tax distinction. A Sub S corporation does not pay federal income taxes. Instead, the stockholders report their share (percent of ownership in the firm) of the corporation's profit for that year on their personal taxes. LLC's are taxed in a similar fashion. Members report their share of the profit or loss on their personal tax forms.

The stockholders pay a tax on the firm's profit rather than on the dividends they receive. In a sense, Sub S stockholders pay the corporate federal tax (and corresponding state income tax) at their personal rate on their federal (and state) returns. If you own one-half of the shares of stock in a Sub S firm that made $80,000 that year, then you would report Sub S income of $40,000 on Schedule E of your personal federal tax return. In a regular corporation, the firm pays a federal tax on its profits and the stockholders pay tax only on the dividends they receive. Some states treat Sub S corporations as regular corporations. These states thereby tax stockholders for the dividends they receive. Many states also charge a corporate income tax.

The Sub S status has certain benefits, but it also has restrictions. The IRS limits the number of people who can own stock in a Sub S corporation. The *S* indicates that only a small number of people can own stock in the corporation. The IRS allows no more than 75 stockholders for a Sub S corporation. Moreover, a Sub S corporation can issue only one type of stock. If you will be seeking angel or venture capital funding, then the Sub S legal form may present problems. Angels and venture capital firms may insist on having preferred rather than common stock. A general corporation may issue common stock and preferred stock, voting and nonvoting stock, cumulative and noncumulative stock as well as convertible stock.

REALITY CHECK

Make sure that the name for the proposed venture is available and that it is registered with the appropriate agencies. It is amazing how many businesses are started without a thorough name search. Failure to register the name leaves the door open for another firm to come in and register that name. This could cause considerable hardship. The same applies to using a name that is already registered by another firm.

Few businesses are created using only the exact name of the entrepreneur. In most states, when you start a business you need to register it with the local Register of Deeds. This is necessary so the owner of the business can be identified and contacted in legal situations. This is commonly referred to as *DBA* or *doing business as*. For example, Jonathan Rand would register his business as Jonathan Rand doing business as (DBA) Rand Enterprises. If the business is formed as a corporation, then it will be registered through the corresponding state agency via its corporate charter.

REALITY CHECK

It is wise to establish an objective basis for valuing your venture. This is particularly true if you plan to have partners, members, or stockholders. By establishing the basis for valuation in advance, it is easier to bring partners, members, or stockholders into the business and for those who are involved in the business to sell their share of ownership back to your venture or others.

REALITY CHECK

It is also wise to establish a buy-back provision before stock is issued so your firm can buy back the stock if a partner, member, or stockholder comes under certain defined circumstances. The buy-back provision (including a basis for valuation) can also be important if a partner, member, or stockholder dies or goes through a divorce. This may reduce the likelihood that a divorced spouse or one's beneficiaries will be in a position to influence the future of your venture.

THE MARKETING PART OF THE BUSINESS PLAN

This part of the plan profiles the who, what, where, how, and why of your venture's effort to create and maintain customers for a profit.

Target market

There is no way that your venture can be all things to all people. Nor can it be some things to all people. Instead, it needs to be exceptional for a specific group of customers. The *rifle approach* to marketing requires that you are able to identify and hit the bull's eye. You will need to describe your target market in specific terms. Your venture can be described by the products/services it offers and the customers it serves. The plan must identify the individuals or businesses that are its target market. Attention should also be directed as to who will be your venture's primary and secondary customers. Your primary customers represent the majority of your revenue. The secondary target market may also represent a significant part of your revenue.

You will need to develop a customer profile that reflects your target market's various characteristics. If your target market is composed of individual consumers, then you will need to describe it in terms of demographics, psychographics, geographics, usage rate, stage of family life cycle, and benefits sought. If your target market is composed of businesses and other institutions, then the target market should indicate the industry, size of the firms, frequency of purchase, price sensitivity, and attributes sought.

You should target customers who are not having their needs met well or at all. They should also be willing and able to purchase what you have to offer. You should try to avoid customers who are fickle or are loyal to other businesses. Amar Bhidé found that 80 percent of the businesses in his study of *Inc.* 500 companies provided products and services to other businesses.[11]

Analysis of Competition

Your plan should profile the nature and extent of competition. Your venture may be based on an opportunity that was identified by constructing a competitive matrix. Chapter 3 profiled how to construct a competitive matrix. A competitive matrix may have been established for each market segment you considered for your new venture. The competitive matrix profiled in your business plan highlights various market-offering dimensions for the market you plan to serve. The competitive matrix profiles the extent each of the existing businesses (who may be direct competitors) is meeting that market segment's expectations. Again, the competitive matrix indicates the gaps in the market where consumers' needs are not being met well or at all. Your competitive matrix should indicate significant gaps for all the existing businesses in dimensions that are valued highly by your target market.

Your venture's competitive strategy in general and marketing strategy in particular should be directed to dimensions that have high value and where existing businesses are not within one rating point of that value. Gaps with at least two points (where the segment's needs are two points greater than what the competitors are offering, which are noted by double asterisks) are noteworthy because it may be easy for a competitor to change what it is doing if its gap is only one point. For example, if a business in Exhibit 7.6 already had a score of 4 on customer service, then it may be possible for it to improve its score by hiring a better staff, providing incentives, and/or improving its information system. Existing businesses that are not meeting the segment's desires are noted by at least one asterisk. A whole row of asterisks indicates customers in that segment are not satisfied and that they are searching for a business that will give them what they want on that dimension. The competitive matrix profiled in Exhibit 7.6 indicates that none of the existing businesses offers the level of quality or the level of customer service desired by consumers in that market segment. If the competitive matrix indicates that numerous rows have asterisks, especially double asterisks, then you may have what the military calls a *target-rich environment* for your venture.

As noted in Chapter 3, if (1) a sufficiently large need is evident and competition does not appear to serve it, (2) you believe you can provide the segment what it wants, and (3) you can generate a level of profit to meet your return-on-investment objective, then this is where you should focus your new venture's attention.

Competitive Factor	Business #1		Business #2		Business #3		Business #4		Business #5	
Price	* 3 x 4 = 12	4	* 1 x 4 = 4	4	** 2 x 4 = 8	4	4 x 4 = 16	4	* 3 x 4 = 12	4
Quality	** 3 x 5 = 15	5	** 3 x 5 = 15	5	** 2 x 5 = 10	5	** 3 x 5 = 15	5	** 2 x 5 = 10	5
Selection	4 x 3 = 12	3	4 x 3 = 12	3	3 x 3 = 9	3	3 x 3 = 9	3	4 x 3 = 12	3
Promotion	3 x 2 = 6	2	4 x 2 = 8	2	2 x 2 = 4	2	4 x 2 = 8	2	2 x 2 = 4	2
Services	* 4 x 5 = 20	5	5 x 5 = 25	5	** 2 x 5 = 10	5	** 3 x 5 = 15	5	* 4 x 5 = 20	5
Customer Service	** 3 x 5 = 15	5	** 3 x 5 = 15	5	** 1 x 5 = 5	5	** 3 x 5 = 15	5	** 3 x 5 = 15	5
Facilities/ Atmosphere	* 3 x 4 = 12	4	5 x 4 = 20	4	** 2 x 4 = 8	4	** 2 x 4 = 8	4	* 3 x 4 =12	4
Location	3 x 3 = 9	3	4 x 3 = 12	3	* 2 x 3 = 6	3	* 2 x 3 = 6	3	3 x 3 = 9	3
Relative strength of this segment	101		111		59		92		94	

```
                                          # ◄──── Importance of this factor to this segment
                                          ┌─ Combined score for the extent the
                                          │  business meets the segment's needs
   Rating of the business                 │  and the importance of this factor.
       on this factor ────► # × # = # ◄───┘
                                    └─ Importance of this factor to this segment
```

* Indicates a gap exists between what this business offers and what this segment wants.
** Indicates a significant gap exists between what this business offers and what this segment wants.

EXHIBIT 7.6 COMPETITIVE MATRIX REFLECTING GAPS IN THE MARKETPLACE

Amazon.com provides an interesting example of the benefits of targeting gaps in the marketplace. Amazon.com's success cannot be attributed merely to its offering of books at competitive rates. Its ability to provide information about books and to suggest books that might interest the customer make a real difference. The ability to order books on a 24/7 basis in an almost effortless manner and to have them delivered to your door gave it a formidable competitive advantage when it opened its *electronic* doors to the public.

Market Offering/Competitive Advantage

Your venture's competitive strategy will be influenced by the number and nature of competitors as well as its target market. Your plan should identify the firms that are vying for customers in the industry in general and the firms that are vying for customers in your target market in particular. Particular attention should be directed to the advantages competitors may have and barriers to entry that may exist. Attention should also be directed to their disadvantages. Elaine Pofeldt noted that studying the successes and failures of your competitors will not only give you a good idea of what works, it may provide a basis for you to develop more innovative marketing strategies.[12]

Your marketing plan should identify the attributes your target market seeks and what your firm plans to offer to create and maintain targeted customers for a profit. The firm needs to have a distinctive competitive advantage. Your firm should direct its attention to offering what targeted customers just cannot get anywhere else. It is important to articulate how your firm will be better than its competitors. Patrick Kelly, founder of Physician Sales and Service noted, "Unless you can answer in fewer than 10 words, you don't really have a competitive edge—which means you'll always be joggling for position in the middle of the pack."[13]

Your plan should show how your offering will be superior to what is already available for your targeted market. To attract and maintain customers, your venture must be superior on the things that matter to your target market. Rob Ryan captured the need to stand out with his five rules of differentiation.[14] The first rule involves *asking the right questions.* He noted that the single biggest thing you can do to build differentiation is to ask the right questions for your business. Most start-ups begin by asking the wrong questions, seeking answers to the wrong problems. They end up selling some knock-off product that's a few dollars cheaper or has a couple extra features. If your product/service offering includes things that customers do not value, then you will be charging them for things that do not add value. If you don't offer what customers really want, then they will have no reason to do business with you.[15]

The more you view your venture as a *customer problem-solver* the greater the likelihood you will find opportunities in the marketplace and bases for differentiating your venture from existing firms. Ryan noted that the following questions posed by Greg Gianforte of RightNow Technologies to prospective customers provide insights for new product/service development:[16]

- What is going to earn you the biggest bonus this year?
- What are you losing sleep over?
- What do you need to accomplish your job?
- What are your challenges?

Ryan also encourages entrepreneurs to identify differentiators that will make your customer look like a hero and factors that could trigger a feeding frenzy for your product.[17]

Entrepreneurs also need to show that their product is a true value proposition to prospective customers. He noted that the more that you can show or measure your product/service's benefit in dollars, the greater the likelihood of securing accounts. Products/services that have very favorable price/benefit ratios and a short payback provide a compelling reason for prospective customers to do business with your venture.[18]

The second rule is you need to try to be a *red polka-dotted zebra*. Your venture must have enough distinctive characteristics that your targeted customers will pick your firm out of a competitive crowd. Ryan noted that most start-ups, like zebras, are herd animals. They edge into crowded industries. Their products and services are variations on black- and-white with a drab distinction—a longer tail, a few more stripes.[19]

The *10 times or better rule* emphasizes the need to be substantially better than your competitors. Your product must be either one-tenth the cost of your competitors or 10 times the performance. Anything less will not derail the incumbent company or technology. Although the 10 times rule may seem impossible for most conventional products or services, it does stress the need for your product/service offering to be markedly superior to what is currently available. If your product/service is just a little better than what targeted customers are already using, then why should they change? Your offering must be a big deal on something that matters to your target market. It must provide a compelling reason, whether it is in time, cost, convenience, quality, and/or resulting profitability to change. The more that you can demonstrate your offering's benefits over what the target market is using in real dollars, real time, and real convenience, the greater the likelihood of getting their business.[20]

The *one year or longer head start rule* emphasizes the need for your business's product or service offering to have a significant head start over its competitors. Ryan also noted that your business model should be difficult to copy.[21]

The *improving with age rule* stresses the importance of continuing your effort to maintain a competitive advantage. A one-year head start and your product/service offering's superiority should not be taken for granted. Your efforts to differentiate your offering should be relentless, and they should be directed at areas that will be difficult for competitors to match.[22]

Ryan stressed the importance that scaling and stickiness can play in your product or service offering. *Scaling* refers to the extent your product or service is used by a customer. If it can be used throughout the customer's organization, then your firm will benefit. Scaling is particularly beneficial if the customer's suppliers and distributors also adopt your product/service offering. Ryan noted that products or services that have the potential to spread like viruses have considerable appeal.[23] Software is the best example of scalability, for two reasons. First, once it is developed, the cost to produce/provide additional units drops due to economies of scale. The extent your business model is able to ramp up without significant additional costs can have an extremely beneficial impact on your venture's profitability and ability to attract investors. Second, the software may become the standard for the customer, market, industry, or world!

Stickiness refers to the extent the product or service can become deeply imbedded into the customer's operations or activities. Stickiness makes it difficult for customers to switch to a competitor's offering.[24] The greater the time, cost, and risk involved in shifting to a competitor, once a customer has adopted your product or service, the more your firm will benefit.

> ### REALITY CHECK
>
> Make sure you check out the degree of scalability and stickiness when evaluating potential market opportunities. If the firms already serving the market under review have established scalability and stickiness, then the odds that you can crack those markets may be stacked against you.

How Will Your Competitors Respond?

The ideal situation for your new venture would be to find markets that are not being served well or at all, where customers have pent-up demand and would be delighted to do business with you with minimal price sensitivity. The ideal business situation would exist if your venture offered the market red polka-dotted zebras that will continuously wow targeted customers to the point that no one will even consider competing against you. You want your product or service offering to be so compelling and addictive once they use it they cannot imagine what life would be like without it. You want your customers, when they hear about your product or service, to drop what they are doing and scream out, "Sold! This will change everything! Sign me up! I want it now!"

Unfortunately, you are not likely to find yourself in the ideal situation. Even if you are highly perceptive and find a lucrative market opportunity, you should approach it with a dose of reality and a fair amount of paranoia. Your competitive strategy must have offensive and defensive dimensions. Although you are trying to create and maintain customers you should be making a deliberate effort to keep present and potential competitors from stealing your thunder.

It is important for entrepreneurs to not be overly optimistic about their competitive position or potential target market exclusivity. "Visionary entrepreneurs must guard against making competitors rich from their work. Many concepts are difficult to prove, but once proven, easy to imitate. Unless the pioneer is protected by sustainable barriers to entry, the benefits of a hard-fought revolution can become a public good rather than a boon to the innovator."[25]

You need to be able to identify how competitors will respond to the new venture, and how your new venture can respond to their response.[26] Even if your products or services are really better, then you need to expect imitation and competitive retaliation through price competition, an advertising blitz, and so on.

> ### REALITY CHECK
>
> It's a cold, hard world out there. Never underestimate your competition. Competitors may also do whatever it takes to cast doubt on your firm's credibility and to discredit your firm's offering to keep their customers. Leslie Brokaw noted, "Your competitors aren't dumb. ... Business strategy is like a chess game ... you do something, then your competitors respond. This is why discount pricing is so dangerous."[27]

> ### REALITY CHECK
>
> Nothing stays the same and nothing exists in a vacuum. If you're not giving customers exactly what they want, then they are still looking for a competitor that will tailor its offering to their needs. Customer loyalty exists only to the extent that you meet their needs. Don't put the welcome mat out for competitors by taking your customers' continued business for granted.

The Name of Your Business

The whole issue of what should be the name for your new venture has not received much attention so far in this book. The lack of attention is not intended to convey that the name of your business is not important. The name is important, and it should be the product of thorough consideration. Every aspect of your venture projects an image and sends a message to your target market. Its name must project the *right* image and send the *right* message. The right name will capture the distinctiveness you want to project. It should also be easy to remember. The last thing you want is a name that doesn't make sense and cannot be remembered. Your new venture will have enough challenges; do not select a name that works against it.

Computer Literacy found after it had been up and running that its target market misperceived its service offering to be classroom training and could not remember its name.

Computer Literacy hired Interbrand Group to help it come up with a new name. The Interbrand Group generated an initial list of 25,000 names for consideration. After legal clearances, only 20 percent of the names were viable given that the name had to have a matching URL. The Interbrand Group came up with the name Fatbrain.com. Although the new name did not please everyone, research indicated that 100 percent of the people tested remembered it a week later.[28]

Your name should be easy to say and easy to spell. It should also reflect your vision for the venture. Also, make sure the name does not have negative connotations or interpretations in other languages and countries. It is amazing how naive some firms have been when they try to enter foreign markets. Either their name does not translate or it projects an image that was not intended.

Product/Service Strategy

Almost every business is classified primarily by the types of products or services it offers and the types of customers it serves. Products may be classified as specialty, shopping, convenience, or impulse purchases. Customers are generally classified as institutions (including businesses), the stage they occupy in the channel of distribution, or as individual consumers. Some businesses are classified as *b-to-b businesses,* or businesses selling to businesses. Other businesses are classified as *b-to-c businesses,* or businesses selling to consumers. Some businesses will sell to businesses as well as individual consumers. One of the things that catapulted eBay's growth was when it went from just being a *c-to-c business* into a venture that provided *c-to-b, b-to-b,* and *b-to-c business.* If you plan to offer more than one product and target more than one type of customer, then your business plan should indicate the relative percentage for each group.

Your venture's product/service offering may be the most important component of its marketing mix. If you do not offer what people want, then it will not matter how you price it, how you promote it, and how you distribute it. W. Keith Schilit noted that your competitive advantage could include performance, durability, versatility, speed and accuracy, ease of operation or use, ease of maintenance or repair, ease of cost or installation, size or weight, and/or styling and appearance.[29] Rita Gunther McGrath and Ian MacMillan noted that the goal of your product/service strategy is to discover the bundle of features that your customers perceive to be worth a lot more than the price you are going to extract from them, as well as a lot more than the competitors are offering.[30]

Amar Bhidé stressed the need for entrepreneurs to make sure their offering provides a significant performance benefit. He noted, "Whereas, established companies can vie for (market) share through line extensions and marginal tailoring of their products and services, the start-up must really wow its target customers. A marginally tastier cereal won't knock Kellogg's Cornflakes off supermarket shelves."[31]

Gunther McGrath and MacMillan provide an interesting way of looking at your product/service strategy. They noted the distinction between exciters, tolerables, dissatisfiers, enragers, neutrals, and negatives. *Exciters* are attributes that so delight the customer that they constitute the overwhelming reason for making a purchase. Exciters are often technically simple, relatively low-cost advances that greatly add to the offering's convenience or ease of use. *Tolerables* are negative basic features that customers are willing to put up with, even though they don't like them. *Dissatisfiers* are factors that customers consider negative discriminating attributes. Ironically, a competitor can turn your tolerable into a dissatisfier if the competitor can eliminate the tolerable in its product. *Enragers* exist when a firm is not on the same wavelength as customers.

You need to look at every product or service your company plans to offer through the customers' eyes. Customer expectations may be different from what you anticipate, and it is their expectations that matter. For example, Honda's market research found that consumers valued drink holders and Southwest Airlines found that its customers were willing to forgo seat reservations if they could get to their destinations sooner and if it would lower their air fares.

If you cannot eliminate an enrager, you may have to avoid that target market. *Neutrals* are *so what?* attributes that do not affect purchasing decisions. Entrepreneurs should make every effort to eliminate factors that add cost to the products that customers do not value. Gunther McGrath and MacMillan also stressed the need to distinguish between *must-have* and *nice-to-have* product/service attributes. Nice-to-have features may have value, but they may collectively drive up the price to the point where price exceeds the product/service's value.[32]

Progressive Insurance's success can be attributed to its ability to differentiate its product/service offering as well as its target market. Progressive's initial success was attributed to its focus on drivers whom conventional insurance providers considered to be too high a risk. Progressive researched that segment and developed a product/service strategy to take advantage of it. Instead of choosing to ignore that market segment or serving it reluctantly, Progressive capitalized on the gap in the market. When Progressive decided to expand into the market segment occupied by regular drivers, it found it could differentiate itself in terms of the services it provided before and after the sale. Progressive provides prospective customers quotes over the phone and the Internet. It also provides fast resolution of claims when there is an accident. Progressive's accident hotline and "adjustment offices on wheels" give it an unparalleled level of customer responsiveness. In many cases, the adjustor can provide a settlement check at the scene of the accident.[33]

First-time entrepreneurs frequently underestimate the role that services and intangibles can play in differentiating their products. Remember, customers do not want products, they want to have their needs met and problems solved. The ease with which customers can buy and use your products before, during, and after the sale may be just as important to them as the product itself. Going the extra *service mile* may be your most significant differentiating factor.

First-time entrepreneurs also fail to plan for subsequent product improvements. Make sure you do not rest on your laurels. Consumers' needs and interests will continue to change and competitors will try to steal your customers by imitating your products. Plan and budget for continued research and development from the very beginning of your venture.

First-time entrepreneurs who are inventors tend to get too caught up in the technical side of their product offering. "If the business plan is page after page of technical information and devotes little attention to the business side of the proposed venture, then that can be a turn off. The plan needs to articulate what the product/service is, how it can be made/ provided, that there is a market, that there is a valued and tangible advantage, and so on. Technical information can be provided in the appendix or available on request."[34]

Price Strategy

Pricing your product/service offering is more of an art than a science. The price you charge for your product/service offering is contingent on numerous factors. *Market skimming* and *market penetration* are the two most common pricing strategies. You may consider a skimming strategy—which involves charging a higher price—if your target market considers your product to be clearly superior and they have the desire and ability to pay a premium for it. The level of their demand and your competitive superiority may provide considerable latitude in your price strategy.

If skimming seems appropriate, then two questions need to be answered: "How high a price should I charge?" and "How long should I maintain that price? Skimming strategy is closely tied to the concept of price elasticity. *Elasticity* refers to the extent that demand fluctuates with price changes. Elasticity projects the extent that the percentage increase in price is greater or less than the percentage change in units purchased. If the percent of price increase is greater than the percent decrease in the units purchased, then total revenue will increase. If, however, the projected percent reduction in units purchased is greater than the percent increase in price, then a price increase will result in lower sales.

Unfortunately, you usually have to rely on projections rather than actual facts. You will not know how the market will respond until you actually offer your products or services to the market. The situation becomes more complicated because you will not know in advance how your competitors will respond. The higher the markup, the easier it will be for competitors to steal your customers by offering lower prices. Skimming is also risky because it might strain your relationship with your customers. Just because customers will pay a premium price does not mean that they will be grateful.

Market penetration strategy is different. Instead of trying to skim the cream off the top of the market, you price the product so that as many customers as possible will be able to buy your product or service. This strategy also tries to minimize the extent that competitors will be tempted to enter the market and steal your customers. The penetration strategy requires a solid grasp for the cost-volume-profit equation. Obviously you cannot price below your costs. The penetration strategy may also not be viable in some markets if larger competitors have economies of scale. Generally speaking, you should not consider entering markets where consumers are very price sensitive. Other firms in their desperation to postpone bankruptcy may be willing to cut their prices to levels you cannot and should not match.

If you plan to start a service business, then your pricing strategy may also be based on a skimming, penetration, match-the-market, or cost-plus approach. Many service businesses charge their customers three times the hourly rate they pay the people on their staff who provide the actual services. The first third is for the staff's salary. The second third is for the staff's payroll-related expenses and the firm's overhead. The final third is to contribute to profit.

Extending credit to your customers should be considered a form of price strategy. Extending credit makes a product or service more affordable. If you consider extending credit, then proceed with extreme caution. The failure to manage credit has been the downfall for too many businesses. Extending credit drains crucial working capital. Collecting your accounts receivable may also strain your goodwill with customers. If you choose to extend credit, then make sure you qualify who will be eligible for credit and set limits on how much you will extend to each person as well as altogether.

Promotion Strategy

Your marketing plan should not be based on the *Field of Dreams* mentality. If the customers you are targeting do not know about your firm and how it is superior to other businesses, then they cannot become your customers. Your promotion strategy must indicate how you plan to communicate with your target market. It must indicate the *who, what, when, how much,* and other factors that will get your message across.

The proverbial question, "Which type of advertising works best?" does not have a simple answer. Your promotion strategy needs to be based on thorough research because it must reflect your unique situation, and you do not have unlimited funds. Most entrepreneurs are reluctant to spend much money on promoting their products/services because money spent on promotions does not have a specific cost-benefit ratio. It would be nice if you knew that for every thousand dollars you spend on advertising you would get 15 new customers. One of the rules of thumb about advertising is that only one-half of your advertising dollar will get results—unfortunately, you do not know in advance which half it is. Some of the money you spend on advertising will not provide any return. Other promotions will provide a high return. Your promotion strategy will require some experimentation and adjustment. The term "guerrilla marketing" is frequently used to describe innovative and inexpensive promotional efforts.

REALITY CHECK

When you hear the voice inside say, "Our product/service is so great, we don't need to spend any money on advertising," recognize that in most cases the failure to advertise can lead to business failure. You will need to attract customers as soon as possible. If you want sales, then you will have to ante up. This is not a time to rely on hope rather than funding. As someone once noted, "Hope is not a business strategy."

You will also need to recognize two other factors when developing your promotion strategy. First, most promotions have to pass a cumulative threshold before they have much effect. You may not see much benefit until your message has been heard a number of times. Second, there may be a time lag between when prospective customers learn about your firm and when they inquire about it. Promotion Strategy 101 teaches us that prospective customers usually have to go through the four-step AIDA (awareness, interest, decision, and then action) process. The amount of money and time it takes to get prospective customers to the action stage will be contingent on your unique situation.

If your product or service is truly revolutionary, then you may be able to get considerable publicity from the media. This will give your firm considerable visibility. It could also give it credibility because coverage by the media may be more believable than your advertisements. Almost any company can get publicity in a trade journal or in the local media. He also noted that trade journal publicity may come in handy when the firm is looking for investors and customers.[35]

Distribution Strategy

Your venture's success will also depend on the availability of your product or service to your target market. You should approach your distribution strategy by starting from the prospective customer's point of view. Attracting customers is like fishing. You have to put your products/service offering where the fish are rather than expect the fish to come to where you are.

Some products may require extensive personal selling and/or a demonstration. Other product or service offerings can be handled on a self-service basis. Some businesses go to the customer. Other businesses have customers come to them. Some businesses never come into direct contact with their customers. They use either the Internet or other distribution channels to connect with customers. Gary Cadenhead, senior lecturer at the University of Texas, noted, "Anyone who's selling any product and who's not looking at Internet opportunities is stuck in the last century."[36]

Your distribution strategy, like your pricing strategy and promotion strategy, is an optimization issue. You need to find the right amount of money to spend and be savvy to the other ways your funds can be spent. Your strategy may also need to reflect supply-related issues. Jeff Bezos chose Seattle for Amazon.com partly due to the availability of a high-tech work force, low sales taxes, and the proximity to a major book distribution center.[37]

Getting Your First Customers

The saying that *all journeys must start with the first step* applies very well to a new venture. You need to identify the best prospects for generating your venture's first sales. Initial sales are crucial for three reasons. First, your venture will need cash to cover expenses. Second, you will need to learn what actually appeals to your target market. Market research is nice, but learning why a customer actually buys your product or service will provide valuable information. Third, your first customers may serve as the lead dominos as you try to attract more customers. Your first customers may provide referrals to prospective customers.

Your effort to attract your first customers must be handled in a systematic manner. This is not the time to use a shotgun approach by trying to attract every possible customer. Instead, you must use the rifle approach. You must focus on high-potential prospects. You do not have the time to wait for the masses to learn about your business and you don't have the money it will take to appeal to the masses. Identify the people who are most frustrated with what has been available and seek them out. Attracting your first customers may take a lot of prospecting, relationship building, salesmanship, resourcefulness, and flexibility. Amar Bhidé notes that entrepreneurs need to make sure they interact with the people who will actually be driving the purchase decision. He noted that while purchasing specialists may place the actual order, you need to deal with the person who will be initiating the order. Bhidé noted, "Selling is about building a relationship. It's about getting in early, defining the playing ground and the rules of the game, creating a sense of urgency, and building toward a conclusion."[38]

A recent article offers some interesting insights into getting your first customers. Desh Deshpande, who cofounded Sycamore Networks, believes that the process starts on day one. If you find the right first customer you'll build the right first product. You need to look for a first customer who will share your vision and who will be engaged early on in the development of your products. This customer needs to be demanding, but also appreciative of the time and effort it takes to bring a new technology to market. And the customer needs to believe in you and become your champion in the marketplace. At the start, it may be hard to convince this customer to do business with your start-up.[39]

Despande, noted that in high-tech, your first customer may be a new company or one that is outside the mainstream. First customers are the early adopters that are willing to accept a completely new technology because it will provide a distinct advantage in the marketplace. They are often willing to stick out their necks by entering a business no one has thought of before.[40]

Joseph and Jimmie Boyett noted, "Contrary to the fantasy of the movies, if you build it, they will not necessarily come—at least not initially, and not without some prodding."[41] The Home Depot's founders sent their kids into the parking lot to pass out dollar bills. Their idea was to lure customers into the first stores in Atlanta by giving them the opportunity to win prizes by matching serial numbers on the bills to numbers posted in the store.[42] Debbie Fields had to go out on the street and give cookies away to get her first customers![43]

It is important for your new venture to get *quick wins*. You should do whatever it takes to get your first customers. Keep an open mind and be flexible in what you actually offer prospective customers. You may need to modify the product's attributes or offer additional services to get the first sales. You may consider providing a money-back guarantee to reduce a prospect's resistance. If your product can be provided on a trial-size basis, then this may also help reduce a prospect's apprehensiveness.

Remember, your products and services are not ends in themselves. They are the means for creating and maintaining customers for a profit. Do not view modifying your product or service to be making a personal concession or something that compromises your venture; view the changes as to build goodwill. Remember, your business will need to have a cadre of satisfied customers to attract new customers. Also remember that your business's success may depend on repeat purchases. You cannot have repeat purchases without initial purchases.

You need to ask yourself, "Who would want to be an untried start-up's first customer?" When Bob Din was starting En Point Technologies Inc. he ran into the usual question from prospective clients. When GTE asked Din for references for his new company, he responded, "YOU are going to be my first reference because I will service the hell out of you."[44] Try to get customers at whatever cost so they can be referrals, then go for some blue-chip customers for additional credibility. Then try to create a *demand pull situation* by putting your firm in a position where prospective customers invite you in rather than you having to make a cold call.

Proprietary Position

If your venture has a proprietary position, then it should be stated in the business plan. A *proprietary position* exists when the venture has something that gives it a competitive advantage. The proprietary position may be the result of having a legal position or some type of exclusive position. The most common proprietary positions come from intellectual property, including patents, copyrights, trademarks, trade names, and trade secrets. The firm may have a proprietary position if it has a license to a certain process, product, and/or trade name. The firm may also have a proprietary position if it has a unique location or the exclusive rights to a supplier or a distribution channel.

Three things are clear about proprietary positions. First, they may be difficult to create. Second, they may be difficult to keep or enforce. Third, they may not be worth the time and money. "Among the sins committed by business plan writers is arrogance. In today's economy, few ideas are truly proprietary."[45]

A *patent* is a contract between the government and an inventor. The government grants the inventor exclusivity for a utility patent for 17 years and a design patent for 14 years. The patent prohibits anyone from making, using, or selling your invention. A *trademark* may be words, symbols, or designs that identify the source of certain goods. Trademarks can last indefinitely. You file your request with the U.S. Patent and Trademark Office. Obviously, you should seek the services of an attorney who specializes in intellectual property law if you will be seeking protection for your product or service.

The patent search process should be two-dimensional. First, you should check to make sure what you are developing will not be infringing on someone else's patent. Second, the search process may reveal patents held by competitors. If the search reveals that a patent exists, then you may be able to learn from the patent and come up with your own improved version. Robert D. Hisrich and Michael P. Peters noted, "Many businesses, inventions, or innovations are the result of improvements on, or modifications of, existing products. Copying and improving on a product may be perfectly legal (no patent infringement) and actually good business strategy. If it is impossible to copy and improve the product to avoid patent infringement, the entrepreneur may try to license the product from the patent holder."[46]

MicroPatent's website (*www.corporateintelligence.com*) offers an online patent exchange with thousands of listings. Its database has 33 million downloadable patents. Its Trademark.com provides a searchable trademark database. MicroPatent's website also provides patent forms, and other information.[47]

REALITY CHECK

Patents are a Catch 22. You may be better off not taking the time and spending the money on filing for a patent. In order to get a patent you need to submit a diagram that identifies the exact design of the product. By filing for a patent, anyone who wants to compete against you can check the design, which is a public record, and then introduce a product that is a modification of your product.

REALITY CHECK

Don't rely too heavily on a proprietary position. Al Miller, cofounder of Accolade, a company making games for Nintendo, noted, "Any start-up going up against large companies should expect to be sued and forced to pay their attorneys up to $2 million over a few years to defend the suits. … Even a company with the law on its side can be crushed by the legal system. High-tech start-ups are particularly vulnerable. Large, deep-pocketed companies have more resources to devote to legal and patent issues, and as a result, they have the power to obstruct, or even halt outright, the progress of smaller companies by embroiling them in legal disputes. At a large company, an IP (intellectual property) lawsuit is a mere setback; at a small one, it can be a crippling blow. And when it comes to IP law and the process of patenting new ideas, small and mid-size companies are often unprepared to defend their territory."[48]

REALITY CHECK

It may be better to go ahead and launch your product than to go the patent route and rely on its patent to protect your company against competitors. If you stay ahead of competition, then they will be imitating what you have done, rather than what you are currently doing. If you go the patent route and go after a firm that is violating your patent, then make sure it is big enough to have the money to get compensation from it.

REALITY CHECK

In your zeal to get your product off the drawing board, use caution when disclosing information about it. Robert Hisrich and Michael Peters noted, "Before making an external disclosure of an invention at a conference or to the media, or before setting up a beta site, the entrepreneur should seek legal counsel since this external disclosure may negate a subsequent patent application."[49]

REALITY CHECK

As soon as you start thinking about starting your own business and quitting your job, you should double check to make sure you did not sign a noncompete agreement and that your proposed venture will not be using any proprietary information that may be covered by a nondisclosure agreement.

REALITY CHECK

You should also make sure your employees sign a nondisclosure and noncompete clause as a condition of employment. The nondisclosure agreement will prohibit them for disclosing trade secrets, including client lists, to anyone outside your firm. Noncompete agreements have to be drafted carefully. They can restrict an employee from competing against your firm, but the agreement cannot keep them from earning a living in their field. The agreement must have a reasonable time limit and not cover too broad a geographic area.

THE FINANCIAL PART OF THE BUSINESS PLAN

The marketing part of the business plan highlights how your new venture will create and maintain customers. The financial part of your business plan highlights how your venture will make enough money to justify the time, risk, and investment. The financial part of the plan thereby links the top line of the business to the bottom line of the business. The plan's financial projections will also influence the venture's ability to attract funding.

The financial plan is like a jigsaw puzzle. It has numerous pieces, and they all have to fit together if the venture is to get off the ground. The financial part of the plan identifies eight key elements:

1. How much money will be needed to start the venture
2. How the venture will be funded
3. Projected income statements
4. Projected balance sheets
5. Projected cash flow
6. Key financial ratios
7. The sources and uses of funds
8. Future funding needs for expansion, and so on

The ability to estimate revenue, expenses, profit, and corresponding level of investment are essential because when these estimates are taken together they serve as a litmus test for the venture. The projections will reflect the relative merit of the venture. If the numbers are favorable, then you should proceed with the venture. If the numbers are not favorable, then your effort to start the venture may come to a screeching halt.

Projecting Sales

Developing the financial part of the business plan for a new venture can be very challenging because most of the data are not readily available, accurate, or applicable to your business concept. The greater the uniqueness of your business concept, the more difficult it may be to make financial projections. This is particularly true when it comes to forecasting sales. Few questions in business are more difficult to answer than, "What will sales be for my new venture in each of the first few years?"

Sales forecasts are the weakest feature of most business plans. "A fortune teller with tea leaves and a copy of Lotus 1-2-3 could do better. For example, Mitchell Kapor, founder of Lotus, projected first-year sales to be $6 million. Lotus posted first-year sales of $53 million."[50]

The difficulty in projecting first-year sales is not limited to high-technology products and services. When Ben Cohen and Jerry Greenfield sat down to write a business plan for an ice-cream parlor they wanted to open in Vermont, they found they needed a loan. When they approached the Small Business Administration (SBA), they found that the SBA would not give them a loan guarantee unless they had projections. Ben and Jerry exclaimed, "How were we supposed to know how many people were going to patronize a home-made ice-cream parlor in a town that never had one?"[51] Both entrepreneurs projected first-year sales to be $90,000. Cohen admits that at that time he believed it would be impossible to do that level of volume. They started the business anyway, even though they only got $4,000 rather than the $20,000 they were seeking. Instead of $90,000, their ice cream parlor, which was located in a former gas station, had sales of $200,000.[52]

Unfortunately, these two examples are not typical for most new ventures. Most new ventures are far less successful than Lotus or Ben and Jerry's. Most entrepreneurs are overly optimistic about the level of sales their new ventures will generate in the first years. This is one of the reasons why the financial projections should be based on three different levels. Projections should be based on optimistic, most likely, and pessimistic sales levels. The *optimistic* level of sales is based on what the venture could do if everything worked out. This level would be the case if the market embraced your venture's product/service offering, if competition does not retaliate, and your venture has the wherewithal to actually meet market demand. The *most likely* estimate should be realistic of what may be possible. The *pessimistic* sales estimate is crucial because it forces you to do a serious reality check. It represents a worst-case scenario. In many cases, the optimistic estimate could be anywhere from 20 to 100 percent more than your most likely estimate. In many cases, the pessimistic estimate could be anywhere from 20 to 80 percent of your most likely sales estimate. There have been instances when a new business did not have any sales!

Your sales estimate is based on a simple mathematical equation. You multiply the number of units (of product or service) you expect to sell times the price per unit. This is where the challenge begins. Most entrepreneurs' sales forecasts are based on your new venture's projected share of the market. If the market had sales last year of $300 million and it is expected to grow by 5 percent to $315 million this year, then you need to estimate the share of the $315 million you expect your venture to capture. In some cases, you may narrow the overall market figure to the specific market segment you plan to target. If the targeted segment represents 20 percent of the overall market, then you would base your estimate on your share of the $63 million segment. If your most likely projection is for 5 percent market share, then your sales estimate would be $3,150,000. Your optimistic estimate may be for an 8 percent market share; then sales would be $5,040,000. If your pessimistic estimate is for 2.5 percent market share, then sales would be $1,575,000.

The mathematical calculations in the preceding example were very straightforward. Unfortunately, things usually are not that simple. The number of units sold will be affected by your pricing strategy. Your sales estimate must take into consideration the issue of elasticity. It should also take into consideration competitive response, as well as the effectiveness of your promotion and distribution strategies.

In a perfect world, you would know how many people (or businesses) will be your customers, how much they will buy, and the exact price they will pay for your products and services. If your venture is being created to provide products or services to specific customers who have approached you to solve their problems, then you may be in a much better position to estimate sales. You will also be in a better position to get a realistic estimate of sales if you get letters of intent or at least tangible indications of interest from prospective customers. Your business plan will be much more credible if you can support your sales estimates with data rather than hope.

Five other sources of data may be helpful in developing your sales estimates. Trade associations frequently compile information about their members. If there is a trade association for your type of venture, then it may be able to provide you with information about industry sales, average sales for its members, and an estimate of the projected rate of growth. *Gale Directory of Associations* provides a listing of numerous associations. Robert Morris Associates' (RMA's) *Annual Statement Studies* may also be a good source of information. It provides various financial ratios for various types of business. As noted earlier, many banks and accounting firms have departments that specialize in new ventures. They may be in a position to provide useful information. Census data may also be a useful source of information. Census data may be available regarding the amount that is spent on certain types of products and services altogether and in various locations.

Suppliers and distributors in your industry may also be in a position to provide information that can be used in developing your sales estimates. They are closely involved with businesses already serving the market and the ultimate consumers so they may provide useful information. They may also be in a position to identify opportunities for creating a competitive advantage for your venture. Their proximity to the market places them in a position where they may see market segments that are not being served well or to hear customers who ask, "Is there any firm out there that ...?"

Projected Income Statements

You should prepare income statements for the first three to five years. Income statements should also be prepared for the optimistic, most likely, and pessimistic sales estimates. Income statements play a critical role in the business plan because they force you to look at the relationship between sales, expenses, and profits. Income statements estimate the costs associated with the corresponding level of sales. Some expenses will vary in direct relation to the level of sales. If you sell tangible products, then your cost of goods sold should vary with the level of sales. If you provide services, then your payroll expenses for the people who provide the services to your customers may vary to some degree with the level of sales. Some expenses will correspond with what it takes just to keep your business going. These expenses include insurance, utilities, and management salaries. Other expenses like advertising and rent will have a chicken-and-egg nature to them. It will take a certain level of advertising to generate a certain level of sales. You will also need a certain amount of square feet to support a certain level of sales.

Projecting the income statements for the three levels of sales will play a major role in whether you go ahead with the venture. The optimistic estimate will indicate the level of profit that may be possible if everything goes well. The projected optimistic income statements will also indicate that you should not expect anything beyond that level. The projected most likely income statements are helpful because if they do not indicate the level of profit to justify the risk and investment associated with the venture, then it may be hard to justify starting the venture. The projected pessimistic income statements are useful because they force you to take a hard look at what could happen. If you cannot afford the low level of profit or loss, then it may be better to look for a more profitable opportunity. The pessimistic projections, however, may actually encourage you to start your venture. If the three- to five-year projections are based on a worst-case scenario and the projected income statements indicate a reasonable profit, then this may signal that the venture is worth the time and money.

The income statements should be done on a monthly basis for the first year and a quarterly basis for the second year. Doing the first year income statements on a monthly basis will force you to project how sales will ramp up. Doing the projection on a monthly basis will also force you to consider seasonal factors that could affect your business. The projected income statements should be done on an annual basis for subsequent years.

Projected Initial Capital Requirement

Estimating the amount of money you need to start your venture may be one of the most important aspects of your business plan. Your initial capital requirement is closely tied to your sales estimates. The sales estimates were based on certain assumptions. Your sales estimates were based on the amount allocated to your promotion strategy and its effectiveness, the amount of inventory available to sell or the number and nature of personnel to provide the services, the amount and quality of space for your proposed facility, and so forth. The sales estimates were also based on the assumption that your venture has a certain amount of funding to support those levels of sales.

The best way to estimate your initial capital requirement is to take your most likely sales estimate for the first year and work backward to figure the type and amount of cash outlays it will take to generate that level of sales. The initial capital requirement will be the amount of cash you need to start the business until it reaches the point where its cash receipts start to exceed your cash disbursements.

Estimating your initial capital requirement relies on your cash flow projections more than the income statement. Your income statement may include sales using the accrual (rather than cash) method and various noncash expenses like depreciation. Your initial capital requirement will need to reflect loan payments, the purchase of inventory, fixtures and equipment, deposits with utilities, and other cash outlays that may not be reflected on an income statement. It will also need to reflect whether you plan to sell your products/services on credit. Generally speaking, any amount that you have in accounts receivable will increase your initial capital requirement, because you will not be receiving cash at the time of sale. Therefore, you will need to have money in reserve to pay for the products you sold or to pay your staff for the services they provided.

By tracking cash receipts from sales and the cash disbursements for each month for the first year you should have an estimate of the amount of money needed to start the venture. Your calculations should also reflect the difference between when you start your business and when you actually open your business to customers. You will probably have to start your venture months before you actually offer your products or services to your target market. Consequently, your venture may not have revenue for some of its first 12 months. This is why your projected cash flow should be done on a monthly basis for at least the first year.

REALITY CHECK

It may be wise to also run your initial capital requirement using your pessimistic estimate. The pessimistic estimate may be a better basis for estimating your initial capital requirement because things involving cash rarely go as planned. The first things entrepreneurs learn about cash is that cash outlays often are twice as fast and twice as large as expected. They also learn that cash receipts often come in twice as slow and twice as low (half) as what was expected. This means that you need to increase your initial cash position so you have some cash in reserve if you need it. Having some extra cash on hand is far better than trying to rustle up some cash when you are on the verge of running out.

REALITY CHECK

When you start your venture you have money but no customers. The challenge is to get enough customers before you run out of money. Leslie Brokaw noted, "No founder has ever overestimated the amount of capital necessary to get started or the amount of time it will take to be legitimated by the marketplace. A lot of entrepreneurs miscalculate the sales cycle—the time between the first sales pitch and that customer's actual purchase. The lag can cause serious cash-flow problems."[53]

REALITY CHECK

Don't plan on divine intervention or expect to win the lottery when you need additional funds. You may have heard stories about entrepreneurs who took their remaining cash to Las Vegas to see if they could make enough money to meet payroll or other pressing obligations. First, don't put yourself in that situation. Second, don't count on winning when you get there!

Projected Cash Flow

The process for estimating your initial capital requirement illustrates the importance of projecting cash flow. Although your venture's profitability will be important, its cash flow may be even more important. Cash is like oxygen; without sufficient cash your business will die. Numerous new ventures go out of business because they run out of cash before their revenue hits the point where cash receipts cover cash disbursements. Some of these businesses were making great strides in increasing their sales, but they ran out of cash before they could make ends meet.

Cash flow needs to be projected beyond the first year so investors have an idea about the venture's ability to pay dividends. The cash flow projection will enable creditors (including banks) to see the venture's ability to pay off its loans. Your business plan should project cash flow on a monthly basis for the first year, quarterly for the second year, and annually for the following years. It may be particularly useful to plot cash flow and the cash on hand monthly on a bar chart for the first year. The bar chart is like a gas gauge. It will indicate in advance when your venture will be getting close to running on fumes so that you can have a reserve tank of cash on hand.

Projected Balance Sheets

The projected balance sheets are important because they reflect the income statements and projected cash flow. A balance sheet indicates the venture's assets, liabilities, and owners' equity. In layperson's terms, it indicates the extent that the venture's assets are owned (equity) versus owed (debt).

Your business plan should include your opening balance sheet and the year-end balance sheets for the first three to five years. The opening balance sheet will indicate the configuration of the venture's assets, liabilities, and the stockholders' investment. Each of the projected year-end balance sheets (each year should have a balance sheet for each of the three estimates) will provide a picture of the venture's financial position. The balance sheets will also indicate if the venture is building wealth for its stockholders as well as if it is paying off any loans that were used to fund the venture.

The projected balance sheets will also be useful if you plan any major expansion for the venture. The balance sheets will reflect the availability of cash for funding expansion. They will also indicate the extent the venture's assets are funded by debt. Generally speaking, the greater the equity to debt ratio (the more the assets are funded by equity), the easier it will be to get debt-based funding.

The projected balance sheets for the first few years will be particularly important if you are seeking a loan from a bank because banks usually will not provide start-up funding. They prefer to wait until the venture is up and running before providing a loan. Banks are risk averse so they reduce their risk by waiting until the venture has sales and a reasonable cash flow. Banks look more favorably and provide better terms to ventures that are demonstrating their ability to pay off a note.

REALITY CHECK

Although bankers may seem interested in your venture's success, they usually are not willing to ante up when you are a start-up and the venture is not much more than an untested concept that is based on a set of assumptions that were developed by an overly optimistic entrepreneur.

Entrepreneurs need to project the amount of cash they will need at various stages in the venture's evolution. Jerry and Jimmie Boyette, authors of *The Guru Guide to Entrepreneurship,* noted that getting money—whether it is debt or equity—is going to be hard and you are going to have to do it repeatedly. They noted, "You will need money to get started; you will need another influx of money when your business starts to grow; and you will need another as you try to expand your business and become even bigger. The whole task of money raising isn't going to end."[54]

Key Financial Ratios and Indicators

Key financial ratios and indicators can be computed from the projected income statements, balance sheets, and cash flows. Numerous ratios can provide insights into the venture's financial position. The following ratios may be particularly useful: profit as a percent of sales, contribution margin, return on equity, return on assets, inventory turn, and debt to equity. Each of these ratios reflects the venture's relative health.

The projected statements may also be helpful in computing certain financial indicators. Key indicators include the breakeven point in both sales dollars and units, the point where the venture has positive cash flow, and the point where the venture can pay off its liabilities. The projections may also be useful in figuring the overall value of the venture by using a price-earnings ratio.

Sources and Uses of Funds

The business plan should indicate the sources of funding at various stages. It should indicate how the venture's start-up will be funded. It should also note when and how additional funding will be sought. Few emerging ventures are able to fund major growth from revenues. The plan should indicate when an infusion of additional capital will be sought. If additional investors will be sought, then the plan should indicate how the funding will be structured. Attention should be based on valuation, the type of stock to be issued, and the resulting ownership structure. If your venture will be seeking debt funding, then the plan should indicate how the loan will be used as well as the terms of the loan.

REALITY CHECK

Be careful when you seek outside funding. Your optimism can come back to haunt you. Mark S. Deion, a business planning and strategy consultant, noted, "There's no question that business plans are used to sell a business and its management. But there are serious drawbacks to hawking a company's financial prospects too hard. If your loan is approved, many banks will make the plan part of the loan document. If you don't make the ratios you promised, the bank can put you in technical default."[55] He also noted that banks in the Northeast have used the default process to get out of entire markets in a downturn.[56] Investors may also have escape clauses if your venture fails to meet certain milestones. Venture capital firms may also use the failure to hit financial targets to remove you as the venture's chief executive officer.

Budgeting and Financial Management

The business plan is not just a blueprint for projecting funding needs; it also provides the basis for managing your venture's operations. The plan becomes the basis for developing your venture's budgets. Budgets tie planning and control together. From a planning perspective, the budget identifies in advance where the firm should be. From a controlling perspective, the budget lets you know if you are where you should be at that point in time.

The budgeting process also helps you focus your attention on the things that matter. Every expense should be subjected to the questions, "Do we really need to spend money on this?" "Will this item really add value to the firm?" and "Is there some way we can lease it or outsource it so we do not have to commit funds to it?" Chapter 8 provides numerous examples of how your new venture can use bootstrapping techniques to reduce your capital requirements and other cash outlays.

OPERATIONAL ISSUES

The business plan should highlight key operating issues and how they will be addressed. The business plan should include a timeline that indicates the key activities associated with starting the venture as well as noteworthy events and milestones once it is up and running. The timeline is crucial, not just because there are a multitude of activities that must be initiated and completed, but also because few activities act in isolation. Most activities are interrelated. Some activities have to be completed before others are begun. Some activities should be done concurrently. The plan should identify key activities, when they are to be initiated, how long they will take, and when they will be completed. The network of activities, events, and milestones should be tied to specific dates so they can be scheduled and resources can be committed to them. The timeline will let you know when things are going as planned. It will also let you know when you are behind schedule so you can do what needs to be done to get back on track.

The need for developing a comprehensive business plan has been the subject of some discussion in the last few years. It is clear that life has become more complicated and that the business world is changing on all fronts. Yet it is also clear that business success today is not just about identifying market opportunities; it is contingent on the ability to keep things from falling through the cracks. Starting and growing a venture is a world where entrepreneurs and their management teams have to *keep the plates spinning!* It is a world where execution may be the difference between success and failure.

When Tom Smith was president of Food Lion, a chain of grocery stores, he was asked how his firm had outperformed it competitors. He noted that Food Lion was 1 percent better on 1,000 different things. Ray Kroc, who made McDonald's a great company, did not want to leave any aspect of his franchises to chance. He noted, "The french fry has become almost sacrosanct for me ... Its preparation is a ritual to be followed religiously."[57]

Goals, timelines, and budgets are essential components for establishing an effective management information system. A well-prepared business plan will help the management team focus its attention on the things that matter the most. It will also make it possible to establish a management by exception system where key metrics indicate which things are not going as planned. Michael Dell noted, "We were fascinated to learn how the 'little things' became 'big things' to the people who really mattered."[58]

The operational plan should indicate the timeline for articles of incorporation, selecting and leasing a site for your business, getting your website up and running, hiring staff, doing grand opening advertising, and the myriad other things that cannot be ignored. It should also identify key suppliers and distributors.

KEY RISKS AND HOW THEY WILL BE ADDRESSED

The business plan should also include a section that identifies the risks associated with the venture and how they will be addressed. This part of the plan underscores the point that planning forces you to take the mental journey before you take the physical journey. This part of the plan identifies key issues for the management team to address. It also lets potential stakeholders know that you are aware of potential risks.

This part of the plan is the result of a risk audit for your venture. The risk audit or analysis tries to identify every point where the venture may be vulnerable. Risk analysis may include the risks associated with not meeting sales projections, cost overruns, problems with suppliers, problems with distributors, not meeting production deadlines, unfavorable industry trends, competitive price cutting, technological developments, running out of cash, loss of key staff, environmental problems, and so forth. It may be helpful to construct a risk table that identifies each major risk, estimates of the probability it will occur, how it will be monitored, and how the issue will be addressed.

Some risks may be addressed by outsourcing certain aspects of the venture. Some risks can be addressed by having the other parties sign contracts specifying performance. Some aspects can be handled via insurance policies. Because of the prevalence of Murphy's Law, it is wise to have contingency plans available in advance so you can respond proactively and quickly to potential setbacks.

EXIT STRATEGY

One of Steven Covey's seven habits of highly effective people is "Begin with the end in mind." The same principle should be applied to how you start your venture. No plan would be complete without some discussion of possible exit strategies. Prospective employees will want to know before they quit their jobs if the venture is being created for a quick sale to the highest bidder or whether you are in it for the long haul. Investors will want to know how they will get their money out before they will put their money into your venture.

The plan should indicate your exit strategy and time horizon. The plan should indicate if your goal is to turn it over to your children, let management buy you out, have the firm be acquired by another firm, or cash out by taking your firm public. Each exit strategy will affect how the venture is started, how it will be funded, and how it will be run.

REALITY CHECK

Having the end in mind makes sense, but so does keeping your intentions confidential. If you want to build a great business, then you will need the support of various stakeholders. Business is about relationships, and relationships are based on trust. Make sure that your exit strategy does not undermine your ability to build a great business. And make sure that the way you approach exiting does not burn any bridges before you get to them. You should also make sure you do not burn any bridges after you cross them. You may need some of those relationships in future ventures.

SUMMARY OF THE BUSINESS PLAN

Even though the business plan begins with an executive summary, it should have a brief and concise summary at the end of the plan. The summary reminds the reader of key points. It also provides a sense of closure.

APPENDICES

The appendices serve two purposes. First, they provide useful supporting material. Second they keep the text of the plan from being too long and cumbersome for the reader. Most plans have a number of appendices. Each appendix will contain supporting information that was either too lengthy, too detailed, or not substantive enough to be included in the text of the plan.

Each appendix will provide information about a factor that may be considered a *driver for success*. Each appendix can be seen as a vehicle for reducing the venture's risk by providing supporting documentation. One appendix will include the resumes of key people including the entrepreneur and management team. Another appendix will include the financial projections that were summarized as tables in the text of the plan. Additional appendices may include schematics of the product, a list of potential clients, names of accountants, attorneys, the lease agreement, as well as the names and correspondence with suppliers and distributors.

CONCLUSION: THE PLAN IS NOT AN END IN ITSELF

The business plan should not be considered an end in itself. It should be a vehicle for increasing the odds that your new venture will be successful. Yet the plan is a bit of a paradox. It should be comprehensive enough to address the key issues, yet it should not be so comprehensive that it takes so much time to prepare that it is out of sync with market realities by the time it is completed. It should have enough details so that it can be implemented, yet it should not try to dot every *i* and cross every *t*. It should provide a sense of direction, yet be flexible enough so that it can be modified to meet the multitude of changes that will take place every day. In a sense, the plan should be your effort to hit a moving target. It should also serve as an early warning system when things do not go as expected.

If the plan is done right, then it will do at least three things. First, it will indicate that a market opportunity exists. Second, it will provide a blueprint for creating a successful venture. Third, it should demonstrate that you and your management team have a plan for turning the opportunity into a successful venture. Fourth, it should provide prospective stakeholders with a compelling reason to become involved in your venture.

Plans are nothing; planning is everything.[59]

—Dwight D. Eisenhower

ENDNOTES

1. David M. Anderson, "Deadly Sins," *Entrepreneur,* August 2001, p. 108. Reprinted with permission of Entrepreneur Media, Inc.

2. Mark Van Osnabrugge and Robert J. Robinson, *Angel Investing* (San Francisco: Jossey-Bass, 2000), p. 134. Copyright © 2000, Jossey Bass. This material is used by permission of John Wiley & Sons, Inc.

3. Erik Larson, "The Best-Laid Plans," *Inc.,* February 1987, p. 60.

4. William A. Sahlman, "How to Write a Really Great Business Plan," *Harvard Business Review,* July–August 1997, in Annual Editions Entrepreneurship 99/00, p. 125. Reprinted by permission of *Harvard Business Review.*

5. Amar Bhidé, "How Entrepreneurs Craft Strategies That Work," *Harvard Business Review,* March–April, 1994 in Annual Editions Entrepreneurship 99/00, p. 126. Reprinted by permission of *Harvard Business Review.*

6. Sahlman, "How to Write a Really Great Business Plan," p. 126.

7. Jeffry A. Timmons, "Growing Up Big: Entrepreneurship and Creating High Potential Ventures," *Texas A&M Business Forum,* Fall 1985, p. 12.

8. Edward O. Welles, "15 Steps to a Start-Up," *Inc.,* March 1994, p. 78.

9. Timmons, "Growing Up Big: Entrepreneurship and Creating High Potential Ventures," p. 12.

10. Leslie Brokaw, "The Truth About Start-Ups," *Inc.,* April 1991, p. 57.

11. Amar Bhidé, *The Origin and Evolution of New Businesses* (Oxford; Oxford University Press, 2000), p. 52.

12. Elaine Pofeldt, "The *Success* Start-Up Guide," March 1999, p. 63.

13. Patrick Kelly, "The Mystery of the Empty Truck," *Inc.,* October 1997, p.35.

14. Rob Ryan, *Smartups: Lessons from Rob Ryan's Entrepreneur America Boot Camp for Start-Ups* (Ithaca: Cornell University Press, 2001), pp. 93-95. Copyright © 2001 by Rob Ryan. Used with permission of the publisher, Cornell University Press.

15. Ibid., p. 96.

16. Ibid.

17. Ibid., p. 101.

18. Ibid., pp. 86 & 87.

19. Ibid., p. 94.

20. Ibid., pp. 96 & 97.

21. Ibid., p. 97.

22. Ibid., p. 98.

23. Ibid., pp. 98 & 99.

24. Ibid., p. 100.

25. Bhidé, "How Entrepreneurs Craft Strategies That Work," p. 70.

26. Sahlman, "How to Write a Really Great Business Plan," pp. 127 & 128.

27. Leslie Brokaw, "The Truth About Start-Ups," *Inc.,* April 1991, p. 56.

28. Cheryl J. Willson, "The Name Game," *Red Herring,* January 2000, pp. 196–198.

29. W. Keith Schilit, *The Entrepreneur's Guide to Preparing a Winning Business Plan and Raising Venture Capital* (Englewood Cliffs, NJ: Prentice Hall, 1990), p. 52.

30. Rita Gunther McGrath and Ian MacMillan, *The Entrepreneurial Mindset* (Boston: Harvard Business School Press, 2000), p. 24. Reprinted by permission of Harvard Business School Press.

31. Bhidé, "How Entrepreneurs Craft Strategies That Work," p. 70.

32. Gunther McGrath and MacMillan, *The Entrepreneurial Mindset*, pp. 34 & 35.

33. Ibid., p. 38.

34. Patrick Kelly, "The Mystery of the Empty Truck," *Inc.,* October 1997, p.35.

35. Edward O. Welles, "15 Steps to a Start-Up," *Inc.,* March 1994, p. 78.

36. Elaine Pofeldt, "The Success Start-Up Guide," p. 63.

37. Lesley Hazleton, "Jeff Bezos," *Success,* July 1998, p. 58.

38. Bhidé, *The Origin and Evolution of New Businesses*, p. 109.

39. Desh Deshpande, "Chose Your Customers Wisely," *Red Herring,* March 2001, p. 134

40. Ibid.

41. Joseph H. Boyett and Jimmie T. Boyett, *The Guru Guide to Entrepreneurship* (New York: John Wiley & Sons, 2001), p. 131.

42. Bernie Marcus and Arthur Blank, *Built from Scratch: How a Couple of Regular Guys Grew Home Depot from Nothing to $30 Million* (New York: Random House, 1999), p. 80.

43. Debbi Fields, *One Smart Cookie* (New York: Simon & Schuster, 1987), pp. 80 & 81.

44. Sharon Churcher, "A Point Well Taken," *Success,* May 1998, p. 50.

45. Sahlman, "How to Write a Really Great Business Plan," p. 131.

46. Robert D. Hisrich and Michael P. Peters, *Entrepreneurship* (New York: McGraw-Hill, 1998), p. 203.

47. Don Steinberg, "Corporate Intelligence.com," SmartBusinessMag.com, April 2001, p. 71.

48. Luc Hatlestad, "I'm Goona Sue Your Ass," *Red Herring,* May 1999, p. 66.

49. Hisrich and Peters, *Entrepreneurship,* p. 203.

50. Larson, "The Best-Laid Plans," p. 60.

51. Ben Cohen, Jerry Greenfield, and Meredith Maran, *Ben & Jerry's Double Dip* (New York: Simon & Schuster, 1997), p. 90-93.

52. Larson, "The Best-Laid Plans," p. 61.

53. Brokaw, "The Truth About Start-Ups," p. 67.

54. Boyett and Boyett, *The Guru Guide to Entrepreneurship,* p. 89.

55. Brian McWilliams, "Garbage In, Garbage Out," *Inc.,* August 1996, in 99/00 Entrepreneurship Annual Editions, p.139.

56. Ibid., p. 138.

57. Walter Guzzardi, "Wisdom of the Giants: A Directory of the Laureates," *Fortune,* July 3, 1989, p. 80.

58. Michael Dell and Catherine Fredman, *Direct from Dell* (New York: HarperBusiness, 1999), pp. 206–207.

59. Louis E. Boone, *Quotable Business* (New York: Random House, 1992), p. 34.

8

SOURCES OF FUNDING

There has never been a time when the supply of capital did not outrace the supply of opportunities.[1]

—William Sahlman
Harvard Professor

This chapter highlights the facts of life for funding a new venture. It profiles various sources of funding, the importance of bootstrapping, and the need for a funding plan. Chapters 9 through 13 provide an in-depth analysis of raising money by getting a loan, as well as attracting angel investors, seeking venture capital, and doing an initial public offering.

ENTREPRENEURS NEED TO KNOW THE FACTS OF FUNDING LIFE

The following sections will provide insights that will help prepare entrepreneurs in their quest for capital.

Fact of Funding 1: Entrepreneurs Have to Accept Risk

The entrepreneurial journey and financial risk go hand in hand. You will have to boldly go where you have not gone before. You and your management team will have to quit your jobs to start the venture. Customers and distributors will have to take a risk when they buy from your untried firm. Suppliers will have to take a risk when they provide credit to your new venture.

REALITY CHECK
If you want others to risk their money, then you must be the first person to ante up.

David Evanson and Art Beroff believe the entrepreneur must finance the venture with whatever funds he or she has available—whether it is $5,000 or $500,000. They note that by doing so, the entrepreneur makes the venture viable to outside investors. They offer the following hair-raising tips when trying to raise money:[2]

1. *Liquidate savings: If you've got it, give it up.* There's no way an investor is going to put in tons of capital that's totally at risk while all or part of your nest egg sits safely in CDs and blue-chip stocks.

2. *Take out a home-equity loan.* Investors love this one because they know that nothing makes an entrepreneur work harder or smarter than the prospect of the bank repossessing his or her home.

3. *Get a bank loan.* If you can actually get a bank to lend you money, you'll be demonstrating the kind of chutzpah investors like. Why? Because any bank will require a personal guarantee, or the guarantees of friends or family members, which tells investors that somebody else is at risk, as well.

Entrepreneurs need to recognize that they are gambling. They are betting their own money—and probably others' money—on the venture's success. Before they embark on the entrepreneurial journey, they need to identify how much they are willing to put at risk. Personal financial risk can be seen in two ways. The first risk is actual dollar risk. If you put $300,000 into the venture, then you are risking $300,000. The second type of risk is relative risk. It looks at how much of your total wealth you are risking. If you commit $300,000 from a total net worth of $2 million to the venture, then you are risking only 15 percent of your wealth. If the venture goes down, then your financial situation has not been dealt a devastating blow. If your $300,000 commitment involves liquidating all your savings, tapping into your 401K, and taking out a second mortgage, then you have put yourself at total risk.

Putting yourself at significant relative risk should not be taken lightly. If you are in a situation like Michael Dell when he was a freshman in college, then you may have little downside risk. He risked only a few dollars and could reenroll the next fall if things didn't work out. The same applies if you are single, have minimal financial obligations, and are so marketable that you could find a great job in a short time if things didn't work out. Most people, however, have a lot to lose.

REALITY CHECK

The rewards for embarking on the entrepreneurial journey and the likelihood of success should more than outweigh the risks associated with the journey. Know the difference between taking an acceptable risk and being reckless.

REALITY CHECK

If you are married, then make sure your spouse is truly committed to the venture. You may have to liquidate part or all of your portfolio, get a second mortgage, tap your 401K plan, and draw from your kids' college fund. He or she may be expected to cosign for a loan and various other things. Your spouse will also have to make other sacrifices. You may become a stranger in your own house as you commit whatever time it takes to get the venture up and running. Dinners together, weekend trips, and vacations may have to be put on hold until a management team is in place and the venture generates positive cash flow. Even when you are at home, you're really not there. Your mind will be jumping from one entrepreneurial challenge to another.

Fact of Funding 2: Determine if You Are Credit/Investment Worthy

Entrepreneurs need to step back and take a look at themselves. Investors invest in people who can make money for them. Banks lend money to people who will make decisions that will repay the loan. Potential lenders and investors will investigate the trustworthiness and creditworthiness of the entrepreneur. If your credit history, employment history, or legal history is tarnished, then the ability to attract funding will be jeopardized. Entrepreneurs who have had to declare bankruptcy, have been the target of major litigation, or who have a criminal record are not likely to engender the level of trust needed to attract funding.

Character flaws can lead even the brightest entrepreneur down the dark road to bankruptcy. "From the venture capitalist's point of view—and from the point of view of bankers, partners, suppliers, customers, and even friends and family tapped for investments—it is not the entrepreneur's products but his personality that can make that critical difference. Even as you're pitching your goods, you're pitching yourself, your professionalism, your competence, and your aura of authority—all become part of the sale."[3]

REALITY CHECK

Run a credit check on yourself before you even begin the venture or seek funds. Check it in advance to see what it says, and get it corrected if it is in error. If you have a checkered past, then forget trying to raise external funding!

Fact of Funding 3: Entrepreneurs Need "Other People's Money"

Very few entrepreneurs have sufficient funds to finance a high rate of growth. Sales receipts rarely provide enough money to fund the increases in inventory, staff, systems, R&D, and so forth that are needed to support a high rate of growth. The challenge is amplified if the firm allows its customers to buy on credit. The venture almost always needs an infusion of external capital to take it to the next level. The money can be in the form of a loan and/or from the sale of stock. Most entrepreneurs have an aversion to issuing stock to attract funding. They do not want to have their ownership position diluted, to have others challenge or second-guess their decisions, or to run the risk of ultimately losing control of their ventures.

REALITY CHECK

Dilution of ownership is the price one usually has to pay to foster a high rate of growth. Entrepreneurs need to ask, "Would I rather have a 100 percent stake of a $400,000 firm, a 60 percent stake in a $2 million firm, or a 25 percent stake in a $10 million firm?"

REALITY CHECK

If your venture can get extended credit from its suppliers and has an extremely high net profit margin, then you will have less need for an infusion of external funding.

Fact of Funding 4: Raising Money Takes Considerable Time

Getting a loan or attracting investors is not like getting a hamburger at a drive-through window. Raising money takes considerable time, information, and effort. It cannot be relegated to "when time is available" or postponed until the last minute. It may take months of prospecting to generate legitimate investor interest. Then it could take another month or two to close a deal if things work out. Getting a bank loan also takes time. Banks do not provide commercial loans with the same speed and certainty as they do with financing a car or a house.

REALITY CHECK

Veteran entrepreneurs stress the need to start the search for funding well before you need it, to have back-up plans because life is full of surprises, and to never assume the deal is done until the money is actually in your bank account.

Fact of Funding 5: Seeking Funding Is Not Fun and It Takes Resilience

Joseph and Jimmie Boyett note that the money entrepreneurs have or can get from someone else makes all the difference in their ability to start a business and keep it going. They stated, "All entrepreneurs learn that lesson and almost all entrepreneurs hate it. Of all the activities entrepreneurs hate the most, raising money and managing money are at the top of the I-can't-stand-to-do list. The fun for entrepreneurs is thinking up ideas, taking prudent risks, winning and losing, wooing customers, inspiring employees, creating, and innovating."[4]

REALITY CHECK

If you have a real aversion to selling, then forget starting a business. Entrepreneurship involves selling people on the merit of joining the venture, of buying its products and services, and of forming alliances.

REALITY CHECK

Raising money also takes considerable resilience. You must have the ability to handle rejection—especially when it comes to getting a loan or attracting investors. Howard Schultz recalls that, in the course of the year he spent trying to raise money for Starbucks, he spoke to 242 people and was turned down by 217 of them. Schultz noted, "Try to imagine how disheartening it can be to hear why your idea is not worth investing in."[5]

Fact of Funding 6: Seeking Funding Is Rarely a One-Time Occurrence

High-growth ventures have an unquenchable thirst for money. Each stage of growth may require an additional infusion of capital. Expanding into new geographic markets, investing in R&D, upgrading computer and information systems, and myriad other cash outlays place new demands on funding.

REALITY CHECK

Entrepreneurs must be willing to ante up for a highly competent person to oversee the firm's accounting and financial dimensions of the firm. They must also be willing to pay for a good accounting system and to use the services of an accounting firm that has experience helping emerging ventures grow and attract funding. It is almost impossible to raise funds without good people, good systems, good information, good connections, good relationships, and good advice.

Fact of Funding 7: Each Funding Source Has Its Own Set of Expectations

Attracting funding is like fishing. You just cannot go out and throw your line into the water and expect to catch a fish. Each source of funding is unique with its own expectations as to the amount available, the length of time it will be available, the level of return expected, as well as specific terms and conditions. Entrepreneurs must identify the type and amount of funding needed at that stage of the venture's evolution and seek the source of funding that fits the venture's circumstances at that particular time.

REALITY CHECK

Funding sources are like the ocean's tides. You cannot change them or swim against them. You must study them, tailor your approach to them, and time your funding search so that your firm fits their criteria.

Fact of Funding 8: There Is No Such Thing as Truly Patient Money

Timing plays an important role in raising money. Start-ups face the greatest challenge in raising funds. They require a leap of faith because, in the eyes of others, they are little more than a concept in search of funding and customers. Emerging ventures that are looking for funding for an extended period of time also face a formidable challenge. Beth McGoldrick, as a contributing editor for *CFO,* noted, "For every young company, the search for capital is an urgent, and sometimes traumatic, task. And the longer the lead time until the investment pays off, the more difficult it can be to raise money."[6] The length of time funding will be provided varies with the funding source.

REALITY CHECK

Entrepreneurs must be in a position to provide most of the start-up funding and must be willing to make certain sacrifices to attract long-term funding. Bankers and investors abhor uncertainty. If you are seeking funding for more than a year or two, then you will need to provide them with a compelling reason to be at risk for an extended period of time.

Timing also applies to the venture's ability to fulfill the funding source's expectations. Bankers and investors will expect their money back—and with a sufficient return to justify the corresponding level of risk. Banks will insist on a specific and regular stream of payments. They will structure the loan to minimize their risk. Banks will attach certain covenants that allow them to intervene and seize the venture's assets if it is delinquent in its payments. Angel investors and venture capital firms will expect to harvest their investments within a certain period of time. Even friends and family will expect to get their money back with a reasonable return.

REALITY CHECK

Gifts are what people give people who they care about at birthdays and other holidays. When you start a venture you enter the world of expectations and accountability. When it comes to money, it's all business. Don't expect favors or extensions. If a loan payment is due, then it is due. If your investors were led to believe the venture would produce certain returns, then the venture better meet or exceed those expectations. The same also applies to paying your suppliers and employees.

Fact of Funding 9: Know the Difference Between Dumb Money and Smart Money

Entrepreneurs need to recognize that all money isn't the same. Some money is smart and some money is dumb. The person from whom you raise money can be more important than the terms. William Sahlman noted, "New ventures are inherently risky; what can go wrong will. When that happens, unsophisticated investors panic, get angry, and often refuse to advance the company more money. Sophisticated investors, by contrast, roll up their sleeves and help the company solve its problems. Often, they've had lots of experience saving sinking ships."[7]

REALITY CHECK

Entrepreneurs who have a big ego or who want to run their own business frequently seek funding from friends and family. In a sense, they just want their money. This is what is known as *dumb money* because nothing else comes with it. *Smart money* is value-added money because it comes with experience and contacts. If the funding comes from a bank that has extensive experience in that industry or market, then the bank might be able to help the emerging venture by tapping its database or network of contacts. *Angels* and *venture capitalists* are also sources of smart money. If they are in tune with that market, then they might be in a position to recommend people for the management team, suppliers, distributors, prospects for joint ventures, and/or additional funding.

REALITY CHECK

Entrepreneurs need to recognize from the very beginning that they do not have a monopoly on wisdom. They should recognize their limitations and seek smart money. Smart money can open doors that will accelerate growth. The ability of smart money to stay cool under fire when the venture encounters inevitable turbulence will also be valuable.

Fact of Funding 10: If It's Not Your Money, It's No Longer "Your" Business

Money always comes with strings attached. Banks will expect periodic reports and financial statements. They may also require the firm to maintain certain balances and comply with certain covenants. Investors may insist on a seat on the board of directors and the right of approval on various business activities. If the venture fails to comply with loan provisions, the bank could shut your business down. If the venture is funded by investors and it fails to meet performance targets, they may even be in a position to replace you or sell the business.

REALITY CHECK

If you don't want anyone looking over your shoulder, then you'll have to fund the venture by yourself. Even if you get your funding from friends and family, they will want to know how the firm is doing. To make matters worse, although they might not have a clue for what it takes to run a successful venture, they will still offer their own suggestions for making it a success.

Fact of Funding 11: There Are Various Ways to Raise Money

This chapter profiles more than two dozen sources of funding and ways to find funding. Entrepreneurs need to be aware of them as well as their benefits and drawbacks. Some of the sources are very straightforward; others are very complicated. Some entrepreneurs are sophisticated enough to seek funding on their own. Some entrepreneurs may be able to tap their network of contacts to open funding doors for them. A few entrepreneurs may need to enlist the help of an intermediary to secure funding.

REALITY CHECK

Funding is like a foreign language. Funding sources have their own vocabulary and customs. They use terms like *prefunding valuation, IPO, burn rate,* and so forth when communicating with each other. You should learn about the sources of funding before even starting a venture. Familiarity with the types of sources and their corresponding criteria will put you in a much better position to secure funding. If you wait until your venture needs funding to learn about the various funding nuances, then you will be placing your firm in jeopardy.

Fact of Funding 12: Entrepreneurs Need an "F-Plan"

It should be clear by now that raising money cannot be left to chance. The need for entrepreneurs to have a business plan for starting and growing their business was stressed in the last two chapters. The business plan needs to include a *financing plan,* or what will be referred to for most of the remainder of this book as the *f-plan.* The f-plan must identify how much money is needed at certain stages of the venture's evolution. It must also identify what it is needed for, where it will come from, and what conditions will be attached to it.

REALITY CHECK

Like most plans, the f-plan will not be foolproof. There is no way that it can project all of the firm's financial needs or the exact timing of the needs. Its value lies in identifying issues in advance that need to be addressed. It also gives you lead time so you can find the funding source that best fits the venture's needs.

REALITY CHECK

It should be clear that all the "accounting and finance stuff" cannot be delegated to your controller/ chief financial officer (if you have one) or your CPA. As your firm's chief executive officer, you will not be able make good decisions without a good understanding of financial statements. If you don't understand the cash flow, income statements, balance sheets, and how they are interrelated, then learn about them before your ignorance causes you to make the wrong decisions.

DEVELOPING AN F-PLAN FOR YOUR VENTURE

Although it is true that a business cannot survive without a sufficient number of customers, it is also true that most high-growth start-ups cannot grow unless they have a supply of sufficient funds to enable their growth. The need for funding is so important that numerous authorities draw a parallel to funding being like our need for air or water. Rob Ryan, who runs a high-tech start-up boot camp, asserts, "Money is the water that keeps your company alive; without it the company will whither and die. But if you start your search the wrong way, you risk ruining your entire water supply. It could take years before the water is clean enough to go back and try again."[8]

Entrepreneurs need to develop an f-plan that assures the venture that it will have the right amount of funds at the right time. The f-plan needs to be anticipatory and proactive. It should identify the stages when the venture will need to have funds and project the amount needed to get the firm to the next level. The f-plan should also reflect the need to have alternative sources of funding if things do not go as planned—which they rarely do! You will enhance your chances of getting funding by starting early, by prospecting for solid funding sources, by being an effective salesperson, and by having the supporting documentation available.

High-growth start-ups usually have the need for external funding in three stages. First, as a new venture they will need a considerable amount of money to get up and running. Second, they will need funding to cover the period when sales are just beginning to ramp up. Although the firm may have revenue, the venture's burn rate usually continues to exceed its revenue stream. Third, if the firm continues to grow, then it will need one or more additional cash infusions to fund major growth initiatives. The third stage is particularly noteworthy. While the firm may even be generating some profit, the need for additional funds to finance geographic expansion, the development and introduction of additional new products and services, and/or even the acquisition of new technology or other firms will exceed the venture's supply of cash.

Money is like water; if you have too much you can drown—if you have too little, then you die of dehydration. The fall of overhyped, overfunded Internet dot-coms indicated what can happen with the influx of too much funding that came in too soon, with too little planning, and too little frugality. Too much money can cause you to develop bad spending habits and to not watch every dollar as if your business depended on it.

Entrepreneurs need to approach cash as if it was water in a well. There must be enough water in the well in the beginning to enable the venture to be launched. There must be a sufficient supply of water in the well to enable the venture to fund each stage of growth. The water analogy is appropriate because any time there is not a sufficient supply of water, the firm will be in jeopardy. If funds are not available to provide the infrastructure (people, facilities, hardware, working capital, etc.) for growth, then the firm might miss the corresponding window of opportunity. If money is not available to fund the venture's operations, then the business might be like grapes in a draught that die on the vine.

REALITY CHECK

You have to start with even more money than you think you will need and you will probably have to seek more money as the firm evolves than you thought you would need. Accept this reality and build it into the f-plan. The need for more money, more often, is not necessarily an indication the venture is in trouble. Quite the contrary—if the firm is one of the fortunate few that has the potential to really take off, then it will need a considerable infusion of money.

REALITY CHECK

Assume the money will go out quicker and in greater amounts than originally projected. Assume also that revenue will come in slower and lower than projected. Then make sure you have enough water in the well to handle this situation.

REALITY CHECK

There will never be enough money to do all the things you want to do. There will always be opportunities to pursue, people you would like to hire, information systems you want to use and upgrade, and so forth. You must approach your venture from a capital budgeting perspective. You need to identify the activities, products, services, territories, customers, and so forth as value-added investments. The f-plan needs to identify areas that have the highest yield per dollar invested over the life of that action and then you need to allocate the venture's limited funds accordingly.

THE AMOUNT, TIMING, AND TYPE OF FUNDING PLAY A CRITICAL ROLE IN THE F-PLAN

The f-plan needs to reflect the various funding challenges the venture will face. It should identify *strategic funding gaps*. It should also project when these gaps will occur and how they will be addressed. Each strategic funding gap will have its own particular funding needs. Early funding gaps may require angel funding. If your venture is about to take off but desperately needs money, then it may seek venture capital funding.

REALITY CHECK

The younger the firm, the harder it is to project your numbers and to make them—your business plan is still evolving.

The f-plan also needs to identify the specific uses for the funds sought and the type of returns the funds will generate to the corresponding source of funding. If debt financing is sought, then the f-plan will have to show how the money will be used as well as when and how the interest and principal will be repaid. If the venture is seeking equity funding, then the f-plan will have to show potential investors the type of return they can expect. Investors, whether they are angels or venture capitalists, will also be looking for a *liquidity event* when they can get their money out with a substantial return. The three most common liquidity events are the acquisition of the venture by another firm, a management buyout, or an initial public offering.

The f-plan needs to demonstrate a degree of finesse. Seeking funding is like having one's hand on the throttle. Although some of the preceding reality checks paint a pessimistic picture about the amount of money needed and the need to avoid having too little money, you also need to be careful not to seek too much money or to seek funding too soon. If you seek funding too soon, then it may cost you more. If you seek more than you need, then it will cost you more in terms of its interest rate or dilution of ownership. If you seek too little or get it too late, then the firm's growth may be slowed or its existence placed in jeopardy.

The type of funding also has to be carefully thought through. As the saying goes, "For everything there is a season." The same applies to the types and sources of funding. Each stage of funding has distinct features. Some stages or needs lend themselves to debt financing. Other stages or needs may best be addressed by equity funding. Developing the f-plan is like constructing a decision tree. The plan should identify critical funding junctions. It should also reflect which funding alternative/source will be most appropriate for meeting that challenge.

REALITY CHECK

Life is full of surprises, and few things will go as planned. The f-plan should be based on a series of scenarios. It should include at least three scenarios: (1) a best-case scenario, (2) a worst-case scenario, and (3) a most-likely scenario. The f-plan should also incorporate back-up sources of funding in the event the expected source(s) of funding or amount of funding do not materialize. The back-up sources may include: (1) the entrepreneur keeping some of his or her money on the sidelines in reserve for unanticipated shortfalls, (2) a line of credit with a bank, (3) untapped credit cards, or (4) an angel investor. The need for contingency plans may also include courting numerous angels or venture capital firms (even if one seems prepared to sign the term sheet) to avoid last-minute surprises if the angel or VC wants to renegotiate the terms or backs out of the deal.

The need for a keen sense of timing cannot be overemphasized. Rob Ryan captured the role timing plays when the venture is in its formative stages. He noted entrepreneurs need to seek friendly angels like mom and dad or good friends to help them finish the prototype and get a beta customer who will test their product.[9] He also captured the importance of choreographing the need for funding with the type of funding when a firm is seeking venture capital. He stated that you aren't ready unless: (1) you have built a product or a prototype or a demo, (2) you have talked to customers and they like it, and (3) you have talked to a manufacturer and it can be manufactured. He also noted that you aren't ready until you can show how you are going to make money—"buckets of money."[10]

Balance also plays a key role in seeking funding. While most entrepreneurs will stress the need to be flexible and take money any way you can get it, the f-plan should try to maintain the appropriate balance between debt and equity funding. This does not mean that the venture should seek a 50/50 spilt between the two sources of funding. Debt has its merits at certain stages of the venture's evolution. Equity has merit in other stages or circumstances. The merits and drawbacks of each source of funding will be discussed later in the section on funding sources.

REALITY CHECK

Too many entrepreneurs spend money like it was inherited, rather than earned. There is no free lunch! The days are gone when drawing a concept on the back of a cocktail napkin could produce easy money from one or more investors. Investors are more diligent and banks are more cautious. Banks will not lend money out of the goodness of their hearts, and investors are less likely to invest on a leap of faith.

REALITY CHECK

The old saying, "The time to seek funding is when you don't need it" has a ring of truth to it. Actually, the time to seek funding is *before* you need it. Although bankers and investors may not have ESP or Ph.D.s in body language, they can tell when a firm is facing a funding shortfall. "When you are low on cash, you tend to look desperate. That can cost you more. People may be reluctant to do business with you, hurting cash even more."[11] By having an f-plan, seeking money at the right time, with some room to spare, and having back-up sources available, entrepreneurs may at least appear to be cool, calm, and collected.

REALITY CHECK

Few things can derail an emerging venture quicker than running out of money, even if it is just for a few days. The employees' faith and trust in the entrepreneur can be destroyed if he or she misses payroll, regardless of the circumstances. The failure to make a loan installment will cause the bank to take a much closer look at the venture's finances and operation. The bank may even call the loan if a payment is missed. Investors also expect the venture to hit certain performance targets. Failure to hit a target could trigger a situation where the entrepreneur would have to buy back the investor's stock or even result in the board of directors replacing or firing the entrepreneur.

PROACTIVE WAYS TO RAISE AND CONSERVE CASH

Having a sufficient amount of money to start and grow a venture involves a two-pronged strategy. The first strategy involves raising the cash. This is usually a multi-iterative process where additional cash may need to be raised to meet projected strategic funding gaps. The second strategy involves conserving the cash. The first strategy can be seen as adding wood to the fire to keep the venture going and growing. The second strategy tries to control the fire so that it does not burn up the wood at too fast a rate. The rate at which a venture goes through cash on a daily basis—known as the *burn rate*—plays a critical role in the need for funding and the corresponding amount of funding.

Because most new ventures are undercapitalized, they must get the greatest mileage per dollar available. The term *bootstrapping* reflects *resourceful* efforts made by the entrepreneur and management team to raise and conserve cash. The first part of this section highlights a few ways to conserve cash. The remainder of the chapter will then highlight various ways to raise cash.

THE BENEFITS OF BOOTSTRAPPING

Bootstrapping is about thinking things through, being resourceful, and being diligent in spending money. It involves anticipating funding gaps. It also involves being liquid by keeping a lid on inventories and receivables. It is about resisting the temptation to spend money on things that do not bring value to the venture and contribute to the bottom line. It is about spending money as if it was your first dollar and your last dollar. It is about investing rather than spending. It is about spending money as if the venture's very survival depended on it ... because it will!

Almost every entrepreneur will have to resort to bootstrapping at some point in the new venture's evolution. Bootstrapping is particularly important in the start-up and early growth stages. It plays a key role in the success of the venture, for at least five reasons. First, it may be the only way to get the funds needed to start the venture. Second, it forces the entrepreneur to be more frugal in using funds. When you have to scrap for each dollar of funding, you develop a keener appreciation for each dollar and are more cautious before spending it. In theory, for every dollar you can cut from your cash outlays, you save a dollar that you will need to raise to pay for operations and/or expansion.

Third, bootstrapping may make the entrepreneur a better businessperson. In addition to being more frugal, operating with a hand-to-mouth cash flow forces the entrepreneur to have good financial controls in place and to monitor operations more closely. When you are operating at the edge, you tend to see things more clearly. You also tend to deal with things right away rather than postpone them.

Fourth, bootstrapping may allow the venture to grow to where it is more attractive to lenders and investors. Bankers are more willing to lend money to businesses that have a track record. Bootstrapping may also pay big dividends when the venture seeks outside investors. Generally speaking, every effort should be made to postpone seeking outside investors as long as possible. The greater the value of the business, the easier it is to attract investors. Higher valuation is particularly beneficial because it means more money can be attracted and the entrepreneur will not have to give up as much of the business to get the money.

Fifth, while bootstrapping may take some of the entrepreneur's time, it may take less time than securing a loan or doing a deal with one or more investors. Entrepreneurs need to focus their attention on getting the business up and running. This means hiring and directing personnel, creating and maintaining customers, having the proper systems in place, and dealing with the nearly endless problems/challenges that pop up. If the entrepreneur must also devote considerable time to courting bankers and investors, then the other dimensions of the business may suffer. If the entrepreneur can bootstrap the venture without taking a lot of time, then his or her time and energy can be invested in the business.

There are seven rules for conserving cash:

1. You need to have your financial act together. If the overall business plan has addressed the crucial who, what, and where questions, then the f-plan should project funding needs. Having your act together reduces the trials and errors that burn cash.

2. Don't spend it unless you have to. Every cash expenditure/outlay should be subjected to the "Is it really necessary?" test. Entrepreneurs must make every effort to ensure that every dollar of cash goes into areas and activities that add value to the venture.

3. If you do need that item or activity, then make sure you are getting it at the lowest reasonable cost and on the most favorable terms.

4. Lease rather than buy

5. If you can get it used, then don't waste valuable cash.

6. If you have to buy it, then finance it for the longest period at the lowest rate so it places the least drain on your monthly cash outlays.

7. Establish your own set of rules and create your own ways to conserve cash.

Conserving cash requires considerable diligence. Diligence helps avoid excesses. Having good financial projections, budgets, and controls will reduce the amount of money tied up in cash, accounts receivable, inventory, fixtures and equipment, payroll, and overhead. The f-plan should reflect diligence that fosters frugality. The f-plan should also reflect just-in-time funding that reduces the likelihood that funds will be idle. Working capital needs to be just that—it needs to be working. The same applies to funds generated by loans and investors.

Wayne Huizenga, who founded Waste Management, started with just a beat-up pickup truck in Fort Lauderdale. Numerous entrepreneurs who received bundles of venture capital during the heyday of the dot-coms spent money like it was growing on trees. Jeff Bezos demonstrated his frugality when he started Amazon.com. Instead of buying the typical mahogany desk for his office, he got an old door and put it on 2x4s. Even when he was worth more than $10 billion, he drove a Honda sedan.

Entrepreneurs should avoid succumbing to the *wheel of retailing syndrome* highlighted in Chapter 7. There is a tendency over time for management to slowly upgrade nonessential items. In the early days of retailing, a number of retailers wanted to take some of Sears' market share by offering lower prices. To offer lower prices, the retailers would pick a site on the outskirts of town, have no landscaping, and have minimal amenities. The stores had few offices, used linoleum floor covering rather than carpet or ceramic tiles, and did not offer special services like gift wrapping or food services. The intent was to keep costs down, but after a while management egos would prevail over frugality. More amenities were added, which in turn caused the stores to raise their prices. The increase in prices not only reduced their competitive advantage over Sears; the price increases also opened the door for firms like Wal-Mart, with its bare-bones warehouse-like stores, to steal their markets.

Although it is true that image does make a difference, when you are looking for money, make sure you present an image of someone who is responsible. There is a big difference between building a venture and just enhancing one's ego. Every effort should be made to avoid nonessential outlays like flying first class, leasing premium office space, purchasing luxurious office fixtures, paying for an expensive logo design and letterhead, and other types of ego-enhancing frills.

Two entrepreneurs demonstrate two different attitudes about how money should be spent. The founder of a bio-tech firm, in an effort to conserve cash and impress bankers and investors that he was committed to getting a return on the money invested in the venture, had a car that was so old and run down that the local movie studios used it as a prop. He was known to fill his tank only halfway when taking a 300-mile round trip if he could get gas for a lower price in the other city.

The other entrepreneur demonstrated that he did not have what it takes to be frugal. When the business plan for his specialty-products firm revealed a significant opportunity, he went right out and leased a Mercedes. He was raising the overhead and corresponding burn rate before he even had his first dollar of funding in the bank.

REALITY CHECK

Be resourceful and frugal, but don't be obsessive. Entrepreneurship is not about winning the award for being the world's best bootstrapper. Entrepreneurship is about creating a successful venture. The clock is always ticking. Don't let your bootstrapping efforts divert your attention from building your business. Your zeal to bootstrap should not allow you to take your eyes off the market or to let it slow you down. When it comes down to spending your time creating and maintaining customers for a profit or trying to reduce one more dollar out of your burn rate, then err on the side of building your venture. You should make an effort to eliminate superfluous expenses, but make sure you don't confuse cutting overhead and committing resources to the things like hiring competent people and building a performance-enhancing infrastructure that are necessary to build your business.

Bootstrapping and Early Positive Cash Flow Can Make a Difference

The media frequently paint a picture that it will take a substantial amount of external funding to become an exceptional firm. For every firm that went public not long after securing one or more rounds of venture funding, there are hundreds of emerging firms that have been very successful–yet not on the same level—without requiring significant external funding.

Amar Bhidé's research provides a ray of hope for entrepreneurs whose ventures may not meet the expectations of venture capital firms. Bhidé found that most of the founders on the 1989 *Inc.* 500 list bootstrapped their ventures with meager personal savings and borrowing or funds raised from families and friends. His research indicated 26 percent started with less than $5,000 and only 21 percent raised more than $50,000. It is also worth noting that just two of the founders raised more than $1 million. A quarter tried to raise venture capital funding and failed. His study of the founders who made the 1996 *Inc.* 500 list indicated only 4 percent raised money from professional venture capitalists and 3 percent from the so-called venture angels.[12]

Data for the firms that made the *Inc.* 500 in 2003 indicated that 80 percent were funded by the founder's personal assets, other founders' personal assets, and assets of friends and family. The data also revealed that 8 percent of the funding came from a bank via a loan or line of credit, 4 percent came from private equity investment, and 4 percent came from suppliers and/or customers. Only 2 percent came from the SBA or other government agencies. Only 2 percent of start-up funding came from a formal venture capital fund.[13]

His research also revealed some interesting insights into how the *Inc.* 500 companies funded their growth. The research indicated their growth was financed primarily through retained earnings. In addition to bootstrapping their ventures with modest personal funds, fewer than a fifth had raised follow-on equity financing in the five to eight years they had been in business. About half had raised bank financing but, reflecting the poor creditworthiness of most start-ups, this had usually been in modest amounts that could be collateralized by the firm's assets three or more years after start-up.[14]

Although the *Inc.* 500 firms may not be the type of firms that capture Wall Street's attention and dominate national markets, their rate of growth is noteworthy. The 25 fastest-growing firms in the *Inc.* 500 in 2003 grew by 8,250 percent on the average during the preceding five years. The largest 25 firms in the *Inc.* 500 in 2003 had an average sales of $230 million, with an average of 624 employees.[15] While their overall valuation might not be in the same league as an eBay or Amazon.com, the relative lack of ownership dilution of the *Inc.* 500 means the founders enjoy an enviable return on their sweat equity and personal investment.

Bhidé's research demonstrates two additional points. First, it shows the value of having quick positive cash flow and profitability. This is particularly true if the firm is not able to attract patient money. If the firm can be started with a minimal amount of cash, if it can keep its burn rate to a minimum, and if its products can garner a substantial profit margin, then it should be able to generate the level of cash that will reduce the need for external funding.

Bhidé's research also demonstrates the existence of the *Missouri factor*. Although entrepreneurs may believe they will succeed and that failure is impossible, investors, bankers, suppliers, and distributors know failure is possible—and quite common. Entrepreneurs should assume potential stakeholders are from Missouri, and that you'll have to "Show them" the venture is a good bet. Actual results beat rhetoric when it comes to raising money.

Bootstrapping Tips/Insights

Insight 1: Money Is Selective.   James Sheldon and Burt Alimansky noted, "Money follows good people who are pursuing good opportunities with good abilities."[16] Entrepreneurs need to demonstrate that the opportunity is there and that the entrepreneurial team can capitalize on it.

Insight 2: Timing Funding Is Essential.   George Gedron of *Inc.* magazine offers the following insights: (1) think strategically about the process of raising money, (2) get all the money you need via loans and so forth before you quit your job … if you look for funding after you quit your job you may be considered to be unemployed rather than an entrepreneur, (3) start looking for money before you need it, and (4) cut back on your personal budget so you can live off an austerity budget.[17] Mark Van Osnabrugge and Robert J. Robinson echo Gedron's point about austerity. They noted how postponing external funding can pay off. They stated, "Clearly, the longer an entrepreneur is able to survive on personal funds and hard work (sweat equity) and internally generated funds, the lower the cost of external risk capital and the more sovereignty the entrepreneur has."[18]

Insight 3: Bootstrapping Is the Norm, Not the Exception. Few entrepreneurs have all the money they need. Do not consider bootstrapping to be a sign of weakness. View it as the way new ventures should be run, especially in their early stages.

Insight 4: Balance Sweat and Real Equity Between Yourself and Your Team. If you want to have a highly motivated management team, then give them the opportunity to invest in your business. You may also consider providing stock options to all your employees.

Insight 5: Not all "Good" Deals Get Funded. Remember, you are competing with other ventures for funding. Your business must stand out in terms of its return-risk ratio. Established businesses have a track record and the stock market is always an alternative to friends, family, and angel investors.

Insight 6: Don't Expect a Healthy Paycheck for a While. Your salary may be the most expendable cash outlay when things get tight. Everyone else will expect/demand to be paid. Make sure you have enough money on the sidelines before you start your business so you can pay your bills.

Insight 7: Don't Expect Others to Pay You on Time. First-time entrepreneurs tend to be too trusting. If you are going to sell your goods or services on credit, then make sure you have additional funding to pay your own bills. Stay on top of your accounts receivable: Slow-paying accounts and nonpaying accounts destroy businesses each year.

Insight 8: Don't Assume You Have the Funding. Too many deals fall through at the last minute. You have funding when you have the money in your bank account.

Insight 9: Funding Takes Time. Raising funds today is not as easy or quick as it was in the era of irrational exuberance. Simply putting .com behind the name of your business will not guarantee that people will provide your firm with financing! Each type of funding source is demonstrating more due diligence.

Examples of Creative—Even Desperate Financing

If necessity is the mother of invention, then bootstrapping may be the national anthem for most entrepreneurs. Entrepreneurs need to recognize three things about raising money. First, it may be the most difficult aspect of starting a venture. Second, resilience and creativity may make the difference between success and failure. Third, most people who are involved in funding ventures are not entrepreneurs. They look at things differently and are risk averse. Wilson Harrell noted that while "risk" is a way of life for entrepreneurs and they eat risk for breakfast, to the financial community risk is synonymous with Black Friday, AIDS, the Bubonic Plague, and getting fired.[19]

Numerous well-known ventures were the product of minimal funding and resourceful bootstrapping by their entrepreneurs:

- Steve Jobs and Steve Wozniak started Apple Computer with $1,350.
- Ross Perot started EDS with $1,000.
- Ben Cohen and Jerry Greenfield started Ben & Jerry's with $12,000.
- Michael Dell started Dell Computer with $1,000.
- Phillip Knight started Nike Inc. with $1,000.[20]

Ted Turner went on the air with a television station he purchased in Charlotte and asked viewers to send in money via a "beg-a-thon." He raised $50,000 for his ailing station. He repaid the 35,000 contributors eight years later when he sold the station.[21] Fred Smith went to Las Vegas with $100 in his pocket. The $27,000 he won helped him make payroll and buy fuel for his planes.[22] Ben & Jerry's offered a carpenter and a plumber membership in their "Ice-cream-for-life club" if they would make the repairs needed to fix the gas station that served as their first location so it could be open for business.[23]

Edward DuCoin started Impact Telemarketing at the age of 18 with $100, a used desk, and a cheap answering machine. His first office was his bedroom in his parent's home. By 1997, his company generated $12 million in revenue. That year, his firm merged with four other collections and mailing services to take the firm public on the NASDAQ as Compass International (CMPS).[24]

SOURCES OF FUNDING

There are a variety of funding sources for start-ups and emerging ventures. Entrepreneurs should be aware of the merits and drawbacks of potential funding sources so they can be in a position to seek the right funding source for the right amount of money, at the right cost, at the right stage of the venture's evolution. The following list of funding sources provides a brief overview of various ways to fund a venture or to reduce its need for cash:

Founder Funding

Entrepreneurs should make every effort to have enough money to get the venture up and running. Every dollar the founder can put into the venture is one less dollar that needs to be borrowed or raised from other sources. While using other people's money (OPM) may have merits, OPM always comes at a cost.

REALITY CHECK

Entrepreneurs should avoid committing their last dollar to the venture. They should keep some money or liquid assets on the sidelines in case of emergencies or unanticipated funding gaps—which are almost inevitable. When time is of the essence, having some money on the sidelines can mean the difference between staying alive and dying on the vine.

Diligent Purchasing and Budgeting

Every dollar saved through diligent spending is one less dollar to be raised. Veteran executives know that reducing expenses or cash outlays by a dollar has far greater impact than increasing sales by a dollar. Reducing a dollar in expenses may be equivalent in its impact on profitability to increasing sales by $10 to $20. If profit is 5 percent of sales, then you have to sell $20 to make a dollar. If you reduce your expenses by a dollar, you gain a dollar profit.

REALITY CHECK

Being resourceful, frugal, and budgeting your money is important, but don't let the window of opportunity close or competition leapfrog you while you are trying to save a few pennies.

Friends and Family

Friends and family represent one of the most common sources of funding. Funding from these sources is frequently referred to as *love money*. Friends and family often lend money or invest in a venture because of their relationship with the entrepreneur. Friends and family play a key role by providing funding when the venture is in the start-up stage when there usually is nothing more than an untested concept. Although they may consider the loan or purchase of stock to be a business deal, they usually do not demonstrate the degree of due diligence or level of expectations used by other funding sources. Numerous ventures received crucial funding from friends and family. Jeff Bezos's parents played an instrumental role in getting Amazon.com off the ground. Peter Buck's desire to have a shop that would provide submarine sandwiches and $1,000 funding helped Fred DeLuca start Subway.

REALITY CHECK

Document the terms and conditions of the loan from friends and family. Make sure you clarify if the loan is to you or to the venture. You should also be sure you charge a fair rate of interest. The IRS has strict rules about loans from family members, and even from the entrepreneur to the venture. The issuance of stock also needs to be carefully documented. Failure to carefully structure and document the loan or issuance of stock could come back to haunt you when you approach other funding sources later on. Other funding sources will be far more diligent. The way you handle funding from friends and family will reflect your professionalism.

Third-Party Guarantees

Friends and family frequently open doors for the venture by cosigning notes or guaranteeing payment for goods and services. When the venture is at an early stage and it has limited credit history and few assets to serve as collateral, it is critical that someone who is creditworthy be willing to cosign or guarantee payment.

Credit Cards

Credit cards may play a crucial role in getting the firm up and running. While they may charge a painful rate of interest, they are often the only means of bringing money into the venture. Entrepreneurs who consider going the credit card route should look for credit card companies that offer very low interest rates as special promotions. Although these rates may only be in effect for a few months, their lower interest rates may actually be lower than commercial loan rates.

Jack Chen and Fernando Espuelas formed StarMedia Network, an Internet network targeted to Latin America, by using 18 credit cards. They raised $200,000 via credit cards until they could get VC funding.[25] Bob Din brought all new meaning to the phrase "charge it" when he was ready to start En Point Technologies Inc. in 1993. Din lacked the capital to make his *electronic shopping service* come to life. He had already mortgaged his house and almost every other source of personal capital he had at his disposal to start his venture. Yet he needed working capital to buy the products that he would find and sell to his clients. One of the company's first orders was for hardware that he could acquire for $550,000 and then sell to the client for $750,000. Unfortunately, the seller would not provide Din any credit. Din then asked the company's credit manager if she would take American Express. The credit manager said yes! Din said, "Charge it!" and to the credit manager's surprise, the charge went through. The ability to explore every possible avenue for financing a new venture is one of the reasons En Point Technologies has grown from a tiny, home-based enterprise into a public company with earnings of more than $5 million.[26] One study indicated that credit cards are also used well after the start-up stage. The study indicated credit cards are a source of financing for 34 percent of America's small- to medium-sized businesses.[27]

REALITY CHECK

Credit cards look like easy money where you can get a few thousand dollars for just filling out a simple form. The application form, however, usually requires full disclosure of all debts. Make sure you do not violate the law or the lending agreement's disclosure requirements in your quest for funding.

REALITY CHECK

Banks, investors, suppliers, and prospective members of your management team may run a credit check on you. Don't jeopardize the future of the venture by creating a bad credit history at this time.

REALITY CHECK

Most of the special low-interest credit cards stipulate that if you fail to make a payment by a certain time or to pay off your balance, then the balance will carry a significantly higher interest rate as a penalty. Be sure you read the fine print and pay the card off before the higher rates kick in.

REALITY CHECK

Carrying a lot of credit card debt even if your accounts are in good standing may affect your ability to get a loan from a bank or attract investors.

REALITY CHECK

Recognize that interest rates affect the cost of doing business. Don't use credit-card financing unless you have reasonably large profit margins and can get other funding in the near future.

Leasing

Leasing equipment and other assets is usually preferable to buying them. Purchasing assets takes up valuable capital and it reduces flexibility. Leasing can be viewed as the opportunity to try something to see if it works before having to make a major commitment.

Sale/Leaseback

If the venture is started with tangible assets or the entrepreneur or others contribute assets as a form of investment in the venture, then it might be worthwhile to enter into a sale/leaseback arrangement. Selling the asset frees up valuable capital. This arrangement may also allow for flexibility in the payment schedule. Asset sales (and leaseback) to relatives or friends can offer a neat and relatively simple alternative to either loans or equity deals. In this arrangement the venture sells one or more assets to someone the entrepreneur trusts and then that person leases those assets back to the business at a price that seems fair to both parties. That person gets regular income stream and a tax deduction for depreciation. The venture gets a one-time infusion of capital, and presumably better leasing terms than it would have received if it had been dealing with an independent financier. The best part of this arrangement is that the business's capital structure remains clean.[28]

Discounted Fees or Fee-for-Equity Propositions

Entrepreneurs are learning that many things are negotiable including fees for professional services. If the venture has considerable growth potential, then it may be possible to negotiate lower fees and favorable payment terms from top-notch accounting firms, consultants, law firms, banks, public-relations firms, and other service providers. These firms want to get their feet in the door, so they may be willing to make certain concessions if they believe they will benefit from the venture's growth.

There is a growing trend for some service providers to take stock in exchange for their services. Michael Perkins states that stock is the new currency for high-potential ventures. He noted that Dennis Crow, of Pierce & Crow, a California-based executive search firm, takes as much as 50 to 100 percent of a customer's fee in equity. Typically, recruiting payments are made in three equal installments. Pierce & Crow asks for the first two installments in cash and the third installment in stock.[29] Public relations firms have also gotten into the equity-for-services game. Pam Alexander, President of Alexander Ogilvy, noted, "We see our clients like VCs see their investments—they're our portfolio companies. We don't take on a client that we would not take equity in."[30]

Law firms, investment banks, and consulting firms have also jumped into the equity-for-services game—especially when it involves high-tech firms. It should be noted that the SEC prohibits accounting firms from taking an equity interest in firms they audit.

Supplier Financing

Credit terms should be considered to be a major factor when selecting suppliers. Entrepreneurs should talk to all their potential suppliers about financing and extending credit terms. The ability to get extended terms on inventory is particularly valuable. If you can sell the inventory and collect the cash before the supplier needs to be paid, then you will need far less capital to run your venture. Jeff Bezos found this very helpful when he started Amazon.com. By having his customers purchase books with a credit card, he was able to get cash for the books before he had to pay the publishers for them. This reduced his need for working capital.

REALITY CHECK

Make sure you meet the credit terms with your suppliers. Few suppliers will put their businesses at risk with accounts that are questionable. Treat them as if your venture's life depended on honoring your commitments. If you try to jerk them around, they may choose to collect in court.

Customer Prepayment or Investment

Customers may help fund your venture in four ways. First, they provide critical cash flow by purchasing products and services. Second, if they are willing to pay cash or pay their payables to the venture earlier, then you may not need to borrow as much money or owe as much to your suppliers. Third, if customers can prepay, that is even better. If they are provided an incentive (a small discount, free shipping, preferential treatment) to pay in advance, then that can be extremely helpful. Fourth, customers may actually be a *source* of funding. A few emerging ventures have generated funds by asking their customers if they would like to invest in them. By owning stock, the customers may gain *most preferred customer* status. This may be particularly beneficial to the customer if the venture has limited capacity.

Factoring

Emerging ventures may consider *factoring* their accounts receivable. A number of firms will buy all or part of a venture's accounts receivable. Factors will pay cash for a percent of the value of accounts receivable. This source of cash is rarely the preferred avenue, but it does represent one way to free up capital. The amount of money provided depends on the extent the accounts receivable are collectible by the factor. Factoring should be viewed as a stopgap measure rather than a regular source of funding.

Bartering

Some emerging ventures barter their products or services as a form of payment for what they need to buy. A start-up service firm may offer to provide its service to one of its suppliers in return for the goods or services it needs to buy from that supplier. Occasionally, the barter arrangement may involve third parties who have common interests.

REALITY CHECK

Ventures considering bartering should consult with their accountant to make sure that such cash-free transactions will not violate IRS regulations.

Management Team Taking Pay Cuts in Exchange for Bonuses or Stock

Emerging ventures frequently rely on stock options and/or performance bonuses as ways to attract and reward members of their management teams and other key employees. To conserve cash, they will offer stock options in return for lower salaries. Performance bonuses also represent a way to hold off paying key people money until it has been earned.

Economic Incentives

Numerous states and municipalities provide economic incentives for firms to locate in their areas. The incentives may encourage ventures to locate in *enterprise zones.* These zones may involve discounted financing as well as lower rates for rent, utilities, taxes, and so forth. In some cases, a cash incentive and/or subsidized employee training may also be available.

REALITY CHECK

Although states and municipalities may dangle these carrots, there is usually a reason or a catch. Either these areas are economically distressed or certain conditions must be met. Nothing is truly free. Don't let the temptation to save a few bucks put your venture in a place where the lack of a good quality of life could hurt your effort to attract talent and conduct business.

Banks

Borrowing money from a bank for a start-up is entirely different from getting a mortgage for your house. Banks rarely provide funding for start-ups. The risks are just too high to justify their involvement. Banks should be seen as a source for growth funding. George Dawson, President of Growing Your Business, notes "Bank loans should be like the frosting on a cake—something that comes at the end, on top of everything else."[31] The nuances of bank financing will be addressed in Chapter 9.

Small Business Administration (SBA)

The U.S. government has been a major player in funding new ventures for decades. The SBA has various lending programs where it actually serves as an underwriter for loans from commercial banks. In most cases, the venture must approach a bank seeking a conventional business loan. If the venture comes close to meeting the bank's lending criteria, then the bank may suggest the venture seek an SBA loan. If the venture meets the SBA's lending criteria, then it will turn around and indicate to the bank that it will underwrite the majority of the loan. By reducing the bank's downside risk, the bank may provide the loan. SBA loans are discussed in more detail in Chapter 9.

Government Grants

The federal government and numerous states provide funding grants for various types of businesses. Small Business Innovation and Research (SBIR) grants may be the most common sources of funding for firms in technology-related fields. These grants come with strings attached and may include an equity interest in the venture. The Small Business Guide to Federal Research and Development Funding Opportunities provides an agency-by-agency breakdown of federal R&D programs. Entrepreneurs should check with their state's Department of Commerce to see if there are state-sponsored programs.

Incubators

Government agencies and corporations have established business *incubators*. Incubators are designed to assist start-ups and emerging ventures. Government sponsored incubators usually provide a lower rent rate, some form of management assistance, and a common infrastructure (secretarial services, meeting rooms, etc.) to help ventures in their first year or two. For-profit incubators like Idealab! (*www.Idealab.com*) frequently provide these benefits, more sophisticated professional services, as well as equity investment. These incubators function like a vertically integrated venture capital firm. They provide considerable support for promising entrepreneurs and ventures. Their assistance accelerates the venture's growth by helping it ramp up operations and get funding. Bill Gross's Idealab! may be the most proactive incubator. Its team of highly talented people try to identify high-potential business opportunities. If an opportunity has merit, Idealab! creates a venture to capitalize on that opportunity.

Strategic Alliances and Corporate Partnerships

Emerging ventures with promising technology may consider establishing an alliance or forming a corporate partnership with one or more firms. Alliances and partnerships are very appealing today because they represent an avenue for funding and other forms of support for ventures that may not be in a position to secure a loan or attract investors at favorable terms.

Alliances and corporate partnerships are formed when an emerging venture and another firm believe it is possible to have a mutually beneficial relationship. Alliances and corporate partnerships are formed for at least three reasons. First, the emerging venture is usually seeking funding and other forms of support to accelerate its evolution. An alliance or corporate partnership can be particularly beneficial to an emerging venture if it enables the venture to get to the commercialization stage sooner where it can generate sales. James Goldberg, CEO of Theta Resources, and Stan Yakatan, CEO of Biosearch, noted the importance of being able to ramp up operations. They indicated, "Success increasingly hinges on how fast a company can get its products into a market segment. Acting quickly provides an opportunity to establish a defensible position and consolidate a prime customer base."[32]

Beth McGoldrick, as a contributing editor of *CFO*, noted the synergistic/symbiotic relationship that may take place between an emerging venture and an established firm. She stated, "The senior partner can provide access not only to capital, but also to marketing expertise, research and development, customers, or production capability. In return, the partner can receive any combination of equity, technology, marketing rights, and manufacturing rights."[33]

Although the established firm may be in a position to open a lot of doors for the emerging venture, allies or partners are different from venture capitalists. Their relationships tend to be far more flexible. They evolve to meet the needs of both parties. Corporate partners are not driven by *liquidity events*. Allies and partners tend to be more patient when it comes to the long lead time it takes to go from conceptualization to commercialization. Corporate partners are also not as prone to seek control when things do not go as expected. Instead, they will try to make the changes that keep things moving forward.

The ability of the ally or partner to provide capital either in the form of revenue or a loan/investment cannot be overemphasized. Allies and partners may be in a position to tailor the funding package to the needs of the emerging venture. The alliance or partnership may also provide the emerging firm with the credibility needed to secure additional debt or investors. By satisfying the established firm's due diligence, the emerging firm demonstrates that it has merit.

Second, the arrangement may be prompted by the established firm's desire to outsource one or more of its internal operations. Outsourcing will enable it to focus its attention on capitalizing on its core competencies. As noted earlier in the book, the movement to outsource internal activities has been the basis for employees who were involved in providing the service for their employers to create a business to provide that service to their former employer when they learn they will be losing their jobs. If the emerging firm can provide the service in a quicker, cheaper, more convenient, or more reliable manner, then it will benefit from the move to outsource.

Allies or partners can play a significant role in the development and growth of an emerging venture. They can be the emerging venture's beta site and first customer. It is easier to get a second customer once an emerging venture has its first customer. The ally or partner plays a symbolic role by being the first customer. The same reasoning applies to quality certification. If the ally or partner is certified, then it may help the emerging venture in its efforts to be certified. Working closely with an established firm that is known for quality not only will reduce the tendency to learn by trial and error, it will also provide credibility for the emerging venture if firms known for demanding quality are a customer.

Third, the relationship may be based on investment purposes. The more established firm may be looking for firms as partners or allies that have the potential to be lucrative investments as part of their overall business portfolio. In this instance, the established firm's value will increase if the emerging venture is successful. If the emerging venture has a liquidity event, then the established venture will also be a beneficiary. In some cases, the established firm may buy the emerging firm.

The established firm's strategic, technical, and operational experience may expedite the emerging venture's move up the learning curve. This may reduce the time it takes the emerging venture to get its products/services to market. The established firm is usually in a much better position to provide insights and information. This could give the emerging firm a real advantage over other start-ups that it may be competing against. The established firm may be able to open distribution doors—including foreign markets—for the emerging firm.

The established firm benefits in many ways as well. It gains access to valuable technology that might otherwise take years to develop. It also may gain most favored customer status as a result of the alliance.

Alliances or corporate partnerships may have other benefits. The corporate partner may be the source of ideas for additional products or services. If the emerging venture considers itself to be a customer problem-solver then it may be in a position to develop and provide products or services to the established firm and other firms including the established firm's customers. The emerging firm may even be in a position to sense what the established firm needs before that firm even knows it. If being close to one's customers is important, then being an ally or partner represents a way to be very close. Atlantic

Corporation, based in Wilmington, North Carolina, has grown on numerous occasions when its customers asked Atlantic's management if it could do certain things for it. In some instances, Atlantic had limited experience doing those functions, but it seized the moment by quickly learning how to do that function and to do it well.

Larger firms may partner or seek an alliance with an emerging firm for another reason. In addition to funding emerging businesses to access their technology, they may do it to reduce the likelihood that the emerging firm will become a competitor.

There are a number of ways for emerging ventures to find the right ally or corporate partner. According to Venture Economics, a Newark, New Jersey, private equity research firm, there are 117 active corporate venture programs (including actual funds) in the United States.[34]

Entrepreneurs may consider checking corporate Web sites to look for firms that have business development offices and indicate they have corporate alliances. Industry conferences may also be an avenue for learning about firms that do alliances or corporate partnerships.

REALITY CHECK

Entrepreneurs should not limit their search for corporate partners to large and established firms. Emerging firms may also offer mutually beneficial relationships, especially when it comes to sharing technology. Although larger firms may have more resources, they may also be more bureaucratic. Their corporate culture may also clash with the opportunistic and agile nature that is characteristic of start-ups.

REALITY CHECK

Due diligence plays an important role in going the ally or corporate partner route. Nothing is free or easy. Make sure you protect your venture. If the relationship sours, litigation may follow. Larger firms have more resources to go the distance in court even if they are at fault. Make sure you have contingency plans in the event the alliance or partnership crashes before it even begins. Having contingency plans reduces your risks and time delays; they put you in a better position to negotiate. John Baker, senior vice president at Alan Patric Associates Inc., a venture capital firm, noted, "Don't give away your birthright. Know what you want to get out of the deal and make sure that you really get it."[35] Finally, make sure the ally or partner doesn't run off with your technology, your customers, key employees, or your business.

Licensing or Royalties

A number of emerging ventures have found that offering licensing or royalty arrangements can be a good way to get an infusion of capital. Emerging ventures that do not want to go (or may not be in a position to go) the debt, equity, or ally/corporate partner route may consider attracting capital by offering a licensing or royalty arrangement to one or more parties. The arrangement is rather straightforward. The emerging venture receives cash from the other party in return for a commitment to provide the other party a percentage of the venture's revenue.

This approach has considerable merit. It does not dilute the entrepreneur's ownership and it is not the same as a loan because it does not require payments on a fixed-interval basis. The emerging venture's financial obligation is paid as it generates sales. Ellen Spragins noted, "It provides a way of getting money in the door without having to send any out again until business can afford it."[36]

This funding avenue is appealing because every aspect is negotiable and the funding and conditions can be tailored to the unique situation. For example, one company provided a three-stage investment of $700,000 in an emerging venture. The emerging company had to meet certain preset conditions at each stage. The first third was provided if the company was able to take the prototype and get it to the preproduction model that demonstrably worked. The second third was provided when the company began real production. The final third was provided when the company actually began shipping the product to distributors or customers.[37]

Another company used royalties to help finance the development of its product. Because the venture didn't have the money, the venture team didn't have the ability to develop software the company needed. The entrepreneurial team knocked on the doors of technology companies and invited them to participate based on the potential rewards via royalties rather than via equity in the company. A telecommunications company accepted their invitation because it wanted to get into the sports market.

REALITY CHECK

Royalty financing has drawbacks. The venture must have sufficient mark-up on its products/services to enable it to pay the royalty. The investor may also place certain covenants on the deal. The deal will almost certainly have some targets and/or timelines. If the venture does not provide a specified stream of income for the investor by the deadline, then the investor may be eligible to full payment, an equity interest, or some other form of compensation. Make sure you don't place the venture or your ownership share at risk when you seek this type of financing.

Small Business Investment Companies (SBICs)

SBICs provide emerging ventures with an avenue for funding their operations. SBICs are licensed and regulated by the SBA. They are privately owned investment firms that are backed by the federal government. Many banks also have their own SBICs which function as the bank's "venture capital" fund. Most SBICs provide funding via convertible subordinated debt or loans with options for an equity interest. Some SBICs will do equity deals. SBICs function like venture capital firms. Over the years SBICs have been early investors in Callaway Golf, Outback Steakhouse, Staples, Federal Express, Apple Computer, America Online, and Intel.[38]

Issuing Stock to Individuals

Stock may be issued in many ways to various types of investors. It can be issued to friends and family, to members of the management team, and to the venture's employees. Stock can also be issued to customers, suppliers, corporate partners/allies, angels, venture capital firms, investment banks, and SBICs. It can also be sold to the public if certain conditions are met.

The major advantage of selling stock is that it is not a fixed liability. Unless it is a condition at the time of issuance, the venture does not have any obligation to pay dividends or redeem it. The major drawback of issuing stock to others is that it dilutes the entrepreneur's ownership position and possibly control of the business.

Angel Investors

Angels are wealthy individuals who invest in emerging ventures. Most angels are very flexible when it comes to the type of ventures they will invest in and the amount they are willing to invest. They may also become involved in the management of the venture. Angels can play a critical role in funding ventures that have growth potential. They help fill the *equity gap* that exists between what the founder is able to invest and what venture capital firms are willing to invest. Chapters 10 and 11 profile the process for seeking funding from angel investors.

Venture Capital Firms (VCs)

VC firms may be the most controversial and least understood form of funding. The phrase, "I'll get venture capital funding," is freely bantered about by entrepreneurs. Few firms meet the lofty expectations set by VC firms. VCs will only consider funding firms that have hockey-stick projections and that offer the potential for lucrative liquidity events. VCs expect to have 20 to 40 percent interest in the emerging firm in return for their risk in funding an early-stage venture. Although VCs rarely try to take a controlling interest in an emerging venture, the terms and conditions they attach to a deal have given them the less-than-endearing label of *vulture capitalists*. Most VC firms will not consider deals than involve an investment of less than $500,000. Many VC firms will not consider a deal that involves less than $3 million. Most venture capital firms also tend to focus on a particular industry or market.

VC firms were hit hard by the irrational exuberance associated with the wave of dot-com disasters a few years ago. Most VCs avoid investing in start-ups because of the uncertainty of untested concepts, technology, and markets. VCs are particularly reluctant to fund at the start-up stage that is being created by a first-time entrepreneur. Instead, they fund early-stage and later stages of growth. Chapter 12 profiles the nature of venture capital and the process of seeking venture capital funding.

Private Offering

The idea of simply selling stock to the general public is not that simple. The U.S. Securities and Exchange Commission is charged with protecting the public from investment scams. The SEC has relaxed some of its rules in the last few years so that smaller businesses can issue stock. Entrepreneurs who are considering the possibility of issuing stock should consult with an attorney who specializes in the issuance of stock.

Investment Banks

Investment banks represent a hybrid source of funding. They help firms put together major funding deals. They may provide debt as well as equity packages. They may be the primary investors and/or lenders or they may put together a syndicate to provide the package. Investment banks play a critical role in putting together initial public offerings.

A few investment banks are well known and respected. Some investment bankers, however, operate at the fringe and do deals that are considered too risky for the more respected investment banks. One investment bank became one of the largest funding firms in the country by lending at five points over prime and insisting on warrants (at no cost to it) that provided it with an equity interest in its clients' firm. Another investment bank put together a package that should have been in *Ripley's Believe It or Not!* When a software firm desperately needed $500,000 to take its new product to market, the investment bank included a $500,000 loan-processing fee as part of the deal. The investment bank crafted the deal so that it did not violate the state's usury laws. The entrepreneur was so desperate that he accepted the deal. The software entrepreneur got the $500,000 he sought as part of a $1 million loan at 20+ percent interest!

Initial Public Offering (IPO)

Doing an IPO is a big deal. Although a few entrepreneurs have tried to do it using Internet technology, most emerging ventures that attempt to do an IPO will have to use a printing company that specializes in doing IPO documentation and a team of specialized accountants, attorneys, and investment bankers. Some entrepreneurs consider the IPO as the culminating point of their entrepreneurial journey. Few emerging ventures go public each year. Most IPOs involve raising tens of millions of dollars with only 80 to 90 percent of the funds raised going into the emerging venture. The associated fees and charges can easily exceed 10 percent of the offering. Today, entrepreneurs may consider adding a magician to their IPO teams. The unpredictable nature and wild swings in the stock markets heighten the uncertainty and valuation associated with an IPO. A number of firms have gone through all of the IPO gates only to have their IPO efforts stopped just before going public because of market volatility.

REALITY CHECK
Unless your venture has the potential to capture a large part of a high-growth market and to garner a pre-IPO valuation of at least $100 million, then do not even think about it.

REALITY CHECK
There is no such thing as patient money in a publicly traded company. Stockholders will expect your company to perform at a level that justifies their risk.

Financial Intermediaries

A number of individuals and firms specialize in finding funding sources for emerging ventures. Entrepreneurs should heed the words *caveat emptor* (let the buyer beware) before using an intermediary. Some intermediaries are very credible and can be instrumental in finding worthwhile funding sources. Credible intermediaries are well connected with funding sources. While banks focus almost exclusively on collateralized lending and angels and VCs invest in high-growth ventures, intermediaries are in a better position to explore various funding sources. If the emerging venture has tangible merit, then it may be able to find a value-added funding source in a short period of time. The ability to attract the right funding, from the right source, with the right terms can expedite the emerging venture's development.

Jill Andresky Fraser noted that a skillful intermediary with valuable contacts at a wide range of capital sources can be the best friend a business owner has. She provides two suggestions when considering an intermediary. First, you should do your homework and talk to absolutely every businessperson you respect and ask each to recommend an intermediary who typically handles companies similar to yours in size and industry. When you've generated a short list, ask each intermediary for 10 business references, including satisfied customers, bankers, lawyers, and so forth. Second, you should be leery of intermediaries who charge up-front fees, since that's a typical scam technique. She does acknowledge, however, that there are some very credible and successful intermediaries who insist on up-front fees.[39]

Internet Search Engines

A number of search engines are designed to help entrepreneurs find funding sources. Some of these Web sites provide information. Other Web sites use search engines to screen and match ventures with potential funding sources. Commercial Finance Online claims to be the "world's largest business finance search engine." It lets you look for financing and investors to look for companies to invest in. Entrepreneurs enter how much they are looking for and where you are located.[40] Some of the Web sites are tied to specific industries. Other Web sites are directed to specific regions of the country.

REALITY CHECK

Entrepreneurs should demonstrate a considerable level of due diligence when considering going the Internet route and doing a deal with anyone listed on the Internet.

CONCLUSION: FUNDING SHOULD BE TAILORED TO YOUR UNIQUE VENTURE

There are as many sources of funding as there are facets on a diamond. The same applies to the terms or conditions associated with a funding package. The need for a comprehensive funding plan cannot be overemphasized. There is no one best source of funding for all ventures—one size does not fit all ventures! Each stage of the emerging venture's growth has particular needs. The challenge for entrepreneurs is to find the source of funding that fits their particular needs at that particular point in time. What is right at one stage in the venture's evolution may be totally inappropriate for another stage. The key is sensing in advance what is needed and having the time, contacts, information, and skills to put together the best funding package.

A few points may be helpful in closing this introductory chapter on funding a venture. First, make sure the process of seeking funding is approached with the highest integrity. Everything you do must foster trustworthiness. If there is any indication that you are not forthright with information and/or that you or members of your team have questionable integrity, then the whole process will come to an abrupt halt. The need for openness and integrity also applies after you get funding. Edward Welles noted that more investor relations fail because of poor communications than for any other reason. Investors expect to see some bad news about companies they are considering. They also realize that any investment or loan has risks. Welles stresses that you should not ignore those risks or try to hide them.[41]

Robert Brown echoes Welles's emphasis on being forthright after getting funding. He noted that most investors and bankers know that not everything will go smoothly. According to Brown, they understand that problems will arise. When problems do happen, talk with investors immediately. The worst thing you can do is to have to go crawling to your investor or bank after a problem has been festering for a long time while you had been assuring them that all is well. Similarly, you do not want to embarrass your principal contact at the venture fund or bank. Their careers will be affected by you and they will not be pleased if they feel they have been betrayed or misled.[42] If your integrity is questionable, then word will get out that you and your venture do not warrant funding.

Second, you have to understand the financials. You need to show to prospective lenders/investors that you know the numbers, that your projections are well founded, and that you will be able to manage your venture's funds and operations. You might have a top-notch accounting firm do various activities, but you still need to be able to demonstrate that your decisions will be based on good financial/accounting information.

Third, assume nothing will go as planned. Remember, your sales-costs, profit, and cash flow projections are based on assumptions. If any of your assumptions are off—and some will be—then your projections will also be off. Also assume that your funding plan will not go as planned. You need to start the process early, to develop relationships with potential funding sources well in advance of the need for funding, to have back-up funding sources and to even have back-up funding sources for the back-up sources.

Fourth, try to keep some money in reserve to cover unforeseen opportunities or problems. Don't commit all of your own money to the venture in the beginning and don't commit every last dollar in the venture to its operations. It would be a tragedy for the venture to go down for the lack of a few dollars. If you get in a situation where you desperately need external funding and can get it, the cost will be very expensive.

Fifth, be realistic with your projections. The old adage, "God watches out for children and drunks," does not include businesses—especially start-ups. You may get to a point in developing your business plan where the projections just don't provide much hope for profit and positive cash flow. This is where emotions like rationalization and denial often overpower good sense. If you cannot be assured up front that you have or can raise the money you need, then maybe you should not pursue the venture. The same reasoning also applies to having your requests for funding being turned down—even with what may sound like encouraging words. Although resilience may be an important quality for starting a venture, it can also keep you from acknowledging the message that others have not been forthright in telling you—your venture just does not have a chance, or you might not have what it takes to make the venture successful. Resist the temptation to say, "Well, it's just one more credit card; I'm sure I will be able to pay it off."

Sixth, the best deals are simple, fair, are based on trust rather than legal stipulations, and are not blown apart when the venture's actual performance varies slightly from the plan.[43] Make sure you are funded by people who understand the turbulent and often precarious nature of emerging ventures. Look for smart and patient funding. If you are going to be seeking "other people's money," then look for people who can add value to the venture via their ideas, insights, and contacts, as well as their ability to hang in there when things get tough.

Seventh, remember that you will probably be the last person to be paid. Your employees, suppliers, and bank will demand that they be paid—even if it means you have to go without a paycheck or getting any return on the money you have put into the venture. Entrepreneurs need to remember Harry Truman's words, "The buck stops here!"

Eighth, don't drain the venture. If you are one of the fortunate entrepreneurs to have bucks start rolling in, make sure you don't drain the venture of the funds that will be so critical to its growth and continued success. Lillian Vernon noted there are three rules to keep in mind to starting a business and keeping it going. They are, "reinvest, reinvest, and reinvest."[44]

There are only two ways of raising money: the hard way and the very hard way.[45]

—Anita Roddick
cofounder of The Body Shop

ENDNOTES

1. William A. Sahlman, "How to Write a Really Great Business Plan," *Harvard Business Review,* July–August 1997, in Annual Editions Entrepreneurship 99/00, p. 131. Reprinted by permission of *Harvard Business Review.*

2. David Evanson and Art Beroff, "Your Butt on the Line," *Entrepreneur,* July 2000, pp. 70–73. Reprinted with permission of Entrepreneur Media, Inc.

3. James Sheldon and Burt Alimansky, "8 Demons of Entrepreneurship," *Success,* March 1986, p. 54.

4. Joseph Boyett and Jimmie Boyett, *The Guru Guide to Entrepreneurship* (New York: John Wiley & Sons, 2001), p. 81.

5. Howard Schultz and Dori Yang Jones, *Pour Your Heart into It: How Starbucks Built a Company One Cup at a Time* (New York: Hyperion, 1997), p. 73.

6. Beth McGoldrick, "Taking on a Corporate Partner," *CFO,* February 1989, number 2, p. 50.

7. Sahlman, "How to Write a Really Great Business Plan," pp. 98–108.

8. Rob Ryan, *Smartups: Lessons from Rob Ryan's Entrepreneur America Boot Camp for Start-Ups* (Ithaca: Cornell University Press, 2001), p. 104. Copyright © 2001. Used with permission of the publisher, Cornell University Press.

9. Ibid., p. 14.

10. Ibid., p. 30.

11. George Gedron, "Where the Money Is," *Inc.,* March 2001, p. 13.

12. Ibid., pp. 37 & 38.

13. *Inc.* 500 special 2003 issue, p. 89.

14. Bhidé, *The Origin and Evolution of New Businesses,* p. 29.

15. *Inc.* 500 special 2003 edition. Data collected from throughout the issue.

16. James Sheldon and Burt Alimansky, "8 Demons of Entrepreneurship," *Success,* March 1986, p. 57.

17. Gedron, "Where the Money Is," p. 13.

18. Mark Van Osnabrugge and Robert J. Robinson, *Angel Investing* (San Francisco: Jossey-Bass, 2000), p. 38. Copyright © 2000, Jossey Bass. This material is used by permission of John Wiley & Sons, Inc.

19. Wilson Harrell, *For Entrepreneurs Only* (Hawthorne, NJ: Career Press, 1994), pp. 134–135.

20. James Morrow, "Secrets of a Start-Up," *Success,* September 1998, p. 68.

21. Porter Bibb, *Ted Turner: It Ain't as Easy as It Looks* (New York: Crown, 1993), pp. 83–84.

22. Vance Trimble, *Overnight Success: Federal Express and Frederick Smith, Its Renegade Creator* (New York: Crown, 1993), pp. 161–162.

23. Fred C. Lager, *Ben & Jerry's: The Inside Scoop* (New York: Crown, 1994), p. 18.

24. Martha Visser, "Phone-omenon," *Success,* September 1998, p. 62.

25. Elaine Pofeldt, "The Success Start-Up Guide," March 1999, p. 62.

26. Sharon Churcher, "A Point Well Taken," *Success,* May 1998, p. 46.

27. Morrow, "Secrets of a Start-Up," p. 68.

28. Jill Andresky Fraser, "How to Finance Anything," *Inc.,* March 1999, p. 48.

29. Michael C. Perkins, "Cash Is for Dummies," *Red Herring,* August 2000, p. 310.

30. Ibid., p. 314.

31. Morrow, "Secrets of a Start-Up," p. 68.

32. James Goldberg and Stan Yakatan, "Why Two Can Speed Products to Market Quicker Than One," *Chief Executive,* January–February 1989, p. 36.

33. Beth McGoldrick, "Taking on a Corporate Partner," *CFO,* February 1989, number 2, p. 50.

34. Cynthia E. Griffin, "Corporate Collateral," *Entrepreneur,* July 2000, p. 38. Reprinted with permission of Entrepreneur Media, Inc.

35. McGoldrick, "Taking on a Corporate Partner," p. 50.

36. Ellyn E. Spragins, "A New Deal," *Inc.,* January 1991, p. 121.

37. Ibid., p. 122.

38. Debra Phillips, G. David Doran, Elaine Teague, and Laura Tiffany, "Young Millionaires," *Entrepreneur,* November 1998, p. 119. Reprinted with permission of Entrepreneur Media, Inc.

39. Jill Andresky Fraser, "20 Tips for Finding Money Now," *Inc.,* March 1999, p. 48.

40. Robert McGarvey, " *www.cfol.com*," *Entrepreneur,* March 2001, p. 61. Reprinted with permission of Entrepreneur Media, Inc.

41. Edward O. Welles, "15 Steps to a Start-Up," *Inc.,* March 1994, pp. 72–80.

42. Robert Brown, "Musicians Reveal Secrets to Raising Venture Capital," *American Venture,* July–September 2000, pp. 11 & 12.

43. Sahlman, "How to Write a Really Great Business Plan," p. 130.

44. Lillian Vernon, *An Eye for Winners: How I Built One of America's Greatest Direct-Mail Businesses* (New York: HarperCollins, 1996), p. 66.

45. Anita Roddick and Irene Prokop, *Body and Soul: Profits with Principles—The Amazing Success Story of Anita Roddick and the Body Shop* (New York: Crown, 1991), p. 73.

9

DEBT FINANCING

*A banker: The person who hands you an umbrella when the sun is out
and wants it back the minute it rains.*

—Mark Twain

Debt financing can play a major role in the evolution of a business. When you talk about debt financing, you are usually talking about getting a loan to help you start a business or to facilitate its growth. Chapter 8 highlighted a few of the funding avenues for starting a venture. This chapter focuses almost exclusively on the role banks play in funding emerging ventures.

Entrepreneurs may consider getting a loan or some form of credit from various sources, including friends and family, credit card companies, and/or credit unions. They may also consider getting an advance, which is considered a loan, from the cash value of their life insurance and/or pension. They may ask their suppliers to allow them to purchase goods or services on credit. They may even consider refinancing their house to free up funds for their venture. In most cases, obtaining a loan from a bank seems to be a logical avenue for funding a new venture.

REALITY CHECK

Most first-time entrepreneurs assume banks will help fund their new ventures. This is not the case. While bankers may seem courteous and wish you the best, they rarely provide loans to start-ups. Banks are the most risk averse source of funding. Banks can play an important role in funding, but they prefer to provide growth-related loans to businesses that already have customers, assets, and better balance sheets.

Most first-time entrepreneurs assume getting a loan from a bank to start a business is like getting a mortgage to purchase a home. While banks may provide a mortgage for 90 percent of the value of the house and give you the option of paying it off over 15 to 30 years, commercial loans bear no resemblance to mortgages. Even if you could qualify for a commercial loan, it would be for a much smaller percentage of the value of the assets used to secure the loan and it would be for a much shorter duration.

REALITY CHECK

If you go to a bank looking for a business loan to start your business, don't be surprised if the bank suggests refinancing your house instead. Mortgages have far less risk to bankers.

REALITY CHECK

Pardon the pun, but entrepreneurs should not bank on bank funding. If you need debt funding to start your business, then you should look to friends and family as well as other sources of debt, credit, or cash advances.

Entrepreneurs who seek loans from friends and family should make sure they approach it in a business-like manner. First, it must be clear whether the money is being loaned to the business or to the entrepreneur. Second, the loan must be structured like a contract. It must identify the various rights and responsibilities. Particular attention must be directed to the amount, interest rate, payment schedule, what may be used as collateral, and any other conditions of the loan. Third, the loan agreement should be notarized. Fourth, the interest rate must be fairly competitive. If the money is provided as a personal loan to the entrepreneur, then the interest rate must be fairly competitive or the IRS may consider it to be a gift rather than a loan. This distinction is particularly important if the loan is for more than $10,000. Fifth, banks may be required to notify the IRS of deposits that are more than $10,000, so it is important that loans be documented well.

The old saying, "Banks lend money to businesses that don't need the money," is not exactly the case. Banks must lend money. That is one of the primary ways banks make money. Banks are merely very selective to whom they lend money. They prefer to lend money to businesses that are up and running rather than start-ups.

Banks can play a valuable role in helping a venture grow once it has proven itself—and reduced some of the risk to the banker. It is ironic that once an emerging venture starts growing, the whole lending game is reversed. As soon as a venture shows true merit, bankers come out of the woodwork in hopes of putting together a loan that will let the same entrepreneur (who could not get funding a year or two earlier) grow his or her venture even more!

While it may be very unlikely that a bank will provide a loan to most start-ups, especially to first-timers, entrepreneurs still need to know from the very beginning how banks approach the lending process. It is for this reason that this chapter on bank funding is provided in this book. Entrepreneurs need to adopt Wayne Gretzky's approach to hockey when seeking a loan. When he reflected on his success, Gretzky noted that part of it could be attributed to anticipating where the puck would be and skating to that point on the ice. You need to know what it takes and when it will be possible so you can position your firm to be in the most favorable position to get a loan when you seek it. This chapter profiles various facets of securing a loan when it becomes a possibility or necessity.

ADVANTAGES OF DEBT FINANCING

Debt financing has two major benefits. First, loans do not dilute the ownership structure of the venture. This has real appeal compared to raising funds by issuing stock to others. Second, interest payments, unlike dividends, are treated as an expense. As an expense, they reduce the venture's tax obligation. This, in turn, reduces the cash outflow for taxes. For example, if the venture sold $200,000 in stock and paid a 10 percent dividend of $20,000 on its earnings, then there would be no tax benefit. If the venture secured a $200,000 loan, then its 10 percent interest payment of $20,000 would be treated as an expense. The reduction of taxable income by $20,000 would reduce the amount due in taxes by $7,000 or so, depending on the venture's federal and state income tax rate.

DISADVANTAGES OF DEBT FINANCING

Debt financing has two major drawbacks. First, loans are contracts. They represent a legal commitment to pay the lender the principal and interest. If the venture is unable to make its payments on time, then it can face serious consequences, including foreclosure. Foreclosure can result in the liquidation of your business. When a business is liquidated, government agencies and creditors are at the front of the line when the business's assets are converted into cash. The owners of the business get the table scraps if any exist when the liquidation is completed.

Second, loans come with strings attached. Loans include covenants that place restrictions on how the venture can do business. These covenants may specify certain balances that must be maintained. They may also require approval from the lender before certain activities may be undertaken by the venture.

COMMERCIAL LOANS ARE TIED TO THE CONCEPT OF LEVERAGE

Entrepreneurs need to recognize the concept of equity leverage. Bankers want to reduce the downside risk of their loans. The more that the venture's assets are funded by equity, the less risk to the bank. When bankers look at the venture's balance sheet, they want to know what percent of the business's assets are *owned by the venture* and what percent of the assets *are owed*. If entrepreneurs want to get a loan, then they need to show that they (and possibly others) have put money into the venture. The picture will look even brighter if the venture is generating a tangible profit. Generally speaking, the greater the amount and percent of equity in the venture, the higher the likelihood the bank will consider a loan and the larger the amount for the loan that may be possible.

REALITY CHECK

Bankers are quick to point out that if the entrepreneur is unwilling to put his or her money into the venture, then the bank has no motivation to risk its money. When the venture gets up and running, then the bank may consider providing a loan based on the value of the assets that are owned by the venture. The amount of the loan and the length of the loan will be contingent on how the funds will be used.

REALITY CHECK

Remember, commercial loans are not like mortgages. Even if the emerging venture qualifies for a loan, the amount of the loan will be for a much smaller percent of the value of the assets that are used as collateral.

WHAT ENTREPRENEURS NEED TO KNOW ABOUT BANKS

Banks need to be viewed like customers. You need to know how bankers think, what they want, and how they do business. It is always unwise to stereotype people, but certain generalities about bankers will be used in this chapter. Entrepreneurs should make an effort to ascertain the specific nature of particular banks and the loan officers within those banks when seeking a loan.

As noted before, bankers are risk averse. Bankers focus on two particular types of risk. The first risk involves the stage of the venture's evolution. Entrepreneurs need to get their venture across the risk *threshold* that is associated with a start-up. The sooner the venture demonstrates its legitimacy via sales, respectable cash flow, and even profitability, the sooner it can garner attention from bankers. The second type of risk involves the nature of the business. Certain types of businesses have higher degrees of risk than others. The type of business, the extent of competition, and various other factors affect the degree of risk.

Not All Banks Are Alike

Certain types of banks are more likely to be receptive to funding emerging ventures. Basically, banks can be classified as large, regional, and local. Large banks tend to focus their attention on large accounts. They usually are not interested in emerging ventures until they are worth their time and attention. If the large bank has regional and local offices, then commercial or business bankers in those offices may be willing to look at smaller ventures. Regional banks may be worth pursuing. They are big enough to have specialists on their staffs who have access to valuable databases. Regional banks also tend to be in a position to offer various services that can help emerging ventures. Local banks tend to have more empathy for start-ups and emerging ventures. They are more in tune with local conditions and appear to have a more genuine interest in developing lasting relationships with entrepreneurs.

Local banks, however, tend to not be in a position to make substantial loans. The larger the loan will be as a percent of the local bank's loan portfolio, the more reluctant the bank will be to commit funds to one particular venture. Banks recognize the value of diversifying their loan portfolio.

REALITY CHECK

Some banks are more committed to local ventures than others. Some banks are also more in tune with technology firms.

Banks Prefer Certain Types of Loans

Banks offer various types of loans. Each type of loan has a certain level of risk and corresponding conditions. Most loans are provided for a specific purpose. Some loans are provided to cover working capital. They are usually for a small amount of money for a limited time. Working capital loans are usually designed to help ventures cover temporary cash deficits when the burn rate exceeds cash receipts. Most banks provide this type of loan to existing accounts because they already have financial information for those ventures.

Emerging ventures frequently seek a *line of credit* from a bank. With a line of credit the venture may be able to draw up to a specified sum as needed over a prescribed period. The period may run from a few months to a couple of years. Inventory loans are similar to a line of credit. The venture repays the loan when the inventory is sold and receivables are collected. Emerging ventures may also seek financing for accounts receivable. A temporary loan allows the company to receive in advance a maximum of approximately 65 to 80 percent of the face value of its receivables that are less than 60 days past due.[1] These types of short-term loans are important because they help emerging ventures deal with seasonality and enable incremental rather than substantial growth.

Most commercial loans are provided to pay for the purchase of major assets. The loans are called *asset-based* or *collateralized* loans. Asset-based lending can be viewed as a situation when the bank provides a loan for the purchase of assets that will, in turn, generate the money needed to pay off the loan. The loan is usually for specific assets like fixtures and equipment that may be needed for major expansion. The amount and time frame for the loan are tied to those assets. The assets then serve as collateral to *secure* the loans. Banks prefer this type of loan because the collateralized nature of the loan reduces the risk for the bank. The bank is in a position to repossess the assets if the business fails to honor its loan obligations. Working capital loans do not offer the same degree of security for the bank.

Entrepreneurs of service businesses need to be particularly savvy about the nature of business loans. Although service businesses usually take less capital to start than businesses that need durable assets, they usually find it harder to get a loan for that reason. Most of their operations are payroll related. The lack of durable assets restricts their ability to get commercial loans. Emerging ventures that are seeking loans for highly marketable assets are in a better position to obtain a loan.

Banks Do Not Like to Make Small Loans

Banks sometimes get criticized because they are not willing to provide small loans. Some entrepreneurs have difficulty understanding why banks may be reluctant to consider a loan request for less than $100,000 or even $200,000. A little math indicates why banks are less than enthusiastic to do relatively small loans even for businesses that are not that risky. Banks usually charge a four-point spread in commercial loans. If their money costs the bank 5 percent, then the bank will try to charge 9 percent interest. The bank, however, does not make a four-point profit. The bank has to pay for the commercial loan officer's time and the corresponding overhead. The bank hopes to make a two-point profit on the four-point spread. If the bank provides a $100,000 loan, then it hopes to make a profit of $2,000 on the $4,000 spread. In a sense, the bank is risking $100,000 for just a $2,000 profit. In most cases it takes the same amount of time and effort to review a $200,000 loan as it takes to review a $100,000 loan. All things being equal, the bank will prefer to do a $200,000 loan. Using the same cost structure, banks consider most loans less than $100,000 to be losers.

Larger banks frequently place a higher threshold when considering commercial loans. Some banks may be willing to do a smaller loan if they can get a higher spread, if the loan has minimal risk, and/or if the bank wants to use the loan to get its foot in the door to establish a relationship with the emerging venture so it can be its primary banker when it seeks larger loans, seeks additional services such as its credit card funds, or when it has significant cash balances that it can manage.

Most large and regional banks divide their business lending operations into three categories. The first category is *corporate* lending. Corporate lending usually involves loans in excess of $2 million. The second category is *commercial* lending. Loan officers involved in this category do loans between $200,000 and $2 million. When people refer to *retail banking*, they are usually talking about banks that are actively involved in making loans of less than $200,000 or have lower thresholds or minimums than larger banks. Most small banks do not do large loans because the loans reduce their efforts to keep a diversified portfolio.

There has been a trend, however, toward *relationship banking* for large and mid-size banks. Relationship banking reduces or eliminates the categorization of loan officers. With relationship banking, loan officers are trained and authorized to provide loans of various sizes so they can develop a better relationship with businesses.

REALITY CHECK

Don't immediately rule out all larger banks. Some of the larger banks do retail banking. Check with other entrepreneurs to see if they have loans from larger banks. Large banks can provide valuable services (exporting advice, pension planning, SBA funding, etc.). They may also be in a position to provide valuable links to other entrepreneurs and established firms; also, Small Business Investment Companies (SBICs) are frequently associated with large banks. They provide long-term debt and equity funding. SBICs, however, tend to favor existing businesses that are expanding rather than those that are starting operations.

REALITY CHECK

Don't confuse investment banks with conventional banks. Investment banking firms may provide debt financing, but their expectations are similar to venture capital firms. They are interested in businesses that have the potential to at least double or triple in size each year. Few new businesses have that potential.

WHAT DO BANKERS LOOK FOR WHEN REVIEWING A LOAN REQUEST?

Bankers want to know the *who, what, where, how much,* and *when* of your business. Entrepreneurs need to have answers to the following questions:

1. How much money do you need?
2. What do you plan to use the money for?
3. How soon can you repay the loan?
4. What terms are you looking for in the loan?
5. How do you plan to pay off the loan?
6. What will happen if the business has trouble repaying the loan?

The first question may be a Catch 22 for the bank. The bank needs for the loan to be large enough so it can make money, but it also wants to make sure that the loan will be manageable for the emerging venture and the bank's loan portfolio. Entrepreneurs need to demonstrate that the amount sought is appropriate and that it can be repaid.

The second question may be just as important as the first question. If the loan will play a key role in enhancing the growth and success of the venture, then the bank will look favorably at the loan request. Two particular uses of loan funds are a turn off for bankers. First, banks avoid lending money to bail out businesses in trouble. If the venture needs a working capital loan because it has excessive accounts receivable or sales have been declining, then the bank will not be receptive to a request. Second, banks want to be sure the loan will not be used in non-value-added ways. Earl Graves and Robert Crandall noted, "Count on a rejection letter if you tell the banker the money will be used to increase your salary or buy a fancy new vehicle."[2]

The duration of the loan is usually tied to the purpose of the loan. Loans tend to be tied to the life of the assets that are being funded by the loan. Working capital loans are for a very short period of time. Loans for durable assets will be for a period of time not to exceed the useful life of the assets. Unless the loan involves real estate and buildings, most commercial loans will be for no more than five years.

The terms of the loan usually involve the rate of interest, the schedule of payments for interest and principal, and any covenants. In some cases, the terms of the loan may be just as important as the amount of the loan. If the loan can be tailored to the venture's projected cash flow, then it should be in a better position to pay off the loan.

Entrepreneurs need to be able to demonstrate how their ventures will be able to repay the loan. The loan request should indicate if the loan will be repaid by offering new products/services or whether it will be from expanding the business into new geographic markets.

The final question, "What will happen if the business has difficulty meeting its loan obligation?" also needs to be addressed. The entrepreneur must demonstrate there is sufficient collateral to minimize the bank's downside risk. The bank may also expect the entrepreneur to personally guarantee payment if the business gets into trouble. The willingness to provide a personal guarantee must be addressed well before seeking a loan—or even before starting the venture. Loan officers will expect you to pledge your assets. If you aren't willing to do so, then why should the bank commit its depositors' assets? They also note that the entrepreneur's spouse must also be supportive of the venture—he or she must be willing to commit your personal assets.[3]

Documentation—Documentation—Documentation

Documentation plays a crucial role in seeking a loan. The entrepreneur's ability to document how the venture will be able to repay the loan will reduce the bank's aversion to risk. Having a well-prepared and thoroughly documented business plan will pay big dividends when seeking a loan. It will provide the answers to many of the questions that bankers want to know before seriously considering the loan request.

Tom and Cherry Householder, who started Staffing Resources, demonstrated that it may be possible to get start-up funding if you can reduce the degree of risk. When they needed a loan to open their first office, they recognized the need to reduce their loan officer's perceived risk. They submitted more than 15 letters of reference from various professional colleagues (e.g., police chiefs, politicians, and other customers) in support of their venture. Their company was able to secure a $135,000 line of credit that was instrumental in establishing a $10 million temporary staffing company.[4]

Entrepreneurs need to make sure the information provided to the bank is presented in a manner that demonstrates the merit of the loan request and in a manner so it is easy for the banker to understand. The business plan that you provide the bank should be modified so that it serves as a funding vehicle rather than an operational blueprint. Particular attention should be directed to the venture's ability to repay the loan and how various risks will be addressed. The loan request and business plan should also minimize the use of jargon and reference to technical details that are not relevant to the loan review process.

REALITY CHECK

You should assume your loan request will be turned down unless you give the bank sufficient reason to provide the money. You must assume the burden of proof is on you to show the merit of the loan. If the banker does not understand how your business works and how it will repay the loan, then there is little chance he or she will approve the loan request.

REALITY CHECK

Don't be surprised or take it personally if the bank asks for a *compilation* of your financial statements. This means that a CPA must review them. There are three levels of accounting analysis: the compilation, a review, and an audit. Each of these levels involves a certain level of analysis, statement of accuracy by the CPA, and cost. Even the audit does not mean that 100 percent of your records and procedures have been analyzed.

PREPARE TO ENTER THE WORLD OF BANKERS

The entrepreneurial world is different from the world of banking. While entrepreneurs are optimistic and focus their attention on capitalizing on opportunities, bankers are risk averse and prefer to review tangible financial statements. Entrepreneurs should make an effort to learn how bankers review loan applications.

Bankers frequently refer to the Cs of commercial lending. Each *C* represents a criteria they use in reviewing a loan request. The number of Cs may vary from bank to bank, but they usually cover the same issues. The following Six Cs capture most of the factors that are important to a banker:

1. Entrepreneur's *character*
2. Entrepreneur and team's *capability* to manage
3. Business's *capacity* to pay off the loan
4. *Conditions* or terms of the loan
5. *Context* surrounding the venture
6. *Collateral* to reduce downside risk

Entrepreneur's Character

The first and foremost thing loan officers look for when reviewing a loan proposal is evidence of your trustworthiness. Someone once defined character as, "Doing what's right, when nobody's looking." Bankers want to have faith that the venture will be conducted the right way and that the information provided to the bank will be accurate.

Character is crucial. If there is anything in the entrepreneur's background that indicates any lack of integrity, loan officers will usually reject the loan application without even reviewing the proposed business idea. Loan applications usually include a section that permits the bank to initiate a thorough credit check of the entrepreneur. Banks place a premium on integrity because they will rely on your statements about the business and the corresponding financial projections. If the financial projections or statements or your professional or personal background has any significant blemishes, then the chances for borrowing money from a bank are diminished.

The bank will also check out the principal officers, key members of the management team, and directors for the business. In any event, be prepared to identify all the people who will be an important part of your new business. In baseball, when you get three strikes, you are out. In commercial lending, the lack of integrity almost automatically means you are out!

REALITY CHECK

Run a credit check on yourself and any other key people well before applying for a loan to see what it looks like. By doing this in advance you will have time to have any errors corrected before you apply for the loan.

REALITY CHECK

When it comes time to actually apply for the loan, make sure you do not provide any negative surprises. If sales have fallen off or if you just lost a major account, then it should be noted. The same applies if you are a bit behind schedule with the introduction of a new product or adding someone to your management team. Bad news is bad enough; to deliberately withhold bad news is not just unprofessional; it may be illegal.

Entrepreneur and Team's Capability to Manage the Business

Bankers know that mismanagement is the primary reason for a new business to fail. Your loan proposal must demonstrate that you and everyone else who will be making the various decisions have what it takes to start and manage. Banks are more likely to lend money to a business that will be managed by people who have extensive business experience, particularly in the type of business being proposed. Loan officers are very reluctant to lend money to first-timers who may be using a trial-and-error approach to managing.

REALITY CHECK

The quality of the venture's business plan says a lot about your ability to deal with strategic and operational issues. The plan should reflect your thoroughness and that you truly recognize what it will take for the venture to succeed in the years ahead. Documentation shows you have your act together and that you base decisions on information, not hunches. Any errors, omissions, and inconsistencies in the plan will undermine banker confidence. Bold claims and the lack of documentation will also undermine the likelihood of securing a loan.

Loan officers want to know the professional background and success of the entrepreneur and management team. They want to know the levels of experience and relevant education for each person involved in running the business. The business plan should indicate how each person is suited for his or her position. A biographical sketch and a resume for each key person should also be available. Alex King, senior vice-president for Wachovia Bank, noted, "The most important item in lending is the management team—If you've got the right team, they can make anything happen. ... We have to be convinced the business has a competent management team and that it is trustworthy.

The team is more important than the business."[5] Kenneth W. Olm and George G. Eddy echo Alex King's emphasis on having a solid management team. They note, "No lender will agree to finance a venture that is understaffed in needed skills."[6]

REALITY CHECK

If you have limited experience running a business, then your chances of getting a loan are also limited. It is advisable to have the business up and running before seeking a loan.

REALITY CHECK

Having people on your team, board of directors, and advisory committee who have been successful will increase the odds for getting a loan. Having top-notch professional service advisors (accountant, attorney, etc.) will also help.

REALITY CHECK

While your enthusiasm and sales skills may play an important role in attracting investors, employees, and suppliers, you should recognize that banks want to see professionalism and documentation rather than a spiel. Anita Roddick, founder of The Body Shop, noted, "I found that you don't go to a bank manager with enthusiasm—that is the last thing a banker cares about."[7]

Capacity to Pay Off the Loan

Banks operate under the very simple rule: "We make money only if we lend money to businesses that make money." If the loan officer feels comfortable with your personal background and your ability to make the right business decisions, then the officer's attention will be directed to the extent to which your business will be able to pay off the loan. Kenneth Olm and George Eddy note, "Lenders almost always insist on being given details of the market and the strategy intended to exploit it."[8]

The financial part of your business plan will be an integral part of your loan request. The loan officer will be looking for the business's ability to pay the monthly interest (and in some cases, principal) as well as its ability to payoff the loan when it comes due. Entrepreneurs need to recognize that bankers are not like investors. They are more concerned about cash flow than profitability and the overall value of the venture.

REALITY CHECK

Your ability to prepare, present, and support your financial projections is an indication of your capability to manage a business. If you have an accountant help you prepare the financial part of the business plan, be sure that you understand the nature and logic of the financial projections. This is one of the reasons why you should have knowledge of accounting and finance. If every time the loan officer asks you a question about the basis for certain figures you respond by saying, "I don't know, you will have to ask my accountant," you reduce your chances for getting a loan.

Entrepreneurs need to be savvy to the type of information bankers look for when reviewing a loan proposal. First, bankers prefer actual numbers. This is why they prefer businesses that have been around for a few years versus start-ups. Existing firms can provide various financial statements. Start-ups can merely offer numbers that reflect their hopes and expectations. In addition to the income statement, balance sheet, and cash-flow statement, you should provide a one-page summary that explains your assumptions about revenue growth, cost of goods sold, operating expenses, interest expenses, turnover of accounts receivable, inventory, and accounts payable, capital expenditures, dividend policy, and income-tax rates. Entrepreneurs need to identify the assumptions that served as the cornerstone for the projections. Entrepreneurs also need to be able to explain and defend the projections.[9]

The loan proposal needs to indicate the sources and uses of funds. It also needs to identify the nature and amount of debt as well as the nature and amount of equity invested in the venture. The debt-to-equity ratio will have considerable impact on the amount of the loan because it indicates the level of risk for the bank.

REALITY CHECK

You need to make sure your projections are realistic. Paul Broni cautions entrepreneurs against being too optimistic about sales growth, operating margins, and cash flow. According to Broni, "All bankers and investors want to do business with ambitious entrepreneurs, but there's a big difference between a realistic business plan and fantasy."[10] The amount of the loan is usually a multiple of the firm's cash flow. Alex King of Wachovia Bank noted, "I have never seen a business plan that didn't project good cash flow."[11] Make sure your firm's projected cash flow makes sense because it will be the source of loan repayment.

REALITY CHECK

Bankers carefully analyze the financial information. Make sure your statements reconcile and projections do not include dumb math mistakes.

REALITY CHECK

Each bank is different, so don't rely on ESP when it comes to figuring out what information to provide. Ask the banker in advance what information should be provided and how it should be presented. Ask which ratios should be reported, as well as the number of years for projections and for past statements. Bankers do not always agree on the number of scenarios that should be run for the financial projections. Some rely on a single most likely scenario. Other bankers also want to see optimistic and pessimistic scenarios.

REALITY CHECK

Bankers expect loan recipients to be frugal with their money. When you are developing the compensation package for the venture make sure each person's salaries and fringe benefits are not out of line.

Conditions or Terms of the Loan

Even if the loan officer is satisfied with the first three C's, the nature of your loan request will also influence the bank's willingness to lend you money. Bankers do not like to take excessive risks. They reduce their risks by limiting the amount of the loan to a certain percent of the business's assets, using those assets as security, and being as close as possible to the front of the line to get their money out of the business if it is unable to meet its financial obligations.

Two other "conditions" also need to be kept in mind when borrowing from a bank. First, the business will have to carry enough insurance on its assets so they are covered in the event of a fire or other types of loss. Second, the bank will also place various restrictive covenants on the operation of your business. The bank may not technically be a partner in the business, but it may seem to be the "senior partner" in certain instances. The banks will expect to see certain financial records on a regular basis that reflect the financial health of your business. Your venture will need to maintain certain levels of inventory, receivables, and cash. The restrictions may include getting prior approval from the bank before making any major changes in your balance sheet via the sale or purchase of assets or altering the business's equity or debt configuration.

Context Surrounding the Venture

Most loan officers have their own perceptions and preferences. Lending is not a science. Loan officers have to exercise judgment when lending money to an emerging venture. There are myriad factors that have to be considered when sizing up the merit and risk associated with financing an emerging venture.

Loan officers also have attitudes about most types of businesses. Some loan officers get excited about manufacturing or high-technology businesses. Other loan officers seem to favor retail or service businesses. This may also be true for banks. Smaller banks tend to be more "retail" oriented. They actively seek opportunities to lend to promising local businesses.

Banks that have had successful lending experiences with certain types of businesses are more open-minded when they review a loan proposal for a similar business. If the loan officer has extensive experience in the emerging venture's field it may also be beneficial. Conversely, the relative newness or nonmainstream nature of your new venture may cause the banker to be apprehensive about the viability and growth for that type of business.

REALITY CHECK

Ignorance is *not* bliss! In the investment field, the absence of information implies risk. The same is true in banking. You will be better off finding a bank that has a track record for providing loans to businesses in your industry and a loan officer in that bank who has experience with your type of business. Recognize that the less someone knows about something, the less they are willing to become engaged in it. If your venture is very "foreign" to the loan officer then you may be better off looking for another loan officer or approaching a different bank.

REALITY CHECK

Some banks and loan officers have had bad experiences with certain types of businesses. If you are planning to start a similar business, you may encounter considerable skepticism by the loan officer. Some banks will not even consider making loans to certain types of businesses. Make sure the bank and/or loan officer you plan to deal with has not mentally blackballed your type of business before you seek the loan. The last thing you want to do is seek a loan from a banker who already has the attitude, "I'll be darned if I will ever lend any money to that kind of business again!"

No business exists in a vacuum. Loan officers look at the context in which the venture operates. They may pay particular attention to potential economic, legal, employee, supplier, or environmental problems. While the venture's financial projections may demonstrate its "capacity" to pay off the loan, loan officers will also look at the local, regional, and national economic picture. Their feeling about whether there will be inflation, a recession, tight money, high unemployment, and so forth, will influence the likelihood of getting a loan. Loan officers can get "cold feet" if the overall economic outlook is not good.

Loan officers may still have "cool feet" even though your venture's industry and target area may have growth potential. Ventures that appear to be recession-proof and inflation-proof may be viewed more favorably.

Loan officers are also interested in whether your business is vulnerable to competition and if its products or services are susceptible to obsolescence. They will be particularly interested in whether the market is already saturated with too many businesses competing for too few customers. They will also be interested in whether the venture is or will be competing with larger, more established businesses or if it is or will be up against other emerging ventures. Loan officers tend to look more favorably on ventures if: (1) they have a fairly new product or service that people already want to buy, (2) there is little competition, (3) the competition is made up of small independent businesses, and (4) few businesses of that type have failed recently. Loan officers don't seem to be bothered if other similar businesses are starting as much as when similar businesses are starting to fail. They prefer the situation where a growing opportunity exists, even with competition, than one where the market is already showing signs that it is waning. Loan officers frequently contact their headquarters to learn about the success rates for certain types of businesses. The bank's staff at its headquarters usually has access to trade data as well as the track record for similar businesses in the bank's loan portfolios.

Loan officers also look at the barriers to entry. If the venture is the type of business that requires extensive experience, rigorous licensing requirements, and/or considerable capital, then the bank will be more willing to lend it money if it is one of the only ventures that meets all the qualifications. Conversely, if almost anyone could start that type of business with no experience and a minimal investment, then this would be disconcerting to a loan officer.

Legal issues also concern loan officers. Certain businesses have come under closer scrutiny and regulation in recent years. Businesses providing medical-related products or that are involved in various forms of health care are expected to encounter additional licensing requirements and regulations in the years to come. The potential for employee accidents and the business's liability may also affect the loan officer.

The loan officer may be concerned about your vulnerability to suppliers and distribution channels. Numerous emerging ventures fail because their suppliers went out of business or failed to continue providing for the needs of those businesses. Numerous emerging ventures have failed because they could not access or lost distribution channels. The same reasoning applies to customer vulnerability. Banks may be very apprehensive if the venture has a limited number of customers. The loss of a major account or a few accounts can kill profitability and jeopardize the very existence of an emerging venture.

REALITY CHECK

Restrictive covenants between one of your venture's competitors and a supplier or distribution channel that restrain trade are illegal, but informal "practices" continue in many fields. The same also applies to patent infringement, theft of intellectual property, and predatory pricing practices. Although you may have a legitimate case, you probably don't have the time and money needed to pay for the attorneys to weather the years of legal battles.

Insurance coverage is another area that concerns loan officers. Insurance premiums for some businesses have more than tripled in the last couple of years. Some businesses have had to reduce their coverage or go without coverage because the costs have increased so much. A few businesses have even closed their doors because they could not get insurance coverage. Some of these businesses did not have a checkered past. The insurance companies simply decided to discontinue coverage to that kind of business. The prospect of an emerging venture dying on the vine because insurance carriers may discontinue providing coverage increases the likelihood the loan officer will not approve the loan request.

Environmental factors may also make the loan officer apprehensive about financing your business. If your business can be adversely affected by the weather (water park, car wash, etc.) or damaged by a tornado, a hurricane, or a flood, then the loan officer may not want to take that risk. Loan officers like to finance businesses that are influenced by their managers rather than by mother nature. Loan officers also tend to shy away from any business that could be involved in any type of ecological disaster. If your business will be dealing with anything that is flammable or toxic, or has the potential to be a pollutant, then the loan officer may steer clear of your proposal.

The fifth C indicates that your loan proposal may be rejected because of the nature and context of your business, regardless of the strength of the other Cs. In such a case, the business plan will have to provide even more documentation to substantiate the venture's viability. For this reason, it may be advisable to set up an appointment with the targeted loan officer well in advance of when you will be seeking the loan. An early meeting may provide an initial impression of the loan officer's interest in the venture and his or her perceptions about contextual factors. Hopefully, the loan officer will be interested in reviewing a loan request. If so, the loan officer may be able to get or recommend some sources of data to help you provide the documentation needed to be seen more favorably. This may pay off later. The more the loan officer is involved early on, the more he or she may be an advocate for the loan.

Collateral to Reduce Downside Risk

Most entrepreneurs place too much emphasis on collateral. Collateral is important, but loan officers do not put it at the top of their criteria when reviewing a loan request. They consider collateral to be like a parachute—it's nice knowing that it is there, but they hope they never need to use it. If the loan officer has reservations about potential profitability and the venture's cash flow, then a large amount of collateral may be required to compensate for the risk. Nevertheless, banks tend to operate with the policy, "If it takes a lot of collateral to cover the bank's position, then don't approve the loan."

The loan request will need to reflect what assets can be used as collateral for the bank loan. As with parachutes, the bank will look for collateral that is large enough to break the fall. Banks also prefer collateral that is marketable and that can be easily converted to cash if the loan goes bad. There are a number of rules of thumb used in the valuation of assets as collateral. Inventory, based on its marketability, may be valued by the bank for as little as 25 percent of its value. Accounts receivable, based on the size, creditworthiness, and recency of the accounts, may be valued at 50 percent. If the venture's collateral will be custom manufacturing equipment that may be difficult to resell and has minimal value once used, then the loan officer may place little value on it. The same may also be true if the entrepreneur provides a personal guarantee using a 200-acre family-owned farm in Kansas as collateral.

If a loan recipient is unable to meet its obligations, then your venture and the bank are placed in three awkward situations. First, direct involvement by the bank does little to develop goodwill with the venture's stakeholders. Employees, investors, suppliers, and creditors frequently jump ship even if the venture is experiencing just a temporary financial setback. Bank intervention, even if it is just a rumor, can be the first domino falling in a string of dominos. Second, the loan officer has to admit to not exercising good judgment by approving the loan. Third, the loan officer has to go through the process of converting assets into cash to recover the bank's money. This takes time and diverts the bank from what it is in business to do.

REALITY CHECK

Don't treat collateral as the primary selling point of your loan request. Collateral rarely makes up for a weakness in any of the other five Cs.

DEVELOPING A FAVORABLE RELATIONSHIP WITH THE BANK AND BANKER

Entrepreneurs need to recognize that while the bank may provide a loan to the business, the bank is really basing its decision on the people who will be making the decisions that will determine if the loan will be paid off. The first two Cs emphasize the need for the entrepreneurs to have integrity and to demonstrate that they have what it takes to make their ventures successful. Trust and business acumen are of paramount importance.

Entrepreneurs need to be savvy to how critical it is to develop a favorable relationship with the banker from the very start. First impressions are particularly important. Holly Hitzemann, president of Great American Stock, a company that provides photographs, stressed the need for entrepreneurs to convey (1) a sense of realism rather than pie-in-the-sky optimism, (2) openness rather than self-defensiveness, and (3) calm self-confidence rather than arrogance.[12]

"How you approach the bank is a reflection of how you run your business, manage your people, and deal with your customers and suppliers."[13] Entrepreneurs need to recognize the banker is both a supplier and a customer. If the banker doesn't buy into the entrepreneur's ability to make the right decisions, then the bank will not be willing to supply the venture with a loan.

Entrepreneurs can increase the likelihood of developing a favorable first impression through various means. First, it never hurts to have a highly respected businessperson serve as a reference. Personal referrals can open doors. This is where having a network of contacts can pay big dividends. If that person has a relationship with a bank, then he or she may open the doors by recommending that the bank contact the entrepreneur or be aware that the entrepreneur may be contacting the bank.

Second, first-time entrepreneurs who have a track record for being successful in business before starting their ventures may garner more interest from a bank than people with limited business experience. Entrepreneurs who have an established track record should be in a position to provide letters of reference from customers, employers, and so forth who can testify to the entrepreneur's integrity and ability. Again, entrepreneurs who have developed such a strong presence in the business community before starting their ventures may garner bank attention.

When a successful real estate agent decided to start his own firm, the bank actually loaned him more money than he had originally requested. The bank, which had been working with him in providing mortgages to his clients, knew his new firm would be successful because of his visibility and professionalism. The bank also recognized that his firm would not really be starting from scratch—he already had tremendous goodwill. His visibility and reputation enabled his venture to hit the ground running. This goodwill enabled him to attract customers and bring other agents on board much faster than if he did not have such a background.

A similar situation occurred when the executive director of a chamber of commerce decided to take the entrepreneurial plunge and start a business brokerage business. Like the realtor, he was so visible and well networked that he could be considered to be a *brand*. The Realtor's and former Chamber of Commerce executive's reputations for making good things happen were like rocket boosters—they provided their new ventures with additional lift from the very beginning.

PROSPECTING: FINDING THE RIGHT BANK AND THE RIGHT BANKER

Finding the right bank and right banker can be a major challenge. "If there is a list out there of entrepreneurial frustrations, selecting the right bank is somewhere near the top."[14] It has already been noted that banks vary in size and their propensity to do business loans—especially to new ventures. Banks also vary in the type and amount of services and assistance they provide emerging ventures. The right bank for one new venture may not be the right bank for another venture. Entrepreneurs need to determine what their particular needs are and then search for the type of bank that has a track record for providing that type of loan.

The first rule of thumb to use when looking for the right bank is that it needs to be large enough to provide the loan and other services and assistance you need. Yet, it also needs to be small enough to provide the personal attention that may help your venture grow.

The size of the bank may also be an issue if you live in a state with branch banking. Although the overall bank may be large, most branches and even city offices for the bank may have loan limits. If the loan sought exceeds that limit, then higher-ups from the bank's headquarters may need to be involved. This has three drawbacks. First, it takes additional time to get attention and approval from the bank's headquarters. Second, the loan officers at the bank's headquarters may not have a real feel for the business climate in the community where the venture is located and/or operating. Third, even if the loan is approved, the entrepreneur will probably not have as good of an ongoing relationship with the bank as it would if the loan was approved at the local level. The moral to the story is to seek a bank that has a track record for making the size and type of loan being sought.

The same applies to choosing a bank that can provide various forms of assistance after the loan is approved. Banks can be far more than just sources of funds. They can provide *smart money*. The extent the banks can provide valuable financial services and assistance should also be considered when prospecting for lenders. Entrepreneurs of technology ventures can benefit from banks that "get" technology. The same applies to health care, electronics, manufacturing, and service organizations. These banks may have access to considerable trade information. They are also in a position to provide valuable business contacts.

REALITY CHECK

It will be worth your time to approach a few banks, not just the one you are using now. Some banks are more receptive to emerging ventures than others. Also, loan terms may vary from bank to bank. You may be able to find a lower interest rate, a more flexible payback schedule, or fewer restrictive covenants if you approach a few banks.

REALITY CHECK

When checking out a bank, find out if your industry or market is on its "do not lend money to this type of business list." Make a point of asking prospective bankers if the bank has provided loans to similar businesses recently.

REALITY CHECK

Most bankers are ill-equipped to assist emerging ventures in getting equity funding. Although a few larger banks may have their own small business investment companies that may do debt and equity deals, most commercial bankers are not in a position to provide links with angels and venture capital firms. Try to establish a relationship with a bank (or banker) that has connections with SBICs, angels, and venture capital firms.

Finding the right banker can also be a challenge. In some cases it may be better to start the search for a bank by first searching for the right banker. Entrepreneurs should look for a banker who (1) truly understands the nature of the venture, (2) wants to develop a close working relationship with the venture, and (3) is in a position to get the loan approved.

Interpersonal and organizational networking may help identify the right banker. Entrepreneurs should ask fellow entrepreneurs which banker and bank they would recommend. Involvement in local or regional entrepreneurial organizations may also provide opportunities to meet accountants and attorneys who are in a good position to recommend bankers who "get it" and who have developed good relationships with their clients. Bankers who get it are usually actively involved in the entrepreneurial organizations.

Finding the right banker is like finding the right physician. First of all, if you need a specialist, then look for a specialist. Second, the duration of the banking relationship (not just the first loan) can have a bearing on which banker may be best. Make sure the banker will be around long enough to help the venture grow. If the banker is outstanding, then he or she may be promoted or transferred to a new area where he or she cannot help the venture. Favorable relationships make things happen quicker and easier. The same also applies to whether the banker may be approaching retirement. Although a veteran banker may be in a position to provide a wealth of knowledge and/or contacts, if he or she will be retiring in the near future, then it may be advisable to look for a banker who will be around to help the venture over the years.

The right banker is simply the one who can get the loan approved. Make sure the banker either has the direct authority to approve the loan or is in a position to get it approved through channels with minimal delay. The founder of a rapidly expanding entertainment business was emphatic in the need to have a banker who has the authority to approve loans for the amount of money sought. He got so frustrated dealing with a local loan officer that he called the president of that bank, who happened to be a former fraternity brother, and demanded that someone come down who had the authority to make the loan or he would take his banking elsewhere! When the vice-president of corporate lending sized up the venture, he immediately approved the loan. The vice-president was not only comfortable with the nature of the business and the amount of the loan, but he also had the authority to do a loan for that amount and duration.

REALITY CHECK

Check to see if the designated loan officer has experience lending to the type of business you are considering and whether the loan officer has the authority to make that type and size of a loan. In this case, familiarity may not breed contempt. The more knowledge and experience a banker has with a certain type of business, the less the loan may be risky in his or her eyes. This experience may be particularly beneficial after the loan is approved. Experienced loan officers are more prone to maintain their cool if the venture encounters some turbulence. They know that even solid ventures have periodic setbacks. Their willingness to hang in there during those times—when less experienced loan officers might bail out—could prove to be worth their weight in gold.

REALITY CHECK

Veteran entrepreneurs know life is full of surprises. The best way to deal with surprises is to have contingency plans to deal with them. This applies to banks and bankers. Bankers move, get promoted, change banks, and do other things. Banks change lending policies too. Don't put all your eggs in one basket. Develop a relationship with at least two bankers and two banks so that you can move ahead if things fall through with the primary banker and bank. The additional time it takes may pay off not just in terms of having a contingency plan; it may enable you to get better terms on the loan. If you place your funding hopes on one banker and bank, they may change the terms at the last minute. The greater the need for funding, the greater the need to have a back-up bank in reserve.

TIMING: ADOPT THE GRETZKY APPROACH

Entrepreneurs should make a deliberate effort to develop a relationship with the right banker in the right bank well in advance of the need for a loan. Alex King of Wachovia Bank noted, "Develop a relationship early with the banker and bank—don't just appear one day asking for money."[15] Keith Schilit goes one step further on the timing issue. He noted, "The worst time to ask for a loan is when you need it. By that time, it is often too late. Thus, you should develop a relationship with a banker as early as possible."[16]

REALITY CHECK

Be prepared to borrow more money than you think you will need and earlier than you think you will need it. The need to borrow may be for good things like higher-than-expected consumer demand or for bad things like slower-than-expected collection of receivables or a requirement for advance payment when ordering inventory. You should also assume that something could derail or delay the loan process. The moral to the story is to start earlier, have money in reserve to cover operations if there are delays, and have a back-up bank that is prepared to provide the funding. If your loan is in the form of a line of credit, then you will only have to pay interest when you actually use it.

COVENANTS: THE BANK'S TEN COMMANDMENTS

Loans almost always have strings attached to them. The strings are called *covenants*. There are affirmative and negative covenants. Affirmative covenants indicate the venture will do certain things. These covenants may include the frequency that the venture must submit financial statements to the bank, that the venture will maintain certain operating ratios and balances, that it will comply with all laws, and that it will make all of the loan payments on time. Negative covenants indicate the business will not do certain things. These covenants may prohibit the sale of major assets, securing additional debt, or the distribution of funds without bank approval.

SBA FINANCING MAY BE A POSSIBILITY

Ironically, the federal government may be a possible avenue for funding. The U.S. Small Business Administration (SBA) may be in a position to help emerging ventures that need additional funding. The SBA is often called the "lender of last resort." This is not the case. The *last resort* label arose from the SBA's policy that it would not consider a loan request unless a bank had already turned down the corresponding loan request. The last resort label and the belief that applicants had to jump over all sorts of bureaucratic hurdles made entrepreneurs reluctant to explore SBA funding.

The *lender of last resort* label was also a misnomer because the SBA really does not lend money. The SBA merely underwrites a substantial part of the loan made by banks in most of its loan programs. Entrepreneurs should not embark on their funding journey with the intent of securing SBA funding. While the SBA may have a few programs where it may provide direct loans, entrepreneurs need to begin their funding journey with a conventional bank.

If a loan officer for a conventional bank sees merit in a loan proposal but has sufficient concerns to turn the loan down, then he or she may recommend that it be considered for a SBA loan. In a sense, the proposal has to be good, but not good enough for a conventional loan. SBA loans often fill the gap between what bankers would like to do and what bankers are willing to fund. This is particularly true for emerging ventures that have considerable merit, but not enough of a track record or collateral to satisfy a bank's *cautious* lending policies.

A number of banks have developed close relations with the SBA that speed the loan review and approval process. The SBA considers some banks as *certified* lenders. This classification means those banks can review loans for the SBA. This classification aids the loan process, but the SBA still needs to provide final approval for the loan. Other banks are classified as *preferred* lenders. These banks, which have been certified, have been elevated to the point where they are authorized to prospect for loans, review them, and approve them without final approval by the SBA. The SBA (*www.sba.gov*) provides a list of certified and preferred lenders.

REALITY CHECK

It is worth your while to contact the SBA to learn which banks have preferred status with the SBA. Those banks may be more receptive to your loan proposal to begin with because they may have an individual or whole department devoted to funding small businesses and emerging ventures.

The SBA has attempted to further streamline the lending process for businesses that meet certain criteria. It has a micro-loan program for start-up, newly established, or growing small businesses. Under this program, the SBA makes funds available to nonprofit community-based lenders, called *intermediaries,* which then make loans to eligible borrowers in amounts up to $35,000. The SBA Express program involves less paperwork hassles and less time. Bank-qualified business owners can borrow up to $250,000 without going through the standard SBA application process and are guaranteed a loan decision within 36 hours. The SBA's 7(a) Guarantee Program and its 504 loan program are also noteworthy. In the 7(a) program the loan can be up to $2 million, with the SBA guaranteeing up to $1 million. In the 504 program, growing businesses can get up to $1 million in long-term financing for major assets including real estate, equipment, inventory, and machinery. A business may qualify for the 504 program if its tangible net worth is less than $7 million and it does not have more than $2.5 million in net income after taxes for each of the preceding two years.[17]

CONCLUSION: BORROWING MONEY IS POSSIBLE IF YOU KNOW WHAT YOU ARE DOING

Borrowing money is one of the facts of life for most emerging ventures. It lets you use someone else's money to make money for you. The best of all worlds—provided that you can pay off the debt—would be if lenders financed most of your business. You would not have to put much money into your business and you would not have to dilute your ownership position by issuing stock to others. When your business eventually paid off its debts, you would get all its profits and own all its assets. As you create and maintain customers for a profit, you will be transforming debt into net worth.

The key to getting a loan is to be in a position where the bank *wants* to do business with you. The ideal situation would be to have banks lined up to do business with you. That is not likely to be the case in the beginning, so you will have to have your act together to develop the type of track record and relationship that will foster the level of interest where banks actively pursue your business rather than the other way around.

In some instances, it may be advisable to borrow money or to get a line of credit even if you believe you have enough money to finance the venture by yourself. This way you have some of your money on the sidelines if you need it. The ability to access money on short notice may enable your venture to capitalize on growth opportunities as well as handle the turbulence associated with unanticipated events or setbacks.

Perceptiveness and flexibility play a key part in securing debt funding. You need to recognize what banks expect of loan applicants and you must be willing to do what it takes to meet their expectations. You also need to be prepared to scale down your request, accept certain covenants, or even modify your business's strategy to fit the bank's lending criteria. This also includes being willing to put more of your own money into the business or guaranteeing the loan with your personal assets.

You must also be willing to explore all avenues for debt financing. This means tapping friends and family, investigating the use of trade credit, approaching Small Business Investment Companies, capitalizing on government-supported technology funds, and/or seeking SBA underwritten loans. Having back-up plans is a must today. Assume there will be delays, surprises, and setbacks. Accordingly, you should start your search earlier, develop alternative funding sources, and avoid burning any bridges if things don't work out with a particular lender.

The importance of establishing good relationships and demonstrating integrity cannot be overstated. The need to provide accurate, timely, and complete information to your bank is essential to getting your first loan and subsequent loans. When people are asked, "Why do people pay off loans?" most respond, "So they fulfill their legal responsibility." Veteran entrepreneurs frequently provide a different response. They say, "So you can borrow money again."

It is important for you to keep your banker informed about how your business is doing, especially if it is not going to meet the projections provided the bank as part of the loan request. Relationships are built on trust. Make sure the banker is not the last person to hear that your business is in trouble—or does not hear bad news first from other people.

Bankers are the keepers of the keys to success for an entrepreneur.
They can help you more than anyone else. They can also hurt you the most,
because all creditors and potential creditors check with the bankers first.
A negative word can stop all your plans. In times of trouble,
it's doubly important to have a good relationship with your bank,
because you must be able to write checks to stay in business.[18]

—Tom Monaghan, founder of Domino's Pizza

ENDNOTES

1. W. Keith Schilit, *The Entrepreneur's Guide to Preparing a Winning Business Plan and Raising Venture Capital* (Englewood Cliffs, NJ: Prentice Hall, 1990), p. 212.

2. Earl G. Graves and Robert L. Crandall, *How to Succeed in Business Without Being White: Straight Talk on Making It in America* (New York: HarperBusiness, 1997), p. 163.

3. James Sheldon and Burt Alimansky, "8 Demons of Entrepreneurship," *Success,* March 1986, p. 54.

4. Ilan Mochari, "Hot Tips" *Inc.,* December 1998, p. 121.

5. Alex King, presentation to a New Venture Management class, University of North Carolina at Wilmington, 2003.

6. Kenneth W. Olm and George G. Eddy, *Entrepreneurship and Venture Management* (Englewood Cliffs, NJ: Prentice Hall, 1985), p. 53.

7. Anita Roddick and Irene Prokop, *Body and Soul: Profits with Principles—The Amazing Success Story of Anita Roddick and The Body Shop* (New York: Crown, 1991), p. 71–72.

8. Olm and Eddy, *Entrepreneurship and Venture Management,* p. 51.

9. Paul Broni "Persuasive Projections," *Inc.,* April 2000, pp.163–164.

10. Ibid.

11. Alex King, presentation to a New Venture Management class, University of North Carolina at Wilmington, 2003.

12. Jill Andresky Fraser, "Money Talk," *Inc.,* September 1999, pp. 109–112.

13. Sheldon and Alimansky, "8 Demons of Entrepreneurship," p. 54.

14. Wallace Weeks, "Making the Cut," *Entrepreneur,* July 2000, pp. 84-85. Reprinted with permission of Entrepreneur Media, Inc.

15. Alex King, presentation to a New Venture Management class, University of North Carolina at Wilmington, 2003.

16. Schilit, *The Entrepreneur's Guide to Preparing a Winning Business Plan and Raising Venture Capital,* p. 217.

17. SBA website, *www.sba.gov,* March 2004.

18. Tom Monaghan, *Pizza Tiger* (New York: Hyperion, 1997), p. 249.

10

SEEKING INVESTORS

Money matters, but raising it is the activity that entrepreneurs hate most.[1]
—Joseph and Jimmie Boyett,
Authors of *The Guru Guide to Entrepreneurship*

In a perfect world, entrepreneurs would have all the money they need to start and grow their companies. Unfortunately, most entrepreneurs are undercapitalized. They encounter a funding gap that forces them to pursue loans and/or to seek investors. This chapter addresses how entrepreneurs can fund their ventures by attracting individual investors.

Chapter 11 provides an in-depth profile of angel investors. Chapter 12 profiles the nature of venture capital and the process for seeking venture capital funding.

This chapter answers the question, "Why should entrepreneurs consider seeking "equity" funding? Three reasons stand out. First, you may not have enough money. Financing a new venture often involves bringing in investors to supplement the entrepreneur's investment until the venture generates sufficient revenue and positive cash flow to internally fuel its growth.

A new venture is like a rocket; it needs to have enough fuel to clear the launch pad and escape the gravitational pull of the Earth. If the venture does not have sufficient initial capital, then it has little chance for survival. Likewise, once launched, it needs to have enough money to cover its daily burn rate and to support its growth. Like the space shuttle, a new venture needs to have external fuel tanks until it reaches an altitude where its own tanks can power its journey.

The second reason is that banks rarely provide start-up funding; the risk-return ratio is too great for banks. The cautious nature of banks usually keeps them from taking the risks that are associated with a start-up. In the risk-return formula, state usury laws prohibit banks from charging high enough rates to justify the risks. Chapter 9 noted that the ability to secure a large amount of money from a bank for a start-up is the exception rather than the rule. Only under certain instances—the loan is a small amount of the total amount of money being put into the business, the entrepreneur has a successful track record, the business looks like it is destined to succeed, and the business has assets that can serve as collateral to secure the loan—will entrepreneurs be able to secure debt financing to help them start their ventures. Banks are far more willing to provide a loan if the business is already up and running and has the assets to secure the loans.

The third reason is that debt service drains the business of critical cash. Interest and principal payments take cash out of the business that needs to be used for growing the business. Almost every entrepreneur will exclaim, "Cash is the lifeblood of a new venture!" Although banks need to lend money so they can make a profit, their risk-averse nature forces them to limit the amount of the loan and its duration. The sooner it has to be paid off, the greater the drain on the venture's critical cash position.

This chapter reflects the bad news/good news nature of entrepreneurship. The bad news is that entrepreneurs might have to spend considerable time seeking one or more investors to fill the funding gap. Seeking equity funding can also be costly. Generally speaking, the earlier you need external investors, the more you have to give up in stock to get it.

Although entrepreneurs are encouraged to use other people's money to start their businesses, the process of seeking outside investors as well as the time it takes being accountable to them has its own trade-offs. Finding and courting investors usually take a considerable amount of time. This time also has considerable opportunity cost. Every moment spent seeking investors represents one less moment available for the entrepreneur to be spending time developing new customers, fine-tuning operations, modifying the venture's strategy to be in sync with evolving realities, as well as prospecting for talent and developing a first-rate management team.

Now the good news. Entrepreneurs who are unable to get their friends and family to invest in their ventures to bridge the funding gap may have an opportunity to seek *angel investors*. Angel investors are individuals who are willing to invest part of their personal wealth in entrepreneurial ventures. The term *angel* goes back to the early years of Broadway, when wealthy individuals helped launch new shows by investing in them.

Angels have played a key role in the development of numerous noteworthy ventures over the years. Henry Ford could not have created Ford Motor Company without the investment of $40,000 by five angels.[2] Angels also helped Amazon, Apple Computer, and The Body Shop. H. Ross Perot, founder of EDS, invested in NeXT, a firm started by Steven Jobs when he left Apple Computer.[3]

Nearly every community has wealthy individuals who may be interested in investing in new ventures that show considerable profit potential. There are between 2 and 4 million people in the United States who have the discretionary net worth to make angel investments. These people play the role of venture catalysts by providing funds, advice, and contacts at a very critical time for new and emerging ventures.

Entrepreneurs face two major challenges when seeking angel funding. First, they need to be able to locate prospective angels. Second, they need to be able to present an investment package that appeals to the prospective angel's risk/return expectations. Jeffery Sohl, University of New Hampshire's Center for Venture Research, noted, "We're seeing a big influx of cashed-out entrepreneurs who have the money and the know-how."[4] He also noted, "80 percent of angels say they would invest more if they were approached with quality deals."[5]

REALITY CHECK

Most entrepreneurs—even of high-potential ventures—fail to recognize that venture capital firms rarely invest in start-ups and that their investment criteria far exceed even the best-case growth scenario for most new ventures. This chapter and the following chapter are important because they encourage entrepreneurs to seek angel funding rather than venture capital funding. The time may come for seeking venture capital, but that time is usually later in the game if the emerging venture is able to demonstrate it meets lofty venture capital expectations.

CLOSE TIES BETWEEN THE STAGE OF NEW VENTURE EVOLUTION AND FUNDING

Finding investors tends to follow a fairly straight and logical path. Most entrepreneurs are the initial investors. If they have enough money to get their ventures up and running, then they are in the enviable position of having more time to direct their attention to managing their ventures rather than beating the streets looking for funding. Most growth-oriented ventures, however, require additional investors.

Angels can provide a boost at a critical time in the evolution of a new venture. An angel investment may help a start-up get its operations up and running. Conversely, angel funding may be timed to help the firm get to the point where it has sufficient cash flow to internally fund its growth. An angel investment may help the firm develop a track record and gain sufficient assets to secure a loan from a bank. Angel funding may be a bridge that enables the venture to the point where it has the potential to attract venture capital funding.

The process for gaining investors involves many dimensions. The entrepreneur must answer the classic *who, what, when, where, how much,* and *how?* questions. Finding investors should not be a haphazard process. It needs to be an integral part of the business plan. It needs to be deliberate, systematic, and flexible. Finding investors is like looking for gold. You need to look in the right places, have the right tools to mine the gold, and have the tenacity to keep mining until you strike it. Veteran entrepreneurs know that few things go as planned. The need for tenacity and perseverance should not be underestimated. Howard Schultz, CEO of Starbucks, noted, "I was turned down by 217 of the 242 investors I initially talked to. You have to have a tremendous belief in what you are doing and just persevere."[6]

The first step in seeking capital is to know how much is needed in the evolution of the new venture. This is one of the times that having a well-prepared business plan can pay big dividends. The plan's financial projections should identify cash flow gaps that will require additional money. The gap may exist from the moment the entrepreneur contemplates starting a new venture. The financial plan should also indicate gaps that may occur due to growth and seasonality well after start-up.

Some emerging ventures are able to finance their growth via their own revenue and retained earnings. High-growth firms, however, almost always need one or more infusions of additional funding to enable them to capitalize on market opportunities. Just as new ventures tend to go through stages of evolution, the need for funding also tends to go through particular stages. Successful new ventures generally go through the following stages:

1. Seed stage (conception)
2. Start-up stage (birth)
3. Early stage (adolescence)
4. Later stage (adulthood)

Seed Stage (Conception)

The seed stage is usually nothing more than an exploratory stage. The business isn't really a business yet ... it is just a concept that needs to be flushed out and analyzed by the entrepreneur. This is the time the entrepreneur mentally explores one or more business concepts or opportunities. Most of this stage is devoted to looking at a business opportunity from

various perspectives. If the opportunity has merit, then the entrepreneur may decide to proceed with developing a comprehensive business plan for starting a venture to capitalize on
the opportunity.

Start-up Stage (Birth)

The start-up stage represents the actual launch of the new venture. It begins when the decision is made to create the new venture all the way through the venture's first full year of
operation. This stage usually involves the first commitment of resources to starting the
business. The venture's products and/or services must be developed. Systems must be
established and operationalized. People must be hired. Marketing plans must be developed
and executed.

Although the seed stage may have indicated that the opportunity may be worth pursuing, this is the first moment of truth for the new venture. If the entrepreneur didn't quit his
or her job in the seed stage, then he or she almost certainly has to take the leap of faith and
jump into the new venture on a full-time basis at this stage. The level of risk grows dramatically because the entrepreneur's finances and personal life are now tied directly to the
success of the new venture.

Early Stage (Adolescence)

Many ventures do not survive the first year. There are numerous reasons why they do not
make it to this stage. First, the opportunity may not have been sufficient at that time to support the new venture. Second, the venture lacked a sustainable competitive advantage and
could not garner enough customers to keep its head above water. Third, it had insufficient
funds to cover its burn rate and the inevitable surprises and setbacks. Fourth, the entrepreneur or entrepreneurial team did not have the skills and experience needed to beat the
odds.

The start-up stage determines whether the venture has a successful launch. The early
stage is like adolescence. In the early stage the venture may be poised for considerable
growth. If the market opportunity has considerable potential, if the venture is pointed in
the right direction, and if the entrepreneurial team has its act together, then the new venture may be able to experience a high rate of growth. Although their rate of growth may be
enviable to most firms, the high rate of growth associated with early-stage ventures puts
them in a fairly precarious position. Profits may still be on the distant horizon and their
growth frequently exceeds their available cash position.

Additional financing is usually crucial at this stage. Without an infusion of new money,
growth may be slowed and opportunities missed. If growth is not in sync with available
cash, then the venture may self-destruct. This is one of the reasons that high-growth ventures are also considered high-risk ventures. Early-stage ventures can be like a house of
cards. One wrong move and the venture may collapse.

Later Stage (Adulthood)

Most ventures that make it to this stage have the potential to continue growing if they are
in an expanding market and/or pursue additional growth opportunities. A major difference
between the early stage and the later stage is that the entrepreneurial team evolved into a

proven management team. Later-stage ventures are also different because they have established a more solid financial foundation. Although the early-stage venture may have been really scrambling—even bootstrapping—to finance its growth, later-stage ventures usually have an established financial position.

EACH STAGE OF EVOLUTION HAS ITS OWN FINANCING CHALLENGES

Each stage has different financial requirements. Each stage can also be characterized by different risks and rewards for investors. Each type of investor has risk and reward expectations. Entrepreneurs need to recognize which type of investor needs to be sought at each stage of the new venture's evolution.

Seed Stage

This stage usually does not require much money unless the entrepreneur decides to devote his or her full time to exploring the various dimensions of one or more opportunities. The primary need for money at this stage usually goes to covering personal expenses and/or for out-of-pocket research expenses while analyzing the merit and feasibility of pursuing the targeted opportunity.

Investors are rarely sought at this stage because it may last for only a few months and the amount should be manageable for most entrepreneurs. It is also difficult for other people to invest in the business because it may be nothing more than a concept. People are usually reluctant to invest in the entrepreneur's time because there is nothing to salvage if the entrepreneur doesn't proceed with the venture.

Friends and family may lend the entrepreneur money in the form of a personal loan at this stage. Furthermore, it is impossible to invest in the venture until it is formed as a general partnership, limited partnership, a limited liability company, a Sub S corporation, or a general corporation. Occasionally, entrepreneurs who envision starting high-growth ventures will actually start the venture at this stage so they can attract investors.

Start-Up Stage

The start-up stage represents the first major expenditure of funds. This stage requires considerable capital because the firm rarely generates a positive cash flow and/or profitability.

Most new ventures that have significant growth potential, however, are formed as corporations by the time they reach the start-up stage. Although the entrepreneur may be the sole or primary investor for a start-up, the corporate legal form opens the door to seeking outside investors. This chapter will direct its attention to new ventures that are started as general corporations, Sub S corporations, or limited liability companies rather than general partnerships, limited partnerships, or sole proprietorships.

The extent that investors are sought is contingent on the amount of money needed to start the venture and the amount of money the entrepreneur has available to invest in the new venture. If the entrepreneur needs additional funds, then he or she usually seeks funds from friends and family. These funds may be provided in the form of a loan to the business and/or the purchase of stock. Funding for the start-up stage is often not-so-reverently referred to as coming from the *four Fs* (i.e., Founder, founder's Friends, founder's Family, and other Fools).

In some cases, the entrepreneur might be able to attract the interest of one or more angels. Angels are private investors who may not know the entrepreneur prior to being courted as an investor. An in-depth profile of angels will be provided later in the section that profiles the types of investors and in Chapter 11.

Early Stage

The early stage of a venture frequently requires a significant amount of capital. This stage is known as the ramping-up stage. If the start-up stage was successful in demonstrating considerable demand for the firm's product or service, then the early stage is known for committing substantial funds to increasing the scale of the firm's operations. The early stage may also include expanding the firm's geographic reach as well as offering additional products and services. If the demand for the firm's product(s) or service(s) takes off, then it may be positioned to start its climb up the envied hockey-stick growth curve. The ability to climb the hockey stick will be contingent on whether the venture has the capital needed to enable rapid growth. The availability of capital is critical at this stage because most high-growth ventures are not able to finance their growth through operating profits. The firm must either have considerable cash in reserve or be able to attract the capital needed in advance to fund growth.

Although it still may be possible to attract money from the other three Fs at this stage, the early stage frequently relies on professional investors for funding the venture's growth. Professional investors are much more prepared for the fast-moving, yet precarious, nature of early-stage ventures. The venture may also be in a position to garner a commercial loan if the venture's financials look good or if the loan can be secured with tangible assets.

Professional investors can be divided into two groups: angels and venture capitalists. *Angels* seem to be best suited for funding the venture as it enters the early stage; whereas *venture capitalists* may be a viable source of funding if the entrepreneur can demonstrate that the venture can achieve an extraordinary return within a few years. If the venture is not expected to have extraordinary gains and/or expected to have a lucrative liquidity event, then venture capital firms are not likely to express an interest in an emerging venture. A liquidity event can occur if the firm is bought back by the entrepreneur/team, acquired by another firm, or taken public. Each of these events allows venture capitalists to cash out—or gain liquidity on their investment. Venture capital funding will be described in depth in Chapter 12. Most angels are more flexible and more patient than venture capital firms in their expectations for getting a return on their investment.

Later Stage

Later stage ventures tend to be more established. Accordingly, most of the questions about their ability to capitalize on a market opportunity for a profit have been answered. This reduces some of the risk associated with investing in later stage ventures. The uncertainty dust associated with emerging ventures has settled to the point that investors who are looking for a reasonable return for a more moderate risk may find later stage ventures to be more appealing. The lower level of risk explains why banks are attracted to later stage firms more than earlier stage ventures.

If the firm has considerable growth potential and a lucrative liquidity event on the horizon, then venture capitalists may express an interest in investing in the venture. If a substantial amount of money is sought to enable dramatic growth or the acquisition of other firms, then an initial public offering (IPO) may be considered. The merit and process for an IPO are discussed in Chapter 13.

THE NATURE OF THE NEW VENTURE WILL AFFECT ITS ABILITY TO ATTRACT INVESTORS

The entrepreneur's intent and ambitions can have a considerable effect on the ability to attract investors. New ventures may fall into one of the following five categories:

1. *Level-one firms.* These firms are typically lifestyle firms. They are created to provide employment for the entrepreneur and tend to be businesses tied to the entrepreneur's personal interests. These firms may have a number of employees, but entrepreneurs try to keep them to a manageable size so they can stay in their comfort zones. Lifestyle firms rarely experience high levels of growth and/or profitability. Their lack of growth and limited amount of capital needed limits the amount of risk and returns associated with the business. Not surprisingly, entrepreneurs usually have to rely on their own funds to start and operate a lifestyle business.[7]

2. *Level-two firms.* These firms are fairly successful lifestyle firms. Although the entrepreneur may have wanted to enjoy the benefits of having a lifestyle firm, the business opportunity prompted the business to grow to a higher level than expected. Level-two businesses grow, but they do not grow to their potential because the entrepreneur does not want to deal with the corresponding complexities. Most level-two firms do not seek outside investors. They grow through the use of internally generated funds.

3. *Level-three firms.* These firms are like rabbits. They have growth prospects of more than 20 percent annually and five-year revenue projections between $10 million and $50 million. Their founders usually rely on various bootstrapping techniques. They may be funded via personal savings, credit cards, second mortgages, customer advances, vendor credit, and the business's ongoing operations. These firms are the backbone of the U.S. economy. Yet they represent less than 10 percent of the one million start-ups each year in the United States. Their sustained rate of growth and profitability may appeal to angels who are not looking for major near-term liquidity events.[8]

4. *Level-four firms.* These high-growth firms are frequently called gazelles. They are committed to sustaining a high rate of growth. They are also innovative, willing to take risks, and able to change. They have five-year revenue projections in excess of $50 million and expect annual growth rates in excess of 50 percent.[9] These firms are particularly appealing to angels. Research into *Inc.* 500 firms, however, indicates that many of these firms are able to grow without outside investors. Their sustained rate of growth and profitability enable them to fund growth via internal funds and/or debt funding.

5. *Level-five firms.* These firms soar like eagles. They have experienced extraordinary growth and are expected to dominate their markets. Angels may have funded them early on, and they may go through one or two rounds of venture capital funding before going public or being acquired by another firm. These firms are the one in ten

thousand of all start-ups. Some people may have considered them to be high-risk ventures in the beginning, but their rate of growth and level of profitability make them exceptional enterprises and very appealing investments. They are the ones that leave everyone else in their dust and become household names.

PROFILES OF INVESTOR CATEGORIES

Entrepreneurs need to recognize that investors can be classified into a number of categories. Each type of investor has different objectives, expectations, and time horizons. Exhibit 10.1 reflects the sources of funding a venture may seek as it grows. Because there are so many forms of funding, careful attention must be directed to the types of stock to be authorized by the firm when it is formed. If only one type of stock is authorized, then the entrepreneur may have less control over the venture. If two types of stock—voting and nonvoting—are authorized, then the entrepreneur may still be able to maintain control over the venture while raising additional funds. The commitment to dividends and whether they are cumulative—will be paid when the firm makes money—will also affect the ability to attract investors.

Founder Funding

Entrepreneurs are the primary source, if not sole source, of funding for most new ventures. This is particularly true for sole proprietorships. Entrepreneurs who lack sufficient funding frequently seek one or more partners to bridge any funding gap.

Friends and Family Funding

Entrepreneurs frequently look to friends and family for funding the launch and growth of their ventures. Friends and family tend to have very different objectives and criteria from professional investors like angels and venture capitalists. Friends and family tend to be at one end of the helping out versus making significant returns scale. Their primary reason for investing is to help the entrepreneur start or expand his or her business.

Their investment tends to be limited to a few thousand dollars. In most cases, they do not expect much of a return in terms of dividends or stock appreciation. They may not admit it, but their investment may be more of a gift than a true investment. It is not unusual for friends and family to prefer lending the entrepreneur or business money rather than investing in it. Loans can be structured to provide interest payments when the business achieves positive cash flow and/or profitability. Loans also provide friends and family with the opportunity to get their money back at a certain time provided that the business has the ability to pay off the loan.

Two things may help entrepreneurs raise funds. First, if the entrepreneur is able to establish a basis for valuing the stock—whether sales or earnings—that investors' friends

Founder	Friends and Family	Angels SBICs Banks	Venture Capital Firms	Initial Public Offering

EXHIBIT 10.1   POSSIBLE SOURCES OF FUNDING

and family can agree to, then it may be possible for investors to have their shares bought back or redeemed at a later date with a reasonable return at long-term capital gains tax rates. Second, loans can be structured so that they can be converted to stock if the business blossoms. This strategy may provide friends and family with a stream of interest payments with the prospect of capital gains if they choose to convert their loans to stock.

Angel Funding

Angels are playing a more significant role in funding start-ups and emerging ventures than at any time in the past. They contribute more funding to more entrepreneurs than any other source. In many cases, they may be the most important players in our entrepreneurial landscape today.[10] Angels, however, may be the least understood of all sources of funding.

Angels, unlike friends and family, are considered professional investors. Although many angels have a genuine interest in helping entrepreneurs, it should be clear from the beginning that they do not put their money at risk out of the goodness of their hearts. They invest to make a significant return on their investments. They should not be mistaken for a government agency that wants to create jobs. Nor are they like a charity that wants to encourage the spirit of entrepreneurship.

Most angels prefer to operate behind the scenes. Their low profile makes them more difficult to locate and contact than banks and venture capital firms. Recently, some angels have formed or joined angel networks. Angel networks will be discussed in Chapter 11.

Angels can be characterized as being smart, value added, and patient. Angel funding is considered to be smart money when compared to funding from friends and family, for two reasons. First, angels tend to be more diligent before investing in a business than friends and family. Like most people, they may be impressed with a product, service, or entrepreneur, but they judge ventures according to their merit and not their emotional appeal. They are not like the people who invest in brew pubs or minor league baseball teams where ownership may have its privileges. The opportunity to be a part owner of a business is not what drives them. Capital appreciation is the name of the game.

Second, most angels have a business background and possibly an entrepreneurial background. They understand the ups and downs and various challenges associated with running a business. They can handle the roller coaster and often-precarious ride associated with new ventures. The tendency for angels to accept the risk and uncertainty has given them the title of adventure capitalists.

Angels do more than fill the equity gap. They frequently help fill the management gap. Angels are considered value-added investors because they frequently invest their time as well as their money in new ventures. Angels can provide valuable and timely management assistance to an emerging firm. As an investor, an angel frequently goes beyond just being an active member of the venture's board of directors. Angels may be involved directly in the management of the venture on a part-time basis. Some angels actually become full-time members of the management team at a nominal or reduced salary until the business gets to the point where it can afford hiring the talent it needs. Most angels also add value to an emerging venture by providing contacts, critical skills, and advice.

The value-added nature of angel involvement is particularly important because most businesses seeking angel investors have not developed a strong management team. Angels can help the entrepreneur establish the strategies, systems, and contacts needed to take the business to the next level. For example, an angel with a strong financial background may help establish the proper financial planning and accounting systems so the venture operates in a more professional manner until it can hire a full-time controller or chief financial officer to oversee those dimensions. The same would apply if the angel has extensive marketing experience. The angel may help the venture make the transition to a marketing-driven business rather than a sales-driven business. The transition to being a marketing-oriented business is critical if the business is to deliberately explore growth opportunities and offer additional products or services.

Angels are also noteworthy because they provide patient money. Their investment time horizon may be longer than most banks and venture capital firms. Their willingness to commit their funds for more than a few years to a venture allows the business to grow without having to pay off a note from a bank or be pushed into a liquidity event by a venture capital firm. Entrepreneurs usually appreciate the patient nature of angels because, unlike friends and family, angels are less likely to start a conversation with, "How's the business doing—and when can I get my money back?" every time they see them!

TYPES OF ANGELS

Most friends and family who invest in a new venture are not acting as investors. They are not angels. Although they may want to get a fair return on their investment, they buy stock and/or provide a loan because they want to help the entrepreneur. They rarely invest more than $100,000 in their friend's or family member's business.

When Jeff Bezos needed a couple of hundred thousand dollars to get Amazon up and running he sought out a pair of angels—his parents. He noted that his parents invested because they had faith in him, rather than his innovative business concept. His father did not even know what the Internet was. Jeff Bezos believed there was a 70 percent chance his parents would lose their investment. He noted, however, that he thought the odds were actually 80 to 90 percent, but that gave him an additional incentive to make good—he wanted to be able to come home each year for Thanksgiving. Later, when he needed another round of funding for $1 million, Bezos found 20 angels who were willing to invest $50,000 each. It took him nearly four months to secure that round of funding.[11]

Angels can be classified by the amount of money they commit to emerging ventures. The first type of angel usually limits his or her involvement to just one business. The limited commitment may be due to a limited search for investments, a modest personal portfolio, the desire to limit risk, or the limited amount of time available to be involved in a business. This type of angel rarely invests more than a total of $50,000.

The second type of angel limits his or her investment to no more than a few businesses. Their total investment might not exceed $250,000. This type of angel usually is not an investor in a venture capital fund.

The third type of angel is more active, commits more money, possibly more money per business, and demonstrates a higher level of due diligence before investing. These angels play a key role in the development of a large number of emerging firms because they are willing to invest in firms that may not qualify for venture capital funding in the near term or at all. These angels may also be limited partners in one or more venture capital funds. Most angels invest about 10 to 25 percent of their wealth in emerging ventures.

The superangel is the fourth type of angel. Angels are frequently cashed-out entrepreneurs who invest from $250,000 to $500,000 or more per deal to help companies get off the ground.[12] Paul Allen, cofounder of Microsoft, Jim Barksdale, founder of Netscape, and Ross Perot, founder of Electronic Data Systems, have provided substantial investments in numerous emerging ventures.[13]

ANGELS HELP BRIDGE THE EQUITY GAP

Angels are like bridges. They help bridge the equity gap that continues to widen for most new ventures. The equity gap can be characterized as the gap between point *a* and point *b*. Point *a* represents what the entrepreneur can put into the business, what can be raised from friends and family, and what can be raised from various loans or types of credit. Point *b* represents the amount of capital needed to launch and/or grow the new venture to the point that it is able to fund itself through internal operations. Robert Robinson noted that this gap typically falls in the $50,000 to $500,000 range, which is a perfect target for angel investors.[14] Keith Schmidt noted that in certain cases, angels might act as a farm system for venture capital firms who may do a later round of funding.[15]

The equity gap can kill a new venture if it isn't bridged before it can achieve critical mass. Most new ventures face an equity gap in their first or second year. Mark Van Osnabrugge and Robert Robinson noted that even profitable firms growing in excess of 20 percent annually are typically unable to sustain growth with retained earnings and cash flow. The more rapid their growth, the more severe their equity and cash problems.[16]

People standing on the sidelines might say, "Why not slow down and let future cash flow fund growth?" One of the facts of entrepreneurial life is that the marketplace waits for no one. If the firm is not positioned to seize the opportunity, then it will be relegated to watching the opportunity pass by. Entrepreneurs either find a way to bridge the gap or they live a life of regret where they hear themselves say, "If I had the money I could have ..." To them, they either find a way to finance their firm's growth or are left watching it die on the vine.

Unfortunately, the equity gap has widened over the last few years for three reasons. First, it usually takes more capital to establish a market presence and a sustainable competitive advantage. Second, it is more difficult to get funding from venture capital firms. Venture capital firms are more cautious in their funding and they tend to be focused on only a few types of business opportunities. To make matters worse, most venture capital firms have raised the minimum amount for a deal package. Most venture capital firms rarely do a deal for less than a million dollars. The costs for analyzing potential deals and monitoring each firm in their portfolio make it uneconomical for many venture capital funds to make smaller investments.

The selectivity, narrowness of focus, and minimum deal threshold for venture capital firms constitute formidable funding barriers for relatively new firms. Without angels, emerging firms—particularly high-growth ventures—would not be able to grow to their potential. There are trade-offs, but for most firms it is the only way to finance growth.

Angels play a critical role by being the major source of funding because they are willing to invest in emerging firms when banks are reluctant to provide a noncollateralized loan and when venture capital firms are not willing to take the time or to accept the risk associated with a relatively untested venture.

Collectively, angels are the oldest, largest, and most-used source of outside funds for young high-growth firms.[17] The total investment from angels has been estimated anywhere from $20 billion to $50 billion, as compared to the $3 billion to $5 billion per year by venture capital firms. The substantial amount invested is matched by the large number of new ventures that are funded. Angels fund roughly 10 times as many businesses as venture capital firms. Industry data indicate angels fund about 60,000 businesses each year and that venture capital firms fund less than 6,000 firms each year.[18] Mark Van Osnabrugge and Robert J. Robinson indicate the multiple of angel investments to venture capital investments may

be much greater than 10 to 1. They note that angels fund 30 to 40 times more entrepreneurial firms than do venture capital firms.[19]

Angels may be the most flexible source of funding. Banks and venture capital firms
have fairly specific criteria. Most angels are willing to tailor their investment to the specific venture. The flexibility is evident in the stage of the venture they will invest in, the
amount of money they will invest in a new venture, the industries they will invest in, their
investment time horizon, and the terms of the deal.

Angels are also more willing to invest in the earliest stages of a venture. Angels boldly
go where most banks and venture capital firms fear to tread! Although they prefer investing in firms that are in their early-growth stage, they are often willing to invest in ventures
that are in their start-up stage or even seed stage.

Leonard Batterson refers to these angels as *seed investors*. He notes that they are willing
to invest in things that others won't touch and that they are as much motivated by the creative urge of sculpting companies as they are to make large returns. He noted that the seed
investor will give the company an incredible amount of personal time and will guide the
growing company in a nondirective, empathic, constructive style. The amount of time a
seed investor spends is significantly out of proportion to the funds invested because a good
deal of the seed investor's satisfaction comes from growing companies and executives. He
believes that seed investors are one of the best things that can happen to a company.[20]

Angels are in the business of providing risk capital. New ventures face formidable challenges. They offer little performance history, no collateral, illiquidity, uncertain growth
rates, weak access to supply and distribution markets, and low survival rates.[21] Robert
Robinson provides an interesting profile of an angel's willingness to accept risk. According to Robinson, "If you think watching the roller-coaster ride of a start-up as it lurches
from one crisis to the next (with your hard-earned cash irretrievably locked up in its treasury), constantly flirting with running out of money, would keep you awake at night sucking antacids for all you're worth, your risk tolerance is too low. This isn't a character flaw,
it's a kind of sanity the rest of us might want to emulate. Put your money in public stocks,
mutual funds, and municipal bonds, and sleep well at night.[22]

Robinson noted that while angels hope they will be investing in the next Amazon.com,
the reality is that the average rate of return on angel investments is in the 15 to 20 percent
range. This rate may be better than the historic market rate of return for publicly traded
stocks, but angels are taking a much higher risk due to the high level of uncertainty and the
lack of liquidity. He noted that this is about the same rate of return that VCs get, despite
inflated claims and hype from that industry. Robinson also noted that about 40 percent of
all angel investments will have negative overall returns and that only 10 percent or so will
double the original investment.[23]

WHO ARE ANGEL INVESTORS?

It is ironic that one of the most important sources of funding for a new venture is so hard to
identify. Angels have been around for some time, but they have such a broad range of
backgrounds, expectations, and levels of involvement that it is difficult to specifically
identify them. Their experience in investing in emerging ventures also varies. Some are
virgin angels who have just entered the angel game. Other angels are veteran angels. Some
angels prefer to go it alone while others team up with other angels or work through an
angel syndicate. Some angels are lead angels. They help orchestrate the investment with
other angels in an emerging firm. Other angels are follower angels. They let the lead angel

put the package together and they choose to co-invest if the package meets their expectations. Angels can be highly involved, somewhat involved, or just investors in the emerging venture. Some angels prefer to invest in one particular type of business. Other angels are willing to invest in a variety of areas. Some angels are generalists who can help the entrepreneur see the forest through the trees. Other angels are functional specialists who provide assistance in more specific areas.

Entrepreneurs should note four particular characteristics about angels. They are professional, reasonably wealthy, tend to become actively involved in the firms they invest in, and rather elusive. Although there are occasions when they may actually be a friend or relative of an entrepreneur, they view their funding first and foremost as a serious investment where they expect to get a return to justify the associated risk. Angels tend to have enough wealth so they can afford to roll the dice and invest in a new venture.

SEC Rules Relating to Angel Investors

Entrepreneurs need to recognize that any strategy for raising equity is subject to covenants established by the Securities and Exchange Commission (SEC). The SEC differentiates between two categories of investors. The differentiation is based on the investor's income and net worth.

The first category is called *accredited* or *qualified investors*. They represent a small part of the population. According to the SEC's Rule 501, an accredited investor is any natural person whose individual net worth or joint income with that person's spouse exceeds $1 million or who had an individual income in excess of $200,000 in each of the two most recent years or joint income with that person's spouse in excess of $300,000 in each of those years and has a reasonable expectation of reaching the same income in the current year. The SEC's definition is based on the assumption that these people have enough money or income that they can afford to take the risk—and can afford to lose their investment if the business fails.[24]

The second category is composed of people who do not meet Rule 501's income or net worth criteria. People do not *have* to meet either of the SEC's criteria to be angels, especially if they are investing a relatively small part of their income or net worth. A person may be considered a sophisticated investor if he or she considers himself or herself to be very knowledgeable in business affairs. The Center for Venture Research noted that the average angel is a 47-year-old, college-educated male, who has been self-employed with an annual income of $90,000 and a net worth of $750,000. The Center's research also indicated that the average angel invests $37,000 per venture.[25]

The SEC limits the activities that entrepreneurs are allowed to do in soliciting equity funding from this group. It usually places a limit on the number of people who can be sought, the way funds can be solicited, and the amount that can be sought from John or Jane Doe. Entrepreneurs are in a safer position from a legal perspective if they deal with people who meet the SEC's criteria. In any event, entrepreneurs should seek legal counsel if they will be seeking investors.

Degree Of Involvement

Most angels are not passive investors. They prefer some degree of involvement in the direction or management of their investments. Angels can play a critical value-added role in an emerging venture. They contribute their time and brains to the venture. Their involvement may range from serving on the board of directors all the way to being involved in daily operations. Their involvement can be valuable, because most emerging ventures cannot afford consultants or hire full-time professional managers.

Each angel has his or her own criteria and foibles because they are individuals. Almost all want a board position and possibly a consulting role. Some want monthly updates, others want weekly updates.[26] About 25 percent of angels are involved in running a venture on a daily basis. The degree of involvement tends to be tied to the venture's stage of development. The younger the venture and the less complete the management team, the greater the involvement by the angel in the venture. The number of investments also affects the degree of angel involvement. If the angel has numerous investments, then that will limit the time that can be devoted to each firm. In any event, there is a tendency for angels to focus their attention on specific strategic or operational issues.

REALITY CHECK

It would appear that entrepreneurs welcome the assistance that can be provided by angels. Stephanie Gruner noted, "Ask cash-strapped entrepreneurs what their companies need and they'll likely speak wistfully of angel investors. Translation: they're hoping some wealthy individual will invest money in their companies without raising a lot of questions."[27] Some entrepreneurs prefer a more passive angel. They want the money but not the meddling. Entrepreneurs need to step back and make sure that the preference for a passive angel is not an unwillingness to take advice. The unwillingness to seek and accept advice will be crucial in the development of a management team.

Entrepreneurs need to determine the type of angel that will provide the most value to the venture. Many angels, especially cashed-out entrepreneurs, look forward to the excitement associated with emerging ventures. As someone once observed, "You can't play golf every day of the week!" Brian Bernier noted, "Angel investors want to be part of the excitement and adrenaline rush that accompanies the push to bring a new product to market."[28] The opportunity to be a mentor can be a form of vicarious entrepreneurship for some angels. It is the best of both worlds for them. They get to share their wisdom, but they don't have to work the 70-hour weeks.

Angels Can Leverage Their Positions

Angels may also help the venture secure additional debt and equity financing. If the angel is a highly respected member of the business community either as a veteran executive or successful entrepreneur, then his or her reputation may bring additional credibility to the emerging venture. The angel's equity investment or guarantee may also provide the funds needed to secure a bank loan. For example, the angel who helped Apple Computer get off the ground in 1977 invested $91,000 and guaranteed another $250,000 in credit lines.[29]

One study found that 9 out of 10 investors provide personal loans or loan guarantees to the firms they invest in. This is significant for cash-strapped firms because on the average, the angel's commitment increases the venture's available capital by 57 percent.[30]

Beware Of Strangers Bearing Gifts

Although an angel can be a real asset to an emerging venture, not all angels are so angelic. Some angels can actually be a liability. Entrepreneurs should also beware of the many potential drawbacks associated with inviting an angel into the firm. The following points should serve as reality checks.

The Distinction Between Helping and Micromanaging. The angel's role in the direction and operations of the firm needs to be clear. There is a big difference between the angel being a valuable mentor providing timely advice and unwelcome meddling. It also needs to be clear that the angel is there in an advisory capacity and that the entrepreneur is still in charge.

Having the Metal and Patience to Go the Distance. A number of people who have a high level of income or net worth have entered the angel game in the last few years. People without extensive business experience like doctors and attorneys rarely make good angels. They usually have difficulty with the precarious nature of new ventures. Experienced entrepreneurs tend to be good angels. The phrase, "It takes one to know one," may apply because veteran entrepreneurs know that emerging ventures have more ups and downs than a roller coaster. They also are in a better position to anticipate and deal with the next challenge.

Adding Value. The process of seeking an angel raises the question, "Which is worse, an angel that knows little about the nature of the business or an angel that insists on providing advice and provides wrong advice?" The entrepreneur needs to be sure the angel's knowledge, experience, and contacts are really value added. If the angel's experience and knowledge are not in sync with the emerging venture's needs or are out of date, then the angel's recommendations could actually hurt the venture. How the angel may have done it is not the issue; what needs to be done in the here and now is the issue. The same applies to the angel's contacts. The angel will be of value only to the extent he or she can open the doors that are critical to the venture's success. Entrepreneurs need to beware of good old boys who talk a good story but cannot deliver the goods. The entrepreneur and emerging venture will be judged by the company they keep. They also need to make sure the angel's reputation is an asset.

Wearing or Not Wearing the Halo. Entrepreneurs need to make sure the prospective angel is not the devil in disguise. First-time entrepreneurs are often too trusting of people who want to provide money and assistance. Entrepreneurs should make every effort to be sure the angel is committed to helping the venture rather than looking for a way of taking control of it. Selecting the right angel and structuring the deal in the proper manner can reduce the risk of a hostile takeover by an angel who lacks scruples.

Expectation of Performance. When angels invest in emerging ventures they do not consider their efforts to be philanthropic. The time and money they invest in an emerging venture is not a gift. The best angels approach their role in a very professional manner and hold the entrepreneur accountable for performance.

It should be noted that angels invest in an *offensive* rather than *defensive* manner. Angels rarely invest when the firm is in trouble. They bridge equity gaps that are associated with growth. They should not be viewed as the Cavalry that rides in to rescue a failing firm. Few angels look for turnaround situations, and those that do usually seek ownership and management control of the firm.

HOW ARE ANGELS DIFFERENT FROM VENTURE CAPITALISTS?

Entrepreneurs need to recognize the differences between *angels* and *venture capitalists*. The old saying, "For everything there is a season," applies to the difference between these two sources of funding. The differences may affect whether venture capital is sought instead of or in addition to angel investors. The differences also affect when venture capital may be sought.

The differences between angels and venture capitalists are noticeable, particularly when it comes to the stage of the emerging venture, the breadth of investments, amount of money per investment, the number of investments, the extent they tie into other vehicles of funding, the length of time for the investment, the propensity to do additional rounds of funding, the amount of due diligence, the criteria used in analyzing an investment, the amount of time committed to helping the emerging venture, the conditions placed on the operations of the emerging venture, and the exit expectations. Mark Van Osnabrugge and Robert J. Robinson developed Exhibit 10.2 to profile the differences in angels and venture capitalists.[31]

Stage of the Emerging Venture

Angels tend to invest in ventures that are smaller and in earlier stages of development. Angels provide management assistance and contacts when the emerging venture needs that type of assistance the most. Venture capital firms rarely fund true start-ups. Most venture capital firms target businesses that are positioned to take off, but need help in generating hockey-stick growth. Research indicates that they invest in less than 300 start-ups each year and that they have a one-third to two-thirds ratio for investing in early stage versus more mature ventures.[32]

Entrepreneurial Experience

Angels have more entrepreneurial experience than venture capitalists. Research indicates that 75 to 83 percent of angels have start-up experience and that only one-third of venture capitalists have start-up experience.[33] Angels with start-up experience have more empathy for the highs and lows of entrepreneurship. They also have valuable street smarts that are not found with some of the MBAs who are part of venture capital firms.

Specific Nature of Firms Considered

Most angels tend to invest in industries they are familiar with, but they may consider other industries if a venture has merit. Industry experience is an important factor for two reasons.

Angels and VCs rank their priorities in a deal very differently.

Business Attributes	ANGEL	VC
Investor's possible involvement	1	3
Investor's strengths filling gaps in business	2	5
Local venture (geographically close)	3	6
Potential exit routes (liquidity)	4	1
Investor's understanding of business or industry	4	2
Presence of (potential) co-investors	6	4

EXHIBIT 10.2 WHAT'S IMPORTANT?
Source: Angel Investing, by Mark Van Osnabrugge and Robert J. Robinson. Copyright © 2000, Jossey-Bass, p. 135. This material is used by permission of John Wiley & Sons, Inc.

First, it makes it easier for the angel to analyze the venture. In this case, familiarity does *not* breed contempt. It allows the angel to size up the merit of the investment quickly. Brokerage houses are famous for rating a firm as speculative if its brokers have little information about the nature of the industry and that particular firm. Angels are the same way. The less knowledge they have of an industry, the more they will see investing in a new venture as risky. Second, the experience may be very useful after the investment is made in terms of the management assistance and contacts in the field.

If the angel has general management experience and is a quick study, then he or she may help the entrepreneur develop an effective business strategy and establish sound business practices for the venture. Angels with specific industry experience are in a better position to hit the ground running and provide substantive and specific assistance. It should be noted, however, that when taken as a whole, angels make investments in virtually all industry sectors and they are not averse to funding technology. Their major concern is investing in ventures with high-growth potential.[34]

Most large venture capital firms invest in a particular industry. They also focus primarily on business-to-business firms and high-technology firms. Smaller venture capital firms may consider a broader range of firms but they still have a tendency to focus on a common theme. Angels are more willing to invest in various fields. As long as the venture has the potential for high growth and high returns, angels may be interested. Angels look at the firm, the market, and then the industry.[35]

Although the industry focus may give a venture capital firm additional insights and investment savvy, it also causes *myopia* or *tunnel vision*. Angels may be more willing to look at smaller markets and untried technology. Bob Glorioso, president and CEO of Marathon Technologies Corporation, observed, "VCs generally don't see the hidden markets, the diamonds in the rough."[36] Brian Bernier, a principal in StoneGate partners, elaborated on the more conservative approach that the venture capital firms employ. According to Bernier, "Venture capital firms tend to be 'formula' investors. … Frankly, the VCs don't always understand the mechanics of early-stage companies."[37] Venture capital firms are more inclined to follow major industry trends in order to satisfy their investors.[38] Professional angels, especially those working in a network or established angel organization, may be more willing to dig a little deeper, to root out the opportunities that may not be readily visible to venture capital firms. The venture capital firm's due diligence may rule out many of the companies that are ideal for angel involvement.[39]

Amount of Money per Investment

Although angels may invest just a fraction of the amount of the typical venture capital deal, the role they play becomes more important as the equity gap continues to get wider. Kenneth Wolfe noted that the angel market fills a void created by the very success of the venture capital market. Angels prefer to make smaller investments than venture capital firms. Research by Mark Van Osnabrugge and Robert J. Robinson indicated that business angels provide 84 percent of rounds under $250,000. They also note that for deals under $500,000 angels provide four times as much money as VCs.[40] Most venture capital firms are unwilling to invest less than $250,000 or even $500,000 in an emerging business. Brian Bernier noted, "Many venture firms won't even look at a business that needs less than $2 million."[41]

Jeffery Sohl, a professor who heads the University of New Hampshire's Center for Venture Research, noted that the space between the ceiling on angels' deal sizes and the floor for venture capital investment widens every year. In 1994, the gap was between $100,000 (the average angel investment) and $2.7 million (the average VC investment).[42] By 2003, the average venture capital investment was over $6.5 million. The increase in the average investment reflects the widening gap caused as venture capital firms raise the minimum they set for investing. Hopefully angels and angel groups will increase the amount they will invest per firm so emerging ventures can get the funding they need for continued growth.

Number of Investments

Angels can choose what percent of their portfolio to invest. They can choose not to invest. They are also free to explore other investment vehicles. If the stock market is booming, then they may commit a significant percent of their portfolio to it. Venture capital funds, however, strive to be fully invested.

Length of Time for Investment and Concern with Liquidity Event

Angels are more concerned with helping the firm grow than with expediting a liquidity event. Venture capital firms must focus their attention on a firm's liquidity event. They must provide a cash return to their investors, and the only way they can do that is through a liquidity event during the limited duration of their fund.

Follow-Up Funding

Angels tend to make a one-time investment in a firm; venture capital firms may do more than one round of funding. Venture capital firms have more funds available and may find it in their best interests to provide additional rounds of funding either to help prop up an ailing business, to help it get to a liquidity event, or to capitalize on a lucrative opportunity.

Aggressiveness and Breadth of Search

Most angels invest when the time and the opportunity are right. Few angels are involved in a continuous search for investment opportunities. Angels are free to choose whether they invest, when they invest, and how much they invest per deal and all together. Venture capital firms need to invest the portfolio within a certain interval. The clock is always ticking. If they are not fully invested, then their money is not generating a sufficient return. Venture capital firms are in an awkward situation today because they have more money than deals that meet their risk/return expectations.

Most angels do not pursue investments in an aggressive manner. It has been observed that most angels tend to rely on random discovery more than deliberate search.[43] Although angels may explore investment opportunities on a periodic basis, venture capitalists' radar screens are always scanning the environment for worthy deals. They have full-time staffs that seek and review potential investments.

Geographic Availability of Funding

Angel funding is available in more locations than venture capital funding. Angels can be found in every metropolitan area in the United States. They also live in smaller communities. As noted earlier, millions of households in the United States have a net worth of more than $1 million. Venture capital firms are concentrated in less than a dozen major metropolitan areas including Boston, Austin, Silicon Valley, and the Research Triangle Park in North Carolina.

If the angel is to be an active investor, then he or she may limit his or her consideration to firms within an hour commute. Venture capital firms show a similar preference for investing in firms that are in close proximity to their offices. Although venture capital firms may be more willing to invest in emerging ventures that are located elsewhere, their desire to meet with the entrepreneurial team and to view and review operations in a face-to-face manner means that venture capital firms place a premium on firms in their neighborhood.

Amount of Due Diligence

Angels are notorious for not doing extensive due diligence because firms in their formative stages do not have much financial information or much of a track record. Angels rely more on their impressions of the entrepreneur, the entrepreneur's game plan, and the market opportunity. Angels might want to review the venture's business plan, but they also recognize that the financial projections are just that—they are projections based on very little hard data. Angels are more willing to invest in a venture if they feel it is a diamond in the rough. There is a growing trend, however, for angels to be more deliberate in the due diligence process.

Angels are more flexible in their financial decisions than venture capital firms. Angels have longer time horizons, shorter investment processes, and lower targeted rates of return.[44] The average amount of an investment frequently places a limit on the amount of money angels are willing to spend for professional services in the due diligence process. This benefits entrepreneurs because it means angels don't have the front-end fees associated with investigating angel investments. This makes it easier for angels to look at potential investments. It also enables them to close a deal quicker than venture capital firms.

Venture capital firms are far more deliberate. They want to make sure the venture has the potential to be lucrative. Venture capital firms spend considerable time analyzing a potential investment. They usually have a member of their staff do a preliminary analysis. If the venture has merit, then a committee will review the potential investment from many perspectives.

Criteria Used in Analyzing an Investment

Angels are less risk averse and have lower expectations than venture capital firms.[45] Although angels may not be as deliberate in their analysis of potential investments as venture capital firms, they do expect the venture's return to meet or exceed the corresponding risks associated with angel investing. The expected return is closely tied to the relative stage of the venture. Robert Hisrich and Michael Peters profile the varying levels of expectations in Exhibit 10.3.[46]

Stage	Expectation
Start-ups	5-year capital gain of 10 times
Firms under 1 year old	5-year capital gain of 6 times
Firms 1 to 5 years old	5-year capital gain of 5 times
Firms more than 5 years old	5-year capital gain of 3 times

EXHIBIT 10.3 RISK-RETURN EXPECTATIONS

Amount of Time Committed to Helping the Emerging Venture

Almost all angels and venture capital firms expect to have representation on the board of directors. Angels usually commit more time to assisting the emerging venture in its early stages when the management team has not been formed. Venture capital firms tend to invest in later-stage firms when they have more a established management team. Angels tend to help the entrepreneur position the firm so that it is pointed in the right direction, it has the right systems, and that it is properly rolling out its product/service. Venture capital firms tend to help the firm ramp up its operations by opening doors for the entrepreneur.

Conditions Placed on the Operations of the Emerging Venture

Angels may expect to get certain assurances about the role they will play in the management of the emerging firm, but the restrictions tend to be limited. Venture capital firms place far more restrictions on an emerging firm. The term sheet provided by the venture capital firm tends to cover numerous areas and contains various covenants.

CONCLUSION: ANGELS FILL A CRITICAL VOID

Angels play a critical role in the development and growth of emerging ventures. Their funding, flexibility and value-added management assistance can provide a timely boost. Few emerging ventures have the track record and collateral to qualify for a loan from a bank nor do they meet the lofty expectations of venture capital firms. The growth rates demanded by venture capital firms are normally way beyond what most businesses can realistically achieve. Angels are a much more suitable and realistic funding option.[47] They are more willing to accept the risks associated with earlier stage ventures and are more willing to invest in a broader range of businesses. The next chapter is devoted to courting angels and getting funding from them.

Money, it turned out, was exactly like sex. You thought of nothing else if you didn't have it and thought of other things if you did.[48]

—James Baldwin
American novelist

ENDNOTES

1. Joseph and Jimmie Boyett, *The Guru Guide to Entrepreneurship* (New York: John Wiley & Sons, 2001), p. 127.

2. W. Keith Schilit, *Dream Makers and Deal Makers: Inside the Venture Capital Industry* (Englewood Cliffs, NJ: Prentice Hall, 1991), p. 61.

3. Ibid., p. 42.

4. Stephanie Gruner, "Conversations with Angels," *Inc.*, October 1996, p. 86.

5. Jeffery Sohl, "Fast Tracking," Angel Advisor website, January/February 2001, pp. 79–80.

6. Scott Smith, "Grounds for Success," *Entrepreneur,* May 1998, p. 126.

7. Mark Van Osnabrugge and Robert J. Robinson, *Angel Investing* (San Francisco: Jossey-Bass, 2000), p. 20. Copyright © 2000, Jossey Bass. This material is used by permission of John Wiley & Sons, Inc.

8. Ibid., p. 20–22.

9. Ibid., p. 20.

10. Ibid., p. xi.

11. C-SPAN, "American Perspectives," *www.c-span.org*, May 19, 2001.

12. Paul Brown, "Rome's Burning. The Nasdaq's Falling. Dot-Coms Are Still Dying," *Inc.,* October 2001, p. 76.

13. Van Osnabrugge and Robinson, *Angel Investing*, p. 43.

14. Robert Robinson, "Excelling: Wings of Desire," Angel Advisor website, January/February, pp. 42–47.

15. Schilit, *Dream Makers and Deal Makers: Inside the Venture Capital Industry*, p. 41.

16. Van Osnabrugge and Robinson, *Angel Investing,* p. 11.

17. Schilit, *Dream Makers and Deal Makers: Inside the Venture Capital Industry,* p. 40.

18. Robinson, "Excelling: Wings of Desire," pp. 42–47.

19. Van Osnabrugge and Robinson, *Angel Investing*, p. 69.

20. Leonard A. Batterson, *Raising Venture Capital and the Entrepreneur* (Englewood Cliffs, NJ: Prentice Hall, 1986), p. 47.

21. Van Osnabrugge and Robinson, *Angel Investing,* p. 34.

22. Robinson, "Excelling: Wings of Desire," pp. 42–47.

23. Ibid.

24. Loren Fox, "Heaven Can't Wait," *Business 2.0,* March 20, 2001, p. 1.

25. Stephanie Gruner, "Conversations with Angels," *Inc.,* October 1996, p. 86.

26. "What Does an Angel Investor Expect?" entrepreneurs at *www.about.com*.

27. Gruner, "Conversations with Angels," p. 86.

28. Wolfe, "StoneGate Guides Angels Where VCs Fear to Tread," p. 20.

29. Van Osnabrugge and Robinson, *Angel Investing*, p. 66.

30. Gruner, "Conversations with Angels," p. 86.

31. Van Osnabrugge and Robinson, *Angel Investing*, p. 135.

32. Ibid., p. 49.

33. Ibid., p. 108.

34. Ibid., p. 65.

35. David Newton, *www.entrepreneur.com*.

36. Wolfe, "StoneGate Guides Angels Where VCs Fear to Tread," p. 20.

37. Ibid.

38. Ibid.

39. Ibid.

40. Van Osnabrugge and Robinson, *Angel Investing,* p. 41.

41. Wolfe, "StoneGate Guides Angels Where VCs Fear to Tread," p. 20.

42. Sohl, "Fast Tracking," pp. 79 & 80.

43. Van Osnabrugge and Robinson, *Angel Investing,* p. 46.

44. Ibid., p. 4.

45. Ibid., p. 41.

46. Robert D. Hisrich and Michael P. Peters, *Entrepreneurship* (New York: McGraw-Hill, 1998), p. 390.

47. Van Osnabrugge and Robinson, *Angel Investing,* p. 52.

48. Louis E. Boone, *Quotable Business* (New York: Random House, 1992), p. 161.

11

GOING THE ANGEL ROUTE

May the angels be with you.[1]

—Paul Brown
Editor-in-Chief of DirectAdvice.com

In a perfect world, either the entrepreneur would be able to finance the whole venture with other people's money, but maintain 100 percent of the ownership, or the entrepreneur would be able to finance the venture through every stage of its development. We do not live in a perfect world. Most new high-growth ventures must attract investors. Entrepreneurs need to recognize that investors will want a piece of the action and they will also want to have a say in the future direction of the business. Angel investors may represent a *reasonable* source of funding. Angels provide funding and additional forms of assistance at a critical time for an emerging venture. They also allow the entrepreneur to keep majority ownership and to run the business.

Going the angel route has its benefits and its drawbacks. There may have been a time when an entrepreneur with a good concept could get angel funding with a brief presentation and a handshake. Times have changed. What used to be a very informal meeting of the minds has evolved into a more deliberate process for entrepreneurs and angels.

Although their due diligence process may not be rigorous or their expectations as high in terms of capital appreciation and cashing out through a lucrative liquidity event as venture capital firms, angels are far more sophisticated than in the past. This chapter provides numerous insights into the processes, criteria, and nuances entrepreneurs should know if they might be seeking angel funding at some point in time.

HOW DO YOU FIND ANGEL INVESTORS?

Angels may be the most elusive source of equity financing. Although it might be more difficult to secure venture capital funding, at least venture capital firms can be identified and contacted either directly or indirectly. Most angels operate behind the scenes and are not that readily accessible to entrepreneurs seeking funding. Angels are not listed in the yellow pages, nor are most angels identified in published guides.

REALITY CHECK

Most angels prefer to operate on their own. Their desire to be selective and not be besieged by numerous overtures by entrepreneurs keeps them in the shadows. Although they are interested in investing, they want to be the ones who decide if the time and the investment are right. They are not like venture capitalists who are constantly scanning the horizon for high-growth prospects and who have to do deals during the fixed duration of their funds. Although banks must lend money to survive and venture capital firms must do deals to provide their investors with a worthwhile return, angels can abstain. Angels are only accountable to themselves, and they tend to invest only when something comes along that gets their attention.

REALITY CHECK

Entrepreneurs who are seeking one or more angels need to learn the rules of the angel game. The game's most fundamental rule is, "You have a higher probability of getting an angel's attention if you don't try to contact the angel directly." Angels usually work through a network of personal and/or professional contacts. Entrepreneurs have a much better chance of getting the attention of an angel if a person trusted by the angel refers them to the angel. The same applies to seeking venture capital funding.

Entrepreneurs who are not well connected to the angel/investor community should make a deliberate effort to meet potential investors or the people who are in a position to provide referrals to angels. Attorneys, bankers, investment bankers, consultants, accountants, and entrepreneurs are often the best source of referrals.

REALITY CHECK

Although referrals frequently come to angels via bankers, attorneys, and accountants, veteran angels recognize that these people have vested interests in helping entrepreneurs who are their clients. Angels, therefore, are more likely to place a premium on referrals made by entrepreneurs they know personally, whom they respect—and who might also be interested in investing in that venture.

The value of networks and one's reputation cannot be overemphasized. Entrepreneurs are judged by the company they keep. If they are known and respected by people in the business community, then they enter the angel-seeking process with valuable goodwill. Establishing visibility and credibility will pay big dividends when seeking investors because it will speed the process and limit the need for cold calls and referrals. Entrepreneurs should tactfully create a situation or *buzz* where angels seek them out.

Professional associations and nonprofit organizations may be good vehicles for meeting people who know the angels as well as angels. Most metropolitan areas have entrepreneurial associations or councils that sponsor events that are designed to bring entrepreneurs, service providers, banks, and potential investors together.

Entrepreneurs who have their acts together may explore the possibility of presenting their venture to a group of angels rather than prospecting on an angel-to-angel basis. There has been an effort by various people and groups in the last few years to establish *angel networks*. Angel networks come in all shapes and sizes. Some networks are fairly large and structured. Others are merely informal networks that are nothing more than a list of contacts.

Most networks have three things in common. First, they are designed to provide a vehicle for entrepreneurs to meet potential angel investors. Second, they are designed to provide a vehicle for angels to learn about potential investments. Third, they are designed to provide a vehicle for angels to meet other angels. The angel-to-angel network may serve as the basis for two or more angels to invest in an emerging venture. Here again, referrals may play a key role in getting funding. According to David Amis and Harold Stevenson, most angel networks won't take cold calls, so entrepreneurs will need to get a referral. They note being invited to present one's business to an angel network may provide substantial exposure in a very short period of time. The invitation represents a unique opportunity to present your company to anywhere from 10 to 110 angels in one throw.[2] Angel networks are discussed later in this chapter in the section that addresses seeking investors via intermediaries, networks, and electronic listing services.

TIMING PLAYS AN IMPORTANT ROLE WHEN SEEKING FUNDING

As the saying goes, "Timing is everything." Timing may not be everything, but it plays a critical role in raising money. Getting angel funding is not like going to get a cheeseburger through the drive-up window. It takes preparation, time, and finesse. Relationships and trust take time to develop. Entrepreneurs need to recognize the need for having sufficient lead time when seeking angel funding. They should make every effort to meet and develop relationships with potential angels well before they will need to actively seek funding. If the angel has met the entrepreneur before the time the entrepreneur seeks funding, then there is a higher probability that the angel will be more receptive to the referral or a direct contact by the entrepreneur.

The value of establishing a network of contacts early was demonstrated when Tom Scott and Tom First, who founded Nantucket Nectors, were at the point where their cash position was so low that they had to sleep in their car. They contacted Michael Egan, who started Alamo Rent-a-Car, to see if he would be interested in investing in their firm. They had met Egan when they had cleaned the deck of his yacht years earlier. Their prior contact paid off. He invested $500,000 for half interest in Nantucket Nectors at a very critical time.[3] Michael Egan later provided $1.5 million when they needed additional capital.

Cliff Ennico, co-host of *Money Hunt* on PBS, provides an interesting avenue for contacting potential investors. He suggests putting together a list of people you could ask to serve on your board of advisors, then sending them your business plan. He indicates that some of these people might want to invest in your firm. He also suggests meeting entrepreneurs who have sold their businesses. They frequently have money to invest and are looking for a constructive use of their time.

Timing Is a Catch 22

There are two rules of thumb when it comes to seeking an angel. Unfortunately, they seem to contradict each other. The first rule of thumb is, "Try to postpone outside investment as long as possible because funding costs less in later stages than in the earlier stages." The second rule of thumb is, "Bring the angel on board as soon as possible to capitalize on his or her advice and contacts."

Tom Weldon, principal founder of Novoste Corporation, emphasized the first rule when he stated, "Most entrepreneurs don't want to let outside investors in on the first round. They fear it will dilute them too much.... The key is to get your company up and running to a level that can attract outside investors when additional capital is needed."[4]

Robert Hisrich and Michael Peters noted that an entrepreneur should strive to maintain as large an ownership as possible, particularly in the start-up financing stage. As the business develops, more funds will probably be needed, which will require more ownership to be relinquished. Every entrepreneur should give up each piece of the venture only after every other alternative has been explored. Not only must alternative suppliers of these resources be identified but also their needs and desires. By understanding their needs, the entrepreneur can structure a deal that enables the resources to be acquired at the lowest possible cost and loss of control.[5]

The second rule of thumb that encourages entrepreneurs to bring an angel on board as soon as possible has an upside and a downside. On the upside, the angel may be able to provide a real boost at a critical stage of the venture by providing advice, contacts, and funding that the entrepreneur could not get by himself or herself. On the downside, angels usually prefer to provide start-up and early-stage funding for self-serving reasons. They get more bang for their buck. As a venture matures and develops a track record, its valuation goes up, which means its stock is worth more and the angel has to put up more money per share of stock. Angels may be less receptive to investing in a later-stage venture for this reason.

The angel's management experience and contacts may also be less critical as the venture matures. This is the "Catch 22" part of the equation. If the angel only wants to be involved as an investor, then the stage of evolution may not be as much of an issue. If the entrepreneur is merely looking for the angel to be an investor rather than a value-added member of the organization, then the entrepreneur should wait as long as possible, as long as it doesn't slow the evolution of the venture.

If the angel wants to be actively involved and the venture needs his or her value-added skills and contacts, then the angel could be one of the best things that could happen to a new venture. Angels can give the venture a crucial boost by finding people to fill key positions in the management team and by contacting suppliers and distributors.

Many angels are in a position to provide the wisdom and experience that most entrepreneurs lack. Many angels have made their relative fortunes in other businesses where they had an active role in managing and directing. They typically understand business risks, competition in the proposed venture's industry, and the kind of structure necessary to ensure operational success.[6] Angels who have been successful entrepreneurs and/or executives can help first-time entrepreneurs. Their *tolerance for the turbulence* and recognition of the need for management systems will make rapid growth more likely and less intimidating.

Leonard Batterson noted that some angels are as much motivated by the creative urge of sculpting companies as they are with making large returns. He also noted that the amount of time is significantly out of proportion to the funds that the angel has invested because a good deal of the angel's satisfaction comes from growing companies and executives.[7] It would be a shame if the entrepreneur's desire to avoid dilution prompts him or her to wait too long in seeking a value-added investor.

Someone once defined luck as "what happens when preparation meets opportunity." Entrepreneurs should view seeking funding in the same way they seek to capitalize on a market opportunity. Securing angel funding is like trying to capitalize on the window of opportunity. If the entrepreneur seeks funding too early, then he or she will have to wait, get less than what is needed, get it at a higher price, or will have to give up more control. If the firm is painfully undercapitalized and appears to be desperate, then the angels have the upper hand.

Timing plays a key role when seeking funding. Entrepreneurs need to seek funding at just the right time. If the entrepreneur seeks funding when the market may have already lost its luster or when the venture no longer has the potential for hockey-stick growth, then angels may not see a compelling reason to invest.

REALITY CHECK

Waiting until the last possible moment, or, as they say in combat, following the advice of "Do not fire until you see the whites of their eyes.," sounds good in theory, but it may not be advisable. Life is full of surprises, and few things go as planned. In business, as in combat, *just-in-time* strategies only work if the system is very predictable and it is highly choreographed by all parties. Emerging ventures live a precarious enough existence; attempting to do just-in-time funding falls somewhere in between dumb and stupid on the entrepreneurial intelligence scale. Start early, have a buffer of time and money, be prepared, and expect the unexpected.

This chapter started off with a characterization of a perfect world for entrepreneurs when it comes to funding. It should be clear by now that being undercapitalized raises the venture's cost of capital. The best way to prevent or minimize ownership dilution is for the entrepreneur to make every effort to start the venture with sufficient capital. Timing incorporates the *golden rule*—whoever controls the gold rules! If the entrepreneur can delay the need for angel funding until he or she is in a position to negotiate from a position of relative strength, then the entrepreneur may be able to have his or her cake and eat it, too.

Having sufficient capital from the beginning to go the extra mile will not only allow the venture to handle setbacks and surprises in stride; it will also put the entrepreneur in a position to be selective, have a lower cost of capital, higher valuation, and less dilution of ownership. Having the time to develop the venture to the point where the entrepreneur can show that a management team is in place will also enhance the value of the business.

Entrepreneurs need to time the funding so that it occurs when there is a legitimate and beneficial need rather than out of desperation. Rapid-growth ventures almost always need additional funding because demands of growth exceed the venture's cash flow. If the funding will serve as a catalyst to growth, then additional funding may be possible. If funding is sought in an attempt to salvage a dying venture or to compensate for the lack of management acumen, then seeking funding will be an exercise in futility.

Keith Schilit noted that it is always easiest to obtain funds when you do not need the funds; investors seem to be abundant when you are in sound financial position, capable of managing your growth. They tend to be unavailable when your funds are scarce.[8] The timing issue can be viewed as a battle between absolute value and relative ownership/control. Entrepreneurs must accept the fact that unless they have an unlimited amount of personal funding they will have to give up some of the ownership of the firm. They need to step back and determine which is the lesser of the two evils: to give up a piece of the equity or to slow the venture's growth to the point where its operations will be able to fund growth.

Entrepreneurs who seek funding at the most opportune time and are willing to give up one or more pieces of a pie usually end up with far more pie than entrepreneurs who are unwilling to give up a piece of the pie. Schilit noted, "As your company grows, its value continually increases, thereby making it an attractive investment opportunity. At the same time, however, your personal equity stake is increasing, thereby tempting you to delay giving up part of your equity until a later time when it will be worth even more. Of course, as your business grows, it will continually require additional capital, thereby diluting your equity position in the company."[9]

Entrepreneurs Need to Plan Ahead

David Evanson and Art Beroff offer entrepreneurs two noteworthy insights. The first tip is that entrepreneurs should not take angels for granted. They note that investors can wait forever or look at other deals; it's the entrepreneurs who'll have to move first, and take any worthwhile angel investment they can get in the game.[10] Angels don't have to invest; there is no real sense of urgency for them. Entrepreneurs need to seek funding at a point in the venture's evolution where the angel's desire to invest is greater than their urgency and need.

They also note the need to start early and be prepared to commit considerable time to the search. According to Evanson and Beroff, raising money from a standing start can often take six months or more. For a company in the throes of a growth spurt, six months to find money just doesn't cut it. For some companies, especially fast-growing Internet companies, the game is over in six months.[11] Entrepreneurs need to calculate their venture's burn rate using a couple of different revenue and expense scenarios to determine when the venture will need additional funding.

TO ATTRACT AN ANGEL, THINK LIKE AN ANGEL

Entrepreneurs need to know what angels look for and what gives them a compelling reason to invest in a new venture. As noted in the preceding section, angels can afford to be selective and patient. Their livelihood and lifestyle rarely depend on doing deals. If deals don't appeal to them, they let them pass them by.

REALITY CHECK

Santa Claus is dead. There is no such thing as easy money any more. Veteran entrepreneurs refer to the latter 1990s as *the good old days*. In that time of *irrational exuberance* securing funding was easier and quicker. A lot of good money was thrown after a lot of bad deals. Most angels are a lot wiser today, and deals are subjected to far more scrutiny.

Robert Robinson notes that *due diligence* is frequently misunderstood by entrepreneurs. According to Robinson, "Most people think that due diligence involves finding out as much as possible about what makes the proposed deal a good one. Wrong. It's designed to reveal the flaws, dangers, and problems in a business plan, and to help develop a healthy understanding of everything that can make this investment go sour."[12]

Angels look at numerous factors when considering a deal. Chapter 10 noted their preference for geographic proximity, the amount of time they want to commit to a venture, and the relative breadth of industry preference compared with venture capital firms. This chapter focuses on the nuts and bolts of investment criteria. Particular attention is directed to (1) the entrepreneur, (2) the team, (3) the opportunity, (4) the business plan, (5) and the structure and terms of the deal.

Although it is natural for entrepreneurs to be excited about the market opportunity, the venture's innovative product or service, and hockey-stick growth projections, they also need to recognize that angels are driven by the ability to get their investment back with a multifold return in 3 to 10 years. Although the entrepreneur's attention may be focused on creating an exceptional enterprise, angels focus their attention on getting an exceptional return for their money.

Criteria 1: Can the Entrepreneur Take the Venture to the Next Level?

Angels are asking tough, often embarrassing questions, including, "What right do you have to run the business?" and "How the hell do you know what you are doing?"[13] The saying, "Just showing up with the ball doesn't mean you should be the pitcher," also applies to entrepreneurs seeking angel funding.

Most angels go through a quick screening process to size up the entrepreneur and his or her ambitions. David Amis is an angel who has invested in 15 start-up companies. According to Amis, within seconds of shaking the entrepreneur's hand for the first time, he has already put the entrepreneur in one of three file folders. He states that no matter what the venture does, no matter how charming and smart the entrepreneur may be, the entrepreneur is one of the following:[14]

- *A lifestyle entrepreneur.* You simply enjoy owning your company, working for yourself, and living your self-directed lifestyle. Making sure your pleasant existence continues is more important than creating the next billion-dollar company.

- *An empire builder.* You love your company's growth rate and being the master of your domain. You wouldn't sell your company if your life depended on it. They will carry you out with your boots on.

- *A serial entrepreneur.* You'll expand your company to the best of your ability, sell or go public, then start another company. Then you'll do it again and again.

Amis will only consider investing in companies run by the third type of entrepreneur—the serial company builder.

Entrepreneurs seeking angel funding should be somewhere in between empire builders and serial entrepreneurs. If they plan to cash out, then they should focus on building an exceptional company and then cashing out; not cashing out by building an exceptional company. Positioning a venture to cash out usually involves cutting corners and not building great goodwill. Building an income statement is not the same as building a great company. If you build a great company, then others will seek you out. If potential and existing customers, corporate allies, and employees believe the venture is up for sale or is about to be harvested in some other way in the near future, then they may keep their distance.

Criteria 2: The Team Must Be There or Be on the Near-Term Horizon

No entrepreneur can be all-knowing and ever-present. The abilities to attract talent and to delegate key decisions are crucial if the venture is to grow and develop. An entrepreneur's unwillingness and/or inability to let go may be the greatest constraint to sustained growth for an emerging venture.

The entrepreneur must recognize the need to hire professionals who have the ability to take the venture to the next level and to have them function as an integrated management team. If the team is not already in place, then the entrepreneur needs to be able to indicate the positions to be filled, the timeline for filling the positions, and the compensation—including possible stock options—in their compensation package. The strength and track record of the management team will also indicate areas where the angel may add value to the venture.

Criteria 3: The Opportunity Must Have Considerable Upside Potential

Angels are not interested in wild-eyed claims by overly optimistic entrepreneurs. They know that the venture cannot be larger than the market(s) it is targeting. The market opportunity must be significant, relatively tangible, and open to an emerging venture. If the market has a limited number of potential consumers, is difficult to articulate, or is locked up via proprietary position of established firms, then the opportunity may not offer much potential or be too uncertain to attract angel investment.

Angels value markets that are good and destined to get better. If they cannot see the window of opportunity, then they will not invest in the venture. They also know the difference between sales and profits. Large markets may provide revenue opportunities, but they do not assure profits. Entrepreneurs need to demonstrate that the window of opportunity is substantial, that it will be open for a considerable time, and that it is open for an emerging venture that has a sustainable competitive advantage.

Criteria 4: The Business Plan Must Demonstrate the Ability to Capitalize on the Opportunity

The business plan is a reflection of the entrepreneur. The quality of the business plan is particularly important for entrepreneurs with limited business experience. This is particularly true for young entrepreneurs and first-time entrepreneurs. Patrick Byrne, who was a young entrepreneur, noted that young entrepreneurs can make up for their age by having a really solid business plan. Byrne also notes that before meeting with investors, he and Shawn Griffen had a lot of written correspondence with them. The correspondence gave them a chance to build a reputation of being very professional before the inevitable face-to-face meeting. He indicated that by the time they had face-to-face discussions, investors were "too far down the road for them to do anything about it." Byrne also noted that their venture was able to overcome investor concerns about their lack of experience by having a board of advisors with a "bit of gray hair."[15]

REALITY CHECK

This example illustrates the role the plan can play in establishing credibility. You also have to show that you are the right person for the venture ... you have the ability to make the plan's projections a reality ... that you can get the venture to the critical mass stage. Hopefully, it will also identify customer, supplier, potential key employee, and distributor interest. If the plan also contains a list of respected professional references, then it will garner a higher level of credibility.

If criteria 3 demonstrated there is a considerable market or the credible potential for a considerable market, then the plan has to demonstrate the firm is or will be a position to capture a significant part of the market. Simply stated, the plan must demonstrate that customers will buy the venture's products and services. Schilit noted that the plan needs to demonstrate that a target market exists and that users have been pleased with the venture's product or service, even if it is only in the prototype stage. Market research, letters from users, and other documentation will certainly support projections provided in the plan.[16] The plan also needs to demonstrate that the venture has a sustainable competitive advantage and if it has any proprietary position. It should also indicate timing issues that apply to the window of opportunity.

The comprehensive plan serves as the entrepreneur's blueprint for creating a successful venture and directing its first year or two. The venture's funding plan (*F-plan*) should show the venture clearly passes the return-to-risk test. Angels may be more interested in the business model and certain logistics than venture capitalists, but they do not want to have to wade through page after page of *who, what, where,* and *when* issues. Angels do not need to—or even want to—know every last operational detail. Their willingness to invest their time and money will be determined by whether the venture will be profitable and provide them with a substantial return to be pivotal.

REALITY CHECK

If the angel wants to know every detail at the initial contact stage, then that may be a bad omen. Due diligence has its place in the investment decision. Overemphasis on details at the initial stage may indicate that angel's propensity to micromanage or his or her inability to see the forest through the trees.

The F-plan should be less than 20 pages, and every effort should be made to keep it to less than 10 pages. A concise F-plan will also provide the foundation for developing the one-page executive summary, a two-minute phone summary, and/or the often overhyped 30-second *elevator pitch.*

Generally speaking, the more sophisticated the investor, the more he or she expects to see a compelling executive summary and a business plan that demonstrates the venture's ability to achieve high returns. The executive summary, when provided with the F-plan, serves a similar function as a cover letter and resume when an individual is seeking a job. It should give the prospective employer a compelling reason to contact the applicant. If the angel is genuinely interested and wants to learn more, then the complete business plan may be provided.

REALITY CHECK

Although the F-plan may be a marketing vehicle, it should also be credible. The F-plan must be reality-based for at least two reasons. First, if the plan makes astronomical projections, then the failure to fulfill the claims may provide fuel for lawsuit by investors. Second, experienced angels will cut through all the smoke; there must be a fire to get their interest. Few things can destroy entrepreneurial credibility quicker than marketing hype and unsubstantiated claims. Attracting investors is not about hype, eyeballs on the screen, hits on an Internet site, banner ads, or field-of-dreams claims that if we build it customers will come. Attracting investors takes more than hockey-stick revenue projections; it's about positive cash flow, profits, and return on investment—creating wealth!

The plan must clearly demonstrate the venture is rooted in a profitable business model, not just a loosely defined concept. The plan must demonstrate that the venture's success is not tied to too many assumptions and external contingencies. Too many if-then assumptions and contingencies will make the venture look like a house of cards.

REALITY CHECK

If you want to make sweeping assumptions, then become an economist. If you want to be an entrepreneur, then focus your attention on showing your venture can make money.

The F-plan must demonstrate the venture has considerable merit from a financial perspective. Although the entrepreneur may be excited about the product and service's competitive advantages, its sales projections, and market share, investors do not get caught up in all that marketing smoke. Investors chant the classic line from the film *Jerry MaGuire,* "Show me the money!" The F-plan must demonstrate key elements:

- The salient points in the return-to-risk ratio
- Profitability, cash flow, and return on investment
- The type of funds sought
- The uses of the funds
- The terms of the deal
- The basis for valuation
- How investors will be able to harvest their investment

Three more points should be made about the F-plan at this point. First, even though considerable thought and industry/market data may have gone into formulating the plan's financial projections, entrepreneurs need to recognize angels will not take them on face value. John Ason, who has invested in numerous ventures, notes, "I have never seen or heard about a start-up meeting its 'conservative' projections. If you try to crunch numbers you will fail, because you will be constantly dividing by zero."[17] Although Ason's comment may seem extreme, it should be clear that claims of quick profitability and substantial returns are not likely to be taken seriously.

Second, the plans should indicate the type of nonfinancial involvement being sought from the angel. If an angel is being sought for value-added talents and contacts, then the angel must feel he or she has the talents and contacts—and that the venture is still at a stage where those talents and contacts can be a real catalyst to the venture's growth and success. The plan should indicate that the angel's nonfinancial involvement can make a difference.

Third, the business-plan and its corresponding F-plan need to be viewed as ever-evolving documents. Both plans are of value only to the extent that they are current. Entrepreneurs need to keep them up to date and in sync with changing realities. They must reflect where the firm is and where it is headed. Keeping the plan current may seem like a diversion of the entrepreneur's limited and valuable time, but shopping around an outdated plan will be a waste of time.

Criteria 5: The Angel Must Find the Investment to Be Compelling

If the entrepreneur and the business plan have been successful in generating angel interest, then the prospect of getting funding is now at a critical juncture. Up to now, the angel may have been doing nothing more than window shopping. Generating interest is one thing; doing a deal is something else. If angels are going to invest, the investment must be more than good; it must be compelling.

If the angel is looking for a purely financial involvement, then his or her criteria will be primarily financial in nature. If the angel will be investing considerable time in the venture, then less tangible factors will also determine whether the investment of time, attention, and money will be compelling. If the angel is to commit considerable time and tap his or her network of contacts, then the venture must offer the type of challenge that appeals to many angels. Angels rarely make investment decisions based on their emotions; this is a time when the venture's products, services, technology, and markets may truly come into play. Financial worthiness clearly takes center stage, but the final decision may come down to whether the angel is excited about playing an integral role in the direction and operation of the venture.

The chemistry between the entrepreneur and the angel will also be a critical factor at this stage. If the angel will be spending considerable time working with the entrepreneur and be involved in substantive issues, then it is important that the angel welcome the time they will spend together and the challenges they will face. If the angel believes he or she can be a welcome catalyst, then that might make the difference between expressing interest and making the investment.

DOING THE DEAL: HOW THE DEAL MAY BE STRUCTURED

The moment of truth has arrived. The deal has to do more than make sense to the angel; it must be structured in such a way that the angel welcomes the investment opportunity. The flexible nature and terms of angel investments are among its major attributes. There is no standard template for angel investing. Everything is subject to negotiation. The financial and nonfinancial conditions of the investment can be whatever the entrepreneur and angel agree to.

The funding side of the deal is usually structured in one of three ways. First, the angel may provide a loan for a specific period at a specific rate of interest. Although a loan may appear to reduce the angel's risk compared to buying stock, the precarious nature of seed, start-up, and early stage ventures also places creditors at risk. Having the entrepreneur personally guarantee the note rarely limits the angel's risk. Many entrepreneurs prefer having a loan because it does not dilute their ownership position. The nondilution nature of a loan, however, may be more than offset by the obligation to make principal and interest payments as well as the angel's ability to call the note if certain conditions are not met. Angels frequently negotiate the provision for warrants into loan packages. A warrant is the right to buy stock in the future at what could be a very favorable price to the angel. A warrant provides an angel with an avenue for reaping the benefits beyond the amount of principal and interest if the firm is very successful.

Second, the deal may be structured in terms of debt with the option of converting the amount of the loan into equity. Like the loan noted in the first instance, funding may initially be in the form of a loan with very flexible interest and principal payment terms. The loan may then be converted into stock at some point so the angel can benefit from capital appreciation and possibly a liquidity event. Convertible debt also gives the angel investor the option to convert to stock ownership if the company is sold or goes public.[18]

A note from the angel may take the form of a *bridge loan.* A bridge loan is designed for companies that are so close to some value-hiking milestone they can taste it and consequently don't want to sell shares on the cheap. In financial terms, a bridge loan is a convertible note in which the principal and interest convert to stock upon the completion of the next round of financing. Andrew Raskin notes, "In metaphorical terms, a bridge loan is to a cash-poor start-up on the verge of a breakthrough as a Power Bar is to a marathon runner about to bonk at the 20-mile mark. It's the last ounce of fuel that propels you toward the finish line."[19]

Third, the investment may be in preferred stock. Preferred stock gives the angel first claim even over the entrepreneur on the firm's assets after the creditors get their share if the firm gets into trouble. If the stock is a cumulative preferred stock, then the angel may be the first one to benefit from the firm's profitability when it has the cash to pay a dividend.

With convertible preferred shares, angels switch them for common stock if the company is bought or has an IPO. Preferred stock can protect the angel's investment if the founder raises additional funds in another financing round. As preferred shareholders, angels have to receive their entire investment back before the founders see one penny of profit from a sale or acquisition.[20] If the preferred stock is not convertible, then the angel may insist on registration rights. Registration rights allow the angel to convert the preferred stock into common shares if the company goes public.

Fourth, the angel may receive common stock. Common stock appears to be a rather straightforward deal, but angels usually look for some special provisions to separate their investment from the other holders of common stock—including the founder. Angels rarely want to be at the back of the line when things sour.

Angels who hold an equity interest almost always insist on a having a seat on the board of directors and the opportunity to influence key decisions. They may also insist on the establishment of performance targets. If the targets are not met, then the firm may be required to buy the stock back at a predetermined price. Being a director gets the angel investor inside, where he or she is more able to make sure the entrepreneur sticks to the business plan and exit plan. In fact, directors have a say in mergers, partnerships and alliances, or plans to go public.[21]

Warrants can also be provided as part of an equity deal. The entrepreneur might make the following offer to the angel, "If you buy one million shares, I will give you the right to purchase more shares for the price of $2 apiece for a period of three years."[22]

The provision for a warrant is not free on at least three counts. First, it will dilute the founder's share of ownership if it is exercised. Second, the amount that it can be exercised for, known as the redemption rate, may be at a much lower rate than the stock is worth at the point that it is exercised by the angel. This represents an opportunity cost to the founder and firm. The shares exercised could have brought in more money and resulted in less dilution of ownership in a follow-up round of funding. Third, the existence of warrants complicates matters if the firm wants to attract venture capital or take the firm public.

Angels frequently negotiate other provisions in the deal. They may ask for the right of first refusal. This gives angels the right to buy additional shares from the owners before other investors in subsequent financing rounds. The same concept applies to antidilution rights where the angel has the right to buy more stock in subsequent rounds of funding to maintain the same ownership percentage.[23] Angels may include *put options* in their contracts, even though they are rarely exercised. Put options give investors the right to ask the company to buy their shares back (redeemed) at a set price and/or after a certain amount of time.[24]

VALUATION CAN MAKE OR BREAK A DEAL

The ability to attract angel investors is directly related to the valuation of the company's stock. The value of a business is determined by numerous factors, including how the entrepreneur and angel perceive the venture's future. Just as the terms of the deal are subject to negotiation, the basis for valuation is subject to one's perceptions. The valuation will be affected by the stage of development for the venture, the rate of growth, the profit margin for the business, the amount of funding sought, the type of stock available, and the terms for the stock. If the entrepreneur and angel can agree on a basis for evaluating the relative worth of the venture and the corresponding share and value of the investment, then doing the deal will be expedited dramatically.

Jason Ason notes that the single biggest deterrent to fundable start-ups getting the money they need is their stubborn insistence on unreasonable valuations.[25] Entrepreneurs should try to see their business through the prospective angel's eyes. According to Ason, angels frequently face this problem: "How do you value one or two strangers with a great idea and boundless enthusiasm, but no revenues or true business experience?"[26] A venture's valuation increases with the entrepreneur's ability to demonstrate the venture has merit and is moving forward. The less it is merely a concept, the lower the corresponding uncertainty. The lower the uncertainty, the higher the venture's valuation.

Paul Brown, as editor-in-chief for DirectAdvice.com, a firm that facilitates online financial planning, places considerable weight on the stage of the venture. According to Brown, each milestone may be worth $1 million in valuation. Exhibit 11.1 profiles the various stages and their corresponding valuation. The venture's valuation may range from $1 million if it has a sound idea all the way to $6 million if it is on the verge of rolling out its product or service. [27]

Ason offers similar guidelines. According to Ason, "If the company has just a good idea but not much else, I set it at $1 million. A working prototype will get them a valuation of up to $2 million. Management is key, and if I think the people involved are outstanding, they could deserve up to $3 million. If there are meaningful revenues, then the valuation goes up to $4 million. If they have all that plus strong relationships in the industry and with potential clients as well, it raises them up to $5 million."[28]

Ason notes that while a venture may have strong points that enhance its valuation, some ventures may also have valuation weaknesses or *demerits*. According to Ason, the biggest demerit is a weak management team. Other demerits will be assigned if the entrepreneur and/or team lack a marketing focus, have no business sense for making alliances and negotiating deals, are secretive and suspicious, and lack respect for angel capital, thinking of it as *dumb money*. He notes that some of these demerits can be fatal.[29]

In Exhibit 11.1 the only constant is that the company has to have a great idea; the other criteria are quite variable. You can view Exhibit 11.1 as a template. If the entrepreneur has an intended valuation of $1 million to $5 million, map the company on this template and modulate the valuation between these two numbers.

Although Brown and Ason's valuation guidelines seem rather nebulous, they do underscore the fact that valuation is not a science. Entrepreneurs are perennial optimists. Angels are tempered realists. A deal will only be struck if both parties can reach agreement. Each

If you have this:	Add this to your company's value:
Sound idea	$1 million
Prototype	$1 million
Quality management team	$1 million to $2 million
Quality board	$1 million
Product rollout or sales	$1 million
Total potential value	$1 million to $6 million

EXHIBIT 11.1   WHAT'S A FLEDGLING COMPANY WORTH?

deal will have its unique points that will also affect the valuation process. The entrepreneur should try to find comparable situations so the basis for valuation does not seem arbitrary and unfounded. If a similar firm has been valued recently, then that firm's valuation may provide a useful benchmark. If other early-stage growth companies in the communications technology industry are being valued at three times revenue, then an emerging venture with $1 million in revenue may be worth $3 million. If it is seeking $1 million in capital, then the entrepreneur should be willing to give up about one-third of the company.[30]

The preceding example reflects another factor in the valuation of an emerging venture. Most deals are valued so the angel or group of angels secures 20 to 40 percent ownership in the firm. This leaves the entrepreneur with control of the firm, but it also gives the angel a significant stake in the firm when it has a liquidity event.

If the venture is in the start-up stage, then the uncertainties will keep the valuation to under $1 million. If the entrepreneur is looking for a rather modest angel investment of $50,000 to $100,000, then the entrepreneur will have to give up at least 10 to 20 percent ownership to attract angel interest. Although an individual angel may invest less than $50,000, it is really not worth their time and money to do so. The same is true if the emerging venture has growth potential but is not likely to be a real blockbuster. The more lucrative the business opportunity and the higher the likelihood the venture will achieve lucrative returns, the more an angel may be willing to do a deal for less of a share of the ownership.

Ason sees more than 1,000 executive summaries and hears at least 150 presentations a year. Yet he only invests in two or three companies. He notes that potential investments have to hit the angel *sweet spot* that places their valuation in the $1 million to $5 million range. He notes that start-ups with a market value of less than $1 million are usually boot-strapped and are frequently funded via friends-and-family money. Ason also notes that emerging ventures that may be valued above $5 million may be better off seeking venture capital funding.[31]

Mark Van Osnabrugge and Robert Robinson provide a number of helpful observations in their book, *Angel Investing.*[32] They note that valuation may be based on a price/earnings ratio, discounted cash flow, key assets, or the value of comparable firms. If the valuation is based initially on projected price/earnings ratios, the investor's required rate of return, and the discount rate, then the valuation and corresponding investment may be computed via the Valuation/Investment formula in Exhibit 11.2

Van Osnabrugge and Robinson note that when the P/E ratio is used as the basis, the higher the investors' required rate of return, the lower the company valuation and the higher the investors' equity. They also noted that a 40 to 70 percent discount rate is not unusual for angels or venture capitalists when valuing start-up and early-stage ventures.[33]

(value of the firm = value including investment infusion x P/E ratio) / (1 + discount rate)*

* = the exponent represents the number of years discounted

Example:

($1,000,000 x 15) / (1+50%)* = 1.98 million

* = the exponent used here is 5 years

Calculation:

$500,000/$1,980,000 = 25%

EXHIBIT 11.2   VALUATION/INVESTMENT FORMULA

The price/earnings ratio when based on after-tax earnings may be more appropriate for determining the valuation of more established ventures. Van Osnabrugge and Robinson note that most entrepreneurs project a hockey-stick shape in their projections, so P/E doesn't work well if there is little if any profit at present time.[34] According to Van Osnabrugge and Robinson, the discounted cash flow method may be more appropriate for the valuation of early-stage ventures because they have little or no income stream or assets.[35] Angels are also leery of hockey-stick-shaped projections of future cash flows.

John Ason points out that when he sees an executive summary that interests him, the first thing he does is check the valuation of the company. If it's not provided, he calls the entrepreneurs to get one. The valuation plays a critical role because he usually wants 20 to 30 percent of the company's equity. According to Ason, an angel that buys into the idea behind the company will do a due diligence review, and only then do the valuation negotiations commence. The vast majority of his negotiations have lasted less than an hour.[36]

Valuation is influenced by many factors, most of which involve perceptions about how successful the venture will be in a very uncertain future. Valuation boils down to the quality of the entrepreneur's presentation, how eager the entrepreneur is to do the deal, and the quality of other investment opportunities—including the stock market—for the angel.

The phrase, "You don't have a business until someone buys your product," applies to attracting angel investment. You don't have an angel's investment until a deal is struck. The valuation of the business, whether the investment will be in common stock, preferred convertible stock, or a convertible note, as well as the terms—board positions, limits on salaries, and so forth—of the deal comes down to what the entrepreneur and the angel agree on.

TIPS ON PROSPECTING: LOOK FOR GOODNESS OF FIT

Entrepreneurs need to recognize that the process of prospecting for angels is contingent on numerous factors. The size of the deal as well as the nature and relative tangibility of the venture will have a bearing on the type of angel to seek and their corresponding expectations and due diligence process. If the amount of funding sought is relatively small, then entrepreneurs should seek angels who do smaller deals. Two types of angels fit this profile. The first type of angel has limited experience with the process. There has been an increase in the number of *virgin angels* in the last few years. Less-experienced angels may invest without much due diligence. The second type of angel has considerable experience and has a portfolio of investments in emerging ventures. Sophisticated angels are accustomed to doing deals and should be able to close a deal quickly if their due diligence shows the venture has merit from a risk–return perspective.

Entrepreneurs seeking sizable investments should seek out sophisticated angels. Sophisticated angels do larger deals and may be networked with other angels. Their angel contacts may enable them to syndicate a deal with other angels. Entrepreneurs need to recognize from the beginning, however, that sophisticated angels tend to operate like venture capital firms in four particular ways. First, they will have higher expectations than less sophisticated angels. Second, they will be reviewing numerous deals, Third, they will be far more thorough in performing due diligence. Fourth, they will place more emphasis on building a business that will provide the opportunity for a liquidity event within three to seven years.

PROFILE OF THE IDEAL ANGEL

Angels and venture capitalist firms often pride themselves for their diligence in analyzing potential deals. Entrepreneurs should also be deliberate in their search for and evaluation of potential investors. David Amis and Howard Stevenson offer the following guidelines for entrepreneurs who are looking for a value-added angel:

1. *Contacts.* You want angels who can help you locate suppliers, customers, and employees. Ideally, your angels will know important players in your industry.

2. *Industry experience.* You want someone who understands your business and worked in your industry. Such an angel can help you anticipate some problems and deal with others that arise.

3. *Entrepreneurial experience.* Angels who have previously raised money for their own companies tend to be easy, quick, and direct to work with. They can also detect likely trouble spots in your company. That way, they won't be surprised when that 12-month project stretches out to three years.

4. *Angel experience.* It's four times easier to deal with someone who has been an angel before than it is to work with an investment first-timer. Everything moves much quicker.

5. *Deep—but not too deep—pockets.* The ideal angel has a personal net worth of $2 million to $50 million. If an angel has more than that, the $50,000 your company needs may fall beneath his or her radar. But if your angel has less, you'll be out of luck if you need to go back for follow-up financing.[37]

PROFILE OF THE IDEAL INVESTMENT

Most of the material in this chapter has focused on attracting an angel. Entrepreneurs need to be sure they court the right angels. They also must tailor their presentations to prospective angels. Although entrepreneurs may have a picture of the ideal angel, angels also have a mental model of what would be an ideal investment.

The following dimensions characterize an ideal investment. It is unlikely that any emerging venture will meet any of these dimensions. Entrepreneurs should note, however, that the more their ventures meet the criteria, the greater their ability to attract investors and the more favorable the terms will be for the entrepreneurs.

Entrepreneur

The ideal entrepreneur has already started at least one successful venture—and shepherded it through a liquidity event. The entrepreneur has the vision to see a lucrative emerging opportunity and the operational ability needed to execute courses of action to make the vision a reality. Although most entrepreneurs enjoy talking about the sizzle of their venture, veteran angels want to know, "Where's the beef?" Veteran angels know that ideas without execution are about as lasting as smoke without a fire. The entrepreneur has already demonstrated the ability to attract quality people and to craft them into a high-performing team. The entrepreneur also has demonstrated the ability to delegate key decisions. The goodness of fit or supplementary nature of the skills between the entrepreneur's and the team's skills and angel's skills can also be a significant factor in angel investing.

Management Team

The complete team is already in place. They have worked together and done successful start-ups before. They also have experience in the industry. Team members are old enough to have developed the wisdom of experience, but young enough (at heart) to challenge the status quo and have the energy to go the distance. There appears to be a good chemistry between the angel and the entrepreneur and team. David Amis and Howard Stevenson noted that angels want you to have a team of at least five senior executives in place. At this point potential investors are really evaluating the people behind the company, not the vitality of the company itself.[38] Veteran angels draw an interesting distinction between the need for a strong management team and having a wow product, service, or technology. They prefer to fund a venture with a strong management team and good technology than with a good management team and superior technology. If the entrepreneur and team aren't strong, then the angels may not be able to make the personnel changes needed to capitalize on the technology.

Market Opportunity

The window of opportunity is open enough to show there is demand. The market is expected to grow substantially within the next three years. Competition, if it exists, is composed of small firms that are targeting small niches. Angels look for ventures that have the potential to generate at least $20 million in sales within the next few years. The $20 million in sales benchmark is important for two reasons. First, the overall market must be big enough for the firm to gain at least a $20 million market share. Markets that are expanding rapidly and that have considerable growth potential enable firms to grow without getting caught in intense price competition. Markets that are destined to remain small or are already saturated will not provide the level of profits needed to provide substantial financial returns. Second, the $20 million sales mark is critical from an absolute dollar perspective. Generally speaking, if the firm makes a profit of only 5 percent of sales, then sales of less than $20 million will not generate at least $1 million in profit. Although the return on investment equation is usually stated in terms of percentages, the absolute dollars must be large enough to attract reasonably sized investments.

The market opportunity will also have merit if no major firms are in the market or expected to enter the market for the foreseeable future. Barriers to entry are also important. There should be sufficient barriers to entry in terms of a proprietary position and/or access to critical resources—including key people—to deter potential competitors.

Product/Service Offering

The venture's offering is clearly superior to what is available—and the venture's competitive advantages are sustainable. The venture also has a proprietary position that will deter future competitors. Potential customers have already expressed considerable interest or intent to purchase the product/service. Amis and Stevenson stress the importance of the venture's ability to generate sales. They note that the longer it takes to get the product into the marketplace, the longer it will be until the angels get their money back. All things being equal, angels would rather get their cash out sooner than later. According to Van

Osnabrugge and Robinson, angels expect the product to be unique and be in a profitable niche market. The product has to be something that no one else is doing, not a me-too product.[39]

Business Plan

The plan demonstrates that the firm will be able to provide the product or service. It demonstrates management has identified and addressed mission-critical issues. The plan is comprehensive enough to be executed by the team. Brian Penney, who is a full-time investor, notes that entrepreneurs certainly will not scare potential angels away if their business plans are well prepared.[40]

Financials

Financial projections indicate quick positive cash flow and profitability. The projections also take various factors into consideration. Although angels may not have as high expectations as venture capital firms, they look for investments that enable them to get 3 to 5 times their investment in five years. Angels rarely consider ventures that will not provide at least a 25 to 30 percent annual return on their investment.

Location of the Venture

The location of the venture may play a major, minor, or insignificant role in angel investing depending on the amount of face time expected by the angel. Generally speaking, angels prefer ventures where they can be involved and home that night. Seventy percent of angel investments are made within 50 miles of the investor's home or office.[41] If the angel expects to be actively involved in the management of the firm, then the angel may only consider ventures in the immediate area. Some angels may even expect to be involved in the daily management of the firm. Although they might not be there every day of the week for eight hours a day for years, their expected involvement will limit the firms they will consider. Other situations may call for periodic rather than continuous involvement by the angel. If the angel expects to be involved for one or two days per month, then the angel may consider ventures in more distant locations. If the angel expects to be involved mainly via financial statements and operating results, then periodic electronic communication and phone conversations may reduce the need for physical presence. Yet angels have been known to drop by occasionally to kick the tires to make sure that financials reflect reality. In any event, angels expect to be involved in regular and special occasion board meetings.

The Deal

The deal has to make sense and be compelling to the angel. The terms of the deal must fit the nature of the emerging venture, and they must be clear. The deal must be structured so that each party's rights and responsibilities are clearly stated and that various contingencies are identified and avenues are available for them to be addressed.

WHY DO ANGELS REJECT DEALS?

If the angel has serious reservations about the emerging venture and the corresponding deal on any one of the preceding criteria, then the angel usually walks away. Doing a deal is not a matter of meeting three out of five criteria. Although it may be impossible for an emerging venture to fit the ideal for even one of the criteria, every angel has a threshold or minimum level that must be met before they will do a deal. The following list highlights a number of issues that can be considered deal-breakers:

- Lack of integrity
- Lack of entrepreneurial and management prowess
- Lack of interpersonal chemistry
- Questionable coachability
- Lack of commitment
- Weak or incomplete management team
- Limited appreciation potential
- Unfavorable valuation or terms
- Lack of interest or experience in the venture's market

Lack of Integrity

The information provided by the entrepreneur plays a crucial role in the investment decision. Start-ups and emerging ventures are not able to provide angels with the level of tangible information that is available with more established ventures. This makes the due diligence process very challenging for angels. Angels have to rely a lot on the entrepreneur's credibility and integrity. The entrepreneur must be extremely trustworthy. Nothing can break a deal quicker than questionable integrity.

Lack of Entrepreneurial and Management Prowess

One of the major differences between angels and venture capital firms is the extent they rely on the entrepreneur. Angels must be confident that the entrepreneur has what it takes to be the venture's chief executive officer. They don't want to run the firm or get caught up in trying to remove the entrepreneur. Venture capital firms are far more willing to replace the entrepreneur if the entrepreneur is unable to meet expectations. In some cases, venture capital firms insist on bringing in a new chief executive as a condition of the deal.

Lack of Interpersonal Chemistry

The potential for a good working chemistry must also be there between the entrepreneur and the angel investor. Chemistry is particularly important if they will be working together closely. A high level of synergy between the entrepreneur and the angel can provide a valuable catalyst for an emerging venture. Chemistry is hard to put into the business plan. Angels frequently have to rely on their intuitive abilities to determine whether a synergistic relationship will develop between the angel and the entrepreneur and management team. If the angel has concerns about the chemistry, then the angel won't go forward. Chemistry is particularly important if there are other good investment alternatives that may have better chemistry and goodness of fit for the angel.

Questionable Coachability

Angels look for entrepreneurs who can make good decisions and welcome the input of others—including the angel. Entrepreneurs who are competent as well as *coachable* have real appeal. Coachability is particularly important when the entrepreneur has limited experience and a management team is not in place. Coachability is particularly important in the early stages of an emerging venture when many of the make-or-break decisions are made. Entrepreneurs who are not open to ideas and constructive criticism and who keep information to themselves not only turn off angels—they rarely make good chief executives for emerging ventures. The entrepreneur must recognize he or she does not have a monopoly on wisdom! Entrepreneurs who know what they don't know and who actively seek advice when they need it will be in a position to tap the right angel's knowledge and contacts.

Lack of Commitment

Entrepreneurs who are unwilling to invest or leverage a significant part of their personal assets will have a hard time finding an angel. Angels are not willing to risk their own money if the entrepreneur is not willing to put his or her financial security on the line. Angels are also very reluctant to do a deal if the entrepreneur does not seem to be committed to going the distance. If the entrepreneur views the venture to be nothing more than an interesting experiment in capitalism or something that seems cool to do, then angels will walk. Entrepreneurs who do not have the resiliency to hang in there when the going gets tough, which it will on numerous occasions, will not attract angels. Although angels may welcome the opportunity to provide management assistance, the last thing angels want to do is to have to take over an emerging venture because the entrepreneur had a mental breakdown or skipped town. Angels will also look for a corresponding level of commitment by the members of the management team if they play an integral role in the venture and are hard to replace. The mobility of people in Silicon Valley years ago indicated that company loyalty exists only if stock options look rock solid and no other firm can beat the venture in the let's-make-a-deal-for-talent game.

Weak or Incomplete Management Team

This is another difference between angels and venture capital firms. Angels do not expect the entrepreneurs to be veteran chief executives. They also do not expect the venture to have a complete management team. Angels frequently add value to the venture by providing management assistance or specific functional assistance until the venture gets to the point where it can hire or develop from within the talent needed for a productive management team. Venture capital firms move very quickly in replacing people who are not qualified or finding professionals for positions that need to be filled to support rapid growth. Angels are turned off by entrepreneurs who are unwilling to let people go who are unqualified. Entrepreneurs who staff positions according to family ties and/or strong personal relationships also represent red flags. Entrepreneurs who are not willing to develop a team or who insist on micromanaging also turn off angels. Angels know that ventures will grow only to the extent entrepreneurs are willing to develop a good team and delegate key decisions to the team. Start-ups and early-stage ventures live at the edge. A weak entrepreneur and/or team adds to their precarious nature. Angels avoid weak management teams and avoid being involved in turnaround strategies because most turnaround efforts are unsuccessful.

Limited Appreciation Potential

Although a 20 percent rate of growth would appeal to most firms listed on Wall Street, it will not be sufficient to attract angel investors. Angels expect to get a substantial return on their investment. A 20 percent annual growth rarely provides the types of returns needed for a lucrative liquidity event.

Unfavorable Valuation or Terms

Although it is human nature for people to want to hang on to what they have, especially if it represents their blood, sweat, and tears, entrepreneurs must be willing to give up some of the ownership. If they need additional capital for their firms to capitalize on lucrative opportunities, then they must be willing to give up something to get something. Entrepreneurs need to recognize that they will have to give up a larger piece of the action when the venture is at its earliest stages. If they put too high a premium on the worth of their ventures, then angels will have to ante up more and get even a smaller piece of the action. The same applies to the terms of the deal. The deal must provide the angel with a compelling reason to accept the risk. Overvaluation by the entrepreneur or the absence of sufficient checks and balances in how the venture is to be run—including specific expectations for performance—by the venture and entrepreneur will keep most angels away.

Lack of Interest or Experience in the Venture's Market

If the angel fails to express interest in the venture because he or she does not like the market or lacks experience in the market opportunity, then this may not mean the venture's prospects are limited. The lack of interest may be the result of inappropriate angel prospecting. Although angels may be more willing to invest in a broader variety of markets than venture capital firms that focus their attention on one or two specific industries, that doesn't mean that angels will invest in any market. Angels are reluctant to invest in areas that they know little about. Risk is often equated with lack of familiarity. It is natural for angels to place a higher level of risk on markets where they have limited knowledge and/or experience. This is particularly true in newly emerging fields and ventures that are trying to introduce radically different and untested technology. If the venture fits either of these profiles, then the entrepreneur should target angels who are more knowledgeable in these areas and who have a track record for investing in emerging firms that operate at the edge. These angels know the difference between being at the *leading edge* and being at the *bleeding edge.*

REALITY CHECK

If angel after angel keeps rejecting the overtures for one particular reason such as the valuation of the deal, then the entrepreneur should step back and reappraise the nature and terms of the deal. If, however, angels identify various reasons for rejection, that should be taken as a vote of no confidence in the entrepreneur. It is a lot easier for an angel to say he or she was not interested because the market's future is still unclear or that the firm lacks sustainable competitive advantage than it is for them to openly state the entrepreneur does not have what it takes to take the venture to the next level. The entrepreneur needs to find out if he or she is the reason angels will not do a deal. This is one of the times when having an advisory board or professional board of directors may be helpful. A well-connected board member may be able to tap his or her network of contacts or even the angels who were courted to get the real story.

USING INTERMEDIARIES, ANGEL NETWORKS, AND ELECTRONIC LISTINGS

This chapter began with the statement that angel investors may be the most elusive source of funding. Fortunately, three vehicles for getting angel attention have surfaced in the last few years. Entrepreneurs may now consider using an intermediary, an angel network, and/ or an electronic listing service.

Some investment specialists offer their services as intermediaries. They will help locate angel investors for a fee of 5 percent or more of the funding deal. Most entrepreneurs have reservations about paying an intermediary to package the deal and find an angel. Using an intermediary is like having a broker list and sell your house. Although the homeowner may be able to sell the house, the odds are much better that it will sell for a fair price if it is handled by a full-time professional. Like a realtor, the intermediary should be in a better position to package the deal and attract angels who are likely to invest in the venture.

Most first-time entrepreneurs underestimate the time and effort required to attract an angel and to do the deal. Thomas Long, founder of Maricultura, a biotech firm, noted that he spent nearly 50 percent of his time looking for funding.[42] By using an intermediary, the entrepreneur is able to spend his or her limited time and attention on the venture. If the intermediary can help the entrepreneur put together a realistic package, find the right value-added angel, and help facilitate the closing of the deal, then the 5 percent fee can be seen as an investment in the firm's future rather than as an expense.

Intermediaries may play a crucial role if time is of the essence. Ventures with a high burn rate and limited cash may be better off using an intermediary than hoping that the right angel investor will appear in time. Even if time is not of the essence, using an intermediary has its merits because it will enable the entrepreneur to direct his or her attention on building the venture.

REALITY CHECK

Entrepreneurs should use caution when considering the intermediary route. Intermediaries are still salespeople who are prone to make all sorts of claims. Entrepreneurs should network with other entrepreneurs who have had success with an intermediary if they are considering the intermediary route. Intermediaries who know the venture's industry may be particularly worthwhile.

REALITY CHECK

Although the concept of *just-in-time* business processes may be in vogue, it does not apply to seeking an angel. An entrepreneur who does not know the ropes should not leave the search to a trial-and-error process.

More than 100 angel networks have been established in the United States. They are located in most entrepreneurial havens. These networks take many forms. Some are merely a listing of entrepreneurs who are seeking funding and angels or professionals who deal with angels. Other angel networks provide a vehicle for entrepreneurs to present their plans to potential angels. Some angel networks provide a breakfast format where an entrepreneur can present his or her business plan to a dozen or more angels. A few angel networks provide more formal forums where numerous entrepreneurs profile their firms to hundreds of investors including venture capital firms. A study by Jeffry Sohl indicates that around 40 percent of those presenting at venture forums get funding.[43]

REALITY CHECK

Making a presentation at an angel forum does not guarantee funding. Forums have varying degrees of sophistication, industry preferences, and successful funding rates. Entrepreneurs seeking angel funding should contact the angel networks to learn the criteria used by the forums when selecting ventures to do presentations. Effort should also be directed to learning the extent to which firms that have presented at the forum received funding. Entrepreneurs should also contact firms that have made presentations at forums to learn about whether they provided a sufficient level of leads and potential investors. Entrepreneurs need to view their time as the precious commodity that it is. Although it may enhance one's ego to be featured at a forum, making a presentation is worthwhile only to the extent that it produces funding.

Sophisticated angel networks provide at least six benefits for angels. First, they provide visibility for deals for angels. Robert Robinson noted that 80 percent of angels say they would do more deals if they could find more quality deals.[44] Second, many angels prefer to co-invest. Robinson notes that about 80 percent of angels involved in networks express a preference to co-invest, usually with three other angels on average, although he has seen as many as 25 in a single deal. He also notes that these syndicates typically take about 25 percent of the firm's equity in exchange for about $300,000, as opposed to the much smaller amount a solitary angel can command.[45]

Networks provide a vehicle for angels to meet other angels. Some angels have taken the network concept to a higher level by forming angel syndicates where a group of angels pool their money like a venture capital fund and invest in numerous ventures. The Band of Angels in Los Angeles is a good example. Each of its members invests small amounts of money in companies that are typically too small or at too early a stage to attract venture capital funding. The Band of Angels has about 150 angels. It invests an average of $1 million per year in each of 25 start-ups.[46]

Third, networks may provide some form of initial screening. Networks usually require certain information from entrepreneurs who want to make a presentation about their firms. Even the most preliminary level of screening and profiling saves angels time. Some networks also make an effort to prequalify angels to make sure they are viable and reputable investors. Although the prescreen of members may be helpful, entrepreneurs should not assume its members are above reproach.

Fourth, angels can access the expertise and contacts of other angels. These contacts not only help them in their due diligence process, the contacts may be useful after an angel invests in an emerging venture. Fifth, the network may provide leads for additional investors if a venture seeks additional rounds of funding. Many emerging ventures need a second round of funding. The second funding gap usually involves $1 million to $3 million. Angel syndicates are better equipped than many venture capital firms to do this level of funding. The ability to do additional rounds of funding by angels may actually reduce the need for an emerging venture to seek venture capital. If the emerging venture is able to attract multimillion-dollar funding from a superangel or an angel syndicate, then it may not have to make the concessions associated with venture capital funding. Sixth, if the venture eventually seeks venture capital funding or goes public, funding via an angel network may provide the emerging venture with additional credibility.

REALITY CHECK

Superangels, angel networks, and angel syndicates are not sources of ongoing management assistance. Although these angels may be able to provide funding and tap a network of contacts to open doors for an emerging venture, they are rarely in a position to invest a lot of time in it. If an angel funds more than a couple of ventures at one time, then it is difficult to spend large amounts of quality time with each venture. Entrepreneurs who are looking for ongoing management assistance should look for angels who have the interest, time, and ability to work closely with the entrepreneur.

REALITY CHECK

The primary drawback for a forum is that it is a public venue even if it is open only to its members. The entrepreneur should not provide any information that should remain confidential.

The National Association of Venture Forums (*www.ventureforums.org*) provides information on venture forums, conferences, and angel clubs. Its Website also posts proposals, an e-newsletter, and a resource guide with tips on making presentations.[47]

REALITY CHECK

Tom Siegel, president of the National Association of Venture Forums, noted that entrepreneurs should not expect investors to be so dazzled by your presentation that they rush up, checkbook in hand and pen poised.[48] Forums are just what the name implies; they are a venue for putting an emerging firm on the radar screen for potential angels.

Although the development of angel networks is encouraging, the larger and more sophisticated networks frequently have investment criteria that bridge matchmaking intermediaries and venture capital funds. David Freedman noted that the odds of an entrepreneur finding funding are nil unless the venture is a hot start-up in high-tech, biotech, or health sciences. He notes that in addition to the 5 percent fee on the money raised, Garage.com buys a small stake in the company at the *predeal valuation* price.[49]

The Internet has changed the economic landscape for the free enterprise system. It has provided a vehicle for entrepreneurs to list their ventures and angels to look for deals. Electronic listing services have knocked down the walls of proximity that have characterized entrepreneur–angel prospecting. It's now easier for small companies to shop their business plans around or advertise for potential backers.[50] Robert Robinson, a Harvard professor and veteran angel investor, believes the emergence of a number of online introduction services to be one of the most promising recent developments in bringing entrepreneurs and potential investors together.

Although some local and regional intermediaries and angel networks have taken their efforts online, a number of national listing services have sprouted up. Even the federal government has become involved. It established the Angel Capital Electronic Network (ACE-Net), which is sponsored by the U.S. Small Business Administration (*www.sba.gov*) as a listing service for companies that have completed the paperwork that are seeking up to $5 million. Companies that meet the ACE-Net listing requirements satisfy many states' securities regulations. The ACE-Net limits solicitation, however, to accredited investors who view the businesses anonymously. Research indicates that 20 percent of the 140 companies listed in ACE-Net's national database had received financing.[51]

It is just daybreak in the brave new world of online venture financing, and there seems to be a new player entering the online financing fray each week. Online matchmakers are multiplying because there are tens of thousands of companies that can't get financing today. Clay Womack, CEO of Direct Stock Market, noted that there are more than 80,000 businesses in the United States that are growing by at least 50 percent per year, and venture capital firms are doing only 2,000 deals at any point in time. His research indicates not even 1 percent of the 300,000 or so companies that are growing 20 percent a year are backed by venture capital firms. The fact that venture capital firms and investment banks are habitually understaffed and overwhelmed by business plans that come in means they simply can't keep up with demand.[52]

REALITY CHECK

The increase in the number and types of matching services, including electronic listing services, seems to open doors for entrepreneurs in search of funding. Entrepreneurs should remember one of the reasons Furniture.com was not successful. Doing a deal is not like ordering a book over the Internet. People, including angels, like to press the flesh and to deal with people they know. Doing a deal is still a high-touch endeavor involving numerous iterations of contact. The less face-to-face contact between the entrepreneur and potential investors, the lower the likelihood a deal will be consummated. People may buy stocks electronically, but angels still want to kick the tires. Although matching services (venture forums, computer matching, breakfast meetings, and various kinds of publication) get a lot of press, research indicates that they account for less than 10 percent of angel deals. Research also indicates that 20 to 30 percent of matching service subscribers are virgin angels who tend to stay on the sidelines.[53]

DON'T FORGET ABOUT LEGAL ISSUES WHEN SEEKING INVESTORS[*]

Entrepreneurs need to recognize that when they solicit investors they are opening the door to a whole host of securities and tax laws. Although the articles of incorporation may have identified the number of shares authorized and initially issued as well as whether there

---

*Entrepreneurs considering issuing securities should seek legal counsel about current statutes. The information provided in this chapter is subject to change and may not apply to specific businesses and situations.

would be more than one type of stock, the process of seeking investors usually is not part of that package. Entrepreneurs should seek legal and accounting advice well before starting the firm so they do not create a minefield when they seek investors. The number of shares available for investors as well as the type of stock they can purchase will affect the ability to attract angel funding and venture capital. The ACE-Net Website provides useful information on issuing stock.

Entrepreneurs may find merit in issuing what is known as 1244 stock. This special class of stock is allowed for small businesses. The IRS allows the stockholders to treat the business's losses as ordinary losses rather than as capital losses. The IRS will only allow up to $3,000 to be deducted for regular stock on a stockholder's return as a capital loss. With 1244 stock, the loss is not limited to $3,000. The stockholder's share of the entire loss can be treated as an ordinary loss. The IRS stipulates that no more than $1 million of stock can be issued, that it must be common stock, and that sales of the stock must be sold subject to a written business plan.[54]

Entrepreneurs should view the process of seeking an angel investor as if the firm is doing a *private placement.* The Securities Act provides guidelines for issuing stock. Regulation D of the Act highlights a number of alternatives available for issuing stock. The following rules indicate some of the circumstances that may be considered when seeking investors:

Rule 504 allows the issuer to sell up to $1 million of its securities during a 12-month period regardless of the number or sophistication of the investors.

Rule 505 permits the sale of up to $5 million of a company's securities in any 12-month period.

Regulation D stipulates the types of investors (accredited, unaccredited, and institutions) and corresponding limits on the sale of securities.

Rule 506 also clarifies the amount of securities that can be sold to *sophisticated* and *accredited investors.*[55]

Years ago, the SEC eased registration requirements when it created the small-corporate-offering registration (SCOR) and Regulation A. SCOR and Regulation A offerings involve little or no scrutiny by the SEC. Emerging ventures can raise up to $1 million in a 12-month period with a SCOR, or up to $5 million with a regulation A offering.[56]

If the entrepreneur is particularly enterprising, then he or she may consider going the private offering route. A private offering is different from a public offering because the entrepreneur is usually soliciting a smaller amount of money. If the offering meets SEC guidelines, then far less time, expense, regulations, and paperwork will be required than is required of an initial public offering. Ed Palmer, founder of SolarAttic Inc., chose to do a private offering when he learned that brokers were not interested in handling a deal of less than $5 million because their commissions (usually 10 percent) would not give them a sufficient return.[57]

There are numerous other online and offline avenues available for doing a private offering, including Direct Stock Market and firms like OffRoad Capital. Direct Stock Market is a listing for direct public offerings and private placements. It provides an online environment in which investors can discuss offerings. Potential investors, however, must do their own due diligence. Direct Stock Market also helps companies to put together Web-based virtual road shows. OffRoad Capital is a placement agent for established private companies seeking growth capital of $3 million for $15 million.[58]

TIPS WHEN SEEKING ANGEL FUNDING

Although each angel investor may be a unique individual, there are some similarities in what they look for in potential investments. Mark Van Osnabrugge and Robert J. Robinson, authors of *Angel Investing,* offer the following observations about angels:[59]

- Angels are overwhelmingly male and average in their late 40s.

- Angels tend to be entrepreneur-manager types, whereas VCs tend to be financial-investor types.

- Angels invest in about 22 percent of the deals that they seriously consider; the acceptance rate is much higher for referrals.

- Few angels fund firms with sales over $5 million.

- First-time angels tend to be too generous.

- Many angels spend less than a week on negotiations.

- Angels may each invest almost $145,000 per deal on average (median: $75,000), although the range was anywhere from $25,000 to $500,000.

- Entrepreneurs usually need a second round of financing, even though they may say that they never will.

- Angels invest when the equity is relatively cheap.

- 60 to 65 percent of angels' investments lose money or break even.

- Angels expect about a 30 percent or more rate of return in start-ups and early stage, and a 20 percent return for more established firms.

- The majority of angels are not involved daily in running the business.

- 23 to 39 percent of angels work full-time or part-time with their investments—the younger the venture and the less complete the management team, the more time angels spend with the venture.

- Generally, angels prefer to be a minority shareholder.

- Angels usually receive about 20 percent of the company equity. When investing as a syndicate, they get 32 percent on average.

- Angels allocate on the average 10 to 24 percent of their wealth.

- The average investment for a six- to eight-person angel syndicate is $600,000 with a typical range of $100,000 to $1 million.

- Angels often use relatively simple investment contracts, agreeing primarily on the price, number of shares for the invested amount, terms, the salary of the entrepreneur, and buyback options for the entrepreneur.

- Only 47 percent of angels in the United States provide for liquidation in their investment contracts.

- Serial angels conduct far more extensive evaluations of their investment opportunities.

- Angels make two or three investments every three years.

- Most angels hope to quintuple their money in five years; only a few actually do.

- Angels tend to scan investment opportunities until they find one of interest, conducting little serious comparison with other deals still coming in.

- Most business angels deals are conceived through professional and personal network contacts.
- 41 percent of angels have experience in the sector they invest in.
- 89 percent of venture capital firms have experience in the sector they invest in.
- One study found that four times as many offers are made by angels than are accepted by the entrepreneurs.
- Most angels limit their risk by limiting their investment—and do not do follow-up investing. They prefer a portfolio rather than having all their eggs in one basket.
- Angels are not likely to do follow-up rounds unless there is a positive and compelling reason, rather than throwing good money after bad to keep the venture afloat.

REALITY CHECK

Robert Robinson noted that angels do not do as much due diligence. Research indicates only 15 percent of angels report doing *extensive* due diligence and that only 50 percent report doing *some* due diligence. He also found only 38 percent of angels report using legal or professional help in drawing up agreements or reviewing deals and that 80 percent of angels said they spent no money for due diligence on their last investment![60] The lack of extensive due diligence and the limited use of outside professionals may explain why angels decide much quicker than venture capital firms whether they will do deals. His research also found that most angels write a check in less than a month after the first meeting with an entrepreneur while venture capital firms usually take about two and a half months.[61]

The following tips represent reality checks:

1. Bootstrap from the beginning as much as possible. Minimize major cash outlays and ongoing cash obligations. By minimizing the venture's burn rate your initial capitalization goes farther.

2. Start the venture with as much cash as possible to postpone the need for and cost of early funding.

3. Make sure you know what you want to give up in terms of ownership, controls, and voting rights before you even consider going the angel route, and make sure you have reasonable expectations.

4. Identify when you will need the money, how much you will need, and what you will need it for.

5. Remember the Gretzky concept of timing; have your act together before you need to seek funding.

6. Start preparing for going the angel route early—earlier than you think.

7. Assume things will not go smoothly or on schedule. Have contingency plans including backup angels or an angel syndicate if things don't work out.

8. Remember, the funding deal isn't done until you actually have the money.

9. Know when to seek outside funds—not too soon and not too late.

10. Recognize the Catch 22 nature of timing. If you start too soon, your valuation will be lower and you will have to give up more of the firm. If you wait longer, then your valuation will be higher and it will cost you less, but you must have the funds to be able to get there. Also, if you wait as long as possible, then the angel has

considerable power because he or she may be able to walk away from the deal. Conversely, you may not be in a position to walk away from the deal if you have reservations about the terms.

11. Surround yourself with people who provide credibility and stature to your venture. Having a high-caliber advisory board or board of directors says a lot about the venture. The same applies to the management team and the firms and people who provide professional services.

12. Be frugal, but hire the best people. Negotiate with the best service providers to discount their rates with the understanding that they may be first in line if the venture grows.

13. Be selective when seeking angels and do your homework before contacting them.

14. Check out potential investors.

15. Avoid cold calls. Expand your network of contacts and use respected individuals for referrals.

16. Make sure you have met the investor before doing any serious prospecting.

17. Develop a high profile for you and your firm so you are known in the entrepreneurial and investor community. Create the type of buzz and reputation where people want to know what you are doing and want a piece of the action.

18. Start your search in the immediate area. Angels prefer investing in firms within a short drive.

19. Find out which angels serve as lead investors. They may bring in additional investors.

20. Beware of virgin angels. Experienced angels make funding decisions quicker and with fewer surprises. Virgin angels may back out when they get cold feet.

21. Seek angels with start-up experience. They understand the roller-coaster nature of emerging ventures and keep their cool under fire.

22. Angels with the same industry experience are in a better position to provide assistance.

23. Determine what value-added dimensions you want from the angel. Identify what perspectives and skills you need to have on the board of directors and what you need from an active angel on a daily basis.

24. Seek angels who can make a profound difference via wisdom and contacts/connections. Angels who can move the venture toward value-enhancing events or milestones are particularly beneficial.

25. Seek angels who can supplement the entrepreneur and team's perspective, skills, and experience. Their ability to anticipate problems and prevent them can help a lot.

26. Avoid angels who have a reputation for micromanaging.

27. Avoid angels who don't get the new rules of the game—particularly information technology.

28. Match funding needs to investor profiles. If your firm is in high technology, then seek angels who get technology. If you will be looking for more than $100,000 in funding, then seek angels who have done $100,000 deals. If you will be seeking additional rounds of funding, then seek angels who have deep enough pockets and who will do additional rounds.

29. Target angels with the same time horizon. If you are not looking for a quick liquidity event, then look for angels who invest patient money.

30. Recognize that angels will not wait forever for a return on their investment. Agree on exit strategy in advance.

31. Avoid angels who are looking for quick liquidity events; their interest in cashing out may undermine the venture's ability to grow by compromising key issues and cutting corners.

32. If you are looking for additional rounds of funding, particularly venture capital funding, then make sure you structure the initial round(s) with that in mind. Follow-up rounds of funding may dilute angel ownership.

33. If you are planning to have stock options available for attracting and rewarding members of the management team, then make sure stock is available in reserve for those purposes.

34. Do not just take the first offer that comes along.

35. Be persistent. If turned down, ask for recommendations of other investors and for feedback about your business plan, and so forth.

IT'S A WHOLE NEW BALLGAME

Entrepreneurs need to recognize that the moment they accept angel investment, their role and their firm change in at least three fundamental ways. First, the entrepreneur's level of accountability to others increases dramatically. "It's often an unpleasant shock when entrepreneurs realize that they have received more than just money as part of the bargain. Once the money has been accepted, it's no longer your business anymore—now you have a partner. .... You must begin thinking about your business as something that is an entirely new entity."[62] This is why it is so important to agree in writing on the rights and responsibilities for both the entrepreneur and angel well before the deal is finalized. Decision-making issues, performance expectations, and exit conditions that are not addressed before the deal is signed can undermine what is supposed to be a mutually beneficial relationship.

Second, entrepreneurs need to recognize that they are trustees of other people's money. How they spend the firm's money is now subject to the angel's scrutiny. Most entrepreneurs are accustomed to making on-the spot financial decisions. They may also have spent some of their venture's funds on personal enhancements. Angel money brings angel scrutiny. Angel funding is different from funding from friends and family. They may have put money into the business to help out the entrepreneur more than as a business investment. Angel funding is also different from venture capital funding. Venture capital firms invest their investors' money. Angels take their investments seriously because they invest their own money!

Third, angels expect their investment to be a catalyst for the venture's growth. They expect their funding to be used to ramp up operations that will take the venture to the next level. Angels will rarely do a deal if their funds will be used to pay off debt or earlier investors, for raising the entrepreneur's salary, or to pay for anything that is not mission critical.

EXIT STRATEGY: BEGIN WITH THE END IN MIND

Most entrepreneurs seek angel funding because they are looking for *patient money*. Jeff Bezos noted, "It is hard to do what needs to be done if you want to build a business that will satisfy your customers in the long term if your investors are only concerned about the short term."[63]

Fortunately, most angels do seem to direct their attention to building the venture more than cashing out. Louise Witt offers an interesting explanation for why angels do not dwell on cashing out. She believes angels recognize investing in start-ups is a high-stakes gamble. According to Witt, "Out of ten angel investments, they'll only hit the jackpot on three or four. Maybe fewer. Two or three will be complete busts. The rest? Known as the living dead, these are mediocre companies that aren't bad enough to fail but not good enough to have an exit, either."[64]

Entrepreneurs also need to recognize, however, that angels only date emerging ventures; they do not marry them. Entrepreneurs need to demonstrate there will be a payoff for the patient money. Angels must have some liquidity event if they are to get a return on their investment. The entrepreneur's financing plan must project whether the angel's investment will be for as little as two years or as much as 7 to 10 years. The expected duration of the investment will affect the venture's growth as well as the type and nature of angel funding.

Entrepreneurs need to let prospective angels know when they will get their money out, how they will get their money out, and what type of return they should be able to get for their investment. Even if the angel does not specify it, the deal should have a provision specifying whether the entrepreneur or firm will redeem the angel's stock if there is not a major liquidity event. The deal should state the terms for valuation and circumstances that could trigger a redemption.

REALITY CHECK

Attorneys always advise their clients to put it in writing. Angels are expected to increase their due diligence and to protect their investments even more in the years ahead. Entrepreneurs need to make sure that redemption provisions do not come back to haunt them. The same applies to performance targets. Entrepreneurs need to be sure that they are not forced into a situation where they will have to find the money to buy the angel's interest before they or the firm can afford it. Attention also needs to be directed to making performance claims in the business plan or the solicitation of funding. If meeting projections is a condition for the funding, then the entrepreneur may be forced to buy the angel out or even to be replaced if the targets are not met. Although projections and/or targets may garner angel interest, they also create a level of accountability that could be very constraining.

A FEW REMINDERS WHEN SEEKING ANGEL INVESTORS

Three particular points need to be emphasized as this chapter comes to an end. Entrepreneurs need to recognize the value of leverage, empathy, and due diligence when prospecting for angels. First, creating and leveraging a strong network of highly respected contacts can pay big dividends when seeking angel funding. The saying, "If you get their heart, then you get their money," is worth noting when seeking angel investors. Entrepreneurs who can attract highly respected people to their advisory committee or board of directors should leverage their visibility and connections. They may be able to open doors for the venture. They may be able to contact a prospective angel whom they know and say, "I'm serving on the board of XYZ Company, and I think you should take a look." If the board members have also invested in the venture, that will also increase angel interest.

Keith Schilit noted that if the entrepreneur is looking for multiple investors, then an excellent way to attract investors is to demonstrate that other investors—particularly, the existing management team—have already invested in it. Showing prospective investors that people have already anteed up reduces the prospect's perception of the risk. There is a story of Frederick Smith, who in his quest for $90 million to launch Federal Express used the tactic of asking all of his potential investors for the last million rather than for the first 89 million.[65]

Leverage also applies to utilizing the angel once he or she comes on board. David Amis and Howard Stevenson noted that entrepreneurs only get 5 percent to 10 percent of what they could out of the relationship. Entrepreneurs should seek their help to find potential customers, additional investors, key staff, and distribution links.[66] They also noted angel investors can also help the venture move toward what investors call value events. Those are anything that can improve the real or perceived monetary worth of the venture by signing deals with strategic partners, lining up venture financing, and landing a well-known account.[67]

Second, most entrepreneurs are so wrapped up in their ventures that they fail to see the venture through the prospective angels' eyes. Angels do not have ESP, nor are they emotionally attached to the venture. Entrepreneurs need to be sure they provide the information angels need and they need to be sure the venture meets the angel's investment criteria. The entrepreneur needs to make sure the elevator pitch, executive summary, business plan, and any other supporting information highlight the most salient points for the prospective angel.

The entrepreneur's sales pitch should not ramble on and on about things that are not on the angel's criteria radar. Supporting documentation must also be readily available, so the angel's questions can be addressed and not require unnecessary iterations. The entrepreneur needs to emphasize the venture's unique selling points that make it the investment of choice. Particular attention may be directed to the potential to dominate a market, to garner a high profit margin, that its people are highly qualified, and that it has a number of sustainable competitive advantages.

Third, due diligence is a two-way street. Investors are always encouraged to look before they leap. Entrepreneurs also need to practice due diligence when looking for an angel. Not all angels have halos. Angels are not immune to misrepresentation. A few angels may even be looking for the opportunity to take the firm over if it fails to meet performance targets. If possible, the entrepreneur should attempt to learn about the angel's past investments and involvement in emerging ventures, whether the ventures were successful, whether the angel truly added value to the ventures, whether there was a good chemistry between the angel and the entrepreneurs, and whether the angel has sufficient funds to do an additional round of funding and to hang in there if things get tight.

REALITY CHECK

Although due diligence makes sense today, angel–entrepreneur relationships must be built on a foundation of trust and respect. Entrepreneurs have to exercise finesse when courting angels. Prospecting should foster goodwill with every potential investor, even if it does not generate a deal. Entrepreneurs need to be thorough, but they also need to remember when doing due diligence and negotiating the deal that they will be working together for a number of years. Even if the angel is seeking a passive investment, he or she will be providing advice, serving on the board of directors, and monitoring the firm's performance.

CONCLUSION: ANGELS CAN ACCELERATE GROWTH

If the emerging venture has merit and the entrepreneur is proactive in seeking funding, then it is very likely that there is at least one angel out there who will invest in the venture. If the entrepreneur has extensive experience and is looking for a passive angel, then there are angels who merely want to add emerging firms to their portfolio. If the entrepreneur is a first-timer with limited experience, contacts, and capital, then there are angels who can play a crucial role in the firm's evolution.

A number of today's most successful firms would not be household names if their angels were not willing to take the risk. Angels were willing to step forward and fund first-time entrepreneurs with limited business experience. Hans Severiens, director and cofounder of the Band of Angels, stated, "We're much more comfortable giving our money to someone who's run a business before. ... But somebody had to fund Steve Jobs ... Steve Jobs had a hard time getting money at first. As did Bill Gates."[68]

Angels also demonstrate considerable flexibility when it comes to the funding package. Angels may provide a very modest investment of a few thousand dollars to a start-up all the way up to hundreds of thousands of dollars to help an early-stage venture ramp up its operations. Angels are also flexible in their financial expectations. Bob Craine, chairman of the Oklahoma Investment Forum, noted that while angels would love to get involved with the next eBay, they're also a pragmatic bunch.[69] He also noted that if you show them a good solid deal with the opportunity for a 25 percent or 30 percent return, they'll probably want to get involved, whatever the industry.[70]

Entrepreneurs may also need to show commensurate flexibility. If they start the process with, "It's my way or the highway," and go into the process with a term sheet set in stone, then they are likely to come up empty-handed. Although entrepreneurs should not give equity away, they need to do what it takes to provide the fuel for growth. By giving up a little, entrepreneurs have the opportunity to gain a lot.

Take the money ... and run

—Woody Allen

ENDNOTES

1. Paul Brown, "Seven Steps to Heaven," *Inc.,* October 2001, p. 81.
2. David Amis and Howard Stevenson, *Winning Angels: The 7 Fundamentals of Early-Stage Investing* (Englewood Cliffs, NJ: Financial Times Prentice Hall, 2001), p. 78.
3. Stephen Rebello, "Visionaries," *Success,* February 1998, p. 41.
4. Edward O. Welles, "15 Steps to a Start-Up Investors Will Buy," *Inc.,* March 1994, p. 74.
5. Robert D. Hisrich and Michael P. Peters, *Entrepreneurship* (Homewood, IL: Irwin, 1989), p. 33.
6. David Newton, *www.entrepreneur.com.*
7. Leonard A. Batterson, *Raising Venture Capital and the Entrepreneur* (Englewood Cliffs, NJ: Prentice Hall, 1986), p. 47.
8. W. Keith Schilit, *The Entrepreneur's Guide to Preparing a Winning Business Plan and Raising Venture Capital* (Englewood Cliffs: Prentice Hall, 1990), p. 30.
9. Ibid., p. 30.
10. David Evanson and Art Beroff, "Your Butt on the Line," *Entrepreneur,* July 2000, p. 73. Reprinted with permission of Entrepreneur Media, Inc.
11. Ibid., p. 71. Reprinted with permission of Entrepreneur Media, Inc.

12. Robert Robinson, "Excelling: Wings of Desire," Angel Advisor, *www.angeladvisor.com*, January–February 2002.

13. Paul B. Brown, "Seven Steps to Heaven," *Inc.,* October 2001, p. 76.

14. Amis and Stevenson, *Winning Angels: The 7 Fundamentals of Early-Stage Investing,* p. 79.

15. James Morrow, "Age Before Booty?" *Success,* May 1998, p 53.

16. Schilit, *The Entrepreneur's Guide to Preparing a Winning Business Plan and Raising Venture Capital,* p. 50.

17. John Ason, "One Valuation System: A Serial Angel Gives His Ideas on the Toughest of Tasks," Angel Advisor, *www.angeladvisor.com.*

18. Louise Witt, "Where's The Exit?" Angel Advisor, *www.angeladvisor.com.*

19. Andrew Raskin, "Bridge Financing Over the River Scared," *Inc.,* June 2000.

20. Louise Witt, "Where's the Exit?," *Angel Advisor, www.angeladvisor.com.*

21. Ibid.

22. David Evanson and Art Beroff, "Many Golden Returns," *Entrepreneur,* March 2000, p. 66. Reprinted with permission of Entrepreneur Media, Inc.

23. Witt "Where's the Exit?" pp. 49–54.

24. Ibid.

25. Ason, "One Valuation System: A Serial Angel Gives His Ideas on the Toughest of Tasks," pp. 71 & 72.

26. Ibid.

27. Brown, "Seven Steps to Heaven," p. 79.

28. Ason, "One Valuation System: A Serial Angel Gives His Ideas on the Toughest of Tasks," pp. 71 & 72.

29. Ibid.

30. Evanson and Beroff, "Many Golden Returns," p. 66.

31. Ason, "One Valuation System: A Serial Angel Gives His Ideas on the Toughest of Tasks," pp. 71 & 72.

32. Mark Van Osnabrugge and Robert J. Robinson, *Angel Investing* (San Francisco: Jossey-Bass, 2000), p. 221. Copyright © 2000, Jossey Bass. This material is used by permission of John Wiley & Sons, Inc.

33. Ibid.

34. Ibid., p. 220.

35. Ibid., p. 216.

36. Ason, "One Valuation System: A Serial Angel Gives His Ideas on the Toughest of Tasks," pp. 71 & 72.

37. Amis and Stevenson, *Winning Angels*, p. 78.

38. Ibid., p. 79.

39. Van Osnabrugge and Robinson, *Angel Investing,* p. 127.

40. Kevon Yarr, "A Good Angel Is Hard to Find," *Atlantic Progress,* January–February 2002, p. 32.

41. Stephanie Gruner, "Conversations with Angels," *Inc.,* October 1996, p. 82.

42. Interview with Tom Long.

43. Van Osnabrugge and Robinson, *Angel Investing,* p. 80.

44. Robert Robinson, "Excelling: Wings of Desire," *Angel Advisor, www.angeladvisor.com*, January–February 2002.

45. Ibid.

46. Bonnie Azab Powell, "Band of Angels's Hans Severiens Wants to Know, Are You Experienced?" *Red Herring,* January 2, 2000.

47. Cythia Griffin, "Venture Capital," *Entrepreneur,* June 2000, p. 154. Reprinted with permission of Entrepreneur Media, Inc.

48. Cynthia E. Griffin, "In Good Forum," *Entrepreneur,* July 2000, p. 98. Reprinted with permission of Entrepreneur Media, Inc.

49. Susan Greco, "A Match Made in Cyberspace," *Inc.,* September 1999, p. 49.

50. Jill Andresky Fraser, "Where Has All the Money Gone?," *Inc.,* April 2000, pp. 101 & 102.

51. David H. Freedman, "We're from the Government and We're Here to Help," *Inc.,* September 1999, p. 45.

52. David H. Freeman, "Virtual Road Show," *Inc.,* September 1999, p. 45.

53. Van Osnabrugge and Robinson, *Angel Investing*, p. 72.

54. W.K. Schilit, *Dream Makers and Deal Makers: Inside the Venture Capital Industry* (Englewood Cliffs, NJ: Prentice Hall, 1991), p. 123.

55. U.S. Securities and Exchange Commission Website, *www.sec.gov* (March 2004).

56. David H. Freedman, "Got Money?," *Inc.,* September 1999, p. 45.

57. Ibid.

58. Susan Greco, "The IPO Classifieds," *Inc.,* September 1999, p. 48.

59. Van Osnabrugge and Robinson, *Angel Investing.* The data provided are from various parts of the book.

60. Robert Robinson, "Excelling: Wings of Desire," *Angel Advisor, www.angeladvisor.com,* January–February 2002.

61. Ibid.

62. Kevon Yarr, "A Good Angel Is Hard to Find," *Atlantic Progress,* January–February 2002, p. 33.

63. C-SPAN, "American Perspectives," May 19, 2001, *www.c-span.org.*

64. Witt, "Where's The Exit?" pp. 49–54.

65. Schilit, *The Entrepreneur's Guide to Preparing a Winning Business Plan and Raising Venture Capital,* p. 15.

66. Amis and Stevenson, *Winning Angels,* p. 79.

67. Ibid., p. 81.

68. Powell, "Band of Angels's Hans Severiens Wants to Know, Are You Experienced?" p. 48.

69. Andresky Fraser, "Where Has All the Money Gone?" p. 109.

70. Ibid.

12

VENTURE CAPITAL FUNDING

When you approach a venture capitalist you should not approach him with the thought
that you are seeking only money. When you acquire venture capital you are acquiring
additional brain power to help your corporation achieve the goals you have established.[1]

—David Gladstone

Venture capital is probably the least understood form of funding. It has always had a
certain mystique to it because very few businesses meet venture capital funding criteria.
Bob Zider, as president of the Beta Group, a firm that develops and commercializes new
technology, noted that venture capitalists have been romanticized almost as much as
entrepreneurs. According to Zider, "The popular press is filled with against-all-odds
success stories of Silicon Valley entrepreneurs. In these sagas, the entrepreneur is the
modern-day cowboy, roaming new industrial frontiers much the same way that earlier
Americans explored the West. At his side stands the venture capitalist, a trail-wise side-
kick ready to help the hero through all the tight spots—in exchange, of course, for a
piece of the action."[2]

Prospective entrepreneurs are frequently heard saying, "Oh, I'll just go out and get
some venture capital to get us up and running." It needs to be noted right now that getting venture capital funding is not like ordering a pizza over the phone or a book over
the Internet. Chapter 1 provided a strong dose of reality in profiling the qualities needed
for entrepreneurs to have a chance to beat the odds. This chapter profiles the realities
associated with trying to secure venture capital funding. A few statistics may provide a
sobering dose of reality. Prospective entrepreneurs should remember the following numbers, *l/1,000, 30 seconds, 2/100,* and *2/10* when they think about seeking venture capital. These numbers represent a few of the facts of life for entrepreneurs seeking funding.

1 IN 1,000: START-UPS RARELY QUALIFY
FOR FUNDING

Venture capital is rarely available for start-ups. Most venture capital firms slammed the
door to funding start-ups when the dot-com bubble burst. It is only recently that they

have begun to consider funding even the most promising start-ups. Venture capital firms generally avoid seed funding altogether.

Venture capital firms prefer to hedge their bets by investing in firms that are much more tangible than an entrepreneur's *concept* or a business that exists only as a *plan.* Nearly a million businesses are started each year, but less than 2,000 of all businesses— new and not so new—will receive venture capital funding this year. The odds that a relatively new venture will be funded by a venture capital firm are less than *1 in 1,000.* To make matters worse, most businesses that are funded have been operating for at least three years. According to a study by Amar Bhidé, 77 percent of companies receiving VC funding were three years old or older. The figure does not even take into consideration the fact that some of the firms that are funded this year are securing follow-up funding rather than initial funding.[3]

Few new businesses fit the venture capital investment criteria. Bhidé's research indicates the venture capital industry typically disburses about two-thirds of its funds to post–start-up or *later-stage* companies.[4] The high proportion of later-stage investments reveals a strong preference for funding businesses after entrepreneurs have reduced the high uncertainties of the start-up stage and demonstrated the potential for large payoffs.[5]

30 SECONDS: GONE IN THE BLINK OF AN EYE!

Venture capital fund managers do not spend much time reviewing business plans submitted by entrepreneurs. It is said that a professional thief can steal a car in less than 60 seconds. Entrepreneurs need to recognize that most venture capitalists take no more than 30 seconds to decide whether to review or reject a request for funding. This is the amount of time it takes the venture capital manager to read the business plan's Executive Summary. If the fund manager finds that the business as profiled in the Executive Summary does not fit the fund's criteria, then the plan will be returned without being read.

The plan will also be returned if the Executive Summary indicates a weak management team, a product/service that doesn't seem viable or appealing, a target market that has not materialized, or a funding request that falls outside the fund's parameters. The business plan may even be returned in some cases without the Executive Summary even being read. Numerous funds will not review it if it was not solicited or referred to the fund by someone affiliated with it or with a key reference.

2 IN 100: MANY SEEK FUNDING BUT FEW ARE CHOSEN

Less than 2 in 100, or 2 percent, of the business plans submitted to a venture capital fund will receive funding. Venture capital and due diligence go hand in hand. Although some venture capital funds may have chased some really bad deals in the dot-com *leap before you look funding frenzy* in 1999 and 2000, most venture capital firms are very deliberate in their analysis of businesses seeking funding. Entrepreneurs need to recognize that seeking venture capital funding is very different from the practice of U.S. courts. A business seeking venture capital funding is guilty (will not be funded) unless it can prove it is innocent (worthy of the risk). The section on venture capital criteria highlights the most salient factors when venture capital firms review funding proposals.

2 IN 10: OF THE FEW THAT ARE CHOSEN, EVEN FEWER WILL SUCCEED

Businesses that make it through the scrutiny of the venture capital fund's due-diligence process and receive funding are not assured of success. There is a Grand Canyon between getting funded and being a truly successful business. Venture capital firms live by the *20-60-20 rule*. On the average, only 2 in 10, or 20 percent, of the businesses funded by a venture capital firm make enough money for the venture capital firm to justify the risk incurred by the overall fund. Sixty percent of the businesses funded by venture capital firms are so marginal that they are called *the living dead*. At least 20 percent of the businesses funded go broke.

Life in the venture capital and emerging venture *fast lane* is full of peril, setbacks, and surprises. The due-diligence process is far from foolproof for even the most respected venture capital firms. Due diligence can only go so far because most business plans for relatively new ventures are based on assumptions about the management team's ability to develop a sustainable competitive advantage and the business's ability to generate a highly lucrative return for its investors.

HOW DO VENTURE CAPITAL FUNDS WORK?

People who invest in venture capital funds occupy a specific place on the investment *risk–reward continuum*. Wealthy individuals are the most common investors in venture capital firms. Insurance companies, investment houses, and pension plans may also invest a portion of their portfolios in venture capital funds.

Venture capital funds are usually formed as limited partnerships. Each fund is managed by individuals who screen funding requests, determine which businesses are funded, and negotiate the terms for the funding. Most funds are established for a 10-year term. At the end of the 10-year term, the fund's management sells the illiquid holdings of the partnership for cash or converts them into marketable securities and returns the proceeds to their clients.[6] For the services they provide, VCs receive a flat annual fee (usually 1 to 2 percent of the assets managed) as well as a *carried interest* or share (on the order of 20 percent) of the profits generated for clients.[7]

Venture capital funds are created to benefit from *liquidity events*. Liquidity events usually take two forms: acquisition of the funded business by another business, or an initial public offering in which the business goes public. If neither of these events occurs, then the venture capital firm may try to find another business to acquire the business or find some other way, including selling its shares to other investors or the funded business's management team. In any event, entrepreneurs need to recognize that a venture capital fund's clock is always ticking. Every prospect for funding is carefully analyzed in terms of how lucrative its liquidity event could be.

Although angels may show some emotional attachment or inherent interest in businesses they fund, venture capitalists see prospects the way people raise cattle view their herds. They are assets that are there only for one purpose—to be converted into the greatest amount of cash in a relatively short time.

REALITY CHECK

Today, only a few funded businesses have an initial public offering. So venture capital firms try to position the funded business so that it can be acquired. Generally speaking, most funded businesses just linger or go bankrupt.

VENTURE CAPITAL FIRMS PROVIDE
SMART MONEY

Most of the businesses seeking venture capital do so because they have little capital left and they need a major infusion of cash. They have little staying power and they have tapped just about every source of conventional financing. In most cases, they need a significant amount of working capital. They do not qualify for collateralized debt so banks are reluctant to put any more money into the business. The entrepreneur and entrepreneurial team have been bootstrapping for a while so they do not have any money—and probably have been taking minimal, if any, salary. The infusion of venture capital permits the emerging business to proceed; without it, the business may have to change course and seek any sort of revenue stream—even if it is not the best one for the future of the business. Without venture capital, the business may need to cut back in payroll, product development, or sales efforts rather than move forward. Without the infusion of cash the business may have to make major concessions in the price it charges for its products/services and/or payment terms with its customers.

Venture capitalists are committed to helping the businesses they fund succeed. They provide more than funding. The best funds also provide valuable advice, resources, and connections. Andy Marcuvitz, a venture capitalist, noted that raising money from random rich people is usually bad. He said, "It's dumb money, and it takes too much time to service. ... We (venture capitalists) don't want to control you—we just want to make money."[8]

Venture capital firms can play a critical role in the evolution of an emerging business. Without funding many emerging firms either would not be able to get to the next level or they would have to wait a considerable time to get there on their own. When the entrepreneurial team gets to the proverbial fork in the venture capital road, it has to decide if it wants to deal with all the issues associated with seeking and having venture capital financing or if the business would be better off trying to finance its growth internally on a hand-to-mouth basis. The latter course places the business in a rather precarious position. Few emerging businesses have the type of cash flow needed to finance rapid growth. Internal financing may cause the business to miss the window of opportunity for significant growth. Potential customers and competitors will not wait for an emerging business to get its financial act together.

Venture capital can provide the business with the funds needed for various critical stages of growth. Venture capital can help the firm go from the prototype stage to commercialization. Emerging businesses frequently need significant funds to launch a new product, process, service, or application. Venture capital can also help a firm that is already in the marketplace to secure a dominant competitive position and to capitalize on the most lucrative part of the growth curve.

Qualifying for venture capital funding may be the most significant milestone in the ever-precarious evolution of an emerging business. Firms that qualify for funding can move ahead. Their funding becomes a barrier that may keep lesser competitors on the sidelines. Amar Bhidé indicates that the capital, ideas, and expertise enable start-ups to leapfrog into the middle region of the investment–uncertainty–profit diagram—a place that takes promising businesses several years to reach.[9] He noted that venture capitalists helped turn Cisco from a small, struggling enterprise into the world's leading supplier of the routers that link computers in different locations.[10]

Venture capital firms can assist emerging businesses by contacting key suppliers, bringing in additional investors, establishing relationships with distributors, and bringing in key talent—including a new chief executive. The venture capital fund may also help the management team by providing valuable objectivity, formulating its strategy, improving its operating systems, exploring the merit of establishing strategic alliances and/or forming joint ventures, as well as determining the relative merit and appropriate timing for a liquidity event.

SECURING VENTURE CAPITAL IS NOT JUST A FUNDING EVENT

Securing funding marks the beginning of a two-dimensional relationship with the venture capital firm. The venture capital firm provides valuable assistance. It will also monitor the business's performance.

The venture capital firm's assistance and scrutiny in monitoring performance may vary with the stage of the business. The earlier the stage, the more time and effort will be devoted to assisting the business. The same also applies to monitoring its performance. Since earlier-stage businesses represent higher risks, venture capital firms have more leverage in negotiating the terms of the funding package. They try to structure deals so they will have a higher return to cover the higher risk. It is interesting to note that after the dot-com funding debacle, most venture capital firms are leaning more toward a little less risk and a little less return than before.

Venture capital firms generally exert the most influence over start-ups (if they fund them) and early-stage ventures. They spend considerable time with management. They may even play an integral role in recruiting the management team. William Sahlman noted, "Partners in venture capital firms usually visit each company they have invested in about 19 times per year and spend a hundred hours in direct contact (either on site or on the phone) with the company. They help recruit and compensate key individuals, work with suppliers and customers, help establish tactics and strategy, play a major role in raising capital, and help structure transactions such as mergers and acquisitions."[11]

Venture capital firms also influence the direction of emerging ventures by advising them via the people they place on the venture's board of directors as well as through the venture capital firm's staff and investors. The venture capital firm can thereby help the entrepreneurial team and board of directors make important business decisions. The same people may also provide assistance through their contacts with other individuals and organizations. Venture capitals firms may also play an integral role in positioning an emerging venture if its plans include an initial public offering. They often assume more control by changing management and are sometimes willing to take over the day-to-day operations themselves.[12]

REALITY CHECK

Venture capital funding is nice if you can get it, but the smart part of smart money may not be as available as it used to be. Although there may be more funds than in the past, venture capital representatives are spread thinner than ever. One article provides the following calculation: If you assume that each partner has a typical portfolio of 10 companies and a 2,000-hour work year, the amount of time spent on each company with each activity is relatively small. If the total time spent with portfolio companies serving as directors and acting as consultants is 40 percent, then partners spend 800 hours per year with portfolio companies. That allows only 80 hours per year per company—which averages less than two hours per week. The popular image of venture capitalists as sage advisors is at odds with the reality of their schedules. In fact, *virtual CEOs* are now being added to the equity pool to counsel company management, which is the role that VCs used to play. Moreover, the average fund today is 10 times larger than those in the past and each partner manages two to five times as many investments. Not surprisingly, then, the partners are usually far less knowledgeable about the industry and the technology than the entrepreneurs. It is for this reason that the entrepreneurial team should look for venture capital funds that are in tune with their technology and markets. The entrepreneurial team should then make every effort to ensure it gets the partner or representative from that fund to serve on its board of directors.[13]

REALITY CHECK

Most venture fund managers and partners have even less time today to spend with businesses that receive funding. By necessity, they are devoting more time to saving the firms in their portfolios that received funding earlier.

EMBARK ON THE VENTURE CAPITAL JOURNEY WITH BOTH EYES OPEN

Seeking venture capital is not for the faint at heart. Entrepreneurs need to proceed with caution because venture capital is a double-edged sword. Under the right conditions, it can play an instrumental role in helping an emerging business accelerate its growth. Yet getting funded is not without its costs. To some entrepreneurs, the process of seeking venture capital funding seems like they are making a pact with the devil. Getting funded not only takes time and considerable effort. It always comes with a number of strings attached.

Entrepreneurs, like venture capitalists, need to take a close look at themselves and their businesses to determine whether the advantages associated with venture capital funding are greater than the conditions that are associated with the funding. Although funding may provide the opportunity for accelerated growth and the rewards of a corresponding liquidity event, it comes with dilution of ownership, performance expectations, considerable and ongoing management scrutiny, as well as the potential displacement of the entrepreneur as the business's chief executive officer.

REALITY CHECK

Before you proceed with seeking VC funding, ask yourself, "Am I the right person to be the business's CEO for the next few years?" Your ability to take the business to the next level and position it for a liquidity event will be questioned by VCs. If not, then you may have to step down as CEO as a condition of funding!

Timing is Everything: Vcs Rarely Fund a Business Before its Time

The stage of development for your business has a lot to do with whether it will get funded. It will also affect the terms that will be tied to the funding. The preceding statistics indicate that only an elite group of emerging businesses get venture capital funding. Venture capitalists are very selective. They focus on certain markets, certain types of entrepreneurs, and certain types of business models.

The newer the business, the lower the odds for funding and the lower the level of funding provided by the venture capital firm. The due-diligence process used by venture capitalists places a premium on businesses that are up and running. Rob Ryan noted on his website *(www.entrepreneur-america.com)* that most first-time entrepreneurs meet with VCs too early. Getting a meeting is not the goal. Getting a good partner and a check should be your goal. He advises entrepreneurs to not talk to venture capital firms until they have their ducks aligned. Your ducks are aligned when you meet these criteria:

- You have critical mass in an excellent founding team.

- You have talked with customers and qualified interest.

- You have references from customers plus work colleagues.

- You have a business presentation of 20 to 30 minutes that answers all appropriate business questions.[14]

He also noted that the following questions, "Do you have a customer?" and "Do you have a working prototype?" are of paramount importance in approaching venture capital funding. According to Ryan, "Until you have a product and customers, you aren't ready to raise money with top-tier venture capital firms, and those are the only ones to deal with."[15]

Amar Bhidé noted that the low likely profit and the high uncertainty associated with most start-ups seem incompatible with the structure and decision-making process of the typical VC firm.[16] It is for this reason that venture capital firms prefer firms that are positioned for hypergrowth. More than 80 percent of the money invested by venture capitalists goes to companies that are in the adolescent phase of a company's life cycle. It is at this stage of development when an emerging business begins to commercialize its innovation.[17]

The hypergrowth or adolescent stage appeals to venture capitalists for two reasons. First, most of the uncertainties associated with a start-up have been resolved so the risks of failure have been reduced dramatically. It is for this reason that venture capitalists invest a multiple of the amount of money in adolescent businesses that they would invest in businesses that have a way to go before they take off. Second, later-stage businesses are much closer to a liquidity event. This means the venture capital firm's investment can be *turned over* or *cashed out* quicker. Although the venture capitalist may not be able to negotiate as favorable a set of terms as it would with a business that is at the preadolescent stage, the higher probability and shorter period until a liquidity event usually outweigh the risks and time associated with a preadolescent business.

Venture Capitalists Fill a Gap in the Financial Marketplace

Venture capitalists occupy an important position in the risk–return funding continuum. Although most entrepreneurs would rather not deal with venture capitalists, entrepreneurs that lack sufficient capital quickly recognize that without outside funding—including venture capital—their business will not be able to fulfill its potential. In some cases, their business's very existence could be in jeopardy without the infusion of venture capital.

Banks may play a modest role in funding new ventures, but they cannot take the risks associated with start-ups and early-stage ventures. Most banks are either unwilling or unable to provide the amount of funding needed by preadolescent or adolescent businesses. Bob Zider noted that astute venture capitalists operate in a secure niche where traditional, low-cost financing is unavailable.[18] The tendency for venture capitalists to occupy a position in the funding chain where they are able to negotiate a significant piece of the ownership and control of a new venture after the entrepreneur and management team have already committed their blood, sweat, and tears to the business has contributed to venture capitalists being labeled *vulture capitalists*.

Angels may be willing to take a noncollateralized or equity position in an emerging business, but there are limits to how far they are willing to invest. Most angels do not have deep enough pockets to provide the funding needed by an adolescent business or they are unwilling to invest that amount of money into a single business. The desire to diversify one's risk is one of the reasons well-capitalized angels invest in venture capital funds. Venture capital funds relieve them of the time and skills it takes to do due diligence. The typical venture capital fund invests in at least 10 emerging businesses.

Venture capital firms have a number of other advantages over dealing with angel investors. Venture capital firms are usually in a much better position to provide additional rounds of funding. An angel may draw the line with the first round of investment in an attempt to cut his or her losses. A venture capital firm is more likely to jump in with both feet and use its financial and nonfinancial resources to help the business. Angels and individual investors are considerably less liquid and have much less tolerance for putting in more capital down the road.[19]

REALITY CHECK

The key to dealing with venture capitalists is to get as much money up front from individual and angel investors. If venture capital funding is to be sought, then it should only be used to get the funding you cannot get from other less-invasive sources. David Evanson, a principal at Financial Communications Associates, noted, "But with professional venture investors, you shouldn't raise too much more funding than you actually need. There's plenty of money left in their till—and if you succeed, you'll get it the second time around at a much better price."[20]

Venture capital also plays a key role for firms that have the potential to move toward their initial public offering (IPO). Although a few firms in the past decade were able to go public without paying their dues in the venture capital stage, the vast majority of firms that are not corporate spin-offs that go public do tap the venture capital market before embarking on their IPO journey. Venture capital firms not only provide funding, they serve as a finishing school by getting promising businesses ready for liquidity events. In essence, the venture capitalist buys a stake in an entrepreneur's idea, nurtures it for a short period of time, and then exits with the help of an investment banker.[21]

Venture capital firms also play a critical role in the development of innovative technology, products, and processes. Although large businesses may pride themselves with their R&D head counts and budgets, it is clear that most established businesses are somewhat cautious in the projects they pursue and the financial thresholds that must be cleared before they will fund an innovative project. Venture capitalists may be more willing to take a chance on new markets and technologies than large corporations. Venture capitalist firms are also more willing to pursue smaller opportunities than larger businesses are willing to fund.[22]

Although IBM, 3M, and Merck allocate far more money on their R&D budgets each year than is available through all the venture capital firms combined, they must seek projects that have the ability to generate returns that are commensurate with their R&D investments. Venture capital firms are different from large organizations because they are more willing to invest in emerging niches where the window of opportunity may just be opening. Larger firms tend to look for opportunities in more established mass markets where the window is more visible and large enough to meet their return on investment targets in relative and absolute dollars. Established firms also look for the windows of opportunity to stay open for an extended period of time. Venture capitalist firms look for windows that will stay open long enough to facilitate a liquidity event. As long as venture capitalist firms are able to exit the company and industry before it tips out, they can reap extraordinary returns at relatively low risk.[23]

Show Me the Money!

Entrepreneurs need to recognize that the investment criteria used by venture capitalists are different from the criteria used by most angels. David Evanson noted that while both sets of investors are looking for a healthy return, the angel's required rate might be somewhat more moderate. Venture capital firms are interested in managing the fund and reporting to their investors. Unlike angels, venture capitalists are investing other people's money. That can have a dramatic impact on their behavior.[24] The accountability to their investors who have very high expectations elicits an even higher level of due diligence by venture capital fund managers.

Angels differ from venture capitalists in the criteria used in selecting businesses to fund. As noted in Chapter 11, most angels tend to invest in businesses that they relate to and that are in their immediate geographic area. Most angels also seem to include some *emotional* metric in their selection process. They are interested in the business's products, services, and/or processes. They may also be interested in what that business can do for the community as an employer. Some angels see their investment as a form of *vicarious parenting* of the aspiring entrepreneur and his or her enterprise. As an angel, they may serve in an advisory role to help the business grow. If the angels were entrepreneurs, then they can experience some of the challenges of entrepreneurship again without having to put in the hours. Angels will be quick to point out, however, that their investments are not gifts. They expect a good return on their investment and they will hold the entrepreneur accountable if their investment sours.

Venture capitalists are not known for including the emotional factor in their deliberations. To venture capitalists, it's pure business. Products are just products, and the business's relative impact on the community is not a factor. The projects that have the best chance of having a lucrative liquidity event are funded. According to Evanson, "The difference between these two types of investors can be tantamount to the difference between an alumni booster at a homecoming football game and a nuclear power plant inspector. There's little you can do to overcome this reality except to expect it and not be offended by it."[25]

REALITY CHECK

Although most venture capitalists indicate the funding decision does not include the emotional factor, the fact that they invest in a particular industry indicates a predisposition for certain types of products, processes, and/or technology. The industry-specific nature of most funds indicates a belief by the fund that there are worthwhile opportunities in its corresponding markets. All things being equal, a business that has some *wow* appeal may garner more interest than a nuts-and-bolts type of business that offers little pizzazz when it comes to spending time working with that business or in describing businesses in the fund to its investors.

The length of time venture capitalists fund an emerging business also reflects the non-emotional side their funding strategy. Venture capital funding is like an agreement between the fund and the entrepreneur to date each other for just a few years. At no time should the relationship be considered a marriage! The venture capital firm and the emerging business will spend some time together and both will benefit, but the intent from the beginning is to make the most out the relationship and then move on by cashing out so the VC can date other emerging businesses that need what the venture capital firm has to offer.

The deliberately limited duration of the relationship needs to be reflected in how entrepreneurs seek venture capital funding. The difference is particularly evident in the 30-second elevator pitch entrepreneurs use when they attempt to attract interest from potential investors. Evanson notes that when an entrepreneur directs the elevator pitch at an angel, the pitch is directed to business issues. The pitch to the venture capitalist, however, must be directed to how much the venture capital firm can make and how quickly it can get out.[26]

VENTURE CAPITAL CRITERIA

The preceding comments make it seem like venture capital firms are cold and calculating and that they prey on the innocent and the needy. This is not the case. Venture capitalists are willing to take a higher level of risk only if there is the prospect of a high enough return to justify the risk. Entrepreneurs need to remember the 20-60-20 rule. Most of the firms that receive venture capital funding either go bankrupt or eke out only a modest return.

Venture capital fund managers must use criteria that create a fairly high threshold to qualify for funding. Although they may not know which of the 2 in 10 businesses funded may be star performers, each business to be funded must look like it has the potential to be a star. The stars represent the lifeblood for a venture capital fund. The few stars have to cover for the businesses that do not soar.

Venture capitalists really are not as greedy as they are portrayed in the media. The high-risk nature of their investments forces venture capital funds to look for businesses that have the potential to have liquidity events at 3, 5, or 10 times their investment in that business. The few stars (if there are any) must not only cover the losses or modest gains in the majority of the funded businesses in the portfolio, they must bring the overall portfolio's value to at least the 30 percent annual return for the duration of the fund.

A little math accentuates the need for the fund to invest in stars. If the fund is started with $20 million, then a 30 percent annual appreciation expectation will necessitate that the fund be worth $80 million (four times its original value) in 10 years when it is distributed to its investors. If each business in the portfolio receives $2 million, then each of the two stars will have to increase in value to $34 million. The two stars combined will be worth $68 million. The six living dead investments, which did not appreciate, will represent an additional $12 million in the portfolio. Of course, the two bankrupt businesses force the stars to make up for their losses. These calculations are simplistic, but they do show that the stars must appreciate between 10 and 20 times their original investments if the overall fund is to hit even a 30 percent annual return on investment.

The following criteria highlight what it takes to attract venture capital interest. At first glance, the criteria sound like the description of Superman. Although entrepreneurs may not have to be "faster than a speeding bullet, more powerful than a locomotive, and able to leap tall buildings in a single bound," they must have certain qualities and their businesses must have the potential to be truly exceptional. With few exceptions, businesses must demonstrate at least a certain level of each of the following criteria to be considered for funding. Being particularly strong on one criterion will not make up for a deficiency in another area.

Criteria 1: Lead Entrepreneur/Team

By understanding how venture capital actually works, astute entrepreneurs can mitigate their risks and increase their potential rewards. Many entrepreneurs make the mistake of thinking that venture capitalists are looking for good ideas when, in fact, they are looking for good managers in particular industry segments.[27]

The role of the entrepreneur changes when it comes to seeking venture capital. The entrepreneur's vision, experience, preliminary projections, personal collateral, and sales ability may have played major roles in attracting funding from friends and family as well as a loan from a bank. Those factors, however, will not be enough by themselves to meet the expectations of venture capital firms.

Venture capital firms recognize that while the entrepreneur plays a critical role in the success of a start-up, they also recognize that a one-person show may be risky. Venture capital firms insist that the business have a solid management team. According to the folk wisdom of the VC industry, a great founder cannot compensate for a mediocre team.[28]

If the business has considerable appeal and lacks one or more key members of the team it is not unusual for a venture capital firm to do what is necessary to make sure it has a solid team in place. Amar Bhidé noted that the high rate of growth and corresponding profit usually come with a corresponding complexity that exceed most entrepreneurs' ability and experience. It is not possible for even the best entrepreneurs to be all knowing in all the issues that need to be addressed and all the decisions that need to be made. He also noted that even Bill Gates probably would not have qualified for venture capital funding at the beginning of Microsoft.[29]

Venture capital firms distinguish between entrepreneurs with *ideas* and entrepreneurs who have a *proven track record*. Bhidé noted that experienced entrepreneurs significantly increase a venture's chances of attaining large scale quickly. Some untrained or inexperienced individuals may be able to learn how to manage rapidly growing firms, but it is difficult, before the fact, for VCs to identify entrepreneurs with this latent capacity.[30] In most cases, venture capitalists do not have the patience or the faith that an untried entrepreneur will rise to the occasion. This is one of the reasons why John Sculley was brought in from Pepsi to direct Apple Computer's growth.

There is no question that Steven Jobs was a great inspiration to his people and that he had a keen sense for innovation. These qualities and being a cofounder of Apple were not enough when it came time to take Apple to the next level. Apple's board recognized the company needed an executive at the helm who had the education, skills, and experience needed to make Apple a world-class company. Steven Jobs recognized he needed Sculley's help to chart the future course for Apple and to improve its ability to execute its plans via state-of-the art management systems. Steven Jobs' ego and inability to grow as an executive at that time led to his downfall. Fortunately, he returned to Apple a few years later with more seasoning to reinvigorate the company he cofounded.

REALITY CHECK

A number of venture funds include *coachability* criteria when evaluating a business. The extent the entrepreneur (or chief executive if the entrepreneur is not the chief executive) seems receptive to taking advice from the venture fund's manager or the fund's representative who serves on the business's board is important. If the entrepreneur seems to be *my way or the highway,* then that close-mindedness will be a serious detriment to funding. The coachability factor is not just important from the venture capital fund's perspective, it may also serve as an indication of the entrepreneur's ability to form a first-class management team and capitalize on its perspectives and talents. Coachability may also indicate the entrepreneur's willingness to delegate key decisions to others in the business. The business's ability to grow is closely tied to the extent the entrepreneur is willing to grow with the business and to let go.

Savvy entrepreneurs have the ability to sense the areas where they are not strong. They put together a team that has the talents needed to foster accelerated growth. Rob Ryan notes, "An entrepreneur knows how to build a strong team, balancing his or her own weaknesses with others' strengths. The team is the first company element investors assess. They know that a hardy team can overcome staggering obstacles, quickly whipping up new products, outsmarting competition, recovering from problems, and make impressive investor presentations."[31] Primus Venture Partners, an Ohio-based private equity partnership that funds private companies with exceptional growth potential, places a premium on the value of the management team. Its first core requirement in its investment criteria is "competent management with deep experience in the industry or markets they address."[32]

REALITY CHECK

It should be clear that venture capitalists are naturally reluctant to fund first-time entrepreneurs. They are even more reluctant to fund first-time entrepreneurs who lack top-level management experience. If you do not have entrepreneurial experience and lack the type of management experience needed to lead your business to a liquidity event, then you should seriously consider the role you should play as a member of the entrepreneurial team where you could provide value rather than the leader of the entrepreneurial team. Before seeking funding it may be necessary for you to bring in a person to take the helm who has the attributes that venture capital firms value. Funding odds go up dramatically if your venture has an exceptional entrepreneur or CEO and an exceptional team. If you were a venture capitalist, why would you take the risk with an untried entrepreneur when there are a number of growing ventures looking for money with founders who have already demonstrated they have what it takes to take a business to the next level?

If the business does not have an experienced management team, then the venture capital managers may be in a position to locate the needed talent. If the business is funded, then it will be able to attract quality people by offering higher salaries than it could afford prior to funding. It will also be able to lure key people with stock options. The opportunity to secure stock options may also make it possible to have them accept lower salaries for higher stock options. Lower salaries for key people reduce the business's expenses and cash outflow. Stock options may also cause higher levels of motivation and the tendency to stay with the business over the long haul.

Criteria 2: Rapid Growth: Industry and the Market

If new venture success is viewed as a horse race, then the entrepreneurial team is the jockey and the market opportunity is the horse. Criteria 1 stressed the need for the venture to have a capable jockey. Yet it takes more than an exceptional entrepreneurial team for a venture to be an outstanding success; it also takes, among other things, an outstanding market. The jockey may be very skilled in directing the horse, but the speed of the horse will also be determined by its potential. The same is true of a new venture. Its growth will be influenced by the size, nature, and growth of the industry and the venture's target market(s). Remember, no jockey has ever carried a horse over the finish line!

Andrew Verhalen, general partner of Matrix Partners, noted while many venture capitalists scout for investments by looking for the right entrepreneurs of the killer product, he looks for the right market. According to Verhalen, "If the management team isn't perfect, well, that's something he can help fix. But, if the market isn't ready and accessible, you can't be successful."[33] Entrepreneurs will increase their chance for success if they pick the right markets. Bob Zider noted, one myth is that venture capitalists invest in good people and good ideas. In reality, they invest in good industries. He estimates that less than 10 percent of all U.S. economic activity occurs in segments projected to grow more than 15 percent a year over the next five years.[34]

Venture capitalists consider the business's potential for dramatic growth and achieving a high level of sales and profits is crucial for funding. Dramatic growth and profitability are not possible if the overall market cannot support it.[35] Bob Zider noted that venture capitalists focus on the middle part of the classic industry S-curve. They avoid both the early stages, when technologies are uncertain and market needs are unknown, and the later stages, when competitive shakeouts and consolidations are inevitable and growth rates slow dramatically.[36]

Although established markets may provide the stability sought by banks and large firms, venture capitalists look for expanding markets where growth does involve zero-sum competition. Venture capitalists look for businesses that have the capacity to *scale up* and grow at an exponential rate.[37] Venture capital firms focus their attention on markets that are large or have the potential to be large within a couple of years that will support high levels of profitability. Small market niches and established markets that are waning markets rarely provide the type of growth and profitability required for venture capital funding.

Going back to the horse race analogy, venture capitalists focus their attention on one or two particularly fast tracks (industries or markets) and look for fast horses (emerging businesses) that will be ridden by highly competent jockeys (entrepreneurial teams). The challenge faced by venture capital firms is trying to sense which emerging businesses will be the winners, the also-rans, and the losers. Bob Zider noted, "During this adolescent period of high and accelerating growth, it can be extremely hard to distinguish the eventual winners from the losers because their financial performance and growth rates look strikingly similar. At this stage, all companies are struggling to deliver products to a product-starved market.[38]

REALITY CHECK

If your business's growth is targeted for a particular niche in a medium-sized market, then forget venture capital funding. The same holds true if you are targeting a larger niche in an established market with moderate growth expectations. Venture capitalists place a premium on businesses that will serve markets that offer the potential for a high rate of growth, a high level of revenue, a high rate of profit, a high rate of return on investment, and a high-valued liquidity event. Industries that offer little prospect for growth or that have questionable technology are avoided by most venture capital firms.

Criteria 3: Proprietary Position and Sustainable Competitive Advantage

Growing markets obviously appeal to venture capitalists. Emerging businesses that have the ability to gain market share in a growing market are even more appealing. Venture capitalists are particularly interested in emerging businesses that have a *sustainable competitive advantage*. Businesses that are able to provide what the market values and can do so with competitive superiority are likely to enjoy pricing latitude that should generate a higher level of profitability. Competitive superiority enhances market share and discourages potential competitors.

Venture capitalists place a premium on emerging businesses that have a proprietary position. Primus Venture Partners' second core requirement is the company's potential to become "a leader in its chosen market" by providing "distinctive products with a proprietary edge" or "unique services with strong customer appeal."[39]

In the middle part of the S-curve, growth is easier because the overall market is growing dramatically. Venture capital firms look for emerging businesses that are positioned to capture the growth stage and have the competitive advantages that will enable them to attract customers from other businesses as well. Kleiner Perkins, one of the largest venture capital firms, seeks to back ventures that are the first or second entrants in their markets, so speeding the product to market in advance of competition is absolutely critical.[40]

A proprietary position gives the business an edge in attracting customers or reduces its operating costs. The proprietary position does not have to be intellectual property that is protected by law. It can simply be having something that the competition does not have and/or cannot acquire. A proprietary position can take many forms. It can be brand identity, a unique location, sole access to a critical raw material or source of supply, a patented design or process, or an operating system that cannot be duplicated. The key to having a proprietary position is that it must provide value to potential consumers or the firm.

REALITY CHECK

The market does not reward firms that are not different from other businesses. Having something that makes your business different is not the issue. A lot of businesses have things that are unique. To have a competitive advantage you have to be different from your competitors in the areas that the marketplace values. The test of a business's proprietary position is whether it provides the business with an edge that enhances performance. A lot of inventors create products and may even have them patented. If their products do not have the potential to wow potential consumers or to have a major impact on productivity or efficiency, then they are of little value. The litmus test for being different is not whether it is different; it is whether it is better. It is better if it makes your business more profitable than its competitors. Venture capitalists look for products/applications that will give their investors the 7 to 10 times (not percent) return on investment they are looking for.

Businesses that have a proprietary position that are difficult or impossible to duplicate are particularly noteworthy and command a premium when it comes to determining the business's value as it approaches a liquidity event. Rob Ryan noted the best businesses are monopolies where the compelling force lasts essentially forever.[41]

If the entrepreneur's idea is not proprietary, then it can be imitated. Venture capital firms want to identify big winners. Rarely will they invest in ventures that are driven primarily by the drive of the founder. They are looking for ventures with something inherently proprietary in their products or processes.[42]

Yet most venture capitalists distinguish between firms that have a patented product and firms that have proprietary technology. This distinction is the same as having a fish versus a unique capability to catch fish. Venture capitalists place a premium on businesses that have a core technology that fosters the development of numerous proprietary products and applications. The core technology will also be valued if it has the potential for follow-up generations so subsequent products and services will be in sync with an evolving marketplace.

Although venture capitalists may value a business that has one or more proprietary positions that will give it an edge in the marketplace, they are always looking for paradigm-shifting businesses. Paradigm-shifting businesses do not come along very often. They are truly exceptional for one of two reasons. Either they have the ability to change the way the competitive game is played so what other businesses do is obsolete, or they are able to do what has been considered impossible. By changing the way the game is played, they become (at least for a period of time) a monopoly.

REALITY CHECK

Although it might seem the ultimate situation for an emerging business is to have a technology, product, process, or service that gives the venture a legal monopoly, success is not assured. Entrepreneurs need to recognize four things about having what appears to be a monopoly. First, having it and capitalizing on it are different situations. The entrepreneur or entrepreneurial team may have developed (or acquired) the proprietary position, but it is of little value if it is not harvested to its potential. Second, having a proprietary position can lead to arrogance. It is easy for a business that has an advantage to try to take advantage of consumers because it is the only game in town. Third, having a proprietary position can lead to complacency. The business may not continue its effort to improve its position or to scan the market for additional opportunities. Fourth, nothing lasts forever. There is no such thing as a permanent monopoly. At best, the business will have a temporary monopoly.

Criteria 4: A Business Plan that Makes Sense and Can Be Executed

When entrepreneurs are asked, "Do you have a business plan?" most respond, "Of course!" If they are asked to show it, many have difficulty presenting an actual written plan. Most entrepreneurs start their businesses with a fundamental concept and a general game plan. Most entrepreneurs do not prepare a comprehensive business plan. They may get by without a comprehensive business plan if they provide their own funding, if they are pointed in the right direction, have good judgment, make the right decisions, surround themselves with a professional team, are in a forgiving market, and have a lot of luck.

Entrepreneurs hit the proverbial wall when they seek funding without a comprehensive plan. Venture capitalists review the plan and its logic as part of their due diligence process. Entrepreneurs who do not have a comprehensive plan or submit a plan that is full of errors, gaps, and/or inconsistencies are just wasting their time.

A well-developed and well-documented business plan does two things. First, it is an indication of the entrepreneur's ability to manage a business. If the entrepreneur is not able to draft the plan, then he or she may not have a clear idea where to take the emerging business or he or she may lack the basic business skills needed to take the business to the next level. When it comes to dealing with venture capital firms, the statement, "Trust me, I know what I am doing," will not get the time of day from a venture capital fund. Entrepreneurs need to assume all venture capital fund managers and investment committees are from Missouri, you have to *show them.* Second, venture capital firms are prepared to take risks; but they are calculated risks as a result of considerable due diligence. A well-developed plan may reduce the uncertainty for an emerging business to the point where the venture capital fund is willing to invest in it.

Venture capital firms do not expect the business plan to be perfect to the last detail nor do they expect the plan to be implemented exactly as it is presented. They know the marketplace is a constant state of flux. Consumers frequently change their minds, market research is frequently misleading, competitors retaliate in unorthodox ways, good things take twice as long as expected, bad things happen in half the time expected, sales projections probably won't be hit, and expenses will come in higher than expected. Venture capitalists want to see that the management team has a handle on the key issues, is savvy enough to anticipate what may be possible, and has the ability to make the changes needed to keep the business moving toward a liquidity event. The business plan may not need to have every *i* dotted and every *t* crossed, but it does need to identify and profile each *i* and each *t* that is critical to success.

REALITY CHECK

Three things should be noted about business plans. First, while venture capitalists expect plans to include financial projections, they know from experience that businesses do not hit their revenue and profit projections. Entrepreneurs are usually overly optimistic and expect the market to grow like a virus in a Petrie dish. Be sure the projections have some justification and documentation. Second, their due-diligence process frequently reveals that the formulas used in electronic spreadsheets contain errors that then provide erroneous financial projections. Entrepreneurs need to have their accountants double check the formulas to make sure they are appropriate. Third, don't subcontract out the development and preparation of the business plan. A number of firms offer turnkey services. This might seem like a great idea and save the entrepreneur considerable time and agony. However, boilerplate-driven plans that merely throw a few numbers into an electronic spreadsheet and template format are a dead giveaway to venture capitalists that the entrepreneurial team does not have the ability to drive the business to a lucrative liquidity event.

Criteria 5: Great Profitability

From a venture capitalist's perspective, it comes down to, "Will the business lead to a lucrative liquidity event?" Entrepreneurs seeking venture capital need to see their business through the venture capitalist's eyes. The entrepreneur may have a vision for a paradigm-shifting business. The entrepreneur may believe he or she has what it takes to lead the business. The entrepreneur may believe he or she has assembled a team of first-class talent. The entrepreneur may believe the business is standing at the threshold of greatness. All of this sounds exciting, but entrepreneurs need to recognize that in the eyes of the venture capitalist, these conditions are merely means, not ends. To a venture capitalist, it all comes down to does your business have the ability to generate truly outstanding profits. The ability to generate extremely high returns on investment is what drives liquidity events.

REALITY CHECK

Entrepreneurs also need to put their business in context. The whole process of fund creation to the distribution of its proceeds is usually done over a 10-year time frame. An outstanding business may generate a 30-plus percent return on investment on an annual basis for a period of years. As noted earlier, venture capitalists are not looking for outstanding firms; they are looking for truly exceptional firms. Your business has to make enough money or show enough promise for its liquidity event to provide the venture capital with a return that will cover the fund's marginal businesses and losers. It will also have to generate at least a 30-plus percent average annual return on its overall portfolio when the portfolio is liquidated and the fund's proceeds are distributed. A truly exceptional business generates a multiple of that. Amar Bhidé noted, "Every venture they invest in must hold the promise to provide returns in the tens of millions of dollars, rather than in the tens or even hundreds of thousands of dollars."[43]

If the average venture capital fund does not have two exceptional businesses in its 10-business portfolio, then it probably will not generate the level of return to justify the level of risk it takes on relatively new and untested businesses. The 20-60-20 rule might, in fact, be too optimistic. A study by Venture Economics, Inc. found about 7 percent of the investments accounted for more than 60 percent of the profits, while fully one-third resulted in partial or total loss.[44]

The exceptional business commands a premium in the financial market if it is courted as a candidate for acquisition. It also attracts investment bankers who want to take it public. If the business is exceptional, then it usually does not stay in the fund very long. Exceptional businesses that are venture-capital funded usually go public within four years.

The business plan must make it clear how the business makes money. Rob Ryan noted that venture capitalists like to see a nonlinear model that reflects an exponential ramp-up like the curve in Nike's trademark. He also noted that the plan should be clear about how many months or years it will take for this to happen and what the exact *trigger event* will be.[45]

Entrepreneurs also need to recognize that venture capitalists aren't just looking for a high percent return on investment. They are looking for high profitability in terms of absolute dollars as well. Venture capitalist firms invest considerable time in the due-diligence process. They also spend considerable time working with the business if it is funded. This time comes at a high price. The amount of time it takes for the due-diligence process and the fund's ongoing involvement is not that different for a $500,000 funding project as it is for a $2 million project. Businesses seeking less than $1 million have to show a level of profits and the prospect of a liquidity event to make it worth the fund's time and attention as well as its capital.

EXCEPTIONAL BUSINESSES BEAT THE ODDS!

Even in the best situations, the odds are stacked against success for businesses seeking venture capital. Bob Zider indicated that on average, good plans, people, and businesses succeed only 1 in 10 times. The Event/Probability Table profiled in Exhibit 12.1 indicates the resulting probability of success even if the probability of success for each of the key dimensions for entrepreneurial success is fairly high. Zider believes the best companies might have an 80 percent probability of succeeding at each of them. Even with these odds, the probability of eventual success will be less than 20 percent because failing to execute on any one component can torpedo the entire company.[46]

Individual Event	Probability
Company has sufficient capital	80%
Management is capable and focused	80%
Product development goes as planned	80%
Production and component sourcing goes as planned	80%
Competitors behave as expected	80%
Customers want product	80%
Pricing is forecast correctly	80%
Patents are issued and are enforceable	80%
Combined probability of success	17%

*Reprinted with permission of *Harvard Business Review*. From "How Venture Capital Works," by Bob Zider, *Harvard Business Review*, November–December 1998, p. 131. Copyright © 1998 by the Harvard Business School Publishing Corporation.

EXHIBIT 12.1 EVENT/PROBABILITY TABLE

Zider noted that if just one of the variables drops to a 50 percent probability, the combined chance of success falls to 10 percent. The companies funded need to be real winners to provide a sufficient return to cover the losers and lack of high-level profits by the firms that do not go bankrupt but just muddle along.[47]

CHOOSE THE RIGHT VENTURE CAPITAL FIRM(S)

Entrepreneurs need to recognize that finding and securing venture capital funding takes longer than expected. Most veteran entrepreneurs indicate you should take any money you can get. They also stress the need to be selective and persistent. It pays to start the search well before you need the funding. Your financial projections in your business plan should indicate when you will need major external financing. Entrepreneurs need to identify that time in advance so that they don't have to rush it. Entrepreneurs also need to build in an *advance buffer* in the event that things take off and go better than expected. Some things can't be rushed. This is one of them.

Starting early is important, for at least three reasons. First, it increases the odds that you will find the right firm. Second, once you have found the right firm, it will be to your advantage if you have some elbow room timewise to negotiate terms. If you are desperate and they see you sweat, it could hurt your chances for funding and the corresponding terms. Third, the venture capital firm may suggest that at least one other venture capital firm be involved. This will slow the funding process.

Getting a venture capital firm's attention may be more difficult than getting funding if the fund sees merit in your business. The typical venture capital firm sees between 1,000 and 3,000 proposals each year. The average fund will invest in just 1 or 2 percent (between 10 and 30) of these business plans.

Venture capital firms are about relationships, not just money. Entrepreneurs have a much higher chance for being considered for funding if a relationship exists prior to actually submitting your funding request. Although there continue to be examples of emerging businesses that used the business pages of the phone book to find a venture capital fund, the majority of funded projects start with a referral by someone who knows the venture capital fund's manager or investors in a particular fund.

Finding the right venture capital fund should not be a random process. Venture capital funds usually focus on one or two industries. They also have a particular project profile. The *Directory of Venture Capital* by Kate Lister and Tom Harnish[48] provides the following information about venture capital firms: industry preference, stage of funding preference, geographic preference, minimum investment, and capital under management. You should check to see the average size of the investment, whether the fund does multiple rounds, if it does follow-up rounds of funding, and if it is usually the lead fund if multiple funds may be involved in the funding. Bob Zider noted that VC firms protect themselves from risk by co-investing with other firms. Typically, there will be a *lead* investor and several *followers.* It is the exception, not the rule, for one VC to finance an individual company entirely.[49]

Although the *Directory of Venture Capital* may be helpful in developing a list of potential venture capital firms, Rob Ryan notes that entrepreneurs should research whether the VC has an investment portfolio in your area or whether the VC invests in your competitor. He recommends targeting three VCs that invest in your type of product/service/technology and do not invest in your competition.[50] It will be particularly beneficial if the venture capital firm is located nearby. Most venture capital firms want to fund businesses in close proximity because they will be involved on an ongoing basis as board members after the funding is provided.

John Hershey and Jamie Earle have observed, "Over the last several years, VCs have become *sellers of money.* In this competitive venture environment, entrepreneurs should be choosy and find potential venture backers whose goals align with their own goals as well as those of the company."[51] They also note, "The entrepreneur is banking on just one investment—his own company—so he wants to partner with a VC who has a track record of consistently backing winners. Therefore, he would likely be more interested in partnering with a VC who, in a portfolio of 10 companies, delivered 10 IPOs, rather than with a VC who, with the same size portfolio, delivered one blockbuster IPO while watching nine companies disappear down the Internet industry drain."[52]

REALITY CHECK

Although the idea of targeting venture capital funds that have a track record for investing in your field makes sense, the explosion of emerging businesses seeking funds in related fields can have an adverse effect. David Evanson noted, "The professionals are chasing more deals and are being chased more actively by entrepreneurs. That means they're more likely to say, 'I saw one of those yesterday—no thanks.'"[53]

Once the appropriate venture capital firms have been identified, it is important to establish a personal link to the funds. Charles Ferguson, who wrote *High Stakes and No Prisoners* and cofounded Vermeer Technologies Inc., stresses the importance of knowing someone who can serve as an introduction or referral for the venture capital firm. He noted, "Unless you have an introduction from someone they know, most venture capital firms won't even talk to you."[54] Jeff Tannenbaum, cofounder of EnhanceNow, stated, "Who you know is vital, which is why we should spend time trying to expand our own network. When we've gotten introductions, it has led to a much better initial meeting."[55]

Getting venture capital can be a rough process so entrepreneurs would be wise to check out the *people-side* of the targeted venture capital firms. Rob Ryan noted, the personal dynamics of a venture capital fund's board members are important. If your company is going to grow successfully, you're going to be in bed with these people for many years to come.[56]

Venture capital firms frequently list funded firms on their websites. *Red Herring* magazine also lists firms that have been funded. Funding is supposed to be a mutually beneficial relationship. Entrepreneurs seeking funding should contact the entrepreneurs who have been funded to see if their relationship with the venture capital fund has met their expectations in terms of the time it took to close the deal, its terms, ongoing assistance, and progress toward a liquidity event.

KNOW THYSELF AND WHAT YOU WANT
OUT OF THE DEAL

Entrepreneurs need to step back and be sure they have a clear picture of what they want to happen when they seek funding. They should have a clear picture for the valuation of the business going into negotiations, whether they want to continue being CEO, whether they want the business to be acquired or to go public, and the amount of return they want from the liquidity event.

Robert Brown notes that most entrepreneurs believe that they can raise money without having to give up much control or ownership. He stated, "Think again. New money is going to cost you."[57] Scott Albert, general partner with Aurora Funds, a venture fund that focuses on early stage technology and life science companies, advises entrepreneurs to have clear objectives about what they want out of a deal with a venture capitalist and what they are willing to offer. The message is clear—this is not free money. According to Albert, "The VC wants to be in a position to control a company to a certain extent. That means equity, board seats, and some measure of control over decision making."[58]

Entrepreneurs should do their homework on that particular venture capital fund before they submit their plans. David Evanson noted, "Armed with this information, you're in a better position to take certain things off the table before they become a part of the negotiation. A good way to find out how past deals have been structured is to contact the founders of companies that the VC has funded. You may be surprised at their willingness to talk.[59] Bob Zider noted that in a typical start-up deal, the venture capital fund will invest $3 million in exchange for a 40 percent preferred-equity ownership position. The preferred equity provision offers downside protection for the venture capital firm. If the venture fails, the venture capital firm is given first claim (among its investors after its creditors are paid) to all the company's assets and technology.[60]

The funding contract will be designed to protect the venture capital funds in other ways as well. Venture capitalists set performance targets for the business. Venture capital firms will also set performance targets for the founders. If they are not met, then they may renegotiate the terms and further dilute the founder's equity position.[61] The contract is also likely to contain downside protection in the form of antidilution clauses, or ratchets. Such clauses protect against equity dilution if subsequent rounds of financing at lower values take place. If this happens, the venture capital firm will be given enough shares to maintain its original equity position.[62]

SUBMITTING THE REQUEST FOR FUNDING:
DON'T SELF-DESTRUCT

Phil Garfinkle, president of Yazam, which provides seed-stage funding and business development services to emerging Internet and technology start-ups, makes an interesting observation. According to Garfinkle, "The money is there. What amazes me, as an investor, is that many companies are unable to secure financing—not because of a flaw in their business, but because of flaws in how they approach the capital formation process." He provides the following list of some of the most common gaffes—and the steps entrepreneurs should take to avoid them:[63]

1. *The deal has been overshopped.* Venture investors talk. They know when a deal has made the rounds, and they shy away from it. Remember, investors want to be on the leading edge—not the lagging edge.

2. *No cash.* It takes money to raise money. Even though you might be running on fumes, you've got to be ready to spend money to meet with investors and close deals. Investors love to hear how you have put direct cash into the opportunity. Legal, accounting, promotion, and travel expenses are part and parcel of every fundraising effort. Without the walking-around money to get the deal done, it won't get done.

3. *The valuation is too high.* Valuation is obviously a sticky issue. The entrepreneurs holding out for sky-high values, for unproven concepts, with no customers and no track records, are the ones that are *unfundable*.

4. *Unrealistic projections.* Financial projections that have the hockey-stick curve can make a company unfundable. You might be able to fool friends and relatives into believing your company will have $350 million in sales by year three, but a sophisticated investor, who has actually run a company, will believe you're foolish and move on. The worst mistake you can make in formulating projections is to simply increase them 25 to 40 percent per year. Anyone with a spreadsheet can do that. The best projections are those that are based on some real-world interaction.

5. *Arrogant management/founders.* Equity investors will tolerate a lot of unusual personality quirks in the pursuit of good investment opportunities. However, one trait that often makes a company unfundable is arrogance among the founders and senior managers of the company.

6. Remember, equity investors see themselves as partners. Our attitude is, "If our money is in the company, the founders have got to be able to take our input constructively. If they can't, we can't do business."

PRESENTATION TO VENTURE CAPITALISTS

There are two ways to make presentations to venture capitalists. The first way involves making a presentation at a venture capital forum. These forums provide an avenue for emerging businesses to appear on the radar screen for interested venture capital firms. Tod Loofbourrow, founder of Authoria, found this type of approach to be helpful and efficient. According to Loofbourrow: "There were a lot of companies that day at Venture Market East presenting technologies in search of a market. Authoria stood out by having both a strong, unique technology and a clear market with a defined need. We had an existing product, a sales model, and potential customers who were enthusiastic about what we were doing. After the program, representatives from 23 venture capital firms wanted to talk about investing in Authoria. That put us in the rare and fortunate position to prune our list of investment firms down from 23 until we came to agreements with Fidelity Ventures and then with Norwest Ventures."[64]

Dealing directly with one or more venture capital funds is the second way to prospect for venture capital funding. It is still the most common avenue for attracting interest.

Although this process may involve more prospecting and referrals, it allows your business to maintain far more confidentiality than making a presentation at a venture capital forum.

Most entrepreneurs submit lengthy business plans to the prospective venture capital fund. The Executive Summary, however, determines whether the venture capitalist takes the time to review the plan. As noted earlier, the business plan will play a critical role in the venture capital firm's due diligence process, its deliberations, and funding decision if it is read.

The business plan submitted to a venture capital firm must highlight the areas that will demonstrate your business meets the fund's criteria. The plan needs to profile the product/service's superiority, the size of the market opportunity, as well as the other critical factors. Particular attention must be directed to profiling the following issues:

1. How much money you are seeking
2. What the money will be used for
3. If additional rounds of funding will be sought and for what purpose
4. Profile of your product/service and how it is superior to everything else in the market
5. Projected growth in revenue and profitability
6. A projection for downside risk for the venture capital firm

The plan should include as much documentation as possible for the projections. Industry data are helpful, but testimonials from real-life customers and distributors supporting your business's claims of market opportunity and product/service superiority will be more credible. Ultimately, the entrepreneur needs to show the venture capital firm that his team and idea fit into the venture capital firm's current focus and that his equity participation and management skills will make the venture capital firm's job easier and the returns higher.[65]

If the fund is interested in your business, then you and your team will be expected to make an oral presentation. Three things are under scrutiny in the oral presentation. First, can you provide a compelling reason for the fund to invest in your business? Second, do you demonstrate the ability to make your plan's projections a reality? Third, will it give the venture capital fund manager a chance to get information not provided in the plan and to probe deeper into the assumptions and projections?

Entrepreneurs should not make the mistake of assuming that funding is assured if they are invited to make an oral presentation. The entrepreneurial team will need to have its act together when it makes its presentation to the venture capital firm. Jeff Tannenbaum noted, "You are not given the opportunity to present your deal for an hour and a half. You get the feeling that you have about five minutes, and, if you don't capture their imagination, it's over."[66]

Bud Whitmeyer, a partner with Research Triangle Ventures, a seed-stage venture capital partnership, puts it bluntly: "You have 5 to 10 minutes to grab me." He said, "Tell me your story. It is your task to clearly articulate the problem you are tackling and the solution." According to Whitmeyer, "You need to excite the venture capitalist with your vision, your story—you have to prove you have enough potential customers out there to build a substantial business."[67]

Rob Ryan noted that you also need to come to the table with a clear, concise answer to the one overriding question: "How are you going to generate revenue?" This ties into the other big questions that venture capital firms want to know: Can you execute? Do you already have relationships with customers or partners? What is your pricing strategy?

What are the milestones you have already reached? What prior experience do your people bring to the table that proves they have it in them to drive the company to a favorable exit?[68]

Scott Albert advises entrepreneurs to be realistic. He noted that overinflated optimism can eat away at your credibility. He also noted that revenue projections are usually completely without merit and that entrepreneurs frequently underestimate the time it takes for the business to ramp up sales.[69] Tom Weldon, principal founder of Novoste Corporation, noted, "Pie-in-the-sky numbers won't do it for you. You need an established history with highly qualified people." Before releasing his business plan for review by VCs, Weldon had it reviewed by his consultant, professionally edited, and reviewed further by industry peers. That ensured conservative projections.[70]

Albert also stresses the need to provide the venture capitalists with materials such as references, an overview of your technology, industry norms, and so forth. He stated, "You want to make it as easy as possible for the venture capitalist to move forward with due diligence."[71] The plan needs to be carefully prepared so it has few errors or omissions. The oral presentation must also be rehearsed so the critical information is provided in the most concise and effective manner. Ryan noted, "You want to get investors on your side so they want to fix the holes in your plan, instead of using them as an excuse to turn you down."[72]

WHAT HAPPENS NEXT?

If the venture capital firm believes your business has the potential to provide the 7 to 10 times its investment, then it will assign someone to continue its due diligence process. If the due diligence process is fruitful, then the venture capital firm will provide a *term sheet*. The term sheet is a one- or two-page statement that summarizes the key elements for the proposed funding deal.[73] If no one is assigned to oversee the due diligence process right away, then assume you have received a *soft no* from the venture capital firm.

Pre-deal valuation tends to be the major stumbling block at this stage of the negotiations. The pre-deal valuation has a major impact on the extent of ownership and control that the venture capital firm will have over your business. Entrepreneurs want to make sure their blood, sweat, and tears are recognized. The lower the valuation by the venture capital firm, the greater the firm's ownership per dollar invested by the venture capital firm. Entrepreneurs who place too high a valuation on their business will not even have their plans reviewed, so the issue at this stage is finding a set of terms that are agreeable for both parties.

Ryan noted that after the term sheet is submitted there are a couple of weeks of *getting to know you* dancing. Your goal is to secure one person within the firm to act as your company's sponsor—someone who is willing to push the other partners to make the investment.[74] Entrepreneurs should expect the final negotiations to be fairly tough. In most cases, the deck is stacked in the venture capital firm's favor. Although the firm would like to invest in a star, the length of the duration of their funds permits them to be thorough and a bit patient. They may be in a position to drag the negotiations out. Entrepreneurs, however, tend to be in a position where they get funding or they die on the vine. This is where picking the right time to seek funding, having lead time, selecting the right firm(s), and having a compelling business proposition pay off. This is also one of those times when it pays not to have your business's future tied to just one venture capital firm. The major issues at this stage are ownership and control.

Joseph Boyett and Jimmie Boyett, authors of *The Guru Guide to Entrepreneurship,* noted, "You'll have to decide how much control you are willing to give up to get the money you desperately need."[75] They also stressed the need for entrepreneurs to fight as long as they can and as hard as they can to maintain as much control as they can.[76] If you can't maintain majority ownership, then negotiate conditions where you can influence major decisions.

CONCLUSION: LEAP FORWARD

If you get venture capital funding, then you should be congratulated. You made it over a funding hurdle that few emerging businesses clear. Now, you have enough money to take your business to the next level. Don't fall prey to the post–venture capital funding cognitive dissonance syndrome. Don't look back and agonize over the time it took, the concessions you made, and the final terms of the deal. Take the money and keep moving forward. You and your business will be much better off if you use the money as well as the connections and advice provided by the venture capital firm than if you second-guess yourself.

> *To a gardener there is nothing more exasperating than a hose that just isn't long enough.*[77]

—Cecil Roberts
English author

ENDNOTES

1. David Gladstone, *Venture Capital Handbook* (Englewood Cliffs, NJ: Prentice Hall, 1988), p. 3.

2. Bob Zider, "How Venture Capital Works," *Harvard Business Review,* November–December 1998, p. 131. Reprinted by permission of Harvard Business Review.

3. Amar Bhidé, *The Origin and Evolution of New Businesses* (New York: Oxford University Press, Inc., 2000), p. 163.

4. Ibid., p. 143.

5. Ibid., p. 142.

6. Ibid., p. 144.

7. Ibid.

8. Charles H. Ferguson, "True Finance: The Education of an Internet Entrepreneur," *Fast Company,* October 1999, p. 286.

9. Bhidé, *The Origin and Evolution of New Businesses,* p. 165.

10. Ibid., p. 163.

11. William A. Sahlman, "The Structure and Governance of Venture-Capital Organizations," *Journal of Financial Economics,* vol. 27, 1990, p. 508.

12. Ibid.

13. Zider, "How Venture Capital Works," p. 136.

14. Rob Ryan, "How to Avoid Self-Destructing in Front of VCs," *Entrepreneur America* website, *www.entrepreneuramerica.com.*

15. Rob Ryan, *Smartups: Lessons from Rob Ryan's Entrepreneur America Boot Camp for Start-Ups* (Ithaca: Cornell University Press, 2001), p. 14. Copyright © 2001 by Rob Ryan. Used with permission of the publisher, Cornell University Press.

16. Bhidé, *The Origin and Evolution of New Businesses,* p. 165.

17. Zider, "How Venture Capital Works," p. 134.

18. Ibid., p. 132.

19. David R. Evanson, "The Graduates," *Entrepreneur,* March 2001, p. 61. Used with permission of Entrepreneur Media, Inc.

20. Ibid.

21. Zider, "How Venture Capital Works," p. 137.

22. Bhidé, *The Origin and Evolution of New Businesses,* p. 153.

23. Zider, "How Venture Capital Works," p.134.

24. Doug Hood and Art Beroff, "The Graduates," *Entrepreneur,* March 2001, p. 60. Used with permission of Entrepreneur Media, Inc.

25. Ibid., p. 61.

26. Ibid., p. 60.

27. Zider, "How Venture Capital Works," p. 133.

28. Bhidé, *The Origin and Evolution of New Businesses,* p. 159.

29. Ibid., p. 141.

30. Ibid., p. 147.

31. Ryan, *Smartups: Lessons from Rob Ryan's Entrepreneur America Boot Camp for Start-Ups,* p. 27. Copyright © 2001 by Rob Ryan. Used with permission of the publisher, Cornell University Press.

32. Bhidé, *Origin and Evolution of New Businesses*, pp. 145 & 146.

33. John Hershey and Jamie Earle, "The Capital Gang: Ranking the Best Venture Capitalists," *Business 2.0,* October 24, 2000, pp. 155–170.

34. Zider, "How Venture Capital Works," p. 135.

35. Ibid., p. 133.

36. Ibid.

37. Bhidé, *The Origin and Evolution of New Businesses*, p. 16.

38. Zider, "How Venture Capital Works," p.133.

39. Bhidé, *The Origin and Evolution of New Businesses,* pp. 145 & 146.

40. Ibid., p. 146.

41. Ryan, *Smartups: Lessons from Rob Ryan's Entrepreneur America Boot Camp for Start-Ups,* p. 115.

42. Bhidé, *The Origin and Evolution of New Businesses,* pp. 145 & 146.

43. Ibid., p. 145.

44. Ibid.

45. Ryan, *Smartups: Lessons from Rob Ryan's Entrepreneur America Boot Camp for Start-Ups,* p. 134.

46. Zider, "How Venture Capital Works," p. 136.

47. Ibid.

48. Kate Lister and Tom Harnish, *Directory of Venture Capital* (New York: John Wiley & Sons, 2000).

49. Zider, "How Venture Capital Works," p. 135.

50. Entrepreneur America, *www.entrepreneur-america.com.*

51. John Hershey and Jamie Earle, "The Capital Gang: Ranking the Best Venture Capitalists," *Business 2.0,* October 24, 2000, pp. 155–170.

52. Ibid.

53. Doug Hood and Art Beroff, "The Graduates," *Entrepreneur,* March 2001, p. 60.

54. Charles H. Ferguson, "True Finance: The Education of an Internet Entrepreneur," *Fast Company,* October 1999, pp. 294–296.

55. Hood and Beroff, "The Graduates," *Entrepreneur,* March 2001, p. 60. Used with permission of Entrepreneur Media, Inc.

56. Ryan, *Smartups: Lessons from Rob Ryan's Entrepreneur America Boot Camp for Start-Ups,* p. 140,

57. Robert Brown, "Musicians Reveal Secrets to Raising Venture Capital," *American Venture,* July–September 2000, pp. 11&12.

58. Ibid.

59. Hood and Beroff, "The Graduates," p. 60.

60. Zider, "How Venture Capital Works," p. 134.

61. Bhidé, *The Origin and Evolution of New Businesses,* p. 155.

62. Zider, "How Venture Capital Works," p. 134.

63. Phil Garfinkle, "Show Me the Money!" *Success,* November 2000, p. 60.

64. Tod Loofbourrow, "My Company Was Born in the Delivery Room," *American Venture,* July 2001, p. 31.

65. Zider, "How Venture Capital Works," p.139.

66. Evanson, "The Graduates," p. 60.

67. Presentation at a venture capital conference sponsored by the Council for Entrepreneurial Development.

68. Rob Ryan, *Smartups: Lessons from Rob Ryan's Entrepreneur America Boot Camp for Start-Ups,* p. 9.

69. Brown, "Musicians Reveal Secrets to Raising Venture Capital," pp. 11 & 12.

70. Edward 0. Welles, "15 Steps to a Start-up," *Inc.,* March 1994, p. 78.

71. Brown, "Musicians Reveal Secrets to Raising Venture Capital," pp. 11 & 12.

72. Rob Ryan, *Smartups: Lessons from Rob Ryan's Entrepreneur America Boot Camp for Start-Ups,* p. 129.

73. Ibid., p. 133.

74. Ibid., p. 135.

75. Joseph H. Boyett and Jimmie T. Boyett, *The Guru Guide to Entrepreneurship* (New York: John Wiley & Sons, 2002), p. 109.

76. Ibid., pp. 108 & 109.

77. Louis Boone, *Quotable Business* (New York: Random House, 1992), p. 31.

13

INITIAL PUBLIC OFFERING

*America is the only country in the world where you can raise your
first $100 million before you buy your first suit.*[1]

—Lawrence H. Summers
former Secretary of the Treasury

Going public is considered by many entrepreneurs, angels, venture capital firms, investment bankers, as well as the business media to be a glamorous event and the most noteworthy affirmation of an emerging venture's stature. Some entrepreneurs consider it to be the business equivalent to winning the Super Bowl or the World Series.

Initial public offerings have experienced a wild roller-coaster ride in the last decade. Initial public offerings (IPOs) were common during the *dot-com frenzy* in the latter 1990s. During that period, too many new ventures went public before they demonstrated any true merit. A few of the firms have been successful and benefited from going public, but most of the dot-coms that went public failed or were acquired by other firms for a few cents on the dollar.

Far fewer firms are going public today because investors and financial institutions have a lot of embarrassment from when they forgot to check to see if the emperor actually had clothes! Investors and financial institutions are now demonstrating more due diligence. Although the door to going public may not be closed completely, few emerging firms have what it takes to meet the criteria associated with going the IPO route.

REALITY CHECK

There have been many times while I was writing this book that I considered not devoting a chapter to discussing the merits, drawbacks, and process associated with an IPO. The odds for a new venture becoming a publicly traded firm on a major exchange are so remote that I wondered whether it was worth a chapter in this book. The odds are better than winning the New York lottery, but it should be clear that while many entrepreneurs may dream about taking their firms public, few will see that day. The odds are similar to a high school quarterback making it into the NFL Hall of Fame. Only a couple hundred of the nearly one million ventures started this year will be listed on one of the stock exchanges. It is for this reason that this chapter will just highlight certain facets of the IPO process rather than provide an in-depth analysis and blueprint for it.

REALITY CHECK

It should be noted that as the final draft of this book was being written, the capital markets were becoming more receptive again to IPOs following the dot-com meltdown at the beginning of the century.

The pendulum has swung back to the point where firms that are contemplating going the IPO route have to show they are more than concepts. Some investors are still prone to jump on the investment bandwagon for an emerging venture that claims it has a killer application, a significant proprietary position, or some other major breakthrough that has the potential to garner substantial profits, but most institutional investors want to see a few years of solid financial performance before they will even consider investing in an emerging venture.

REALITY CHECK

About one-half of IPOs are the result of established firms taking one of their divisions public.

Entrepreneurs of emerging ventures that experience a high rate of growth and have the potential to grow exponentially frequently get to the point where going public becomes the topic of discussion. Few aspects of growth generate stronger opinions among entrepreneurs than taking their firms public. The process of doing an IPO and selling the firm's stock to individual and institutional investors has benefits and drawbacks. Some entrepreneurs who have taken their firms public are quick to state, "Avoid it at all costs." Other entrepreneurs claim the process of going public strengthened their firms.

There are as many reasons for going public as there are pitfalls to avoid. Entrepreneurs considering the prospect of going public have to answer a series of questions. The first question is rather elementary: "Should I do an IPO?" If the answer is yes, then the *who, what, when, how, where, and how much?* questions naturally follow. This chapter primarily addresses the first question. The more detailed questions that follow are for the myriad accountants, lawyers, and investment firms to sort out.

TAKING THE FIRM TO THE NEXT LEVEL

Each stage of new venture growth has its corresponding needs for external funding. Slow-growing yet profitable firms may be able to fund their growth via their revenue streams and retained earnings. Moderate-growth firms may be able to secure commercial loans to finance their expansion. High-growth ventures almost always have to seek large sums of money from external sources. If the firm is looking for funding in the range of a few thousand dollars to a few hundred thousand dollars, then it may seek one or more angels. If it is looking for $500,000 to $10 million then it may seek one or more venture capital firms. If the firm is poised for dramatic growth and is looking for more than that, then it may consider doing additional rounds of venture capital funding or going public. The IPO route might be the only way to go if the firm is looking for at least $100 million in external funding.

IPO: ITS BENEFITS

IPO funding is usually sought by firms to accelerate their growth by broadening their product/service/customer/technology portfolio, to build facilities, and/or to expand geographic reach. Funds may also be used to acquire other firms.

Although those involved in the IPO process may say they are doing it to enable the emerging firm to seize a substantial opportunity, it should be clear from the beginning that the primary purpose of an IPO is to enable those who started the venture, those who joined the management team, and the outside investors who may have invested in the venture at various stages to garner significant financial returns.

Ultimately, it will provide the entrepreneur with an opportunity to sell some or all of his or her stock. IPOs provide angels and venture capital firms with the liquidity events they sought from the very beginning. IPOs give investment banks the opportunity to make a considerable amount of money in fees and by taking an equity position in the firms they take public. Who knows—the people who invest in the firm once it is publicly traded may even make money!

REALITY CHECK

The IPO process does not provide you with an immediate opportunity to sell stock in your firm. The IPO is usually accompanied with a lockup agreement. The agreement initiated by the investment bank prohibits the shares owned by the founders, employees, their friends and families, and venture capital firm(s) to be sold for up to 180 days following the IPO. You should see the IPO process as a vehicle for your firm to generate cash by selling some of the stock it has not issued. Once you get through the lockup period, you can enjoy your own liquidity event by selling your own stock.

Going public has other benefits beyond raising funds and providing a vehicle for investors to sell their stock. It offers a number of opportunities that are not available to firms that keep a tight grip on their stock. An IPO can provide the following benefits:

- *Ego enhancement.* It represents a major rite of passage for entrepreneurs and others who are also involved in a high-growth venture. An IPO is something that is achieved by few firms. To be the founder of a publicly traded company has stroked a lot of entrepreneurs' egos.

- *Leveraging debt.* Firms that have been unable to get additional loans because of their debt-to-equity limit may be able to secure additional debt financing by bringing in additional equity.

- *Human resources.* The fact that the firm's stock is traded may elevate its stature in its staff's eyes. Stock options and stock incentives may put the firm in a better position to attract, motivate, reward, and keep talent. Bill Gates noted that he did not take Microsoft public because he was seeking funding; he did it so Microsoft's employees could have a vehicle for selling their stock.

- *Enhanced stature.* Firms with traded stock also cast a positive shadow on suppliers, customers, distributors, and the public. Going public means that the firm has been able to demonstrate a fairly high level of sophistication in meeting investor expectations.

IPO: ITS DRAWBACKS

Entrepreneurs need to proceed with caution when they consider going the IPO route. The first thing they must recognize is that the entrepreneur's world will change dramatically. The following factors should be considered in the decision process:

1. *Going public changes the entrepreneur's life forever.* The entrepreneur's relationship with friends, board members, and investors must change. Becoming a publicly traded firm means that the entrepreneur can no longer talk to his or her friends about the opportunities the firm plans to pursue. The entrepreneur, management team, and board of directors must make sure that the firm's plans are properly disclosed so everything is done above board.

2. *Privacy.* Going public means that the firm will be like a glass house. Anyone has access to the firm's financial statements. This could have a major impact on the firm because it means that competitors may learn the firm's operating ratios and expansion plans. Analysts will want to know what is going on. They will be constantly researching your firm, your competitors, your customers, and your industry. As a private company, your mistakes are not public. In a publicly traded firm, every dimension of the firm is under the magnifying glass. Your mistakes and faults are visible. The SEC and investment community will also pay attention to compensation (salary, performance bonuses, stock options, etc.) for key executives.

3. *Corporate governance.* Board and investor expectations also add pressure to the entrepreneur's job. Meetings will have to be documented better. Salaries and fringe benefit packages for the executives will need to be disclosed, discussed, and justified. The entrepreneurs will also need to take time throughout the year to field questions from investors, analysts, and the media.

4. *Accountability and vulnerability.* Even if the entrepreneur has been able to attract private investors in the past, the IPO process raises people's expectations about who is running the firm and with what level of performance. If the entrepreneur does not have what it takes or the venture fails to meet investor expectations, then the board of directors may replace the entrepreneur with someone who can get the job done.

5. *Learning.* The entrepreneur will have to learn a whole new vocabulary. Going public has its own jargon. The entrepreneur has to learn about exempt versus nonexempt offerings, green shoes, waiting periods, road shows, blue sky laws, and various ways of classifying investors. There is a joke on the street that goes, "There is good news and bad news for those who go public. The good news is that you get to meet a whole new group of people. The bad news is that they are attorneys, accountants, and analysts!"

6. *Time demands.* The entrepreneur may have operated with some latitude in his or her schedule before embarking on the IPO journey. The IPO process takes time away from running the firm. Going public puts the entrepreneur on such a tight timetable that it will preempt many of the activities that received quality time in the past. Time that has traditionally been spent (or invested) in strategic thinking, developing relationships with prospective clients, and managing by walking around will be reduced and/or postponed.

7. *Time horizon.* Being a publicly traded firm means that investors expect results, and they expect them soon. There is no such thing as *patient money* when a firm is publicly traded. While the entrepreneur may be accustomed to doing what it will take

for the firm to do well in the long term, most investors dwell on quarterly and annual performance and stock appreciation.

8. *Focus.* The process of going public redirects the entrepreneur's attention away from the marketplace. Instead of directing one's attention to developing innovative products and services, the entrepreneur will be trying to meet a whole host of financial inquiries and regulations. The entrepreneur's efforts to create and maintain investors may jeopardize the firm's efforts to create and maintain customers. The entrepreneur's dream of having an infusion of new cash could be rudely awakened by the loss of customers who constitute the ultimate source of capital.

9. *Preparation.* Going public is not an overnight proposition. It takes considerable preparation and lead time. It may take up to three years to get the firm to be properly positioned for an IPO. The investment community looks far more favorably (in terms of valuation) on firms that demonstrate profitability and an even better future than on those that try to seek investors with hopes and dreams.

10. *Costs.* The IPO process is an expensive undertaking. The firm must have a highly competent chief financial officer. The firm's accounting system and financial records must be above reproach. The actual IPO process involves considerable expense. The investment bank's fees are usually 6 to 8 percent of the gross proceeds. When you include the fees for your accounting firm, legal fees, printing fees, and various other expenses, costs could easily exceed $1 million. The overall costs could take up to 10 percent of the gross proceeds of the public offering. The costs might be an even greater percentage if the firm is trying to raise less than $20 million. The costs of going public continue after the IPO. A general rule of thumb is that it costs at least $1 million a year to deal with investor relations, to comply with government regulations, and to have the accounting information prepared. Moreover, this estimate does not include the additional costs for board compensation and associated expenses. If you go the IPO route, executive compensation will go up dramatically. Executives of public companies are paid a lot more than private companies. Director and officer insurance cost will also go up dramatically. Board compensation will also increase. The firm may also have to offer more stock options.

11. *Uncertain funding.* The amount raised by an IPO will not be known until it actually happens. Numerous factors that affect the ability to do an IPO are beyond the firm's control—including the overall state of the stock market, investors' attitudes about that particular industry, and the overall economy. These can all affect the amount of money raised. The investment banker may change the targeted offering price right up to the day it is listed.

12. *Constant surprises or last-minute changes.* The IPO process is not a simple process, nor is it perfectly predictable. There will be surprises, areas that need to be negotiated, and last-minute crises.

REALITY CHECK

Some firms that went public have purchased their shares and gone private again so they have the freedom to move freely and do not have to pay the costs associated with financial documentation and investor relations.

WILL YOUR FIRM FIT THE IPO PROFILE?

Few entrepreneurs would object to having a major infusion of cash. There always seem to be more uses for cash than cash on hand. Yet most entrepreneurs should not consider going public. Only a select group of emerging firms fit the IPO profile. The size of the firm, its rate of growth, and the amount of money management seeks to raise have a lot to do with whether it should consider going public.

Chapter 12 noted the lofty capital appreciation expectations held by venture capital firms as well as the due diligence process they go through when reviewing firms. If the firm has been able to secure venture capital funding, that might be an indication that the firm could have the potential for an IPO. As noted earlier, venture capital firms invest in ventures that they believe have the potential for a liquidity event—including an IPO.

The IPO process is more rigorous than the due diligence process used by most venture capital firms. The investment banker will pay particular attention to the business opportunity, the management team, and the firm's competitive advantages. The firm must represent a compelling investment opportunity. This is where the IPO process varies from seeking venture capital funding. Although a venture capital firm may have been willing to work with an emerging venture to help it get its act together in terms of its management team, marketing strategy, management systems, and so forth, the firm must have its act together *before* it starts its IPO.

Doing an IPO is like lowering the water in a rapids. Rocks that were not visible now stand out. Management must be able to demonstrate that the firm's strengths give it a formidable and sustainable advantage, that a first-class team is in place, and that the firm has few, if any, weaknesses or vulnerabilities. Management should also be able to demonstrate that major economies of scale exist that will enhance profitability and stock value. It should also be able to demonstrate that the firm's offering poses a significant barrier to entry to potential entrants. The firm will be viewed more favorably if management can demonstrate that the firm's offering places its customers in a position where the costs for switching to a competitor or doing it themselves are prohibitive.

TIMING PLAYS A KEY ROLE IN GOING PUBLIC

Firms that seek IPO funding do it for offensive or defensive reasons. From an offensive perspective, they do an IPO to capitalize on an opportunity and to take the firm to the next level. From a defensive perspective, they seek IPO funding because if they don't have an infusion of funds, the opportunity will escape.

Timing is important for two reasons. The firm must be ready to do an IPO, and hopefully it will be going public when investors are seeking that type of investment. If the firm seeks funding too soon, then its valuation will be lower. Some firms may need to do additional rounds of venture capital funding, or what is called *mezzanine funding,* to get it to the point where an IPO will be most beneficial.

REALITY CHECK

Timing can be a Catch 22. If the firm waits too long, then it risks not having the money when the market opportunity is most lucrative. If the firm holds out, waiting for an even higher valuation, then it could miss the window or be forced to play catch-up.

Going the IPO route needs to be considered and planned well in advance. Ideally, the prospect for an eventual IPO should be considered from the inception of the venture. External funding has an effect on the type of stock the firm should authorize. Angels may prefer one type of stock. Venture capital firms may require another type of stock. The IPO process will also have considerable bearing on the number and type of shares to be issued.

It may take two to three years to prepare for an IPO. Firms usually need to provide audited financial statements for at least the last three years so investors know how the firm is doing. It usually takes about four to five months to do an IPO if the firm is properly prepared for it. This includes the two to three weeks for road show after filing with the Securities and Exchange Commission (SEC). It usually takes the SEC about 40 days to review the IPO documentation. Firms are usually required to go public within three to four months after their last annual audit. Data become dated quickly and are of little value for firms that are experiencing rapid growth.

Timing may also be important in terms of the mood that investors have toward the stock market in general and new equity offerings in particular. If the stock market is declining or depressed, then investors tend to look less favorably at new offerings. Conversely, if the market is full of lucrative yet less risky investment alternatives in established firms, then new offerings may encounter resistance. One firm had the misfortune in 2001 of trying to go public the day terrorists attacked the United States.

VALUATION: ART AND SCIENCE COMBINED

Chapters 10 through 12 noted that valuing an emerging business can be a real challenge. In almost all cases, the value of a firm is what people are willing to pay for it. The same principle applies to valuing a firm in the IPO process. Valuation usually boils down to multiples and percentages. Most IPOs are designed to raise about 25 percent of the firm's overall post-IPO valuation. If the firm is trying to raise $100 million, then it needs to be worth at least $300 million for the new money to be worth about 25 percent of post IPO valuation. For the IPO to be successful, the emerging venture must demonstrate it is worth the pre-IPO valuation and that the investors who participate in the IPO will get a worthy return on their investment.

INVESTMENT BANKERS: TAKE MY FIRM PUBLIC, PLEASE!

Investment bankers play a crucial role in the IPO process because their job is to create the conditions where the firm can raise the largest amount of money per share issued. The investment banker will influence whether investors are lined up to participate in the IPO. Fortunately, institutions and investors are always looking for exceptional opportunities. Hopefully, the firm is positioned to generate exceptional returns.

The investment banker's job, among other things, is to run the road show and get together a syndicate of investors. Investment bankers target a number of institutions and individuals to buy the stock. Institutional investors are particularly important because they may represent 80 percent of the investment with individual investors providing the balance.

CHOOSING THE INVESTMENT BANKER

If the venture is being courted by numerous investment bankers, then it will have the opportunity to hear each investment banker's presentation in what is called the *bake-off*. In the bake-off, each investment banker presents its case for why the emerging venture should hire it.

REALITY CHECK

In most cases, entrepreneurs do not select the investment banker. Most emerging firms cannot be that selective. Unless the venture has phenomenal appeal and investment bankers are lined up to do the deal, the investment banker is the one who does the selecting. Investment bankers are selective because they are in a sense buying the venture's stock so they can sell it. In many instances, the investment bank is underwriting the sale of stock.

The following tips should be incorporated when selecting an investment banker:

1. Check the investment banker's reputation. Your firm will be judged by the credibility of the investment banker doing the IPO.
2. It is also important to have trust in the investment banker, so try to establish a relationship in advance.
3. Check what types of deals the investment banker has done.
4. Make sure the investment banker's staff who will be involved in your IPO has an in-depth knowledge of your industry, market, technology.
5. Make sure the investment banker's staff is prepared to develop an in-depth understanding of your business.
6. The size of the deal will affect whether more than one investment banker is involved.
7. Make sure the investment banker is committed to the IPO business.

Alan Zimmer and James Rouse, as CEO and CFO of Reeds Jewelers, respectively, offered the following advice:[2]

1. Don't take the process too seriously; there is not as much mystique as the players like to perpetuate.
2. Don't believe everything the investment bankers tell you.
3. Negotiate and monitor all fees closely.
4. Don't give a blank check to the investment bankers, lawyers, auditors, and printers.
5. You can pay a lot, or you can pay a lot more; stay on top of the bills everyone will be running up.
6. Know, and be able to explain, your business, your niche, and your strategy—thoroughly.
7. Make up your mind to enjoy the process; you're paying the investment bankers, lawyers, and auditors to worry and plan for you.
8. Expect that the proposed price of offering may be dropped the night before the deal is done.
9. Raise the capital you expect to need for the next five years.
10. Get the managing underwriter to solicit analysts' coverage from members of the syndicate.

11. Don't expect the business to run on its own while you are in the IPO process.
12. For the smaller business, the aggravation of being public will most likely exceed the reward.
13. There will be days when you wish you were private.
14. Whether a public or private company, the ethics of your company and its associates will be a major key to sustained success; you should understand that the public will perceive that those ethics will be a reflection of your own personal integrity. Model the behavior that you want to see in your associates.

SELLING TO THE PUBLIC VERSUS DOING
AN INITIAL PUBLIC OFFERING

Chapter 8 noted there is a difference between selling stock to the public and doing an IPO. This chapter has been directed to IPOs. If your firm does not fit the profile for raising tens or even hundreds of millions of dollars through an IPO and it is seeking less than $1 million, then you should consider doing your own stock offering. The SEC's conditions are less stringent for firms that want to sell less than $1 million.

LEGAL COUNSEL: AN IMPORTANT PART
OF YOUR IPO TEAM

This chapter has emphasized the importance of having a qualified management team in place and making sure you have the right investment banker doing the deal. The need for the right legal counsel has not been addressed. It should be clear by now that each player in the IPO game has his or her interests in mind. The investment banker wants to make a lot of money. If a venture capital firm invested in your venture, then it wants to have a lucrative liquidity event. Your legal counsel plays a critical role because it is that firm's job to protect your interests throughout the whole IPO process. There will be times when there are different views about how things should be handled. Legal counsel will need to make sure each party recognizes and respects your firm's rights.

REALITY CHECK

Make sure your firm's legal counsel has gone through a successful IPO before so the lawyers know how to deal with the underwriter and the underwriter's attorneys.

CONCLUSION: THE IPO PROCESS IS NEITHER
SIMPLE NOR EASY

Don't even think about doing an IPO unless it has really strong merits. Doing an IPO is like opening Pandora's box—you cannot tell in advance exactly what you will encounter. If you have your act together, surround yourself with trustworthy and capable individuals and firms, are positioned to generate considerable wealth, and the investment market is supportive for IPOs, then you should proceed.

An IPO is a double-edged sword. It may be the only way for your firm to seize the moment. Yet it will also change your venture and the role you play in it. Life will never be the same. Finally, it should be noted that while an IPO represents a milestone experienced by an incredibly small number of firms, it does not guarantee that the firm will be success-ful. Money is merely a means to an end. If it is not used properly, then the venture will miss the opportunity to be an exceptional enterprise.

> *It's best to remember that IPOs have a lot in common with high school proms.*
> *A lot depends on who takes you there. And sometimes it's best to stay home.*[3]

—Emily Barker, *Inc.*

ENDNOTES

1. Business 2.0, May 2000, p. 462.

2. Some of these points originally appeared in Stephen C. Harper, *The McGraw-Hill Guide to Managing Growth in Your Emerging Business* (New York: McGraw-Hill, 1994), pp. 323 & 324. The points were updated to reflect recent thoughts by the two executives of Reeds Jewelers.

3. Emily Barker, "The Road to Wall Street," *Inc.,* June 2002, p. 86.

EPILOGUE

ENTREPRENEURIAL *DOS* AND *DON'TS*

If you have gone through all the steps of analyzing the market, identifying opportunities, and developing a business plan, then you have made substantial progress toward preparing yourself to start your own business. However, if you are like most people, you probably found that for every question you answered, more questions surfaced that needed to be answered. At this point, your situation is similar to when a person graduates from college. You've learned a lot but you still don't know all you need to know. There is a lot more to learn if you want to increase the odds for starting a successful new venture.

The preceding chapters provided numerous helpful insights, examples, tips, guidelines, and reality checks. It is easy for people to be overwhelmed, however, when presented with so much information on so many different dimensions. The following list of *dos* and *don't*s has been provided to help put things in perspective and to highlight many of the most salient points you need to keep in mind as you continue the entrepreneurial journey.

The following tips were provided by interviews with more than 210 entrepreneurs from a wide range of businesses. It may be helpful, however, to provide a few noteworthy observations by a few of the entrepreneurs before reading the list:[*]

I was fed up when I realized that I knew what to do, but I couldn't convince my boss to do it. I felt like I was living at home, with my parents still telling me what to do... I was just getting too old for that.

—Founder of a marketing research
and communications firm

---

[*]The 600-plus tips provided in the epilogue are an expanded and updated version of the 200 tips that originally appeared in the second edition of *The McGraw-Hill Guide to Staring Your Own Business* by Stephen C. Harper, published in 2003. Permission to use that material has been provided by McGraw-Hill Publishing Company.

Life in a start-up is similar to the cycle of manic-depressive behavior
where you feel you are on the top of the world one day and wake up
terrified in the middle of the night on the next.

—Founder of a technology firm

You should [be able] to eat what you kill. I was tired of getting such a small piece of the
money that I earned for XYZ Company [actual name of company withheld].

—Founder of a software services firm

If I have to live by a dumb decision, then at least I will be the one to make it.

—Founder of a construction firm

Be bold. Make sure you aren't running with self-imposed limitations.
In the early phases of starting a company, the trials and tribulations can cause
you to question the value of your skills, your product, and possibly your mission.
This doubt can lead you into self-imposed limitations. An entrepreneur should constantly
reexamine the limitations, looking for ways to break them down or change the rules.
Human beings tend to follow rules and seek order.

—Founder of a software technology firm

Failure is an orphan, success has a million parents. You never hear about
the 99 percent that are duds.

—Founder of a medical technology firm

READER BEWARE

Three notes of caution should be recognized before reading the list of more than 600 *do*s and *don't*s. First, the ideas are from various entrepreneurs who have had varying degrees of success. Following their suggestions will not guarantee your success. Second, some of the recommendations are situational. They may apply in some entrepreneurial situations and settings, but not others. Third, like most people, entrepreneurs have their own opinions. You will find that some of the *do*s provided by one or more entrepreneurs may also appear as *don't*s by other entrepreneurs. Your job is to determine which ones apply to your situation.

TAKE THE MIRROR TEST: LOOK AT YOURSELF, YOUR LIFE, AND WHAT IS DRIVING YOU

- Be able to answer why you want to be in business for yourself.
- Don't regard the new venture as a way to get rich quick.
- Don't start a business just because you are tired of working for someone else.
- Don't do it for the money. Do it for the passion and self-satisfaction.
- The level of passion and commitment is one of the distinguishing factors between successful and unsuccessful entrepreneurs. It is easy to see who is committed to the business for personal reasons, and who is in it simply because it seemed like a good idea at the time.

- Don't start a business venture with the main goal of getting rich fast, regardless of how lucrative it appears.

- Don't forget that you are running a business. It is not supposed to be a welfare agency or a hobby.

- The business, whatever it is, really should be something that the entrepreneur would do if money were no object. The levels of effort, risk, and commitment required are so high that the business needs to be something that fulfills more than economic issues.

- Think about and be clear on what your motivation is for starting the venture.

- Be prepared to lose all of the money that you invest in the business.

- Set a minimum before you start. Realize what return will be acceptable before you start.

- Starting and managing a business is very hard on everyone involved.

- Realize your business is a 24/7 adventure. You can't call timeouts and there are no real vacations.

- Recognize the impact on your family and social life. Your family is part of the venture. You will need their support, especially when things are stressful. Recognize it will cost them something—time, and money, too.

- Don't venture into a business on a spur-of-the-moment decision/desire to become an entrepreneur.

- Make sure your personal life is in order. You cannot afford to let personal problems interfere with the business.

- Do something that you are not enthusiastic about.

- Don't expect to maintain your same lifestyle and standard of living. Cash flow may not be what you expect, and some sacrifices may need to be made in order to remain in business.

- Forget about having a life or money in the opening phases of the company.

- Save enough money to live on for the first two years that your business is open, so that you can take all profits made and put them right back into your business.

- Make sure that you and your family can recover from the financial setback if things do not go as well as planned. Things normally don't go as well as planned.

- Don't go too far with the personal sacrifices. Try hard to maintain some balance in your life.

- Don't dive in half-heartedly. Go all out, or go home!

- Have your heart and soul in the business. If you don't believe in it, no one else will.

- Don't just go into a venture because you are tired of what you are doing.

- Don't start a business because someone else has been successful at the same business. You will never be able to copy their decisions (good and bad) or luck.

- Make sure you really want to be an entrepreneur. Too many hours, too much stress, too many tasks that have to be done that you may dislike.

- Don't expect that life will be much easier now that you are your own boss.

- Be prepared to work harder than you even thought.

- You must be willing to do most of the work when starting out.

- Realize you will wear many hats. Especially when first starting. You will do a variety of tasks that you never envisioned and would not do working for someone else (e.g., mounting towel racks in the bathroom, buying a coffee maker for the office, etc.).

- Don't think you will be your own boss.

- Don't expect there to be less pressure than working for someone else.

- Don't think it is going to be easy. The life of an entrepreneur is one that requires a lot of self-imposed discipline. You will not have a boss to call it a night or to give you needed encouragement when things are rough.

- Don't underestimate the power and importance of having prior experience or knowledge.

- Don't assume that expertise in one area will easily translate into business savvy in another area.

- Don't go into business as a get-rich-quick scheme. This will generally backfire.

- Do not let other people's skepticism scare you away from accomplishing your own goals and dreams.

- Always be willing to take a chance.

- Don't let the fear of failure hold you from something you want to do.

- Don't burn bridges when you leave a company.

- Don't alienate people in the process of considering your venture.

- Don't share ownership with your spouse because you both will have different job styles and different ways of doing things. If you disagree at work, you will most likely take those disagreements home with you.

- Don't get married; opening up a business takes up a lot of your time. You don't have as much time to delegate to your social life.

TIME IS YOUR ENEMY: YOU WILL NEVER HAVE ENOUGH TIME

- It takes at least three years to get a concept to really take off. Running a company is like working two jobs for three years. Your new venture will become your life. Get used to not having a vacation.

- Don't underestimate the amount of time that it is going to take being an entrepreneur.

- You must be able to manage and budget your time carefully.

- You will work harder and longer hours than ever before.

- Don't think success will come quickly or easily.

- Spend a lot of time building relationships with suppliers and sources of customers, to develop a presence in the market.

- Focus on those things that are important to the business. Don't spend a lot of time on office paperwork instead of meeting prospects or improving the network of contacts.

- Don't spend months trying to understand the technology and how to setup the Web site architecture. Outsource it and spend your time where you can add the most value.

- Don't forget about running the business while you are out generating new business.

- Have patience and dedication, because it will take time in the beginning.

- Time is your enemy.

- When it comes time, stop talking about it and do it.

PREPARATION: STACK THE ODDS IN YOUR FAVOR

- Don't look back. If you have recently been fired from a job, looking back will only stall you.

- Don't get into things you know absolutely nothing about.

- It takes more than a degree to be successful in business, especially new ventures.

- When you jump off the big company boat, be prepared to be shocked by the lack of (support) talent available to you.

- You have to go with a 100 percent commitment or not at all. If you go, run like hell. There's more to starting a business than you can imagine and more than you could ever learn in business school.

- Get business advice early. Take advantage of the many groups that provide assistance to small ventures.

- Talk to many other individuals who have launched their own businesses and keep track of what they perceive the pitfalls to be.

- Don't be too proud to ask for help.

- Never try to be an expert at all things. Hire professionals with specific talents.

- Get a lot of advice from people who want to help. Their experiences and advice will keep you from making mistakes they have made and point out opportunities you may not recognize. This is particularly true in the areas of finance and law. Hire the best accountant and lawyer you can afford.

- Work your way into the business by rubbing elbows with the big dogs.

- Join a network referral group.

- Form or join coalitions that will give you access to information.

- Do a lot of networking. Network with suppliers, competitors, and customers. Information sharing is the key. Involvement in the local chamber of commerce and the business community can yield important contacts.

- Contact professional advisors before anything else.

- Set up some type of advisory committee or board composed of experienced business-people well before you start your business. These advisors can go beyond providing advice. They can provide introductions to other companies, identify opportunities, and may become investors themselves.

- Surround yourself with a great professional team.

- Hire professionals that know what you do not know.

- Network, network, network. Develop as many contacts as you can. You will need all of the help you can possibly muster.

- Talk to other entrepreneurs in the area.

- Work for a successful similar business in order to learn which systems work and which ones may be improved on while spending someone else's dollar to do so.

- Learn from others who have gone before you. Learn from successful people by examining both their successes and their failures.

- Visit people in other cities who have started similar ventures like the one you are considering. Pick their brains.

- Take advantage of the many groups that provide assistance to emerging ventures.

- Join industry groups to share best practices and leverage the Small Business Association for new ideas and funding.

- Have a mentor. Find someone who can help you with knowledge of your business or running a business in general. You need a reality check from time to time.

- Take every opportunity to build relationships with customers, suppliers, employees, and the community at large. Many positive outcomes, big and small, will flow from relationships you've invested in.

- Seek to cultivate relationships with established players in complementary fields. This will help to build some credibility for a reputationless start-up.

- Don't quit your full-time job until you know you can make a living at the new enterprise.

- Don't mix friends with business because they will always want something for free.

- Don't wait to learn it all before you start—be prepared to learn and change as you go.

- Create a set of go and no-go conditions such as performance metrics.

- Don't underestimate the business potential of your idea and look at it as a sideline.

- Make sure you make the right impressions; demonstrate professionalism in everything you do.

- You need to be at least 40 years old to have enough experience to start, but if you're older than 40, you won't have enough energy to persist.

- If you are starting a new venture early in life, leverage your enthusiasm; if you are starting it later in life, leverage your experience.

- Know the business that you are starting, inside and out.

- Go into business with as much experience as you can.

- Know your strengths. As long as you are humble enough to recognize that you can't do some things, you may find someone to help you with what you lack in experience or simply can't do.

- Do not assume that expertise in one area will easily translate into business savvy.

- Don't take yourself too seriously.

- Don't work 16 hours a day.

- Don't wander from one idea to another.

- Don't reinvent the wheel; do what works.

- Know your threshold for risk. Don't be afraid to push the bubble, but do it in baby steps and always know how much you are willing to lose or gain.

- You should invest considerable time finding new business.

- Expect dishonesty.

- Don't share your idea with everyone. Be discreet with whom you talk to about your idea.

- Have the ability to work long hours.

- If possible, work within the business before starting a venture. The best way to research a business is to work within that business for a while.

- Find an idea or industry that excites you. It will help with the long hours associated with a new business venture.

- Don't start a business based on something you like to do or want to do just to have a business of your own. Make sure there is a market for the product or service.

- Don't be afraid to start the new venture. If your planning and research are thorough, and you feel confident about its prospects, then start your own business.

- Get a good accountant. An accountant can tell you areas in which to save money that a simple bookkeeper cannot. This is especially important with taxes and deductible expenses.

- Attend to financial and legal matters before you start your business.

- Be sure you've researched your product or service idea and make sure a market exists.

- Know the answer to the question, "How am I going to make money?" before you start your business.

- Don't wait for the perfect opportunity to present itself. If you wait for the home run ball, you'll never make it to the plate.

- Don't overextend yourself—opening a business is a gradual process.

- Trust yourself, but remember, you don't know everything.

- Don't piss off anyone. You don't want to make too many people angry right when you open up a new business.

MANAGEMENT: WHO EVER SAID IT WOULD BE EASY?

- Don't just be the entrepreneur and manager; be a leader.

- Think of yourself not as just a CEO, but as a chief cheer officer, chief sales officer, and chief strategy officer.

- Create your own company culture on purpose; don't leave it chance.

- Be the first person to arrive and the last to leave as well.

- Don't come into the venture without the desire and know-how to complete the task at hand.

- Have a vision of what success would look like and a vision of what failure would look like.

- The most important characteristic of a successful entrepreneur is an understanding that making other people see your vision, share your dream, and strive toward the goals of the firm is the only real road to success.

- Don't let your vision run wild.

- Entrepreneurs need to focus on those things that are important to the business. Some entrepreneurs get lost focusing on the wrong things. Examples included spending a lot of time and money on promotional materials, and spending time on office paperwork, instead of meeting prospects or improving the network of contacts.

- Take a stand, learn from the experience, and adjust.

- Don't be a dreamer; implement your ideas.

- Sweat the small stuff.

- Be open to new ideas and ways to accomplish them.

- Be known for your strong ethical and reliable business background.

- Be proactive, stay ahead of situations.

- Expect the unexpected.

- Network with everyone, all of the time.

- Try not to rely on voice mail for your business; people want to talk to a real person.

- A characteristic of successful entrepreneurs is their ability to handle multiple things at the same time. These are parallel people in contrast with serial people who need to complete something before moving on to the next thing.

- Develop an understanding of what the critical success factors for the business will be.

- Seek input and ask a lot of questions. Listen to what people say, but you should not necessarily follow every bit of advice. Always remember, however, that this is your business and you must make the final decision.

- Don't take someone's word on anything; always make sure it is correct by finding it out yourself.

- Do what you think you should do instead of what everyone else thinks you should do, but don't get so cocky that you think you do not need the help and advice of experts.

- Don't rely too heavily on previously learned behaviors from previous life, in Corporate America.

- Don't be afraid to make a major decision on gut instinct when there is no other choice.

- Be prepared to have big responsibilities, make quick decisions, and resolve problems.

- Do be prepared. You can never be too prepared.

- Do your homework—research the variables and perform due diligence.
- Don't place all your trust in the hands of accountants and lawyers.
- Consensus is a good thing—especially when it's among smart people who will give you their honest opinions.
- Don't make major decisions without alternatives, but don't let analysis paralysis overtake your decision making.
- Don't be afraid to make wrong decisions; only some of them need to be correct.
- Don't wait for all the data to make a move or decision.
- Seek out diversity of opinion; this may give you a better perspective in business decisions.
- Don't try to identify or solve all the problems at once; do it in steps.
- Take risks and make decisions quickly.
- Seek statistical backup for hunches and intuition.
- Don't let emotions drive decisions.
- Get help from someone who has done this or something similar before. They will point out things that should be obvious to you. Often you will not see them.
- Don't make quick irrational decisions.
- Don't be afraid to ask stupid questions.
- Seek advice, but remember, it's your business. You are the one who has to decide the *who, what, when, where,* and *how much.*
- Get advice from experts and be sure to get all of the facts before making any big decisions.
- There is a time to stop analyzing, to check your gut barometer, and then to make a go/no go decision.
- Don't treat the risks of business like a gamble. Business success is not a game of chance, it is a game in which careful preparation can lead to significantly better outcomes.
- Don't hesitate to take action. Don't wait to have all the answers.
- Don't wait too long to act on ideas.
- Don't subscribe to *not invented here* syndrome.
- Don't think you will survive just because you are smart.
- Don't think you know everything, because you don't.
- Recognize and understand how much you know, and how much you do not know.
- Challenge your assumptions.
- Don't overestimate the big things.
- Don't underestimate or overlook the little things. What you took for granted when you worked in a well-established company does not exist in the new business.
- Don't throw in the towel at the first sign of adversity; be prepared to face tough times.

- Don't panic when something doesn't work the first time.

- Don't believe everything you hear.

- Timing may be everything, but it's not something that we can easily control.

- Hard work only carries you so far—you need resources to be successful. Recognizing what those resources are and finding a way to get them is a critical aspect of any new venture.

- Set long- and short-term goals for your venture.

- There is no lack of great ideas, just lack of execution.

- Don't believe the old adage, "If you build a better mousetrap, the world will beat a path to your door." Ideas are a dime a dozen; it is skilled people and a well-thought-out plan that will turn a good idea into a business success.

- Concentrate on details. Execution is often key, and the details are what get you ahead of the competition.

- Solid implementation also requires having the right people in place and giving them the right motivation to meet their goals or objectives.

- Thorough analysis and careful planning do not guarantee that you will get desired results. More important, entrepreneurs must remain flexible and responsive to the signals of the market.

- Continuously analyze where you are and where you should be going in business.

- Know the early warning signs of failure.

- Be perceptive and flexible. Be willing to adapt your strategy. The marketplace can change. Preconceived ideas can be disproved. New opportunities can develop. Unless you have a frame of mind to be flexible, you will miss these opportunities and changes that can negatively impact your success.

- Learn to say no.

- Don't be afraid to make mistakes and own up to them. You must create an environment that rewards risk taking.

- Learn from your mistakes and the mistakes of others.

- Establish your positive reputation in the business community.

- Be ethical with your employees and customers. Once compromised, this is hard to recover.

- Don't compromise your integrity.

- Honor your commitments. Don't promise anything you can't deliver.

- Do the right thing, even when it hurts.

- Never lie to customers or employees. Lies will always come back to haunt you.

- Communicate relentlessly with your management team.

- Communicate thoroughly and openly with the board of directors (they must be the first to know).

- Make a big bet on your board of directors. Vest them immediately so that they have a vested interest in your company from day one.

- Use the board of directors to acquire financing and recruit good people.

- Don't hire a board of directors who only look good on paper.

- Don't get directors who are just figureheads. You need people who are innovators, who have extensive contacts, and who have good networks across many businesses.

- Stay informed in your field. If you are isolated from other people who do the same thing that you do, join a professional organization, and attend the meetings. This is a good way to find potential good employees, too.

- Continuously cover all of the bases. A new venture is fragile. Employee morale, cash flow, customer relations, finances, everything needs to be monitored constantly. Any problems that arise need to be addressed immediately.

- Listen to customers'/employees' complaints and ideas.

- Don't bite off more than you can chew. Know your limits and pace yourself.

- Don't assume your way is always right.

- Don't trust another person's estimates on revenue or profits unless you can be sure that they do not have a vested interest in you starting the business (franchises come to mind). Do the analysis yourself if you can, or hire an independent consultant.

- Don't get discouraged when you hit obstacles or things do not go as planned. There will be bumps in the road.

- Be flexible.

- Don't get frustrated by the down times.

- Don't get overly optimistic in the good times.

- Don't think you can do it by yourself.

- Stay humble no matter what successes you have.

- No matter what mistakes and setbacks you have, learn from them.

- Be prepared to motivate yourself because you will be your own boss and there will be no one there to tell you what needs to be done.

- Don't take on a partner unless you absolutely must.

- If you plan to have partners, partner with individuals with skill sets that differ from yours.

- If you plan to have partners, then objectively evaluate your own motives and those of your partners. The overall vision (objectives of the enterprise) and core values (including business ethics) must be shared by the entrepreneurial partners.

- If you plan to have partners, don't assume that your partners have the same definition of success that you do.

- If you plan to have partners, don't assume that your partners have the same expectations of you that you do.

- Never be satisfied with your current state, but always look for ways to improve the business.

402   ENTREPRENEURIAL *DOS* AND *DON'TS*

- Track key operating and performance metrics carefully.

- Hone your management skills and have people available to you who are good managers.

- Your job will need to evolve as your business grows. Be prepared to learn, to change, to delegate, and solicit constructive criticism.

- Use technology to improve performance and enhance your personal productivity.

- There are new technologies every day that can help improve efficiency, yield, throughput, and so on. Look for ways to exploit technology to improve the business.

- If there is new technology, get in early.

- Recognize the criticality of reliable IT (information technology).

- Don't keep advisors that you don't feel are doing a good job.

THE BUSINESS PLAN: THE MENTAL JOURNEY MUST PRECEDE THE PHYSICAL JOURNEY

- Prepare a real-world business plan. Period!

- Plan up front. Don't wait until your business is open to decide how you're going to do things.

- Take time to create a stellar business plan.

- Prepare a business plan so that you understand the issues, risks, and costs.

- Develop a business plan, even if you will be investing only personal funds.

- Plan strategically but do not overplan.

- Set up targets/metrics to assess your growth periodically.

- Have 1-, 3-, 5-, and 10-year plans as to how you want the business to grow and develop over time, and adjust them as time moves on.

- Don't build a business plan that is rigid or inflexible.

- Don't rely on home-run plans. If everything has to happen exactly as planned for the venture to be successful, it will probably fail.

- Prepare beforehand for seasonal pitfalls.

- Factor in the slow times and prepare for them.

- Don't overlook the effects of local and national economy.

- Don't expect that your business plan will be 100 percent complete. It is not realistic to expect to be able to plan for all possibilities. However, play the chess match in your head and try to anticipate as much as possible and what your response might be.

- Develop contingency plans for major decisions.

- Don't get blindsided; know every little possible detail that you could ever imagine.

- Don't assume that mishaps won't happen; they will, and when you least expect it or need it.

- Think about failure; be prepared that it might happen and for how you would handle it.

- Identify the potential pitfalls and risk of the venture and build a risk management plan around those. Focus more attention on the risky areas than on the no-risk components.

- You must have a plan. It might be wrong, and you might change it, but you must have something to manage to. If things don't work, go back to the plan and try to understand what it is that isn't working.

- Embrace risk in pursuit of returns, but do so after careful analysis and planning.

- Remember to consider federal and state regulations, taxes, and human resources issues.

- Spend a lot of time planning. It helps convince yourself and others that you are pursuing a real opportunity.

- Know the business you're in and stick to it. Resist the temptation to be everything to everyone. Rather, differentiate on quality, level of service, and value-added functions of the core product set. Build a reputation for product excellence.

- Plan for changes in your marketplace; the more dynamic your firm is, the more advantage it will have against established competitors.

- When it is time to grow, do not grow too fast.

- Have an expansion/growth plan in case the business takes off.

- Prepare a business plan that spells out prospective customers and the likelihood of their actually providing revenue to the venture.

- Don't try to grow faster than your market or your ability to provide the service or product. Don't overcommit.

- Do not accept more customers than you can handle. Quality service is the most important attribute of launching a business. During the initial stages of the business, concentrate on service, not on revenues.

- Study and understand the industry you plan to enter and determine where your new venture would fit in.

- Excel in the execution of the business plan.

- Set your own reasonable benchmarks.

- Do a significant amount of research in your field such as trends, competition, and so on.

- Don't jump into any business blind. Make sure you research what you are doing and look at all of the aspects of the business.

- Get it right the first time—you don't get a second chance.

- Have realistic goals that are tough enough to make you try really hard to achieve them.

- Think strategically. Ask yourself how the industry will change in the next 10 years.

- Follow your business plan. If you have to change it along the way, then fine, but you need an outline of the main goals that you are trying to accomplish.

- Don't write your business plan for survival only. You should look further into the future and plan for greatness, not mediocrity.

- You shouldn't feel confined to a business plan. You may need to stray far from your original draft.

- Don't let your plans collect dust; make sure you execute them.

- Translating a good idea into a profitable business is the key.

- Just because something looks good on paper, doesn't mean it will work in a competitive environment.

- Be realistic. Don't expect reality to match your initial concept.

- Make up the best, worst, and real scenarios that this business would probably face.

- There is no fixed formula for success in a new business. No *blue light special* is ever going to be offered guaranteeing success, because each business is different. The critical success (or failure) factors will vary between businesses, even those operating in the same industry. Some businesses are successful in spite of themselves simply because someone steps up to deliver an unmet need.

- Don't fall into the *idealism trap.* Murphy's Law applies (if something can go wrong, it will, and at the most inopportune time), even with thorough planning and preparation. Things cost twice as much and take twice as long as you expected.

- Don't overanalyze potential opportunities; the window of the opportunity could be closed by the time you are ready to launch the venture. You will lose your competitive advantage.

- Hard work only carries you so far. You need resources to be successful. Recognizing what those resources are and finding a way to get them is critical to any new venture.

- Don't scrimp on mission-critical needs.

- Plan, plan, plan, plan, and then when things do not go as you have planned, start over and reevaluate the situation.

- Have a clear idea of what your goals are and how you are planning to achieve them.

- Secure resources (people, money, etc.) before you need them.

- Perform a detailed technological analysis to gain an understanding of the latest manufacturing and operations techniques.

- Begin with the end in mind. Develop your exit strategy first. When going into business, always have an exit strategy.

- Know your exit point, both on the upside and the downside—when you will exit, under what conditions. On the up side, understand what you have to do to get there. If you want to IPO, understand what a company looks like that does a successful IPO.

- Set a time frame and success measures so you know when to call it quits.

- Make sure that you set yourself up for the worst-case scenario, or what you can expect to be your worst nightmare.

- Don't forget to allow for lag time when planning, because everything will not arrive when expected.

- Develop the awareness to see when you have a total loser on your hands and *get out!* Know when to raise the white flag. Life is too short to keep bailing out the ship; you want to be rowing, not bailing.

STRATEGY: HOW DO YOU PLAN TO GAIN SUSTAINABLE COMPETITIVE ADVANTAGES?

- Be original. Differentiate yourself from everyone else so that you will not be forgotten.

- Formalize a business strategy, even if only done as a mental exercise. Although mid-course corrections are certainly to be expected, starting operations by the seat of your pants will probably not produce a sustainable business.

- Don't be first in a market. Educating the market can be very time consuming and expensive.

- Don't attempt to compete in a mature industry unless you have particularly strong experience, creativity, or contacts.

- Don't hire a sales team until the prototype's features and benefits are known, it is ready to sell, and the infrastructure is in place.

- Don't commit to a project that is too big, too early. Developing a solid reputation is critical.

- Never sacrifice quality for financial gain.

- Don't position your business to be nonflexible when surprised by unanticipated events.

- Don't expect strategies to remain constant.

- The critical success (or failure) factors will vary between businesses, even those operating in the same industry. Some businesses are successful in spite of themselves simply because someone steps up to deliver an unmet need.

- Do not be afraid to imitate. Look at what similar companies are doing in the marketplace. There is no reason to reinvent the wheel on some factors.

- Look at the industry you have experience in; it may be a good avenue to get your foot in the door.

- Perform industry and market analysis; figure out the size of the pie and the opportunities to obtain a piece of the pie.

- When developing your strategy you need to know the targeted market, the opportunity, the goals, the requirements, the challenges, the competition, and so on.

- Establish a barrier to entry. This may be through a product that is hard to copy or a service that is unique to your company.

- Look for new or additional opportunities in unexpected places.

- Look for a niche that is not serviced in an existing market.

- To maintain a sustained competitive advantage, your firm must ensure its resources are rare, they are valuable, they are hard to copy, and they have no substitute. A deficiency in one or more brings into question the long-term viability of the firm.

- Differentiate your business. Your competitive advantage should be based on service, quality, and value-added functions.

- Focus on the one thing that will differentiate you from your competition and do all you can to be the best at that one thing. Lots of times, entrepreneurs put their fingers into more projects than they can handle and none pans out.

- Be flexible if the business does not go in the direction that you want it to go. Rapidly changing technology may move your business in new directions, also.

- Invest heavily in new business development/product development skills initially.

- Don't think that you can manage everything that needs to be done: Don't be afraid to outsource. Understand your core competencies and outsource everything else. Focus your attention on satisfying your customers; outsource sidetracking tasks such as accounting.

- Take imitators and inelastic demand into consideration.

- Recognize that in some businesses, not-for-profit entities may be direct competitors.

- Don't enter an industry without a significant product innovation/advantage.

- Prioritize and analyze resources in terms of sustained competitive advantage.

- Establish barriers to entry (technology, intellectual knowledge, expertise).

- Know your competition. A key problem with many new start-ups is that they get so focused on developing their product that they don't know what's going on in the marketplace. This is especially true for underfunded, resource-strapped start-ups in high-tech industries. Such mistakes can prove costly. You may end up with a cool product that nobody really needs, or your competition might have already come up with a better gadget.

- Build a brand name to deter competitors (particularly for products that are easily copied or imitated).

- Be creative and innovative: look to new markets and new products.

- Don't spend your time working on business segments that are not profitable.

- A diversified business or portfolio of businessess will help insulate the ups and downs.

- Be prepared for change. Nothing remains the same. Even if you do everything right, your business can still fail.

- Think about different scenarios and how you can handle them. Always have contingency plans.

- Don't jump into situations too late.

- Don't underestimate the competition.

- Don't steal your clients or customers from previous employers.

- Don't be afraid to change your strategy to meet changing times and needs of the customers.

- Don't have any one customer responsible for more than 10 to 15 percent of your revenue.

- Don't have a narrow focus; go after the best you can do and let the others handle what you cannot do.

- You should always have alternative strategies for the rapidly changing environment. If an exit strategy is required, you must be able to make that jump.

- Know what your core competency is and what it isn't.

- Be ready to change your business model on a dime.

- Be able to respond quickly if what you are doing isn't working (e.g., when ad campaigns are not producing expected revenues).

- Make sure that it is the right time to enter the market.

- Dare to be different! Those businesses that are different are the ones that stand out. Sam Walton said, "Break all the rules, swim upstream, and go the other way."

- Know the business you're in and stick to it. Resist the temptation to be everything to everyone.

- Don't get distracted. You'll see lots of interesting ideas, but to be successful you must stay focused.

- Be opportunistic, receptive to feedback, and flexible when launching a new business. It may not be until you are in business that you fully understand the business you are in.

- Don't cut corners. Build a reputation for excellence. Quality and service might cost more upfront, but they pay back over time multifold.

- Most products work because of one or two simple features. Figure out those features and execute those extremely well.

- Start small, obtain some experience, and then expand.

- Don't expand too rapidly or grow for growth's sake.

- Be committed to continuous improvement and continuous innovation.

- Expect to spend most of your time attracting new business.

- Don't expect that the rest of the world is like the United States.

- Don't forget that human motivations vary across cultures.

- Success is less about strategy than about people. Strategy can always change.

HUMAN RESOURCES: YOU WILL ONLY BE AS GOOD AS YOUR PEOPLE

- Don't forget that people are your most important resource.

- Don't expect to hire employees that have the same level of passion.

- Outsource to the best service providers and hire the best talent for what you don't outsource.

- Choosing the right employees to hire is the most important thing. The difference between good and great is the difference between success and failure.

- Make sure that early hires are especially good hires, since these employees will help to jumpstart the company.

- Your second or third employee should complement you. If you're an engineer, hire an office manager. If you're an accomplished manager, hire a salesperson or engineer. It is important to round out the company.

- Try to find up-and-coming people in the industry.

- Hire employees who are smarter than you.

- Make sure you hire people who are doers.

- Hire people who are willing to take risks and encourage risks by taking them.

- Hire people with track records.

- Hire people who have done something similar before and who can help you take your firm to the next level and beyond. This also applies when seeking people to serve on your board of directors.

- Hire people with cross-functional skills, including project management skills.

- Hire employees with good ethical standards.

- Look for people who want to invest in themselves.

- Invest in hiring top talent to help run the business as it expands.

- Don't allow friendships to cloud hiring decisions; try to hire people as hungry as yourself. Don't allow your partner to hire anyone he has the "hots" for.

- Don't hire family or friends unless they are already in the field.

- Surround yourself with good people. You need to find people who are committed and passionate about their work. You have to give these people ownership and freedom to operate. Give all employees an equity stake in the company.

- Trust your instincts when dealing with people.

- Don't settle for a warm body. That approach will undoubtedly cause problems. In the event you do invest the time and an individual still doesn't work out, make the decision in an expeditious manner to let that person go.

- Don't hire people who are incapable of projecting a good image for your business.

- Don't just hire people with traditional or old-fashioned ideas. Having creativity is very important.

- Don't hire solely on education and skills. You can teach skills but you cannot teach values.

- Don't hire/raid from your previous employer's employee base to staff your business.

- Don't hire cheap—hire the best you can find and afford.

- Don't hire in-laws.

- Don't hire people because you know them or owe them something; hire based on experience and expertise.

- Avoid hiring people you can't afford and don't necessarily need.

- Remember that 20 percent of your employees will do 80 percent of the work.

- Don't hang onto marginal employees. You don't have time to rehabilitate an employee that isn't performing. Don't be afraid to quickly fire an employee that is not working out. Delaying dismissal only prolongs the agony and lost productivity. Mediocrity is the death of a new venture.

- Don't let employee problems go on long without dealing with them.

- Don't let animosity fester in a small company. Bad morale is tough to cure.

- Don't overwork yourself or your people. You make bad decisions when tired.

- Do not take employees for granted.

- Get to know your employees and their families.

- Understand what motivates your employees. People are motivated differently.

- Recognize there is a big difference between the owners running the operation and paid employees.

- Offer attractive compensation packages to attract an A team and marquee talent.

- Invest early in a human resource infrastructure especially if you will be in a service business.

- Never start a project with partners or employees who are not dedicated to it as well.

- Clearly document employee positions and responsibilities.

- Have an evaluation system that your employees consider to be fair.

- Be a leader. A high level of energy and a high level of infectious enthusiasm are essential.

- Your persona becomes the persona of your business. Your drive, stamina, attitude, and behavior become the attributes of your business. Any action you take in front of employees or customers is a representation of your business. Always put your best face forward.

- Don't go into business with friends because you think it will be easier. It might be hard when you have to tell your best friend he/she is wrong or fired.

- Create an environment that is differentiated in order to attract, develop, and retain top talent.

- Don't neglect to spend plenty of time finding the right people to help you.

- Complement and reward employees when good jobs are performed.

- Keeping good people is a challenge—have incentives so that employees see value in being a part of your organization and so that they are vested in the venture.

- Motivated people are your primary asset. Treat them well. If the people believe in the mission, they will work harder than any amount of money could induce. Find other ways than money to motivate and reward them.

- Pay a little more for the folks that deal directly with the customer. Your customers are valuable assets and you can't afford to lose one because of a worker that doesn't care or feel rewarded.

- Pay your people on time.

- Remember, when unemployment is low good employees are hard to find and keep.

- Compensate your employees well so they stay.

- Don't neglect to spend plenty of time and money to train and retain those people that you spent so much time finding.

- Make sure to have background checks on employees to make sure they are reliable and don't have a record.

- Set guidelines for your employees such as hours to be worked, sick time, flexibility, and what you expect from them.

- Have patience in training employees.

- Cross-train your people and have back-ups.

- Develop people so they are capable of running critical parts of the business.

- Demand more than you are willing to do yourself.

- Make sure you are the chief salesperson and do not delegate that.

- Treat your employees as well as your customers. When your employees enjoy working, they will serve your customers much better.

- Know your own strengths. Hire talent to fill in your weaknesses.

- Delegate. Delegate. Delegate.

- Delegate based on your shortcomings.

- Learn to keep your mouth shut and let other people talk.

- Listen to what employees have to say to ensure that everyone in the organization is satisfied with their jobs.

- Find someone you trust to help with the business. You will want days off, and most people do not want to be a slave to their business.

- Don't take on a partner unless you absolutely must. If you do, make sure he/she is as committed as you are.

- Whoever your partners are, make sure you define your partner issues.

- If you can't trust your partners, you are finished.

- Do drug testing for critical jobs.

- Don't keep employees that do drugs.

- Create checks and balances to limit dishonesty.

- Don't let people get away with stealing.

- Avoid becoming emotionally attached to long-term employees as well as family employees.

- Don't keep employees and advisors that you don't feel are doing a good job.

- Don't keep employees that do not fit in with your company's strategies or goals.

- Learn to deal with employee problems because there will always be at least one or more a day, and hire a good and experienced staff.

FINANCIAL SIDE: MONEY IS LIKE OXYGEN—YOU NEED IT TO LIVE

- Scrape up as much capital as possible before you start.

- Have the ability to sustain yourself for two years if giving 100 percent.

- Forecast how long your business will have negative cash flow before it will have a positive cash position. Arrange financing so you can last that long. If you think you are going to have negative cash flow for six months, be prepared for nine.

- Estimate how much financing (cash) you feel you need and double it.

- Get the necessary capital in the beginning. The last thing you want to worry about is how you are going to pay for everything while you are working hard at getting your business off the ground.

- Use as little capital as possible to start your business. Work your way through progressively, starting small and building slowly and steadily. Build up a business as quickly as your cash flow allows you to. Not faster.

- Don't invest all your money at the start of the business. Save some for growth or survival.

- Don't risk or jeopardize all of your life savings by investing in your business.

- Get the necessary capital in the beginning. The last thing you want to worry about is how you are going to pay for everything while you are working hard at getting it off the ground.

- Don't start a business without some reserve for the slow periods.

- Start the venture with an achievable cash flow plan for at least one year.

- Establish clear financial objectives.

- Don't think that the money will never run out; it does.

- Don't try to finance everything yourself even if you can. This leads you to become super cost conscious and less business oriented. There is something about using other people's money that gives you clarity of business thought.

- Don't let undercapitalization stop you. Getting money is not your problem. If you have a good business idea, there's always a way to raise money.

- Having people on your board of directors with proven track records and insights is invaluable in accessing funding from venture capitalists and gaining other sources of early mezzanine funding.

- Don't have only one way to finance your venture. Have startup financing alternatives—or a rich father-in-law.

- Don't undercapitalize. No matter how much you try to anticipate your expenses in the first year, there are always unexpected expenses. Costs are rarely less than you would have guessed.

- Don't take money early on. Tier it because it tends to be less diluted over time when demonstrated milestones are met.

- Look for investors that would help grow the business so you do not have to cover all the expenses.

- Find strong financing partners, whether it is the bank, VCs, investors, or others.

- Cultivate a variety of funding sources, which can help you more fully execute your business plan and prevent (or at least limit) resource constraints.

- Don't underestimate the amount of time it takes to raise money.

- Don't stop raising money. It needs to be a continual process, and in the best-case scenario, you want to have competing potential investors.

- There is a temptation to pitch the company that you think the investors want to buy. Not every investor is for you, and you will only find the right one if you pitch the company as it is and as you envision it.

- Don't give away too much equity in the beginning just being a good guy. The more you give away, the more fragmented your ownership is and the less power you have to do what is best for the company later. If you delude yourself, it is easy for the outside investors to run the company in their interest and not yours. At the same time, make sure everyone in the organization owns a piece of it.

- The window for financing can be very narrow. You must be able to capitalize on funding when it is available. To obtain capital, one must have a dominant position in the field or some defined market niche, a good product, a well-written business plan with a defined mission, and a management team with a track record, because it is the *what* and *who* that investors are looking at. Remember, due diligence goes both ways.

- If given the choice, take smart money over dumb money: Your investors' experience and connections can be as important as their cash.

- Attract angels who can invest and can work to help you because they know your industry.

- Ask for bigger investments rather than what you think will be approved. Although a bit counterintuitive, requests for larger amounts of capital are more attractive to investors than requests for smaller, more humble amounts. Private investors know it will take significant amounts of money to get a business started. The large request indicates an understanding of the resource requirements and the low probability that the entity will be requesting subsequent incremental amounts of capital.

- Why go to a VC versus an angel? The color of money is the same. A good VC has done it successfully many times before, brings skills to the table that you do not possess, and asks for an appropriate percentage so that there's enough to motivate a growing firm's future employees. An angel usually has been an entrepreneur so he understands what you are going through. Angels usually just have money and ask for a little less.

- When seeking capital, don't waste a lot of time arguing about how to divide up the pie. Focus your energy on growing the pie.

- When selecting a VC firm, do in-depth due diligence on them as much as they do on you.

- Choose a location that is accessible by major VCs (rule of thumb = 1 hour flight, 1 day trip).

- Understand the background and expectations of the venture capital group that you choose (or that chooses you).

- Eliminate the phrase *dilution of ownership* from your vocabulary when it comes to obtaining funding. VCs are a strategic component of any financing strategy. You need their money in the early stages. As CEO you should not worry about dilution. Your aim is to grow the business, get to value points.

- Don't end up working for your investors; always maintain control.

- Don't give up equity to the extent you lose control of your venture.

- Don't get too many investors. Managing them is very time consuming.

- Keep options open on all deals: there is no such thing as a done deal.

- Don't forget that bankers are not entrepreneurially minded.

- Don't expect the bank to lend you money to start your business.

- Don't go to just any bank. Research a number of prospective banks.

- Have a good standing relationship with at least two banks.

- To establish business and obtain funding quicker, partner with someone who is already known by lenders.

- Get a line of credit immediately. You never know when you will need it. You cannot get money when you need it, because of that very reason. You will need money, and banks hate cash-flow problems. That is the reason you will need it.

- Don't try to run your business off of debt.

- Don't commit excessive collateral to obtain the financing.

- Don't mortgage your life away for a single opportunity. Credit cards and second mortgages are not a good financing alternative.

- Cash is king. Have as much cash on hand as possible. Most bad situations can be resolved with cash.

- Don't ever lose sight of cash flow.

- Cash flow management issue points to keeping very close tabs on the condition of the business. It is not healthy to leave reviewing the financial condition to other people. Certainly, do not to put it off for a significant period of time.

- Make sure you have enough working capital for growth.

- Manage your accounts receivable. Get customers to agree to net 10-day terms. Minimize late payments and nonpayments.

- *Undercapitalization* can actually be good. It helps you stretch and be more creative. It keeps you from being wasteful and squandering your resources.

- Most employees can deal with the fact that their CEO is watching the dollars like a hawk because it gives them some peace of mind about the survival of the firm.

- Don't spend any more money up front than you absolutely need to.

- Have enough sense not to grasp for things beyond your reach, have plenty of capital, and be very careful with your expectations—you always spend at least double what you imagine.

- Make sure that you have the proper funds to cover unexpected spending.

- Don't spend money foolishly in areas that do not bring value to generating revenue.

- Limit your fixed costs. Run your business leaner than you really want.

- Don't try to get by with cheap equipment—find stuff that works and stick with it; good equipment does not cost much more than low-end equipment. If you buy low-end equipment, then you end up losing in the end when you have to come back and fix or replace it for free; your reputation is all that you have.

- Find out the hidden expenses by talking to other business owners.

- Establish a good credit line now.

- Keep the company lean. Do not have too much overhead.

- Resist the temptation to buy things.

- Anticipate incidental out-of-pocket expenses and work them into the financing up front. Be sure to have cash available for the unexpected.

- Continue to reinvest the profits back into the business for continued growth.

- Have a cushion of money to fall back on—you will probably not have the cash flow you project to begin with.

- Make sure that you have company credit cards to use in case of an emergency.

- Pay bills on time and build credit rapidly.

- If you want to be big you have to act big without spending big.

- Growing too rapidly can be fatal, unless cash flow is positive.

- Learn to budget. Once your budget is set, do not stray from it. Watch the numbers carefully.

- Things rarely go exactly as planned. Have a backup financing plan just in case you go over budget.

- Keep a close eye on your business's cost structure; don't let expenses get out of hand in the name of growth.

- Keep your personal finances separate from your business finances.

- Don't mix home and business bills.

- Don't try to do your own accounting unless you are truly capable.

- Be liquid with your finances and be prepared to take a big hit in the beginning so that you don't go out of business.

- Keep records of any exchange of money in case you are audited.

- Resist the temptation to buy things that do not add value to your firm.

- Keep a close eye on the finances of the company to ensure that all the money is going where you think that it is and you do not have an excessive burn rate.

- Be realistic about your expectations for income.

- Don't spend money based on promises to do business with you; wait until there are contracts.

- Don't expect to make a lot of money right from the start.

- Resist the temptation to spend profits freely. As you begin to move from the red to the black, do not immediately spend extra cash. Reinvest it into the business as part of your growth plan.

- Don't try to do your own taxes. Unless you're a tax attorney or CPA, it is not worth the time and frustration to try to do your own taxes. You will come out better hiring an expert and concentrating on running your business.

- Don't get behind on your accounting; it will set you far behind.

- Don't try to get away with dishonest financial records; it will never work.

THE BUSINESS OPPORTUNITY AND BUSINESS CONCEPT

- Remember, a good idea does not necessarily translate into a profitable business.

- Quickly sort out unpromising ventures.

- Always know the field that you are working in and know the potential for growth in that field. If you are going to make a considerable amount of profit, there needs to be room to grow.

- Select a business to best suit one's individual characteristics—skills, background, and experience.

- Choose an idea or industry that you like. You're going to give up a lot of your life getting the new venture going.

- Don't choose something *just* because you personally like it or think it might work; know what is needed and what will succeed.

- Fall in love with your initial idea.

- Look for niche opportunities where you can fill a void.

- Find something that people need and want in any economy. If your product and/or service is only attractive when the Dow Jones Industrial Average is breaking new ground, you are in for many long, sleepless nights.

- Be able to clearly describe your customers and exactly why they should care about you. If you cannot clearly communicate what problem you are trying to solve for whom, then no amount of hard work and technical genius will make it successful. Make sure your concept is easily understandable to the wider customer audience, to perspective venture capitalists, and to potential future employees.

- Select an opportunity that has the potential for plenty of growth and high margins.

- Most service businesses have low barriers to entry. Anyone with previous experience may be able to get into the game.

- Don't get distracted. You'll see lots of interesting ideas but to be successful you must stay focused.

- Fill a real need. Making the best widget in the world is to no avail if no one is buying widgets.

- Do market research to see if there truly is a need for your product or service.

- Select a business that is preferably an established concept to the customers in the industry.

- Don't choose a business where you must educate the customer in a new technology.

- If you offer a complex product or service, then you must be able to translate your product/service offering's value to one that is easily and clearly understandable to customers and potential investors.

- Recognize that changes in the environment, government regulations, and so forth all have the potential to produce new business opportunities.

- Don't start a business because someone else has been successful at the same business. You will never be able to copy their decisions (good and bad) or luck.

- Weigh the incremental cost of entering a niche with the value perceived by the potential market base.

- Don't attempt to service an industry without deep knowledge of that industry's needs, issues, and problems.

- Don't wait for the perfect opportunity to present itself. If you wait for the home run, you'll never make it to the plate.

- Don't think that your ideas are unique and move forward without research.

- Stay focused on a narrow range of opportunities.

- Identify and weight key criteria for success.

- Assess the entry and exit barriers.

- Don't choose a business with high exit barriers.

- Analyze the market for bargaining power of buyers, bargaining power of suppliers, threat of substitutes, and rivalry among existing firms.

- Look for markets in which other firms are profitable.

- Don't attempt to compete in a mature industry unless you have particularly strong experience, creativity, or contacts.

- Look for an industry that is out of step with its customer's needs.

- Exploit opportunities in emerging or changing industries.

- Favor ventures that require less capital to those that are capital intensive (less capital-intensive businesses lead to a lower initial capital requirement).

- Favor ventures that have simple operations (avoids impacts of technical delays and cost overruns).

- Don't buy a successful business assuming that you will have similar or better results. The business will be different once you own it.

- Start a business that someone else would be willing and able to buy.

MARKET OPPORTUNITY: ANALYZE THE MARKETPLACE AND DO THE RIGHT MARKETING

- Don't limit your definition of what a market is.

- Don't assume that your market will always stay the same as it is today.

- Select a product or service that has demand in the area where you are establishing your business.

- Don't enter a market with a product that is readily available and inexpensive (like a commodity).

- Don't compete directly with larger companies.

- Look for a niche that is not serviced in an existing market.

- Look for existing markets that need revitalizing or where existing firms may have become stagnant in a market with new needs.

- Make sure you have a product that has a defined market.

- Make sure you research the client base, and make sure that there actually is a base to buy your product.

- Don't overestimate customer demand. Have an idea of what the market might be like, but do not deceive yourself; you can't create the market if it is not there.

- Don't get into an oversaturated market. Make sure you offer your customers a unique product or service. It's easier to be successful if you are the only one offering a certain product or service in town.

- What holds true for one geographic market does not necessarily hold for another, even one in close proximity.

- Do not simply hang out your shingle. It is a good idea to have one or two clients lined up prior to opening your business.

- Get commitments from several key prospective customers before you actually launch your business.

- Be willing to start with small contracts and lower hourly fees while you build a roster of clients and build your reputation. Remember that potential clients are taking a chance by trying your business. Make the decision easier for them by reducing their risk or cost.

- Find a unique service to offer.

- Don't assume everyone will love your product or service.

MARKETING PLAN

- If you plan to start a service business, the key to profitability is billable hours. You need to get over the feeling of not wanting to charge for less value-added work (unpacking/repacking equipment, etc.).

- If you start your business out of your home, then get out of your home. Large clients are skittish if they know that you're working out of your home.

- Know your customer. If possible, work with a well-reputed customer and seek their advice to improve your product. This approach will not only help you build a better product, it will also give you a good reference in the future.

- Ask people what they want, but give them what they need.

- Don't overpromise and underdeliver.

- Provide better service than expected—go beyond the customer expectations.

- Define very clearly who your targeted customers are, focus on who may be your best customers, and provide them with superior service. A well-serviced customer is going to be loyal and very profitable.

- Never compromise quality.

- Develop a product or service that keeps the customer coming back for more.

- Develop a realistic timetable for product development and beta testing.

- Map out the marketing of the product before development. What will the ads look like? What are the salient features?

- Have a variety of different products/services.

- Don't do your own marketing.

- Get your name known in the public.

- Be creative in advertising.

- Advertise and promote your business in advance so that it can hit the ground running.

- Don't assume that customers will find you. Always assume customers have never heard of you.

- Make sure your Web site has faultless execution. Most customers will not return if they do not have a good experience when conducting a transaction.

- Don't think that because you have a Web page that clients will come to you.

- Recognize your Web site will need to be updated and improved.

- Don't believe that everything that matters is price; you can win a lot of customers with good service.

- Don't put too many things on sale—many customers will start to believe that the product will eventually go on sale and will wait until that time to buy it.

- Location is very important in the retail business. Don't go for the first vacant facility you find.

- Don't locate the business in a certain place just because *you like* the location.

- Research your location thoroughly, including vehicular and pedestrian traffic.

- If possible, locate your business close to important resources. For a software company, for instance, locate near a well-trained, reasonably priced, and plentiful technical labor pool.

- Talk to all of the other business owners in the area that you plan to open up in before you consider locating there. Find out about problems they might have had with leasing and maintenance, and discover what type of customers live in the community and shop in the area.

- Avoid relocating at all costs, especially if you have a small company.

- Don't ever get caught without a business card.

MARKETING: COMPETITION

- Unearth and understand who the competitors are, their size, and their clientele.

- Take into consideration who your current competition is and who might be your competition in the future.

- Don't be overly worried about the competition you are about to face; identify their weak points and excel at them.

- Find your competitor with the best customer service and figure out how to do it better.

- Research your current and potential competition. Find out everything you can to be well informed.

- Know your competitors—what services they offer and what rates they charge. How do you compare?

- Take into consideration who your current competition is and who might be your competition in the future.

- Analyze the firms already in that field—are they doing well?

- Analyze the firms already in that field—there will be relationships between them. If they are adversarial, there might be something you should investigate further.

- Don't target all competitors. Instead, go after a few competitors.

- Don't trust competition but do respect them.

- Always be aware of where you stand in the market and where your competition stands relative to you.

- Don't underestimate your competition. Identify potential retaliatory threats from them.

- Don't yield to unscrupulous competitors—keep your values and be respected in your community.

- Find something to offer that your competitors can't offer.

- Focus on the one thing that will differentiate you from your competition and do all you can to be the best at that one thing.

- Build barriers to entry and competitive advantages. Don't share your creative ideas with your competitors.

MARKETING: CUSTOMERS

- Consider customers as your first priority.

- Know your customer base. Having an idea of whom you are trying to sell to is much better than guessing after you have already started.

- Don't expect that your customers will understand your product as easily as you think.

- Don't assume that your friends will buy your services.

- Don't expect your customers to come to you—you need a strong marketing and sales plan.

- Don't expect a prospective customer to close the deal.

- Try to establish a good customer base, especially in the beginning. You need to get regular customers. When you get them, don't lose them. Keep your customers satisfied.

- Spend as much time with your customers as possible. It will take you three times longer to sell a new product over an existing and functioning product.

- Look for a big initial customer.

- Don't send confusing or mixed signals to the customer base or business community.

- Get commitments from several key prospective customers before actually launching the business.

- Find a customer evangelist.

- Don't miss opportunities to make new customer or business acquaintances.

- Be honest with your customers, and if you don't know an answer, find out and get back to them.

- Ensure frequent customer follow-ups.

- Do the little extras that people notice.

- Be willing to do some work for free in order to get a contract or save a contract.

- Be willing to start with small contracts and lower hourly fees while you build a roster of clients and build your reputation. Remember that potential clients are taking a chance in hiring a new consultant, so help make the decision easier for them.

- Don't depend exclusively on one client.

- Don't become vulnerable to customer concentration. Avoid having only a few large customers.

- Don't sit around waiting for customers to walk in the door.

- Make a lot of cold calls.

- Follow up on every lead.

- Don't fall into the trap of thinking, "I'm busy trying to run this business …the customers won't leave me alone!" Customers always come first.

- Know that if you are not delivering the right service, someone else is.

- Look up the chain and determine who is making the buying decisions.

- Be prepared to constantly revise your timelines and project schedules to meet the needs of big customers. Large businesses can be very bureaucratic.

- Treat everyone as a possible lead for your business.

- Don't invest time and resources on sales leads that have a low probability of closure. The current lengthy process has been modified to more deeply probe the prospect up front to assess technical needs, degree of interest, and the commitment to purchase.

- Don't rush the cultivation of potential customers if your product is expensive or your ultimate customer base is relatively small (hundreds or thousands versus millions).

- Choose your customers very carefully; don't be shy about dropping customers who don't pay.
- Trust your gut instinct about clients. If you don't trust a client, don't take the job, as it will be more trouble than it is worth in the long run.
- Don't allow the customer to take advantage of you.
- Sales always take a longer time to develop than you initially expect them to, especially when you are dealing with a quasi or fully public entity. Sometimes it can take up to six months to win a new contract.
- Don't dismiss customer complaints. Complaints can be learning opportunities.
- Get feedback from your customers after the sale. Ask clients for feedback. Ask how you can serve them better.
- Always gladly accept any recommendations for making your business more attractive to your target market. You do not have to implement every idea, but you should consider each suggestion.
- Recognize customer base may vary at different times of the year and know the specific needs of each set of customers.
- Quality service is the most important attribute in launching a business.
- Don't jeopardize your reputation or customer relationships for short-term gains.
- Don't get so busy running your business that you lose sight of your customers.
- Make sure you don't lose clients once you have them.
- Don't go on vacation during the busy season, and when you do take a vacation, notify your customers weeks in advance.
- Don't accept more customers than you can handle.
- Don't ever lie to a customer.
- Don't fail a customer's request.
- If you don't know an answer to a question posed by a customer, then find out and get back to the customer.
- Don't ever forget to thank your customers.
- Don't extend credit, but if you must to be competitive, then don't give extended credit to customers if you are unsure of their ability to pay.
- Don't hold a grudge against your former employer. Your former employer could become your largest customer, and you'll know it better than any other potential customer.
- Think twice about accepting work from lawyers. They tend to be cheap and they will sue you faster than you can say "It's a faulty router."

SUPPLIERS: YOU CAN'T LIVE WITHOUT THEM

- Make sure that you have all of your vendors lined up in advance.
- Value and establish mutually beneficial and trusting relationships with your suppliers.

- Keep an open line of communication with your suppliers.
- Don't be penny-wise, but pound-foolish. Invest in the long term with education and quality equipment.
- Buy used equipment. Don't think you need the newest technology. If you buy it a year old you get better pricing and financing.
- Shop around for suppliers and vendors.
- Don't become vulnerable to supplier concentration.
- Don't tie your whole business to any one vendor.
- Don't assume your current insurance company is the best for your company.
- Don't assume your current bank is the best for your business.
- Don't be afraid to ask your suppliers for a lower cost and volume discounts.
- Don't go with a software application without conducting thorough financial due diligence on the software vendor.
- Don't keep a large inventory on hand; use just-in-time inventory to keep your storage costs lower.
- Don't sign contracts with vendors if you don't understand the fine print.
- Don't wait too long before setting up your accounts with the telephone company.

LEGAL: IT'S A MINEFIELD OUT THERE!

- Consult legal counsel when starting a business. Make sure that all of the details of starting a business are covered.
- Don't do anything without hiring a lawyer first.
- Don't seek to represent yourself in legal matters.
- Write standard contracts and use them.
- Make sure that you have the proper licenses and permits if you are selling to the public.
- Check zoning laws before signing any lease or agreement.
- Don't underestimate the power of fire marshals and building inspectors.
- Follow all regulations.
- Don't make verbal agreements with clients. Make sure that you have written work agreements with clear expectations of the work to be accomplished. This will ensure that there are no misunderstandings later.
- Don't rely on anyone else (i.e., a partner) when starting the new venture without a formal legal agreement.
- Be sure that you incorporate. This way someone can only sue the business, not the partners as individuals.

- Don't skimp on resources. If you need legal counsel for the high-tech industry, do not choose a general counsel, thinking you can get by. The right resources are worth the time and effort.

- Have a good computer program to store all of your company records and accounts.

- Make sure that your insurance company covers liability as well, because if you damage someone's property, you can be sued for everything that you have.

- Store all of your contracts and important financial records in a fireproof safe deposit box.

- Establish a buy-back provision when issuing stock.

- Have a basis for valuing your business in the event you have to buy back stock.

- Carry key-person insurance so your business has the money to buy back the stock of key individuals if they die.

THINGS TO REMEMBER AFTER YOU HAVE STARTED YOUR BUSINESS

- Nothing stays the same. Don't quit researching your field, competition, and so on. Think constantly about how the industry is changing and how the market is shifting.

- Don't ever let your guard down or stop paying close attention to quality and details.

- Don't allow yourself to get sidetracked and lose sight of your business plan.

- When you are growing, watch your costs, but when business is waning, spend money and do the things that drive growth.

- Have a strong vision for what you want in the long run. Examine and reevaluate it periodically to make sure that it still holds for the current situation.

- Revisit plans and strategies regularly.

- Keep looking over your shoulder, and be prepared to act.

- Paranoia is good. Eventually you will be copied or someone else will do the job better. So continually look for ways to do a better job. Look for ways to reinvent your business.

- Focus on how the company is doing, rather than only how much money it is making.

- Always be looking for ways to add value to your business.

- You always have to strive to do better.

- Give every detail about your business your attention, but try to see the forest in spite of the trees.

- Recognize mistakes and be willing to make changes quickly.

- Step back and ask yourself periodically, "Am I the best person to take this company to the next level?"

- Realize that in most cases a new skill set equates to a new person leading.

- Don't expect that any one set of skills can lead the company through every stage of its development. The same skills that get you started may not get you funded and will not get you through to financial solvency.

- Get up from your desk every day and walk the floor. Speak to everyone within the firm.

- It's critical to identify and maintain your competitive advantage. Recognize every prospective customer has figuratively tattooed across his or her forehead the question, "So what?" This is even more important as competition increases.

- Don't expand for the sake of expansion; grow only when it makes strategic sense.

- Don't get cocky. Don't let your successes lull you to sleep at the wheel. Remember that past success is no indication that you will avoid future disasters.

- Maintain a big picture perspective.

- Don't forget to plan for the future.

- Constantly develop new strategies to sell your product.

- Come up with new ideas constantly and apply them to your business.

- Don't overstretch your plans. Be future orientated, but be realistic, too.

- Expect the unexpected all the time. Every day be ready for new problems, new people, and different challenges.

- Don't be satisfied with how good things were yesterday; it won't pay the bills today.

- Remember that too much of a good thing can be bad. Celebrate your successes. Enjoy the wins along the way, but don't become complacent. Don't take your eye off the ball.

- Take care of your health.

- Take vacations every once in a while to reward yourself and recharge your batteries.

- Don't rest on your laurels. Continue to raise the bar.

- Reinvest profits into business instead of supporting your lifestyle.

- Avoid getting caught in a rut.

- Don't let failures at the beginning get you down.

- Don't let minor setbacks deter you.

- Don't wear *technical superiority blinders*—you'll be caught off guard and lose market share.

- Don't lose track of keeping your accounting records current or your taxes.

- Don't begin an expansion project without enough preparation.

- Know when and how to expand.

- Avoid expanding too quickly because overhead could eat you alive.

- Use the down times in business to prepare business for the up times.

- Keep your skills up to date.

- Keep up with modern technology.
- Constantly look to catch the big waves.
- Don't do anything half-way
- Don't be afraid to take on a loan to help your business expand, but know how much of a loan you can handle so that you are able to keep the business finances healthy.
- Learn to get energy from the good days so that you can make it through the bad days.
- Be loyal to the people who take the best care of you.
- Don't be afraid of change. You should continuously question your most cherished assumptions.
- Take incremental growth steps.
- Have and plan your resources for managing growth.
- Don't try to get too big, too fast. As businesses grow, there are various inflection points along the way, which require action/organizational change. Success will depend on how these inflection points are managed.
- Always stay focused on the long-term objective, because if you don't, things will not go as planned.
- Don't exceed your capital and go into too much debt.
- Don't expand beyond what can be managed to your satisfaction.
- Don't be afraid to admit when you are wrong.
- Learn from your mistakes and move on.
- Don't leave the business to someone else too early in the game.
- Keep business and personal life separate, and definitely have a personal life outside work.
- Make sure you take personal time. Work hard but do not forget to take vacations as well, even short ones. You need some time to recharge your batteries if you expect to be profitable.
- Make sure to have balance in your life. Take one day a week for nonbusiness activities.
- Don't forget about the people who got you where you are. Don't neglect your family and loved ones; not everyone understands your drive. Don't build your entrepreneurial house and lose those close to you, or get divorced and lose half your assets.
- Don't fall prey to every organization that wants a charitable donation.

CLOSING POINTS

- Keep your ego under control.
- Don't lose your entrepreneurial spirit.
- Know when to exit. Don't invest too much time or money into the business if it is failing. Knowing when to quit and minimizing your losses is very important, since this may determine if you'll have anything left for the next venture.

- Know when it is time to sell your business. Sell it when things are good or to get out when things cannot be fixed.
- Don't spend the rest of your life doing something you don't like.
- Have fun and enjoy the ride.

Remember the very first tip: Don't forget why you started this thing in the first place.

INDEX